Latin America
Made in Canada

Library and Archives Canada Cataloguing in Publication

Latin America Made in Canada
©2022 Alter / Lugar Común Editorial
Diseño y maquetación ©2022 Lugar Común Editorial

For information and order write to:
Lugar Común Editorial
67 Norice St. Ottawa, Canada. K2G 2X7
www.lugarcomuneditorial.com
info@lugarcomuneditorial.com

Maria del Carmen Suescun Pozas, PhD
Associate Professor, Department of History, Brock University

Alena Robin, PhD
Associate Professor, Department of Visual Arts, Western University

ISBN 978-1-987819-67-0

Printed in Canada

Latin America
Made in Canada

Maria del Carmen Suescun Pozas
and Alena Robin, Editors

To the memory of J. E. Suescún Hernández (1936-2019), S. M. Lara Flores (1949-2019) F. Robin (1941-2017), R. Morgan (1944-2017), C. Ward (1955-2017), Earl Pearce (1937-2015), J. L. González Chagoyán (1917-2009), N. R. Peddie (1935-1998), and M. E. Rodríguez de Martínez (1914-1993).

Wishing Joaquín Antonio and Amalia María, Aaron and Amanda, Ewan and Johanna, Gerónimo, Ernest Eugene, Lenna and Ellie, and Elena a bright future on our beloved planet Earth.

To María del Carmen Pozas Gómez and Régis Robin for the gifts of life and continued support.

Contents

Preface

The seeds of the scholarly collaboration embodied in *Latin America Made in Canada* were planted in 2010 at the Canadian Association of Latin American and Caribbean Studies (CALACS) Congress in Montreal and at the Universities Art Association of Canada (UAAC) Conference in Guelph. It was in the "Imaging Memory Across Political and Disciplinary Boundaries" (CALACS) and "Latin America Made in Canada" (UAAC) panels, more specifically, that the ideas for this project were initially developed. Beginning in earnest in 2012, our collaboration crystallized at the 2013 CALACS Congress in Ottawa with a panel entitled "Research and Teaching on Latin American and Caribbean Art and Visual Culture in Canada" and, in 2015, all of the authors involved in the volume had the opportunity to get together to read their contributions, engage in conversation with one another, and offer and receive feedback in a workshop setting. As editors, we have had the privilege of accompanying the contributors on their creative journey. We wish to thank all of them for keeping their work fresh during each stage of the writing and revision process.

This volume is testimony to the patience, commitment, resilience, persistence and hard work that are required to build a community of knowledge across academic disciplines, professional associations, community networks, and other formal and informal networks that transcend national boundaries. The articles in this collection developed over time, with most of them starting out as papers that were delivered at conferences in various parts of Canada (Alberta, British Columbia, Ontario, Québec) as well as in Costa Rica (San José) and Japan (Tokyo). Numerous organizations were also instrumental in the successful realization of this book. In particular, we would like to acknowledge CALACS, the UAAC, the Canadian History of Education Association, the UTokyo Latin American & Iberian Network for Academic Collaboration, the Seedling for Change in History Brock Collective, Seedling for Change in Society and Environment, the Niagara Military Museum, and the History Lab.

We are grateful to students in the undergraduate and graduate History programs at Brock University and to the Department of Languages and Cultures at the University of Western Ontario for embracing themes and methodological approaches that connected the histories of Latin America and Canada in ways that were largely new to them. Our sincerest appreciation also goes to "Seed" student researchers with Seedling for Change in History, Laura Lee Burey Morgan, Ryan Laxton, Chris Mcgivern, and Saeeda Ali, Jonathan (Jono) Bond; and to dedicated students, Nikki Pruden, Tabitha Lewis, Sarah Rangaratnam, Jacob McIntosh, Ayelet Ishai and Jimena Zambrano, who offered various kinds of assistance, serving as so much more than sounding boards for ideas and approaches informing this book. For their enthusiasm and the generosity with which they engaged in conversation with us and continuously helped us stretch our imaginations, we are indebted to Lesley Bell, David Sharron, Elizabeth Vlossak, William Straw, Victor Armony, Hugh Hazelton, Jorge Nallim, Catherine LeGrand, Cameron and Susan Ward, Rick Morgan, Penny Morningstar, Gordon Sisler, Jim and Kathy Doherty, Mike Ashford, Berndt Meyer, Victor Packard, Julia Rose Simone, Ann Sperling, Chris Lowes, Lucas Spinoza, Jeffrey W. Edmunds, Salomé Torres, Annie Holtby, Stella Muñoz, Phil Hall, Ann Silversides, Joël Marier, Constanza Burucúa, Marjorie Ratcliffe, Frédéric Robin, Régis Robin, Natalia Suescún, Jorge Suescún, Nicolás Palau van Hissenhoven, Paulina Suescún, and Belén Samper. We also thank the anonymous readers of the manuscript for this volume, which is all the stronger for their recommendations. We are fortunate to have found Lugar Común Editorial, a gem of a Canadian publishing house and the perfect match for this undertaking; to our colleagues there, Luis Molina, Christel Kopp and Trish Van Bolderen: *gracias infinitas* for making a dream, long in the making, finally come true. And lastly, loving gratitude goes to César Rafael Maldonado Mercado and Raúl Manuel López Bajonero, who are tireless companions in our scholarly journeys, and champions of our transcontinental and transhemispheric adventures.

We wish to acknowledge the generous support we received aid-to-publication grants from the Humanities Research Institute at Brock University and from the Rosslyn Swanson Humanities Fund through the University of Western Ontario's Faculty of Arts and Humanities. We also wish to recognize the kind support of the Government of Ontario Multicultural Community Capacity Program, the City of Niagara Falls Cultural Development Fund, and Brock University's Co-op, Career and Experiential Education, its Experience Works program and its Service-Learning course-incentive grants.

Very special thanks go to the late Jorge Eliécer Suescún Hernández and Françoise Robin, both of whom continue to be sources of inspiration. In life, they were champions of Latin American culture and history beyond the region's current geographic boundaries. Françoise's volunteer work with new immigrants arriving from the Latin America and Caribbean region to the Trois-Rivières and Cap-de-la-Madeleine area in the 1970s, and her love of and passion for the cultures of many Latin American countries, have left an indelible mark. Jorge's commitment to teaching, scholarship and engaged citizenship, his insatiable curiosity and *joie de vivre*, and his firm belief in Latin America's leading role in lifting humanity out of the depths and into a brighter future for the entire planet, continue to point the way.

Niagara Region & London, Ontario; Montréal, Québec; Zipacón, Cundinamarca (March 2022)

Introduction:
Writing the Cultural History of Canadian-Latin American Relations Through a Cultural Production Lens

Maria del Carmen Suescun Pozas
Alena Robin

In 1943, Spanish-Uruguayan artist Joaquín Torres-García drew an upside-down map of South America, placing the southern tip at the top to signal that "the South is our North." His *América Invertida* remains an open invitation for people in both the north and south to revisit their relative positions and explore their mutual conditioning and embeddedness in history (Fig. 1). One can only but marvel at the simplicity with which Torres-García rendered in visual form the complexity and nuance of this shift in orientation. Whereas ideas and culture from the north were historically a primary point of reference for artists, writers, technocrats and politicians, Torres-García called on his contemporaries to look, instead, to the outer and inner landscapes of the south for transformative, creative inspiration. The time had come for the south to become the muse of the future. The sun and the moon, and the boat sailing along the line of the horizon line of Torres-García's map identify the south as the guiding northern star. Navigators could safely set out on a new course using this map as their nautical chart.

In the new ideational landscape that emerges from turning the world upside down, we find ourselves in a hall of mirrors where north and south merge endlessly into one another. The act of upending the map does not point to a condition of north and south opposing one another, nor does it call for a severing of their ties. What results instead is that the south, now designated as north, evokes a *unifying* consciousness. In this new geography of the mind, north and south extend beyond their own physical geographies and spill onto one another's terrain, thus giving birth to a new relational field. Although this field may still be as transnational in nature as it had always been, the new journey involves each entity seeing itself reflected in the other. Inside the hall of mirrors, the logic of interdependent, non-linear expansiveness rules.

Figure 1. Joaquín Torres-García, *América invertida*, 1943, ink on paper, 22 x 16 cm. (Courtesy of the Estate of Joaquín Torres-García)

The present volume broadens the history of Latin America so that it also accounts for what happens beyond the region's geographical limits.[1] Specifically, the collection adopts a multidisciplinary approach, drawing on contributions from emerging and established artists and scholars alike, to consider representations in cultural production coming out of Canada. For the purposes of this book, culture is defined as those ways of seeing, thinking, doing and relating that are readily agreed upon to be distinctive and salient to a given human collective and that inform both internal relations (how members relate to one another within the collective) and external relations (how one human collective relates to another). Human collectives vary in nature: there are groups of people who self-identify as communities and those that exist within and/or as organizations, just as there are administrative and political entities, such as governments and nations. Likewise, cultural production is understood as encompassing a full range of literary, performing and visual arts, all of which are considered to be means through which everyday life is enacted. *Latin America Made in Canada* considers Torres-García's intriguing proposition of an imaginary geography, using historical and cultural studies lenses to map out Canadian-Latin American history within a single volume. It examines the role of creative practices within Canada from the early part of the 20th century through to the present. It explores the ways in which fragments of tangible and intangible Latin American cultural history have made their way to Canada and contributed to Latin America becoming a cultural artifact in this country. The *making* of Latin America manifests itself through a plurality of practices involving diverse social actors who work across different economic sectors. Each chapter in this collection should be read as an interpretive framework, an appreciation of cultural production that branches out into other cognate experiences which find a place within our proposed narrative.[2] By examining these practices as snapshots of everyday life, this volume sheds light on a history that is simultaneously visible and elusive to the storyteller.

Besides being geographical and territorial spaces, Canada and the region of Latin America are also institutional, discursive and political entities that exist beyond the realm of mere categories of thought and lend themselves well to historical analysis. Following in the steps of cultural history and political science, which delve into intercontinental relationships, this volume explores cultural production as part of Canadian-Latin American relations, with a particular focus on how Latin America is rooted in Canadian soil. Ultimately, we hope this volume will contribute to disrupting persistent tendencies to oversimplify the relationship between Canada and Latin America, where the regions are presented as two different worlds, often split into two (English, Spanish) or three (English, French, Spanish) language groups, and where Latin America serves as a placeholder for culture and values that inherently set it apart from Canada.

Latin America is here in Canada and all around us in this country-in the food we eat, the music we listen to, the languages we speak at home or hear in the streets, the spiritual and religious rituals we practice, the current events we discuss, the advocacy work we engage in, and the rich repertoire of cultural products we create. In addition to the Latin America that is embodied in the people and goods that come from the near and distant south, there is another Latin America that is located closer to home, intimately linked to the Canadian context in terms of the way it manifests itself and is (re)presented in policy, media, business and a whole variety of cultural products.[3] Latin America speaks to us *from within* Canada, insofar as local and transnational awareness is incorporated into Latin American poetics and traditions that are mediated by those who—regardless of their birthplace—are based in Canada.[4] Instead of dwelling on the geographical and abstract distances that separate Canada from Latin America, or continuing to reproduce such distances by leaving them unquestioned, this book invites readers to explore the *making* of Latin America as part of the ever-changing and expanding cultural heritage and repertoires of both Latin America and Canada. The case studies presented in this book offer examples of how to grapple with disavowed dimensions of Canadian experiences, and open pathways for expanding Canada's cultural history.[5]

Framing the cultural history of Canadian-Latin American relations through a cultural production lens

Any attempt to use culture as a prism for historicizing the engagement between Canada and Latin America involves exploring the ways in which cultural production is bound up in and conditioned, determined and/or otherwise informed by processes of production and reproduction that are specific to particular national and regional settings and that make manifest, in more or less tangible ways, the idea of that nation/region. Even if national/regional frameworks do not exhaust the possibilities for producing meaning, and even though nation and region are not the sole categories one can draw on to understand or explain cultural production, perceptions of "us" versus "them" materialize though the repetition of sense-making repertoires. Canada and Latin America are concrete geographical entities as much as they are the result of iterative acts. Cultural products, which are examples of such iterative acts, keep national and regional identities alive from within as well as from beyond, with political, geographical and/or similarly powerful imaginary borders that stem from repeated assertion both rejecting and inviting difference. What comes from an imagined "beyond" serves to affirm national/regional identities, while cultural repertoires that originate from diverse geographical locations meet and interact "within," identities are negotiated and ultimately transformed. Nations and regions might be limiting as categories of analysis; nevertheless, they are productive. An alternative to completely abandoning national or regional approaches to understanding cultural production is—at the risk of reproducing distance and oppressing distinctiveness by omission—to engage with the materiality of nationhood and regionalism in cultural practices.

Over the past couple of decades, an emphasis on what unites peoples across and "in between" national borders, in spite of any differences, is what has helped situate Canada (and Canadians) in relation to Latin America, and advance knowledge about Canada's engagement with these regions.[6] Such engagement involved Canada and individual Canadians turning their attention inwards as much as outwards: as a sociopolitical entity, Latin America initially resided beyond Canada's national borders, but since the mid-20th century, as a result of exile, immigration, and diasporic and transnational solidarity, it has also and increasingly been found *within* those borders.[7] Examining cultural production as a site of engagement undoubtedly contributes to knowledge about the relationships that exist between Canada and Latin America and that, while operating across national borders, are "embedded, place-specific, material, and historical" in nature.[8]

Perhaps the most exciting and challenging aspect of discussing Canadian-Latin American relations, in terms of cultural production, is finding a way of thinking and talking about them that appropriately captures the specificities of Canadian and Latin American history, including what both entities have in common and what might make their shared story troublingly "American." An intriguing term, found throughout literature on Canadian-Latin American relations, is "discovery." Authors Jean Daudelin and Edgar J. Dosman use it as an operative word,[9] meaning that they expect readers who come across the term to pause and consider its legacy of colonialism so as not to be unreflective about reproducing ways of thinking.[10] Exploration, discovery and encounter belong to a narrative that we may inadvertently rely on in order to make the unfamiliar (Latin America, in this case) familiar.[11] Acknowledging the limits of what is known is the first step towards preventing imperialist and colonialist ideologies from introducing themselves into this collection.

When used in contemporary discourse, language associated with colonial projects such as the formation of the "New World" is expected to evolve from notions of exploration and expansion to those of decolonization and, eventually, the consolidation of new, transcultural communities to follow from each other. José Antonio Giménez Micó refers to such a process when he speaks of "Latin-Americanizing Canada," which he defines as a "process of transculturation that occurs through the inclusion of Latin American identities into Canadian culture, and the consequent transformation of the latter."[12] The sense of belonging that stems from this process leads us to view connectedness as an important pathway to forging new communities and experiences.

Historical underpinnings

In 1976, historian J. C. M. Ogelsby noted that "[i]t was easy in the past to say that Canadians have not had much contact with Latin Americans, but after historical investigation the record clearly indicates that while Latin America has not had an overwhelming importance in Canadian foreign relations, it has been exceeded in its historical importance to Canada only by the British Commonwealth, western Europe, and the United States."[13] His book contains essays on Canadian diplomacy, trade, banking and investment, on religious issues and Canadian missionaries, and on Canadian emigration. Ogelsby acknowledges that culture is missing from his work, saying that "[a] significant area that has not been granted importance in Canada's relations with Latin America has been the realm of culture."[14] Although his understanding of culture (largely restricted to literature and the fine arts) might be narrow, he noted the intriguing absence of engagement with the topic,[15] commending the "Canadians who did try to come to grips with the language, culture, and prospects of a particular [Latin American] country" and who "found their efforts rewarding," but ultimately bemoaning the fact that these Canadians were few and far between.[16]

As one of Ogelsby's interests lay in diplomacy, he noted that "[n]either the Latin-American embassies in Canada nor the Canadian embassies in Latin America did very much in the cultural sphere."[17] In his view, this could be explained by the fact that, "[t]he promotion of culture has few initial economic benefits. Therefore, it is hard to justify expenditures on it."[18] For the purposes of this volume, it is especially relevant to note two points that Ogelsby raises. First, he identifies culture as playing an important role in international relations, insisting that "[i]t is through cultural exchanges and involvement that nations develop an understanding of each other that facilitates contacts in other fields."[19] Second, he points out that Canada remained "of little attraction to Latin American intellectuals,"[20] with evidence suggesting that relations were premised, instead, on trade and investment opportunities. He considers this situation short-sighted on the part of both Latin America and Canada, for "[o]ne can only speculate what might have happened if the promotion of culture had received even a modest place in the century-long push for closer trade relations."[21] Since the publication of Ogelsby's book, much has changed in terms of Canada's engagement with Latin America and the study of relations between the two spaces.

Over the past thirty years, foreign policy, aid, trade, investment, immigration and mobility between the two regions feature at the centre of groundbreaking scholarly works.[22] Historians and scholars in diverse disciplines have amply demonstrated that the histories of Canada and the Latin America are connected.[23] Comparative studies have also offered insights into experiences that make the two regions different and also alike.[24] In recent years, studies of Hispanic people and/or *Latino*, *Latina* and Latinx in Canada have shed light on various aspects of immigration and, perhaps most importantly for the purposes of this book, on the capacity for people who migrate to Canada from Latin America to effect positive change across communities by engaging in politics, the arts, print and audiovisual media, and civic life.[25] Once the *making* of Latin America is set in Canada, the national, regional and hemispheric histories of Latin America are usefully problematized.

When one thinks of Canada in relation to Latin America, most generally one immediately visualizes two separate entities. Foreign policy, trade agreements and international law are there to remind us that separation is a matter of fact, not of fancy. The very same features that, in those arenas, serve as evidence for the disconnected nature of nations, regions and hemispheres become, for scholars, evidence of connectedness. For cultural historians, the notion of connectedness underscores how mutual embeddedness is characteristic (if not a precondition for productive and sustainable) international relations. This is the very thing that recent scholarship on Canadian-Latin American relations has set out to explore.[26]

Latin America Made in Canada is situated at the crossroads of studies that have been published in Canada over the past four decades and carried out in the areas of art and literature, performance and theatre, cultural history and visual culture, transnational history and political science, Latino-Hispanic studies, and Canadian studies. Rooting Latin America in Canadian soil challenges the boundaries that divide disciplines and geographies, the nature of what constitutes archival material, and any modes of inquiry that are premised on separation and/or "otherness." For most of the contributing authors, the main theme of this book is the warp and woof of their life and work in Canada, with Latin America being their foundation and their horizon. Canadian-Latin American relations are, for them, the site where inquiry unfolds.

Organization

Using Canada as its point of origin and thematic framework, this volume provides a first glimpse into the narrative features of the cultural production that Canadian-Latin American relations have offered since the late 19th century.[27] The volume is divided into four parts. Although the individual chapters are not strictly presented in chronological order, the chosen sequencing offers unique opportunities for readers to gain insights into patterns of continuity and change.

Part I, entitled "Trans-American Pathways of Neocolonialism," provides concrete examples of how ideologies rooted in colonialism and racism persist in the postcolonial era and in apparently unlikely places. In the introductory chapter, Rosana Barbosa focuses on a migratory episode from Montreal to São Paulo in 1896 and argues that the way that year's major Canadian newspapers portrayed Brazil as inherently inferior was embedded in colonialism and in Euro-North American racialized views of the southern American subcontinent. In Chapter 2, Madeleine de Trenqualye examines a segment of the Canadian tourism sector that promoted travel to Latin America in the 1990s, and she provides evidence of how Latin America was consistently viewed in a way that erased signs of its modern infrastructure and industrial development. The third chapter consists of Mariza Rosales Argonza's study of visual artists who migrated to Canada; in it, she discusses instances of decolonization whereby the artists cross borders and subsequently incorporate a range of cultural and linguistic structures into their work, adopting new ways of thinking and acting amid circumstances that are unstable due to migration.

Part II, "From Outsiders to Insiders," tears down the imaginary cultural and linguistic wall that separates the two regions, and it offers a glimpse into the ways in which people previously perceived as outsiders become insiders.[28] Focusing on Mexican art exhibitions in Canadian museums between 1943 and 1961, Sarah E. K. Smith (Chapter 4) demonstrates that culture played a role in the political and economic exchanges between Canada and Mexico long before the early-1990s impetus in Canada to formally showcase Mexico as an economic partner. In Chapter 5, Jason Dyck analyzes photographs and films of seasonal agricultural workers, i.e., temporary residents of Canada who are commonly known as migrant workers. He argues that this visual history complicates the traditional geographical and cultural borders of Greater Mexico, which is generally confined to Mexico and the southwestern United States, and explains why those borders should be expanded to include Canada. In Chapter 6,

Maria Eugenia de Luna Villalón examines the linguistic landscapes that result from Spanish being used as a language of communication within small, local businesses that cater to people travelling to Canada through the Seasonal Agricultural Workers Program. She contends that these linguistic landscapes, which invite this community of workers into a space that offers them customized information and/or services, represent a concrete illustration of how borders and territories across Canadian rural and semi-rural regions are constructed. Finally, Natalia Lara Díaz-Berrio (Chapter 7) uses photography and testimonials to explore the interface between public and private domains, looking at the ways in which recent Mexican-Canadians recreate Mexican identities in 21st-century domestic spaces.

Part III, "Building Community," considers strategies that people who were born in Latin America have mobilized to root themselves in Canada and organize themselves for political and artistic ends. Exploring the various ways in which Chilean exiles in Canada "performed" Chilean culture as part of a political practice, as a form of collective therapy, and/or as an affirmation of national identity, Francis Peddie (Chapter 8) argues that the period between 1973 and 1990 represents an important moment in Chile's history. In Chapter 9, drawing on her own theatre experience and that of other immigrant practitioners, Andrea Ávila questions the body of dramatic works in Canada that might be labelled "Latin American" and how a Canadian-Latin American identity is constructed through these theatrical performances, and she demonstrates that the fight for Latin American recognition in Canada is ongoing on account of *latinidad* being defined in non-European terms. In Chapter 10, Ana Chiarelli examines 21st -century short stories by Latino-Canadian writers with a view to understanding how they depict Canadian society. John-Alexander Raimondo (Chapter 11) rounds out this section of the book, using a combination of archival and oral history methods to investigate how two Latino newspapers circulating in Hamilton, the Niagara Region, and the Greater Toronto Area between 2003 and 2013 have contributed to community building.

In the fourth and final part of the book, entitled "Hall of Mirrors," we see how cultural production, and more specifically the immersive experiences of creation, of celebration and of inhabiting different spaces, facilitate the dissolution of distances otherwise separating Canada and Latin America. In Chapter 12, Victoria F. Wolff examines how the award-winning music education program that José Antonio Abreu founded in 1975 in Venezuela was introduced to Canada and adapted to fill an important sociocultural gap. In Chapter 13, drawing on her experiences of spending thirteen years in Mexico City and of living in a bicultural household, Dianne Pearce reflects on her own artistic production as a space where languages, Mexican fiestas, and other popular celebrations come together to encourage audience participation and foster conviviality in the Canadian art circuit. In the closing chapter (Chapter 14), Nuria Carton de Grammont explores the possibilities that artist-in-residence programs present in terms of challenging narrow and one-dimensional understandings of national imaginaries and deconstructing cultural stereotypes that inform Canada-Mexico relations through the arts. Together, the four parts of this book demonstrate that, for over 100 years, Latin American poetics and traditions have been integral to cultural production in Canada.

Analysis premised on the significance of chronology opens pathways for identifying patterns of continuity and change and for tracing novel cultural production coming out of Canada. Latin America in Canada lends itself well to discussions organized around a particular theme or analytic framework. To illustrate this point, we offer four examples of how to go about reading the chapters in ways that help advance the study of the cultural history of Canadian-Latin American relations using a wide range of sources. The first analytical framework centres on the word. Essays by De Luna, Chiarelli and Raimondo invite readers to consider the written text as a doorway into understanding how Latin America, when appreciated as a shorthand for particular ways of being and doing, becomes part of Canadian society thanks to creators and consumers of cultural products. In the second framework, the *image* proves central to knowledge production; essays by Dyck, Lara and Pearce offer entryways into understanding images as powerful sites of cognitive activity. Third, authors such as De Trenqualye, Ávila and Carton de Grammont examine everyday rituals and practices that are embedded in cultural production, raising awareness of the importance of remaining alert to performative (i.e. embodied) dimensions of experience that might not be immediately obvious. Finally, the authors in this volume collectively demonstrate how image, word and sounds at the heart of everyday life are interdependent and therefore reflect a connectedness that is fundamental to understanding visual culture not in relation to objects but, rather, in relation to actions that serve a particular goal, that elicit positive and/or negative responses, and that are always, albeit to varying degrees, transformational in nature. These four frameworks offer methodological avenues for developing a history of Canadian-Latin American relations that are mediated by images, words and performance.[29]

Joaquín Torres-García's *América Invertida* challenged conventional understandings of the place of the global and colonized south in relation to the colonizing power of the north (Fig. 1). The way Canada related to and engaged with Latin America over the time period covered in this book obeyed a logic that was established long before its own birth in 1867 as a dominion of Great Britain and that was also integral to that birth. Inasmuch as the ability to make history beyond national borders or continental land masses is not uniquely the prerogative of imperial powers, Latin America can lay claim to a history where notions of north and south dissolve. *Latin America Made in Canada* positions the pursuits of actively engaged men and women in Canada as sites of cultural production that fill an important gap in the history of Canadian-Latin American relations. Furthermore, each of the volume's case studies offers methodological models that are relevant to expanding this historical repertoire. Ultimately, this collection invites readers to explore a story set on Canadian soil that has yet to be told.

Part 1
Trans-American
Pathways of Neocolonialism

Chapter 1

Representations of Brazil in Canadian Newspapers at the Turn of the Twentieth Century

Rosana Barbosa

Introduction

Canadian representations of Brazil in newspapers at the turn of the twentieth century were mostly non-existent except on two occasions. These exceptions came in 1896, when the state government of São Paulo organized an immigration scheme in Montreal; and in the first couple of years of the twentieth century, when a group of financiers began investing in Brazil, giving rise to the Brazilian Traction, Light and Power Company. In 1896, Brazil was bluntly portrayed as inherently inferior to Canada and an unsuitable place for the adaptation of Canadian and Northern immigrants. In the latter case, it seemed that Brazil was beginning to be seen in a more positive light. Instead of words such as "unhealthy" or "unsuitable," this country - especially the São Paulo region - was portrayed as "civilized" and "prosperous." The study of these two moments of Canada representing Brazil shows that the country would be portrayed in a less negative light as long as it supported a profitable relationship, with Canada as an outside investor, in a situation that was historically common in that it was defined as a *superior* country investing in a *less developed* one. Canada - being a white Dominion in the British Empire - would *naturally* accept this role as Brazil was, until WWI, part of the informal British Empire.[1]

Yet a focus on financial investment alone is not enough to comprehend the apparent shift in the way Brazil was represented on the two occasions. It is also necessary to look at the racialized European view of the world,[2] which emphasized Brazil's inferiority due to its mixed-race population. Thus, it was inconceivable that Brazil would try to incite Canadians to immigrate there, or as the *Star* stated, "astonishing that the Government of Brazil should have such a low opinion of the desirability of Canada as a place of residence as to hope to attract Canadians to their country."[3] Still, when it came to investments, it was not necessary to reinforce Brazil's supposed inferiority, because that was implicit in the context of colonialism, in which whites dominated non-whites.[4]

15

1896: Brazil as an unhealthy country

In March 1896, the government of the State of São Paulo hired an Italian steamship company - Angelo Fiorita & Co. from Genoa - to recruit and transport European immigrants to Brazil, specifically to that State, due to its booming coffee economy.[5] The contract, signed by both parties, specified a total of 45,000 Europeans, but it also innovated by including Canadians as prospective immigrants, with the objective of recruiting 10,000 Canadians from Montreal in the summer and from Halifax in the winter.[6] Campaigns such as this one had been common in Brazil since the abolition of the slave trade in 1850 and the end of slavery in 1888. The 1896 campaign in Montreal was the first attempt to engage Canadians (and/or Europeans living in Canada) in immigration to Brazil, and almost 500 individuals boarded the steamship *Moravia* sailing for São Paulo on 14 September of that year.[7] One consequence of this immigration episode was the media reaction in Canada, as it was the first time Brazil had received massive news coverage.

The journalistic reaction was quite marked in Ontario and Quebec, with major newspapers in Ottawa, Montreal, and Toronto covering it extensively both in English and in French. The objective was to warn prospective immigrants not to go to Brazil.[8] Yet this response was an intensely negative one in which that South American country was dismissed as unhealthy and totally unsuited for people of the northern climates. The notion that Brazil was unhealthy began with a letter from the British consul in Rio de Janeiro, George Wagstaff, to a prospective immigrant, Vander Haeghe, who had written to the consul asking his opinion about the scheme. Wagstaff replied negatively, explaining that the immigration agents were "attempting to exploit ignorant agricultural labourers" and that the potential emigrants should be discouraged from leaving for Brazil because of the "illusory and misleading" offers of those organizing the scheme. In addition, he mentioned tropical diseases, such as "foot diseases, different fevers, yellow included, and other maladies indigenous to this tropical region," and commented that the men "would likewise fail disastrously in bettering their lot by coming to Brazil."[9]

Excerpts from this letter were published by several newspapers and taken out of context. For example, *La Presse* had a dramatic headline, "La fièvre jaune et autres calamités les attendent."[10] The *Star* added "that the country where they are going to is entirely unfit for any English man to live in, and that if they were not stricken down by fever they could hardly earn enough to feed themselves."[11] About a month later, it returned to this theme: "It is almost inconceivable that any of our people should desire to emigrate to a country entirely unknown to them, and which they have been assured is unfit in climate and labour for those born in a northern zone."[12]

The notion of the unsuitability of Brazil for English or Northern people had no basis in reality since Brazil, throughout the nineteenth century, had received significant numbers of immigrants from northern Europe.[13] Moreover, although it was not the norm in the state of São Paulo, there were extensive plantations owned by Europeans such as the one owned by English individuals, the Fazenda Dumont, and others owned by the German-born Francisco Schmidt, who had arrived in Brazil as a child in 1856. All of these controlled large plantations - Fazenda Dumont had four million coffee trees and Schmidt had six million coffee trees on his plantations. In addition, the plantations employed thousands of Brazilians and immigrants.[14] Indeed, the British presence in the country dated back to 1808, when the Portuguese royal family had settled in Rio de Janeiro. At that time, several British investors had established themselves in Brazil, where they took advantage of the end of the colonial monopoly and became very influential in the country.[15] Therefore, there were significant numbers of northern Europeans living and profiting in Brazil during the nineteenth century. To be sure, the conditions on the coffee plantations could be difficult, and in that regard the concerns about the scheme had some legitimacy; yet what was presented in the newspapers was an over-generalization of conditions in Brazil, reinforced by the racial assumptions of the time. As a result of this media campaign, many prospective immigrants gave up on the idea of going to Brazil. The *Ottawa Journal* asserted, "[A]s a result fully one-half of them left the ship or did not go on board. Instead of the 1,000 or so who were to sail, probably not more than half remained on board."[16] The *Globe* stated, "The steamer *Moravia* sailed from Montreal to Brazil, carrying about 300 immigrants. The warnings of the officials influenced nearly half of those who intended to go, and they left the vessel before she sailed."[17]

The negative representations continued after the *Moravia* had set sail for South America. The fear now was that a similar campaign would be repeated. A couple of days after the immigrants departed for Brazil, the *Montreal Gazette* published a short article entitled "Brazil is Unhealthy." This was based on an interview with Donald Burns, an animal importer from New York who was participating in an exhibition in Montreal. Burns had spent time in the Amazon and owned a Brazilian snake, a tree boa:

"Why Brazil is altogether unfit for habitation by Northern people," he said. "I have seen Canadians down there; poor, emaciated creatures they were. In the first place they cannot get food; it is not in the country. Fever and the heat soon take the life out of them." Mr Burns added that quinine and whiskey was his diet when on the Amazon. "I know one Canadian woman there, however," said Mr Burns, "who is doing immensely well. She is a French-Canadian, and as sharp as a steel trap; she returns home to Montreal occasionally. She and her husband go up the Amazon in boats, peddling to the natives, taking rubber and other products in exchange, which they dispose of in the market at a good profit. They are making money."[18]

Although the story of the successful French-Canadian woman in Brazil was mentioned, there was no further information about her, and the focus of the article was on the unhealthy nature of Brazil. Moreover, the *Gazette* made no distinction between the Amazon and São Paulo, although the two regions are about four thousand kilometers apart. Then, a few days later, on September 26, the *Globe* published a long article entitled "Emigration to Brazil: A poor place for Canadians to seek fortune."[19] On October 13, the *Toronto Star* stated that "Brazil has evidently not given up the idea of obtaining further ship-loads of Canadians to work on her plantations." The *Star* harshly criticized the government of Brazil for insisting on this immigration scheme, its tone reeking of condescension as it underlined the perceived inferiority of Brazil.[20]

A few weeks later, on 14 December, a correspondent by the name of Allan Maclean wrote from Argentina to the editor of the *Globe* to give some more details about the immigration scheme. Maclean again emphasized the negative image of Brazil. It is unclear who he was and what he was doing in Buenos Aires, although it is apparent that he was a British citizen. He stated, "As far as I can learn the Canadian papers seem to have laid particular stress upon the unhealthfulness of the country in warning intending emigrants, but that is not the worst feature of the matter. It must be remembered that outside of Rio Janeiro itself, there is in Brazil no such thing as enforcement of law, or even handed justice as we understand these matters, for government is simply carried on by a minority for their own benefit."[21] Maclean did not deny that some could reap profits in Brazil, but asserted that within South America, this country was not the best choice for immigrants: "It is quite possible that some Canadians by the exercise of energy and industry might make fortunes in Brazil, as other English speaking people have done, but I do not think that they are more likely to do so here than in Canada by the exercise of the same virtues, without the risks of health and life they would incur in Brazil through fever, revolution and the evils arising from a Government so vicious that British citizens who have not been in South America can scarcely realize how bad it is." He continued by making a distinction between Brazil and other South American countries that had large proportions of European descendants: "If Canadians must emigrate to South America they would be wiser to come to Argentina or Chile, which have the nearest approach to decent government that can be found in South America. But I would not advise anyone to come to South America to settle. The drawbacks are, by far, greater than the advantages."[22]

It is interesting that Maclean mentioned the dangers of "revolution" and "vicious government" since, within Latin America, Brazil had exceptionally stable governance in the nineteenth century. Dom Pedro II was in power from 1841 to 1889 and has been considered by many historians to be a wise and fair leader.[23] It is true that in 1889, a coup had overthrown the monarchy, but it was mostly a peaceful transition.[24] Perhaps the only event that could have raised comments about political violence in Brazil would be the War of Canudos, from November 1896 to October 1897, but this was a localized conflict fought in the interior of the state of Bahia. In addition, his reference to "decent" government reflected an attitude of racialized arrogance. Once again, the racial inferiority of Brazil was implied when Maclean considered Argentina and Chile better settlement options in South America.

As already noted, the representations of Brazil in newspapers did have an impact on discouraging some from emigrating, but they failed to change the mind of almost 500 individuals. The reality was that many were concerned about their situation in Canada, as most were impoverished people.[25] That aspect was not highlighted by the newspapers, although a couple of articles did state that the campaign had been successful because of the social conditions of many Montrealers. For instance, the *Montreal Daily Herald* mentioned that the immigrants who went to Brazil were "poverty stricken."[26] Government officials also commented on the poverty of those who agreed to go to Brazil.[27] Finally, William Darlington, the President of the Canadian Order of United Workmen, while accepting the stereotypical view of Brazil, wrote a letter pointing out that it was "an unfortunate state of affairs when hundreds of our citizens are willing to risk everything for what appears to be a vague and dangerous chance of a living in a foreign and reputed to be fever-stricken land."[28] Overall, however, the difficult situation in Montreal was not highlighted, since the intention of most writers and editorialists was to discourage emigration to Brazil, and not to improve the living conditions of the destitute population of Montreal.

Finally, it is important to note that although this reaction was embedded within racial European views, it was specifically a Canadian reaction, associated with a view of Brazil as a major competitor for immigrants. In the nineteenth century, Brazil and Canada were competing with the United States and Argentina, which were the first two choices for immigrants in the Americas.[29] An article in the Star clearly shows this preoccupation. In regard to Argentina, it stated, "Argentina still continues to attract emigrants by the ship-load, while the people we need for our mines and farms stay away from Canada." When mentioning Brazil, the article alluded to the *Moravia* episode: "Not only does Brazil attract more emigrants than Canada, but she even comes here and coaxes away our people, who are unfitted for both the climate and surroundings which they will find in the Southern Hemisphere."[30] Thus, racialized condescension and Canadian self-interest formed a powerful combination.

Early 1900s: Brazil comparable to the most civilized European countries
Just a few years after the migration episode, the representations of Brazil in Canadian newspapers took an abrupt turn. The intention now was to encourage Canadians to invest in that South American country, and the idea being portrayed was a positive one. For example, on 9 February 1901, the *Globe* published a large front-page article describing the prosperity of the city of Belém, in the state of Pará, at the mouth of the Amazon River. As the first paragraph stated, "Pará, the Queen city of the Amazon valley, situated as it is near the mouth of the river, has a great future before it. Its progress during the last few years has been immense. The rise in the price of rubber and the great demand for it, especially Pará rubber, the product of the Amazon valley, which is the best, being superior to any other kind in the world." The article continued by describing the city in extremely positive terms. For instance, when describing the main downtown square, it asserted:

> There are crowds of people moving about, passing up and down, tram cars loaded with passengers, cabs flying about, bicycles flitting here and there. The cafes and merry-go-rounds and music and crowds of people seated at numbers of little tables on the sidewalks outside and inside the cafes, the clink of the ice and glasses, the busy pleasant hum of conversation, the laughter, the music, the light costumes of the promenaders, all combined to give a delightful and enchanting effect.[31]

It is unclear from the context just what the objective of the article was. It had been written by a correspondent in the Brazilian city itself, and it may have been intended to popularize rubber from Pará, as Canadian companies were using it for the making of shoes. It was common to find advertisements for shoes made of Pará rubber: for instance, the Canadian rubber company of Montreal published a large notice on 11 November 1903 stating that it imported "the finest crude rubber in the world from Pará, Brazil."[32] On another occasion, Granby Buckled Overshoes also advertised that they used rubber from Pará, Brazil, and that because of its quality, "Granby Rubbers have the Canadian people by the heels - so to speak."[33] What is certain is that in the early twentieth century, the state of Pará (as well as that of Amazonas) was experiencing a booming economy, and Belém was the main port for exporting rubber to the world. Thus, there were large investments in the region, although evidence is lacking as to whether there was any direct Canadian investment there. This thriving economy lasted until about 1920, when rubber began to be produced on a large scale in Asia, taking over the world market.[34] Still, even at this time of decline, the region retained a major investment, when Henry Ford decided to found a settlement in the state of Pará in order to produce rubber for his automobile industry.[35]

The change in Canadian attitude at the turn of the twentieth century was further evidenced when Canadian investors established a company in São Paulo which would become the giant Brazilian Traction, Light and Power Company (renamed twice: in 1969, to Brascan, and in 2005, to Brookfield Asset Management). With its head office in Toronto, the company was founded in 1899, its major objective being to invest in public transportation, electric-generation plants, and telephone companies in Brazil's two largest cities, São Paulo and Rio de Janeiro. Accordingly, the associated image needed to be one of security and prosperity in order to attract investors.[36] The media attention was centred primarily in Ontario - the financial heart of Canada and location of the company's headquarters. There, newspapers were careful to give reassurance to potential investors as to the profitability of the company. The reassurance was undoubtedly necessary in order to convince Canadians to invest in a faraway, unknown country which had been portrayed so recently as inferior to Canada. For instance, a prospective investor, C. J. Holman, demonstrated this need for reassurance in a letter to one of the directors of the company, Alexander Mackenzie. He wrote, "I am poorly conditioned to form an accurate estimate of the situation and prospects at Rio de Janeiro. [...] Do you think the Rio de Janeiro affair promises well? I have heard that the country round Rio de Janeiro is a most God-forsaken one, and yet I cannot understand if that were the case, how such a large city exists there."[37]

In order to address this concern based on unfamiliarity, the *Globe* described the city of São Paulo - where the investment began - as "one of the most important centers in Brazil with 202,000 population, splendid public buildings and varied industries."[38] A day later, the *Star* also focused on Brazil. This time there were some traces of the stereotyped view (notably in the headline: "Tell Affairs in Brazil - That Country Very Much Behind the Times"), but the article itself leaned further towards a favourable view. It focused in part on the views of the new American Consul in Toronto, Edwin Norton Gunsaulus, who had previously served in Pernambuco, in the northeast of Brazil. Although Gunsaulus considered the northeast "backwards," the article devoted more of its attention to a positive depiction of the possibility of developing trade. Moreover, it asserted that in comparison to the other republics in the region, Brazil was more stable. Finally, the article ended with the fact that there was "quite a large English colony in Brazil and English capital probably leads in banking, railroads, and cable lines."[39] A couple of months later, the positive image also prevailed. This time, an article in the *Globe* compared the state of São Paulo with Ontario: "The state of São Paulo, which, as we have said, is to Brazil what Ontario is here." The image portrayed of Brazil as a whole was also a positive one: "Brazil is quite as unlikely to suffer from any disturbance of law and order as any of the most civilized countries in Europe, and capital is as safe and the rights of property as thoroughly respected there as anywhere in the world. The constitution expressly protects the persons, rights and properties of foreigners."[40]

On another occasion, the newspaper tried to build the confidence of investors with a two-page article: "It is a far cry from Toronto to São Paulo, and to get there comfortably one must cross the Atlantic twice, as the journey by the regular steamship lines to Great Britain and thence to Brazil is much to be preferred to the uncertain direct connections from New York. When one gets there one finds a large, handsome and prosperous city, somewhat larger than Toronto, but resembling Toronto in many ways."[41] The following month, the *Star* stated that after a meeting in Toronto, it was decided that the capital invested in the São Paulo company was to be increased "by a million-five per cent."[42] A day later, the *Globe* acknowledged a special meeting of the directors, highlighting the company's "splendid" progress and its "most satisfactory growth [...] and the gratifying results of its operations in São Paulo."[43] This reassurance continued later in 1902 and beyond. For instance, the *Star* in October 1902 published an article entitled "São Paulo Revenue Soaring Rapidly.[44] A year later, the same newspaper announced the establishment of the Rio Company, stating that capitalists had "combined in the largest project ever undertaken by Canadians outside of Canada." It concluded by clearly affirming the certainty of a profitable result: "The interest on the bonds at 5 per cent would equal $1,250,000, which would leave $2,852,500 surplus for stocks."[45]

The *Globe* would also provide positive representations of Brazil on issues that were not directly related to financial considerations but would portray Brazil in a positive light and thus, by implication, as a safe place for investment. For instance, in July 1902, the newspaper turned its attention to coffee due to the visit of a coffee planter of Dutch origin from Santos, São Paulo, a Mr C.H. Van der Wens. This article is especially interesting in that the same newspaper that had disparaged Brazil as a destination for Northern immigrants was now giving space to the statement of this individual, who declared, "Brazil offers the greatest opportunities for the emigrant of any country in the world."[46] A few weeks later, Brazil once more received attention from the *Globe*. The occasion now was the upcoming inauguration of the elected president, "Dr Francisco de Paula Rodrigues Alves," who was chosen for the newspaper's "Men of the Day" feature, complete with significant details about his background, education, and political experience.[47] A few days later, the same newspaper gave details of Alves's inauguration in a new article entitled "BRAZIL'S GOVERNMENT. Brilliant Festivals at the Inauguration. An Imposing Procession and a Ball, in Which Officers of Foreign Warships Joined."[48] It is worth mentioning that Rodrigues Alves was a major supporter of the Traction, Light and Power Company and of its expansion in Rio de Janeiro.[49] Therefore, the implied objective of the *Globe* was, once again, to favour an important group of North American investors. In fact, this more positive representation of Brazil did achieve its purpose, as it boosted investment and guaranteed the profitable success of the company. Brazilian Traction remained in Brazil until the late 1970s, providing significant parts of the country with transportation, electricity, and telephone services.[50]

Conclusion

One interpretation of the two episodes discussed above would be that financial interests had pushed successfully for a shift in how Brazil was seen in Canada in the early twentieth century. The crucial context, however, was that the positive view was directly intended to contribute to generating profits and - as was frequently the case in many global regions under the influence of the British Empire - that the search for successful investments in no way precluded the idea that non-Europeans were inherently inferior. Examples of this compatibility are widespread and can be exemplified in a Canadian context in the British Caribbean, where Canadians would see their role as "the Big White Brother" who would protect the "empire's darker subjects."[51] This paternalistic approach was a product of the racial divisions of the European colonial dominance of the world and the directions that investments took in countries populated in great part by non-whites.[52] In the early twentieth century, Europeans, especially Anglo-Saxons, pervasively considered Brazilians - and Latin Americans in general - as inferior, or "ineligible for membership in the White men's club" due to their Spanish/Portuguese ancestry and their mixed-race population.[53] In this context, the two examples of Canadian representations described in this chapter show that there was no real shift, but, in fact, a continuation of the views portrayed during the immigration episode of 1896.

Chapter 2

Depictions of Authenticity and Risk in Canadian Tourism Representations of Latin America

Madeleine de Trenqualye

Introduction

Travel advertisements and brochures have played a critical role in how Canadian audiences come to imagine and understand particular people, cultures, and countries. Without having to go abroad, Canadians become virtual tourists, imagining other cultures through a lens mediated by advertisements, websites, and travel brochures, as well as more traditional sources of knowledge such as films, newspapers, museum exhibits, and history books. Previous critiques of tourism promotion have drawn on Edward Said's work in calling attention to how power relations between tourists and hosts are reflected, constructed, and reinforced through tourism advertisements.[1] This prior research has highlighted the tendency of advertisements to (a) cast foreign hosts exclusively within a "hotel context" or service capacity as entertainers, vendors, or servers;[2] (b) erase signs of the local presence in order to construct visions of "untouched paradise" that exist solely for the benefit of the potential tourist;[3] and (c) omit evidence of poverty or internal political conflicts that may plague the destinations in question.[4]

While this research has been critical in revealing the ways in which travel advertisements function as discursive sites for the articulation of ideas about Others, the growth in popularity of new forms of tourism, spearheaded by Canadian companies such as G Adventures (formerly Gap Adventures)[5] shifted the way Latin American places and peoples were represented in tourism advertising. This chapter considers how Latin America is portrayed in Canadian tourism representations by analyzing promotional materials from 2010 found in a specific Canadian context: a student travel agency. Contrary to agencies selling all-inclusive resort packages for tourists seeking escape to a paradise of sandy white beaches, upscale hotels, and golf courses, the brochures found in the Travel Cuts agency in the early 2010s (Fig. 1) marketed an "off-the-beaten-track" experience that includes an intimate and extended encounter with local cultures. I analyze three key elements in the discourse of these tourism brochures that have not received significant attention in tourism marketing research: (a) an emphasis on immersion into local cultures rather than controlled interactions in which tourists will merely be served by foreign hosts; (b) the marketing of certain regions as "challenging" by calling attention to factors that have long been avoided by the tourism industry, including poverty levels, a lack of access to modern amenities, and recent histories of war and political violence; and (c) an increased value placed on the notion of authentic and traditional Otherness together with a call to experience and help preserve this authenticity before it disappears or is corrupted.

This style of tourism (sometimes called community tourism, cultural tourism, ecotourism, or sustainable tourism) is relatively small in Canada compared to all-inclusive resort vacations, which make up a large percentage of Canadian tourism to Latin America, particularly in coastal Mexico, Cuba, and the Dominican Republic. However, the rate at which it is growing and the promises it makes about its capacity to preserve fragile cultures make it worthy of attention. Its promotional materials reflect a concern about the negative impact of mass tourism and globalization on local cultures, yet include promises about facilitating access to cultures whose surfaces have not yet been scratched. Paradoxically, in their attempts to portray the "real" Latin America, they offer a highly-edited vision of Latin American cultures which erases signs of modern infrastructure and industrial development, and sometimes masks the complex relationships

Figure 1. Top left: Gap Adventures brochure 2010; Gap Adventures brochure 2011; Intrepid Latin America brochure 2010; Intrepid Latin America brochure 2014. Reprinted with permission from G Adventures and Intrepid.

26

between local cultures and the global economy. At times, these Canadian-made or Canadian-circulated representations of Latin America are also at odds with the branding efforts of Latin American tourism boards.

This chapter explores how Latin America is packaged and circulated within a Canadian tourism context. It contributes to an understanding of how Latin America is made visible in Canada by offering insight into a critical piece of the representational framework: tourism marketing. This study contributes to the literature on tourism representations by highlighting new elements in tourism marketing that have received relatively little attention: an emphasis on in-depth immersion into local cultures, the marketing of regions as "challenging," and a call not only to experience but also to help preserve vulnerable cultures by participating in socially conscious travel practices. This chapter's attention to these themes will benefit scholars interested in other representational tools that portray Latin America to Canadians, including film, art exhibits, and media depictions.

Sources and methodology

This is an exploratory study, influenced by semiotic theory, that draws on a wide range of literature spanning the disciplines of anthropology, sociology, and marketing. As part of this study, I interviewed representatives from the Mexico Tourism Board in Vancouver,[6] the account director for the Canadian communications firm responsible for promoting Dominican Republic tourism to the Canadian market,[7] and a Chief Experience Officer at G Adventures in Vancouver, BC.[8] In addition, I analyzed the G Adventures and Travel Cuts websites, the G Adventures 2010 South and Central America brochure, and the 2010 and 2014 Intrepid Latin America brochures[9] (the only two brochures focusing exclusively on Latin America found in a Montreal, QC, Travel Cuts). The brochures and websites were studied to find recurrent themes and visual and literary tropes used to promote Latin America. I draw on communications scholar Arthur Asa Berger's framework for analyzing and decoding commercial texts. Berger approaches advertisements by considering what language and rhetorical devices are used, who the target audience is, what role the product being advertised plays in society, and what values are represented. He encourages the viewer to pay attention to how people are presented and to consider fashion, props, body language, age, race, signs of occupation, educational level, gender relations, and objects in the background. This approach offers a holistic but culturally subjective framework for uncovering the meaning and symbolism of images and text.[10]

In examining Canadian tourism representations of Latin America, I considered the following questions: What words, motifs, and rhetorical devices are used to describe Latin America? What sights and activities are offered up for the potential tourist to see, experience, consume, or photograph? How are relationships or interactions between locals and tourists depicted? What buildings, houses, or objects appear? How is nature, civilization, or modernity portrayed? Perhaps most importantly, who and what has been left out of the promotional material? As William O'Barr emphasizes, the viewer is the "ultimate author of the meaning of an ad."[11] Each viewer interprets an advertisement or brochure in a subjective and culturally bound framework. However, the images in tourism brochures do not exist in a vacuum - they refer and respond to widely circulating symbols and ideologies within Canadian culture. By drawing on or responding to familiar themes about Latin America, advertisements reinforce or challenge existing stereotypes.

Canadian tourism to Latin America

By the early 2010s, over four million Canadians were travelling to Latin America annually. Since 2000, three Latin American countries - Mexico, Cuba, and the Dominican Republic - have consistently been among the top 10 most visited international destinations for Canadians, surpassing European destinations such as France, Italy, and Germany in popularity.[12] All-inclusive package vacations including airfare, hotels, and meals represent a large portion of those visits, attracting tourists lured by sun, accessibility, and low prices - particularly during Canada's winter months. Despite the popularity of all-inclusive vacations, cultural and experiential tourism is growing - especially among university-educated travellers, younger travellers, and solo travellers.[13] A 2014 Canadian Tourism Commission report states that changing social norms in Canada led to "an increased desire to connect with other people and share experiences. Travellers are looking for an authentic experience, and contributing to the local economy and learning about their local surroundings are ways to do that."[14] Gwen Dianne Reimer's study of Canadian tour operators suggested Canadians have a greater willingness than Americans to go to non-English- or non-French-speaking destinations and more interest in in-depth cultural immersion and an "off-the-beaten-track" experience.[15]

Reimer suggested Canada's culture of multiculturalism makes Canadians more open to experiencing cultural difference on their travels.

Representatives from the Mexico Tourism Board in Canada also suggest that Canadians have different travel patterns from Americans and require different marketing strategies. Their research suggests that, while US tourists are primarily interested in sun, sea, sand, and relaxation (a "quick fix,"[16] as one tourism board representative noted), Canadians are more interested in adventure tourism and immersive cultural and nature-based experiences. According to one of their recent reports, "the Canadian market is looking for new experiences involving attractions different than just Sun & Beach such as culture, history, eco-tourism and adventure.... Savvy Canadians are interested in exploring places that can enrich their knowledge of the authenticity of culture in the World."[17] Correspondingly, marketing campaigns designed for Canadian audiences rely more on nature-based and cultural themes. The Mexico Tourism Board's promotional efforts over the past decade have achieved favourable results in Canada: the volume of Canadian tourists more than doubled from 2009 to 2012, with over 1.6 million Canadians travelling to Mexico in 2012. In 2014, Canadians were the second largest group of inbound international tourists to Mexico, following tourists from the United States.[18] Even the Dominican Republic, traditionally a classic sun-and-sand getaway for more than 800,000 Canadian visitors annually, changed its Canadian marketing strategy in 2013 to emphasize what lies beyond the resort, highlighting the island's culture and history.[19]

G Adventures: A Canadian tourism trendsetter in Latin America and the marketing of anti-tourism tourism

Ira Silver's definition of "alternative tourism" offers a fitting characterization of the way G Adventures, Intrepid, and Travel Cuts market Latin America. Silver wrote that alternative travellers define themselves in opposition to mass tourists, believe mass tourism has a negative impact on the Global South, and seek an "authenticity that takes them off the beaten track."[20] He claimed that, "generally, there is no such thing as an advertisement or a brochure for alternative travel, because this type of tourism is premised largely on anti-commercialism."[21] However, the anti-tourist discourse is an integral theme in the marketing campaigns of G Adventures, which earned upwards of $170 million in sales in 2013 and catered to over 100,000 clients worldwide.[22] One example of this new branding approach can be seen in their 2010 South and Central America brochure:

Gap Adventures offers holidays for the traveler seeking an authentic experience. We intend to show you the "real" world. Although we could easily shield you from the less-westernized areas of a country, we choose not to, as it would be an injustice to you and the communities we visit. On occasion, you may not receive the services and standards you are accustomed to at home, however, these lesser visited areas are where you will find the most fulfilling experiences. Open your mind and step outside your comfort zone. You will be rewarded with a once in a lifetime, authentic, travel experience.[23]

G Adventures and its main competitor, Intrepid,[24] were part of a growing subset of the tourism industry marketing the idea that authentic experiences can be achieved by rejecting the trappings of mass tourism, sacrificing comfort, and venturing into remote and anti-modern locales. Both companies list sustainability as one of their core values, with G Adventures stating that "preserving cultural heritage and conserving and replenishing the natural environment, while improving the lives of local people, is the essence of our way of traveling."[25]

The "poster boy"[26] for G Adventures was Delfín Pauchi - an Indigenous Ecuadorian from the Pimpilala tribe whose face appeared in every 2010 brochure (including those for Europe, North America and Asia), as well as on giant wall posters in the G Adventures head office in Toronto. The brochure says the G Adventures founder met Pauchi in the jungles of Ecuador and invited him to host small tour groups in his Amazonian village so that travellers from North America could "experience daily life in the jungle with his family and discover the natural wonders of the Amazon in ways never before imagined."[27] This initial encounter led to the company's first "local living tour" - "Ecuador: Inland and Amazon," which included a homestay in Delfín's village.

The tour to Delfín's community has been offered every month for nearly twenty-five years, during which time G Adventures grew to be the most successful adventure travel company in the world. By 2014, it was considered the industry leader with sales increasing an average of 30% per year.[28] Founder Bruce Poon Tip has been described as "Canada's most successful travel entrepreneur."[29] G Adventures offers trips to over 100 destinations worldwide; boasts partnerships with Air Canada and the Discovery Channel; operates a chain of concept stores in Toronto, Vancouver, Calgary, New York, and Melbourne; runs its own non-profit foundation; hosts a television show for the Outdoor Life Network; and has opened hotels in Ecuador, Peru and Costa Rica. Although the initial market was in Canada, the company has expanded worldwide, and by 2014, over 70% of their business came from outside North America.[30] The company has a strong connection to Latin America. Not only was Latin America host to the company's first tours, but it remained the highest-selling region, with Peru and Galapagos the most popular destinations overall (the company sends over 40,000 travellers to Peru every year alone).[31] After lobbying Peru's Tourism Minister, G Adventures became the first Western tour company granted permission by the Peruvian government to run its own tour operation on the Inca Trail (it did so after finding local operators were failing to deliver a consistent G Adventures-brand experience).[32]

Significantly, Latin America also became the primary site of the company's growing efforts to partner with local NGOs, governments, and international agencies to create new community tourism experiences. In 2013, they announced a $1 million collaboration with the Multilateral Investment Fund and the Inter-American Development Bank to finance and develop a series of community-based tourism programs in Central and South America, including homestays in Guatemala and Nicaragua, a new trek in Peru, and a co-op coffee community partnership in Costa Rica. The company's marketing strategies (which include brochures, their website, social media, event sponsorship, ties with bloggers, and travel

Figure 2. An example of the G Adventures' marketing philosophy: "Engaging customers to a higher purpose" - branding its style of tourism as a vehicle for wealth redistribution, cultural preservation, and environmental sustainability.

guides)[33] emphasized "engaging customers to a higher purpose" - branding its particular style of tourism as a vehicle for wealth redistribution, cultural preservation, and environmental sustainability (Fig. 2).

One of many cultural preservation examples promoted by G Adventures is the company's development of a women's weaving co-op near Cuzco, Peru. The founder recounts his concern about the impact of tourism on the local culture. Peruvians were flocking to cities to cater to the growing tourist traffic (a large portion of whom were G Adventures customers) to find jobs in restaurants and bars while "Peruvian traditions were slowly dying."[34] He describes the establishment of a traditional weaving co-op as an innovative business solution that would allow local women to reclaim an ancient craft and maintain a livelihood, as well as providing his customers with an enriching and authentic cultural experience. The popular Inca Trail tour evolved to incorporate a full-day stop at the weaving co-op for travellers to meet the weavers, learn how to weave, and purchase authentic textiles.

These examples illustrate ways in which the tourist interest in experiencing local culture can have important social, political, and economic impacts on local populations. In the midst of enormous global success, the company's "origin story" with Delfín, framed as a simple, yet culturally sensitive, cross-cultural encounter in the Amazon, helps to anchor the multi-million-dollar company to its grassroots beginnings and encapsulates the company's social-enterprise-branding approach.

An intimate cultural immersion

Homestays in the Ecuadorian Amazon are just one of many experiences that G Adventures and Intrepid offered to cater to the traveller's desire to experience more intimate and up-close encounters with local Latin American cultures. Numerous travel packages offered by both companies include spending a few days in the homes of villagers or farmers, marketed as a chance to gain a rare, first-hand experience of people "whose lives are very different from your own - and who are happy to open a window into a culture that is unique and fascinating."[35] Intrepid's itineraries included visiting open-air markets to "rub shoulders" with natives as they buy and sell flowers, medicinal plants, and handicrafts, or picking up local lingo in the sprawling tobacco fields of Viñales, Cuba, while the G Adventures brochure suggested stopping by a local school to meet children on the plains of Argentina.

Although immersion into local cultures was described as one of the key elements in the travel philosophies of both companies, images in the

2010 brochures avoid showing the interaction between tourist and local, tending instead to use images of locals on their own, removed from the cross-cultural encounter. Alternatively, some brochures feature images of tourists on their own, gazing at natural landscapes or engaged in extreme physical activities. The Intrepid brochures, in particular, feature almost no images of cross-cultural encounters to complement trip itineraries, despite the fact that cross-cultural exchanges are described in almost every trip itinerary. The few exceptions to this rule tend to be images of travellers posing with local children rather than adults. This omission of the tourist encounter has the effect of representing local cultures as sealed worlds of unmodified culture rather than spaces of cross-cultural exchange and foreign influence. These depictions also permit viewers to imagine their own, unique interactions with local cultures, while masking those of previous tourists.

The G Adventures country profiles: Negotiating national stereotypes

In addition to travel itineraries, the G Adventures website offered short profiles of each of its national destinations, aiming to seduce audiences with details about the country's natural and cultural highlights and promising a variety of unique sensory pleasures particular to each nation (Fig. 3). Website visitors could browse through a hundred or so different country profiles from all seven continents, consuming concise characterizations of the landscape and its people. While the profiles often subvert familiar stereotypes, they are ultimately tasked with boiling down a country's essence and its tourist appeal to one short paragraph and accompanying image. In this respect, the country profiles offer a fascinating case study in how the tourism industry must negotiate contrasting ideas about other places and populations. In some cases, positive or nostalgic stereotypes are invoked (Germany is described as "the Europe of postcards and history books [...] fairy-tale landscapes sprinkled with medieval castles," while France is "dripping with romance and bucolic charm"); in others, the profiles confront and reject national stereotypes directly. A viewer who clicked on Canada's profile, for example, was told that "behind the natural stereotype, Canada is young, modern, and sophisticated, with cities that have absorbed the best of the myriad cultures that make up one of the most vibrant multicultural societies on earth," while the reader of the US country profile is warned that "as soon as you try to pigeonhole it, you are blindsided with the sublime, the ridiculous, or both simultaneously."[36]

BRAZIL TRAVEL AND DESTINATION GUIDE

SOUTH AMERICA

Sex, dancing and partying. It seems the Brazilians have made a science of all that is fun in life. The world champions of hedonism were no doubt aided by a lush land and steamy climate, but still there is something different about Brazilians. For one, they are the most diverse country in Latin America, not to mention the continent's only former Portuguese colony. One of the largest countries in the world, Brazil certainly has plenty to see the Amazon and Iguaçu falls come to mind—but then anything it's the Brazilian passion for life, epitomised in Rio's Carnival celebrations, that will make you fall in love and want to return again.

If adventure on the high seas is what you are looking for, visit our Brazil Tall Ship Sailing page for interactive route maps, photographs and details about our sailing tours in Brazil.

Highlights
> Tall Ship Sailing
> Pantanal
> Iguassu Falls
> Rio de Janeiro
> Manaus

TRAVEL GUIDE FOR BRAZIL

COLOMBIA TRAVEL AND DESTINATION GUIDE

SOUTH AMERICA

If there were ever a country that suffered from a case of seriously bad press, it's Colombia. It's not well known by travellers, so the border feels like crossing one of the last frontiers of travel. Colombia is ripe for discovery, and there is a little of everything: green valleys, golden beaches and snow-capped mountains, colonial fortresses and Bogotá's hip-attic energy ... everything it seems, except tourists. From intellectual Medellín to Cali's salsa clubs, birthplace of both humble and fabled Gabriel García Márquez, Colombia is musical and literary in equal measures. Welcoming and intelligent, the spicy, fun-loving Colombians too may surprise you. And while it is true that travel in Colombia demands some extra awareness, care and preparation, the extra energy is rewarded a hundredfold.

Highlights
> Santa Marta
> Isla de Rosario
> San Agustín
> Providencia and San Andres Islands
> Cartagena

TRAVEL GUIDE FOR COLOMBIA

VENEZUELA TRAVEL AND DESTINATION GUIDE

SOUTH AMERICA

A land as stunning as its people, contemporary Venezuela's oil has turned it into one of the wealthiest nations in South America. Yet deep in the countryside, people still live traditional lives. The sandy, uninhabited islands of Los Roques, just north of modern Caracas, epitomise the Caribbean face of Venezuela, while farther south, the country goes from marvel to marvel. Canaima National Park, in an area of colossal sandstone mesas called tepuis, is home to the world's highest waterfall, Angel Falls - 16 times the height of Niagara. Continue south and you reach the Venezuelan Amazon, where stone-age tribes still live their lives largely unchanged since ancient times.

Highlights
> Orinoco Delta
> Ciudad Bolivar
> Angel Falls
> Mochima National Park

TRAVEL GUIDE FOR VENEZUELA

ARGENTINA TRAVEL AND DESTINATION GUIDE

SOUTH AMERICA

It has become cliché to say that Argentina is as much European as it is Latin; yet to arrive in Buenos Aires and discover this is actually true still surprises. Argentina is so much more than this. With the Patagonian Andes as its glacial backbone, it is a land of extreme wilderness, while its vast pampas are still home to roaming gauchos - the original South American cowboys. Had enough of the wild? The birthplace of the tango and the world's 5th largest wine producer has enough high culture to satisfy the most discerning palate, plus a nightlife to match.

Highlights
> Bariloche
> Moreno Glacier
> Iguassu Falls
> Buenos Aires

TRAVEL GUIDE FOR ARGENTINA

NICARAGUA TRAVEL AND DESTINATION GUIDE

CENTRAL AMERICA

It's a pity peace and democracy don't make headlines like revolution and war, because the word overwhelmingly remembers Nicaragua the last time it was in the news, which was decidedly the latter. But no news is good news, and that was 15 years or so news ago. Why Nicaragua? Some might ask. Consider its neighbour to the south, Costa Rica. Not one is saying "Why Costa Rica?" Yet they share much the same geography. Only Nicaragua is cheaper, and bigger. And safer, according to a recent UN survey. It boasts an enormous freshwater lake, with twin volcanoes piercing its centre, and one of Central America's best spoiled colonial cities, Granada, on its shores. And very few tourists. And ... what was the question again?

Highlights
> Granada
> Corn Islands
> León
> Ometepe Island

TRAVEL GUIDE FOR NICARAGUA

BOLIVIA TRAVEL AND DESTINATION GUIDE

SOUTH AMERICA

The poorest country in South America and landlocked in the high Andes, Bolivia is not for the faint of heart. Among its must-see sights number the "world's most dangerous road," and endless desert salt flats; its capital La Paz is the highest in the world. But for the traveller willing to endure a little discomfort Bolivia is a trip back in time. With the most visible indigenous culture south of Guatemala, coca leaves and bowler-sporting indigena are common sights, while its geography is truly extreme: running from the Amazon jungle to the Andes and from the edge of the lowest empire at Lake Titicaca to the edge of the Atacama desert, there is no easy way around.

Highlights
> La Paz
> Potosí
> Sucre
> Salar de Uyuni Salt Flats
> Lake Titicaca

TRAVEL GUIDE FOR BOLIVIA

GUATEMALA TRAVEL AND DESTINATION GUIDE

CENTRAL AMERICA

Smoking volcanoes spin by as a sea of Mayan weaving lurches from one side of the chicken bus to the other. With the Mayan majority on constant display, dramatic geography, and prices a student could love, for some, Guatemala is the quintessential Central American experience. One of its mandatory stops, incredible Antigua Guatemala, was once the capital of an enormous swath of the Americas. Frozen in time for centuries thanks to repeated earthquakes, today it has been impeccably restored in all its rubble and glory ... not to mention it's the best traveller's hub from here to Cusco. From cooler skies to the ruins of Tikal, it's a miracle Guatemala is still off the radar for so many. Let's hope it stays that way.

Highlights
> Chichicastenango
> Río Dulce
> Antigua
> Tikal

TRAVEL GUIDE FOR GUATEMALA

SURINAME TRAVEL AND DESTINATION GUIDE

SOUTH AMERICA

It's all about nature here in Suriname. With most of it's population lying at it's north coast on the Atlantic, the rest of this tiny country is made up of unspoiled rain forest and a host of beautiful sights. With waterfalls, rivers, cliffs, glaciers and an amazing array of flora and fauna, Suriname is a paradise for the adventurous nature lover.

Highlights
> Raleighvallen
> Brownsberg Nature Park
> Central Suriname Nature Reserve

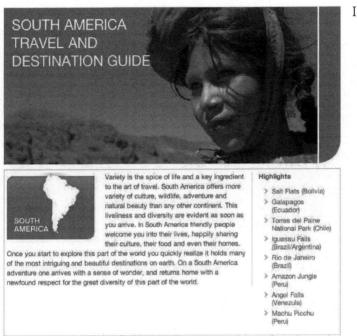

SOUTH AMERICA TRAVEL AND DESTINATION GUIDE

SOUTH AMERICA

Variety is the spice of life and a key ingredient to the art of travel. South America offers more variety of culture, wildlife, adventure and natural beauty than any other continent. This liveliness and diversity are evident as soon as you arrive. In South America friendly people welcome you into their lives, happily sharing their culture, their food and even their homes. Once you start to explore this part of the world you quickly realize it holds many of the most intriguing and beautiful destinations on earth. On a South America adventure one arrives with a sense of wonder, and returns home with a newfound respect for the great diversity of this part of the world.

Highlights

> Salt Flats (Bolivia)
> Galapagos (Ecuador)
> Torres del Paine National Park (Chile)
> Iguassu Falls (Brazil/Argentina)
> Rio de Janeiro (Brazil)
> Amazon Jungle (Peru)
> Angel Falls (Venezuela)
> Machu Picchu (Peru)

Figure 3. Country profiles of G Adventures' nation destinations from their website.

spite of selective attempts to undermine national stereotypes, many of the profiles essentialized national traits. Latin American profiles marketed the attractiveness and personalities of local people to a much greater degree than European ones. Venezuelans were said to be a people as "stunning" as their land, Belizeans were "friendly and easy-going," and Salvadoreans were "unjaded and always quick to make conversation." In some cases, not only was the attractiveness, friendliness, and hospitality of locals highlighted, but also their education or intellect. Colombians were characterized as welcoming, spicy, and fun-loving, but also intelligent, while Costa Ricans were described as friendly and educated. In other instances, the profiles drew from and reinforced long-standing stereotypes, reflecting historical practices of portraying Latin American cultures as exotic and sensuous, as in the characterization of Brazilians as a lascivious and self-indulgent people[37] "Sex, dancing and partying: it seems the Brazilians have made a science of all that is fun in life. The world champions of hedonism were no doubt aided by a lush land and steamy climate, but there is something different about Brazilians."[38]

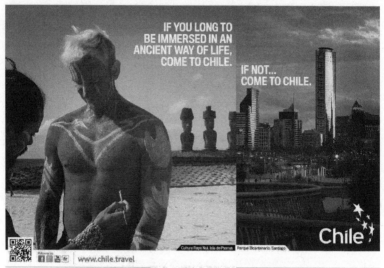

Figure 4. A tourism campaign by Chile's National Tourism Board. Reprinted with permission from the Chile Tourism Board.

While images of local people are used in many of G Adventures' online country profiles, their use was more frequent in Latin American destinations than European ones.[39] This can be seen in the images chosen to complement the written description for each of G Adventures' one hundred plus national destinations appearing on the company's website. The most common images used for South and Central American country profiles are of local people of Indigenous and African descent, often photographed in a rural setting or colourful market scene, closely followed by images of Indigenous culture, art, and architecture (for instance, Mexico is represented by a Meso-American pyramid, Chile by the Moai statues of *Rapa Nui*, and Uruguay by rows of ornately crafted *mate* cups). (Fig. 4) By contrast, only one of the twenty-eight European destinations used a photograph of local people to complement the written description; instead, the most popular visual themes included art and architecture, city squares, and towns.

Table 1. Images Representing Country Profiles in Latin America vs. Europe[40]

South and Central America	29 Country/Regional profiles
Local people	9
Indigenous culture/architecture	6
Natural landscapes	4
Animals	4

Cultural object	2
Beach	1
Colonial architecture	1
Europe	**28 Country/Regional profiles**
Art/Architecture	8
Village/Small town	5
Natural landscape	5
City square	4
City scene	4
Animals	1
Local people	1

Selling risk and challenge in Latin America

Tourism scholar Laurence Wai-Teng Leong once wrote that tourism marketing is similar to international diplomacy in its effort to project "wholesome and 'politically correct' images"[41] and generally omits information about internal political tensions, poverty, or intercultural misunderstandings. Brochures "rarely reveal the endemic tensions and squalid sides of a given country,"[42] he noted. Similarly, Ira Silver observed that, by marketing travel as an escape from the problems of modern life, tourism marketing necessarily portrays destinations as "devoid of problems."[43] However, tourism advertising is not the only medium by which Canadians learn about and come to know Latin America; negative representations of the region (and of certain countries in particular) permeate Canadian media, drawing attention to high levels of drug trafficking, organized crime and violence, human rights abuses, or political unrest. In 2014, the Canadian government advised travellers to exercise a high degree of caution or avoid nonessential travel in certain regions of almost every Latin American country except Argentina, Chile, Cuba, and Uruguay. Reasons for cautioning Canadians included illegal, armed groups and the unpredictable security situation (Colombia); high levels of violent crime or gang-related violence (Ecuador, Belize, Paraguay, the Dominican Republic, El Salvador, Brazil, Costa Rica, Guatemala); armed violence and sexual assault (Nicaragua); illegal drug trafficking, organized crime, and street gangs (Honduras); and social conflicts, kidnappings, and terrorist attacks (Peru).[44] The work of national tourism bureaus has traditionally focused on eclipsing potential concerns by highlighting the positive, safe, and welcoming aspects of the nation in question. The Mexico Tourism Board spends millions of dollars in Canada annually to refashion Mexico's reputation from a land of drug wars and gang-related violence (an image which has found ample ground in Canadian media in recent years), to a safe and friendly destination. These promotional efforts are undertaken with assistance from Canadian public-relations and advertising firms. As destination-branding scholars Morgan, Pritchard, and Pride suggest, "never was the saying 'accentuate the positive and eliminate the negative' more true than in destination branding."[45]

In some cases, negative national reputations are so pervasive that tourism boards are forced to acknowledge them, as in Colombia's tongue-in-cheek 2010 campaign, "Colombia: The only risk is wanting to stay."[46] According-ing to the national tourism bureau's website, the campaign was created in response to concerns raised at international fairs about the risks involved in visiting the country. The website did not specify what concerns were raised, simply suggesting they reflected a "lack of knowledge" about the country: "The goal is to present Colombia to international tourists as a va-cation alternative by showing that the only risk in coming is to fall in love with its landscapes, people, food, fairs, festivals, handicrafts, colors and all the experiences the country can offer a tourist."[47] One way the Colom-bian tourism bureau works to reassure potential visitors is to emphasize the existing popularity of Colombia as a tourist destination. The website boasts that "millions" of foreigners from around the world have enjoyed "the best vacations of their lives" in Colombia. It includes multiple trav-ellers' testimonies and links to flattering media reports from around the world portraying Colombia as an attractive and safe tourism destination.

G Adventures took a different approach to marketing Colombia, how-ever, reformulating the country's negative reputation abroad as a key at-tribute in marketing the region as a challenging, untouched, and exciting destination that is free of tourists:

"If there were ever a country that suffered from a case of seriously bad press, it's Colombia. It's not well known by travelers, so the border feels like crossing one of the last frontiers of travel. Colombia is ripe for dis-covery, and there is a little of everything: green valleys, golden beaches and snow-capped mountains, colonial fortresses and Bogota's frenetic en-ergy [...] everything it seems, except tourists. [...] And while it is true that travel in Colombia demands some extra awareness, care and preparation, the extra energy is rewarded a hundredfold."[48]

The negative international reputations of El Salvador and Nicaragua were also highlighted rather than hidden in G Adventures' profiles: El

Salvador's profile refers to its 1980 civil war, during which time, G Adventures tells its reader, "disappearances and death squads were common," while Nicaragua's profile states that the world overwhelmingly remembers the country for revolution and war. In marketing Bolivia as a travel destination, G Adventures tells its reader that it is the poorest country in South America and "not for the faint of heart."[49]

Calling attention to recent histories of violence and political instability and current levels of poverty not only runs counter to the promotional efforts of national tourism bureaus, but risks deterring potential clients who may not be familiar with these negative reputations in the first place. However, there are advantages to drawing attention to these elements: it provides compelling evidence for claims that the regions are "untouched" by mainstream tourism, and it gives the destinations an aura of excitement and edge. The upshot to Colombia's recent history of drug wars, guerrilla groups, and kidnappings, G Adventures suggests, is that the region has been sealed off from the tourist masses and is now "ripe for discovery." Similarly, by representing Bolivia as a difficult, poverty-stricken destination that has been avoided by other tourists, the brochure promises that Bolivia's traditional culture is still available to be experienced (before other tourists discover, modernize, and "spoil" it). As the website description puts it, "for the traveler willing to endure a little discomfort, Bolivia is a trip back in time."[50] These depictions also help G Adventures position itself as an anti-tourism company that gives travellers the real deal, as opposed to conventional mass tourism operators who keep their guests sheltered in the confines of a resort.

These Canadian-made and Canadian-circulated representations of Latin American regions as challenging or even risky can appeal to Canadians seeking to gain cultural capital from non-conventional or strenuous journeys to remote regions. "There is a growing clamor among sophisticated Canadian travelers to experience and to add to their travel resume, unpredictable, sometimes strenuous vacations,"[51] wrote Gwenn Dianne Reimer in her review of Canadian tour operators. Some consumer research suggests that incorporating messages of risk or challenge may work for Canadian audiences in particular. For example, a 2006 study by Reisinger and Mavondo found Canadians were less "risk averse" than Americans when choosing a travel destination, scored lower on "uncertainty avoidance," and were less afraid of crime, terrorism, or cultural barriers when planning a vacation destination. Their research encouraged tourism promoters in the US context to emphasize low travel risk and suggested the Canadian market could, conversely, be "additionally targeted with messages that incorporate some elements of adventure or challenge."[52]

For some audiences, highlighting poverty, political violence, and revolution can be a seductive marketing strategy. However, these representations may also counter efforts by Latin American nations to build reputations as modern, stable nations, serious political players, or technological powers.[53] As destination-branding expert Simon Anholt notes, countries with a reputation for being poor, dangerous, or corrupt will have trouble exerting influence over more cautious travellers as well as other important target audiences such as international students, trading partners, or multilateral agencies.[54]

Latin America: The myth of the uncivilized and the unchanged

While emphasizing histories of revolution and poverty in textual descriptions, the brochures in Travel Cuts portray an image of Latin America in which almost all signs of modern urban life are absent. They include virtually no images of bustling downtown city centres, upscale restaurants, or modern boulevards. Instead, the visual emphasis is on desolate mountainscapes, pristine lakes, and exotic animals. Civilization is portrayed with photographs of crumbling but colourful rooftops and villages (or as one description on the Travel Cuts website put it, buildings "in picturesque decay"),[55] marketplaces filled with fresh fruit and livestock, and local villagers and townspeople. Instead of staying in international hotels, travellers will stay in "rustic" homes, ride in local chicken buses rather than air-conditioned coaches and, at times, venture into parts of the region that do not even have roads. Here, it is the fact that accommodations will *not* be luxurious and that transportation will *not* be comfortable that is emphasized to seduce would-be travellers who seek a more authentic experience. "Given that this is Latin America after all, creature comforts aren't always readily at hand,"[56] states the Intrepid brochure. The locals selected to visually represent their respective communities play a crucial role in the authenticity discourse - they provide evidence of a world untouched by globalization. Their colourful dress, mysterious rituals, or simple lifestyles are packaged as an enriching experience for modern travellers.

The image of Latin America that emerges from these depictions omits not only modern infrastructure such as paved roads, skyscrapers, or upscale hotels, but also Latin American people who shop in malls, work in corporate office buildings, or go on their own travels abroad. Travellers wishing to "learn more about local life," or pick up local lingo, are not encouraged to rub shoulders with people working at, for example, a department store or law firm, but instead with workers in a tobacco field or vendors selling livestock and plants at open-air markets. This may reflect the brochure maker's assumption that tourists want to encounter cultural differences, or experiences and interactions that cannot be duplicated at home. However, the particular social and economic background of subjects presented as worthy of attention not only speaks to the kinds of communities tourism promoters think travellers wish to encounter, but also what kinds of cultural communities tourism promoters feel they have the *right* to enter. To consider this distinction, we might think about how Canadian audiences would react to a tourism brochure for Canada produced in a foreign country that encouraged travellers to stop by an elementary school in downtown Toronto to meet local children.

Images of Latin America that exclude signs of industrialization or modern infrastructure not only mask the complex relationship between Indigenous cultures and globalization, but may also be at odds with the branding efforts of Latin American tourism boards. Recent promotional campaigns by the tourism boards of Mexico, Colombia, Ecuador, Argentina, and Chile project multiple facets of their countries with visuals and descriptions of modern cityscapes, museums, and high-end shopping in addition to rugged natural beauty, Indigenous culture, and folklore. One striking example can be seen in Chile's recent tourism campaign (Fig. 4), which highlights the duality of "ancient" culture and urban modernity, seemingly in an effort to challenge stereotypes of the region.

Latin America: The land of authenticity

In *The Tourist*, Dean MacCannell argued that the essence of modern tourism is a "quest for authenticity." Tourists travel, he suggested, to recover what they believe is missing in their own lives - the pristine, the primitive, and the natural - and expect to find such qualities in "less developed" places.[57] Heidi Dahles and Lou Keune echo MacCannell's arguments, suggesting that cultural tourism to Latin America is often propelled by the traveller's desire to experience what is deemed to be an authentic way of life which is being destroyed in the industrialized world. In this context, the authentic is linked to myths of primitiveness, exoticism, tradition, and an "as yet 'unspoiled' natural environment."[58] Anthropologist Charles Lindholm makes explicit the connection between the modern understanding of authenticity, the myth of the primitive, and the rise of European colonialism. Lindholm argues that notions of "cultural authenticity" were heavily shaped by early travellers' accounts of encounters with "primitive indigenous peoples," which many European intellectuals used as a means to critique "corrupt Western values":

> Tribes living in isolation (or even peasants living in the countryside) were imagined and portrayed as representative of coherent and pristine rural cultural traditions, integrated with nature, unashamed, communal, loving and close to the paradisiacal Garden of Eden. They were authentic in the double sense of being pure and original and of being without falsity. At the same time, they were regarded as being in contact with mysterious and primordial spiritual forces no longer perceptible to modern humanity.[59]

The effect of this "Noble Savage" myth was not just a benign critique of industrialization - it also provided the rationale for imperial intervention. Lindholm points out that these myths continue to have resonance in the present-day tourism discourse that projects the fantasy of authenticity onto non-Western places and people and promises to take travellers "back in time." This rhetoric, which positions Indigenous cultures outside of civilization and history, was a staple in the promotional materials found in Travel Cuts. For example, G Adventures promoted Venezuela by asserting that "[d]eep in the countryside, people still live traditional lives [...] continue south and you reach the Venezuelan Amazon, where stone-age tribes still live their lives largely unchanged since ancient times."[60] An Intrepid trip itinerary for Mexico to Panama invited potential customers to "feel the hands of time pull you into ancient worlds while exploring Maya ruins."[61] Finally, the online itinerary for G Adventures' "Ecuador: Inland and Amazon" homestay tour (one of its most popular offerings) marketed the journey as an opportunity to "travel back in time."[62] The website for Travel Cuts also exploited the perceived link between authenticity and primitiveness, marketing particular regions on the basis that they have experienced little contact with outsiders: "Travelers seeking authenticity should look no further than landlocked Paraguay. While not on the average tourist itinerary, the country's Jesuit ruins and national parks offer a glimpse of a South America untrammelled by the twenty-first century."[63] Likewise, the potential G Adventures client was told, "If you are looking for an authentic experience and some true adventure, Bolivia is the place," as it is "a traditional country where modern tourism has barely scratched the surface."[64] The fact that these depictions call attention to the negative influence of mass tourism and simultaneously promote intensified contact with Indigenous cultures may seem to be a strange paradox. In this context, however, it is not an unusual one; consider for example the way G Adventures markets Guatemala as an appealing destination: "It's a miracle Guatemala is still off the radar for so many. Let's hope it stays that way."[65] The description suggests, ironically, that Guatemala will become less appealing as a destination if the company's goal of selling travel packages there succeeds. These depictions capitalize on the idea that eventual "discovery" is inevitable (evident in phrases like "*yet* to be fully discovered" or "*still* off the radar"), building a discourse of the disappearing authentic and selling potential customers on the idea that there is only so much time left before a place will be discovered, modernized, and subsequently spoiled. The depictions also evoke a fantasy of neocolonial discovery of final frontiers - a desire to penetrate unknown lands and discover primitive peoples. While it is suggested that the native culture is corrupted by cross-cultural contact, the tourist is apparently enriched by the experience.

Despite recognizing the value of non-Western cultures, the equation of cultural authenticity with a pre-Western-contact state of purity not only obscures the extent to which colonialism and globalization have impacted Indigenous life, but also reinforces the notion that the authentic Indigenous Other can never inhabit the same modern present as the Western Self; the Indigenous present is always the Western "Stone Age." The travel company's claims to provide tourists with "authentic experiences," "authentic accommodations," and "authentic means of transport" as a function of their ability to penetrate remote and untouched regions illustrates how the discourses of authenticity and primitivism not only permeate and interpolate one another, but are ultimately rendered indistinguishable.

Conclusion

In addition to selling flights and travel packages, Canadian tourism promoters articulate regional and cultural identities, challenge or reinforce national stereotypes, and portray appropriate relationships between tourists and hosts. This exploratory study has considered how Latin America is portrayed in Canadian tourism representations by analyzing promotional materials from 2010 found in a specific Canadian context: a student travel agency. It pays particular attention to the promotional materials of G Adventures, a Canadian company with a strong presence in Latin America that is widely considered the industry leader in adventure travel tours. By marketing exploration in lesser-known regions and in-depth immersion into remote and "untouched" cultures, G Adventures packages Latin

America as a venue for the modern and privileged Canadian tourist to travel back in time to be enriched by encounters with primitive cultures in undeveloped and fragile landscapes. In many ways, these representations fit into a Western historical tradition of depicting Latin American cultures and peoples as innocent, natural, and authentic, and reinforce the modern/traditional and nature/civilization binaries that Westerners have historically employed to understand Latin America.

However, this study also reveals that efforts to promote regions as "untouched" or "ripe for discovery" are calling attention to factors that have traditionally been avoided by the tourism industry, such as high poverty rates, a lack of access to modern amenities, recent histories of violence and war, or negative international reputations. Potential customers are challenged to be real travellers, not tourists, by venturing beyond the tourist enclave and experiencing discomfort, poverty, and brushes with recent revolutionary unrest, that are portrayed as authentically Latin American. The portrayal of Latin America as a place of poverty, revolution, and political unrest reinforces opposing constructions of Canada as a modern, industrialized, and stable democracy. It also emphasizes the differences between Canadians who have the power to travel to pre-modern worlds to be enriched by difference, tradition, and risk, and the power to move back to their modern, civilized societies.

This chapter has touched on ways in which these Canadian portrayals can clash with the destination-branding efforts of Latin American tourism boards but has not analyzed in depth how the promotional materials produced by national tourism boards differ from those produced by Canadian travel companies. Future studies could further compare and contrast the image of Latin America that emerges from Northern representations with those coming from the countries themselves. This chapter also highlights the emergence of environmentally and socially responsible travel as a key marketing tool, reflecting the perceived concerns of customers not to participate in mass tourism's contaminating impact on authentic landscapes and cultures. While it has not been the intention of this chapter to assess whether actual commitments to sustainability practices align with marketing rhetoric,[66] this study demonstrates the growing appeal of branding travel as a vehicle for cultural preservation and environmental sustainability.

Chapter 3

Representations of the Latin American Diaspora in Quebec: Latino-*Québécois* Visions

Mariza Rosales Argonza
Translated from the Spanish by Michael William Parker Stainback

> You could live peacefully by simply putting on the immigrant costume when necessary and taking it off when you please, if it weren't for the fact that in order to have a productive, intelligent, and sincere dialogue with the society on the other end, you've each got to know one another.[1]
>
> Ramón de Elía, *La otra bahía de Hudson*

Introduction

Cultural transformations stemming from global socio-cultural processes, immigration dynamics, exiles, and mass media generate intense circulation of material and symbolic culture at the transnational level. Recent Latin American diasporas to Canada invite questions with regard to Latin American artists' symbolic constructions in Quebec, as well as with the dynamics between artistic creation and place. The present chapter seeks to explore identity-construction strategies of immigrant artists as displaced subjects who are nevertheless actively participating in the receiving culture.

Current destabilization of traditional, polarized, "centre/periphery" binaries allows for a scenario of greater plurality when it comes to forms of representation and permits the broadening of spheres of meaning. Artistic practices born from hybridization, manifested in permanent appropriation and re-signification, generate a need to create a new, more flexible dialogic analysis spectrum that responds to the interweaving of cultural symbols, the circulation of multiple realities, and the construction of new imaginaries.

This study outlines an approach to the cross-border strategies used by Latino-*Québécois* visual artists whose work is a reflection on de-colonization as it moves back and forth across borders of identity, Indigenous worldviews, and immigration. It is based on interviews with artists who speak of their experiences and reflections, which unveil a construction

45

of meaning and reveal the circumstances surrounding the possibility of creation and integration within the Québécois context. Such experiences translate into both the meanings and contexts of the artworks discussed below.

The present study largely considers artworks and testimonies from Domingo Cisneros, Claudia Bernal, and Osvaldo Ramírez, three artists whose visual work develops a complex chain of symbolic significance that questions established notions based on the language of the dominant culture (Figs. 1-3). Analysis of such materials is performed on two levels. On a first level, the analysis is based on personal and visual memories that emerge from the interviews. On a second level, I interpret the artworks as discourses in order to understand their referents and formal visual grammars within the framework of individual and collective imaginaries, as well as to understand the ways in which these discourses are created and shared.

The theoretical aspects of the cultural studies to which I refer in the present chapter derive largely from authors who make interpretations based on a transnational vision of Latin America, as for example, Gerardo Mosquera, Walter Mignolo, Néstor García Canclini, Guillermo Gómez-Peña, and Gloria Anzaldúa. For some decades these authors have emphasized Latin America's culturally diverse and complex origins, and have warned us of the risks that come with the idea of a Latin American identity or in speaking of the region as a unified whole. These theorists have evinced special interest in notions of the border. At the same time, they have added complexity to discussions on artistic practice through a post-colonial perspective that goes beyond binary oppositions and unequal relations between the "centre" and the so-called "periphery." These discussions emphasize the articulation of multi-directional relationships that have modified the international culture system.

Here I propose an approach to Latino-*Québécois* visual artists' discourses based on experiences of immigration and of crossing cultural borders. These experiences contextualize work that stages complex identities that resist nationalist hegemonic categorizations. I focus on movement between borders and a systematic incorporation of diverse cultural structures and languages that manifest themselves in specific ways of producing knowledge and that demonstrate a unique conception of the world expressed in a distinct art. This in turn proposes new forms of knowledge and action within unstable contexts.

In light of such a scenario, conditions surrounding the possibilities for a cultural integration of artists and their cultural production, generated from an "extended Latin America," are of particular interest in understanding social mechanisms that are enacted for coexistence in multicultural societies. From this perspective, the interrelationship of artists of Latin American origin in Canadian cultural and artistic life constitutes an example of the complex exchange that comes with the meeting of cultures. Following Zygmunt Bauman's proposal,[2] this study adds to research on the Latin American diaspora in Canada through an exploration of its artistic interactions. Thus, it invites a reorientation of a cultural policy that goes beyond mere multiculturalism and proposes greater cultural inclusion, hence responding to a transforming Québécois society that generates art stemming from diverse cultural origins.

The artists

Among Latin American visual artists who have taken up residence in Quebec, largely starting in the 1960s, most share an interest in actively inserting themselves into cultural life. They do not form a homogeneous group. The purpose here is not to propose any exhaustive reviews or cataloguing, given that different generations and immigrant statuses, as well as excessive and transient movement, render this type of analysis beyond the scope of our study. In general terms it can be noted that a number of artists, such as Manuel Lau, Giorgia Volpe, Andrés Salas, Jorge Aguilar, Carolina Hernández-Hernández, José Luis Torres, Alejandro Maya Anda, Constanza Camelo, María Ezcurra, José Szlam, Pilar Macias, and Domingo Cisneros, began their careers in their native countries, where they exhibited extensively and enjoyed significant renown. These artists quickly connected with different artists' centres or created projects both inside and outside of Montreal.

On the other hand, there are artists of Latino origin who have actively participated in shows largely aimed at the Latino-*Québécois* community, such as Marcela Calle, David Alvarado, Elsa Gallegos, Alicia Hernández de Coll, and Juan Aquino, who have exhibited collectively and have not formed any definitive group or school. A number of these artists work mainly in figurative painting, and their artistic imaginaries are anchored in references to their cultural heritage; their works are populated with a repertoire of themes and references that evoke artistic movements such as Mexican muralism.[3]

There is, as well, a generation of visual artists who undertook their training or artistic careers in Canada. For artists such as Rafael Sottolichio, Osvaldo Ramírez, Paolo Almario, Carlos Rojas, Lucia Barreto, Julian

Palma, Malena Szlam, Juan Ortiz-Apuy, Federico Carbajal, Helena Martin Franco, and Claudia Bernal, among others, who trained at Canadian universities, insertion into the cultural milieu has been easier, and they have actively participated in different arts centres such as the Clark Centre for Contemporary Artists, the Atelier Circulaire print-artists' centre, and the Montreal MU mural-painting cultural project.[4] These artists display an interest in expanding their fields of action beyond "Latino" circuits. Even as some have taken part in cultural events aimed at Latin American audiences, such as the annual *LatinArte*[5] festival, they generally endeavour not to limit themselves to that audience, and they frequently participate in events in other Canadian and US cities, as well as in a number of Latin American nations.

Irrespective of when these artists immigrated or where they trained, it is a fact that artists of Latin American origin residing in Quebec, like all immigrant populations, face Quebec's linguistic duality. Their choices to operate either in French or English to a large degree determine the circuit in which they will move as well as the audiences they will address. Linguistic competency can further influence artists, as some choose to relocate to anglophone cities such as Toronto[6] or Vancouver.

Cross-border artists

As part of the panorama of Latino-*Québécois* artists who cross cultural boundaries, Osvaldo Ramírez Castillo, Domingo Cisneros, and Claudia Bernal endeavour to reconstruct colonization via a number of cross-border strategies. Their works stage critical border-related thinking that accentuates diversity based on context. Their art works toward a deconstruction of representations of Latin America, vindicating its right to different kinds of knowledge and to an exercise of difference, as opposed to the idealism of universal values determined from the North American centre.

While their works hold some questionings in common, they move in very different contexts. Osvaldo Ramírez, originally from El Salvador, immigrated to Canada at a very early age. His family established itself in Toronto, where the artist's basic training was completed; he then moved to Montreal, where he completed a master's degree in artistic creation at Concordia University. He lived in Montreal until 2013, when he relocated to Vancouver, where he currently resides, and from where he manages to maintain an active Montreal presence via numerous galleries and shows.

Domingo Cisneros, from the Tepehuano Indigenous people, was born and raised in Mexico's northern Sonora state, where he began his work as an artist. He immigrated to Canada because of his participation in political activities surrounding the 1968 student movement, which had given rise to a climate of political repression.[7] Once in Quebec, he was linked to the Indigenous community in the Laurentian Mountains, north of Montreal, as an art professor at Collège Manitou.[8] His experience with Indigenous communities has led him to be considered one of the main driving forces behind the revaluation of Indigenous art in Quebec.[9]

Claudia Bernal came to Canada from her native Colombia to study French linguistics. She moved to Montreal and began her artistic training with a BFA from the University of Quebec at Montreal (acronym in French: UQAM). Thanks to support from the Canadian government, she travelled to Mexico City in order to complete a diploma program in art history. Once she returned to Montreal, Bernal undertook an MFA in scenographic arts at UQAM and has maintained an active presence on the Québécois cultural scene as a multidisciplinary artist, as a cultural agent for artists' centres through various arts projects such as *La cobija mágica*, and as an exhibition curator.

Each of these artists' creative strategies is different. While Ramírez makes use of drawing and of a neo-baroque aesthetic to make critical commentaries, Cisneros favours installations and environmental art to pose questions regarding colonization and to revalue ways of knowing the natural and Indigenous worlds. Bernal turns to conceptual performance and video as an act of denouncing violence that dovetails with her vision of the artist as social activist. The works to be discussed below - Ramírez's *Becerrillo*, Cisneros's *La Reconquista* (both completed 2008), and Bernal's *Monumento a Ciudad Juárez*, presented in Montreal in 2006 - share the critical character of artists who create works based on historical memory, while at the same time linking to the immediate context and placing an emphasis on revealing realities that are frequently ignored. All three works evoke the pre-Columbian past as a place of passage that indicates a number of ways of articulating border-related thinking, i.e., an enunciative space that operates from and by means of the margins. Within that atemporal space, they evoke common cultural referents as an amalgam of origins from which they recreate dialogues that celebrate their second-class condition.

Latin American artists in Quebec

Currently, territorial discourses are being questioned around the world, and socio-cultural positions are moving away from territorial, identity-based, ideological positions. Dynamics of so-called "local culture" in relation to "global culture" invite a rethinking of notions of "Latin American culture" and its transterritorial cultural relations in a globalized context.

For art critic Gerardo Mosquera, Latin American diasporas, migrations, and repeated experiences of exile, largely in Europe, the United States, and Canada, are converting cities heretofore distant from Latino denomination, such as Toronto and Vancouver, into distribution foci for Latin American art. These Latino contributions are increasingly becoming an inevitable reference for contemporary art.[10]

This Latino dissemination has managed to expand physical borders and to penetrate in unprecedented ways into circuits previously reserved for northern European nations, the United States, and Canada.[11] It forms a part of intangible cultural heritage, given that the Latin American community expands through transnational cultural exchange circuits and plays an important role in the production, maintenance, and re-creation of cultural practices, thus contributing to an enrichment of cultural diversity and creativity in the cultures of both the artists' home countries and of their destination.[12]

Latin American immigration to Quebec has been a recent regional phenomenon, particularly starting in the 1970s, and is largely due to political and economic factors: dictatorial regimes in Chile, Argentina, and Uruguay, and various economic crises that produced an exodus of emigrants to Canada and the United States. In the 1970s, Canada's federal government initiated an immigration policy that sought to assist economic and refugee immigrants and gave rise to a series of migratory movements to Canada. Quebec, in particular, began to receive large numbers of South American immigrants. The 1980s were marked by an influx of Central American immigrants fleeing wars in El Salvador, Nicaragua, and Guatemala. The Hispanist, Hugh Hazelton, points out that the Latin American community in Quebec formed a fundamental part of the province's immigrant workforce that shaped its capitalist economic expansion as well as its multi-ethnic nature.[13] The 1990s were marked by an increase in immigrants and refugees from Colombia, Peru, and Mexico. These three are among the twenty-five top countries of origin for all immigrants to the province of Quebec.[14] This noteworthy growth in immigration from Latin America represents a new participation and integration scenario for the community.[15]

The integration of Latin American immigrants into Québécois society has been shaped by different factors including age, admissions category, educational levels, and linguistic choices, that affect immigrants' integration into society and the labour market. Recent statistics show that *Latinos* are present in all economic sectors thanks to the fact that they enjoy educational levels above those of the average Québécois.[16] Some researchers point out that their successful integration into Québécois culture is as yet incomplete in that, while Latin Americans do evince active participation in the social fabric, they have not managed to improve their economic conditions, given that their average incomes are well below the provincial median.[17]

Some Latino artists engage in the creation of literary, musical, or visual arts address large-scale audiences. The Montreal region is noted for having the greatest presence of visual artists of Latin American origin, owing to its wide variety of venues and its intense artistic activity in both official and alternative art spaces. However, there are also artists residing in Quebec City, Chicoutimi, Trois-Rivières, Gatineau, and other parts of the province.[18]

The Quebec cultural scene is unlike those of anglophone cities in North America. In the United States, historico-cultural relationships and the Latino community's demographic weight have earned it a distinguished place in the generalized culture. These achievements can in large measure be traced to politico-cultural participation from Mexicans and other Latin Americans, which gave rise to the Chicano cultural movement of the 1960s. Since then, Chicanos from different generations have created and expressed important reflections on immigration, the notion of Latin America, and the role of art and culture as an intercultural social tool in the United States' cultural agenda. At the same time, they have supported the creation of a number of research centres as well as multiple academic studies that have become landmarks in recent cultural investigations.[19]

In Quebec, the French-Canadians' will to survive in the face of a possible loss of their identity in relation to English Canada lies at the centre of a great many of the province's cultural policies on linguistic identity and on the valuing of francophone culture. This leads other cultural communities (such as the Latin American) to perceive their field of action as limited and to lump it in indifferently with that of other "diverse" cultural communities, in organizations such as Diversité Artistique Montréal (DAM).[20] An example of this is the rise of artistic spaces whose mandate includes "favouring intercultural exchange and dialogue," as in the case of the Montréal Arts Interculturels (MAI) Centre, which presents itself as a disinterested showcase of new intercultural practices yet separates "Québécois" local culture from the indistinct totality of "other" cultural communities.[21]

To understand the Latino-*Québécois*, it is essential to identify the challenges artists face in light of the Québécois cultural specificity that is encapsulated in two predominant communities that define the city of Montreal: the French- and the Anglo-Quebecers. This dynamic sets into motion different strategies that directly influence Latino-*Québécois* integration into cultural and artistic life.

The most representative case of Québécois policy centred on culture reaffirmation is that of education. For Charles Taylor, Quebec is a "moderate" example that illustrates taking more or less radical action to avoid the loss of a culture. Québécois linguistic policy insists on sending children of immigrants to francophone schools, "a policy that points to survival [and] seeks to create community members, as for example, when it guarantees that future generations continue identifying themselves as Francophone."[22]

Artists find themselves obliged to move between the two predominant cultures (the French- and English-Canadian), and certain artistic practices pose questions that go beyond that duality. Artists prefer to adopt a critical position. Through their works, they analyze colonial relations and play with identity roles as a discursive strategy in order to generate greater space both inside and outside the Québécois cultural scene.

Crossing borders

Interactive processes in intercultural societies imply a series of multiple negotiations - whether material or symbolic - that are required so that secondary groups' "local histories" can negotiate coexistence with dominant structures, states, and global corporations. Recognition of new cultural referents that are generated and that find expression through symbols formed by means of individuals' internalizing and externalizing processes constitute the social imaginary. The imaginary in this context is an integrating process that, because of its relational dimension, reveals a series of reaffirmations and juxtapositions between different cultures. These symbolic elements are expressed in a differentiated manner via their creators' cultural and artistic production.

Confrontation and dialogue pervade this process. Rethinking this dynamic is a tool for recognizing distinct contradictions and tensions in order to work in a democratic manner towards acceptance. According to Néstor García Canclini, hybridization, as a process of intersection and negotiation between different cultures that allows multiculturalism to prevent segregation, recognizes different kinds of knowledge and makes progress toward interculturalism.[23] The author suggests that true integration of diversity into the social fabric will lead to an inclusion and recognition of difference, i.e., of indissoluble elements that cannot be hybridized.

The visual arts are a realm that makes *addition* possible, in which recognition and integration of difference is encouraged via the creation of bridges as well as of pertinent links between diverse cultures and societies. Through art, therefore, the imaginary is re-created, and mechanisms such as prejudice are exposed: stereotypes can be questioned. A true *territory of dialogue* - an atmosphere of encounters, interaction, recognition, and socialization between individuals - is opened by means of artistic experience.

A polycentric and relational perspective of the various cultures in question is necessary to better understand this process, as is distancing oneself from the traditionally Eurocentric vision of art history. A multidisciplinary outlook is required as a critical tool for broadening intercultural discussions, as well as research that contextualizes each specific discipline and cultural community. Thus, it is necessary to revise the relativist thinking that has informed social research in recent decades. As García Canclini warns,

> It's easy to declare that all cultures, or all cultural modalities in a single nation, are legitimate: but does being Western or Eastern have the same value, and, in and out of the West, does being from the United States, Europe, or Latin American have the same value? Even amid the array of cultures contained within each of those regions, does belonging to one group or another have the same value? When we ask if they have the same value, we need to strip the question of all essentialism. I am not thinking of one culture or society's intrinsic superiorities over another, but rather of conditions with which each endows its members to move through the interconnected world where comparisons and confrontations with regard to socio-cultural developments are constant and unavoidable.[24]

García Canclini proposes a policy of coexistence, citizenship, and human rights, on a transnational scale that gives rise to strategies for managing conflicts and the economic and symbolic remittances that move from one country to another. Analyses and proposals of options for inclusion in response to multiple cultural exchanges require a cross-border vision.

To sketch a frame of reference that offers guidelines for approaching Latino-*Québécois* art, I propose to examine the concept of cross-border thinking, based on a proposal by Walter Mignolo, who re-examines the notion of border in order to re-posit the so-called post-colonial condition through a Latin American lens. He proposes the concept of "colonial difference" as a starting-point for exploring the space in which colonialism and power interact. Recognition of colonial difference makes possible a recognition of the subjects and knowledge that colonial mechanisms put into operation have marginalized from the sixteenth century onward. Colonial difference implies the possibility of dialogic situations in which fractured enunciation is enacted from a "second-class" perspective in response to a hegemonic discourse, emphasizing that it is more a question of knowledge, of a conflict between epistemological positions for seeing the world than of a class struggle. Mignolo defines second-class knowledge that operates from a place of difference as "border thinking" or "border gnosis," a form of knowledge that restores what hegemony effaces.[25]

From the nineteenth century onward, the West has endeavoured to set up national borders as part of an obvious post- and neo-colonial project in which second-class subjects (Indigenous peoples, Chicanos, African-Americans, Latin Americans, etc.) have been diminished and are subjected to the violence of ostracism and marginalization. In light of this, many voices, such as those of Gayatri Spivak, Homi Bhabha, Trin T. Min-Ha, James Clifford, and Stuart Hall, have proposed deconstructing the Western ideologies that continue to dominate the imaginaries of former colonies. In Latin America, writers such as Walter Mignolo, Néstor García Canclini, Guillermo Gómez-Peña, and Gloria Anzaldúa stand out as the most prominent thinkers from the heterogeneous current of border studies and studies of hybridized cultures. A great many of these authors insist on an exploration of what Bhabha describes as "the third space of enunciation," an interstitial and contradictory space that opens up between colonizer and colonized.[26]

Based on this intermediate/border space, it is possible - through the immigration experience - to move from one side to the other. Mignolo suggests that here a secondary enunciative space is made possible in which the imaginary of the contemporary world system "breaks."[27] This intermediate space offers alternatives for approaching Latino-*Québécois* artists' cultural production in express reference to their second-class status, not from a nostalgic position that glorifies or supports the idea of victim, but rather from a deconstructivist viewpoint that seeks to shatter stereotyped imaginaries. This leads the artists to re-create new forms of identity that are subject to a wide variety of displacements and negotiations.

The border is a locus of negotiations still subject to prickly encounters. Gómez-Peña's vision differs from those of other US-based Latino theorists such as Gustavo Pérez-Firmat, who proposes a "life on the hyphen" that casts its lot with fusion; or Gloria Anzaldúa, who proposes the idea of a "third nation." For Gómez-Peña, the idea is not to bind a wound but rather to recognize it and attend to it. It is in juxtaposition - a metaphor for the internal, perpetually volatile "mini-border" - where disparate elements connect. It is a synonym for interaction, a constant process, and movement.[28]

Here I propose to analyze visual art, produced by artists of Latin American origin in Quebec, that moves between different cultural or ideological borders from a cross-border perspective since, as previously mentioned, Quebec's specificity - largely dominated by its anglophone and francophone communities - creates a need among Latin American artists to find strategies that make the opening of a space within the Québécois cultural scene possible. This in turn means that creators circulate in liminal spaces and move among multiple realities via cross-border art that carries out negotiations according to the conditions present within the art system.

Recognition of artists' creation strategies and of their presence in Québécois cultural life can become a tool for finding modes of interaction that give rise to a process that creates integration, democratization, and pluralism, through culture. Study of the visual arts that are created based on this context will contribute to a differentiation and valuation of the singularity of its content, its diverse artistic experiences, and the languages that enrich memory and the collective Québécois imaginary.[29]

What Latin American heritage?

Art produced by artists of Latino-*Québécois* origin frequently evinces a multiple identity that goes beyond geographical parameters and out-of-date concepts that smack of the colonial. A large number of these artists have been strongly influenced by the cultural richness of their places of origin and by the Latin American artistic tradition.

Thus the complex and diverse universe of their artistic heritage is worth bearing in mind. It requires rethinking the dynamics surrounding relationships between cultures and exchange within Latin America, and calls for a revision with regard to the use of terms such as transculturation (Ortiz, 1978),[30] hybridization (García Canclini, 1989),[31] de-bordering (Appadurai, 1996; Hannerz, 1997),[32] globalization (Harvey, 1996),[33] and appropriation and re-signification (Maffesoli, 2005),[34] that have been used to characterize Latin American art and art in general from the post-colonial realm,[35] since they can be useful in creating an image of equitable and harmonious fusion that masks not only differences but also contradictions and obvious inequalities under the guise of an integrated region.

So-called "Latin American" art has been traditionally defined and interpreted from dominant centres as peripheral, folkloric art inspired by popular tradition that seeks to recover oppressed nationality by evoking allegorical or dreamlike representations labelled "magic realism." Otherwise, Latin American artistic production is typically reduced to the creation of militant, socially engaged creation understood as a medium of social transformation linked to the tradition that Mexican muralism kicked off.[36]

According to Nelly Richard, Latin American art has been reduced to the idea that it illustrates the immediate physical world, an immediate reality devoid of deeper reflection, a *practice* that primitivizes it and drains it of content. This essential differentiation removes it from the arena of art as proposed in the centre and remits it to an immediacy, while distancing it from theory. At the same time, the formal and discursive problems presented by art are the concern of the centre.[37]

Critical art that emerges from a Latin America that extends beyond its borders contains both formal and content-related values and often moves from the aesthetic to the political and from the political to the aesthetic as a way of addressing an identity dissolved into innumerable fragments:

> It has been constructing a hybridized meta-archipelago in which the domestic and the global coexist, as do memory and oblivion, fiction and political commitment, the impossible and the real. In such a scenario, the idea of a fixed identity has been transgressed and become obsolete, incapable of taking on the task of differentiation or of portraying the immense, baroque plurality - as profound as it is saturated - that claims both the fragility of its certainty and the urgency of its voluntary destiny.[38]

Artists re-create new territories: their works present imaginary maps as visions that allow cartographies to be refashioned as crossroads and that make a reinterpretation of the meaning of Latin America possible. An evocation of the notion of Latin America is not a mere invocation: it passes through a process of selective remembrance as a function of its present needs. A discovery of new referents and cultural repertories is a link that binds affinities and differences among different cultural groups. The willingness to incorporate these referents becomes an effort to forge connections and build bridges of knowledge and understanding. This is no false unity but rather the search for a deeper union centred on the recognition of possessing a shared destiny and of passing through common situations.

This will to open up space for encounters and interaction with other cultures can be cited as a characteristic of Latino-*Québécois* artists. However, much work remains to be done in order to activate horizontal dialogue, since there is still a great deal of ignorance or stereotyping with regard to interacting cultures.

In Quebec, large portions of the public, as well as many of the players on the cultural scene, have no clear notion of "Latin America," much less of contemporary "Latin American art." This is largely due to the scant existence of specialized courses of study on art from other parts of the world in the curricula proposed by many Québécois universities and art schools. There is also a lack of specialized publications on art emerging from an extended Latin America and of exhibits that can shed innovative light on this art.

This creates difficulties that Latino-*Québécois* artists must face, such as a limited awareness and distribution of their work, which is typically confined to spaces such as artists' centres and cooperatives, cultural centres, consulates, and cultural diversity centres, and is thus effectively cut off from museum spaces. While some artists have benefitted from different fellowship and grant programs,[39] others are confronted by a number of impediments that prevent their full integration into the commercial gallery/collection circuit. Most notable is the fact that there are few collectors interested in acquiring Latino-*Québécois* art and that most galleries focus efforts on the promotion of Franco- or Anglo-Québécois artists.

Furthermore, there are few researchers and insufficient resources for advancing the understanding of the cultural exchange that Latino-*Québécois* artists propose. This takes on relevance because advances toward diverse social practices - that are neither assimilative nor separatist but rather relational - require the search for a new community spirit subject to trust and mutual respect. The role of research is fundamental, given that "[c]omparative study and critical analysis are essential to the development of cross-cultural understanding and progressive social reconstruction. In a liberal democracy, such work can and should be carried on, however, within a framework of mutual respect founded on recognition of the intrinsic worth of all cultures."[40] It is necessary to assemble a history of collaborative efforts that generate transnational academic projects that in turn provide valuation and analytical tools for Latino-Canadian art. As Taylor has emphasized, this does not imply that every difference must survive (as today's multiculturalism enthusiasts claim). In order to make progress toward a true respect for equality, real judgments of equal value applied to cultural customs and differences will be required.

The artworks

Becerrillo

In this piece, Osvaldo Ramírez Castillo reconstructs "coloniality" based on childhood images marked by war in El Salvador by portraying

Figure 1. Osvaldo Ramírez Castillo, *Becerrillo*, 2008, mixed media. Reproduced with permission of the artist.

the image of the colonizer by leveraging an artistic imaginary that verges on neo-expressionism (Fig. 1). Ramírez steps out of the local Salvadoran context and subverts the official and historical notion of Latin America's origin being the result of European "conquest" that usually omits mention of the brutal genocide brought on by colonization as a mode of domination. Ramírez calls to mind the chaos and violence that human beasts cause. *Becerrillo* concerns the destruction brought on by the colonializing project, represented as a half metal-armour, half-emaciated body that lacks any precise ethnicity or skin colour and that reveals its true face as deformed by a lust for power.

The representation of the conquistador emerges from *Becerrillo*, the insurrectionist Indians' hunting dog that makes an appearance in Eduardo Galeano's *Memorias del fuego*.[41] The oppressor, using his numerous hands, condemns subjects to death at the same time as he holds the reins of power, extending historical ties that are projected into the future as a wound. Astride a three-headed beast, he kills the world, and Meso-American Indigenous fire-knowledge - a phoenix that cannot be reborn, constantly oppressed by the imminence of war and the death that comes in its wake - then buries them in clay urns.[42]

Becerrillo is a work that puts a still legitimate dynamic of historical struggle on the table, a struggle that binds and lends a tragic sense to the reality lived in many parts of the Americas in places where the First and Third Worlds live together on a day-to-day basis. Its images, charged with symbols and cultural references of diverse provenance, are permeated with contradictions in which confrontation is a constant dynamic. It constitutes a cartography of the chaos for current-day societies, the labyrinthine, Babel-like spaces of our identity.

Ramírez's work is an act of bringing the past to the present, the explicit desire not to forget, that allows contemplation of the wound and the origin of a culture while still understanding its present-day conditions. It is an attempt to introduce questioning that goes beyond local limits to a global scenario and to recognize a reality that in itself suggests a form of resistance to discourses that seek to homogenize populations and deny community memory.

La Reconquista

Domingo Cisneros' works are distinguished by their interest in exploring the links that exist among Indigenous cultures of the Americas. He dismantles the colonizing project and proposes movement across alternative spaces that transcend cultural borders. He has become an essential part of a renaissance in contemporary Indigenous US and Canadian art through his training workshops, and he is a pioneer in ecological art. His project entitled *Territorio cultural* (*Cultural Territory*), situated in the Laurentides, forms part of his notion of sociological art, an artistic laboratory that creates through dialogue and with natural elements.

Narration is a fundamental element in Cisneros's work. Through it, the artist transmits values and knowledge of Canada's First Nations (i.e., Indigenous groups except Inuit and Métis) as well as of their experiences. Identity-related constructions stand out in his work and emerge from ancestral memory and its relationship to nature, elements that are essential to the process of self-recognition, to building and maintaining relationships with others, and to engaging with environments. His use of installation offers an opportunity to create a space that defines the context and makes silent dialogues possible. In these installations, Cisneros explores common elements among Indigenous communities in different ways, representing them by objects in a *mise-en-scène* in which, through the artistic experience, matter, space, and the spectator are participatory actors.

In his installation *La Reconquista*, Domingo Cisneros places various references from culturally different universes within a dialogue; his work transcends cultural borders by means of a *mise-en-scène* and pastiche that

Figure 2. Domingo Cisneros, *La Reconquista*, 2008, installation. Reproduce with permission of the artist.

become a critical reflection on man's destiny (Fig. 2). Structured through three elements formed by organic materials placed in different areas of the space, *La Reconquista* presents a trilogy that begins with the Catholic religious tradition imposed by the colonizer which determines the "destiny-places" of souls after death: heaven, hell and the intermediate space known as purgatory.

Cisneros recalls the origin that lies beneath every process of domination that passes through culture in its elemental sense of being in opposition to nature: man, the modeller of culture and the master of natural elements.[43] *La Reconquista* posits the construction of culture and its inevitable loss (hell), exiled humanity (purgatory), and the possibility of reinstating the natural order (heaven). When constructing hell, the black colour and stone texture attest to the remains of a civilization: they are the shadow and memory of a fallen culture that leaves behind fossils as well as the remains of the beings who once inhabited it. Purgatory is an arid place which is the result of nature's indiscriminate abuse, domination, and exploitation. From the fallen tree, humanity laments the desert-like destiny that buries its own.

Heaven is presented as a possibility for balance, a return to knowledge and origins. An interwoven recipient symbolizes social construction that surrounds the richness of knowledge thanks to diversity. All manner of elements are united and integrated in an organic, harmonious manner that respects materiality based on a vision situated in another space that values the complex, ancestral knowledge of the First Nations. Cisneros transcends these juxtaposed spaces and cultures, moves across them, reveals a critical deconstruction, and proposes subversion based on border knowledge that overcomes differences and discovers what they have in common.

The work's structure reveals a secondary knowledge by means of elements that recall the Indigenous world and a spiritual world that the evangelizing project sought to displace and that still largely underlies Christian representations and religious syncretism throughout Latin America.

La Reconquista seeks to add the possibility of a spiritual world to public discourse. This world incorporates nature and other forms of "local" knowledge, and re-values and portrays Indigenous cultures as a paradise of ancestral "universal" knowledge or as an alternative that questions paradigms dictated from the centre through formal elements and conceptual content.

Monumento a Ciudad Juárez
Claudia Bernal creates works that explore a wide variety of aesthetics through differing mediums such as installation, video, and performance.

It is through such media diversity that she proposes questions that oscillate between the individual/internal and the social/external. She generates and inhabits spaces that re-signify, using objects laden with symbology into which she inserts social commentary in a sort of visual poetry whose elements are trace-narratives of desperate lives being extinguished before our eyes. Bernal evokes the ephemeral aspect of an action, a memory, an image, or a nameless face that is erased from memory.

In *Monumento a Ciudad Juárez*, "sólo aquellas que mueren de muerte violenta entrarán al paraíso" (in *Monument to Ciudad Juárez*, "only women who die a violent death will enter Paradise"), the artist denounces the city's notorious "femicides." Ciudad Juárez - which lies on the US-Mexico border - is one of the most violent border cities on the planet (Fig. 3).[44] Bernal intervenes in the post-colonial discourse by reflecting on the fundamental role that gender plays in the dynamics of patriarchal power.

In contrast to cultural studies that tend to metaphorize the border, Bernal dismantles the idea of border spaces as a utopia of hybridization. In her work, she identifies, within borderland realities, the difference that exists between the real and the metaphorical, exposing the complexity of borders and most particularly, the violence that is often hidden or ignored. In the *Monumento* installation, Bernal portrays a border that produces monstrous, violent, hybrid subjects and situations. She appro-

Figure 3. Claudia Bernal, *Monumento a Ciudad Juárez, sólo aquellas que mueren de muerte violenta entrarán al paraíso*, 2002, installation. Reproduce with permission of the artist.

priates the border as a place to comment on postmodern dystopia and in which to articulate her denunciations.

The video/installation and performance piece was carried out in different phases. The first took place in Ciudad Juárez and Mexico City and corresponds to the creation phase. Later, a performance was staged in Mexico City's main plaza, the Zócalo, in 2002, as part of a march by the general public to protest the impunity of those responsible for the femicides. Bernal marches in the company of victims' mothers and family members, as well as with women from civil-society organizations. Swathed in black veils, they carry clay urns that bear the victims' names or, in certain cases, the word "disappeared." They put the urns on the ground in the centre of the square so that together they form a spiral at the foot of an extended cloth onto which is projected a video made in Ciudad Juárez and the desert areas where the victims' bodies were discovered.

Through denunciation, Bernal seeks to subvert borderland violence through a funerary ritual that takes up Meso-American tradition. The clay urns, with lids of tortillas, provide a dignified burial for patriarchal power's female victims and bear witness to the state of criminal impunity that thousands of women crossing all manner of physical and cultural borders must face. From her perspective as a resident of Quebec, Bernal seems to suggest that the answer to these gender atrocities is collective involvement that should take place on a transnational level. In *Monumento*, Bernal ultimately bases her acts on border thinking as she reveals all the various ways women can be forgotten.

Conclusion

There is still a great deal to be discovered with regard to the creative strategies of Latino-*Québécois* artists. For example, there is a clear need to look deeper into the ways in which they reconstruct their identities and at the same time contribute to shaping the visual arts in which they variously participate. New figures will continue to arise and blaze fresh trails that move among cultural interstices by means of a reflexive art that involves a distinct aesthetic as well as discursive repertoires. Through their border thinking, Latino-*Québécois* artists have made progress in eliciting dialogue on the Montreal art scene with regard to a number of issues and concerns. Yet it is a fact that, despite the work carried out by different generations of artists, deeper knowledge of their complex identities and of the wisdom that shines through their work is still needed. Greater involvement is needed on the part of specialists who can contribute to the critical interpretation of the mechanisms these Latino-*Québécois* artists have set into motion, in order to present dialogic analyses of their artistic manifestations within a context of intense transnational flows.

In Quebec, the city of Montreal appears as a cross-cultural space in which a discourse about "us" is constructed and incorporated, and in which cultural coexistence is practiced and moulded day by day. There is constant negotiation among multiple realities as well as historical eras, shared social concerns, and cultural as well as symbolic elements that appear intermittently in artistic production. Based on a diversity of visual languages, artists reflect on important questions that respond to a complex historical time that transcends any geographic or national limit.

As mentioned at the beginning of the present chapter, we do not seek any exhaustive interpretations since many of the artists mentioned undertake continuous movement, and these creators cannot be distinguished as a definite, organized group. Each artist's visual work forms a territory that is traced out by relationships and circuits where history, social memory, and personal imaginaries converge. Richness in content, quality, and visual preoccupations moves away from traditional limitations to affirm the existence of a Latino-*Québécois* art in a broad sense that is defined as a true territory of diversity constructed from - as Ticio Escobar would have it - "transitory positions on unstable ground."[45] It is from this condition of constant transit that the artworks are constructed and intervene in Québécois culture based on an integration of discourses and cross-border artworks.

There is much work still to be done to move towards a more inclusive cultural policy. For this reason, it will be necessary to generate access to, and an active participation in, institutional spaces in order to move forward together towards a culture of diversity that incorporates a greater visibility, as well as a real and equitable participation of artists from all cultural spheres of Montreal's artistic milieu. Ultimately, in order to generate a horizontal dialogue in which cultural diversity is based on the inclusion and articulation of an intercultural discourse - as Latino-*Québécois* writer Ramón de Elía affirms - and to cultivate productive dialogue, we must get to know one another.

Part 2
From Outsiders to Insiders

Chapter 4

Exhibiting Mexican Art in Canada: Histories of Cultural Exchange and Diplomacy in the Mid-Twentieth Century

Sarah E.K. Smith

This chapter focuses on mid-twentieth century exhibitions of Mexican art in Canada. I suggest that this history can contribute to understanding the display of Mexican art in the more recent past. Specifically, I refer to the surge of exhibitions at the turn of the millennium, a period that witnessed unprecedented attention paid to Mexican art by museums across Canada. This included *Mexican Modern Art: 1900-1950*, the largest touring exhibition in Canada of Mexican modern art. It comprised approximately two hundred and seventy paintings, sculptures, photographs, and prints, and was shown at the Montreal Museum of Fine Arts in 1999 and the National Gallery of Canada (NGC) in 2000. Mexican art also prominently featured in exhibitions that included Canadian and US artworks - for instance, *Carr, O'Keefe, Kahlo: Places of Their Own*, a 2001-2002 touring exhibition of the work of female art icons from Canada, Mexico, and the United States; and *Baja to Vancouver: The West Coast in Contemporary Art*, a show of works from the transnational coast of the Pacific.[1] In the same period, the Canadian federal government emphasized Mexican art in two online exhibitions - *Panoramas: The North American Landscape in Art*, a trilateral state-sponsored survey exhibition; and *Perspectives: Women Artists in North America*, a survey exhibition uniting partner institutions from Canada, Mexico, and the United States.[2]

These exhibitions facilitated access to Mexican art for the Canadian public and in several cases presented Mexican art and artists in relation to those in Canada and the United States. Moreover, they provided opportunities to cement increasingly public connections among Canada, Mexico, and the United States.[3] For example, *Panoramas* was announced in 2000 at the third annual Trilateral Ministerial Meeting in Santa Fe, New Mexico, by Canada's foreign affairs minister, Lloyd Axworthy; the American secretary of state, Madeleine K. Albright; and the Mexican foreign secretary, Rosario Green.[4] Similarly, the opening of *Mexican Modern Art* at the NGC saw Canadian and Mexican flags hung side by side at the entrance to the exhibition and was feted by distinguished political, corporate, and cultural figures including the Canadian heritage minister, Sheila Copps, and Gerardo Estrada, the general director of Mexico's Instituto Nacional de Bellas Artes.[5]

The artworks on display in these exhibitions were mobilized in the service of political and economic ties cemented in a series of free trade agreements near the end of the twentieth century. As I have argued elsewhere, from the 1990s and into the first decade of the twenty-first century, the governments of Canada and Mexico used art to support the new free trade agreement between the two states and the United States - the 1994 North American Free Trade Agreement (NAFTA).[6] Prior to this deal, both Canada and Mexico focused more on their respective bilateral relationships with the United States than on their relationships with each other. As María Teresa Gutiérrez Haces explains, "When Mexico and Canada decided to negotiate a trilateral free trade agreement with the United States, they suddenly had to confront an undeniable fact: during the past fifty years, neither one had advanced in its knowledge of the other."[7] As such, cultural initiatives were necessary to build public confidence in the new economic integration of North America.

This use of culture as a tool to build state relations falls into the realm of soft power, which Joseph Nye Jr. describes as "attractive power" - a resource that contributes to compliance - "a different type of currency (not force, not money) [used] to engender cooperation, and an attraction to shared values and the justness and duty of contributing to the achievement of those values."[8] Culture offers a key means of facilitating cooperation and conveying messages in part due to Western perceptions of a universal conduit across differences of language, religion, and ethnicity. This conception underpins the historical use of works of visual art as representative envoys in the negotiation of a variety of relationships. Thus, control of cultural goods and their circulation, which often lies in the hands of the state, becomes very important. "If the artworks are of universal significance," Judith H. Balfe states, "speaking across cultural boundaries, so is their discerning patron or owner. That, at least, is the claim."[9] Such constructions of the state can even be creative, depicting new relationships and configurations rather than merely reflecting existing dynamics.[10]

Prior to the end of the twentieth century, Mexican art had a relatively low profile in Canada, making its increased presence at the turn of the millennium even more striking. But if art is such a powerful tool of diplomacy, why had Canada and Mexico not used it before? In fact, examination of cultural exchange between the two states reveals a long history of diplomatic aims underwriting art exhibitions. While the history of Mexican art in the United States has been widely studied by scholars, an examination of this history in relation to Canada is missing from contemporary scholarship. My research seeks to contribute to our understanding of twentieth-century cultural exchange, a topic that speaks to key moments in the history of formal diplomatic and economic relations between Canada and Mexico. I suggest that understanding this longer history will provide a key context for assessing the more recent shows in the 2000s. Additionally, I aim to establish the unique nature of Canada-Mexico relations, with the hope that this analysis will lay the groundwork for further studies of Mexican art exhibitions in Canada, contribute to thinking on this subject within a Canadian setting, and spur the examination of the key Canadian and Mexican historical actors involved.

There were three key exhibitions of Mexican art in Canada in the mid-twentieth century held in 1943, 1946, and 1960-61. I examine these shows in order to suggest a long continuum of culture shaping political and economic exchange between the two countries. While exhibitions of Mexican art in Canada during the mid-twentieth century were few and far between, and had a lower impact nationally than those of recent years, I suggest that their ties to political objectives were just as strong as those in the 2000s. I also speak to reciprocal exhibitions of Canadian art sent to Mexico during the same period, closely tied to exhibitions in Canada, as well as to plans that were ultimately never realized. The results of this survey provide historical context for the more recent iterations of Mexican art in Canada mentioned above and the diplomatic and political interests that shaped them, and help to uncover how art has influenced each nation's understanding of the other over a longer historical time period.

To date, the history of Canada-Mexico relations has not been the subject of extensive study. As José Springer suggests, connections between Canada and Mexico are understudied due to the dominance of the United States in North America. "While the economic and cultural relations between Canada and the U.S. and between Mexico and the U.S. have had a long and controversial history," he states, "the Canada-Mexico link lies virtually unexplored."[11] Nevertheless, Mexico is of central importance to Canada because it has been seen historically as a key to building broader relationships in Latin America. In fact, both Canada and the

United States arguably viewed Mexico as a metaphor for Latin America as a whole through much of the twentieth century and as a symbolic entryway to closer relations with other states. Case studies of visual culture, including exhibitions, provide a means of marking changes in the Canada-Mexico relationship. My research reveals not only diplomatic tactics but also the crafting of an image of Mexico, or of different Mexicos, in Canada, indicating what sort of nation the Mexican state was interested in promoting abroad, as well as what representation of Mexico the Canadian public perceived.

My study focuses on the NGC because this institution played a central role in bringing Mexican art to Canada during the twentieth century, coordinating and hosting many exhibitions that subsequently circulated to other Canadian museums, predominantly in large urban centres such as Toronto and Montreal.[12] The exhibition files held in the NGC Archives contain evidentiary materials including correspondence pertaining to the various exhibitions, photographs, catalogues, planning documents, and press clippings.[13] The role of the NGC as a cultural broker was overt. As the *Ottawa Journal* noted in 1943, "in showing special collections from other countries, the Gallery hopes to forge friendly links between the nations through the medium of art."[14] As a federal institution, the NGC was the site of a great deal of government activity, including partnerships with the Department of External Affairs (now Global Affairs Canada) as well as relationships with various Canadian embassy staff worldwide - relationships that were central not only to the circulation of foreign artworks in Canada but also to placing exhibitions of Canadian art abroad.[15]

Mexican art today

Exhibition files reveal a deep connection between the showing of Mexican art in Canada and the development of diplomatic and trade relationships between the two states. Formal diplomatic ties between Canada and Mexico were only established in 1944, but informal relations date back to the late nineteenth century.[16] The first exhibition of Mexican art in Canada, *Mexican Art Today*, opened in 1943, on the eve of Canada's new formal relationship with Mexico. This touring exhibition, circulated by the NGC, first went on display in Ottawa between 22 July and 22 August, and then travelled to the Art Association of Montreal from 2 September to 3 October. It was subsequently shown at the Art Gallery of Toronto (AGT) from 15 October to 14 November 1943.[17] While the exhibition played a significant role in strengthening connections between Canada and Mexico, it was actually organized in the United States and curated by Henry Clifford of the Philadelphia Museum of Art in collaboration with Inés Amor, a leading gallerist from Mexico City.[18] The fact that the NGC employed an external institution to organize this show indicates a lack of knowledge of Mexican art and access to it in Canada at this time. The exhibition addressed current developments in Mexican painting and raised awareness of a Mexican art scene outside of works by well-known muralists José Clemente Orozco and Diego Rivera.[19] Comprising oil paintings, watercolours, drawings, woodcuts, lithographs, and photographs, all drawn from Mexican and US collections, the show focused on cultural production between 1910 and 1943.[20] *Mexican Art Today* included over two hundred works by roughly sixty artists, representing key painters such as Rivera, Frida Kahlo, Rufino Tamayo, and David Alfaro Siqueiros.[21] The exhibition was extremely popular. The NGC reported over 9,000 visitors during its Ottawa run, a figure it cited as "one of the largest attendances on record at a summer exhibition."[22] In Montreal, the exhibition was likewise well attended; the press took note of the more than 3,000 visitors to the gallery in the first ten days of its run, during which time all of the catalogues were sold.[23]

In the exhibition catalogue, Luis Cardoza y Aragón stressed the need to understand Mexican art outside of the standard Western frame of reference.[24] "What we should appreciate in our own works of art is their resistance to European influences," he explains, "and whatever qualities of their own that they managed to put into obligatory themes, religious or otherwise."[25] In his essay "Contemporary Mexican Painting," he argued that Mexican art did not come into its own until after 1910, when the Mexican Revolution provided a key break from the colonial influence of the West. "Before such a social upheaval Mexican life was not a good basis for art. From having been an art of imitation, born from a society already almost destroyed, it rose to be an art looking toward extreme realism, and not without some creative fantasy. It reached this point of reality though an exaltation of life, through dreams."[26] The Canadian press, however, did not pick up on Cardoza y Aragón's emphasis on the Mexican Revolution, itself in part a comment on the new politics of Mexico since 1910.

Instead, press coverage focused on the aesthetics of the artworks. For example, one reviewer wrote, "The Mexican collection is completely free from propaganda of a political or economic sort, and, when you see Diego Rivera here, you see not the preacher of a system but the draughtsman

71

of Mexican genius."[27] Such rhetoric prioritized the concept of artistic genius and denied any relationship between art and the circumstances of its production, thus depoliticizing the works. While some reviewers did mention the Mexican Revolution, many downplayed its politics, reframing the works in terms of authenticity. For example, Elizabeth Gairdner, writing about the Montreal exhibition, stated, "These artists were not quiescent men - many were soldiers who fought in the terrible struggle of the Mexican revolution. The pain, sensualism, sorrow and horror which gluts their canvases comes from solid truth."[28] By discussing the artworks in terms of their authenticity, the political change that was a key part of the Mexican Revolution was ignored.

The three presentations of *Mexican Art Today* were supported by two collaborators with vested interests in the project: the Canadian Inter-American Association (CIAA) and the Wartime Information Board (WIB).[29] The CIAA provided support specifically to the Montreal edition. A non-governmental group based in the city, the CIAA was described in the press at the time as an organization "founded to promote a closer and more friendly understanding between the people of Canada and the peoples of the other nations of this hemisphere."[30] The WIB, a federal government body based in Ottawa, played a much larger role in *Mexican Art Today*. It provided key funding for the NGC to bring the exhibition to Canada, and correspondence reveals that the WIB's involvement was central to the institution's agreement to take on the exhibition.[31] A letter from NGC Director H.O. McCurry to A.S. Grigsby, Curator at the Vancouver Art Gallery, explains the WIB's strong desire for the exhibition to come to Canada, as well as its financial support, which was essential to the show. McCurry writes, "We didn't feel that we could afford it but the Wartime Information Board, for reasons that would be obvious to you, was anxious that it be held."[32] While McCurry does not state these reasons, the involvement of the WIB suggests that a primary motivation was to demonstrate Mexico as Canada's ally against fascism in the Second World War. To contextualize the Canada-Mexico alliance in this period, Mexico's relationship to Britain must be understood. Following Cárdenas's expropriation in 1938, Mexico underwent a "Mexican miracle," experiencing economic and social prosperity. At the same time, the United States and UK decried this change and supported a ban on Mexican oil. The outbreak of the Second World War ensured that there was a market for Mexican resources, however, and Mexico eventually joined the Allies in 1942. By 1943, the British Council had opened a Mexican outpost.

In October 1943, John Grierson, the director of the WIB, spoke at the Toronto opening of *Mexican Art Today*, which shared a launch event with a concurrent exhibition on tour from the Museum of Modern Art in New York, *Art of Latin America*.[33] Grierson talked about Canada's role internationally and compared it as a "young aspiring nation" with other South American countries also searching for their "character" and "spirit."[34] Press coverage of *Mexican Art Today* also emphasized the aims of the WIB. One review outlined Mexico's alliance for Canadian readers: "Mexico's government encourages creative art, [and] has always been hostile to Fascism and Nazism. Mexican volunteers fought shoulder to shoulder with the forces of Spanish Republican government - two years before 1939 when Hitler and Mussolini were smashing the rising young democracy of Spain ten years ago."[35] In this way, press coverage positioned Mexico as similar to Canada in its moral dimension, that is, as a state that would fight against a common enemy. *Mexican Art Today* was thus mobilized as a political tool to bolster state alliances at the height of international conflict and presented Mexico as united with Canada against the totalitarian governments of Germany and Italy.

The press also noted the exhibition's role in cultural diplomacy by remarking on its connection to the impending establishment of formal diplomatic relations between the two countries.[36] One article described the exhibition as "a further link in the development of understanding and respect between Canada and Mexico."[37] Another presented the Toronto exhibition as "complementary [...] helpful in understanding the Latin American neighbors with whom current circumstances make neighborliness not only the polite thing but essentially valuable."[38] Several reviews talked about good neighbours and the idea of neighbourliness between Canada and Mexico, and between Canada and Latin American nations generally. For example, in reference to the US "Good Neighbor Policy," a strategy of cooperation and trade between the United States and Latin America announced by President Franklin Delano Roosevelt in 1933, a review in the Windsor *Daily Star* identified Mexico as Canada's "nearest 'good neighbor.'"[39] Dina Berger characterizes this period as the "era of the good neighbor," a time "when friendship and cooperation toward Latin America replaced U.S. interventionism by the mid to late 1930s."[40] With its support of *Mexican Art Today*, the Canadian government demonstrated a similar though belated approach to Latin American relations.

The *Ottawa Citizen* noted Mexico's role in building better relations with South America. "Mexico is our North American link with the culture of the South-America's millions who live with us in our one-world of today."[41] The presence of key political figures at the openings of *Mexican Art Today*, where the artworks provided a key site for diplomacy, reinforced this interpretation.[42] For instance, in Ottawa, members of the diplomatic corps attended the opening, as well as J.A. MacKinnon, minister of trade and commerce. MacKinnon introduced another distinguished political guest, Carlos A. Calderón, the consul general for Mexico in Canada, who also attended the subsequent Toronto opening.[43] Calderón expressed the growing ties between Canada and Mexico in his speech at the event, stating, "It is with real satisfaction that I can testify to an ever-growing current of mutual sympathy and brotherly understanding between Mexico and Canada."[44] Furthermore, he spoke of an "inter-American spirit" which draws "us still closer as an integral part of the great American family."[45] Such lofty rhetoric was echoed by gallery officials. H.O. McCurry, director of the NGC, explained the importance of hemispheric unity: "We must realize North America does not stop at the Rio Grande."[46] Similarly, notable government representatives at the Montreal opening included Dr H.K. Keenleyside, the Canadian assistant deputy minister of external affairs.[47] Keenleyside commented on Mexico and Canada's similarities as nations, as well as their status as allies in war.[48] In Toronto, the joint opening of *Mexican Art Today* and *Art of Latin America* was attended by Latin American officials, including representatives from Brazil, Chile, Argentina, Colombia, Peru, Cuba, and Bolivia.[49] The significant presence of diplomatic figures at these openings, as well as the role they played in launch events, reinforced the diplomatic nature of *Mexican Art Today* and its importance as a platform for bringing national representatives together.

If government and other officials saw the exhibition as a chance to show off a new alliance, the press demonstrated the lack of Canadian awareness of Mexican culture at the time. In speaking about the exhibition as a way for Canadians to learn about Mexico, reviewers noted that Canadian audiences lacked proper preparation for understanding Mexican art. In the *Globe and Mail* (Toronto), Pearl McCarthy wrote that Toronto viewers would need to prepare themselves in advance to understand the show because of their lack of knowledge of Mexican culture, a culture she described as possessing Aztec influences, "supernatural" elements, and a preoccupation with death.[50] "Without that attempt," she added, "[viewers] might see nothing but what [they] would label morbid; and morbid suggest[s] something sickly, which Mexican art certainly is not today, although it has much to do with death. That paradox makes it difficult for plain westerners to understand."[51] Such interpretations framed Mexico as exotic, as opposed to the "plain westerners" of the Canadian public.[52] A subsequent article by McCarthy further emphasized the differences she saw between the two cultures of Canada and Mexico. "Some of it will be at first, a little hard to take because the point of view is so different. But it is vitally important that it be taken with full respect even if not always with private preference. The strangeness should not be allowed to obscure the intrinsic worth of the art itself."[53] In fact, anticipating widespread lack of knowledge, the gallery in Montreal announced that an information desk would be set up to provide further details on Mexican culture to visitors.[54] One report even noted that the desk would be staffed by a "Mexican resident in Montreal," who would be available to "explain to gallery visitors the background and surroundings in which these pictures were painted."[55]

In these ways, the press coverage made clear the lack of a close relationship between Canada and Mexico, the differences between the two states, and an ability to understand Mexico only in its contrast with Canada. The *Ottawa Citizen* drew an analogy to each nation's respective national artistic representation: "Unlike Canadian artists, whose trend is toward landscape, the Mexicans concentrate on human beings and their problems for their subjects."[56] Nevertheless, throughout the run of *Mexican Art Today*, press coverage noted the importance of Mexico's art. Mexican art was promoted as being on a par with the art of Canada, making clear that Mexican art was "not [...] a primitive school but a fully matured school of art" and "advanced in the cultural field."[57] Overall, coverage emphasized the difference and separateness of Mexican art but at the same time held it up as equal to the cultural production of Canada. The messages conveyed by the exhibition were ultimately complex: Mexico was Canada's ally, the two united in their fight against fascism. But the exhibition also advanced a narrative that spoke to Canadians' lack of understanding of Mexico, playing up racist preconceptions. As "the most representative showing of Mexican art ever seen in Canada [to that time]," *Mexican Art Today* walked a difficult line between exoticizing and de-politicizing, while showcasing the significance of Mexican cultural production.[58] State support and diplomatic overtures reveal the exhibition as a tool to announce a new formal relationship with Mexico and to create awareness of Mexican culture and promote it amongst the Canadian public. Overall, Canada and Mexico were positioning themselves as distinct but aligned sovereign states. This emphasis on national and cultural difference lasted until the late twentieth century and would only change with North American economic integration.

Contemporary Mexican painting

Only three years after *Mexican Art Today*, the NGC coordinated another touring exhibition of Mexican art in Canada, though on a more modest scale. Titled *Contemporary Mexican Painting*, the show toured Quebec and Ontario in the summer and fall of 1946, appearing at the NGC, the Art Association of Montreal, the AGT, and the Willistead Art Gallery in Windsor.[59] The exhibition comprised twenty-six wall-based works in a range of media - oil, gouache, watercolour, tempera, charcoal, pencil drawing, and ink drawing.[60] Works included pieces by Diego Rivera, David Alfaro Siqueiros, and Rufino Tamayo, among others.[61] The show also included several pieces of furniture - chairs, tables, a loveseat, and a screen -, a grouping described in one review as "essentially functional, but also attractive in appearance."[62]

The exhibition had direct links to another Canadian cultural exchange project with Mexico: the Canadian Pavilion at the 1946 International Book Fair in Mexico City. A significant endeavour for the Canadian government, the pavilion saw many different agencies play a part. One government memorandum suggested the pavilion should be coordinated by a committee with representatives from the Department of External Affairs, the WIB, the National Film Board (NFB), the Canadian Broadcasting Corporation, the Department of Trade and Commerce, and the NGC.[63] Furthermore, a meeting of the Inter-Departmental Committee on Canadian Publicity in Latin America was convened specifically to address Canadian participation in the book fair and included representatives from the Department of Trade and Commerce, External Affairs, the Canadian Information Service, the NGC, and the NFB.[64] This diversity of representation demonstrates not only the Canadian state's investment in building ties with Mexico and promoting the Canadian state abroad, but also the role of culture as integral to these efforts. Correspondence from the time reveals a considerable desire to promote Canada in Mexico. A memorandum to the Canadian ambassador in Mexico City explained, "A first class presentation of modern Canada would undoubtedly be a revelation to Mexico.... So far Canada has engaged in no major project to make herself known to Mexico. To achieve a successful exhibit at the Book Fair, would be to make a positive contribution in this field and one which should open new contacts for Canada of a profitable nature."[65] As this statement shows, the end goal of Canadian representation abroad was trade. Ultimately, the NGC coordinated a display of six Canadian paintings for the book fair pavilion by Edwin H. Holgate, A.Y. Jackson, Jacques de Tonnancour, Goodridge Roberts, Emily Carr, and Will A. Ogilvie.[66]

The connection between the book fair and *Mexican Contemporary Paintings* was largely pragmatic. In February of 1946, Arnold Tucker, a Canadian who was in Mexico City to oversee the erection of the Canadian Pavilion, was asked by NGC director McCurry to look into the possibility of securing an exhibition for the NGC. [67] The gallery was eager to host another show of contemporary Mexican painting. Tucker, in turn, conceived the idea of piggybacking on the shipping arranged to transport the Canadian pavilion materials back to Canada at the end of the book fair.[68] Mexican art could be shipped to Canada at the same time. While in Mexico City, Tucker engaged Inés Amor of the private Galería de Arte Mexicano to select and organize artworks for this Canadian exhibition.[69] She had also been involved in the earlier exhibition shown in Canada, *Mexican Art Today*. Amor (1912-80) was a key figure on the Mexican art scene, known for her promotion of modern Mexican art. Amor's older sister, Carito, opened the first gallery in Mexico City in 1935, and Inés assumed the role of director within five months, going on to become one of the most important gallerists in the city.[70] Amor also developed significant international connections - most of her clients were foreigners, and she built relationships with institutions including the Museum of Modern Art.[71] Coincidentally, J.S. McLean, a Canadian from Toronto, had just purchased several works of Mexican painting from the Galería de Arte Mexicano, which Amor included in the exhibition.[72] In this way, the NGC was able to secure an exhibition of Mexican art much more quickly than anticipated and for a greatly reduced cost.[73]

Even though the connection between the Canadian pavilion and the exhibit seems in hindsight to have been one of good timing, both endeavours were part of developing state relations at the time. After shipping the exhibition to Canada, Amor wrote to McCurry about the success of the Canadian pavilion at the book fair and expressed hope that the exchange would lead to greater understanding between Canada and Mexico: "Things like this and the interest of such fine people as Mr. McLean will undoubtedly help a great deal towards a better understanding of our countries."[74] Reviews of *Contemporary Mexican Paintings*, however, were not entirely positive. In Toronto, one critic wrote in the *Telegram*, "It is not as interesting an exhibition by a long way as that brought here a season or so ago. Still there is much that rewards attention."[75] McLean was very disappointed with the show, writing to McCurry to express his "shock," as he "had expected that [... his] pictures would be an inconspicuous part of a quite important group of Mexican paintings [...] similar to the Mexican show of four or five years ago."[76] Instead, his works comprised the bulk of the exhibition. To placate the lender and ensure he would agree to leave his works in for the duration of the tour, McCurry replied: "I agree that Miss Amor did not go to much trouble to make a representative exhibition but on the whole the collection is interesting and it was enjoyed here. [...] There was no attempt on our part to repeat the Mexican exhibition of 1943 but simply to keep more or less informed on Mexican art by having a small exhibition which will be interesting to all galleries and not too large for the smaller places which were not able to participate in the big exhibition a few years ago. [...] While I agree that Miss Amor could have done better, we are not altogether disappointed in this little show."[77] Due in part to its small size and the calibre of the artworks included, the exhibition was not lauded as a platform for state relationships in the way *Mexican Art Today* had been.[78]

Canadian overtures/Mexican disinterest

For more than a decade after 1946, the NGC did not coordinate any exhibitions of Mexican art. Correspondence nevertheless reveals that both the NGC and the Canadian government were very interested in mounting another exhibition during this time. A key motivation of the Canadian government was an interest in sending Canadian culture to Mexico in return.[79] In 1948, Canadian embassy officials expressed specific interest in a reciprocal cultural exchange between Canada and Mexico. The embassy explained its position in a letter to McCurry: "We continue to feel that one of the most useful things we could do would be to have an exhibition of Canadian art. The Mexicans are becoming fairly well informed on Canada as an industrial country with great resources, through business connections and through general publicity. But it is the opinion of a great many of us that there is almost complete ignorance about our cultural aspect."[80] While the Canadian government was eager to place Canadian culture abroad through reciprocal exchanges, the NGC was more interested in obtaining an exhibition of Mexican art to display in Canada. Other Canadian cultural institutions such as the AGT also demonstrated a significant interest in Mexican art.

Mexico, however, did not reciprocate this Canadian interest, despite its own interest in developing the bilateral relationship with Canada in this period.[81] For instance in 1951, Mexican President Miguel Alemán introduced a Canada-First Trade Policy.[82] Nevertheless, none of the several different entreaties for cultural exchange with Canada made through various official and non-official channels to Mexican representatives between 1948 and 1954 were successful. Overtures came from the Canadian ambassador in Mexico, the AGT, the NGC, and even Canadian artists living in Mexico. A letter to the Canadian Embassy from the undersecretary of state for External Affairs suggests that one reason for the lack of success was the NGC's insistence that any exhibition be reciprocated when the Mexicans were reluctant to accept a show of Canadian artwork to tour their country.[83] Throughout this period, correspondence nevertheless continued to reference the good relations between the two countries. Charles S. Band of the AGT wrote, "Relations between our two countries have never been better.... [But] that for good relations, exhibitions between our two countries are long overdue."[84] Nevertheless, it seems clear that Canada and Mexico were not as close as rhetoric would suggest, demonstrated by the Canadians' inability to secure a tour of Mexican artworks in Canada and vice versa.

At the same time, Mexico was sending exhibitions to Europe. McCurry's correspondence indicates he was well aware of specific exhibitions in locales such as Paris and Stockholm.[85] But by the 1950s, the NGC knew it was making no progress in negotiations with Mexico. McCurry expressed his frustration in a 1951 letter: "I must say that the proposed exchange of exhibitions between Canada and Mexico has been under discussion ever since I was there in 1947 and we never seem to get any further, largely I think because the Mexicans are not specially interested in exchanging exhibitions with us, although they did assure me that it was one of their most cherished hopes."[86] Finally, in 1954 McCurry confirmed that the NGC would drop the issue of reciprocal exhibitions or even an exhibition of Mexican art in Canada due to lack of interest from Mexico.[87]

The reasons for Mexican disinterest in Canadian art are not entirely clear but may have been related in part to the different federal systems of cultural administration in the two countries. Mexico's cultural institutions are highly centralized and have close ties to the federal administration, resulting in increased governmental control over their circulation abroad. Furthermore, as a dominion of the British Empire (although self-governing by this point), Canada may have lacked the international standing and global influence of a country like France. Mexican art had received considerable recognition for its strength since the state's participation in the Venice Biennale in 1950, which featured Orozco, Rivera, Siqueiros, and Tamayo.[88] But it seems that Canada lacked a strong presence in Mexico. Correspondence mentions Canada's reliance on the Anglo-Mexican Institute for Cultural Relations in Mexico, a British institution sponsored by the British Council.[89] As Canada had no cultural centre in Mexico, it used this institution as a base for negotiations. Finally, changing political circumstances at the end of World War II meant there was no longer a pressing need to demonstrate and strengthen military alliances through cultural exchange.

It is clear that Canada was more interested in Mexico than vice versa. Writing to Howard Gamble, editor of *Canadian Business*, McCurry noted the one-way relationship of cultural exchange: "Most of the cultural trade seems to have been from Mexico to Canada so far. Among the showings of Mexican art in Canada have been 'Mexican Art Today,' in Ottawa and Toronto in 1943; 'Contemporary Mexican Paintings,' shown in Ottawa, Toronto, Montreal and Windsor in 1946; a small show of Mexican paintings at Eaton's College Street, Toronto, in 1948; and a show of the work of José Clemente Orozco in Toronto in January-February, 1953."[90] The same letter notes that the only displays of Canadian art in Mexico were a series of silkscreen reproductions of paintings and the screening of the film *Canadian Landscape*, both shown at a UNESCO Conference in Mexico in 1947.[91] Strangely, McCurry did not mention the paintings sent by the NGC to Mexico for the International Book Fair in 1946, perhaps because they were seen as decoration for the pavilion rather than as a stand-alone exhibit.

Then, in 1956, the NGC became involved in an exhibition of Mexican modern art that came closer to fruition. In this case, the NGC collaborated with the arts institution, Arte A.C., in Monterrey, Mexico, which arranged for an exhibition of Mexican paintings to travel to Canada for showings at the NGC and three other Ontario venues. At the last minute, however, the curator, Lupe Solórzano, left the Mexican organization over a disagreement.[92] Then the NGC learned that Mexican artists were removing their work from the exhibition.[93] This was not due to Solórzano's departure; rather, NGC correspondence reveals that this "embarrassing situation" arose because the Mexican artists were hearing that there was a far more important Canadian exhibition of Mexican art being organized, and they wished to transfer their participation to it.[94] Solórzano's exhibition fell apart. D.W. Buchanan, the associate director at the NGC, wrote to A.J. Andrew of the Department of External Affairs to complain, emphasizing the lack of Canadian success in organizing such ventures: "I have a communication from the Canadian Ambassador in Mexico complaining that commercial enterprise has been able to arrange a Mexican exhibition for the Canadian cities of Vancouver, Edmonton, Winnipeg, Toronto and Montreal with the cooperation of the Instituto Nacional de Bellas Artes of Mexico City, whereas government cultural agencies have not been able to do so."[95]

The rival exhibition was funded by Canadian Pacific Air Lines to promote flights to Mexico and was shown at Hudson's Bay department stores across Canada. This arrangement demonstrated the success of private industry in the face of numerous failed government endeavours. However, it also showed that, even in private industry, building relationships is a reason for cultural exchanges. G.W.G. McConachie, president of Canadian Pacific Air Lines, wrote to Buchanan: "We initiated this project as a contribution to better understanding between Canada and Mexico, and also as a means of stimulating Canadian interest for travel to that country."[96] In the end, the exhibition curated by Solórzano for the NGC was cancelled for numerous reasons, including a lack of participating artists, the NGC's lack of power, communication issues, and a lack of interest from Mexico in sending two exhibitions to Canada simultaneously.[97] Nevertheless, the NGC did ensure that the exhibition funded by Canadian Pacific Air Lines circulated to some of the smaller galleries, such as the Public Library and Art Museum in London, Ontario, that were originally to receive the exhibition it had attempted to coordinate.[98]

Mexican Art: From Pre-Columbian Times to the Present Day

In all, over fourteen years would pass between *Contemporary Mexican Paintings* and the next exhibition of Mexican art held at the NGC. As in the past, bilateral relationships again provided the key impetus for Mexican officials to finally loan an exhibition.[99] The show, *Mexican Art: From Pre-Columbian Times to the Present Day*, toured the Vancouver Art Gallery, the NGC, and the Montreal Museum of Fine Arts between 1960 and 1961.[100] The exhibition featured more than two hundred works representing a period of over four thousand years, including pre-Columbian sculptures, colonial sculptures, colonial paintings, twentieth-century paintings, prints, photographs of contemporary architecture, and indigenous crafts.[101] The catalogue emphasized the exhibition's importance in building connections between Canada and Mexico, calling the show "a landmark in the history of cultural relations between Canada and other countries of this hemisphere."[102] And finally, this exhibition was linked to a reciprocal show of Canadian art, which travelled to Mexico City and Guadalajara in 1960 and 1961. Called *Arte Canadiense*, the show consisted of a survey of Canadian art from the eighteenth century to the 1950s, produced by the NGC in collaboration with the National Museum of Canada, and featured French Canadian artworks, Inuit sculpture, indigenous carvings from the west coast of Canada, paintings, and contemporary graphic art.[103]

Governments were involved in *Mexican Art: From Pre-Columbian Times to the Present Day* in several different ways.[104] The origins of this exhibition date to 1957, and correspondence indicates that the show was a high-level diplomatic concern of both Canadian and Mexican officials.[105] A memorandum from Buchanan at the NGC suggests the lengths that the Mexican ambassador in Canada was willing to go to in order to secure an exhibition: "The ambassador of the Republic of Mexico, Dr. Maples-Arce, promised that if no official indication was received soon from Mexico as to the availability of the Mexican art exhibition for showing in Canada in 1960, he then himself would advance discussions personally in Mexico City later that summer. The Ambassador is sternly in favour of the Mexican government touring this exhibition in Canadian cities."[106] Members of the Canadian embassy staff in Mexico were also involved in the early days of the exhibition, facilitating discussions between the NGC and the Instituto Nacional de Bellas Artes (INBA) in Mexico City.[107] The two governments also provided state funding. A cost-sharing arrangement equalized the expenses associated with the exhibitions. This arrangement became quite complicated when unanticipated issues arose in shipping the works abroad.[108] The solution was a complicated system whereby different government agencies funded different aspects of the show. As the funding came equally from Mexican and Canadian partners, it is clear that both exhibitions were well supported by the state and by arts institutions.

New bilateral relationships were also forged through these exhibitions. For example, gallery officials in Ottawa and Mexico held face-to-face meetings. Buchanan, as associate director of the NGC, travelled in October 1959 to Mexico, where he met with several Mexican officials, including the director-general of the INBA, Celestino Gorostiza.[109] The exhibition openings once again provided occasions for the typical political overtures. For example, the Mexican exhibition was opened in Vancouver and Ottawa by the Mexican ambassador to Canada, Rafael de la Colina, and the Ottawa opening featured the Canadian minister of citizenship and immigration, Ellen Fairclough.[110] While not directly discussed in correspondence from late 1950s, both exhibitions would ultimately be promoted as marking the 150th anniversary of Mexican Independence, achieved in 1810.[111] The upcoming 100th anniversary of Canadian Confederation in 1967, in turn, provided an opportunity to market both Canada and Mexico as established nations with strong and distinct national cultures, demonstrated through their extensive and diverse cultural patrimonies.[112]

The Canadian and Mexican exhibitions mirrored each other as large-scale, comprehensive shows featuring artworks in a range of mediums. Additionally, both *Mexican Art: From Pre-Columbian Times to the Present Day* and *Arte Canadiense* featured indigenous cultural production, presenting these artworks within the colonial narrative of the modern nation.[113] In initial correspondence about the exhibition, Miguel Álvarez Acosta, the director general of the INBA, wrote to Douglas S. Cole, the Canadian ambassador to Mexico: "We believe that these exhibits will contribute to strengthen even more the already existing bonds of friendship bettwen [sic] Mexico and Canada and at the same time [...] they will spread the knowledge of the artistic manifestations of the two countries."[114] However, he also wrote of the need to encapsulate the nation's artistic accomplishments within the exhibition: "The main object [...] is to present in Canada a complete picture of the development of our arts."[115] Equally important to the Mexicans was having Canadian culture fully represented for Mexican audiences, as one meeting summary indicates: "Señor Salas desired that the Canadian exchange exhibition parallel the Mexican one as closely as possible."[116] A memorandum confirms, "Mr. Salas wanted the exhibition to include 18th and 19th Century paintings, sculpture and also perhaps a selection of Indian handicrafts as well as Eskimo sculpture."[117]

The NGC was preoccupied with ensuring that the Mexican exhibition coming to Canada was of the same calibre of those that had toured Europe. Buchanan was very clear that he had always wanted a reciprocal exhibition, writing, "From the very beginning the understanding given the Mexicans has been that we only wanted it if it was of the same quality of the exhibition [...] which went to Europe."[118] In other correspondence, Buchanan mentions an exhibition that toured Europe and also went to

Japan, writing that he hoped that "something similar can be re-assembled on a manageable scale" to go to Canada.[119] The NGC even compared lists of objects for inclusion in the Canadian show with lists of those that had travelled to Europe.

The aim of both the Canadian and Mexican exhibitions in 1960-61 was to establish national prestige, serve as a visual representation of binational relations, and buttress each state's autonomous identity and power. This type of cultural diplomacy seems characteristic of the mid-twentieth century in that it focused on discrete national narratives. Despite rhetoric about a close and growing relationship between the two states during this period, as well as Mexico's move to prioritize Canadian trade in 1951, the difficulties of establishing reciprocal cultural exchange shows that the two states were not as close as they professed to be.

Mexican art in Canada at the turn of the millennium

While the NGC subsequently hosted group exhibitions that included Mexican artists, such as the 1994 exhibition *Cartographies: 14 Artists from Latin America*, not until the turn of the millennium did the gallery host another show that focused solely on Mexican art.[120] This exhibition, *Mexican Modern Art*, featured works similar to those that had toured Canada in the mid-twentieth century. It was, however, quite different in the messages it conveyed about Mexican ties with Canada. In contrast to the earlier exhibitions, which were preoccupied with establishing differences between Canada and Mexico as sovereign states, this exhibition promoted continental ties. Exhibitions of Mexican art in Canada during the mid-twentieth century, as the analysis here shows, suggest an uneven relationship between the two states, one in which Mexico often held the balance of power and seemed largely uninterested in Canada. Projects of cultural exchange do not progress in a linear fashion but instead occur in fits and spurts, stopping and starting depending on political developments. Regardless, art was and remains a key to diplomacy, revealing relationships and also furthering political aims.[121]

Chapter 5

Economic Pilgrimage to Southern Ontario: Vincenzo Pietropaolo and the Photohistory of Mexican Farmhands, 1984–2006

Jason Dyck

Introduction

The Canadian countryside has significantly changed in recent decades with the rising dependency on guest workers. Every year thousands of farmhands from Mexico and the Caribbean migrate to Canada to harvest fruits, vegetables, tobacco, and nursery stock. Today the majority of foreign workers come from rural *pueblos* (towns) in the states surrounding Mexico City, and most of them end up on farms in southern Ontario. Over the past forty years, Mexicans have gone from being a relatively small minority that was largely invisible to Canadian society, to a sizeable community whose visibility is starting to change local social relations and economies. They are more noticeable at local establishments; academics and journalists pay more attention to their working conditions; and a larger number of church groups and activists reach out to them through language programs, services, protests, and legal action. But even though a Mexican riding a bicycle down a country lane is now a common sight in many parts of rural Ontario, the visual history of migrant workers in Canada has yet to be written.

A "pictorial turn" in the study of foreign workers in Canada is made possible through the work of the Italian-born Canadian photographer, Vincenzo Pietropaolo (1951-).[1] For over twenty years Pietropaolo followed Mexican farmhands with his camera from their fields of employment in southern Ontario to their home *pueblos* in central Mexico. He published a selection of these photographs in a photo essay entitled *Harvest Pilgrims* (2009), introducing his work with an imaginary letter to a migrant Mexican worker named Fermín. "You are like a harvest pilgrim," he writes, "you return to the same area, often to the same farm, year after year, in an annual pilgrimage. You live between two worlds, North and South."[2] Taking inspiration from transnational and borderlands histories, I argue in this chapter that Pietropaolo's deliberate fusion of agricultural and religious imagery complicates the traditional borders of "Greater Mexico," a region generally understood to be comprised of only Mexico and the southwestern United States. *Harvest Pilgrims* clearly demonstrates that Mexican *pueblos* exist in the Canadian countryside in similar ways to the way they exist in rural America, albeit in temporary and fragmented forms. To demonstrate this, I analyze Pietropaolo's photo essay as a series of uncommissioned *retablos* that, similar to *exvoto* paintings commissioned by Mexican labourers in the United States, provides a visual commentary on transnational labour in rural Ontario and the limits of multiculturalism in Canada.

This chapter is based upon forty-eight photographs of migrant Mexican workers in *Harvest Pilgrims*, all of them shot between 1984 and 2006 in both Mexico and various regions of southern Ontario.[3] All of these photographs are in black and white and, with the exception of a few digital prints, were taken from traditional negatives. My analysis of *Harvest Pilgrims* is divided into three parts. In the first section I provide a brief overview of the literature and visual record of the Canadian Seasonal Agricultural Workers Program (CSAWP), demonstrating that Pietropaolo's transnational perspective mirrors changing patterns in scholarship on migrant workers. The second section looks at images as historical documents and places Pietropaolo's photographic method in the larger context of photohistory and the popular artwork of Catholic pilgrimage. In the last section I compare Pietropaolo's photographs of Mexican farmhands in Canada to ex-voto paintings dealing with migration to the United States.

The Canadian side of "Greater Mexico"

At one exhibition, as he was setting up his photographs from *Harvest Pilgrims*, Pietropaolo recalls being asked "in which country were [his] pictures taken." When he responded that he had shot them all in southern Ontario, his visitors were "incredulous."[4] *Harvest Pilgrims* at times blurs the multiple borders of North America. The agricultural setting of Pietropaolo's photographs can easily be mistaken for the United States which, much like Canada, harvests many of the same fruits, plants, and vegetables and, in certain cases, shares similar physical landscapes with its northern neighbour. For example, Pietropaolo's photograph of Rosario in an open field in La Salette provides no clues that he is working in Canada (40).[5] Completely encircled by tobacco plants, Rosario looks straight into the camera lens, his baseball cap perfectly aligned with the skyline and casting a shadow across his eyes. One can draw a similar conclusion from his shot of Érica Carreón-Acosta on a tomato harvester in Wheatley (116). Érica gazes into Pietropaolo's camera behind the chains, bars, and hydraulic hoses of the machine. Only a few trees appear in the background because the harvester occupies by far the greatest part of the frame. These are Mexicans at work but we are unsure where.

Due to economic necessity, Rosario, Érica, and thousands more are forced to leave Mexico to find employment and higher wages in *El norte* ("the North"). During the colonial period, Mexico was known as New Spain, a viceroyalty of the Spanish crown that also included large sections of present-day Central America and the United States. Although Mexico eventually lost a large portion of its northern territory in the Mexican-American War (1846–1848) and as a result of the Gadsden Purchase (1853), the history of the Spanish borderlands has, in the words of Samuel Truett, always been a "multiplicity of overlapping and competing histories."[6] Given these intimate ties across the Mexico-US border, several historians have moved away from the cartographic confines of the modern nation-state to larger transnational movements and patterns. Inspired by the work of Américo Paredes (1915-1999), scholars have built upon the idea of Greater Mexico by recognizing that there are also "many Mexicos" on *el otro lado* ("the other side") that need to be accounted for to properly write the national histories of both Mexico and the United States.[7] But the concept of Greater Mexico, as Paredes originally envisioned it, signified Mexico in a cultural sense and, as a result, was far more expansive than the borderlands region.[8] Given the increasing numbers of migrant Mexican workers in southern Ontario, visually documented in *Harvest Pilgrims*, I argue that Greater Mexico needs to cross yet another border to include Canada.

Mexicans have crossed the Mexico-US or the Canada-US borders illegally as *mojados* ("wetbacks") or as contracted farmhands through bilateral agreements such as the Bracero Program (1942-1964) and the Canadian Seasonal Agricultural Workers Program (1966-).[9] In contrast to the long tradition of relying upon Mexican labour in the United States, which stems back to at least the mid-nineteenth century, Mexicans only officially started working in Canada in 1974, when the CSAWP expanded its labour pool beyond the Caribbean. The number of Mexican participants in the program grew steadily from 203 in 1974 to 10,777 in 2004,[10] the greatest increase taking place after the signing of the North American Free Trade Agreement (NAFTA) in 1994 and the implementation of neoliberal reforms. Economic opportunities in the

Mexican countryside are few and, as a result, migration continues to form an integral part of the social and economic fabric of many Mexican *pueblos*. Their presence has become so ubiquitous in various parts of the United States and Canada that Ronald L. Mize and Alicia C. S. Swords have argued that North American consumption "rests squarely, though not exclusively, on the backs of Mexican labor."[11]

Pietropaolo began photographing migrant workers in the mid-1980s, roughly ten years after they were incorporated into the CSAWP. "The more I investigated," he recalls, "the more astonished I became at how invisible these migrant workers were in our society."[12] Living in rural areas with limited means of transportation beyond the bicycle, "guest" workers were indeed hidden from most urban Canadians in the 1980s and 1990s. These "invisible workers" were, and still are, primarily married men with families who are landless, poorly educated, and underemployed, and come from the states surrounding Mexico City. They are normally between the ages of twenty-five and forty when they start the program, and several work into their sixties, when they are able to retire with a Canadian pension.[13] More women have joined the CSAWP since 1989 but their numbers are still low given that local farmers normally prefer men, and gender roles in Mexican *pueblos* often confine females to the domestic sphere.[14] Most Mexicans working in Ontario can be found on farms or greenhouses in the Niagara Region, Essex County, Holland Marsh, and Simcoe County, with contracts ranging from six weeks to eight months. By 2004, Mexican farmhands were working on 1,800 farms across the country in nine provinces, and 1,600 of these were in Ontario.[15]

Little had been written on Mexican farmhands in the CSAWP when Pietropaolo first took an interest in documenting their lives with his camera. Although most of the early studies had concentrated on Jamaicans and other Caribbean workers,[16] by the 1990s Mexicans were the primary focus of researchers and social activists. Thanks to their efforts, there is now a growing body of literature on most aspects of migrant Mexican experiences in Canada (particularly in Ontario) that cover a range of topics such as health problems, work experiences, remittances, immigration policy, and questions of social exclusion and inclusion in Canadian society.[17] In large part Canadian farmers, government agencies, and foreign observers have all presented the CSAWP as a "model program" that was far superior to the Bracero Program in the United States. Criticisms, however, have become more commonplace in the past decade as scholars and activists are increasingly describing "harvest pilgrims" as "unfree" workers because they are unable to circulate in the labour market or completely refuse the demands of their employers.[18] They have also claimed that migrant workers in Canada are "like feudal serfs," forced to "enact performances of subordination," bound to their employers in paternal relationships, and suffering several cases of racism and gender biases.[19]

This growing body of criticism is partially explained by a shift in the sources used to interpret the CSAWP and the places where research is now being conducted. Instead of primarily interviewing farmers, bureaucrats, and other Canadian and Mexican officials, researchers have been turning to the opinions of the workers themselves. Since there is very little written by Mexican workers participating in the CSAWP, scholars have been forced to turn to oral histories, conducting interviews in both Canada and Mexico. Some anthropologists have even performed fieldwork at local farms in Ontario, Nelson Ferguson arguing that it is necessary to move beyond the economic systems determining migratory cycles of millions of Mexicans to the "lived experiences" of those involved.[20] Beyond this, more studies are adopting a transnational perspective to interpret migrant work, which has meant contextualizing agriculture in both Canada and Mexico to understand the CSAWP. Pietropaolo has employed this same method in *Harvest Pilgrims*. "Early on," he recalls, "I realized the importance of documenting the workers in the reality of their own homes in their own countries."[21] Indeed, the history of Canadian agriculture in the past forty years is a larger story that must be told from both Mexican *pueblos* and Canadian farms.

Despite the growing literature on migrant Mexican workers in Canada, visual sources are much harder to find. There is good reason for this. Until relatively recently, migrant workers had been largely absent from the local media in Ontario.[22] In the first two decades of the CSAWP, according to Pietropaolo, "fewer than a dozen feature-length articles appeared in mainstream magazines or newspapers in Canada."[23] Not only this, but few Canadian artists have seen migrant workers as worthy subjects, and in most cases Mexicans themselves have not turned to artistic forms to express their work experiences.[24] And nobody, to my knowledge, has attempted a study of Mexican photographs and home videos of their time in Canada.[25] They are not tourists when they arrive in this country, and hence most do not see the workplace as a worthy subject for a picture. The evidence I offer here is clearly anecdotal, but after working for thirteen seasons (1989–2003) at a local nursery in St. Catharines, I remember only one Mexican videotaping during work hours. And although I have several digital pictures of my co-workers in their Mexican *pueblos*, I only possess one photograph of them working in Canada. *Harvest Pilgrims* fills in this pictorial gap on the Canadian side of Greater Mexico, both for me as a former agricultural worker and for the CSAWP more generally, specifically the early history of the program.[26]

The photohistory of migrant workers in Canada

Canada imports thousands of foreign workers to harvest local food given that Canadians generally shy away from agriculture because of the nature of the work and the low salaries. "It is in this context," Pietropaolo says, "that I photographed the workers that I call Harvest Pilgrims, all of whom came to this country as part of the CSAWP in Ontario."[27] Indeed, *Harvest Pilgrims* offers a window onto the fields, orchards, and greenhouses of the province where Mexicans stake, pick, grade, thin, sort, and harvest. Whether it is apples, pears, peaches, carrots, tomatoes, tobacco, or tulips, Mexican hands cling to what Canadians eat, plant, and smoke. In a buttoned-up shirt and baseball cap, Fermín Pérez primes tobacco in Otterville with agility, speed, and concentration; his hands, moving quickly, appear blurred in the frame (42). Another worker in Holland Marsh, elaborately clothed in rain gear, plastic gloves, and a warm toque, gazes emptily upon a conveyor belt of carrots he monotonously inspects, his hands positioned and ready to interject when needed (60). And in an orchard in Beamsville, a farmhand looks straight into Pietropaolo's lens, standing on guard with his hands firmly sustaining a Foodland Ontario basket filled to the brim with peaches (36). *Harvest Pilgrims* visually documents how dependent local growers in Ontario have become on migrant farm workers.

To fully understand the experiences of migrant workers like Fermín, it is necessary to move beyond photographs as mere illustrations to see them as historical documents. Peter Burke, in his study *Eyewitnessing* (2001), argues that images, in whatever medium, are important forms of historical evidence to interpret the past and should be used together with written documents and oral testimonies.[28] Although they have the potential to provide insight into various aspects of social reality that other written sources omit, Burke cautiously guards against the "temptations of realism, more exactly of taking an image for reality, [which] are particularly seductive in the case of photographs and portraits."[29] Photographs, like all written texts, are constructed by men and women who are guided by their own subjectivities and biases. They are taken during a particular time, at a certain angle, and in a given place, and hence need to be understood within their historical context to fully appreciate both

90

their subject matter and authorship. The camera is "not an unbiased witness," as Pietropaolo makes clear, but, as "a good witness," the photographic image "may make people uncomfortable while it is current, but over time, as history recedes further and further into the past, this same image can resurface into the present and evoke the past."[30]

Pietropaolo's photographs, then, are not only historical documents that shed new light on the CSAWP, they are an important contribution to what John Mraz has called "photohistory," which he defines as the representation of history in photographs. Mraz argues that pictures complement written history by providing visual images of material culture, working conditions, popular culture, and larger social relations of race, class, and gender.[31] He claims that one "contribution photography can make to historiography is that of personalizing the past: on seeing individual human beings, we remember that it is people who really forge history, as they make something out of what is being made of them."[32] Not only this, he also suggests, together with Jaime Vélez Storey, that photographs provide a "human face to sociological data and statistics, showing people who actually experienced the events which historians usually research and reconstruct through written documents."[33] "Personalizing the past" is rooted in a larger quest to uncover the lives of ordinary people, those who have been traditionally overlooked by older currents of historiography or by a great-man view of the past. Pietropaolo joins in this quest not only in Harvest Pilgrims, but in most of his photoessays, concentrating on immigrants, workers, and those with disabilities in Canadian society. His goal, especially with workers, is to take "anonymous beings, without identity" and "validate" them through his camera.[34]

Beyond "personalizing the past," Pietropaolo's photographs of migrant Mexican workers reflect his own personal past, which is deeply shaped by experiences of immigration and the search for employment in a transnational context. Born in the small rural village of Maierato in Calabria, Pietropaolo spent the early years of his life in southern Italy where, much like in certain parts of the Mexican countryside, subsistence farming was common practice. In search of a brighter economic future, his family migrated to Canada in 1959, settling in Toronto, where his dad earned a living by working in various construction projects. Although Pietropaolo moved back to Italy with his mother and siblings for a few years, he eventually returned to the provincial capital in 1963 and grew up in the Italian enclave to the west of the Kensington market. As a young immigrant to Canada, Pietropaolo recalls how his father, whom he also describes as a "migrant farm worker," searched for work on tobacco farms during periods of high unemployment in Toronto. "[I]mmigration has been a defining element in my own life," he confesses, and it was "through photography that I have been able to deal with the uprooting nature of the immigration process."[35]

To understand the "immigration process" Pietropaolo follows his subjects - whether an Italian immigrant, a factory worker, or a Mexican farmhand - in both public and private spaces. His goal is to uncover the "collective contributions of ordinary people"[36] in their everyday settings, which has forced him to climb construction sites, visit factories, enter homes and places of worship, follow street processions and protests, and travel down country roads in both southern Ontario and central Mexico. Pietropaolo recognizes that photography involves collaboration between the subject and the photographer, which is why several of his subjects stare directly into his lens, reflecting both their consent and general trust. In preparation for *Harvest Pilgrims*, Pietropaolo arranged to visit several Mexican workers in their own *pueblos*, arriving ahead of time to capture the wide-ranging emotions of their return home. Beyond soliciting permission, Pietropaolo also performs extensive interviews with his subjects, seeking to understand their personal stories through their own words, which he in turn incorporates into his photo essays. He understands that photography "is one of the most universal languages" but that, when "combined with words, the two narratives become fused much like one braid, and each of the intertwining strands impacts powerfully upon the perception of the other by the viewer/reader."[37]

Similar to earlier forms of documentary photography, which developed in Europe and the United States in the late 1800s in response to increasing levels of urbanization and industrialization, Pietropaolo also acknowledges that "photography is very political."[38] By concentrating on changing labour trends in Canadian agriculture, he wants his photographs to serve a social function and sees them as "a gesture of solidarity in [the] struggle for social justice."[39] Much like the American documentary photographer Lewis W. Hine (1874–1940), whom he claims had a "profound effect on [him],"[40] Pietropaolo uses the camera as a "research tool" to uncover the social inequalities of global capitalism.[41] In the same way that Hine photographed child labourers in the United States with an empathetic eye, Pietropaolo views migrant workers through a compassionate lens when taking pictures of them on Canadian farms. Similar to the ways in which Hine admired the "heroes" and "men of courage, skill, daring and imagination" forging the New York City skyline, Pietropaolo pays homage to "the sweat of Mexicans" who "grow our food" in Ontario.[42] And like Hine and other documentary photographers, Pietropaolo has placed his photographs on display in several magazines, newspapers, museums, and exhibits.[43] The photographs in *Harvest Pilgrims*, then, are pilgrims on a journey in much the same way as migrant Mexican workers themselves.

Pietropaolo's pilgrim images draw awareness to Mexican farmhands living "on the fringes of society"[44] through the convergence of religious and secular imagery. He draws inspiration from Eugene Smith (1918-1978), hailed as the "master of the photo essay," and especially his desire to "right what is wrong" through photography.[45] Smith was known for both the aesthetic quality of his pictures and the ways in which he penetrated the lives of his subjects with his camera. His photograph of Ryoko Uemura bathing her daughter Tomoko (1972), who had been severely deformed by mercury poisoning in Minamata, Japan, has been compared to the Pietà of Michelangelo, a Renaissance sculpture depicting Jesus in the arms of Mary just after his crucifixion.[46] Pietropaolo was influenced by this image when he photographed the disabled in Canada, but his camera eye has also been deeply impacted by the religious traditions of his own Catholic past. He confesses that "the idea of people praying in the streets had always fascinated me. Like most children born in Italy I had been exposed to a variety of religious processions, and other public rituals."[47] In following the Italian community in Toronto, Pietropaolo photographed the faithful praying before candles in church and participating in several aspects of the liturgical calendar. One can find similar images of Mexican workers in *Harvest Pilgrims* that, in many cases, bear a striking resemblance to ex-voto paintings.

In the widest sense of the term, an ex-voto is an object offered to the divinity with the goal of completing a promise made for some sort of favour. The practice is ancient, not restricted to Catholicism, and might include offerings such as metal or wax replicas of body parts (*milagros*), crutches, diplomas, toys, trophies, articles of clothing, or even photographs.[48] Although the practice of painting ex-votos (also known as *retablos*) most likely crossed the Atlantic in the 1500s, some of our earliest examples in Mexico come from the first half of the seventeenth century from the elites of colonial society.[49] The artistic genre only became popular among the poorer classes of Mexico throughout the nineteenth century, when tin sheets became more widely available.[50] *Retableros* (painters of *retablos*), who are normally self-taught and leave their works unsigned, found tin to be a cheap, light, durable, relatively rustproof, and adhesive surface on which to paint. After a *retablero* had completed the ex-voto painting, the devotee performed a pilgrimage and deposited the work in a local shrine as a sign of gratitude. A few *retable-ros* still paint at the present time, but the practice has considerably declined from the mid-twentieth century onwards, photography playing a contributing role in this larger trend.[51] It is much easier and cheaper to leave a photograph at a local shrine than to leave an ex-voto painting.

Devotees commission *retableros* to paint, which means they need to listen carefully to the miraculous stories of their clients. Ex-voto paintings detail the hopes and fears of the faithful and reproduce some of the suffering and pain that was characteristic of the lives of many men and women in post-independent and post-revolutionary Mexico. These sheets of tin contain three major elements: (1) the apparition of a Catholic image that is normally surrounded by clouds near the top at either side of the composition, (2) the graphic re-enactment of the miraculous event that takes up most of the space in the middle, and (3) a written description of the miracle at the bottom with information on the place, date, and human actors involved. Pietropaolo's photographs of migrant workers may not include the first element, but in several cases, they mirror the latter two. He may not have listened to the prodigious wonders of his subjects, but he did take note of their economic hardships, emotional displacement, and occupational woes. And even though Pietropaolo was not commissioned by any of his subjects in *Harvest Pilgrims*, through his photo essay he acts as an uncommissioned *retablero* detailing the economic pilgrimages of migrant workers to the Canadian side of Greater Mexico.

Although the farmhands in Harvest Pilgrims did not solicit Pietropaolo's services, several Mexicans returning home from the United States have approached *retableros* for theirs. In *Miracles on the Border* (1995), Jorge Durand and Douglas S. Massey performed a study of *ex-voto* paintings that were either commissioned or painted by Mexican workers in the United States or by their relatives back home. After finding 124 examples, they concluded that "*retablos* capture events as they were experienced by the migrants themselves. The pictures and texts provide a rich source of historical and sociological data."[52] Similar to photographs, which are sometimes used as *ex-votos*, *retablos* "personalize the past" of migrant workers from their crossing of the border to their return home. Durand and Massey divided these experiences into six groups: (1) making the trip, (2) finding one's way, (3) legal problems, (4) medical problems, (5) getting by in the United States, and (6) homecoming. All of the *retablos* in Miracles on the Border "reveal unambiguously and unequivocally the degree to which US migration has become a core part of the collective

Figure 1. Vincenzo Pietropaolo, *A solemn moment during a mass celebrated for migrant workers in Spanish at Our Lady of La Salette Roman Catholic Church*, gelatin silver print, La Salette, Ontario, 1996. Reproduced with the authorization of the artist.

experience of the Mexican people."[53] *Harvest Pilgrims* demonstrates similar trends in Canadian migration for an increasing number of Mexicans.

Visualizing economic pilgrimage in "Greater Mexico"

One migrant worker told Pietropaolo that he did not "know why God created us to be so poor." Plagued by his poverty and weary from his transnational journeys, the man concluded "that God should have made us all equal."[54] *Harvest Pilgrims* provides a visual outlet for these types of unspoken prayers. In a special mass celebrated for migrant workers at a local Catholic church in La Salette, Pietropaolo captures a migrant worker in a solemn moment with the palms of his hands outstretched in worship (106) (Fig. 1). This religious service took place in 1996 during the *fiestas patrias* (patriotic celebrations) honouring Mexican independence from Spain.

In another shot, Pietropaolo focuses on a large group of migrant workers gathered around a lamppost, standing on guard and singing the Mexican national anthem with pride (105). He also follows a procession of Mexican farmhands leaving the aforementioned church carrying a crucifix, the Canadian and Mexican flags, and a statue of the principal patroness of Mexico, the Virgin of Guadalupe (107).[55] These photographs could have been taken anywhere in Greater Mexico, but the maple leaf draws one to the fields of southern Ontario.

Figure 2. Anonymous, *Retablo of Braulio Barrientos*, oil on metal, dimensions unknown, Sanctuary of San Juan de los Lagos, Jalisco, Mexico, 1986. Reproduced with the authorization of Mexican Migration Project, Princeton University.

Figure 3. Vincenzo Pietropaolo, *A Mexican worker arrives in Canada at the beginning of the work season*, gelatin silver print, Pearson International Airport, Toronto, Ontario, 1987. Reproduced with the authorization of the artist.

Comparing the silent petitions of *Harvest Pilgrims* to the written prayers of *Miracles on the Border* highlights important similarities and differences between migrant experiences in Canada and the United States. Included in the category "making the trip" are a series of difficulties, obstacles, and risks that the migrant worker must overcome on both sides of the Mexico-US border to make it to *El norte*. This process starts in Mexico and involves accumulating enough capital to get to the border, which, depending on the individual, might be a long and dangerous trip. Upon arrival, the migrant worker often needs to solicit the services of a *coyote* or *pollero* ("guide") to cross, which might involve traversing the Rio Grande, trekking through the desert of New Mexico, or climbing a fence in California. In all cases, the migrant runs the risk of fraud and banditry and needs to be on the lookout for the border patrol. A *retablo* (1986) commissioned by Braulio Barrientos (Fig. 2), for example, narrates the desert crossing of four migrant workers who, surrounded by cacti and arid yellow sand, are "without hope of drinking even a little water."[56] Through the use of bright colours, a blazing white sun, and long dark shadows, the *retablo* captures the danger, anxiety, and overall stress of making it to *el otro lado*.

Crossing the Canada-US border takes place under significantly different circumstances. Under the CSAWP, Mexicans enter the country legally with working visas, and their flights are partially subsidized by their employers. They do not need to be smuggled across two borders by a *coyote* or *pollero*, because their employers are responsible for picking them up at the airport. On one occasion in 1987, Pietropaolo arranged to be at the Pearson International Airport in Toronto to witness the arrival of migrant workers. In one of his photographs, a Mexican (68) (Fig. 3) patiently waits in line by a Thrifty Car Rental booth and an exit sign lettered in both English and French, the two official languages of Canada. Dressed in slacks, sweatshirt, and a traditional *sombrero*, the man sustains a duffle bag strapped over his shoulders while dangling another bag from his folded hands. Although a few travellers pass by in the background, he stands alone in the centre of the picture and contemplatively looks ahead, seemingly showing no signs of pressing concern. His face of quiet resignation is a stark contrast to the fear and anguish expressed by the four men crossing the desert in Barrientos's *retablo*.

Even though border crossings vary across Greater Mexico, the larger process of travelling to Canada is not without its own hidden expenses and stresses. *Harvest Pilgrims* may not illustrate the anxiety of the entire journey northward, but the accompanying captions certainly do. While in Mexico in 1993, Pietropaolo photographed a man carrying a large package over his shoulders as he triumphantly arrives home at the Benito Juárez International Airport in Mexico City (69). Underneath the picture is a short narrative of the *reservas de aeropuerto* ("airport pools"), workers who wait at the airport to take the place of others who drop out at the last minute.[57] One, in particular, travelled to the capital on several occasions only to find that the "person in the office was very dismissive." After several days of waiting in the airport he "did get lucky, and we were able to come, so we could start working." This account of the *reservas* reflects only a small portion of the costs that Mexicans accumulate to participate in the CSAWP. On average, each worker needs to travel to Mexico City five or six times each season for interviews, medical exams, and other documentary procedures.[58] These multiple trips force many to take out loans, because the Mexican government only started to partially subsidize these costs in May of 2002.[59]

Crossing borders is indeed a source of anxiety and stress for migrant workers, but "finding one's way" upon arrival to *el otro lado* is also fraught with several difficulties, especially for those without relatives or personal contacts. Durand and Massey found two major issues facing Mexicans in the United States: finding employment, and potentially getting lost. With limited language skills, directions, and knowledge of the labour and housing markets, these tasks were daunting for several workers and cause for divine intervention. This was clearly the experience of Isidro Rosas Rivera, a *campesino* (peasant) from a small *pueblo* near San Luis de la Paz in the state of Guanajuato. In his *retablo* (1976), Rivera appears on his knees in blue slacks, a white-collared shirt, and a turquoise jacket before the Virgin of San Juan de los Lagos. Surrounded by white clouds in a plain blue sky, the Marian image hovers above a gated fence attached to a brown wooden barn. The simplicity of colours in the composition complements the solemnity of Rivera's face as he gazes piously upon the Virgin with his hands clasped to his breast. "I give infinite thanks" to the Virgin, the caption reads, because "without me knowing it [you] guid[ed] me to the ranch in Brackettville, Texas."[60]

Unlike Rivera and thousands of other *mojados* travelling to the United States, Mexicans in the CSAWP leave home with established contracts. They are under no stress to commence a job hunt upon arrival and, for the most part, do not run the risk of losing their way. Their employers, as shown above, either bring them home from the airport themselves or arrange for their pickup. One worker noted to Pietropaolo that "when

99

you go to Canada, you know ahead of time for whom and where you'll be working, but when you go to the United States, you don't know. Everything is more certain up there [Canada]."[61] And so instead of a man kneeling before the Virgin and offering thanks for finding work, Pietropaolo captures a shot of a recently arrived migrant worker in a local shoe store in St. Catharines trying on new rubber boots (110). Surrounded by a sea of organized shoes neatly arranged on descending racks, the man concentrates on finding the right size of footwear instead of a place of employment. In fact, on a weekly basis, Canadian farmers are required to take their workers to a local mall so that they can do their own banking and grocery shopping. Some employers pay for taxis, others use company vehicles with designated drivers, while others provide cars for their workers so that they can drive themselves.

Also built into the CSAWP is mandatory housing for Mexican workers, which limits the stress of searching for a temporary place of residence. Billeted in converted storage warehouses, trailers, houses, cabins, or even newly furnished apartments on their employer's property, lodging for Mexicans varies according to the local farm.[62] Although there are set regulations on housing by the Ministry of Health, they are not always properly enforced. After an initial annual inspection before the workers arrive, government agents only return at the request of employers or when there is a formal complaint, opening the doors for some farmers to provide substandard living conditions.[63] *Harvest Pilgrims* provides an intimate tour, then, of some of the homes where Mexicans eat, sleep, cook, wash, and relax while living in Canada. In front of an orchard and behind a barn near a trailer, Pietropaolo snaps a shot of a worker tending his clothes on a makeshift clothesline crossing a pile of skids, farm equipment, and a lawn mower (84). In another, María Isabel Alejandra Hernández Cervantes poses with a smile in front of her small, rustic, temporary home in Whitby (85). "For me," the caption reads below, "my family is very important. Yes, you are full of sadness when you leave, but full of joy when you return."

Through both text and photograph, Pietropaolo captures the isolation of Mexican workers in southern Ontario. Accustomed to living with their families in their own communities, Mexicans board with fellow countrymen in the Canadian countryside, where they are disconnected from their local and national traditions. *Harvest Pilgrims* documents this aspect of migrant work, especially in the initial years when their numbers were relatively small. Scholars suggest that Mexicans have generally been excluded from Canadian society, given their rural seclusion, long working hours, housing arrangements, language barriers, general lack of transportation, and limited "Latino" support networks. Although Kerry Preibisch confirms that social exclusion was still the norm in the early 2000s, she demonstrates that several forms of social inclusion do exist through the work of both church groups and social activists.[64] A similar transition can be observed in *Harvest Pilgrims*. Virtually none of Pietropaolo's photographs from the 1980s and 1990s show any form of integration into Canadian society, a pattern which starts to change in his pictures from the 2000s. A panoramic view of Talbot Street in Leamington during the 2006 Two Cultures celebration is revealing of this trend (108). Through Pietropaolo's lens we can see hundreds of Mexicans dancing in the street with a few other Canadian onlookers of European descent curiously observing.

Although Mexicans have generally "found their way" much more easily in Canada, in some cases they have experienced obstacles, expenses, and living conditions similar to those encountered by their counterparts in the United States. "Legal problems," however, are of much greater concern for the majority of migrant workers in the United States because of their illegal status. Two of the major problems Durand and Massey encountered in *Miracles on the Border* were struggles to acquire official documentation, and run-ins with the law. Ever since the late 1970s, US immigration law has become more restrictive for Mexicans, a factor that makes it much more difficult to acquire visas and hence legal passage into the country. Since thousands of migrant workers choose to cross to *el otro lado* by illegal means, they need to be vigilant of migration authorities, and so they run the constant risk of deportation. Given the challenges of obtaining official status in the United States, several Mexicans have either turned to the saints for help or interpreted their success as divine intervention. In his *retablo* (1990), Juan Sánchez R. appears in black and white, kneeling upon a tiled floor before the Lord of the Conquest, which is centered in circular bright blue swirls on the left-hand side of the composition. Instead of offering thanks for a miracle, Sánchez extends his arms towards the image "to resolve a problem of arranging some papers of importance in the USA."[65]

Obtaining official documentation to work has generally been much easier for migrant workers in Canada than in the United States, notwithstanding the expenses of travelling to Mexico City to acquire them. And since Mexicans come to Canada legally on contracts, run-ins with the law and the fear of deportation are, for the most part, not a general concern.

As one migrant worker stated to Pietropaolo, "You don't have to be watching over your back for the *migra* [immigration authorities]"[66] in Canada. Desertion levels are also extremely low, and few choose to stay in the country after their contracts have expired. The structure of the CSAWP, as Tanya Basok has demonstrated, is designed to ensure their return, as immigration officials make sure that seasonal work does not result in permanent settlement.[67] This is clearly displayed in Pietropaolo's portrait of Rogelio González Martínez's family in Monte Prieto, Guanajuato (92). The migrant worker, after seasons of farming in London, stands in front of the doorway of his home together with his wife and five children. His oldest daughter stands by the threshold with her mother, while the rest of his children appear by the edges of the unplastered cinderblock entryway aligned with potted plants. Beyond documenting Rogelio's family, this photograph illustrates his incentive to return home. The CSAWP targets married men with children so that they have dependents to support.

Migrant workers may enter Canada freely and leave without having to worry about immigration authorities, but this does not mean that fear is entirely absent from the CSAWP. After every season, employers are required to fill out a report for each of their migrant workers which they hand over to them in sealed envelopes. Mexicans, in turn, are required to report to the Ministry of Labour in Mexico City with these evaluation forms. If they have a poor evaluation, they run the risk of being excluded from the program the following year. The CSAWP places significant power in the hands of the employer, who is entitled to "name" the workers he/she wants back each season. Scholars have shown that this practice has tended to foster an environment in which migrant workers, for fear of being sent home before the end of their contract, put up with substandard working and living conditions to make sure they receive a good review. In one photograph, Pietropaolo documents a dark, solitary room in 1984 with three unmade cots, a pair of dangling pants, and a few towels hung out to dry on carpenter nails (74). Below we read that the "conditions where we lived were terrible, and so was the owner. He treated us worse than animals... And I put up with it so that I wouldn't lose the opportunity of coming back to work in Canada."

Suffering substandard working and living conditions can potentially lead to "medical problems," the name of the largest group of *ex-voto* paintings in *Miracles on the Border*. With limited resources and an expensive healthcare system, getting sick in the United States is extremely difficult for migrant workers. Beyond the possibility of suffering an illness or operation without a support network of family and friends, sickness and injuries of any type mean that workers go without pay. One can feel the isolation of Venancio Soriano in the undated *retablo* he commissioned to thank the Virgin of San Juan de los Lagos for "relief" from a "grave illness of the left lung that was thought incurable."[68] With only his head showing, Venancio lies covered in white sheets on his hospital bed, a sharp contrast to the dark, plain green walls encircling him. Closely related to these types of health issues are several daily aspects of "getting by" for migrant workers, who often require medical attention. Two of the most common concerns that Durand and Massey found were work-related injuries and traffic accidents. Senovio Trejo's undated *retablo*, for example, depicts a jeep crashing into a utility pole on the side of a country road. The surrounding cotton fields horizontally cross the composition with a curved road passing through from top to bottom. The orangey colour of the soil, the broken pole, and the squiggly wires strewn on the ground all heighten the "very great danger" Senovio experienced "far from [his] homeland and [his] family."[69]

In contrast to illegal migrants in the United States, Mexicans working in Ontario are covered by the Ontario Health Insurance Plan (OHIP). The Mexican government also requires them to pay for additional travel insurance not covered by the province. But any long-term illness contracted in Canada as a result of a working accident is not covered once

Figure 4. Vincenzo Pietropaolo, *On their first morning in Canada, Mexican workers are taken shopping for food and supplies*, gelatin silver print, St. Catharines, Ontario, 1987. Reproduced with the authorization of the artist.

a farm worker returns to Mexico. Not only this, in several cases migrant workers that have become too sick to work have been sent back home without receiving the medical care they paid into. In other cases, some employers have withheld OHIP cards from their Mexican workers or denied them access to local physicians as is stipulated in the regulations of the CSAWP.[70] None of the photographs in *Harvest Pilgrims* show Mexican farmhands sick, at local clinics, or in operating rooms of Ontario hospitals. This absence is explained not only by the places Pietropaolo chose to visit, but by the silence of Mexicans themselves. Catherine Colby found that, due to language barriers, some migrant workers were unable to express medical problems to their employers. In an effort to avoid causing problems, or out of fear of not being "named" the following year, many Mexicans have avoided reporting illnesses.[71] And so Pietropaolo's photographs of a farmhand pruning a pear tree in Beamsville (32) or another migrant worker staking for apple saplings in Whitby (64) may be silent *retablos* concealing untold medical problems.

There are other possible concerns for migrant workers that are perhaps hidden in *Harvest Pilgrims*. Modern agriculture, after all, is highly mechanized, often involves dangerous work, and has one of the highest rates of accidents in the workplace.[72] In Pietropaolo's photographs, Mexican workers are surrounded by tractors (114), harvesters (117), forklifts

Figure 5. Anonymous, *Retablo of Candelaria Arreola*, oil on metal, 24 x 17.5 cm., Durand-Arias collection, 1955. Reproduced with the authorization of Mexican Migration Project, Princeton University.

(58), and conveyor belts (62). Beyond this, farm work also places one at risk of acquiring long-term injuries or chronic illnesses due to long periods of contact with the sun, exposure to pesticides and other chemicals, bending and heavy lifting, and loud machinery.[73] Pietropaolo's shot of Fermín Pérez in a kiln in La Salette (44) is suggestive of some of these potential medical concerns. Completely surrounded by cured tobacco leaves and clutching them with his two hands, one wonders if Fermín and others like him acquired the symptoms of Green Tobacco Sickness (GTS) through nicotine poisoning. Another major concern for Mexicans is road accidents both on and off their places of employment. Since they are usually isolated on rural farms, their only mode of transportation is the bicycle, and more than a few have been killed on Ontario roads while making their way into local towns.[74] In other cases, migrant workers are carted around in trucks or vans without seatbelts, as is displayed in Pietropaolo's photograph of three Mexicans in the back of a makeshift cab of a Ford pick-up on Welland Street in St. Catharines (72) (Fig. 4). The recently-arrived workers do not show signs of concern as expressed in Senovio's *retablo*, but their precarious position in the back demonstrates that, unlike their employer, their risks as farmhands are often much greater.

"Homecoming" is the final group of ex-voto paintings in *Miracles on the Border* and, similar to "making the trip," is potentially dangerous. Since several migrants return home with cash and gifts for their families, they are potential targets for thieves and self-seeking border officials. They also know that, as soon as they return home, the only way to get back to *El norte* is by undergoing the same process that got them there in the first place. But beyond some of these difficulties complicating the homeward journey, arriving home safely is cause for celebration, one that is mixed with both joy and sadness as relatives are reunited after long periods of separation. In 1955, Candelaria Arreola commissioned a *retablero* to paint an ex-voto depicting the arrival of her son (Fig. 5). Clothed in a white robe with the baby Jesus in her arms, the Virgin of Talpa appears in the sky above as the returning migrant marches forward with suitcase in hand. His other arm pierces the white circling clouds of the Virgin, who guides him home to his mother. At the threshold of her white, red-roofed, adobe home, Arreola awaits with outstretched arms to embrace her son. "I give thanks to the Holiest Virgin of Talpa," the caption reads, "for having brought my son home from the United States, where he stayed for a long time" (75).

Migrant workers in Canada, in contrast to their counterparts in the United States, do not have too many obstacles to overcome to make it home. Although several workers in the CSAWP also fly to Mexico with several gifts, they generally do not need to worry about theft, given that their employers arrange for their departure. In one of his photographs, Pietropaolo snaps a portrait of a Mexican worker at the Pearson International Airport on his way home (71). Dressed up in a suit jacket and a white collared shirt, he softly caresses his leather suitcase with his two hands as his boss looks on in the background. "When I went to the airport, I saw many owners who had accompanied the workers," the caption reads, "and they said goodbye to them warmly, very warmly. But there are differences, some bosses are good, some are not so good. . . ." Whether work experiences were positive or negative in Ontario, many migrant workers know that their time at home will only be temporary. Most Mexicans who choose to work in Canada are caught in migratory cycles in the same way as their fellow compatriots in the United States, a transnational quandary that is often passed on to the next generation. When Pietropaolo visited Monte Prieto, he photographed a young boy pushing a wheelbarrow at a local adobe brick operation (99). The caption below states, "If I don't go to junior high next year, somehow I'll make my way *pa'l norte* [towards the United States] or Canada, like my dad."

The return home for many Mexicans means recognizing that, during their working career, they will spend more time away from their families than at home. Pietropaolo's photograph of Virginia's and Manuel González's home in Monte Prieto (93) documents this sense of separation through a shot of their bedroom wall. Adorned with three pictures and four ceramic plates, the wall is primarily covered by a TV stand and dresser layered with cosmetics. Reflected in the mirror are the mother, four children, and another lady watching television from the bed. "As you can see, my house is not finished," the caption states below, "I spend more time living in Canada than in Mexico." A Mexican who works on an eight-month contract over the course of twenty-five years spends 200 months in Canada and 100 in Mexico, which is equivalent to roughly 16.6 years abroad and 8.4 at home. In those years away, migrant workers miss births, baptisms, first communions, *quinceañeras* (birthday celebrations for fifteen-year-old girls), weddings, funerals, and other, annual celebrations, both patriotic and Catholic. This sense of separation is captured in Pietropaolo's family portrait of Blanca Anaya Castillo (94). Her three boys surround her on the bed, her daughter sits quietly on her lap, and another elderly woman, possibly the grandmother, observes the photo shoot by the doorway in the background. The father, at work in Ontario, is notably absent from the photograph.

Although eight months away from family takes its toll on Mexican farmhands, many prefer this scenario to living illegally in the United States for years at a time. But despite the opportunity to visit home during the winter season, studies have shown that these long periods apart have strained marriages, have led to worker depression, and have also changed the dynamics between fathers and their children.[76] And much like migrant workers who return home from the United States, those arriving from Canada find that their homecoming is a joyous occasion mixed with bitter sorrow. In Monte Prieto, Pietropaolo shoots a scene from a dance in the town square during the Feast of La Santa Patrona de la Concepción, celebrated on December 8, just in time for returning migrant workers. Four couples swirl to the music as they trample the earthen ground beneath their feet (104). The festive mood depicted in this picture differs significantly from Pietropaolo's photograph of Manuel González greeting his sister Beda (67) upon his return home. (Fig. 6) Although the photograph only focuses on their two heads, the scene still captures the same emotions of Arreola's *retablo*. Beda's face is

Figure 6. Vincenzo Pietropaolo, *Manuel González greeting his sister Beda on his return home*, gelatin silver print, Monte Prieto, Guanajuato, Mexico, 1993. Reproduced with the authorization of the artist.

entirely covered with a striped shawl that Manuel, clad in a checkered flannel shirt, firmly grasps to wipe away his tears. The return from an economic pilgrimage, regardless of the destination in Greater Mexico, is a homecoming of mixed emotions.

Conclusion

On 11 June 2014, officials in Toronto from the Mexican and Canadian governments celebrated the fortieth anniversary of Mexico's entry into the CSAWP. Mexican workers shared how their labour in Ontario has helped to support their families back home, while local farmers continued to praise the program as a model for other countries. But despite the benefits the CSAWP provides for thousands of migrant workers, the program is still, to use the words of Jenna L. Hennebry, "a highly racialized system of employment,"[77] designed to exclude Mexicans from the full rights of citizenship. Despite their long years of service and interest in making Canada their home, migrant workers are barred from becoming permanent residents.[78] *Harvest Pilgrims*, as I have argued in this chapter, highlights not only the limits of multiculturalism in Canada but the "many Mexicos" in Greater Mexico. In contrast to the long established "Mexicos" of the United States, the "Mexicos" forming in southern Ontario are primarily male and, thanks to legal impediments, by nature "permanently temporary." Although Pietropaolo's photographs demonstrate a slight increase in social inclusion from the mid-1980s to the mid-2000s, migrant Mexican workers are still largely invisible to the majority of consuming Canadians.

Following the methods of John Mraz, I have also shown that *Harvest Pilgrims* helps to address the invisibility of migrant workers in Ontario by providing a unique photohistory of the CSAWP. Photographs and ex-voto paintings, as Peter Burke reminds us, can be used as historical evidence and hence offer a "personalized" look at migrant Mexican workers in a transnational perspective, a vision that moves beyond statistics and official documentation to the experiences of individual workers. One learns about the living and working conditions they experience while stationed in Canada, together with their familial and domestic life in their pueblos back home in Mexico. *Harvest Pilgrims* also illustrates the reality of modern agriculture in southern Ontario during the neoliberal age, most specifically the dependency of local growers on migrant workers. But Pietropaolo's photo essay is also suggestive of many potential silences - whether medical, spiritual, or emotional - that lie hidden in

Figure 7. Vincenzo Pietropaolo, *Manuel González, a Mexican pear picker*, gelatin silver print, Beamsville, Ontario, 1993. Reproduced with the authorization of the artist.

his photographs, given both the formal structure of the CSAWP and the informal social relations between workers and their employers. *Harvest Pilgrims* does not tell the entire story of migrant experiences in Ontario, but it certainly offers an important starting point for a larger visual history of Mexican farmhands in an expanding Greater Mexico.

Beyond functioning as an archive of historical "documents," I would also contend that *Harvest Pilgrims* is a powerful reminder that the nation state is not the only frame of reference for understanding human experience in the past. Workers have been migrating throughout the Americas for economic reasons or by brute force ever since Europeans arrived in the Caribbean in the late fifteenth century, and this pattern has only been amplified by neoliberal reforms. Ontario boasts of local food, wine, and nursery stock, and rightfully so; but behind the stalls at local markets, TV advertisements, winery tours, and the manicured gardens of public buildings lies a transnational story. For Canada to produce and export local food, it imports foreign workers from Mexico and now, increasingly, from other parts of Latin America. Historians of the borderlands have long recognized that Latin America cannot simply be considered a region to the south of the Mexico-US border. *Harvest Pilgrims*, as I have demonstrated, forces Canadians, albeit in a lesser way, to acknowledge that their history is also intimately intertwined with the region as a result of migrant labour. Pietropaolo's photograph of Manuel González, who struggles to carry four fully-packed Foodland Ontario baskets of pears to a jitney, visually illustrates this shared history (33) (Fig. 7). "Good things grow in Ontario," as the popular jingle goes, but they are often harvested by Mexican hands.

Chapter 6

Linguistic Landscape:
Imagined Borders and Territories
Made By/For Latin Americans in Canada

María Eugenia De Luna Villalón

Introduction

Canada has two official languages, English and French. These two languages are not used in the same way in the public sphere. The use of English, French, or both, will be determined by different factors such as the linguistic policies of the province, region, specific city, or neighbourhood, and the need to inform the population in one language or the other. But Canada is not only anglophone or francophone; Canada is known as a multicultural country where each populous place has its very own configuration, resulting from a mixture of majority and minority ethnolinguistic groups, a result of the country's immigration policy, which opens its doors to international migration on both a permanent and a temporary basis.

The ethnolinguistic configuration of the country is reflected in many ways, the Linguistic Landscape (LL) being one of the most prominent to the public eye. The LL refers to the presence, visibility, and salience of a language/languages on public and commercial signs in a specific area. The LL can be considered a marker of diversity in the Canadian context,[1] a marker of language dominance,[2] and also a symbolic marker of identity. The presence of a bilingual or multilingual LL can help us to construct, understand, and discuss issues related to linguistic areas, urban borders, and ethnic identity, and it may show the vitality of a particular ethnic group in a specific region.[3]

Metropolitan areas, such as Toronto, Vancouver, and Montreal, are the best examples of a multicultural Canada where the LL is a fluid representation of multiculturalism and multilingualism that helps to construct borders between different ethnic neighbourhoods of the cities and that also reflects the mosaic of different voices that may conflict in one particular area. Moving out of the metropolitan areas, one may find a more homogeneous Canada, with the logical consequence of less depiction of minority groups in the LL. However, this is not the case for Leamington, Ontario. Leamington is a small-sized Canadian city that is well known for being an immigrant community. This city has been receiving temporary migrants, mainly from Jamaica and Latin America, since the 1960s and 70s. The LL of Leamington seems to be the typical portrait of a small anglophone city in Ontario where the immigrant population has been assimilated or has less representation than the majority.

However, when one reaches the downtown area of Leamington, the language in the LL turns from texts written primarily in English to texts written in Spanish and a combination of English and Spanish. It is impossible not to notice that the language choice for the LL is different from the rest of the region, and therefore not to acknowledge that there must be a Spanish-speaking group in the area, even without knowing that Leamington is a receiving community for a large, temporary, Latin-American group: Mexicans arriving under the Seasonal Agricultural Workers Program (SAWP). Thus, the main purpose of this chapter is to show the role of the LL in the construction of imagined visual and linguistic borders within a specific small Canadian city and to determine whether the imagined borders and territories are created *by* Latin Americans or *for* Latin Americans - contributing also in this way to the study of Spanish-speaking communities in Canada, a research field that needs further investigation.

Latin Americans in Canada

According to Statistics Canada,[4] the number of people of Latin American origin is growing very quickly in Canada, making it one of the largest non-European ethnic groups and the fifth visible minority group in the country (Table 1). In the 2006 Census, there were 304,245 people of Latin American origin, compared with 244,400 in 2001.[5] The majority of Latin Americans were born outside of the country and arrived in the last few decades - most of them before 2000, with a second big influx from 2001 to 2006.[6] Of the total number of Latin Americans in Canada, 29 % are non-immigrants and 71% are immigrants. Immigrants are landed immigrants in Canada, while non-immigrants are Canadian citizens by birth who reported being of Latin American origin.[7] The countries of origin for Latin Americans in Canada include mainly Mexico, Chile, El Salvador, Peru, and Colombia, with Mexicans forming the largest

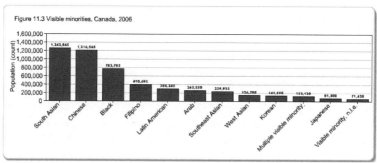

Figure 11.3 Visible minorities, Canada, 2006

Table 1. Visible Minorities, Canada 2006. Source: Statistics Canada.

population (61,505 persons). However, Latin Americans in Canada also come from the following countries: Bolivia, Brazil, Costa Rica, Cuba, the Dominican Republic, Ecuador, Guatemala, Haiti, Honduras, Nicaragua, Panama, Paraguay, Peru, Uruguay, Venezuela, Puerto Rico, and the French West Indies and other islands. Most Latin Americans in Canada live in four main provinces - Alberta, British Columbia, Ontario, and Quebec -, and the majority live in large cities in these same provinces (i.e. metropolitan areas such as Calgary, Vancouver, Toronto, and Montreal).[8]

The construct Latin American provided by Statistics Canada does not take into account Temporary Migrant Workers of Latin American origin; it only includes people with immigrant and non-immigrant status who can be counted in the census. However, there are Temporary Migrant Workers in the country, staying long term, who have been coming to Canada for many years. I will consider all Temporary Migrant Workers who come from Latin America as part of the Latin American construct. At the same time, for this study, this construct will be linked not only to the country of origin (i.e. in Latin America) but also to the Spanish language.

Latin Americans as a temporary migrant population in Canada: The case of Mexican agricultural workers

Temporary labour migration is considered to be the main mechanism to address labour and skill shortages in Canada. Thus, the recruitment of Temporary Migrant Workers (TMWs) or Foreign Workers (FWs) has experienced a noticeable increase in the country.[9] Citizenship and Immigration Canada (CIC) has developed Temporary Workers Programs (TWPs) to "facilitate the entry of visitors, students and temporary workers for purposes such as trade, commerce, tourism, international understanding and cultural, educational and scientific activities."[10] CIC is the department with the responsibility for establishing immigration and citizenship policies in Canada, as well as dealing with, processing, and implementing programs and services to build a strong country. This entity works with Employment and Social Development Canada (ESDC) to admit foreign workers and to ensure that employment opportunities for Canadians and permanent residents will not be affected.[11] In 2012, there were 213,573 temporary foreign workers reported by CIC (and only 141,549 permanent foreign workers). Of the total number of temporary foreign workers, 32,352 were Latin Americans. The Latin American countries considered by CIC in these numbers were Mexico, with 20,984 foreign workers, as well as Guatemala, Brazil, Chile, Honduras, Nicaragua, Peru, Argentina, Colombia, Venezuela, Costa Rica, El Salvador, Ecuador, Uruguay, Bolivia, Guyana, Paraguay, and Panama.[12]

Mexicans come to Canada to fulfill different categories of temporary jobs. The greatest numbers of Mexican foreign workers come to the country as part of SAWP, a bilateral agreement between Canada and Mexico that has been running since 1974. The purpose of this agreement is to overcome difficulties that both countries face. Canada needs to address the shortage of seasonal labour for Canadian producers,[13] and Mexico needs to offer alternate programs for unemployed agricultural workers. The program operates on a seasonal basis (not to exceed eight months) in the following provinces: British Columbia, Alberta, Saskatchewan, Manitoba, Ontario, Quebec, New Brunswick, Nova Scotia, and Prince Edward Island.[14]

Like any other seasonal worker program, SAWP was designed "to add temporary workers to the labour force without adding permanent residents to the population."[15] SAWP has expanded in every direction during the last forty years. More workers, provinces, and farmers, and a variety of crops have been included. It is through SAWP that Canadian farmers have expanded their operations, because they can rely on a source of temporary labour; in consequence, other related industries have also seen a positive growth.[16] In 2012, there were 25,414 TMWs who came to Canada under SAWP,[17] 17,626 of whom were from Mexico.[18] The province of Ontario received half the total number of Mexican TMWs,[19] Leamington being the preferred destination because of the high number of farms in the region and, therefore, the area in greatest need of TMWs.

Leamington: A small-sized Canadian community with a dynamic temporary migrant population

Leamington is one of the receiving communities for Mexican Temporary Agricultural Workers (MTAWs) who work in Canada for a specific period of time, anywhere from 6 weeks to a maximum of 8 months per year. Leamington is located in south-western Ontario (Fig. 1); it has a population of 28,403 inhabitants and is considered to be an immigrant community with people from different ethnic groups such as Chinese, South Asian, Black, Filipino, Arab, West Asian, Japanese, and Latin American,[20] groups considered to comprise the visible minority population of the area. The inhabitants of Leamington are diverse and considered to form a rich mosaic with their diverse ethnic and rural background.[21]

As a consequence of having a diverse population, several languages are spoken in Leamington. According to the 2011 Census,[22] the language of the majority is English (59.9%), and the minority languages are French (1.4%) and non-official languages (36.4%). The non-official languages reported in the 2011 Census (Statistics Canada 2012) were German (18.4%), Spanish (5.0%), Portuguese (4.0 %), Arabic (3.8%), and Italian (2.5%). Only 5.8% of the population reported that they did not know English or French (i.e., the official languages of Canada). It is important to notice that MTAWs are not considered for the census results because of their immigration status, i.e., temporary agricultural workers. For official statistical purposes, only immigrant and non-immigrant statuses are considered to be part of the data.

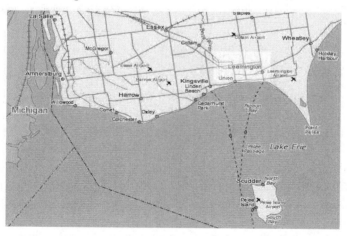

Figure 1. Location of Leamington, Ontario, in Canada. "The Atlas of Canada." NRCAN-Natural Resources Canada.

Leamington has a significant number of farms (351) and receives an average of 4,000 temporary migrant workers each year,[23] the majority of whom are Mexican. The town is better known in this country as the "Tomato Capital of Canada" because it is home to the largest number of greenhouses in North America, with tomato being the principal crop followed by other vegetables, mushrooms, fruits, and nursery products.[24] One of the reasons that make Leamington the Tomato Capital of Canada is the work and effort of the migrant agricultural workers, of which the MTAWs form a part. They are a group that is heterogeneous, although the town's residents identify them as a unit or group without individual characteristics that spends season after season working in the fields of Canada (i.e. as a homogeneous group).

Overall, an MTAW is on average a middle-aged, rural Mexican male with grade 9 as his maximum level of education, someone who has low literacy skills and who probably speaks and understands more than one language: an MTAW has parents that did not go to school, an illiterate, stay-at-home mother, a father who might know how to read and write, and who might have also been an agricultural worker. At the same time, this MTAW is married and has an average of 3 children who go to school and will probably achieve a high-school education and might even attend college. Some of the male children may end up becoming MTAWs too, but the MTAW (as a parent) does not want this for his children because of the difficult situation they will have to experience working away from home, in Canada, and feeling socially and linguistically isolated.[25]

The high numbers of TMWs who arrive every season in Leamington have transformed the town, and it is possible to appreciate this at a glance. Businesses downtown are ethnically oriented with restaurants, bars, nightclubs, global payment service companies, ethnic food stores, religious services, government services, and other businesses that serve diverse ethnic groups, most specifically Hispanics.[26] As with any other migrant community, Leamington has adapted to the different ethnic groups who live in the area because of the market opportunity they represent, among other factors. That is why there seems to be an increase in ethnolinguistic enclaves. The characteristics of an ethnolinguistic enclave are that it sells ethnic products and/or services, and that everyone there, owner, workers, and maybe even customers, are part of a specific ethnic group and share an ethnic language (i.e. minority language) as their mother tongue. These ethnolinguistic enclaves modify the LL with signs and information written in different languages, Spanish included (Fig. 2), and seem to create imagined linguistic borders in the city.

Figure 2. Multilingual Linguistic Landscape. Leamington, Ontario, in Canada. Photograph by the author.

Canada: Language policy

Canada is a country with high rates of immigration; it is officially bilingual (and bicultural) in English and French according to the Official Languages Act (OLA) of 1969. Through the Official Languages Act, English and French have equality of status and equal rights and privileges for all purposes of the Parliament and Government of Canada.[27] Canada is also multicultural, according to the Multiculturalism Act of 1988. This Act promotes respect and support for all the languages and cultures of Canada through anti-racism and affirmative action in support of visible minorities.

The English and French languages have been protected through the Constitution Act of 1982, as well as through the Charter of Rights and Freedoms, which also protects the rights and privileges of any other language (i.e. minority languages).[28] The Official Languages Act is the main law by which languages are regulated. The objectives of this Act are to ensure the respect, equality of status, and equality of rights and privileges of both English and French; to support the development of both languages and advance the equality of status and use of English and French in Canadian society; and to set out the powers, duties, and functions of Canadian Federal Institutions in relation to the Act.[29]

In reality, bilingualism in Canada is institutional. The Canadian language policy consists in the institutional promotion of the French language (i.e. institutional bilingualism)[30] in the francophone areas of the country, as well as a strategic second-language program for immigrants, tailored to Canadian interests.[31] Both languages create language barriers, which become social barriers too, because the primary language of an individual indexes class, educational level, ethnicity, race, and age, while at the same time reinforcing stereotypes.[32] The language used in public spaces in Canada will vary according to the province or territory, and in some cases it will also vary according to the specific region or town.

Linguistic policy in public spaces in Ontario

Ontario has a regionalized language policy. Some regions are bilingual, while others are English-only. In 1986, the French Language Services Act (FLSA) was created to guarantee the language right of francophones to receive services in French from the Government of Ontario's ministries and agencies in specific, designated areas. Also, the FLSA was created to preserve French for future generations in Ontario.[33] However, it is important to mention that in Ontario, francophones are a minority (only 4.1% of Ontario's population), and that they are located mainly along the physical border with Quebec, Ottawa being the largest bilingual city of the province.[34] In regard to public advertising, Advertising Standards Canada[35] regulates public advertisements expressed in any language and in any medium (with some exceptions) through the Canadian Code of Advertising Standards. The Code does not explain if there are language regulations related to language choice in public spaces in Ontario (or Canada), it only explains that if there are complaints related to public advertising in French, the issue will be evaluated by *Le Conseil des Normes*.[36]

Leamington, Ontario, is an English-only region and is not part of the FLSA-designated areas, and therefore services are offered in English only. However, Leamington's population is diverse, so in relation to signs in public spaces, the regulation states that "signs in other languages are permitted but signs in English are encouraged."[37] For bike signage, the written information has to be in multiple languages to ensure that all users understand the information. The Municipality of Leamington also explains that having signs in languages other than English may potentially create a barrier to the integration of visitors and residents, thus recommending the use of English as the preferred language in public spaces.[38]

Linguistic policy in public spaces in Quebec

Quebec is a francophone province in Canada. The province has adopted a language policy since the 1960s that focuses on the maintenance and promotion of the French language. In Quebec, since 1977, The Charter of the French Language, or Bill 101, states that French is the language of government and law, and the normal language of work, instruction, communication, trade, commerce, and business. However, the province explains that it is respectful of the anglophone community in their province as well as of other ethnic minorities whose language is neither French nor English.[39] In relation to commerce and business, chapter VII of the Charter of the French Language explains that French should be the language used for public signs, etc. Law 51 states the following:

> Every inscription on a product, on its container or in its wrapping, or on a document or object supplied with it, including the directions for use and the warranty certificates, must be drafted in French. This rule applies also to menus and wine lists. The French inscription may be accompanied with a translation or translations, but no inscription in another language may be given greater prominence than that in French.

Also, and relevant to this chapter, law 58 states:

> Public signs and posters and commercial advertising must be in French. They may also be both in French and in another language provided that French is markedly predominant. However, the Government may determine, by regulation, the places, cases, conditions or circumstances where public signs and poster and commercial advertising must be in French only, where French need not be predominant or where such signs, posters and advertising may be in another language only.[40]

Finally, Law 68 explains, "The name of an enterprise may be accompanied with a version in a language other than French provided that when it is used, the French version of the name appears at least as prominently."[41] The province wants a French "linguistic face" or a noticeably French Linguistic Landscape for Quebec cities and towns (Fig. 3).

Linguistic Landscape

One of the most noticeable markers of the presence of a minority ethnolingusitic group, other than the people themselves, is the Linguistic Landscape (LL). Landry and R. Bourhis[42] proposed the term "LL" to indicate the written language used on the "public road signs, advertising billboards, street names, place names, commercial shop signs, and public

Figure 3: Linguistic Landscape in St. Rémi, Quebec, Canada. Photograph by the author.

signs on government buildings"[43] of a specific territory where objective and subjective ethnolinguistic vitality is salient. As Huebner[44] states, the LL delimits the ethnolinguistic and social borders of a particular group. There are two kinds of signs, private and institutional. Private signs "include commercial signs on storefronts and business institutions (e.g. retail stores and banks), commercial advertising on billboards, and advertising signs displayed in public transport and on private vehicles," and government signs "refer to the public signs used by national, regional, or municipal governments in the following domains: road signs, place names, street names, and inscriptions on government buildings including ministries, hospitals, universities, town halls, schools, metro stations, and public parks."[45] From a Bourdieuian perspective, linguistic signs are markers of power and status, either public or private; however, they can also portray linguistic, cultural, and ethnic identities, or even effects of language contact and signs of globalization. Signs have two different functions: informative and symbolic. The informative function informs members of linguistic groups that they have entered a territory where they can find information and/or services for a specific ethnolinguistic group, and therefore they can communicate and have access to services and information in their own language (e.g. Spanish in an English-speaking country).

The LL tells us a lot about the sociolinguistic composition and situation of a particular territory; however, it is not a synonym of language demographics.[46] As Coulmas explains, the LL can help to uncover the connection between languages and different social factors such as ethnicity, religion, social status, etc.[47] Through the LL, we can observe the predominance of one language (dominant linguistic group) and the subordination of another (weaker linguistic group), the territorial limits of language use, the power and status of the linguistic groups, and even the economic repercussions of the existence of certain linguistic groups. The bilingual or monolingual writing of a public sign gives us very clear information about the linguistic policies of a particular bilingual or multilingual territory; on the other hand, private signs can give precise information regarding the linguistic diversity, as they can capture the multilingual composition of the area. As Landry and R. Bourhis explains,[48] "the diversity of languages present in the LL can be seen as a concrete manifestation of the linguistic and cultural diversity of the ethnolinguistic groups inhabiting a particular administrative territory or region."[49] The symbolic function is more prominent in multilingual settings, where ethnic identity is important.

What is the effect of the presence or absence of one language, in a multilingual setting, on the Linguistic Landscape?

As Landry and R. Bourhis explains,[50] the presence or absence of one or another language, in a multilingual setting, "can symbolize the strength or vitality of one's own language group on the demographic and institutional control front relative to other language communities within the intergroup setting."[51] In Spain, in the Basque Country or Euskadi, which is an autonomous community in Spain where the Spanish language shares its status of official language with the Euskera language (i.e. they have two co-official languages), Cenoz and Gorter's study shows that there is a multilingual landscape in Spanish, Euskera, English, and other minority languages such as Italian, French, and German.[52] In this region, Spanish is the dominant language used in the LL (with an overwhelming 80 to 95% of use), which shows that it is the dominant language and the language of the majority (with a higher status and power); Euskera is the second most used language in the LL (34-50% presence), which reflects its minority status and power in the region compared to the Spanish language, with which it shares a co-official status at the political level. At the same time, the Cenoz and Gorter results show that the use of English in the LL is spreading in the area (9-28% presence), apparently because of its relevance as a lingua franca, its high status as a world language, and its economic power for tourism, while the other minority languages in the area (i.e. Italian, German, and French) have a small presence in the LL.[53] This also seems to show that the use of these minority languages in the LL is related to tourism and linguistic status, as it may give the idea that the city is modern and diverse.[54]

Likewise, Muñoz explains that in Madrid, Spain, the LL shows a growing multilingualism in the city because of three main factors. One is globalization and its carry-over effect, as the LL shows that there are new businesses with names in the original language of the company, and new Spanish businesses that decide to have their name in English because of the language's high prestige and possible economic repercussions. Tourism is the second factor that promotes the use of English or other languages related to tourism in the area. And immigration is the third factor. Regarding immigration as a factor for a multilingual LL in Madrid, Muñoz explains that the language choice in the LL could be Russian, Romanian, or Chinese, as well as other languages of immigrant communities in the city. The reason for these language choices in the LL is to cover specific needs of those minority ethnolinguistic speech communities, which at the same time may show the high vitality of those groups and their language in the region. Finally, Muñoz concludes, in a very straightforward manner, that a multilingual LL is just the result or reflection of a multilingual society.[55]

Moreover, Pons-Rodríguez found in her study of the use of Hispanic-American Spanish in the LL of Seville, Spain, that the use of this linguistic variety shows the presence of Hispanic-American enclaves in the area (mainly from the Andean region) due to a migratory trend towards Spain in the last few decades. Pons-Rodríguez's results show that the LL in the Hispanic-American variety of Spanish helps to construct a collective identity that fosters the possibility, for this immigrant group, of portraying and maintaining their cultural identity. Also, Pons-Rodríguez explains that the effect of the use of a Hispanic-American Spanish linguistic variety favours the language contact phenomenon among different Spanish varieties (i.e., the Andalusian and the Hispanic-American), which promotes language change with the inclusion of phonological features and new lexical forms, among other traits.[56]

Authorship in the Linguistic Landscape

Scholars have tried to explain the presence of one of the languages used in the LL by analyzing the public signs from a semiotic approach, considering the position of one language with respect to the other. The dominant language will be the one on top, in the centre, or on the left, and the subordinate language will be the one on the bottom, to the right, or in the margins of the sign. In other cases, the dominant language will be the one with the bigger font size and the subordinate language, the one with the smaller.[57]

As for Ben-Rafael et al., the choice can also be that of LL *actors*, considering that the *actor*, or the *one* who decides the need for a public sign, has a voice; therefore, he explains the need to show the behaviours and choices of the LL *actors*.[58] In these lines, Malinowski raises another possibility of explaining the language choice and use in the LL by presenting the term *authorship*. In his study, Malinowski interviewed the local *actors* to determine their language choice in bilingual signs of Korean-American business owners in a specific location in Oakland, CA. Among his results, Malinowksi found that the intentional meanings and motivations of the authors of the LL can remain hidden even to the writers of signs themselves because of previous or historical literary practices, the signs' designers, previous owners of the businesses, etc., thus showing the complexity of *authorship* in the LL and the importance of situating and contextualizing LL studies.[59]

It is important to explain that in the case of places such as the province of Quebec in Canada, where the law regulates the position, size, and prominence of one language over the other in the multilingual LL, it may be problematic to analyze the theme "authorship." In this case, both the semiotic approach and the authorship approach may fail to work as methodology for this analysis or may need to be adapted, also taking into account language policies.

Linguistic Landscape in Leamington: Imagined borders and territories

The significant numbers of TMWs who arrive in Leamington regularly every season have transformed the town. The businesses downtown are ethnically oriented with restaurants, bars, nightclubs, global payment service companies, ethnic food stores, religious services, government services, and other businesses that serve diverse ethnic groups, more specifically Latin Americans.[60] Like any other migrant community, Leamington has adapted to the different ethnic groups that live in the area because of the market opportunity that they represent, among other factors. It is possible to see the adaptation of Leamington to the TMWs through the rise of ethnolinguistic enclaves and other manifestations. Ethnolinguistic enclaves are characterized as being businesses that commercialize ethnic products and/or services, but are also typified by the fact that everyone there (owner, workers, and maybe even customers) are part of a specific ethnic group and share an ethnic language (i.e. a minority, non-official language) as their mother tongue. Consequently, ethnolinguistic enclaves modify the LL of the area where they are located by having signs and information written in minority, non-official languages. In Leamington, the LL of the ethnolinguistic enclaves seems to delimit a territory by forming imagined borders through the use of Spanish, among other languages. But are these ethnolinguistic enclaves created *by* Latin Americans or *for* Latin Americans? Are Latin Americans perceived to have high or low socio-cultural power and status, and high or low linguistic vitality,[61] as a consequence of the use of Spanish in the LL?

The study

This study is the result of a series of visits to Leamington, one of the locations that I visited from 2009 to 2010 and that inspired a larger research project with a Language and Migration Approach related to the Mexican Temporary Agricultural Workers in Canada. For this specific study, I collected data in 2010 on two different occasions, but I visited the region nine times. I designed this study having in mind a lateral research project to investigate the use of Spanish in the Linguistic Landscape of the town. Thus, following an ethnographic research approach to a sociolinguistic phenomenon, I visited twenty businesses that were selected as a sample.

The selection of the sample was made in relation to the use of written Spanish on the public signs and/or information about services and products displayed in the windows. The units of analysis were photographs, interviews, field notes, and observations. The photographs of the signs of the twenty businesses (eighteen private commercial establishments and two institutions, i.e., one non-governmental organization and one community centre) were taken mainly on my two visits devoted to collecting data for this study. I conducted the interviews with the owners or employees (eleven men and nine women) who were working at the time of my visits.

The interviews were carried out using a short questionnaire. The language of the interviews was either English or Spanish, according to the linguistic knowledge of the interviewees. The questionnaire was designed to elicit information related to the language choice and language use in the LL, the authorship of the LL, the language use in the business, the kind of products or services offered in the place, the motivation to use Spanish in the LL, the target market, the origin of the owners and employees of the store, and their mother tongue. All interviews were conducted and transcribed by myself. Finally, the field notes drawn from my observations were made during the interviews and when I was taking photographs of the commercial signs.

As part of my larger project, I also visited the town of Saint Rémi[62] in the province of Quebec and originally planned to collect data to compare Leamington and Saint-Rémi. However, I soon realized that the LL of Saint-Rémi was very different from the one I found in Leamington (even with a very similar number of MTAWs working in the surrounding area). In Saint Rémi, the use of Spanish in the LL is very limited, which could be the result of Quebec's linguistic policy, the size of the town, or because of the small visible minority populations with either a non-immigrant or immigrant status in the area. This phenomenon would need to be studied in more depth.

Results and discussion

The commercial district of Leamington is located downtown, which is also considered uptown. The main streets, Talbot and Erie, have the main concentration of commercial locations that use English and Spanish in the LL and that mark a specific territory through their language choice and use. The LL in Leamington's downtown can be considered a cultural and social practice that establishes an imagined border through the use of the Spanish language (Fig. 4).

This imagined border is not an indication of language demographics,[63] as Leamington's downtown is mainly a commercial district, neither is it a result of globalization and tourism, as Muñoz Carrobles found in his study.[64] In Leamington, there is no Latin American or Hispanic neighbourhood as can be found in Canadian metropolitan areas such as Toronto, Montreal, or Vancouver; and as a result of their migratory status, MTAWs do not settle in the area; they only go to the town to shop or look for products, services, and/or information.[65] Therefore, it is possible

Figure 4. Spanish use in the Linguistic Landscape of Leamington, Ontario, in Canada. Photograph by the author.

to say that the choice and use of the Spanish language in the LL is aimed at targeting a specific market (i.e. MTAWs), even if this is not the case in Saint-Rémi, QC., a town with a very similar number of MTAWs in the region. In Leamington's downtown LL, migration is a deciding factor for the multilingual LL with a conspicuous use of Spanish, similar to Muñoz's[66] and Pons-Rodríguez's[67] findings in Spain.

In Leamington, the use of Spanish can be a double-edged sword. It may be a gatekeeper, leaving this population as outsiders or on the periphery of an imagined border, and/or it may help them to adapt temporarily to the community. The Spanish in the LL may create sociolinguistic barriers that can also reinforce stereotypes,[68] not only of the MTAWs but of the entire Latin American ethnic group in the area.

The MTAWs have low socio-cultural power and status as a consequence of their precarious migratory status (i.e. with no access to the rights - and obligations - that any Canadian permanent resident or citizen has), which keeps them in the role of periodical outsiders. However, the MTAWs do have a strong presence and economic power in Leamington. This is reflected in the existence of diverse numbers and categories of so-called ethnolinguistic enclaves and institutions that provide goods, services, and information for Latin Americans as a target and captive seasonal market. The distribution of the sample in relation to the type of business is 20% restaurants, 15% money transfers, 10% convenience stores, 5% corn tortilla shops, 5% cybercafés, 5% telephone services, 5% barbershops, 5% new and used clothing stores, 5% NGOs, 5% religious centres, 5% restaurants and bakeries, 5% community centres, and 5% a combination of restaurants and money transfer stores. This configuration of linguistic enclaves is unique to this small Canadian city.

As we saw earlier, the characteristics of an ethnolinguistic enclave is that they sell ethnic products and/or services, and that everyone there (owner, workers, and maybe even customers) forms part of a specific ethnic group and shares an ethnic language (i.e. minority language) as a mother tongue. However, these ethnolinguistic enclaves are different in the sense that the owners or workers may not have Spanish as a mother tongue and may not be Latin American. The mother tongue of the people interviewed has a varied repertoire where 10% have English - the official language - as their mother tongue, 5% were not quantifiable because of the type of business (community centre), and the rest (85%) have a minority, non-official language as their mother tongue including 10% German, 5% Arabic, 5% Portuguese, 5% Indonesian, and 5% Italian. Finally, Spanish is the mother tongue for 55%

Figure 5. Spanish choice and use for the Linguistic Landscape in Leamington, Ontario, in Canada. Photograph by the author.

of the sample, which is the majority. Also, the origin of the owners is diverse. Of the total number of participants, 55% are Latin Americans (5% from Guatemala, 5% from Costa Rica, 35% from Mexico, 5% from El Salvador, 5% Mexican-Mennonite), 5% Iraqi-Canadians, 5% Germans, 5% Indonesians, 5% Italians, 15% Canadians, 5% Italian-Canadians, and 5% Portuguese. Therefore, the choice and use of Spanish in the LL is not restricted to ethnolinguistic enclaves in Leamington's commercial district.

Moreover, Leamington is an English-only region that has a diverse population with different minority, non-official languages as their mother tongue. It is possible to find languages other than English in the LL of the area studied. These languages are Arabic, German, Italian, Chinese, Portuguese, and Spanish, among others. The Municipality of Leamington permits the use of languages other than English in the LL; however, this practice is not encouraged or recommended. According to the Municipality of Leamington, having signs in languages other than English can create a barrier to the integration of visitors and residents, and it recommends using English as the preferred language in public spaces.[69] As the results show, in downtown Leamington, the recommendation of English as a preferred language is not followed, and Spanish is chosen and used in the LL in Leamington's downtown area (Fig. 5).

This is totally different from what happens in the province of Quebec, where linguistic policies are taken very seriously and "linguistic police" supervise compliance with the law (i.e. The Charter of the French Language in Quebec), a result of linguistic pride and linguistic panic - i.e. the fear of losing the language of the province's majority, a minority language with respect to the entire country. Thus, the LL in Leamington shows the effects of a more flexible linguistic policy, which at the same time may have favoured the expansion of the choice and use of Spanish.

Figure 6. Use of Spanish in the Linguistic Landscape of Leamington, Ontario, in Canada. Photograph by the author.

The use of Spanish in the LL in Leamington's commercial district shows that businesses and organizations see Latin Americans (MTAWs more than any other group) as a target market (see figs. 5 and 6). The findings show that of the total sample, 80% have a bilingual sign or information where Spanish is present (75% English/Spanish and 5% German/Spanish); 5%, multilingual (English, Spanish, French, Arabic, German and Chinese); and 15%, monolingual (Spanish). Thus, following the explanation in Landry and R. Bourhis[70] of what it means to have more than one language in the LL, it is possible to assume that in Leaming ton the Spanish language has both strength and a high demographic and linguistic vitality in relation to other languages, a situation that usually results in the increase of the language use and the expansion of a sociolinguistic norm, what J. Bourhis and Allen call a *carry-over effect*.[71] This carry-over effect can be perceived as an increase in the strength and vitality of the ethnic group, Latin Americans, and their language. However, in this study, the LL does not provide sufficient information to reach this kind of conclusion.

In Leamington only 5% of the population reported Spanish as a non-official language in the Canadian Census;[72] therefore, the Spanish language has a low linguistic vitality in this area. Yet the use of Spanish in the LL indicates to Leamington's visitors, and maybe even local residents, that the Spanish language in the region has a high linguistic vitality. This high linguistic vitality is only subjective or temporary (i.e. the Spanish language may have a *temporary high linguistic vitality* only due to the temporary presence of migrants). Hence, it is necessary to learn more about the composition of the town, the status of the migrants, and the number of speakers of Spanish as a non-official language among other factors, in order to better interpret and explain the use of Spanish in the LL of the main area of the economic district of the city.

Regarding the LL *actors*, respondents to the questionnaires concurred that their choice for having signs and information in public spaces in Spanish was determined by the type of customers to whom they were directing the products they commercialize and the services they offer. As I have explained before, they have a target market. Of the total number of respondents, 50% said that their target market was Mexicans, 10% said Hispanics, and 40%, Latin Americans; in short, the target market is a Spanish-speaking population. However, it is interesting to see the LL author's construction of a perceived identity, which could be assigned by place of origin and/or mother tongue, thus giving three different representations of the same ethnic group that is socially constructed in this study and that identifies as Latin Americans. This is a collective identity, as Pons-Rodríguez also found in her study in Seville, Spain,[73] where Hispanic-Americans were perceived as a group that helped the members to portray and maintain their cultural identity.

In addition, it is important to consider the LL authorship in this kind of study. The LL has an author, someone who decides the language choice(s), the language use, and the design of the public signs. As Malinowski did with the Korean-American sample of Oakland, CA,[74] I have also witnessed the complexity of *authorship* in the LL, even if it seems to be straightforward (i.e. because of the demand). Authors have intentional meanings and reasons to use Spanish in the LL that go beyond the perceived demand; for example, the owner of one of the businesses, who is from Iraq and does not speak Spanish, bought the business from a previous owner and did not change its merchandise, even though he does not speak Spanish or identify with the ethnic group. The authors of a bilingual or multilingual LL have one main motivation for their choices, i.e. to address a specific ethnolinguistic target market that in this case is a temporary one: the MTAWs, a group forming part of the Latin American community in the region.

Conclusion

In a Canadian setting, the presence of either or both of the country's official languages implies the demographic presence of a particular ethnolinguistic group, as well as the established LL policies derived from the institutional policies regarding language use in public and government signs and spaces. However, within a multicultural and varied ethnolinguistic population, the presence or absence of a non-official language and its visibility in the LL imply the strength or weakness of an ethnolinguistic group within the society, its socio-cultural power and status, and the high or low vitality of the language.[75]

In Leamington, the LL has undergone a significant transformation, and the presence of the Spanish language on commercial and informative signs has become more popular and evident, reflecting the ethnolinguistic and cultural diversity of the city and the *territorial* limits of the language use as indicated by the *imagined boundaries* that create the LL and its economic repercussions. There are monolingual and bilingual signs; however, the linguistic choice and use is not straightforward, as Huebner[76] explains, because many multilingual (or bilingual) signs have a complex language choice and use. There is a bilingual/multilingual LL, and the use of Spanish in different but specific domains manifests the existence of subjective ethnolinguistic vitality of a temporary Latin American migratory group, the MTAWs, who comprise the majority of Spanish speakers in this territory.

The use of Spanish in the LL is evidence of the presence of an ethnolinguistic minority in the area with a collective identity of "Latin Americans" as well as the presence of a flexible linguistic policy regarding language use in public spaces. Also, the use of Spanish in the LL plays an informative role, showing that there exists a possibility of being served in Spanish, but does not represent a high linguistic vitality of Spanish in the permanent population of the city - something that is impossible to know at a simple glance. Therefore, a bilingual or multilingual LL can convey a mistaken impression about the linguistic vitality of minority, non-official languages in Canada, showing the importance of including different, broader visions for the study of LLs. The use of Spanish in the LL is not exclusive to ethnolinguistic enclaves; it is also used in other kinds of businesses that are not members of Spanish-speaking groups, and therefore the function is not merely symbolic. The LL seems to be created *for* Latin Americans, rather than *by* Latin Americans. However, the LL continues to shape and create physical (i.e. linguistic) borders that show the diverse composition of a small Canadian town - a phenomenon that because of its own nature, can change in time with the constantly shifting face of a country of immigrants, both permanent and temporary, and with a tailored immigration system designed to match the economic and demographic needs that may arise in the future.

Chapter 7

Expatria: Natalia Lara Díaz-Berrio's Photographs on the Mexican Diaspora and the Domestic Space (Visual Essay)[1]

Natalia Lara Díaz-Berrio

All around the world, millions of people make one of the most difficult decisions there can be: to leave their home in search of a better life elsewhere. The reasons for this vary, and it is important to note the difference between having the choice (as well as the means) to move to another country versus being forced to do so. People who find themselves caught in the latter scenario are often fleeing from different situations ranging from human rights violations (such as persecution and torture) to armed conflict or other types of crisis. Another option is that people fleeing from home might have been targeted because of their identity (in terms of ethnicity, religion, sexuality, or political opinions/actions). International NGO's such as Amnesty International refer to this group as refugees or asylum-seekers. Migrants or immigrants, on the other hand, constitute a group of people who can move from one country to another and decide to do so. This is often done in order to find work, to join relatives, or to escape natural disasters. Some move away from home because they are fortunate enough to have that choice, while others feel forced to leave because of poverty or other problems. There are additionally regular and irregular ways by which means people obtain official permission to stay in a country, and this is not always granted in favour of those who need it most, in part due to the ignorance that exists around this issue.

Considering some of the latest contributions of feminist thinkers to the world of critical theory, it is important to address the need that our global society has for creating better frameworks for understanding what actual encounters with other/newcomers entail, beyond superficial assumptions rooted in ignorance and discrimination. Without theoretical tools such as intersectionality and oppositional consciousness, the tendency of the conventional academic is to reduce the complexity of an individual to an essentialist/universalized category (or ensemble of categories). Thus, the Canadian host can be either hospitable or hostile, something which is contingent upon her/his relation to how a given immigrant guest might appear to her/him, as either holding promises of economic development or posing a potential threat to the status quo.

Latina/o Studies social anthropologist, Sofia Villenas understands these different dimensions that exist within the immigrant narrative, ranging from the "hard-working 'American dream' immigrants to immigrants who are a drain on the economy." This reductive framework for perceiving otherness is highly detrimental to the social fabric of a nation in the sense that it legitimizes false notions that are (in most cases without due evidence) taken as realities and that impact those who are forced (economically and politically) to leave their countries of origin for the sake of finding greener grass on the other side. At the same time, this kind of arrogant perception solidifies the transformational capacity of the newcomer, meaning that it becomes harder for the immigrant to manifest her/his difference without having to sublate it into a larger ideological paradigm that is hostile to change and that is particularly violent to newcomers.

In Quebec, immigrants are a constitutive part of the social realm and of its political and cultural landscape, in spite of the fact that they are overlooked in a great number of contexts - particularly in the professional sphere. However, one must bear in mind that Canada (as any other nation, to a certain extent) is socially the result of several waves of migration ever since (and even before) the first British and French settlers arrived during the sixteenth and seventeenth centuries, ever since the period that is known as the conquest of the Americas. For Tzvetan Todorov, this moment in history constitutes the genesis of modern-day Western ideology. He writes that *La Conquista de América: El problema del otro* (*The Conquest of America: The Problem of the Other*) reveals the ways in which identity is built by and through the encounter with someone that is not I. He writes, "one can discover the others in oneself, coming to the realization that we are not a homogeneous substance, nor are we radically foreign to that which is the self: I is Other."[2] This is a line of thought that coincides with one of the strongest academic voices of Occidental thought, Jean Paul Sartre. Sartre's philosophical reflections on the topic of selfhood and nothingness conceive that "the Other is the indispensable mediator between myself and me. I am [...] myself as I appear to the Other," which points to the fact that identity is not fixed but is constantly being negotiated throughout the encounters one has with everything else.

There are several ways in which one can encounter something other (or the Other) in the social arena of a country. For Todorov, this can happen internally (facing difference mostly in terms of gender, race, ability, and capital) and externally (across geographic borders or even territories within nations). The aim of these forms of conceptualizing and categorizing immigrants can, on the one hand, help to establish speculative narratives (imaginaries) to empathetically engage with people who are not familiar with the experience of having to move to another country. However, on some occasions, if these categorizations are not contested and reconfigured in terms of responding to the needs of a shifting context, they will run the danger of becoming problematically outdated, which leaves the immigrant in a precarious state with respect to power.

Considering the recognizable damage that a hate-filled and discriminatory rhetoric such as the one that pushed forward the Trump campaign and that also fueled the Brexit controversy in Great Britain, it is imperative for cultural creators to be able to challenge the falsehood behind these stereotypical images of the Other. The way to do so is by reconceptualizing the subverted and reconfigured spaces that exist between individuals and nations inhabited by diasporic spaces; the purpose is to foster constant reflective inquiries addressed to the reality that is presented as such.

Artists who are driven to engage in social justice and community work use their practice as a means to bring this discussion to the fore by creating images that contest the spectacle of "wretched Otherness" (e.g. prejudice against immigrants). The purpose of this kind of work is to develop people's sensibilities in terms of facing the actual complex situation, the hardships of those who suffer the deleterious consequence of prejudice. Villenas recognizes the need to foster more open mentalities that are capable of bravely accepting the necessary shifts that our general perceptions of the Other need in order to attain a better understanding of the power of multiculturalism as a form of collective resistance to power. The goal is to use art, regardless of the medium, as a means to connect isolated existences through the commonality of difference. The purpose is to try to create communities that seek to transcend the political boundaries that are rooted in Patriarchy and Empire. Villenas writes, "In a politically volatile climate around immigration, alliance building across different groups and political orientations is crucial for ethnography in new Latino diaspora communities." This line of thought coincides with the philosophical understanding of art as a means to transform people's perception of their reality in order to change the properties and distribution of reality itself. This constitutes the essence of Jacques Rancière's political-aesthetic project.

Rancière proposes a restructuring of the sensory apparatus in order to problematize the capitalist regime of perception that maintains an agential separation between those who are seen on stage (actors, politicians, immigration officers) and those who remain passive observers of the drama, the audience (spectators, citizens, immigrants). This argument is a direct reply to Guy Debord's renowned theory of the spectacle (the performativity of capitalism as manifested in social relations of individuals, mediated through images of desire to consume/possess commodities); he sees an enormous potential in the arts as a space where the political can be renegotiated in accordance with the practice of emancipation. He writes, "[P]hotography, installation and all forms of art can rework the frame of our perceptions and the dynamism of our affects."[3] Rancière sees the photographic image not as a mere duplicate of a reality, but rather as a complex set of relations between the visible and the invisible. He also warns about artistic work that enforces a particular distribution of the sensory that is reductive and relies upon passive contemplation. Rancière reminds us that "[a]n image never stands alone. It belongs to a system of visibility that governs the status of bodies represented and the kind of attention they merit."[4]

Expatria: photographs on the Mexican diaspora and the domestic space

I conducted *Expatria* as a first attempt, a pilot one might say, in order to delve deep into the identity of the immigrant in Canada, albeit with a particular focus on the Mexican immigrant population in Quebec. Furthermore, throughout this chapter I reflect on the photographic project *Expatria* (2012-2014), which I started while I was completing a BFA in Studio Arts in Concordia University (Montreal, Canada). As a Mexican student in Canada, I realized I was facing a complex challenge in becoming an immigrant myself. This meant that I was to deal with a shift in the perception I had of the world I had lived in and of the one I had moved to. I suddenly found myself belonging to two worlds: first Mexico and then Canada. In this vein, it is relevant to bring up the work of Gloria Anzaldúa, regarded as one of the most influential feminist authors in Chicano studies.

Anzaldúa's writing reflects upon the experience of having to live in a constant "crossover" between different types of realities. Anzaldúa's concept of the New Mestiza is part of a new postnational project built upon the principle of embracing the multiple within one's identity as a form of resistance to dominant and discriminatory identity politics. In this regard, she explained, the mixed-raced woman can subvert the discourse of difference-as-pejorative by taking advantage of the semiotic interstice in which she exists (qua immigrant) in order to perform oneself without the psycho-political restraint of geographic borders or boundaries of the self. Anzaldúa points out: "It is a cultural mestizaje in that we are constantly crossing into different worlds - we go from the ethnic home world to the world of the academy, to the job world, [...] to the different communities of other peoples of color." I had access to travel and study abroad and at the same time in Canada I was, in a way, sharing a reality with other Mexicans who were living there as immigrants (in similar or different conditions).

The term *Expatria* refers to a feeling of displacement; of not belonging to one's former homeland, one that often results from being out of one's country of origin for a prolonged period of time. I conceived *Expatria* as a means to collectively explore the complexity of performing immigration, by positioning myself within that situation. This, I thought was an exercise for introspection, which also worked as a way to reflect on stereotypes in order to creatively resist cultural prejudice in Mexico. The purpose of this is to ultimately promote dialogue by creating spaces for discussion within the microcosm of my show in Montreal.

I interviewed and photographed forty Mexican immigrants in their houses, in different cities in several countries around the world (specifically in Italy, France, Switzerland, Germany, England, Turkey, Canada, and Japan).[5] The project was showcased at Espacio Mexico (the exhibition space of the Mexican consulate in Montreal) throughout March and April 2014. The motivation behind *Expatria* was to exhibit a series of accounts of real people in order to unmask the person behind the generic term "immigrant." The point was to show these testimonies alongside their photographic portrait, a specific pairing up of text with image that was meant to create a dialectical space that would allow for the viewer/participant to unsettle her/his own unconscious biases against Otherness. This was done in an effort to create a space in which people felt not only allowed, but compelled to negotiate newer perceptions they might have towards immigrants rooted in radical hospitality.

This particular kind of art additionally invites viewers to reflect on the ways in which immigrants might be subject to discrimination, sometimes subtly, other times overtly. It is for this reason that, in my work, I seek to explore the relations between these stereotypes and identity. Comparably, photography as a means to critique this issue has been used by the artists Guadalupe Ruiz, Daniela Rossell, and Meera Margaret Singh, among others. I have a particular interest in their work because they are women photographers who explore the cultural identity of specific communities albeit in a personal way, namely from the ambivalent perspective of both *insiders* and *outsiders*.

The project *Expatria* invokes much of what contemporary feminist theory is writing about; namely, reflecting on the performance of race with a perspective that seeks to include non-hegemonic worldviews - which I consider to be paramount. Travelling and studying abroad, I have rendered a crucial reflection: that people engaging in similar, experimental, autovisual ethnographies can come up with creative alternatives with which to negotiate the social parameters of respectful relationality among people with different backgrounds. With this project, I intend to foster shareable processes of embracing diversity as a society. As a caveat, my theoretical and methodological practices in this chapter are informed by my self-identification as an *insider* and an *outsider*, occupying a liminal position in the equation. Liminality alludes to Homi Bhabha's key concept in the theory he developed around the question of the formation of a culture. Bhabha refers to Lacan's third locus (space), which is located in neither speech nor its interlocutor, but situates itself outside of the discourses of individualism. He explains that "[s]uch a disjunctive space of temporality is the locus of symbolic identification that structures the intersubjective realm - the realm of otherness and the social - where we identify ourselves with the other precisely at a point where he (sic) is inimitable, at the point which eludes resemblance."

This hybrid space that I occupy as a multidimensional immigrant constitutes for Bhabha the possibility of a subaltern, subversive agency, one capable of negotiating its own semantic/epistemological authority through iterative, insurgent modes of relinking (the artistic lens of photography). My lived experience of immigration and my Mexican cultural identity allowed me to thus provide a more grounded sense of the issues in question. At the same time, being the photographer, interviewer, and artist led me to experiment with a distance of perception, for I was also an Outsider (a tourist, of sorts) to the private lives of those I interviewed. Over the course of this narrative, I invite the reader to pause and reflect on what this illusory dichotomy entails in their own perception of others.

In 2012, *Expatria* started as my own personal way to attempt to come to terms with the most salient issues of the crisis of identity that comes with the phenomenon of migration. At the time, I was completing a BA in Studio Art, travelling to study abroad in Montreal in 2010. My main concern was to produce aesthetic accounts of how others, or myself, dealt with their own experiences of migration; I was specifically interested in knowing the different strategies people use when adapting to another place. Through exploring experiences, images, and feelings, the portrayal of Mexican immigrants and visits to their houses became a central aspect of the work. Gaining a certain intimacy by entering the home at their invitation, I became aware of how the objects and the space around us reflected aspects of my host's personality. These materials I started to mentally weave, forming a register, an imprint of their presence. The domestic space, in this sense, became a pretext for me to reflect on the specific traits by which the identity of a Mexican immigrant is constructed in Canada and on how difficult it is to define something in constant movement, and to share these reflections with others.

I decided to display the text of the interviews I had conducted with my temporary hosts (Mexican immigrants who were in turn guests of this other territory) next to the photographs I took of their homes. In this way I sought to create a dialogue that would more personally engage those visiting the show with the people in the photographs. This allowed the viewer a wider context surrounding each personal narrative; I was attempting to facilitate a deeper reflection on issues that arose from the dialogue but that did not necessarily emanate from the semiotic arrangement of the image itself.

The connections built between the photographic work and the interviews allowed me to think of myself as an informal artist-ethnographer, for I was engaged in creating ways to translate living practices of other people into art (to be shared with the world). However, being aware that I myself was going through a process similar to that of my hosts allowed me to cross that separating threshold between subject and object of study. Thanks to this humbling experience of active listening, of attempting to truly understand what the other is saying through the filter of one's own lived experience, I now understand how I was transgressing traditional terminological borderlines that would otherwise render my hybrid work (qua self) problematic. This, I specify, would be the case if my work were following the traditional ethnographic method, as opposed to seeking to create a new framework for reception of images in order to reach the sensory fabric of the people themselves. The difference lies in the artistic quality of this project; I collect visual material and interviews that contribute to a more sensitive understanding of a community and also of myself. For I too have faced the bureaucratic and social pledges that dictate who gets to move away and who does not.

Through conversation, the people I talked to express their concerns about having to embody/perform the role of "immigrant." Many of them narrated the specific difficulties that they had had while arriving in their host culture, bearing in mind all they were missing what was left behind. Regardless of the number of years they had spent away from Mexico, there was a sense of a fracture in the territory of their persona. On one hand, they could feel comfortable and well-installed in the new place, but there remained some residue, a feeling of not belonging and maybe of wishing to leave. Liminality was for them an issue in terms of nostalgia, but it also held the promise of being able to thrive on difference.

Sharing issues of immigration can allow one to understand his/her own experiences as well, from the perspective of the multiple. As Robert Clarke explains, "The complexities and paradoxes of migration may best be served by articulating them; of sharing differences; respecting customs; and of making compromises, in the necessary effort of accommodating each other's perspectives and understanding how the others feel."[6] By losing myself in all of those experiences, I slowly became aware of my own reality as an immigrant. The exchange of stories and overall dialogue contributed to the formal construction of the work, but it also played a central part in my coming to terms with my own changing identity. One of the strongest impressions that I perceived was that of Bhabha's in-between or third space, a constant disorientation (with varying degrees) between two countries and cultures (loci). The contradictions of that state seemed to affect all immigrants I have met, regardless of whether they made this conscious or not.

Identity, immigrants and photography

The concept of identity is central in the interviews and in *Expatria*. It refers to the characteristics and aspects that define a person in terms of physicality (under a given politics/regime of visibility) and social function (namely, status and work). This means that it is a way of introducing oneself to others, a way of showing their nature through certain features. There exists a set of visible and invisible, tangible and intangible dimensions within the multifaceted complexity of an individual. Susan Chev-

138

lowe, affirms that "[r]ather than unified or singular, identities are [...] constructed across difference, often intersecting and antagonistic discourses, practices and positions."[7] In this regard, identity is framed as malleable, complex, and flexible, and is created through words, memories, and images. To conceive of that condition in this way is to see it as a living thing, something that cannot be fixed or defined. The words and the collective group of people shape this imagined community, through stories and traditions by which everyone can learn to relate to one another. The Mexican national narrative which has been built over time in stories, in the media, and in popular culture consists of a group of images and symbols that represent experiences, triumphs, and defeats, all of which give meaning to the nation. Stuart Hall explains that the national cultural narrative has been told with an "emphasis on origins, continuity, tradition, and timelessness [...] The essentials of the national character remain unchanged through the vicissitudes of history."[8] Nationalism is then built on characteristics that transcend the present, and that are a result of events from different periods that are assembled in one complex construction.

As immigrants, we build our national identity (the macro scale of our identity) in relation to our personal memories (the micro). We take our strength, in a way, from our powerful imagination. Our individual and collective sense of nationality is performative, meaning that it is constantly being shaped by what happens, in relation to each one's history. However, beyond the limitations of the individual, in order to understand the performative quality of the phenomenon of nationality, one must consider the concepts of "nation" and "native." Raymond Williams explains in his book *A Vocabulary of Culture and Society* that the word *nation* comes from the Latin word *nationem*, which means *race*. The word, in its origin, had an emphatic racial connotation. Over the years, the term has acquired a sense of political consolidation of a people. However, it remains a racially charged term (even if it is not thought of in that way). Moreover, the word *native* refers to a person who comes from a specific place, but the problem with this term is that it also has a negative connotation. Williams mentions, "It was particularly common for 'non-Europeans' in the period of colonialism and imperialism [to employ] the negative use of native to describe the inferior inhabitants of a place subjected to alien political power or conquest, or even of a place visited and observed from some supposedly superior standpoint." Later the author adds: "The negative use, especially for 'non-Europeans,' can still be found, even in writing which apparently rejects ideological implications."[9] Often, discussion about national identity or immigrants has an implicitly negative appeal, and that is why people prefer to avoid conversations that deal with these topics. The concepts "native" and "nation" may seem simple to us in the present, at a superficial level, but actually carry the weight of a specific history that reveals past mentalities regarding segregation and human classification.

Displacement that is caused by immigration creates shifts and changes in identity, but some original elements are kept in the practices/personality traits of a given group or community of immigrants. As Chevlowe mentions, every ethnic group has elements in common with regard to food, religion, customs, and history. Photography can create awareness and help to describe the visual elements that bind a community together. Chevlowe affirms, "[P]hotography is not simply a mirror held up to reality. It shows us what we want to see, framing and shaping the world and the values and history of a particular community."[10] Through the act of taking photographs, there is a deliberate choice made in terms representing certain aspects of a community: the point of view of the photographer becomes determinant.

One of the ways in which photographers have reflected on the identity of a group of people is by looking back at the space in which they live. The domestic space may have an important connection with national identity. Photography explores the privacy of the home by revealing it to the viewer. This process sheds light on the diverse aspects of the person who lives in that photographed space. In addition to this, the task of exploring issues of identity in art is challenging because the concept (and our collective notion) of identity is unstable and multifaceted.

Guadalupe Ruiz and Daniela Rossell are two Latin American photographers who have approached the domestic space in order to reveal important traits that constitute the identity of a specific community. They both also happen to belong to the communities they portray (Colombian and Mexican, respectively). Both express their own personal understanding of their country and their society. Through the pictures they take, they reflect the culture as well as the social and economic situation of certain populations within a country.

Rossell caused great controversy in 2002 with her work. Between 1994 and 2001, she produced a series entitled *Rich and Famous*, portraits of multi-millionaire women in their homes. The scandal arose because she showed them as anonymous, and it was discovered that they were the families of Mexican politicians who revealed an immense opulence in their lifestyle. The photographs showed a part of society marked by government corruption and impunity. For example, one of the families was that of former president Carlos Salinas (who led the country into a huge economic crisis in the 1990s); another was that of Gustavo Díaz Ordaz (who ordered the student massacre of Tlatelolco, Mexico City, in 1968). This event unleashed a great debate about the country's social situation. Rossell deliberately acts as an insider in this project, being the daughter of a distinguished member of the Institutional Revolutionary Party (Partido Revolucionario Institucional) herself. Her privileged status granted her access to these private spaces of the Mexican elite. This was a relevant, historic moment, since very few people (in the general public) had seen those images before. It was a significantly scandalous issue, for it reflected the excesses that these families enjoyed, while the majority of the Mexican population lived in poverty. The photographs are expressive of a context, a social condition, but they also reveal a conflict and pose a contradiction.

Rossell's work is an example of how photographing a person in the domestic space can address issues that transcend the space itself, beyond what the photographer is looking at or can foresee from a close perspective.

Ruiz's work also takes place in the domestic place, although it offers a different point of view. She takes pictures of Colombian people in their homes. At first glance, the photographs seem to have been taken rather spontaneously. However, if observed closely, the viewer can realize that they are in fact staged. The images show stereotypes of the Latin American cultural imaginary as consumed in popular culture. The macho man and the warm-blooded woman appear in hackneyed settings. The portraits are caricatural in a sense and lead us (the viewers) to question our own views of these people. Ruiz chooses parody as an efficient format in which to present her work, displaying stereotyped images which offer a critical spin to the aesthetic eye.

Because she is a member of the same community she is portraying, she is allowed to create that specific kind of work. She is granted a particular power that comes from being an insider. Both Rossell and Ruiz are insiders of a community and use domestic space and portraits to reflect on larger issues. Their work offers a hint of humour. In my work, I am not necessarily aiming to be cynical or humorous. However, I do act as an insider by being part of the Mexican community, and that allows me to have a closer approach to the people I learn with. The works of the two photographers mentioned above provides me with certain insight into strategies one can adopt in order to work as an insider in a photographic project such as *Expatria*.

In opposition to this strategy, other photographers have chosen to detach themselves from, rather than immerse themselves in, their work in order to present it from an (arguably) more "objective" perspective. Photographer Meera Margaret Singh is a renowned Canadian visual artist who acts as an outsider in her series *Farmland*. Her work is an interesting contraposition to the work I am engaging in, and thus provides an interesting alternative for a reflective comparison.

Singh's project titled *Farmland* (2011) deals with the issues that revolve around the identity of immigrants in Canada. She constructed a series of portraits of immigrant workers and farmers labouring specifically in Ontario's Greenbelt. Singh explores "how cultural physical, geographical, and emotional thoughts of displacement and suspension can be explored photographically."[11] Through photography, Singh shows the relationship between people, their workspaces, and the landscape: "[She is] not looking [...] to dissect an issue such as migrant labor in Canada [...] from all angles photographically. As she affirms: I am interested in each individual I photograph."[12] This means that the artist does not concentrate on large-scale situations but rather she focuses on the individual stories, considering that photography is not a way to confirm a hypothesis or a conclusion. The camera gave her access to a community to which she is foreign. This allowed her to become involved with different people who eventually came to trust her through sharing her photography. She operated as an outsider in this case, since she was not part of that specific group of workers she was photographing. She was also keen enough to observe the process of assimilation or social integration of these workers from a closer yet still foreign perspective.

These three photographers work within a community through photography to reflect on issues of identity. They deal with national identity (Rossell and Ruiz), migration (Singh), and stereotypes (Rossell and Ruiz) in specific contexts. Photographs reflect that complex weaving of ideas. Their works are an inspiration for my own project, since they are examples of approaching a community as an insider or outsider, using a particular space (Singh/work, Rossell and Ruiz/domestic space). Since Ruiz and Rossell focused their work on the domestic space, they are using a similar vocabulary to my own. I feel an interest in Ruiz's and Rossell's work because of how they reflect the fact that the domestic space has a power of communication because of what it can convey.

Peter Galassi, Curator of the Department of Photography at the Museum of Modern Art, is someone who has written about artists whose work focuses on the domestic sphere. He considers that "[t]he pictures contain plenty of evidence of what anthropologists call material culture, what people own, how they dress, and the stuff they hang on their walls or pile up on their desks."[13] Galassi affirms that the space where people live reveals precious information about them. In addition to this, the term "material culture" is related to visual anthropology, namely to the study of a culture through images and objects. Thus, choosing to create portraits in the domestic space is a strong way of showing several layers of a person's identity. Objects configure an essential dimension of material culture, and their presence or absence has been extremely relevant in *Expatria*.

Throughout the project I became aware of the subtleties of the Mexican identity abroad, both in terms of stasis/tradition and transformation/adaptation. The more conservative and stereotyped image of what people conventionally take to represent Mexicans was in fact absent in many of the houses I worked in. The specific contact one can make with one's culture can be achieved through non-visible rituals and activities. Myria Georgiou, educator in international communications, expresses in this regard that "shared characteristics - language, religion, family values, food tastes, and so forth - get their meanings and construct images of *We-ness* and *Otherness*."[14] That creation of a delimitation of two groups gives a sense of distance in terms of defining what is close and what is further away. This contributes to people's understanding of the importance of what is truly shared, and cherished, by a community.

Racism and imagination

When executing art projects such as *Expatria* or those done by Ruiz, Rossell or Singh, issues of race and racism intrinsically appear in the process or in the final result of the work. When I addressed this issue in interviews with Mexicans, they noticed that some people had emphatic, determining, and discriminatory ideas about people, like themselves, who come from Mexico. I believe that certain attitudes are founded on unconscious conditionings of a racist ideology. According to Michèle Vatz-Laroussi, doctor in intercultural psychology, who explores the relationship between migration, families, relationships, boundaries, and territories, Quebecers perceive immigrants as four possible figures: minority, different, sub-citizen, or nomad. She reflects on the process that takes place between the in-group ("us") and the out-group ("them").

High tensions often arise in the encounter between these two groups regarding the image of the different ones, "the Others," perceived in terms of the differences they pose to the social norm, whether visible or attributed, as something static: these traits are the bearers of unchanging cultural characteristics leading to stereotypes. The above mentioned are limited and relatively constant definitions applied to a group of people, a way to categorize someone. They can lead to negative behaviours, to the radicalization of the attributes, and to actions inspired by the stereotyped perception. Clarke notes, "[W]e must recognize that thinly concealed behind the rhetoric of economic excuses, voiced as a resistance to migration, are issues of race and racism."[15] Furthermore, Hall reflects on the complexity of that identity and the relationship between different identities. He argues that race has no relation to biology and it is a discursive element which can be invisible because it is often related to nationalism and patriotism.[16] Some of the Mexicans I interviewed have told me they have been discriminated or undervalued at work or in other places without a valid reason, and they have perceived it as a consequence of prejudices that exist and circulate in Canadian society regarding Mexicans.

Race and discussion about race can be considered through photography because of its visual components and because of its connection with the imagination. American cultural historian and art critic Maurice Berger argues that "[t]he visual arts can serve as an important catalyst for the discussion of race, a rare instance where contemporary art can have broad social relevance. This is true because much of what defines race in culture is innately visual."[17] Indeed, visual elements are used to categorize people, and art uses visual vocabulary to create different patterns of meaning to contest those already existing in reality. Art can question the viewer's issues, without having to use words, through images presenting icons, symbols, and images; art can create a dialogue about racism issues. Exploring the idea of race and art, Patricia Williams, a legal scholar, had the same opinion as Hall about the non-scientific value of race but recalls the influence that those ideas still have on us and the power they have as racial categories.

Berger writes, "[I]t's precisely the acknowledgement of whiteness that can help people understand their racist behavior, attitudes, and complicity."[18] He argues that every individual should consider the meaning of their race. Again, race is neither biological nor scientific but an element of the discourse between people coming from different countries. In this context, art can be a means to share and express expectations and experiences. We must be prepared to challenge and question our beliefs.

As a society, we are governed by stereotypes and identities in conflict. This tension between what is authentic and what is prejudice, between what has been lived and what is assumed, between what is real and what is artificial, can be a powerful questioning tool in art. American philosopher and feminist theorist, Drucilla Cornell states that one alone cannot make huge changes because racism is a social, political, and economic problem that cannot be solved by individual decisions. It is essential to take an active part in a movement which struggles for the recognition of the humanity of all those who have been historically repressed. Working together weaves the power of each individual, creating a common fabric of community that is guided by a shared self-confidence. As a consequence, this collective force can help to challenge the stereotypes which oppress all of us humans. We need to be critical about our own way of thinking about others, constantly and emphatically.[19]

As Cornell points out, "our consciousness of what is Other can only encounter another consciousness if we recognize our own freedom [...] Such a task is inseparable from our imagination."[20] We need to reinvent our way of seeing life, and imagination is essential to keeping in touch with others. It is an indispensable function in understanding the world around us: it is a manifestation of reality. Since art is linked to the image, the word, and sensitivity, it arises from the imagination, which is a kind of sensory knowledge. Thus, just like art, imagination is a liberating activity: it suggests more than it shows. It is proleptic more than ekphrastic or mimetic. The artist, the one that imagines, the one that creates and transgresses, can transit from concreteness to abstraction, from particularity to universality, and consecutively until the end of time.

Conclusion

Expatria allowed me to explore how identity is not something that can be easily defined or described. By asking the participants I photographed to dress in Mexican clothes, there is a suggestion of staging a certain identity. The resulting image is a record of an enactment, the result of my asking the sitters to dress in a way that is representative for them. The chosen elements reflect to a certain extent what they keep to remember where they come from. In some cases, as in the homes of Aida (photographs 3 and 4) and Carmelo (photographs 9 and 10), they had only a Mexican flag. Other participants, such as Araceli (photographs 5 and 6), owned several Mexican objects. All those items are material culture, but they don't represent the same thing to all beholders. It should be mentioned that the absence of objects does not reflect a lack of contact with the Mexican culture and community. For example, the love for traditions, regardless of particular objects, is expressed by Norma, a children's teacher and mother who told me, "It is very important for me to celebrate the Day of the Dead (Día de Muertos) and the Day of Our Lady of Guadalupe. I also share with my students the stories and heritage of my country, like pre-Hispanic tales."[21] Through the activities at home and also at work, she keeps in contact with the culture and the traditions.

By means of the encounters with Mexican migrants, it can be seen that it is important to have the feeling of belonging to a community. In some cases, it can be to the Mexican community or to another community, but it is a relevant factor to belong to the place where the person lives. It is important, as Cornell states to be part of a group to feel empowered.[22] In the interviews I conducted, it became evident that many of them kept strong ties in Quebec to the Mexican community and culture, and also with their homeland, establishing the bond of friendship with compatriots, as well as through their activities and preferences. As Rafael pointed out, he has mainly friends who are fellow countrymen, and he is in constant communication with his family abroad. Aida is in contact with groups of Mexicans who support each other in Montreal, and that keeps her in contact with her culture. From a different perspective, Jorge (photographs 7 and 8) does not feel close to the Mexican community, but he is still interested in Mexican culture (for example in music, reading, and food).

Almost all the Mexicans I talked to have seen their migration to Quebec as a formative and transformative life experience in which they learned both about themselves and about a new culture. Many Mexicans have also found opportunities that did not seem available in Mexico. Nevertheless, integrating is not a simple process.

In the exhibition presented at Espacio Mexico, the response of the audience recognized the diversity of characters shown in the photographs. Some people were surprised not to see very many Mexican objects in the houses. Those reactions indicate that the project reveals a vision of Mexicans that does not correspond to preconceived ideas. Several people in the exhibition shared with me their experience as immigrants in Quebec and the way in which they could identify with the participants in the project. Some viewers wanted to know more about the background of the person in the photograph. The project triggered an interest in communicating personal experiences and also generated empathy towards the participants.

The project *Expatria* is meant to invite us to imagine how we see others, and to question ourselves on that vision, not through the accuracy of what I present, but through what the stories and the images reveal, what is implicit in them, and what they do not say, thanks to the rich potential of the imagination. Carrying out this project allowed me to get to know more about Mexico and Mexicans and the process of migration which, though different for each person, has similar facets. In a way, it was a project that corresponded to my personal needs and was fulfilling, by helping others and myself to create bridges of communication. That necessity was only one aspect of the project. The need for expression was also felt by other Mexicans, and it was rewarding to participate in an undertaking in which they could express how they perceive themselves as immigrants, i.e., the psychological, social, and economic aspects involved. I hope that this project can reflect the essence of this project in depicting different aspects of Mexicans.

The reflections that this project kindled in the people who helped shape it led me to face the reality of migration from the perspective of the complex. Reducing the immensity of this phenomenon is to do a disservice to those who are caught in the bureaucratic hardships of being an immigrant from an "underdeveloped" country such as Mexico. Art in this way can help one to grasp the totality of this complexity and can be used as a tool to both communicate this complicated experience and to navigate it better collectively. The goal is to learn how to understand Otherness through radical empathy, namely seeing that there are infinite variables in the situation of others. And therefore, it is extremely important to come up with new ways in which we can help spread these stories so that people can learn much more about what migrating entails, beyond the negative stereotypes that circulate in the mainstream media. Art can help us to challenge our arrogant ways in order to perceive others in need.

As artists, it is our responsibility to create projective realities through the manipulation of images. In this regard, it is understood that the ultimate purpose of this type of art is to bring these discussions to the fore in an effort to bring to reality a different world where empathy can rule over fearful judgment without much paperwork in the middle.

Rafael[23]
Place of birth: Mexico City
Place where he grew up: Cuernavaca
He migrated alone
Living in Montreal for three years
Occupation back in Mexico: Jeweller
Occupation in Montreal: Labourer

"I started university but left it the second semester and started to work. In 2009, Canada didn't ask for visas, so Mexicans could enter the country with just a passport. I came to work for a short period of time and after that I decided to stay in Montreal. While in Mexico, I didn't imagine there would be so many people in Canada from Mexico and other countries. Being in Montreal, I feel it was easy to integrate into the society because I built relationships with Mexicans at work and at home. I speak more Spanish than French or English. I haven't established many close relationships with Canadians, and I feel more comfortable with Mexicans and people from other countries. I feel that what defines me as Mexican is the pleasure of partying. I would like to go back to Mexico: I came alone and miss my family, although I am worried I won't be able to return to Canada afterwards."

Photograph 1. Rafael in his living room wearing casual clothing.
Photograph 2. Rafael with the jersey of the Mexican national soccer team.

Aida
Place of birth: Mexico City
Place where she grew up: Mexico City
She migrated with her husband and her son (who was then four years old)
Living in Montreal for three years
Occupation back in Mexico: Financial advisor
Occupation in Montreal: Financial advisor

"I decided to leave Mexico when my son was born because I began to feel insecure. I had previously been assaulted but did not worry about it at the time; however, I did when I became a mother. My husband and I spent four years in the migration process in order to achieve permanent residence. I don't feel as happy as I had imagined living in Montreal; I don't know exactly why. However, I don't think I would be better off in Mexico and don't want to live there again. I am not attached to traditions, I am not a supporter of any soccer team, and I have never voted. I do not practice any religion, and I was surprised to realize how Catholic the Mexicans I knew in Montreal were; and I realized that Mexican culture was different from the one I remembered in Mexico. I feel I'm committed to Canadian society, working in Canadian companies, and I'm bound to the Mexican community, participating in two support groups for the integration of immigrants in Montreal."[24]

Photograph 3. Aida, husband, and son in their living room.
Photograph 4. Aida, husband, and son with a Mexican flag.

Araceli
Place of birth: Acapulco
Place where she grew up: Acapulco and Monterrey
She migrated alone
Living in Montreal for two years
Occupation back in Mexico: Producer of cultural TV shows
Occupation in Montreal: French Literature student

"I came to Montreal in 2012 to study. I had previously been to Canada and wanted to return. I know that I will go back to Mexico, but don't know when. When I arrived, I didn't have high expectations; I already had an idea of what Montreal was like: an urban place, a mixture of French and Anglo-Saxon cultures, and a North American country. I think that what defines me as Mexican is my calm, friendly character. I try to avoid complicated situations and treat people equally. The idea of Mexico that Quebecers have is the one they see in the news: an economically underdeveloped country where there's a lot of violence. Perhaps the idea they have of Mexico is very similar to the one they have of the rest of Latin America: violent countries, much poverty, and great economic differences. At the same time, they think that they are countries with a lot of sun, and with friendly, fun-loving people. I doubt that Canadians have much information about a particular country. I think they see all of Latin America in a general way."

Photograph 5. Araceli in her terrace, wearing casual clothing.
Photograph 6. Araceli wearing Mexican embroidered clothes.

Jorge
Place of birth: Mexico City
Place where he grew up: Mexico City
He migrated with his parents and his brother
Living in Montreal for seven years
Occupation back in Mexico: High school student
Occupation in Montreal: Music student

"My family and I decided to leave Mexico after my mother was shot in a bank robbery and my father and brother were shot also while strolling on a ranch (fortunately none of them was killed). We applied for Canadian residency and moved to Montreal. The first three years were difficult for me as I had to redefine myself and adapt. I do not have good relations with the Mexicans I have met in Canada. Mexicans do not form a helping community: on the contrary, they want to take advantage of each other. I was disappointed with the Mexicans' image and walked away. Canadians perceive us as people who are refugees, unemployed, live on support from the government, do not speak good English or French, are violent, sexist, alcoholic, homophobic, and uneducated. I had a trilingual school education, and I had been in Canada four times before migrating; I have a privileged status. Still, I consider myself a Mexican ambassador who upholds the fine reputation of his country.[25] I believe that what defines me as Mexican is the music I listen to, the fact that I am a courteous young man, and the joy I feel when listening to mariachis. I don't want to live in Mexico again; I wouldn't have a chance to grow as a musician there."

Photograph 7. Jorge in his dining room, wearing casual clothing.
Photograph 8. Jorge enacting a mariachi, with his collection of Mexican hats.

*The reading of chapters this week provided me with a lot of new intriguing info, but what stuck out to me most was the testimonials of Mexicans living in Canada. I think it was interesting to hear their perspectives and how they felt. Furthermore, I felt it was important to highlight how different they all were/felt from each other especially considering the similarities they share. such as the difficulty adapting and feeling a sense of belonging in Canada which was also something that saddened me.

Carmelo
Place of birth: Tacopan (municipality of Atempan, in the mountains of the state of Puebla)
Place where he grew up: Tacopan and Puebla city
He migrated alone
Living in Montreal for six years
Occupation back in Mexico: Quality inspector in a recycling industry
Occupation in Montreal: Cleaner and activist

"In my town, we all speak Nahuatl, and I learned Spanish in elementary school. I studied chemical engineering and worked in the paper-recycling industry. I had political problems and sought asylum in Canada. Although I didn't speak English or French when I arrived, I felt that it wasn't difficult to adjust to living here. I like to be in touch with people and get involved in society's activities. I take part in a theatre workshop and participate in a radio program on immigrants. I've been well treated in Canada, but there is a problem in regard to the employment agencies and the migration policy. My concern about the treatment immigrants receive inspired me to get involved with the group Mexicanos Unidos por la Regularización, which supports people without papers.[26] My participation in this movement has changed my perspective on my commitment to society, and if I return to Mexico, I will also fight for rights. My experience as an immigrant has given me another perspective of both myself and my place of origin."

Photograph 9. Carmelo swaddled in blanket with the Mexican flag.
Photograph 10. Carmelo in his bedroom, wearing casual clothing.

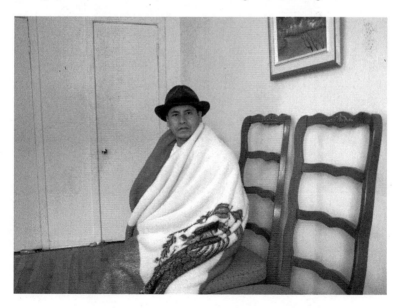

Part 3
Building Community

Chapter 8

Culture for *la denuncia*:
The Chilean Exile Community and the Political
Goals of Cultural Expression, 1973-1980

Francis Peddie

Between 1973 and 1980, the Chilean community in Canada grew from a group numbering in the hundreds to one of over 10,000 people. A substantial part of this wave came as a direct result of the *coup d'état* of 11 September 1973, with Chileans fleeing their country either for reasons of political repression or as a result of economic and social marginalization caused by the policies of the military dictatorship. The regime that replaced the *Unidad Popular* (UP) leftist coalition government headed by Salvador Allende attempted to stamp out all influence they judged Marxist through direct and indirect methods of repression, resulting in the deaths of thousands and the exodus of over one million political exiles and economic migrants displaced by the dictatorship's exclusionary policies and political, economic, and social alterations between 1973 and 1990. The realities of military rule were the direct cause of the growth of the Chilean community in Canada.

In its stage of rapid growth in the 1970s, the Chilean community was predominantly composed of people who self-identified as exiles. The political, social, and cultural activities of this community of exile reflected a continuing focus on events and developments in Chile, where most of the members continued to live in their hearts, even if their bodies were by necessity in Canada. As this chapter will argue, Chilean exiles across Canada used cultural expression and performance for multiple ends: to promote and preserve aspects of traditional culture such as music, dance, and cuisine; to teach Canadians of other ethnicities about their homeland, but also to broadcast their political views, denounce the dictatorship, and raise funds to support political prisoners and victims' solidarity groups back in Chile. For the Chilean exiles, "cultural" meant "political," and the repudiation of the military dictatorship - *la denuncia* in Spanish - was an overarching goal of all community activity.

La denuncia was also therapeutic. Along with the above-mentioned ends, expressing *chilenidad* - Chilean-ness - was one strategy by which Chilean exiles reasserted their national identity in the face of expatriation. Dancing the national dance, the *cueca*, or preparing *empanadas* for sale at a *peña* (a traditional Chilean party) to raise funds for political prisoners and their families back in Chile served both a political purpose and a psycho-emotional one. Excluded from Chile physically, exiles were also portrayed by the military regime and its supporters as unpatriotic, untrustworthy, and ultimately un-Chilean agents of a foreign ideology. However, the exiles in Canada and throughout the world did not meekly accept this depiction. Instead, they used expressions of a particular vision of *chilenidad* to oppose the negative discourse of the regime and present themselves as the true Chileans, in contrast to the military leaders and their supporters, who had violated national tradition by the very act of their *coup d'état*. Exiles in Canada and elsewhere asserted that values such as respect for democracy and human rights, along with the active solidarity shown to other Latin Americans and peoples of the world suffering from repression and inequity, were features that defined what it meant to be Chilean. The exiles' affirmation of their Chilean-ness was political as well as a statement of origin and belonging, serving at once to denounce their opponents and to affirm their national identity in the face of the dictatorship's effort to erase them from Chile.

The use of culture for political ends was not confined to elements of popular or folk culture such as food and dances but encompassed various mediums of expression including photography, painting, film, theatre, and literature. Poetry with political content was a particularly prominent form of cultural expression among exiled Chileans, so much so that by the late 1980s, the prevalence of Chilean poets among Spanish-speaking writers in Canada led one observer to comment that they formed a category unto themselves, with an output that far exceeded other Latin American groups.

Writers of various genres used their voices to condemn what was happening in their country of origin and contributed their artistic skills to the solidarity campaign and its fund-raising efforts. In addition, their exploration of the emotional and psychological impact of exile on identity articulated the anxiety and trauma felt by many of the Chilean newcomers, who had to confront the reality of rebuilding stable lives and careers, learning new languages, and coping with the pain of separation from family, friends, and familiar surroundings. In literature as well as public display, cultural performance by Chilean exiles served a connected dual purpose: to condemn those who had usurped the power in Chile, and to deal with the difficult issues of national and personal identity caused by exclusion from their homeland.

Finally, public performance of *chilenidad* was used to establish a relationship between the exile communities and the general population in their cities of refuge in order to win support for *la denuncia*. While activism was portrayed as a component of *chilenidad*, a purely political approach had limited appeal in English Canada. In a society perceived by the exiles as largely apolitical and uninterested in Latin America, exiles needed to use other methods to broadcast the Chilean cause to the populace. In countries where political mobilization had limited effectiveness, exiles launched appeals for support in ways that played better to the local people, such as through the performance of folkloric Chilean culture and the attraction of food. The political nature of the Chilean exile community, however, did influence the viewpoint of Canadians, in particular the way journalists saw the group, and this situation contributed to the formation of the image of an educated, young, activist cohort that spread to the broader population. As the first Latin American nationality to arrive in such large numbers in a short time and with such a high media profile, the Chilean exiles were a key group in establishing the Latin American presence in Canada. Chileans therefore influenced how Latin Americans in general were seen in Canada, as human links between the country and the region began to grow and deepen after years of mutual ignorance. However, on a practical level, political exiles had to use cultural tools to broadcast their political message to the Canadian public, who had little knowledge of, or interest in, events in Latin America.

Methodology

This study comes out of research on immigration history in which I focused on Chilean exiles who arrived in the 1970s and on how they reestablished interrupted lives in Canada. The current chapter examines one aspect of the process of settlement in Canada which was politically, socially, and even spiritually vital to the exiles and simultaneously helped them broadcast their presence as newcomers in the nation. The primary material for this study comes from interviews I conducted between October 2008 and April 2010 with twenty-one Chileans who were living or had lived in Ontario or Quebec and who self-identified as exiles. The interviews took place mostly in Toronto (sixteen out of twenty-one), along with several others carried out in Ottawa (two) and Santiago, Chile (three). The interviews were conducted in Spanish or English based on the interviewee's preference, and I later translated the Spanish transcripts into English (the original language for each interview cited is mentioned in the notes). All of the interviewees except one had come to Canada between 1973 and 1978, and all but one took up residence in Canada after arriving. In some cases, quotations from these interviews have appeared in other work of mine, while others used in this study have not been previously published. During the interviews, I asked several open-ended questions to gather information about the participants' involvement in Chilean associations along with questions about who had offered assistance to the exiles upon their arrival. The information gleaned from these questions revealed that Chilean exiles based in Ontario and Quebec had a vibrant community life that initially revolved around three core goals: providing orientation and assistance to Chilean newcomers, denouncing the anti-democratic junta that had overthrown the UP government and committed widespread human rights violations, and raising money to help people left behind in Chile who were targeted by the military regime (solidarity campaigns). This study focuses on the second and third goals, as the closely-connected activities of denunciation and solidarity are where we can see the incorporation of cultural expression and artistic performance for larger political purposes, along with the subtler assertion of the exiles' authentic *chilenidad*.

Oral testimony is supplemented by other primary sources, such as the newsletters of Chilean associations and reports of pro-exile Canadian organizations, most of which I accessed in New York at the New School for Social Research, which houses the microfilm archive of the North American Congress on Latin America - Archive of Latin Americana (henceforth, NACLA-ALA). Posters, illustrations, and advertisements in these sources illustrate how activities such as concerts, exhibitions, and film screenings, as well as social events such as *peñas*, were used as vehicles to deliver the political message while also collecting money for those back in the homeland.

While this research relies on numerous secondary sources, three of them warrant particular mention for the contribution they have made to my understanding of the associational life of Chilean exiles in Canada: José del Pozo's "Las organizaciones comunitarias de chilenos en la provincia de Quebec, Canadá"; Joan Simalchik's "The Material Culture of Chilean Exile: A Transnational Dialogue"; and Litzy Baeza Kallens's "Voces del exilio: testimonios orales del exilio chileno en Edmonton, Canadá." These studies illustrate how close the connection was between the cultural and the political in associations founded in the 1970s, how time and changing circumstances led to transformations in the goals of Chilean organizations, and how subsequently Chile and *chilenidad* were portrayed to both the broader Canadian society and within the community itself.

Historical research on Chileans in Canada remains in a formative stage, as it does for other Latin Americans, whether viewed as distinct national groups or part of a broader Latin American Canadian community. There are regional or thematic limitations to studies of the Chilean Canadian community - perhaps better described as plural communities - that are illustrative of the geographical factors that influence group identity and organization among newcomer groups. José del Pozo's monograph, *Les Chiliens au Québec. Immigrants et réfugiés, de 1955 à nos jours*, covers a broad scope of the Chilean experience, exile and non-exile, but only as lived in Quebec. Julie D. Shayne's *They Used to Call Us Witches: Chilean Exiles, Eulture, and Feminism* is similarly geographically confined to Vancouver and focuses on more specific linkages between political and feminist activism among exiled Chilean women. It becomes clear that, when added to the articles mentioned in the previous paragraph and my own research on the topic, studies of Chileans in Canada are province- or even city-specific. While this chapter also relies on primary evidence collected in one area of Canada, the findings and analyses of del Pozo, Simalchik, Baeza Kallens, and Shayne, among others, have helped me form a reasonably complete picture of how cultural activities and expressions were used as a tool of *denuncia* by Chilean exiles wherever they settled in Canada. I would posit that for future research, whether on Chileans or other communities in the country, finding pan-national, shared points of focus such as that represented by *la denuncia* may offer a path to analysis that overcomes the centrifugal forces of language and regionalism standing in the way of a nationwide perspective on Latin Americans in Canada.

Conceptual framework

In my research on Chilean exiles, I borrow Mario Sznajder and Luis Roniger's four-point model encompassing the expelled, the expelling force, the receiving societies, and the transnational networks of exiles and human rights activists who adopted Chile as a cause. However, rather than conceiving of it as a square or rectangle, I view it as a large triangle composed of four smaller triangles, wherein the central triangle represents the exile community and its constituent individual members, and connects to each of the other triangles:

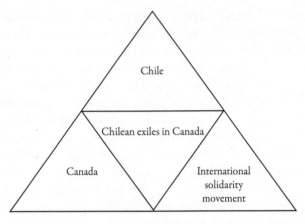

Diagram 1. Conceptual framework for Chilean exiles in Canada and their relationships.

Chilean exiles were physically separated from their homeland but maintained a relationship - albeit a highly antagonistic one - with the military regime that had expelled them. They also continued both overt and covert relationships with family, friends, and colleagues left behind, and directed solidarity efforts such as fundraising toward helping or securing the release of the political prisoners in Chile, who had once been their fellow party members and activists during the years of the UP.[1] By necessity, they had to find ways to relate to other people in Canada beyond those who sympathized with their cause and acted in solidarity with them. At the same time, the community in Canada was only one of many Chilean exile communities around the world,[2] and despite geographic distance, Chileans in exile communicated with each other and sometimes coordinated actions across national boundaries to denounce the regime.[3] International tours sponsored by Chilean solidarity organizations of musical groups whose members were in exile, such as Inti-Illimani and Quilapayún, are an example of how the international solidarity network operated and incorporated cultural expression into the political message.

However, in spite of the transnational network that existed among exile groups, I hesitate to identify Chilean expression and performance in Canada during the 1970s as being part of a broader Latin American movement. While there is evidence that Chilean exiles cooperated, collaborated, and coordinated with other Latin Americans to produce Spanish-language literature, for example, these projects only began to appear in the 1980s.[4] Most of the cultural output of individual exile artists or exile associations was consciously national in character: Chileans presenting their culture, talking about the problems in their homeland, and trying to affirm and maintain a sense of national identity in a situation of forced expatriation. While the question of where Chileans stood vis-à-vis a broader Latin American community in Canada would become more prominent in the 1980s and even more so later on among the 1.5 and 2.0 generations - people who were either born in Chile but came to Canada at a very young age, or were born in Canada to exile parents -, the exiles in the 1970s focused most of their effort and energy on assertion of their *chilenidad* through political action and the cultural expression that went along with it.

The self-consciously national nature of political action and cultural expression relates to the second pillar of the conceptual framework of this study, which is the psychological and emotional importance of community action and affirmations of national identity among groups in diaspora. Whether through willing migration or forced relocation, people who reside and eventually settle in foreign lands feel the need to preserve a connection to a life and a past left behind in the country of origin. In the case of the Chilean exiles in Canada, the performance of *chilenidad* through political activism and cultural activity served as a repudiation of a military regime that declared them bad Chileans or even un-Chilean. As Joan Simalchik observed, Chileans in exile adopted certain overt symbols and practices of *chilenidad* only after being separated from Chile, when the need to demonstrate the authenticity of their identity became acute.[5] Studies and reports by Chilean and non-Chilean psychiatrists treating exile patients in the 1970s and 1980s, whether in Canada or in other countries of exile, underlined the important role played by acts of *denuncia* in helping people forced from their homeland to rebuild a damaged sense of identity and belonging.[6] In a sense, exiles delivered a double-edged *denuncia* to the dictatorship through political activism that included expressions of *chilenidad* by both denying the legitimacy of the regime itself and repudiating the accusation that exiles were somehow unworthy of their national identity.

In concrete terms, the Chilean organizations founded by political exiles used any and all means of cultural expression to broadcast their message of condemnation to the society around them and to raise funds for their comrades in Chile. In the next section, I shall examine the coalescence of groups in various parts of Canada founded by Chileans whose activities focused on *denuncia* and solidarity, using expression and performance of *chilenidad* as a means to these ends.

Denuncia, solidarity, and attracting los gringos

A few political exiles found shelter in Canada in the months immediately after the coup, but their numbers were very small.[7] These early
arrivals received assistance from federal or provincial authorities that was
available to new immigrants and refugees, but they were also welcomed
and helped by the small number of Chileans already resident in various
cities as well as by secular and religious organizations.[8] These groups were
sympathetic to the plight of Chileans victimized by the military takeover
and had often been supportive of the UP programme of revolution by
peaceful means.[9] The Canadian groups became important allies to the
Chilean exiles during their first years in the country and acted as a lobby to pressure the federal government into anathematizing the military
dictatorship and securing the admission of greater numbers of Chilean
exiles under more flexible criteria.[10] Pressure from the groups acting in
solidarity with the victims of the coup throughout the autumn of 1973
eventually led, at the end of November of that year, to the establishment
of the federal Special Movement Chile (SMC), under whose provisions
Chileans who were being persecuted and marginalized for their political
beliefs were given landed immigrant or refugee status under somewhat
relaxed regulations.[11] The establishment of the SMC precipitated an influx of displaced people that caused the number of Chileans in Canada to
balloon between early 1974 and 1978, when the special movement was
discontinued, and it is in this period that distinctly Chilean community
organizations appeared in a number of Canadian cities.

While studies of Chilean exile communities in Canada and elsewhere
have shown that divisions along the lines of political party membership
eventually disrupted the unity of community associations,[12] the members of the early organizations overlooked such differences when working to orient new arrivals, mount campaigns to denounce the regime,
and host events to raise both awareness of the crisis in Chile among
the Canadian population and funds to help those left behind. Toronto
resident Juan Núñez described the goals of the first associations very
succinctly: "First, keep the Canadian public informed about what was
going on in Chile, denounce everything, and secondly send money."[13]
During our interview, S.V.P. described the process of group formation
and the focus of activities:

> When we arrived, we quickly formed the Toronto Chilean Society. It was
> made up of members of all parties. There were Communists, Socialists, people
> from the MIR [*Movimiento de la Izquierda Revolucionaria*, Movement of the

Revolutionary Left, which had not been part of the UP coalition], the whole gamut of the political left. And we had *peñas*, not every weekend but at least two times a month where we got together on the weekend in distinct groups. We had places in churches, we did a few *peñas* in the north side of the St Lawrence Market, the Portuguese lent us their halls. [...] All the profit from these we used to pay for the place, and the rest for solidarity with Chile, which was done through the church network. [...] It was a way to get us together, to pass along information [...] and cooperate economically, to the point we were able, with solidarity in Chile. And this went on for many, many years.[14]

Further testimony underlines how quickly the first Chilean exiles formed associations to denounce what was happening in Chile and organize in solidarity with those still under military repression. Joan Simalchik, a transplanted American in Toronto who worked intensively with the Chilean exiles and their Canadian supporters through the organization *Chile Democrático*, asserted in our interview that the organizational skills that many exiles had acquired during their years of political activism with the UP or MIR helped the Chileans constitute community groups remarkably quickly: "[T]hat's something else that really stands out about the exile community, to see how fast they translated their organizational skill. [...] They found each other pretty fast. And that collectivism held identity to a certain extent. [...] And that kind of thing reconstituted them. People learned how to dance the *cueca* and make *empanadas* here."[15]

Studies by José del Pozo in Quebec and Litzy Baeza Kallens in Alberta show that associations comparable to the Toronto Chilean Society came into being as soon as there were enough exiles to form them. By 1974, the *Asociación de chilenos de Montreal* and *Centro Pablo Neruda* in Quebec City were operating, both dedicated to *denuncia* and solidarity activities, which were carried out in various ways.[16] In Alberta, the first group appeared in 1975, at the height of the SMC, when the federal government was trying to spread the arriving Chileans throughout the country and therefore directing Chilean arrivals to destinations other than Ontario and Quebec.[17] Called the *Comunidad Cristiana de Base* (Christian Base Community), it operated from 1975 to 1978 and focused on settlement and orientation issues as well as solidarity work.[18] In 1977, the *Comunidad Chilena* de Edmonton also came into being and was more aimed at *denuncia* and solidarity work. According to Baeza Kallens, the organization included sub-groups that focused on children's issues, women's issues, media, publicity, the Edmonton Salvador Allende School for language and cultural preservation, and cultural diffusion.[19]

The works of both del Pozo and Baeza Kallens illustrate the political objectives of early Chilean groups, but they also touch on the challenges Chilean exiles faced in mobilizing Canadians to help them. Toronto resident Marlinda Freire underlined that, while there were people like Joan Simalchik who dedicated their time and energy to *la denuncia*, they were a small minority within the broader society: "We did a lot of solidarity work [...]. We tried to talk to people, there were people who helped us [...]. There were always people who wanted to help us, who had social consciousness. But I would say we didn't have a big effect on the general population. The general populace didn't have much idea of what was happening in Chile. There was never very much media exposure."[20] With the exception of Québécois involved in the *souverainiste* movement, Chilean exiles found most Canadians politically apathetic and realized that marches and demonstrations would not be effective on their own in attracting allies and benefactors to help fund solidarity activities and condemn the dictatorship.[21] In addition to the political content of community activities, exile-run associations also integrated aspects of Chilean popular culture, such as *peñas* with *empanadas* and dancing, in order to make solidarity activities more appealing to a broader audience. Carlos Torres, who lived in Montreal for the first part of his time in exile, described to me the range of activities in an exile-led political campaign and the manner in which it incorporated forms of cultural expression: "From organizing [...] a campaign for the defense of political prisoners, organizing tours for the relatives of political prisoners, to develop more awareness of what was really [happening ...]. We also organized cultural events, we used to bring musicians, bands, exhibits of pictures and posters reflecting the struggle, and documentaries, showing movies and documentaries."[22]

S.V.P. also mentioned the need to appeal to Canadians through activities with cultural content such as photo exhibits, peñas that were open to all ethnic groups, *cueca* classes, poetry nights, book releases, and even recreational activities such as soccer tournaments. She commented on the effectiveness of the approach in a country where Latin American political issues had little currency: "I think that we introduced the Chilean community to Canada, because when I got here a lot of people confused Chile with China - I don't look Asian, do I? - or they asked me 'Do you speak Mexican?' What a nightmare [...]. There was a lot of ignorance, a lot."[23] During our interview, another Toronto resident, Nidia Rivera, recalled the close connection between expressing *chilenidad* and the political goals of the groups: "Yeah, we were all the time making *empanadas*, parties to raise funds to send home [...]. The Toronto Chilean Society was the one that was doing everything together, because my children were dancing there, and we were in Harbourfront, we were running all over the place to promote our culture. The *cueca* and everything."[24]

Chilean exiles relocated in Ottawa commented on the connection between culture and politics as well. The late Willy Behrens described *peñas* and literary activities to raise funds for activities of the Ottawa Chilean Association, which at one point confidentially sponsored a member of parliament to go on an observation mission to Chile.[25] Poet Jorge Etcheverry was explicit about the nexus between political activism and expression: "In Latin America, or in Chile at least, culture was always on the Left."[26] The considerable number of Chilean writers who came to Canada in exile had been politically involved in the UP and party politics and maintained this activism in Canada. Etcheverry himself founded *Ediciones Cordillera* in Ottawa in the late 1970s, the first Spanish-language publishing house in Canada, which had a consciously political as well as artistic purpose. According to Etcheverry, *Ediciones Cordillera* was a public space for discussion,

> which was in part to foster solidarity with the Chilean community in Canada through the diffusion of Chilean literary culture. It was a time of folk concerts by Chilean *cantauteurs*, *peñas*, and cultural folkloric dances for solidarity at a time in which, paradoxically, the esoteric, avant-garde texts of the members of the School of Santiago could sometimes be heard along with protest songs and popular art forms. This kind of avant-garde poetry [...] was present in large measure due to the particular composition of the Chilean literary exiles in Canada and to the fact that in some instances, the cultural agents were also members of the solidarity movement and members of political parties in exile.[27]

However, attracting wider support for *la denuncia* using culture as a tool was not confined to solidarity events organized by exile associations. The condemnation of the military regime and presentation of an alternative vision of *chilenidad* sometimes occurred in places where Chilean exiles interacted with Canadians of other ethnicities. These spaces of contact and communication often featured elements of performance and cultural expression. Lawyer and solidarity activist Jeffry House mentioned a live-music house called The Trojan Horse in Toronto, where a band called *Los Compañeros*, composed of Chilean exiles and their Greek leftist counterparts, would perform three or four times a week to audiences of sometimes over 200 people and pass the hat to raise funds for the solidarity campaign.[28] While not formally part of efforts for *la denuncia*, these polyethnic, shared spaces of expression and performance helped to diffuse information about events in Chile and project a positive, alternative vision of *chilenidad* associated with the exile community.

To sum up this section, the evidence from my research, and that of others who have studied Chilean exiles, shows that community organizations quickly emerged in countries where the expatriated found shelter and that in the early years of exile, these associations focused on condemnation of the military regime, solidarity, and orientation for newcomers. The first two goals often involved concrete symbols of *chilenidad*, such as the ubiquitous *empanada*, or expressions of Chilean culture as diverse as dancing the *cueca*, or poetry with a political message to appeal to a broader sector of the host country to add their voices to *la denuncia* and their money to the solidarity effort. Culture was part of the toolbox available to exiled Chileans to combat the military regime that had robbed them of their country.

At the same time, actions that expressed identity and belonging served another purpose. If *la denuncia* and solidarity were part of the external or public face of the Chilean exile community, there was also a more introverted, existential aspect of expressing *chilenidad* which tied into the damage to the self and group identities caused by exile. In the next section, I shall explore how exiles in Canada resisted the dictatorship in another way, by presenting themselves as the authentic Chileans and denouncing the regime as pretenders and usurpers of Chilean identity.

The exile as the authentic Chilean

In her study of Chilean exiles in Alberta, Litzy Baeza Kallens frames part of her work around the question of the political culture of exile and how Chilean communities around the world used this as both a weapon to denounce the military regime and as proof of the authenticity of their own *chilenidad*.[29] The corollary of this assertion was that the vision of Chilean society projected by the authoritarian government was therefore false and a perversion of real national traditions and values. The affirmation of the exiles' authenticity had an element of external appeal to it when dealing with Canadians, but it also served the vital inter-communal function of helping exiles reassert and project their sense of identity as representatives of a politically and socially progressive *chilenidad*.

Exile, for anyone, is a trauma that has severe impacts. As psychiatrist Margarite Perez described it, "Exile is an aggressive term. It means expulsion at a physical level and rejection at a psychological one."[30] Another psychiatrist, writing on Chilean exiles in Great Britain, described the traumas and symptoms resulting from them as akin to bereavement, accompanied by "a profound sense of loss of security, emotional security of family and friends, cultural security, and so on."[31] Chileans were in exile because a political movement and vision of society they had supported had been violently crushed. Rody Oñate and Thomas Wright have shown that exiled Chileans suffered from feelings of guilt, bitterness, trauma, and the sense of being losers, and that this led to high rates of depression, divorce, alcoholism, and suicide. Exile constituted an attack on individual and group identity against which Chileans in Canada and elsewhere had to find methods of defending themselves. Political action that recreated a sense of community and reaffirmed a sense of identity became a strategy to resist a regime that had denied their legitimate *chilenidad*: "Having lost the political battle at home, exiles sought to undermine Pinochet's victory from abroad."[32]

Jorge Barudy, in his study of Chilean exiles in Belgium, and Francisco Allodi and Alejandro Rojas, in their examination of a Chilean housing cooperative in Toronto, connected involvement in *la denuncia* and solidarity work to the question of identity. Barudy, himself both a psychiatrist and an exile, found that "the political movements or party to which our patients belong is an important reference in their readings of themselves and of the surrounding world" and that "these groups organize meetings to denounce the existence of organized violence and its consequences in their country of origin. Additionally, these meetings are important rituals which permit the group to organize and communicate, to reconstruct the atomized and fragmented social tissue which they experience in exile."[33] Allodi and Rojas also found that political activity, while less intense than it had been in Chile, "provided the exiles with important political and social functions" that helped traumatized individuals deal with the emotional, day-to-day difficulties of life in exile.[34]

Community activity also created a space for the exiles to reassert their identity as legitimate Chileans. Echoing Barudy, Joan Simalchik argues that Chileans in exile adopted certain practices that displayed their *chilenidad*, such as singing the national anthem at the beginning of political meetings and displaying the Chilean flag, that had not been part of their political rituals in Chile but became central expressions of identity in Canada. Exiles took ownership of symbols of Chilean national identity such as *peñas*, *cuecas*, and *empanadas*, along with national icons such as Nobel laureates Pablo Neruda and Gabriela Mistral, as belonging to the true Chileans in exile, not the military regime and its supporters, who had derailed the country from its historic mission. Commemorating important dates ignored by the military regime, such as the anniversary of the UP's election victory or the founding of Chile's largest trade union, provided an alternative vision of what Chilean society stood for. At the same time, dates co-opted by the military regime to symbolize the salvation of Chile from the "Marxists," such as National Day on 18 September and the 11 September anniversary of the *coup d'état*, were also used as moments of commemoration for the exiles. Simalchik describes the 11 September events as rituals of remembrance, complete with communal ceremonies to honour lost or absent comrades, and as acts that symbolically defied the dictatorship's claim to true Chilean-ness and allowed exiles to validate their own national identity.[35]

The therapeutic and existential aspects of resisting the dictatorship also appear in testimony from my research in subtle ways. Psychiatrist Ana María Barrenechea opined that the *Escuela Salvador Allende* school in Toronto, while ostensibly founded to transmit Spanish language and Chilean culture to the children of exiles, was in fact more a vehicle for the exiled parents to assert their vision of *chilenidad* and pass it on to the next generation.[36] Marlinda Freire also commented on the affirmative power of collective action, especially for male exiles, describing such involvement as being "based on needing to go out, needing to talk, needing to denounce, you need to help the people who were suffering the dictatorship in Chile."[37] As suggested by psychiatric studies of Chilean exiles throughout the world, the assertion of *chilenidad* and a certain set of Chilean values was an essential part of recuperating a sense of identity in the face of exile.

These values connected closely to the culture of exile discussed by Baeza Kallens for Alberta and del Pozo for Quebec. Juan Núñez described the *chilenidad* expressed within the group, and most importantly to the children of exiles, as one of moral strength and the fight for justice, in contrast to the repressive and unequal society imposed on Chile by the dictatorship. For Núñez, the most important lesson of the exile vision of chilenidad was "[t]hat you can fight for a better society. We were an example for them of social struggle."[38] Marlinda Freire also mentioned the connection between positive *chilenidad* and exile culture, citing social consciousness as one of its hallmarks "[...] according to our set of values, to be a good Chilean you have to act as a good citizen of the world."[39] In the area of literary production, meanwhile, Jorge Etcheverry described to me how works published by *Ediciones Cordillera* promoted a version of Chilean identity that opposed authoritarianism and the violence of the military regime, while also expressing a desire for freedom and justice for all people.[40] The contrast of these values with the austere conservatism of the military regime allowed the exile communities in Canada and around the world to lay claim to a vision of Chilean identity that was a form of *denuncia* in itself and an expression of the true *chilenidad* of the expatriated.

Unlike the explicit expressions of Chilean-ness that were part of the public *denuncia*, the more inward-directed intergroup rituals and practices were a less visible but nonetheless powerful repudiation of the dictatorship and its attempt to demonize the exiles as un-Chilean. The confirmation of their own authentic *chilenidad* among the exiles helped them combat the damage done to their sense of personal and collective identities, and establish a positive alternative vision of true Chilean culture that was being kept alive by the very people who were denied the right to live in their homeland. This culture of exile, however, would not remain static. As I will discuss in the conclusion, changes in the composition of the Chilean community in Canada in the 1980s and in its patterns of associational activity led to transformations in the ways in which identity was expressed and imagined.

Reimagining *chilenidad*

The Special Movement Chile ended in 1978, and in 1979 the short-lived Progressive Conservative government headed by Joe Clark introduced new immigration regulations that curtailed the number of Chileans accepted into Canada. From 1979 until the end of the military dictatorship in 1990, the number of Chileans admitted under any migratory condition fell to about half the number that entered from 1974 to 1978, which meant that exiles continued to constitute the majority within the broad Chilean community in Canada.[41] However, the newer Chileans did not consider themselves political exiles but rather economic migrants displaced by neoliberal restructuring and the devastating recession of the early 1980s, and their sense of identity posed a challenge to the image of *chilenidad* established by the exiles. While some of the newcomers became involved in the continuing efforts of *denuncia* and solidarity, their expressions of national identity and culture more often revolved around apolitical activities such as soccer. Ana María Barrenechea underscored the distinctive sense of identity projected by the economic migrants: "While they weren't necessarily political, or partisan if you prefer, they were more open about how to organize the things we did [...]. They organized dances, competitions, and sports, sports, sports [...]. Now there are two celebrations for the eighteenth of September [Chilean National Day], and there are a lot of people who go to both, but there are a lot of people who prefer to go to theirs."[42]

The changes in how Chilean exiles in Canada saw and expressed themselves are illustrated by the disappearance of some of the early associations they founded and the emergence of new ones with different priorities. Both del Pozo and Baeza Kallens narrate the expansion of the focus of organizational activity in Chilean groups in Quebec and Alberta in the 1980s. While in many cases *denuncia* and solidarity activities continued to have importance, they became less the overriding objectives of the groups and more just two elements of organized community life. *La Asociación de chilenos de Montreal* folded in 1980 due to internal divisions and the waning interest of members; in its place today is la *Asociación de chilenos del Quebec*, which has consciously tried to represent all Chileans in the province, whether or not they arrived as exiles, and focuses on representing the community in dealing with government bodies and assisting in the integration of new arrivals.[43] *La Comunidad chilena de Edmonton* is now la *Comunidad chileno-canadiense de Edmonton*, the Chilean-Canadian Community of Edmonton, which concentrates more on the preservation of language and traditions as symbols of identity, rather than on maintaining the culture of exile.[44] Groups founded in these two provinces since the 1980s also tend to have names that signal a greater affinity with a Latin American identity, such as the AMIGAS Latin American Women's Society in Edmonton or le Centre des femmes d'Amérique latine du Québec in Quebec City, both of which also contain an explicit gendered element.[45] Chilean women form an important part of both groups, but these are open to all Latin American nationalities.

In a similar vein, while many groups continued to be committed to acts of *denuncia*, protest and condemnation were not confined to the question of Chile. Testimony from my research participants reveals that Chilean exiles were active participants in solidarity campaigns against repression and injustice in other Latin American countries and beyond. Carlos Torres described how Chilean exile activists in Montreal participated in solidarity campaigns to denounce the US-backed *Contras* in Nicaragua and the military regime that ruled El Salvador in the 1980s.[46] Jorge Etcheverry talked about how the Chilean exiles in Ottawa contributed to, and assisted with, the campaigns of other exile and refugee groups, such as Salvadoreans and Palestinians, and how *Ediciones Cordillera* participated in a form of Latin American literary solidarity by publishing the poetry of an exile from El Salvador.[47] Toronto resident Patricia Godoy also described how the focus of her activism expanded, while continuing to use expressions of chilenidad from the 1970s to contribute to solidarity and denuncia:

I was always doing thousands of things. I worked with organizations, with the Communist Party, an Italian group, with a group of Caribbean women who were going to be deported. I worked in a lot of solidarity activities. Of course, I was in the women's group here in Toronto [...]. I think all of us who arrived in that era got involved in everything. So I participated a lot with the Uruguayans, the Argentinians, we helped the Madres de Mayo [Madres de Plaza de Mayo], I was involved in all that kind of thing. We had fiestas, and through the fiestas we'd raise money to send to the countries. The last work I did here was with political prisoners in Chile, we had a fiesta. We mostly made food and had dances to raise money for political prisoners [...]. I was very active in everything that had to do with solidarity. I got to know Toronto well because I was walking all over the place![48]

In the final analysis, I would argue that, by the 1980s, the culture of exile described by del Pozo and Baeza Kallens had taken on new dimensions, and that the overt assertion of *chilenidad*, while still vital in activities targeting the dictatorship in Chile, became less of a preoccupation for Chilean exiles in Canada. The values and practices of authentic *chilenidad* that they used in fighting the regime materially and psychologically could be and were applied to helping other national groups and ethnicities that faced repression and expatriation, an action that formed bonds between the exiles and other groups in Canada. The exiles in Canada, and indeed throughout the world, had won the argument with the military regime that had displaced them and had inflicted terror on them and their families and friends. Their *chilenidad* of poems and *peñas* was associated with the acts of solidarity for social justice and *la denuncia* of violence and authoritarianism. In that, they showed the world what it meant to be true Chileans.

Interview questions

The following are the questions from the semi-structured interview template used during my doctoral research that pertain to this theme:

After settling in Canada, were you involved in organizations dedicated to fostering awareness of the situation in Chile at the time? If yes, what organization? Where was it based? What kind of activities did it carry out?

After settling in Canada, were you involved in organizations dedicated to promoting Chilean culture? If yes, what organization? Where was it based? What kind of activities did it carry out?

Upon arrival in Canada, did representatives of any non-governmental organization (i.e. churches, citizen's groups) provide you with any form of material assistance or counselling? If yes, please explain what kind of assistance or guidance was provided.

Were there any organizations that helped you in the settlement process (i.e. finding housing, employment, providing translators or interpreters, helping to find schools for children)?

If yes, please explain which organization(s), and what it/they did to assist in the settlement process.

Were there services available to you in your native language? If yes, what services and who provided them?

Chapter 9

Theatre and the Building of a Latin American Identity in Canada

Andrea Ávila

> Una de las obsesiones recurrentes de la cultura latinoamericana ha sido definir su identidad. A mi juicio, se trata de una pretensión inútil, peligrosa e imposible, pues la identidad es algo que tienen los individuos y de la que carecen las colectividades. [One of the recurring obsessions of Latin American culture has been to define their identity. In my view, it is a useless, dangerous and impossible claim, because identity is something that individuals have but communities lack.]
>
> Mario Vargas Llosa, "Dentro y fuera de América Latina."[1]

The concept of identity is quite new in the social sciences. It started in psychology, as a concept to define one individual's characteristics and ways of identification of the self with regard to the Others. Sociology and anthropology "borrowed" the concept of identity to apply it to the more extensive realm of the community in order to discuss how a group of people defines its own characteristics and peculiarities based on their nationality, religion, language and other common factors. When people share these aspects, they may perceive themselves as belonging to the same group.

According to author Eduardo Galeano, identity is a concept that has changed over the decades and it is now more appropriate to think about living identities, identities in constant movement, as opposed to inherited identities: those that we receive from our parents or the social groups in which we grew up and developed. Galeano establishes that every person chooses his or her own identity, because the foundation of identity relies on places, sites, and values that each individual chooses as his or her own. In those terms, a Latin American identity doesn't exist as a unity. "There are many Latin American identities, varied and diverse," as Galeano says.[2]

Latin American is a concept that until very recently, was still being contrasted to that of Hispano-American, which excluded the presence of the Brazilians, Haitians, and people from Guyana, Surinam and Belize, due to their respective languages, i.e., Portuguese, French, Dutch, and English. Then, the use of Ibero-American (acknowledging the presence of

179

Portugal in the Iberian Peninsula) was adopted, still excluding countries with a French influence, before finally arriving, after visceral discussions, at the more inclusive term, Latin American, which is still being debated.

Anthropologist Víctor Ramos thinks that it is important to analyze whether "Latin American" is a closed topic or, as he states, "a project for the future," a utopia that works as an instrument to imagine, think of, and build up any possible outcome from that reflection.[3] For Ramos, Latin American identity is a contradiction in itself if we try to place it in the context of globalization: while the rest of the world insists on the homogenization of laws, practices, and beliefs, Latin American countries insist on differentiating themselves from the Others.

For Latin American peoples established outside of their country of origin, the issue of national identity rapidly transforms into a personal quest to keep their individual identity. Yasla Yilorm explains that for an educated person who experiences exile (in a forced or voluntary way), adaptation is a key element in the necessary rebuilding of identity. When the exiled person is middle-aged, says Yilorm, once in another country he or she needs to acquire a name and a position, something that he or she might have already achieved in their country of origin. This causes difficulties to these people in becoming used to various factors: the language, where it is different from their native Spanish; jobs, because there is a strong likelihood that they will need to start a new career; their status, as exiles, refugees, or simply newcomers, instead of the place they already had in their society; as well as other challenges to overcome. Nostalgia and homesickness result, then, in a constant revision of the qualities of the "lost land," which in remembrance will always be better and sweeter.

For a person in their early twenties, or a teenager, exile brings more opportunities than losses, and they tend to adapt more quickly to a new environment with new friends, work, or school, where the new land represents to them an important brick in their ongoing construction of an identity. If these two types of people happen to form part of the same family, this is the perfect recipe for a generational collision. However, the young person will find that family values and traditions form part of their own identity and will be searching in their roots for answers to their individual identity problems. In this scenario, the local and personal identities gain more importance than the collective Latinidad, and both generations will start claiming a national identity as opposed to a continental one, i.e., Chilean, Colombian, or Mexican, instead of Latin American.

Theatre and identity

As we can see, Latin America(n) is a concept which is negotiated with some difficulty, whether as a continent, as an individual country that forms part of it, or as the definition for a whole community of people who perceive themselves as very differentiated groups with certain affinities. When these groups start forming communities in a foreign country, they will carry with them their local identity markers, the distinctive signs of their culture and history. Unless they are a bigger group amongst the minorities, all of them will be perceived as part of one category: Latin American.

From a creative perspective, the body of work that emerges from this group of expats in the country they live in is a very lively one that comprises all forms of art. From literature to performing arts, including plastic arts and music, the experience of the (voluntary or forced) exile breaks through the message and struggles to be communicated. One of the main themes will be the experience of living in a new land, which reveals all our own internal and social contradictions - among other things, the need to belong and the decision that has to be taken regarding where to belong.

Theatre and the search for recognition

In his essay about Cahoot Theatre, the theatre company based in Toronto, Ontario, Guillermo Verdecchia cites Charles Taylor in his argument about identity and recognition, the latter being fundamental for people to be able to define who they are.[4] As a culture or as an individual, we need to be able to establish what we believe in and our ways of expression and strive to be accepted and recognized for them. Verdecchia says: "I think theatre can provide both kinds of recognition: the personal or intimate and the social or public," helping individuals and communities to speak out on what they claim to be theirs.[5]

Hybridization, acculturation, and appropriation of cultural practices are some of the ways in which cultures had been coexisting in countries that experienced the process of conquest and independence. In America, the Spaniards in New Spain used theatre, among other cultural practices, to bring a new religion to this continent. The Jesuits used the stage to teach religion to the natives and were clever enough to gradually introduce their language whilst allowing the people to use theirs in the first phase of the cultural conquest. Where words were too abstract to be translated, images and movement helped to communicate the complexities of Christianity to the Indigenous peoples. Subsequently, theatre developed a new language capable of representing the merging of both cultures into a new one. This was the introduction of Western drama to the continent, a style based on text, in Spanish, following the Aristotelian unities of action, place, and time. The locals continued the practice of their own performing arts, based mainly on dance and song, and, in time, the hybridization process took place in such a way that they integrated both practices.

Through the centuries, theatre continued to be a tool for building identities, not only national but community identities as well. In the early twentieth century, Bertolt Brecht used theatre to confront the working class with their historical origins, their ways of behaviour, and, particularly, the ways in which they related to each other and to the bourgeoisie. As Kellner discusses in his essay, Brecht's attempt was to educate the workers about the situations of justice and injustice in history.[6] At the same time, he was helping the workers to build a class identity and to relate to the more powerful classes through awareness of their origins, a sense of belonging, and values.

During the 1960s and 70s, the profound social changes that were taking place in the world were portrayed on the stage as well as in other artistic enterprises. The text-based theatre started fading out as numerous directors, actors, and playwrights decided to experiment with other kinds of performance, as did Eugenio Barba and Odin Teatret in Denmark, looking to South American and African rituals as performing techniques and incorporating them into their shows. This change helped peoples on those continents to re-evaluate their own identity markers and to work with them on stage. The process was completed when, in the case of Odin Teatret, the troupe came back to the countries where they had studied the rituals and presented them integrated in a whole new form of art that combined different traditions.

In many places, the politics of language started to become increasingly apparent. This was the case in French Canada, where the government started supporting playwrights who wrote in French on the basis that this was the best way to reflect the French Canadian identity. However, some artists thought that this support was limiting their artistic expression and their influence in English- (or any other language-) speaking communities. In Montreal, a group of circus artists decided to create a new kind of circus, without animals, that entailed more dramatic aspects: a storyline, for example, but without depending on words to deliver it and thus avoiding the language barrier. This was the origin of Cirque du Soleil, which evolved into a performance company that was based on the circus arts but that explored many other aspects of performance as well.

On the other hand, Robert Lepage decided to make apparent the politicization of language on stage by introducing not only French and English but also other foreign languages without translation or subtitles. This new aspect, namely of a theatre that was not based on a single language and was thus less dependent on the dramatic text, allowed Québécois culture to become known worldwide without the limit of language and, at the same time, to establish a defined identity different from that of English Canada. Something similar happened in Catalonia, with the development of La Fura dels Baus, a theatre company based on acrobatics, dance, and monumental structures for performances on public sites. They also decided to stop using Catalonian as the exclusive language of their performances and, instead, used different languages and different media such as TV monitors, movie projectors, robots, and all kinds of communication devices such as cell phones, to communicate directly with the spectators during their staging, via text message or WhatsApp, regardless of the language.

In this way, these three companies transformed the concept of language as a national identity marker, and this result had two main outcomes: the companies reflected characteristics and values that their groups of origin identified with, and they were better able to make that identity known to the world than if they had continued to use their official national language.

Theatre and the identity quest: Three cases
Chicano
Chicano theatre in the United States is probably the theatrical expression that immediately comes to mind in relation to a community living in a country different from its original one. However, Chicano performance artists consider themselves to be a community that originates in the United States and not in Mexico or any other Latin American country. They claim that the first Chicano play ever performed on US soil can be dated to 10 July 1598 and was performed by Spanish friars. They appropriated the travelling companies that came from Mexico as a precedent to Chicano theatre. There is an old theatrical tradition that belongs to them, with a disregard of the political situation that changed with the sale of former Mexican territory to the United States. They happened to be there when this transition took place, being considered Mexican by the two countries, and they then became either citizens of the United States or illegal immigrants.

The emergence of the company Teatro Campesino in California during the 1960s helped to forge the Chicano identity and to differentiate them from Mexican (legal or illegal) immigrants as well as from other Latin American groups. Their first motive was political and related to the work environment, portraying characters that were peasants, like themselves, and talking about their right to strike. They were a key factor in improving the communication among other Chicano groups in the rest of the country and, after gaining some of the benefits they had claimed in the political movement, they became a more artistic group that incorporated other cultural symbols, such as pre-Hispanic rituals or Catholic images such as the Virgin of Guadalupe. In his article in *Revista Arrabal*, Martín Rodríguez says that contemporary Chicano theatre has turned itself into an urban expression which is "as of today, a bilingual, multicultural, transnational border product and, at the same time, decidedly original."[7] All of it is based on an historical malleability which is both its characteristic and the foundation of its future.

Aboriginal-Canadian

Aboriginal theatre in Canada has the particularity of being thought of as a foreign cultural expression in its own country. In his introduction to *Aboriginal Drama and Theatre*,[8] Rob Appleford establishes that the term "Canadian Theatre" is problematic because it is "less a definition of a thing than a site of debate and contestation."[9] Inside this site of debate, Aboriginal peoples are allowed to perform on stage to deliver a political identity and a "voice" that fits the concept that the dominant culture has of them, "placing undue pressure on Aboriginal playwrights and performers" to portray an Aboriginal community that is unified, homogenous, and political, when the truth is that they are different nations with specific political views and social needs. He offers the case of Tomson Highway, an Aboriginal playwright with a highly political approach to drama. He is one of the most prominent Native Canadian writers, and, whenever a different playwright wants to stage their plays, they are asked to meet Highway's standards because mainstream authors "became a sign of homogenized public ethnicity [...] rather than idiosyncratic, exploratory experiments in cultural (re)construction."[10] This is important because the pre-existing notions of Aboriginality prevent a resistant Aboriginal drama from being effectively staged.

In the same volume,[11] Tomson Highway makes us aware of the fact that theatre written, performed, and produced by Native people in Canada "has been around only about ten years [in 1984]."[12] He states that the Aboriginal literary tradition goes back thousands of years, but his generation, who had a "reasonable grasp of the English language,"[13] was able to transform the oral into dramatic literature more easily than into narrative because drama better suits oral storytelling. No Aboriginal work of art is considered drama in Canada until it can be expressed in English.

Asian Canadian

Asian Canadian theatre in Canada is a concept that gathers the theatres of Japanese, Chinese, Korean, Filipino, and Indian origin, at least, in one group. As with Aboriginal and Latin American theatre, the concepts are the generalization of the characteristics of different groups of people with more differences than similarities, and this generalization is expressed in different ways in their everyday life.

For example, the individuals from the dominant cultures in Canada tend to perceive all Asians as "looking alike," as Karen Shimakawa underlines in her essay on Asian Canadian Theatre.[14] "All Asian women look the same"[15] is a sexualized myth explored on stage by Korean playwright Jean Yoon. Shimakawa analyzes her play Yes Yoko Solo, where the character Helen, of Korean origin, is often mistaken for Yoko Ono, a situation that annoys her extremely.[16] She also analyzes *Miss Orient(ed)*, a comedy by Nina Lee Aquino and Nadine Villasin, where three Filipina women compete in a beauty pageant. Their answers to the questions of the judges reveal what they think about being Filipinas and about their efforts to adapt and blend into a Canadian environment. One of the contestants explains that she had her nose done because it was the only thing keeping her from being a "true Canadian."[17]

Shimakawa concludes after her analyses that Asian Canadian is a category that must be contested on two fronts: first, from its racialized way of approaching either an artistic community, as in the case of Asian Canadian theatre, or a whole group of people who are very different from each other; and second, from the old practices and the keeping of traditions, which may not be the most convenient way to live in today's world. According to the plots of the dramas she analyzed, Asian Canadian women are portrayed as people who have to challenge both their mothers' teachings and the way in which the dominant culture regards them in order to build an identity of their own, integrating the gender factor into the identity equation.

Latin Americans: Where they come from and what they work on. Some context[18]

Latin Americans are one of the most recent immigrant groups to arrive in Canada. However, the number of people reporting a Latin American origin has grown quickly. Fernando Mata has described Latin American immigration to Canada as waves happening from the 1950s to the 80s: the Lead Wave, the Andean Wave, the Coup Wave, and the Central American Wave.[19] "The first wave of Latin American immigrants to Canada arrived during the 50s and 60s," says Mata, "with the arrival of people from the most industrialized countries of the region (Brazil, Argentina, Mexico, Venezuela and Uruguay), linked to Europeans [and] answered to the implementation of the Immigration Act of 1952 that privileged immigrants with European links."[20]

The next wave took place after the immigration amnesty in 1973 as a result of a Canadian movement to regularize the status of immigrants entering the country before 30 November 1972, which particularly benefitted Colombians and Ecuadorians living in Canada at the time. They were skilled and unskilled labourers that Mata describes as having "strong motivations for social mobility."[21] Official figures show that Canada's total Latin American population was less than 3,000 before 1970 and scattered across the country. Between 1969 and 1972, and due to a growing demand for labourers, Canada relaxed its immigration requirements.

The vast majority of Chilean political refugees immigrated to Canada after the overthrow of the Allende regime. From 1963 to 1973, only 2,135 people were recorded as immigrants from Chile; by 1976 there were 4,600 people who had immigrated to Canada as part of the Special Chilean Movement by the Canadian government. During the early 1970s, about 20,000 Ecuadorians in search of a better life immigrated to Canada.

In the 1950s and 60s, the number of Mexican immigrants in Canada was very low, but it increased in the early 70s due to the economic crisis during that period and peaked again in the mid 80s, also due to economic factors. By 1991, the Canadian census registered 16,460 people of Mexican origin. A new wave of Mexican immigrants began in the 2000s due to the "war against drugs" but was stopped in 2009, when Canada started asking for a tourist visa and began reviewing Mexican citizens' applications for refugee status, most of which were refused. It wasn't until 2016 when the visa requirement was changed to an Electronic Travel Authorization (eTA).

The fourth wave refers to those immigrants and refugees coming from Central America in the 80s after a series of civil wars in Nicaragua, Guatemala, and El Salvador. These immigrants were "a mixed conglomerate of individuals who feared reprisal from political enemies or suffered severe social losses."[22]

It can be observed that between 1996 and 2001, the number of Latin Americans in Canada increased by 32%, while the overall population grew by 4% during the same period. According to Statistics Canada, there were almost 250,000 Latin Americans in Canada in 2001 and by 2006 their numbers had grown to over 527,000 (equivalent to the total population of Kitchener-Waterloo in Ontario).[23] The growth of this segment of the population is due to immigration; the majority of people of Latin American origin reported having been born outside Canada.

As Hugh Hazelton has noted in *Latinocanadá*, Latino/a immigrants "settled around Toronto, Vancouver and Montreal, with smaller communities in Ottawa, Winnipeg, Calgary and Edmonton."[24] The first waves of immigrants were exiles arriving in Canada in the form of intellectuals, artists and scholars. Many of the Uruguayan and Argentinian exiles - along with Chileans and Spaniards - were active in theatre in their homelands, and they went on to establish Spanish language theatre companies in Canada.

Although in his book Hazelton focuses on narrative and poetry, his observations are useful for glimpsing the themes and aspects that Latin American groups, actors, and playwrights work on in their life in Canada, whether it is in voluntary or involuntary exile. Hazelton says there is an "initial period in which the homeland is still uppermost in the writer's mind," focusing on themes of political struggle, economic hardship, and family relationships. Then they begin to write about the "loneliness of exile and nostalgia for the native land." And "[a]fter a while [they] start writing about the present. If the impulse is strong enough and the writer has enough linguistic ability, they may move to write in English or French."[25] Hazelton stresses that every artist has their own time frame for passing from one stage to another, and that there are artists who don't move at all, such as Alberto Kurapel, who has developed what he calls "estética de la insatisfacción" ("non-satisfaction aesthetics") or Gloria Escomel, a writer who, 30 years after arriving in Canada, still writes about the day when she is going to return to Uruguay. The weather is a recurrent subject as well. This set of themes and subjects give those authors' work uniqueness in their exile in Canada.

Historically, the *Festival TransAmériques* (the former *Festival de Théatre des Amériques*) was the institution that showed the work of theatre artists from the whole continent. Founded in 1985, the Festival started as a biannual event with Latin American groups invited to perform in Montreal, such as Rajatabla from Venezuela or Teatro Irrumpe from Ecuador. That year the Festival showed the work of five Latin American groups out of the seventeen plays presented.

By 1987, *TransAmériques* showed six Latin American productions out of twenty-two and, by 1989, there were five from Mexico alone. This trend continued into the 1990s with Mexico, Colombia, Chile, and Argentina as the main participants, but by 1997 the only Latin American country invited was Argentina, due to a new policy of inviting more North American groups. It took ten years for the Festival to reclaim its American focus and to begin inviting Latin American groups again.

Another aspect of the relationship of Latin American theatre with Canada is the collaboration amongst institutions to invite artists to writing retreats, i.e. international exchanges for playwrights to come to Canada and work on specific projects, or for Canadian authors to go to other countries to write, translate, or perform. Eve Dumas reminds us that "[t]o date, the Latin American presence in Canada is mainly due to these exchanges. In that way Mexicans, Cubans, Chileans, Argentinians, and others discover Canadian culture and Québécois culture at the same time that Canadians and Québécois enjoy the artistic productions of Latin America in all their subtlety. Furthermore, an important part of the theatre and reality of Hispanic America comes to us through the work of Chileans, Argentinians. or Salvadoreans exiled in Canada many years ago."[26]

Among these collaborative projects is the relationship between the Centre des Auteurs Dramatiques (CEAD) from Montreal and the Centro Cultural Helénico from Mexico. Playwrights from both countries travel to the other nation to work on their translation of plays, attend workshops, and present their latest work. One of the most successful of these exchanges has been the visit to Canada of Mexican director Mauricio García Lozano, who has been working on the plays by Canadian author Carole Fréchette, *Les Quatre Morts de Marie, Jan et Beatrice*, and *La Petite Pièce* en haut de l'escalier, has translated them and has shown them in Mexico City with Mexican actors.

Primary sources and interviews

This chapter discusses two issues about Latino-Canadian theatre. The first is the actual existence of a body of work, homogenous and broad enough to be called Latin American, to which most of the Latino population in Canada can relate and with which they can identify as part of their cultural inheritance. The second is the question of whether theatre is helping Latin Americans to build an identity as a group living in Canada.

In addressing these issues, I started this chapter by giving a definition of identity that could help to outline the characteristics of the vast group of immigrants from Latin America living in Canada. Working from the basis of the explanations from Eduardo Galeano, Gilberto Giménez, and Héctor García Canclini, I noted that identity is an ever-changing category that depends on history and culture as much as it does on context and everyday life, resulting in a continuous process instead of a static concept that can be preserved as stationary.

Having established that identity is always under construction, the following are the arguments of theoreticians such as Jaime Chabaud, María Angeles Grande, and Cirilo Leal about the role of theatre in the construction of national and community identities.

On analyzing the Canadian approach to theatre and identities and the way the country deals with the many cultural influences that coexist on its soil, I reviewed the work of Nina Lee Aquino and Ric Knowles, *Asian Canadian Theatre*, and of Rob Appleford, *Aboriginal Drama and Theatre*, two volumes of collected essays from various authors writing about Asian and Aboriginal theatre. These groups have an older history of work on Canadian stages and of their fight for recognition of that work. Additionally, *"Ethnic," Multicultural and Intercultural Theatre*, a book edited by Ric Knowles and Ingrid Mündel draws attention to the fact that a phenomenon like multicultural theatre has been very little analyzed over a period of twenty years in a country that has an official policy regarding multiculturalism. These experiences and works help to illuminate many aspects of the struggle of Latin American performance artists in Canada.

Landing on the case of Latin American theatre in Canada, I reviewed the literature relevant to the subject, including Natalie Alvarez's *Latina/o Canadian Theatre and Performance*, and Hugh Hazelton's *Latinocanadá*. Due to their comprehensiveness, these books are the foundation upon which to start any study of Latin American literature and drama. Most of the existing works on this matter are short and limited to the analysis of a particular play or playwright, whereas Hazelton decided to represent the landscape of Latin American literature since the arrival of the exiled people from South America, and Alvarez has started calling attention to the theatrical efforts of the community. I found the *Canadian Theatre*

Encyclopedia (a scholarly website by Athabasca University dedicated to the analysis and dissemination of Canadian theatre productions and studies) to be an intelligent and well-documented source of information about multiculturalism in Canadian Theatre. The website was launched in 1996 and is (like one's identity) under permanent construction; but it represents an interesting outline of the subject.

To illustrate how these panoramas are reflected in the everyday lives of Latino Canadian artists, I interviewed three members of the theatrical field based in Toronto, the city that together with Montreal, is becoming the place with the largest Latino immigrant presence and, thereby, with the largest production of Latino theatre. Toronto is considered as well the most multicultural city in the world,[27] and it is where artists make considerable effort to represent different cultures within their cultural space. I decided to interview these professionals because they navigate the academic as well as the artistic community. The interviewees are Guillermo Verdecchia, playwright, actor, and essay writer; Natalie Alvarez, author of two books on Latin American theatre in Canada, an anthology of plays by Latin American authors, and a book of essays on the topic; and Ana Lorena Leija, a Mexican scholar and artist living and working in Canada, with experience as a playwright and director in both countries. Alvarez and Leija have PhDs in Theatre Studies, the former from the Graduate Centre for the Study of Drama of the University of Toronto, and the latter from the Université Laval in Quebec City.

I asked the above professionals about the existence of a body of theatre work that can be called Latin American. Depending on each answer, the interview followed the path of outlining the characteristics this body of work has, or should have, and its effectiveness in reflecting the characteristics of the Latin American community in Canada. I conclude that the combination of both types of experience, academic and artistic, gives the interviewees a distinctive perspective on how the issue of identity is addressed by the groups and individuals that are creating the new plays and productions by Latin Americans in Canada.

How is theatre helping (or not) to build a Latin American identity in Canada?

In 2003, Factory Theatre in Toronto chose a play by a Latina-Canadian playwright, Carmen Aguirre, to be produced and staged by them. It was *The Refugee Hotel*, the story of a Chilean family arriving in Canada after the *coup d'état* in their country. Highly autobiographical, the play is written in English, and it was ideal for performing in a theatre with a grant to produce multicultural performances that reflected Toronto's multicultural tradition. However, Aguirre withdrew the play because she could not reach an agreement with the artistic director, Ken Gass, in the matter of casting. Gass had chosen mainly white actors, with the exception of Latina-Canadian Mariló Núñez, cast as *Calladita* (*Little Silent One*), who had no lines to speak. Six years passed before *The Refugee Hotel* opened at Théâtre Passe Muraille in Montreal, in co-production with Mariló Núñez's own company, Alameda, and with a multicultural cast.[28]

After fourteen years, the situation regarding Latino-Canadian theatre has changed inasmuch as there are now two fully Latino-Canadian professional companies, one being Alameda Theatre, a Latin American theatre company, founded in 2006 by Mariló Núñez, and based in Toronto, Ontario.[29] Alameda Theatre created opportunities for Latin American theatre artists and playwrights, and attracted audiences to their work. Alameda started the De Colores Festival of New Works, Canada's first playwrights' unit and festival dedicated to developing the work of Canadian Latin American writers. Other pivotal programs included *El Barrio*, a national online database of Latin American theatre artists, and *Nueva Voz*, A Latino Youth Initiative."[30]

The other Latino-Canadian professional company is Aluna Theatre. Its website defines it as being "a not-for-profit charitable company that creates, develops, produces and presents artistically innovative and culturally diverse performance work, with a focus on Latino-Canadian and women artists." Their *Festival Rutas Panamericanas/Panamerican Routes* presents theatre artists from the whole continent. The first festival was held in 2012 and from then on in 2014, 2016, and 2018 (the 2020 festival was cancelled due to the health emergency generated by the spread of COVID-19 worldwide).

There are also Latino-Canadian playwrights and theatre artists whose scholarly essays written about Latino-Canadian theatre have been published and some of their plays staged with some Latino-Canadian actors cast in those plays. However, the mainstream is still a glass ceiling reached by only a few, and the themes addressed within Latino-Canadian theatre are seen as being of interest to only a limited audience.

There is some contradiction in concluding whether a play is successful or not because of the size of its audience, just as we assess the success of novels by the size of their readership, for instance. The very soul of theatre is what makes the goal of reaching a vast audience a very complex one. Theatre travels more slowly and along a more difficult path than literature. The differences between a story told in the form of literature and the staging of that story are evident: As creator of an individual work, a writer decides what to say and how, and delivers a story for the reader to read as an individual experience. When a playwright writes theatre, the experience is intended to be collective.

The ritualistic and community essence of performance demands that the compulsion of telling a story involve a group of people with the same aim.[31] Many factors should be common to a group of actors united by the desire of staging a play: they need to like the play, agree on the artistic style of the staging, agree on the political or philosophical point of view from which the text will be approached, and be comfortable with the other people they are going to work with. Even more practical requirements may need to be met, such as schedules, time to commit to rehearsals and/or performances, and touring availability. If everything goes well, and the play is presented in a theatre, it usually targets an audience that shares some of the ideas of the troupe. Then the audience has to suspend disbelief from the very instant they come into the theatre; they also have to agree with the theatre company regarding the values, aesthetics, and subjects, in order to like their work. Theatre is an art to be practiced by and directed toward a community. Both sides need to feel that the message in the play is worth sharing.

Based on these examples and arguments, it can be stated that there are at least two quite recognizable trends among Latino-Canadian playwrights and theatre artists. One of them is based on tradition, on keeping alive the memory of the political events that led to the theatre artists' (or their family's) exile, highlighting Latino values. The other trend is more personal and reflects the efforts of second-generation Latino/a-Canadians to adapt to the new reality to which they feel they don't entirely belong. At the same time, they deal with their heritage values, without totally agreeing with them.

Natalie Alvarez is an academic who, in a scholarly format, has documented plays written by Latino-Canadian playwrights. In her opinion, two of these works by artists of Latin American origin exemplify both trends: *Three Fingered Jack and the Legend of Joaquin Murieta* by Chilean playwright Mariló Núñez; and *Fronteras Americanas/American Borders* by Canadian (born in Argentina) playwright Guillermo Verdecchia, still considered the most visible Latino/a-Canadian play in the mainstream to date.[32] Let's analyse Núñez's play first and link it with the academic work of Natalie Alvarez.

Three Fingered Jack explores Latinidad from a classic dramatic structure, telling the story of a renegade bandit in the time of the California Gold Rush. This character became a benchmark of identity for Latino in the United States and turned into an important figure for Núñez, as his story was told to her to remind her of her own origins. Once in Canada, Núñez went back to Murieta's myth and transformed it into a story where women have much more to say than in the original.

The plot involves Murieta, his wife, Rosita Feliz, Rosita's brother, Manuel Feliz, the bounty hunter, Harry Love, and stage artist and Love's lover, Lola Montez.[33] Murieta becomes an outlaw when Love attacks his house, beats him up, kills his son, and rapes Rosita, all in an attempt to get hold of an important gold source that Murieta has discovered. Love accuses him of being a bandit, and Murieta and Manuel Feliz raise a gang to seek vengeance. Up to this point, the story is the classic gold rush saga with historical characters who had previously been turned into literary characters in works by people such as Chilean author Pablo Neruda, who wrote a play about Murieta. The twist that Núñez gives to the plot is in the action taken by Rosita to reclaim Joaquin's head and bury it. It leads to the killing of Love by her and Lola Montez, who also gains an active role in Núñez's story.[34]

Núñez portrays Latino characters who are humiliated and dispossessed by the dominant group. This group will always be aware of what they actually do, being cruel to people who are not like them. Núñez makes her villain admit that his business of showing Murieta's head in public will succeed for that reason: "*Harry Love*: This is the United States of America! People will pay to see other peoples' sufferin'. Specially if it's the sufferin' of a Mexican [sic]."[35]

At the same time, this character will argue before higher authorities and public opinion that North Americans try to avoid being racist and tend to treat others in the best way possible: "*Harry Love*: We treated Mexicans with nothing but respect. Mexicans own land! They hold positions of power in some counties! Murieta wanted you to believe otherwise."[36] Meanwhile, Rosita, undercover as *Three Fingered Jack*, tells her version of the story as a witness and protagonist, letting the audience know the tribulations that these characters caused them. In the end, the women take revenge both for the killing and discredit of the men and for the mistreatment they have faced because of their gender. It is Rosita who closes the story with a firm statement: "*Rosita*: Rosita Feliz survived all her men,"[37] while Lola kills her lover and gets ready to continue with her own story.[38]

Núñez chooses a Mexican character to reflect a continuous conflict between white Anglos and Latin Americans, starting at the border between Mexico and the United States with the constant crossing of people from one side to the other. She also chooses a dramatic theme that has been used before in order to give continuity to a Latino saga. As a Chilean Canadian staging her work in Canada, we can argue that she is building a bridge from the United States to Canada that shows two aspects: the Latino's struggle to find egalitarian work and living conditions in the United States is similar to their struggle in Canada; and, as a consequence, the outcome of their fight for rights and recognition there is one that the Latino in Canada can relate to as well. If racism and neglect can be found in both countries, as well as the difficulty of becoming a recognized citizen, there are precedents for the fight for Latino rights in the United States that assure Latino people that these rights can be achieved somewhere else also. Núñez is appropriating the re-colonization myths that give Latino people a unified identity in North America.

Núñez's play was developed as part of the Nightwood Theatre's 2003-2004 Groundswell Festival and then produced as part of the 2006 SummerWorks Theatre Festival. Produced by Núñez herself, *Three Fingered Jack and the Legend of Joaquin Murieta* was directed by Natalie Alvarez, editor of the first two books that take Latino-Canadian theatre as a body of work with its own characteristics and idiosyncrasies, *Latina/o Canadian Theatre and Performance* and *Fronteras Vivientes. Eight Latina/o Canadian Plays*, which includes this play.

As a Latina descendant, academic and theatre artist, Natalie Alvarez represents the population of second-generation Latino-Canadians who have decided to keep their heritage even though they were born in Canada. She has reflected on the situation of Latino-Canadian theatre and the issue of identity. Alvarez started her research for plays written by Latino-Canadian authors and then published the anthology *Fronteras Vivientes. Eight Latina/o Canadian Plays*, thinking about "the very active and increasingly growing demographics of Latin Americans in Canada, and a very active community of artists coming from Latin America."[39]

One of the motivations for writing this book and her next one, a compilation of academic essays on Latino-Canadian theatre, *Latina/o Canadian Theatre and Performance*, was to ask the question, what is the theatrical tradition of Latino theatre and performance? Instead of asking questions about specific identity markers, she begins by posing the question, "Why don't we simply say that there are people from Latin

America, that their 'cultural origin' informs their practice and their politics? Why don't we take that as a starting point and then forge a Latino community, following the idea that self-naming is a process of cultural imagining and of identifying the basis of a critical body of work? There is a real strategy in doing that; you can build alliances and gain strength. I didn't look so much for common characteristics but, simply, for those of transnational movements."[40]

After the experience of staging *Three Fingered Jack* and talking to other Latino-Canadian artists, she has reached the conclusion that there is an audience for this work as well. "We witnessed it first-hand with *Three Fingered Jack*, which was performed at the Factory Theatre in Toronto. On some nights, the audience would not be very large, and the next it would be packed, with everybody on their feet, emotional and clapping. Afterwards, you could hear them speaking about how they really connected with the material. And I think that the work creates the audiences too; it generates that audience. For some part of that population, it might be too expensive to go the theatre; that's why Aluna Theatre [company] has decided to have very low-priced tickets, as a political move to reach those sectors of the population that cannot afford to go [to a show]."

Alvarez admits that identifying the emergence of a group and of their body of work implies certain generalizations that theatre artists, in particular, are very sensitive to.

Naming a collectivity is a very delicate process - a difficult and a politically tenuous exercise. Even before doing these books [director] Bea Pizano told me: 'I don't identify [myself] as Latin American. I am from Colombia, but I don't feel that my work is Colombian.' I sympathize with the idea of not wanting to be categorized in terms of one's cultural identity, but, on the other hand, I think there is a strategy in naming a collectivity. Arguably, they are dispersed, but in terms of public and academic recognition, when all these other identity groups have been recognized in the form of a critical collection of their works, why should the Latin American group not be recognized in the same form? Even if it just means that people will say, 'You know, I don't want to be part of this identity politics, it's very 1980s.' That would be a positive outcome. And it's not just about the theatre artists. There has been a group of academics who have been here and there through the years, since the 1970s, and whose analytical work needs to be recognized as well.

For Alvarez, there is a contradiction within the dominant group, at least in English Canada, when they don't recognize other theatrical traditions that grow in their own country. "Canada's theatre tradition comes from England. We were a colony and we have here a Stratford Festival and a Shaw Festival. That has set up a particular theatre tradition and has resulted in the marginalization of anyone who didn't fit into that kind of identity of the Anglo tradition." However, Canada is not a colony anymore and should build its own theatrical world.

At some point in the process of working on the anthology, Natalie Alvarez talked to Guillermo Verdecchia about the future of Latino-Canadian theatre. "Guillermo said, 'I don't think there is such thing.' Then he went to the first Panamerican Routes/Rutas Panamericanas, the festival-conference I have been organizing with Aluna [Theatre], and he saw all these young people that self-identify as Latino. He saw all their work, how active they were politically and he thought, well, there is something [that can be called Latino-Canadian theatre], something is starting."

Actor, director and playwright Guillermo Verdecchia, who was born in Buenos Aires in 1962 and arrived in Canada with his family two years later, has undertaken all his formal education and professional work in Canada. He represents the Latino population that arrived in Canada very young and still had strong emotional links with the motherland. Also an essay author, he is in the process of re-evaluating the Latino-Canadian presence. "Now I think there is the beginning of something that has been identified as Latino-Canadian theatre. It is nascent and taking its first steps. There are lots of Latino in Canada that are making theatre, at the community level, working in Spanish. Some others are Latino artists that have trained at a professional level but they are not necessarily identified as Latino or Latina and are not necessarily working in any way that is identified as Latino-Canadian."[41]

To Guillermo Verdecchia, *Fronteras Americanas/American Borders* was the play that helped him to work out his own identity issues:

> I wrote *Fronteras* 20 years ago, because I wanted to understand why I was here physically, but emotionally and imaginatively, I was somewhere else [Argentina]. And I came to the conclusion that I live on a border, and it is a really good place to be. Now that the years have passed, I have other things in my life that give me another sense of belonging or another sense of place. Perhaps that identification [as Latino-Canadian] isn't as important as it once was, but I understand that it is still important for others. I think that we live now in a world that still has borders, but they are highly mobile, and they are dispersed and networked.

Verdecchia's play tells his own story based on an *avant-garde* dramatic structure, according to the image of a person who considers himself part of a new type of Latino, the Latino-Canadian, or the interstitial, border-type person, who cannot identify himself with one culture or the other.

In *Fronteras Americanas*, Verdecchia portrays and impersonates two characters: himself, Verdecchia, telling his story, his struggle to overcome the fact that he has been different since he was a boy, his idealization of the motherland as "home," and the disappointment of "going home" and not recognizing it at all. He is sweet, melancholic, and sounds a bit depressed. The second character, Wideload, makes fun of Verdecchia, behaves like a Latino gang member, speaks with a very strong accent (represented on the text with phonetic spelling) and makes fun of the white audience as well: "*Wideload*: Espeaking of music, I haf to say dat I love de way you guys dance. I think you Saxons are some of de most interesting dancers on de planet. I lof to go down to the club when my friend Ramiro is playing and just watch you guys dance because you are so free - like nothing gets in your way: not de beat, not de rhythm, nothing [...]. Now, I doan want you to get de impression I'm picking on you, Saxons [sic]."[42]

While Verdecchia's experience of the world becomes more and more nostalgic, Wideload becomes more and more aggressive in his way of approaching the "Saxons." One of his last appearances, called "Latin Invasion" in the printed version of the play, starts, "*Wideload*: It's okay, mang [sic]. Everybody relax, I'm back. Ya, I been lying low in dis act but let me tell you, I'm here to stay [sic]."[43] Then, after some five minutes of speech, it escalates to "*Wideload*: So, what is with you people? Who do you think you are? Who do you think we are? Yes, I am calling you 'you' - I am generalizing, I am reducing you all to de lowest common denominator, I am painting you all with de same brush. Is it starting to bug you yet? [...] Dat has been my mistake, I have wanted you to like me so I've been a funny guy [sic]." This vignette ends with a claim: "*Wideload*: I want to ask you please to throw out the metaphor of Latin America as North America's backyard, because your backyard is now a Border, and the metaphor is now made flesh. Mira, I am in your backyard, I live next door, I live upstairs, I live across the street."[44]

Just when Wideload's attempt to make himself visible starts to sound like a threat, Verdecchia restarts an amiable relationship with the audience towards the end: "*Verdecchia*: I am learning to live the Border [...]. I am building a house on the border that, I hope, others, perhaps my children, maybe yours, will come to live in." But the last word belongs to Wideload: "*Wideload*: And let the dancing begin!"[45] In the recognition that the border is less a place in space than a way of life in a country that embraces diversity, Verdecchia and Wideload establish a relationship with the audience that doesn't have to stop being festive but calls for respect on both sides of the equation.

The way in which Verdecchia is able to combine three different levels of relationship between immigrants in one play is novel and sets the relationship towards facing the future. In that regard, Verdecchia distinguishes himself from most Canadian playwrights of any origin who continue writing plays in the traditional Western style with an orderly, identifiable story and a recognizable structure, where the audience participates just by witnessing the action. Here they are exposed, they are talked to and exhibited (Wideload asks for the room lights to be turned on and rejoices at the presence of white people).[46]

To explain this stylistic choice, Verdecchia highlights the decision of Canadian writers to preserve Canada's colonial cultural tradition and the lesser importance that it gives to theatre as a cultural expression:

> I don't think [Canadian] is a very theatrical culture. I don't think we are a culture where theatre is significantly important. That doesn't mean that people are not doing important things in theatre, but I think that as a culture, Canada values novels [more], because we have been successful writing novels. Particularly English Canada, because Quebec is a different story. In Quebec, people go to the theatre not just because it will be interesting, different from going to a movie, but because they feel there is something valuable there, that they will attain a kind of understanding that they can only attain there. People go to the theatre in Toronto because we have always gone to the theatre, or we have a subscription, or I've heard it is funny. There is very little necessity it seems to me, in the theatre culture.

When asked if this makes things twice as difficult for Latino-Canadian theatre artists, he says,

> I think on one hand everything is open in some ways. You don't have an enormous weight of tradition that you have to resist and rebel against and question or overthrow, because nobody cares that much. At the same time, realistically, many people can't do anything because they don't have access [to the industry]. And we are talking about the professional theatre in English Canada. For some Latino artists, it is going to be harder to have access. But at the same time, I must say the field is wide open, so, in a sense, you can do anything if you can imagine it and bring it into action.

If Latino-Canadian artists are recognizable by their identity markers, there is a difficulty in defining Latin American theatre:

> I suppose it would be theatre made by Latinos living in Canada that has some relation to the markers of being Latino in Canada. Then, what do we do with all the Latino writers that don't have any of the markers of *Latinidad*? I don't know what unifies different theatre artists' work but, somewhere along the line, we

have some connection with Latin America. Our work is very different, so I am not sure how to define it or what is the point of that definition. I proudly identify myself as Latino-Canadian, but I don't think there is anything in my work that is traditional or folkloric or consciously exoticized. I don't think any of the artists I admire are traditional. We are all border crossers, bringing this kind of influence to bear on our work.[47]

The fight for recognition from the point of view of identity is as hard as the gender fight. Ric Knowles, in his essay on Aboriginal theatre, "Translators, Traitors, Mistresses, and Whores: Monique Mojica and the Mothers of the Metis Nations," speaks about the Aboriginal icons of women all through America (Pocahontas and Malinche, for example) usually represented as docile to the conqueror or traitors to their people.[48] The faith of women theatre artists is not very different. Verdecchia is aware of this fact. "For me, at my age, it is different now. I've been here for a long time and I have enjoyed a lot of privilege. I'm white, I'm male, I'm straight, I speak English fairly well, etc. So, my position is going to be different from that of other Latinos asking the same kind of questions,"[49] i.e., who don't share these characteristics.

A good example of those "other Latina" is actress and director Ana Lorena Leija, a Mexican scholar who has settled in Guelph, Ontario, and who has worked with both of the main Latino-Canadian theatre companies in Toronto, Alameda and Aluna. The perspective from which Leija as a newcomer (with "just" ten or so years living in Canada) sees the challenges of Latino-Canadian performance artists opposes that of Canadians of Latino heritage who have lived in Canada, studying and working here most of their lives: "Guillermo Verdecchia and Natalie Alvarez analyze the phenomenon from an 'insider's' point of view," says Leija.[50]

After obtaining her PhD, Leija tried to take "the logical step of finding an academic position," but she felt disappointed about the academic environment and the lack of opportunities in it. However, she was very eager to continue working in theatre. She discovered the Soulpepper Theatre Company, described in the *Canadian Theatre Encyclopedia* as a "repertory company with a three-tiered mandate: to present history's great stories in vital Canadian interpretations; to train the next generation of theatre artists; and to enrich and inspire young people through mentorship and access."[51] Leija continued:

> The company works on classic theatre. I discovered there that it was very difficult for a member of a visible minority, with the issue of having an accent, to be accepted as an actress by a white group. Furthermore, the possibility of

them being directed by an immigrant was almost unthinkable. Then, I realized that I needed to look for other Latino immigrants if I wanted to find my place in the Canadian theatrical environment. [...] As part of the 'Brown group' [everything here is classified by colour], I discovered that the Ontario Arts Council funds most of the professional companies and has the mandate to distribute funds in an equitable way between all the racial groups that work in theatre in Canada. It is the main way that the Brown sector gets any money to produce their plays, and the same is true for Asian, Aboriginal, and other groups. As theatre companies need money to operate, people gather in accordance with their ethnic group. But differences among Latino are very important, and many of them would want their art to be understood in a specific way: Colombian theatre, Mexican theatre, Argentinian theatre, and so on.

In this context, Leija explains that both main Latino theatre companies, Aluna and Alameda, have different ways of approaching theatre and differences in how they work.

Aluna Theatre is perhaps the older of the two, even though they used to be considered contemporaries, and their work is as focused on the aesthetic form of their shows as on the content. Alameda, on the other hand, works in a more political way, and delivering a message about the community is their main concern. Leija continues:

Another, less noticeable, aspect of Latino-Canadian theatre in Ontario, particularly in Toronto, is the work of community companies, which produce their plays without any government help. They are not professionals and, more often than not, they are not paid for their work. Some of these groups can be found in Casa Maíz, a sort of 'house of culture' like those we are used to in Latin American countries. It is hosted in a building owned by a lawyer of Latino origin who has become an art patron by lending rooms on the site so children can attend art classes, groups can hold rehearsals, and some performances can be given.

The latest play co-written by Leija and Mexican actress Andrea Valencia had its first public reading at Casa Maíz in November 2014 and then an opening show before travelling to Mexico. Leija thinks that the work of these community groups will be the basis for a broader, more interesting and culturally-rooted Latino-Canadian theatre.

When asked about the limitations of Latino-Canadian theatre in Toronto, Leija answers, "There is not enough of an audience for plays in Spanish, basically because it is too expensive for most of the immigrants. For those families it is not easy to pay $20 dollars for a ticket to attend a play." In Leija's opinion, Toronto is experiencing the process Néstor García Canclini called *hybridization*, in this case of Latino and Canadian cultures. Latino-Canadian theatre has taken on a very important role in this process, helping immigrants to reflect on their particular motivation for living in Canada and the struggles they face in adapting to the new reality, whilst Canadian audiences get used to the presence of Latino-Canadian artists on Canadian stages.

Ana Lorena Leija also points out that there are many groups of Latino descendants, such as Verdecchia and Mariló Núñez, who feel as comfortable working in English as in Spanish but choose the former in order to reach a broader audience. "However, that choice tends to exclude a significant percentage of newcomers who are still looking for cultural products in their own language."

Identity cannot be built upon decree

Up to this point, we can summarize the theatrical environment in Canada as drawing on multiple traditions thanks to the multicultural nature of the country. However, Western realism is still the most praised type of theatre and, when there is a requirement to stage a classical, high-culture type of play, the option will always be to present Shakespeare or Shaw, for example. In that respect, Canada follows the behaviour of a colony that still turns to the motherland for approval of its cultural expressions. This situation was addressed in the late 1960s by the French Canadians, who have always fought for the validation of their culture as a foundation of Canadian culture. The result of their fight was the biculturalism act, which stated that the country had two official cultures, English and French, and that through their cultural practices, those ethnicities present in the development of the country - immigrants, new Canadians, including second- or third-generation peoples - added a brick to the great building that was Canada.

The acknowledgement of French culture gave way to a new division of cultures vs. ethnicities. In the fine arts, world cultures were perceived as official and highly rated, while ethnicities were incidental and, in artistic terms, always amateur, not fully developed. For a play, a piece of art, or a book to be representative of the ethnicity in which it was created, it was necessary for it to reflect it in a static way, fixed in time and form, unable to change - like artistic crafts that must have the distinctive dragon if they are of Chinese origin, or feathers if Native American, or bright colours if Latin. They were just folkloric expressions of a way of life that was past, if not extinct, and not relevant at all in the modern world.

Biculturalism became multiculturalism in 1971 when the government issued a new statement of the policy on cultures in Canada, officially giving the same status to every community without regard to their language, customs, and practices. But, as theatre artist Guillermo Verdecchia pointed out, the multiculturalism tag could (and in fact, did) result in the division of those cultures into small fractions of the population that then had little to do with each other or with the main official cultures, English and French.

Under the umbrella term of multiculturalism, each group was left alone, essentially in a ghetto rather than in the plural, ideal society that Canadians still want to build. On the one hand, theatre actors, playwrights, and directors are still not incorporated into mainstream productions (for example, you will not see a Latin American actress playing Ophelia in a staging of *Hamlet* for a Stratford performance, or Charity in *Sweet Charity* for the Shaw Festival). On the other hand, artists of other ethnicities want to stage plays that tell their stories as immigrants or new Canadians, and these stories are seen as being only of interest to a relatively small audience.

In the 1990s, Toronto saw the arrival of several theatre companies which had a mandate to promote multicultural theatre with artists, subjects, and contents from cultures other than English or French. One of them was Cahoots Theatre, which started working with playwrights of "visible minorities" and producing the resulting plays, while organizing workshops and readings and writing grant applications to obtain funds from the Arts Council of Ontario, the main organization that promotes the arts in this region.

Quebec and British Columbia have been working since the 1990s to portray the diversity of their bigger cities in a theatrical form. Latino-Canadian theatre artists have been instrumental in achieving this goal. However, it wasn't until 2000 onwards when authentic efforts to develop and integrate a Latino-Canadian theatre were made in Ontario, particularly in Toronto. The struggle is still going on to be considered an original, different group, entitled to a modern artistic style, and funding for its development is ongoing.

Conclusion

Taking the case of Chicano theatre in California, we have compared the emergence of the theatre tradition as the means of expression of a group that defined itself as different from Mexicans and "Gringos," becoming Chicanos and giving to their art specificity in themes, forms, and language. We have argued that Latino-Canadian theatre is in an emerging state, one that will eventually give form to a similar phenomenon representing the image of a group of people that is under construction as well. We have illustrated how being a smaller population within a broader country is a determining factor in the slow rate of integration and self-identification, together with a very different weather from that of their countries of origin, thus presenting challenges that are difficult to overcome for this community, whether the creators of a theatrical performance or the audience that attends it. On the same topic, we have noted that Chicano refers to a community of people that claims pre-Hispanic roots in the United States, who consider themselves to be the heirs of a centuries-old tradition that makes them not a community in exile, but a marginalized community in their own country, with more in common with the Native Americans than with illegal Latin American immigrants.

On the one hand, Latin American is a concept that has never been fully agreed upon by the peoples of the continent. It has been problematic in origin, and many groups reject being tagged as members of this category, placing first their own local and community identities (for example, Mexicans, Colombians, and Salvadoreans fighting to be identified as such instead of as generic Latin Americans). On the other hand, identity itself has become a dubious category because it reflects the stationary characteristics of a minority group as perceived by a majority one. In order to keep to their "pure" and "correct" identity, the minority has to reproduce those characteristics over and over through their art. There is a contrast with and a struggle against the local identity that also affects this process. We have to consider that within the Canadian communities up until the late 1960s, white people avoided producing and attending other forms of theatre that were not white.

Latin American theatre in Canada juggles these problems while trying to gain a presence in a society that Latin Americans perceive as very different from their own. In doing so, their presence is limited not only by the group in power, but also by the presence of many other peoples who claim, and work for, a space of their own.

However, considering the fact that Canadian Aboriginal peoples acknowledge having a theatrical tradition of just 40 years, whilst the Asian peoples in Canada have been practising theatre since the 1950s, we can assert that by comparison, Latin American theatre is a successful, ongoing phenomenon that draws the attention of Canadian and Latino-Canadian audiences.

Latino coming from different parts of the continent are perceived by Canadians as interesting immigrants with a culture and intellectual abilities that are worth knowing. This has its roots in what Hazelton says about the origin of Latin American immigration. There is a precedent of the South American scholars, politicians, or writers, exiled for political reasons, with knowledge and beliefs that make them different from other newcomers. Even if this does not make it easier for these artists to join the theatrical mainstream, at least they do not face the same prejudices as do Aboriginal writers.

The two trends of dramatic approach that Latino-Canadian drama has been showing on the stage have proven to be of equal interest, based on the evidence that there are groups trying to work on each trend. The festivals and contests where emergent playwrights show either way of approaching *latinidad* give us indications about what the community is dealing with and aiming for. Homesickness and nostalgia are still there, but there is also the desire to adapt to and develop within the Canadian culture that might be different but is also perceived as safe, inclusive, and diverse.

The case of Asian Canadian theatre is a good starting point from which to reflect upon the possibilities and challenges of Latin American theatre. This artistic community has faced most of the struggles of the Latino theatre artists and, in observing how this group has solved the difficulties and overcome the limitations to their work, people involved in Latin American theatre should find some answers to their own conflicts.

Chapter 10

Perspectives of Exile in Twenty-First Century Hispano-Canadian Short Narrative

Ana Chiarelli
Translated from the Spanish by Natalia Caldas[1]

Introduction

The following work will explore different perspectives of exile through the analysis of migration short stories written by immigrant and exiled authors and published in Canada in the twenty-first century. Although the first Spanish literary writings by immigrants residing in Canada appeared in the 1940s, with the arrival of Spanish refugees,[2] their study in academia, although it exists, is still scant. Consequently, this chapter aims to contribute not only to the understanding of the phenomenon of exile as a literary concern presented in the short stories I have selected, but also to the dissemination of this literature and a recognition of its contributions to the reality of Canadian culture.

In the last few decades, the number of Hispanic-Americans that have made Canada their home has increased constantly,[3] bringing about an increased interest in diverse manifestations of Hispanic-American culture. Music, festivals, various art and audio-visual exhibitions, and literary productions that include varying genres are being created in Canada today and continue to search for a place within the larger cultural and social mosaic. These works contribute to Canada's society, not only as cultural artefacts, but also as ways to understand social processes such as immigration and adaptation to the host society.

In particular, literature has been written in Canada and published, for the most part thanks to the effort of its authors and the Hispanic community, including in particular the intellectual groups that form part of Canadian universities.[4] Its subalternity with respect to the general panorama of Canadian arts and literatures (in the two official languages) continues to present a challenge to these authors,[5] who number approximately one hundred and fifty and who belong to various levels and literary canons.[6]

The topic of exile has been present in literature since the Greek classics; the study and understanding of exile, the continuous movement of humans between national and international borders, is yet to be exhausted. The reasons for this mobility are as varied as they are changing, and the definition of exile will be drawn from this idea later in this work. Migration influences the society of origin just as much as it does the new, adoptive society, affecting it socially, economically, politically, and demographically. The study of exile has been concentrated in disciplines such as anthropology, sociology, psychology, geography, and history, contributing to its understanding, yet leaving out aspects that bring it closer to the artistic, human side. As a result, migratory literature - and, in this case, the study of exile - allows the phenomenon to be observed from different perspectives that may have remained hidden from the eye of the researcher dedicated to the social sciences. The study of exile, nonetheless, proposes a way to deal with the realities of the migratory subject from an internal, individual perspective, validating and enriching the discoveries of these disciplines, and permitting an interdisciplinary approach that is broader and at the same time more in-depth from the human and the social points of view.

The literary works to be analyzed in this study consist of narratives by Hispano-Canadian authors present in anthologies published in the new century: Rose and Zisman's *Cuentos de nuestra palabra* and Molina Lora and Torres-Recinos's *Retrato de una nube.*[7] In total, ten authors are cited and thirteen short stories that are considered to be representative of the vast corpus of this genre that has been produced in twenty-first century Canada in Spanish. It is worth mentioning that not all texts relating to migration have been included for reasons of space, but rather those for which an opportunity for a more extensive study could open up in future. The short story has been chosen as one of the genres most cultivated within the community of Hispanic authors in Canada from the first waves of Spaniards until the present day (after poetry); in addition, it is generally recognized as an important and well-known genre within Hispanic literary studies in general.[8] As Trish Van Bolderen points out, referring to the Hispano-Canadian literature published after 2007[9] and the genres that this includes, the short story makes itself present (at times exclusively) in various of them,[10] for which reason its relevance to Hispano-Canadian literature is undeniable.[11]

To return to the idea initially proposed, the object of this study is to analyze different perspectives of exile (exile *per se* and immigration) that come out of the reading of Hispano-Canadian short stories produced in the last few years. Exile is seen as a category of analysis that takes a step back from political causes and relates to the physical separation of individuals from their birth country or the place they consider home. Therefore, exile, for this analysis, is first of all the place the author is "writing from." It is not important if the displacement is the result of political, economic, or personal factors. Exile refers to the objective situation of living outside one's country of origin (or from the nation that one considers to be one's native country) and, in this situation of "*transterramiento*"[12] for the Hispano-Canadian authors, writing about the experience of a new reality. Exile, therefore, is understood as a place where a bridge is created between origin and destination, between past and present - a bridge from which the migratory experience is narrated.

Jorge Etcheverry suggests a similar definition of exile when he states, "immigration should not be seen as absolutely separate from exile, since people emigrate for very specific economic, social, and political reasons that in their extreme form lead to civil conflict, dictatorship, or *coup d'état*, thus producing exile."[13] It relates to the experience of a new situation that is the result of superimposing realities, both spatial and temporal, from which the author can narrate the experience of a new locality, a new territoriality that superimposes itself onto the one that already exists in his or her mind, the one that corresponds to the homeland.

However, it is important to establish the separation that exists between the experience of exile in the poetic form of literature and the experience of exile in real life, which are distinct even if they are spoken about in the same situation.[14] That is to say, there is a tendency to see the migrant author and the author's migrant character as the same person, so that it is essential to understand the difference between the real world and that of fiction. Unless it is an autobiography, author and character are always separate. Nevertheless, it is undeniable that the life and environment of the author, especially in realistic themes such as exile, exert an influence on his or her work. Based on this idea, the theory of sociocriticism has been used to approach short stories for this type of analysis. In 1971, Claude Duchet formulated its basis when he proposed, as an object of sociocriticism, the study of what is social in the text.[15] Sociocriticism orients itself toward the interdiscursivity present in the text, that is, toward the different discourses that circulate in society and co-exist in the text.[16] The author selects, from the cultural world that surrounds him (the *pretext* according to Duchet), information and themes that will form the text (*co-text*), which proceeds to become known as *socio-text* once it exists as a literary product in the interaction of the various discourses that the author has taken from the social environment.[17]

In relation to what was briefly touched upon above, sociocriticism permits the verification of certain features in a literary text that are taken from the society in which it was produced and is, in this regard, a theoretical proposition that is used to approach this work with questions such as, what are the main problems that are reflected in these texts? How is the Canadian social space represented? Are these narratives about exclusion, or the opposite, about integration? Can the transnational/translocal be verified in these works? What are the processes of self-identification in the characters? Is this identification related to the context of the original state/nation, or to the new surroundings? Answering these questions will make it possible to approach the experience of displacement and to understand what representation of both Hispanic-American and Canadian societies is presented through Hispano-Canadian literature.

General comments on the short stories and their authors

The authors of the stories to be referred to in this chapter belong to two different generations. One group is made up of authors born in the 1930s and 1940s (Junge-Hammersley, Etcheverry, Rodríguez, Valle-Garay) and the other, of those born in the 1960s and 1970s (Díaz León, Rojas-Primus, Casuso, Saravia, de Elía, and Tarud). The generational differences can also be seen in their immigration characteristics. Immigrants in the first group were more frequently political refugees; in the case of the second group, the reasons for migrating were more of a personal nature, for example, in order to obtain a university education in Canada (more about the migratory waves of Hispanic-Americans to Canada will be presented in the next section). The group is made up of four women and six men and, originally, half come from Chile, the other five from Cuba, Argentina, Bolivia, Nicaragua, and Peru. Geographically speaking, the ten authors settled in four urban centres: Montreal, Ottawa, Toronto, and Vancouver. None is solely dedicated to literary production; most have careers related to academia, arts, translation, and journalism. An important aspect to point out is the literary production, which represents a variety of genres: poetry, novels, short stories, and even theatre. At least four of these authors have published books, not to mention their inclusion in anthologies. Alejandro Saravia and Carmen Rodríguez also write in English and/or French, a factor that is not common among the Hispano-Canadian authors.

In relation to the selected short stories, seven appear in *Cuentos de nuestra palabra* and the remaining six in the anthology *Retrato de una nube*. It is important to note that the stories collected in *Cuentos de nuestra palabra* either were prizewinners or obtained an honourable mention in the short story contest, *Nuestra Palabra*. This competition was created by the Peruvian writer Guillermo Rose and has been carried out continuously since 2004. This contest combines new and experienced authors and has been developing into a space of exchange and recognition among circles of authors, editors, and readers of Hispano-Canadian literature. On the other hand, stories appearing in *Retrato de una nube* are the result of a call sent out by its editors, Luis Molina Lora and Julio Torres-Recinos. The theme of migration was not, in either of these two cases, a condition for submitting the stories. For this reason, diverse topics can be found in both of the anthologies, although concerns with exile, belonging, and displacement run through a large number of the narratives. Finally, even if it is difficult to establish a date of production for each short story, as this information is not provided by the author, all selected stories were, interestingly, proposals for assessment/publication after entering the new millennium, in this case, the year 2007 for *Retrato de una nube* and between 2004 and 2009 for the narratives presented in the competition and later anthologized in *Cuentos de nuestra palabra*.

Brief overview of Hispano-Canadian literature

Before going further into the topic of exile in Hispano-Canadian short stories published in the first decade of the twenty-first century, it is important to review the emergence and development of Hispano-Canadian literature in general.[18] The term "Hispanic-Canadian" is commonly used to name Spanish literary production in Canada. However, use of the term "Hispano-Canadian" is proposed here to incorporate the study of authors who are of neither Hispanic-American nor Spanish origin, but who write and publish in Spanish in Canada.[19] It is important to clarify that the term "Latino Canadian Literature" is not used as it also refers to those individuals from Latin America who speak Portuguese and French and that exclude Spaniards, who have historically been part of the Hispano-Canadian authors.

On the other hand, if referring strictly to the origin of the authors or their characters, this work does not try to look into the debate of the labels "Hispanic" versus "Latino." These labels are related to different meanings in accordance with a particular geographical/social/historical/

demographic point of view, and therefore offer little ground for absolute agreement over its use. In any case, it is important to mention that the demographic and historical repercussions on the residents of Hispanic-American origin in Canada are far from similar to those on the corresponding residents of the United States. In that country, there exists a more polemical debate around the use of "Latino" or "Hispanic" as imposed (or self-imposed) on this group.[20] It could be that the geographic closeness and massive commercial and political relations between the two countries could allow both positive and negative views to permeate Canadian society. However, it should not be forgotten that in Canadian society, concepts such as multiculturalism and cultural mosaic are deeply rooted in the collective consciousness and make up part of what Canada highlights as a primary principle and a government policy, Canada being one of the first countries to incorporate this policy officially as a law in 1971. John Harles outlines the differences between Canadian and American multiculturalism. For him, Canadian multiculturalism refers to the integration of all visible minorities, regardless of whether the individuals are new immigrants or have been in this country for many generations. It is about promoting integration but not assimilation, encouraging the preservation of traditional values, languages, and customs within the framework of life in Canada. In contrast, Harles posits that in the United States the concept was adopted much later (early nineties) and was based initially on an ethno-racial perspective aimed at offering more rights to the African-American community. Despite this, Harles sustains that the key to integration of the immigrant population (both in Canada and the United States) is not found in its views on multiculturalism but in its immigration policies, Canada being much more generous than the United States in anti-discrimination laws and cultural politics of integration in the labour and education sectors, which benefit the voluntary immigrant just as much as they do the exile.[21]

Returning to the historical development of Hispano-Canadian literature, Hispanic authors were producing their works in the country before the 1970s (among them Spaniards, historically the first wave of Spanish-speaking authors exiled in Canada, as already mentioned).[22] However, the true beginning (of production and publication, creation of editorial houses, public readings, and creative writing events) of Hispano-Canadian literature as a cultural phenomenon is due to the reception of exiles from countries suffering under dictatorships. In this regard, the majority of literature in Spanish written in Canada began with the arrival of Chilean poets after the overthrow of Salvador Allende in 1973.[23] Argentinians and Uruguayans later followed in similar circumstances that caused them to seek refuge and, in the following decades, people arrived from countries such as El Salvador, Guatemala, Colombia, and Peru, that is to say, countries that were experiencing national violence and repression.[24]

Political instability leaves an opening for the search of better opportunities, so that Canada began to receive immigrants with motives such as economic ones during the 1980s and 90s, and still does to this day.[25] Nevertheless, Canada has continued to take in refugees from countries experiencing political or armed conflict, such as Colombia.[26] Since then, authors settling in Canada have continued with their career from their country of origin,[27] but others have found their literary voice here, perhaps as a means to deal with the new reality.

As for the theme of this production, it can be said that although this mainly revolves around the experiences of uprooting and exile, not all Hispano-Canadian authors have chosen this path. As Hazelton states, each author has "his or her own internal thematic chronology,"[28] that can go through the various stages of exile and adaptation, as well as the idea of return[29] or of elimination of the migratory condition within the chosen topic. In this last case, Elena Palmero González says that the authors demonstrate a tendency to reflect over two main themes: the body and their own writing.[30]

One of the first efforts to consider the production of Hispano-Canadian literature and other ethnic literatures and their contribution to Canadian culture and literature in general[31] was made at the end of the 1970s and beginning of the 1980s by the Multicultural Sector of the Department of the Secretary of State. Twenty-five years later, the community of Hispano-Canadian writers has grown, and its work has multiplied. Today it is a vigorous body of writing "that experiments with the great development and is present in environments with a specific readership in the Spanish-speaking community, Hispanic academic studies, the field of literary translation, and international solidarity";[32] and yet it still has a long road ahead to get out of its liminal situation.

A few words about sociocriticism

There are various tendencies that have developed out of Duchet's original sociocriticism, disagreeing with his proposition in only a few aspects. The works of Pierre Zima (France), Antonio Gómez Moriana, Marc Angenot, and Régine Robin (Canada) give an account of this divergence, in addition to María Amoretti's (Costa Rica) or the line developed by researchers at the International Institute of Sociocriticism at the University of Guadalajara (Mexico), among others. One of the most prominent schools is that of Edmond Cros, a French Hispanist, who founded the Centre d'Études et Recherches Sociocritiques de Montpellier (CERS) and the journal *Sociocriticism*. For the most part, Cros's work has been dedicated to the study of Spanish and Latin American literature, writing his research in Spanish as much as in French. The relationship between Sociocriticism and Hispanicism, and especially Hispanic literature, in particular the Crosian school with its studies of Spanish literature from the Golden Age, is a close one. However, the application of sociocriticism to migration literature is a field that has yet to be explored, although there are known works that approach the topic with relevant concepts such as Monique Carcaud-Macair's binominal identity/alterity in the 1930s film representation of the Arab in French culture,[33] or Edmond Cros's study on national identities and cultures in post-independences in Latin America.[34]

It is worth remembering that sociocriticism is based on the relation of permeability between the text and the discourse that circulates in society.[35] Jorge Ramírez Caro affirms that "given that the practice of writing is a social practice, all text materializes in diverse voices and sociohistorical and sociocultural contradictions of the social and ideological formation from which they originate."[36] This moves away from the study of the text as the abstract linguistic material of Formalism and proposes to reveal the interdiscursivity within. Sociocriticism, having the literary text as the primary object of study, start from the text and the social discourse contained within. Sociocritical studies have diverse forms of literary analysis (semiotic, rhetorical, narrative, etc.) to access the reflection of society in what was produced and, therefore, charged with ideological content.

In this chapter, a critical analysis of the literary text was carried out in order to search for the different representations of exile. Critical reading was essential to understanding exile as an analytical category, looking into aspects such as identity, alterity, translocality/transnationalism, integration and exclusion, representation of the Canadian social space, and the problems affecting the displaced characters.

From a distance and exile

As migration is a recurrent aspect in human history, it should be of no surprise that literature has manifested the concerns, interests, and creativity of humankind, constituting itself as a channel for the expression of the situations and experiences entailed. Different names have been given to these texts: exile literature (which is written by authors subject to political exile), immigration literature (which describes the complexities of changing cultures and, at times, the linguistic problems that the authors and characters experience), or ethnic literature (whose authors do not share the language or the ethnic background with most of the members of the society in which they live). The authors presented here could be associated with one or more of the literatures mentioned, but what has guided this analysis is their position as authors in exile, living far from the physical limits of their country of origin and writing, under these conditions, of the experience of displacement and of their original and of their adopted societies.

In this regard, the experience of exile is represented from a reality, territoriality, and temporality that superimpose and transversely cross, like a bridge constructed of events. This exile possesses characteristics and qualities that change according to the individual experiences of each author, according to the selection of practices and social discourse that each one operates as a function of their novel. This work posits exile as a course of events with three different phases. The first is one that begins in the same place of origin and that engenders the exile itself. A second stage occurs when the exile becomes a state that accompanies the individual during the journey that takes him/ her to a new place. Finally, in the third phase, exile is then defined as the situation that this individual lives in, in the present, and that is represented in the work of the exiled author (the enunciated subject) through the voice of the subject. Exile makes it possible to look at the "here" and "there," the Hispanic America left in the past and the Canada of the present.

Brigit Mertz-Baumgartner states that the Hispano-Canadian literary production "maintains a concept of dialectic identity conflict perceiving and describing the migratory experience as the confrontation of two opposite cultural worlds."[37] This discourse can be verified in the majority of the short stories involved in this study. Nostalgia for the lost paradise of the place of birth, the sensation of not fitting in, of an "I" as opposed to the Others (Canadians and other immigrants), and some cultural mechanisms that function in different ways from what is familiar, can be read in these narratives. It is important to review the particular case of Alejandro Saravia, author of two of the short stories selected for this work. In his stories, Saravia incorporates elements from the original and adopted societies and cultures in a unifying way. There are no remnants of opposing discourse, but rather coexistence and even interaction between these differences. These works offer a distinct perspective on exile, one in which the multiculturalism that characterizes the Canadian social framework is present and enriches the material of the social discourse prevailing in the tests being read through the lens of sociocriticism.

It is also important to note that this is not about using labels, such as victim, which are often imposed on the émigré because of their position as newcomer in society or the circumstances under which the individual left the homeland. Neither it is about seeking to emphasize a positive or negative representation of the societies shown in the various works. In any case, the present analysis aims to observe in the chosen texts traits of the social discourse about the Hispano-Canadian immigrant that circulates in twenty-first century Canada. Of course, it is vital to remember that it is a two-way process and that as social discourse circulating influences the author and his/her work, this work influences, in turn, the social discourse. As Luis Torres states, "Without giving exile and literature an undue privilege, it is in the artistic representation of this experience that we find an important source for thinking about territorial displacement, attachment to a locality, and the struggle for community."[38] The mental processes and social relations involved in exile, and the references to them in the short stories that are the subject of this work, show this to be true. They are "transplanted discourses," as Jorge Etcheverry calls them, approaches that emigrated writers use in their works when portraying the realities of exile.[39]

But why is it important to study exile in the works of Hispano-Canadian authors? As mentioned above, the topic of exile/immigration is the one most examined by these authors, so that its analysis is vital in order to understand the phenomenon of Hispano-Canadian literature produced in this country. Additionally, the study of literature produced in exile is framed within the need to study the culture from a mobile perspective in a world in which migration is a constant and, therefore, exchanges and cultural artefacts are constantly created. In this regard, the historical and economic moment that each author has experienced in his/her home country and Canada, the importance that notions of nation and patriotism have in the current societies, or the vision of migrations that prevail in communities left and adopted, are aspects reflected in the works analyzed as they are the ideas formed and circulated in the environment in which the author is managing to get along. The understanding of these ideas is an opportunity to grasp the ideological load that these cultural artefacts have as mediators between the two realities the authors have used to produce the literary work and, hence, to understand Hispano-Canadian literature and its most recurrent topic: exile.

The origins, the reasons, and the land left behind

As previously mentioned, there are multiple reasons an individual leaves his/her country of origin. Whether they are of a political, economic, or personal nature, it is interesting to approach these motives from their portrayal in the short stories of exiled/immigrant authors in Canada, as well as the depiction of the country of origin, memory, and processes of self-identification.

One of the most interesting aspects of the representation of origin in these short stories is identity, that is to say, the processes in which individuals participate in order to self-identify within a national community, a particular group, or even a specific race. Noé Jitrik presents the existence of different types of self-identification according to the condition in which they are chosen or not by the subject. Therefore, the *gregarious identity*, refers to aspects such as race, family, or nationality, and the *conceptual identity* is the result of choice (immigration and adoption of a new nationality, for example).[40] The story by Yoel Isaac Díaz Léon,[41] "Miedo viejo," serves to illustrate this idea. In this narrative, Díaz Léon presents the story of a Cuban who returns every December to visit his friends, all in their sixties, and of the fears that the return brings with it. In the story, narrated in first person, the man, also named Yoel, feels distant from the observed reality. Everything to him seems small, precarious, and dirty. His emigration represents a triumph over his friends. "Our conversations are the same as always: the unbearableness of the situation and the unavoidable conclusion that I at least did well to leave; why would they."[42] The character Díaz Léon resolves to join another community, one that he has evidently adopted and that contrasts with the difficult reality filled with the deficiencies of his origin. But even so, Yoel cannot avoid identifying himself with the original society through his friends; they represent what he loves and misses, what he fears losing. His realization of the distance from his origin brings out the fear he will return one day and find that his friends are not there anymore. Beyond "the tension of the people, their rudeness and violence, the unbearable heat in the bus,"[43] Yoel confronts the fact that he has left behind his loved ones. Cuba is depicted in a hostile manner, but as a place where there is affection, his emotions, and this is the reason he returns every year, so that the break will not be complete. "Conceptually" he identifies as Canadian, "gregariously" he is Cuban, to use Jitrik's terms cited above.

However, not all narratives talk of sentimentality when referring to identity. Jorge Etcheverry,[44] in *Metamorfosis II*, digresses on the deforma-

215

tion undergone by the body of the protagonist, a well-known littérateur living in Ottawa and soon to be awarded the Nobel Prize. In examining the characteristics of those in power, of politicians in the rooms of the Canadian Parliament, the man speaks about his theory of metamorphosis and the success produced in those who achieve it, a metamorphosis that "does not seem to be produced in our countries, at least not at the same level."[45] In placing emphasis on his own origin and, intuitively, that of the readers of the short story, Etcheverry appeals to the sense of a collective identity, if not explicitly of Hispanic-Americans, definitely of those who are not Canadian by birth.

But beyond the negative vision that power and success in Canada seem to lend to those who succeed, this story offers the opportunity to look at another aspect, namely, the representation of Hispanic-American countries in narratives. Etcheverry depicts them as places in which power "is never the true, absolute power, and the same happens with culture, an ambiguous fruit with roots who knows where, but whose grafts of European elements often seem grotesque to the man of the world."[46] The Hispanic-American countries are seen by Etcheverry's subject of statement as a faint copy of the large nations of the northern hemisphere, but lacking somewhat the deformation that occurs in the latter. The author also points out the undeniable contact with Europe from the colonization to the present time through the waves of immigrants that were received in the nineteenth and twentieth centuries, as well as the influence that this immigration has had, not only on the process of identity formation on a large part of Hispanic-Americans, but also on their culture.

On the other hand, the ancestral land is also depicted as magical. The Chilean author Constanza Rojas-Primus[47] offers a religious-magical experience in her short story *La iniciación*, in which the author takes the reader through an initiation ceremony in the Palo Monte-Mayombe cult, in an unknown location, but one that is tied to the Caribbean, where the cult is well established. The ethnographer protagonist participates in the ceremony with scientific aims for her work in a research centre in Montreal. The narrative of fantastic situations in which the character engages is a reality completely different from Montreal, in a situation that transcends all that is comprehensible in North American societies. The Hispanic-American territory is presented as magical and, at the same time, definitive, since the ethnologist stays. "I imagine their faces when they find out that I am no longer the same, that I don't even have the same name, and that I dictate the paths for my life from my spirits, my death, my *ganga*."[48]

The magic traps her, that is how the origin triumphs: the roots of African mixed with Hispanic-American win over the positivism of the verifiable. Another aspect of exile is the return to the original land. Here, the reunion with loved ones, with country, customs, and memories, permits the creation of an image of what was left behind through a third element: the idea of going back. Anita Junge-Hammersley,[49] in *Cerrando el círculo*, describes the emotions of the return when a female character goes back to Santiago de Chile in search for her grandfather. After all the adventures in airports and a long journey filled with expectations, the woman arrives in Chile to discover her family at the airport waiting for the hug from those who have been waiting for a long time for it. In this narrative, Anita Junge-Hammersley describes the emotions of returning, the reunion with relatives who are now more white-haired, and the tears of joy - that is to say, the experiences of those living in exile that find themselves on the journey of a whirlpool of emotions upon the return. But the character also relives the experience of the grandmother (who accompanies her to the airport in Canada and also lives in exile): the jail, the tortures, and the vexations that she suffered in Chile and for which the author does not ascribe a historical date. It is worth noting that Anita Junge-Hammersley arrived in Canada in the mid-1970s, a time during which followers of Salvador Allende suffered persecution. Such events may suggest their inclusion in the story of the woman who returns to Chile searching for her grandfather.

In a different tone but with the same basic historical context, the origin, view from exile and memory, is approached by Carmen Rodríguez[50] in her work *Juegos y jugarretas*. A story told through the recounting of a memory, from a conversation without an answering voice, that the protagonist maintains with a childhood friend Pilar Vallejo, takes the reader through the experiences of her youth to a present time of mental and social confinement. The protagonist tells the story to her friend: "I am under another sky and another sun, very far from the port [Valparaíso]. My parents, waiting for the postman in their house in Quilpué and searching for my brother, who disappeared since September 11, 1973. Me, learning how to speak in Canada and trying with all my might to find meaning in life. I work as a cleaner in a skyscraper in downtown Vancouver. From the 32nd floor I can see the boats in the bay, like we saw from the hill in Bellavista, almost 30 years ago."[51] The woman maintains her ties with her parents through letters, and, in her mind, the violence of the dictatorship is still alive through the memory of her missing brother even after the decades that have past. The figure of the bay that is always present, one in

Canada and one in Chile, relates to the physical space that is converted to a thread that gives a sense of belonging to a past and a present, superimposing experiences and images through a bridge that unites them.

The images of the native countries are diverse, as are the processes of identity: the tense, dirty, unbearable Cuba of Yoel Isaac Díaz León;[52] the violence of "our poor countries"[53] by Jorge Etcheverry; Constanza Rojas' land where magic occurs; and the long-awaited hug from those that stayed of Anita Junge-Hammersley. The origin is not always mentioned by name. Sometimes it is described as a grouping of Hispanic countries in general, perhaps with that generalizing vision of the North American academies imposed on Hispanic-America, its people, and its artistic production. Sometimes, in contrast, it is depicted as an image of the past being a parallel to the present, as in Carmen Rodríguez's bay, trying to build a bridge that unites the two stories, memories, and times.

The discourse that co-exists in these texts depicts a reality of the exile/immigrant that is transnational and translocal in which the processes of identification are various. The transnational can be observed not only in the economic relationships (through remittances), but also in the family, social, and political relations between the exiled characters and their native country, which authors echo in their writing. Translocal, in turn, is as much geographic as it is in reference to a community; that is, more than just living in a physical space, the characters also move within the social network in which they work, possess family ties, and engage in all aspects of human life. It is within this framework of transnational and translocal that the individuals presented in the narratives construct their identities, both personal and collective.

Finally, an interesting aspect that appears in at least two of the short stories studied is the placement of parallel realities, Hispanic-American and Canadian, where characters find themselves in one space or the other due to the similarities in the situations they experience. This reproduction of realities or, perhaps, connecting realities suggests the argument of the exile as a bridge between territories and experiences. This connection allows the author to develop this work with the depiction of the Canadian society in the twenty-first century Hispano-Canadian short story.

In search of community: Depiction of the Canadian experience

If the originating society has a central role in the literary production that is reviewed in this work, it is important to approach the representations, perceptions, and patterns the authors have drawn on from the adopted society and the Canadian experience. As mentioned above, the use of a sociocritical perspective to view the representations allows for awareness of the different ideological positions adopted by the exile/immigrant with respect to the host society and makes up the social framework in which the author (this same exile or immigrant) is coping.

One of the most frequently found aspects is the sense of not belonging in the host community. In his short story *En la habitación*, the Peruvian Luis Casuso[54] reveals the violent face of Toronto in relation to gangs and immigration. The protagonist is a young man whose roommate is a Black girl who is part of a gang. He dislikes the activities and friendships of his roommate, and he does not receive support from the landlord. According to him, "in Canada immigrants are worth less than fires,"[55] when the Russian landlord decides to intervene only after finding out that the young woman smokes marijuana in the home. The young man is trapped in the house because he cannot afford anything better. She threatens to press charges if he calls the police again "so that you lose your visa, damned immigrant,"[56] she tells him. Casuso depicts a character who is in a losing situation because of his immigrant status, as this situation is perceived not just by others, but by him as well. However, it is interesting that the other characters are not natives of Canada either. The antagonistic representation of the Black girl and the Russian landlord confronting the protagonist suggests an opposition between immigrants or, at least, the inability to unite these diverse cultures that inhabit the city. It is about opposing identities that collide. Immigration is portrayed as difficult and the environment, hostile. Violence, drugs, economic deficiency, solitude, and fear are revealed in the lines of the short story. But the protagonist at rare times finds his roots in the past through music, childhood, and happiness. The songs that the main character listens to speak to his identity, one that is not at all shared by his roommate nor by his landlord.

Pastor Valle-Garay,[57] from Nicaragua, takes part in the anthology *Cuentos de nuestra palabra* with his short story *Mi arce en Arce (Maple, Ontario)*. It is about a maple tree belonging to a Hispanic family living in a typical suburban community, a "series of homes, rushed architecture, monotonous residences in the undefined Neo-Canadian style,"[58] in which the maple tree occupies a special place. It is small and delicate and has not grown at the same speed as the others in the area, like a "metaphor of the malnourished Third World children," as the narrator states.[59] One day, little bones appear in the roots of the plant and the police spring into action. The tree is pulled out, various officials come around, but when the mystery is solved (it was an old native cemetery), the maple tree never comes back even after all the demands and requests by the owners. Pastor Valle-Garay portrays Canadian society as extremely structured, ordered, and repetitive. In society, each individual has a certain role and conforms in an automated manner. The tree that holds so much meaning for the Hispanic family, perhaps as a reminder of past times, seems not to be important in the exaggerated bureaucracy of the organized society exhibited in Valle-Garay's short story.

A perhaps harsher reality that reveals the discourse of not belonging is the one sketched by Jorge Etcheverry in *Camas paralelas*. It is a narrative of two female immigrants living in a society that does not seem to be made for them. Adela cleans shelves in the kitchen "made for tall people, that her hands could not reach";[60] María Eugenia misses sex constantly that the "little blond boys"[61] deny her in order to give to the "gringa girls"[62] at lunchtime, sex which her ex-husband used to give her daily. Adela's husband pressures her to send money, while she observes her separation, disconnection, and excuses for coming to Canada. Personal relationships between the immigrant and Canadians are distant, if not non-existent. The couple of relationships left behind are portrayed as broken, lost. It's a narrative of the disillusionment, struggles, and hopelessness of these two women who share a room with two parallel beds.

In one of the Nuestra Palabra prize-winning stories, *La orureña*, Alejandro Saravia[63] creates a singular narrative that breaks away from the uprooting and threatening vision of a new environment witnessed in the short stories so far presented. The journey begins with a Canadian engineer from Toronto who goes to work in the Bolivian mines in a city called Oruro and who brings with him a record of the musical group, *Four Lads*. María Isabel, the protagonist, has several children after her marriage to the Canadian and is imprisoned for opposing the Bolivian government. She arrives in Toronto at seventy years of age to make a new life for herself. Saravia portrays the city poetically, recalling its multicultural and cosmopolitan nature. It is described as a "swollen, polyglot metropolis. Through its streets the streetcars ran like muscular, red-coloured horses. City of a thousand languages and kitchens. Lion smell in the metro."[64] Another topic that is emphasized is the English language. María Isabel wants to learn English, so she attends night classes for immigrants in which a debate is sparked on the pronunciation of the city's name: "Thronah" some say. "Tronto" say others. The most convincing response comes from a Mexican woman who says to María Isabel, "[D]on't worry about your accent, we don't speak like the Spanish, nor do the Torontonians speak like Londoners. [H]ere we all have accents, Ms María."[65] Saravia reflects a multicultural society, open to differences, in which relationships between Canadians and immigrants are established, and between immigrants from different origins as well - in which the journey does not goes south-north. Saravia gives an account of the intercultural that is not seen in other Hispano-Canadian short stories.

However, *La orureña* offers another side. In search to improve her English, María Isabel converses with an elderly man who suffers from Alzheimers and who turns out to be one of the *Four Lads*, from the record of her youth. "Tuesday and Thursday mornings, María Isabel continued to speak with James, who is slowly but surely losing his memory. She tells him over and over what Oruro was like. Sometimes, she talks to him of her view of Toronto, which she invents using her new language. And James continues to become *orureño* by walking through the same streets and going to the same parties."[66] Spanish and English form the bridge between these two people and between them and their memories. James learns Spanish and learns about the city in which María Isabel was born; she, for her part, becomes part of Toronto, of its past and its present through this man who she helps to remember in his own language, thereby building a perfect symbiosis. Perhaps this unique representation of Canadian society is due to his position as an immigrant author in Canada. As Norman Cheadle points out, Saravia writes "with mastery,"[67] not only in English, but also in French. "Such mastery of the languages used in Canada goes hand in hand with the determination, quite unique in his generation, with which Saravia has approached what Canada is, delving into its story, its literatures and cultures."[68]

Los osos de Port Churchill, another short story by Saravia, provides a similar panorama. In this narrative the author describes the Canadian Artic and its incomparable landscapes. The story has as protagonist a language professor who moves from Montreal to Port Churchill for work, who suffers for not being able to bring his most prized books with him. However, the magic of a potion sold to him by a Mohawk native in Kahnawake is the solution. The professor, like a hamster with seeds, is able to fit in his cheeks all the books he wants to bring with him on his trip. He surprises the polar bears at his arrival, who ask themselves "what kind of animal was he that is able to put two bear cubs in the sides of his mouth."[69] Saravia is able to give an account of a Canada in which different cultures coexist and interact: francophone, anglophone, First

Nations, and immigrant. The choice of a language professor who accepts a position in a secluded Canadian region; who has to drink a potion, given to him by a Native, with which he can turn into anything he wants; and who, thanks to it, is able to open his mouth so wide that he is "able to swallow all languages possible and devour the world whole,"[70] is a metaphor of the Canadian mosaic, referring to the multiculturalism on which Canada builds its foundation.

The Chilean author, Anita Junge-Hammersley, returns to the complex ethnographic configuration of Canadian cities, in the case of her narrative, Ottawa. With obvious testimonial traits, she describes the events that occur while she is on the bus in relation to the similarity with something that could be experienced "in Santiago, or another Latin American country":[71] people who have left their offices, others that talk on their cellphones or read, all engrossed in their daily activities that are only different in the fact that it is about "people of the entire world, chewing gum, spitting on the ground, women with strollers, all in different languages and in a variety of clothing, the characteristic cultural behavior, and the corresponding gestures."[72] It is an image of multiculturalism, but unlike Saravia's, this short story does not reveal the idea of interaction but rather the idea of coexistence in the way the differences are marked and definitive. Another important aspect of Junge-Hammersley's short story is the construction of an image that could be representative of the country of origin just as much as of Canada. It is a way to connect the past with the present and, perhaps, to observe what in both realities is common to the human species.

Other authors have also depicted Canada as a place where the fantastic can occur, but it is important to note that behind the fantastic anecdote hides the experience of exile, all that is left behind, the memories that are unwanted. This is the case for Ramón de Elía's[73] narrative, Las doce noches, in which the island of Montreal and particularly the eastern part of the city are the settings for the succession of events. The trip through Saint-Denis, Notre-Dame, and other city streets takes the protagonist and his friend, Leopoldo, to the Pointe-aux-Trembles, where a tree has the power to "speak" about the past. The mushrooms on the tree bark, with psychotropic powers, invite the character - without knowing beforehand - on a journey of twelve nights to relive his past filled with suffering from the death of his wife, the torture and disappearance of his father in his youth, and other events that are part of his memory. This tree revives the past with the full impact of the experience, and the shock accompanies the man to his apartment where he confesses,

I raised my eyes and looked towards the east: Point-aux-Trembles was at some point on the horizon, beyond the smoke of the refineries, beyond the reasonable, far beyond what an immigrant who has left everything behind hoped he would find in the city. I thought of her and the agonizing night that, like the stripped painting of a Renaissance fresco, had been restored to its bright, outrageous, original colours. I thought of those twelve nights that were given back without even having exercised my right to choose."[74]

Within this narrative, there is a message. In it, Leopoldo, a friend of the main character and, as can be deduced, also an immigrant in Canada, brings him there to ask him if he would return, "like myself and so many others, or if you will reject, as some do, the possibility of knowing how things happened. If you will avoid the responsibility that the future will inevitably look like [...] that past. And that that past is you."[75] The character's message is clear: one cannot forget who one is, or what one's experiences are, and experiences of the past remain there despite one's having crossed a physical border. In the short story, De Elía presents an opportunity to verify the idea of exile as a bridge connecting to the past through a position, a person, or a present event as in the case of the immigrant.

However, the exile often adapts to the adoptive Canadian society, as seen in the short story *La orureña* by Saravia. This occurs partly, in the case of immigrants in particular, because it was their own decision to leave their country. In the case of political exiles, perhaps because they arrive in Canada to continue with a life that, although it is not the same as the one they had in their country of origin, manages to fulfill their aspirations. In *La caja del falte* by the Chilean Denise Tarud,[76] the protagonist remembers the houses of her grandparents, who were immigrants in Chile, and their difficulties in struggling to start and raise a family. She also immigrates, but it is a different situation. "I arrived in Toronto half asleep, after more than thirteen hours of flying. Despite having the three seats in the middle row of the plane, I slept only a little. Here I was, another emigrant in the family. I came in a comfortable airplane, not by third class on a boat. The trip took only thirteen hours, not months. At my destination, a taxi was waiting for me, not a mule. And I wasn't fleeing from a war."[77] It is an interesting story because it compares the migrations to America of the past century with the migration from south to north within the same American continent, one that became stronger in the last third of the twentieth century and has continued into the twenty-first century. The narrative is a reflection of the migratory reality that has gone through different stages and at present responds to a policy of an economic nature.

This woman is not a victim, but a woman who begins a life in exile, outside of her community and far from her family, with the hope of getting ahead by following the example set by her immigrant grandparents.

Therefore, the host territory is seen from varying perspectives throughout these different narratives: as a violent terrain (the gang, different from the violence of a dictatorship or the impunity of the Hispanic countries); as a coldly organized, prefabricated, but prosperous destiny; and as a multicultural land in which immigrants from a wide range of backgrounds coexist. In the texts, there is a tendency to present a social reality that, despite being plural, does not indicate an interaction between the immigrant and the Canadian characters who populate the short stories (except for Alejandro Saravia's texts).

The discourses that are extrapolated from these readings express a feeling of not belonging in a Canadian society, in which a large number of cultures coexist but without exchange or interaction among them. The I/Other discourse is also perceived, in which Canadian multiculturalism is presented but segmented, that is to say, is such that each individual closely relates only "to one's own people." In this way, the representations seem to transcend the limits of the two generational groups to which the chosen authors belong. The difficulties involved in integrating into the new society and understanding it, and thus becoming part of the social fabric of Canada, can be seen in the chosen texts, with only one exception. As demonstrated above, the two short stories by Alejandro Saravia put forward a different portrayal of characters, those who integrate into society both through working, volunteering, mastering the language, and through their relationships with other immigrants and with Canadians. Or, at least, they do not make migration the main part of their story.

Conclusion

Canadian society is defined by the diversity of its social fabric, and it is in this diversity that a variety of experiences, realities, and cultural mechanisms coexist and give birth to multiple discourses. Exile can be included among these ideologies and discourses, which shape notions about social dynamics prevailing at a given time. The perspectives on this subject, as witnessed in the stories that form part of this work, involve a myriad of issues and provide an opportunity to understand the realities of exiles/immigrants in Canada in the twenty-first century.

In sociocritical terms, there exists, in the literary works presented, an interdiscursivity in which one can see evidences of transnational relations, social networks that go beyond local limits, the struggle to develop an identity, and the difficulties in finding a sense of belonging within a multicultural society. It is possible that the way in which these issues influence the vision of exile or, better yet, the way in which exile influences these issues, could change depending on the reasons that gave rise to exile in the first place. In this regard, the opportunity to see how integration depends on whether one arrived in Canada as a political refugee or as an economic immigrant, the command over the official languages, the ability to identify with new groups or with an acquired citizenship, the ability to distance oneself from the polarization or victimization that sometimes accompanies immigrants, are presented as areas that lend themselves to future study.

In the short stories presented, the representation of Hispanic-America was established through historical-political events such as the Chilean and Argentinian dictatorships in the last century (with the violence involved in such events) and the lack of opportunities in the poorer countries. But other qualities also described are the value placed on the family, the candour and struggle of the people, the affections they have retained, and the fantastic, magical component that has been linked to Hispanic America since its "discovery." There is a "We" in opposition to the "Other" and on occasion the name of the country is omitted to be substituted by a word that gives a sense of "unity" among Hispanic-American countries. Memory is another notion that appears consistently throughout the narratives. The remembrance of places, experiences, and people from the birthplace are recurrent in the texts. In any case, it can be claimed that the works studied give a variety of perspectives of Hispanic America: of the magical/fantastic land where the supernatural becomes ordinary; the territory that is identified with suffering from political struggles and armed action that affects the individual, to the family environment and its national context; and the representation of the place of possible return.

Canada is represented as a place to make a better life, although the path is depicted as difficult and intricate. Frequently, though not in all cases, the exile is presented in a losing position that could be inflicted from the outside or adopted by this character, bringing a reinforcement of the uprooting, of not belonging. The Canadian mosaic seems to be often shown, not as an interconnected set, but rather as a segmented one. Opposite identities, not only in the binomial foreign/Canadian, but between immigrants of different origins, can be observed in some of the short stories. The country is also represented as a medium for economic production that provides for remittances but ultimately cuts the emotional connections between the displaced characters and the people they have left behind. Even so, the exile in Canada is seen as having the ability to learn how to live again. The organized society, structured and repetitive, is, therefore, in opposition to the improvisations often associated with the native countries. Alejandro Saravia deserves special attention in his representation of Canada. The direction of the immigrants' voyage is not always south-north, nor is the language a barrier, but rather an opportunity to learn about the Other and live the Other's reality. The Canada of Saravia is a large mosaic that incorporates the diverse cultural and linguistic possibilities.

In this regard, and in response to the initial questions proposed in this chapter, the main problems encountered in these narratives refer to the processes of self-identification as exile/immigrant and the difficulties they put forward in the possibility of adaptation. It is not important if they are about direct identification with a country in particular or with a "we" that contains the Hispanic people in general. In most cases, it is about narratives that may not be strictly called "exclusionary" but that are accounts of uprooting and estrangement. However, the relationship with the origin is never lost. An object, a memory, a geographic point, or the existence of loved ones can reinforce this relationship; the immigrant/exile is a transnational subject that tries to form a community beyond spatial borders.

Specifically, in the representations of the origin and destiny, there are a couple of things to add. In the first place, there is no specific view of Hispanic America that differs from the perspective that could have a Hispanic émigré in any other part of the world. This representation is based on political, social, economic, and cultural aspects that are found at the root of the Hispanic-American people and their history. It is important to note the particularity of Canada's representation as a social space made up of different ethnographic origins in which different languages and customs co-habit and relate to one another. This coincides with the discourse of multiculturalism that is found at the heart of Canadian society, whether or not it is effective in practice.

New questions arise from this study. Are the processes of self-identification different for a political exile or an immigrant with different motives of displacement? How do transnational relations change according to remittances, political participation, and family contact? Is it assumed that multiculturalism is a group formed by diverse and unrelated segments, or can it be shown that there exist intercultural relations? What aspects influence the possibility of adaptation or integration? What are the most recurrent discourses involving exclusion, integration, origin, and host society? Literary works, in their ability to contain social meaning, approach these questions and many more, shedding new light on the migratory processes and their human aspects.

From the reading of these short stories, other research possibilities can be extrapolated, for example, objects that evoke memories of one's origin. Books by Borges and Argüedas, Alejandro Saravia's language professor, the tree cut down in Pastor Valley-Garay, Anita Junge-Hammersley's airport, or Denis Tarud's portable display case, all suggest this. Also, there is the possibility of evaluating the presence of a political discourse implicit in the narratives produced by political exiles in the country, as opposed to the narratives produced by voluntary immigrants.

Ultimately, the stories studied allow a wide audience to access the realities of the Hispanic-American exile in Canada, either for the enjoyment and identification of a Latin American readership, or the curiosity of a Canadian audience. What is important is the literary contribution of the aforementioned authors, and others not mentioned, to Canada's cultural heritage and to the understanding of the associated phenomenon of migration.

Chapter 11

Ethnic Media in Canada: Latino Newspapers in the GTA, Hamilton, and Niagara, 2001-2015

John-Alexander Raimondo

The Latin American experience in Canada differs greatly from that in the United States and the rest of the world. According to the 2011 Canadian census, there are 544,380 Latinos in Canada, a figure that represents 1.6 percent of the country's total population.[1] The Latin American population in Canada is predicted to increase exponentially in the next ten years. Based on the 2011 census, and accepting the narrowest qualification of a "Latin American" as any person born in a Latin American country, it is perceived that this group represented 5.7 percent of all immigrants in Canada. The importance of studying the situation of Spanish-speaking Hispanics in Canada is significant in understanding the changing multicultural landscape of the nation. Media is a powerful tool that defines events, but most usefully to this chapter, defines identity. Therefore, media as a means of communication, such as radio, television, newspapers, and magazines, can reach and influence people on a wide-ranging scale. Latino media in Canada has allowed Latino Canadians to maintain contact with their native Latin American region and to develop a sense of community in Canada, fostering an identity locally and on a national level.

According to historian Maria del Carmen Suescun Pozas, the history of a country or region can happen beyond its boundaries.[2] In her view, immigrants from Latin America living in Canada are part of a process of integration in which Canada and Latin America can find their own respective pasts in each other's histories.[3] The importance of ethnic media in connecting minority groups should not be overlooked in her hypothesis. The concept presented by Suescun Pozas is applied in this chapter. Ethnic media plays an important role in Canadian society as a useful tool for learning and connecting, a role this chapter seeks to highlight. This research intends to examine ethnic media, with a focus on Latino print media in Canada, combining archival and oral history methods. Oral interviews, conducted in English, will provide first-hand accounts of the history of the two Latino newspapers for the Greater Toronto Area, Hamilton, and Niagara, between 2001 and 2015. *Correo Canadiense* and *Presencia Latina* stand out as the only newspapers producing original journalism. This chapter will aim to do the following: (1) document and describe the making of two newspapers that have the Latin American community in mind; (2) analyze *Correo* and *Presencia* and their scope and role in the community in order to get a sense of the role they see themselves playing; (3) speak to the "unifying" term Latino; and (4) establish the relevance and possible applications to the Niagara Region. Using Benedict Anderson's notion of "imagined communities,"[4] this chapter argues that these two newspapers have created an "imaginary" community of Latinos in the GTA, Hamilton, and Niagara that is neither physical nor unreal but connects Latino beyond geography and their vast ethnic diversity. This research fills an important gap in the scholarship on ethnic media in Canada.

Diasporic groups have been developing networks of communication through media outlets that have had important social implications. Cultural identity, which is the feeling of inclusion in a group or culture, is one such effect of proper ethnic media.[5] The ability for cultures to transcend geographical boundaries and become a "new" group in a foreign country, encompassing traditional cultural traits and values, is nothing novel, yet there appears to be a connection between ethnic Latino media in Canada and the creation of a unified Latino cultural identity that is uniquely Canadian. The state of the field at the current moment has a focus on Latino media in the United States and its growing misrepresentation and underrepresentation. In addition to this, it is known that the media can act as a powerful tool in shaping attitudes and either reinforcing or reducing possible pre-existing stereotypes. The United States is receptive of such studies of ethnic media because of the sizeable, widespread, Hispanic population. This chapter takes a different approach to the topic of ethnic media by focusing on Latino print media in Canada for Latin Americans.

Latino print media acted as an umbrella under which Latin Americans in the GTA, Hamilton, and Niagara were united in a larger hybrid community; this can be seen more specifically with *Correo Canadiense* and *Presencia Latina* newspapers, in which they were able to construct a new, inclusive, Latino identity that is uniquely Canadian. The majority of the primary information received for this chapter is from interviews I conducted with two editors of Hispanic newspapers in and around the Greater Toronto Area, Hamilton, and Niagara, John McTavish and Freddy Velez. John Mc-

Tavish, coordinator at Niagara College in Niagara-on-the-Lake of the Academic and Liberal Studies Division, ran the *Presencia* paper for eight years after its inception. Freddy Velez is currently the editor-in-chief of *Correo Canadiense* in Toronto and has been part of their team since 2001. The interviews reveal the ways in which Hispanics in Canada have challenged common notions of Latinos and created a hybrid identity by using ethnic print media. *Presencia Latina* is a newspaper in magazine format that is published monthly in the Hispanic community in and around the Greater Toronto Area as well as in the Niagara region.[6] It seeks to represent and showcase Latin culture to Latinos in Canada and Canadians, and to promote a sense of community among all Hispanics.[7] *Correo Canadiense* is a weekly Spanish newspaper distributed around the GTA, Vaughan, Richmond Hill, Mississauga, Hamilton, and the Niagara Peninsula.[8] Its objective is to promote the "progress of the Hispanic community in Canada" and provide its members with relevant news.[9] This chapter approaches newspapers drawing from Anderson's notion of creating an "imagined community" to describe the ways in which print media has affected the Latino community in the GTA, Hamilton, and Niagara.

There are a number of different terms that exist to describe ethnic media. Anna De Fina reminds us that the term "ethnic media" is used widely in literature to include "media by and for (i) immigrants, (ii) ethnic, racial and linguistic minorities, and (iii) indigenous populations across different parts of the world."[10] Luisa Veronis presents terms such as "immigrant media," "minority media," and "diasporic media."[11] She chooses to use the term "multicultural media" to refer to media "largely produced by and for particular ethnocultural communities [...] including immigrants, visible minorities, and refugees."[12] Yet studies have shown that ethnic media serves an important role. Veronis indicates that ethnic media is a "product of these minority groups" and attempts to organize, communicate, and facilitate their successful transition into Canadian society.[13] Similar debates have been adopted by other academics. As noted by Veronis, one main debate centres around the idea of multicultural media as a tool to assimilate, facilitate, or hinder acculturation of immigrants in their society. She looks at several sources that demonstrate how ethnic media has allowed migrants to maintain and tighten "links with their own culture while mediating their integration and recognition within the host society," a factor of utmost importance.[14] This chapter seeks to engage in conversation with Canadian academic Luisa Veronis and her focus on Latin Americans in Canada.

Latino communities are not just visible in Ontario along the Golden Horseshoe. This area has one of the largest Latin American populations in all of Canada. Hispanics make up one of the top five visible minority groups in the city of Toronto. Here there are 64,860 individuals of Latin American origin, making up 2.6 percent of the city's population, according to Cassandra Eberhardt.[15] Also, thirty-one percent of all of the "Latin American" diaspora lives in Toronto.[16] Yet, the question is, How does the experience of this group compare to the experiences of other Latino groups in Canada? Can they all be integrated into a pan-ethnic Hispanic experience in Canada? This question also emerged in the research process. It can best be explained by the interesting case of Quebec and Montreal. Victor Armony shows that Quebec City is different in Latin American population from the rest of Canada, specifically when compared to the GTA, Hamilton, and Niagara.[17] Armony looks at how studies of immigration carried out on Canada should include the "Quebec variable." This is best described as Quebec province's "intercultural" policy, closer to assimilationist European models, which focus on more collectivist, state-centered public culture.[18] Quebec's situation is unique and found nowhere else in Canada. Armony points out that, in 2012, for the first time, Quebec was the main destination for South and Central American immigrants. Some 11,322 individuals from Latin America settled there, compared to only 9,762 in Ontario.[19] Between 2009 and 2013, Latin Americans would account for 34,177 individuals or thirteen percent of all immigrants to Quebec.[20] This is significantly larger than the rest of Canada. Armony attempts to explain why this is the case in Quebec in his article. Interestingly, by the end of the article, Armony leaves the reader with more broad questions left unanswered. Can Latin Americans be tied to a single, extensive nation-state as happens in the United States? From several surveys, Latin Americans in Quebec are aware that community ghettos, or too much multiculturalism, are not socially acceptable in Quebec, as integration is considered a civic duty.[21] Latin Americans are happy with their cultural affinity in Quebec and are generally met with positive stereotypes about Latinos being hard-working, law-abiding citizens.[22] Essentially, Quebec handles its own immigrant policy. In comparison to the rest of Canada, Quebec looks at "skilled workers," while Canada's federal government is based on a points system - open to all applicants - but with an emphasis on economic factors. The important role Latinos can play in Quebec's future is to be noted. The notion presented by Armony of "three different Latino societies" in North America: Quebec, the rest of Canada, and the United States, was examined in depth. By looking into the Canadian Multiculturalism Act, the differences become apparent.

In Canada, attitudes towards multiculturalism vary from region to region. In Quebec, many people express uneasiness about, or even resistance to, federal multiculturalism since its inception.[23] In a Library of Parliament paper from 2009, Québécois have viewed multiculturalism "as a ploy to downgrade the distinct society status of Québécois to the level of ethnic minority culture under the domination of English-speaking Canada."[24] In addition to this fear, the idea of reducing the rights of French-speaking Canadians "to the same level as those of other ethno-racial minorities" for multicultural purposes is "inconsistent with the special compact between the two founding peoples of Canada."[25] The article also goes on to mention Quebec's immigration policy, touched upon by Armony as well. Quebec's "interculturalism" is best described as

> policy mainly concerned with the acceptance of, and communication and interaction between, culturally diverse groups (cultural communities) without, however, implying any intrinsic equality among them. Diversity is tolerated and encouraged, but only within a framework that establishes the unquestioned supremacy of French in the language and culture of Quebec.[26]

Immigrants' experiences in Canada, especially Latin Americans', differ in Quebec and Ontario. The creation of the Multiculturalism Act in Canada was a fairly quick process. In the late 1960s and early 1970s, Canada officially approached ethnic groups in a new and improved way. Michael Dewing writes, "the adoption of a race-neutral admissions criteria, known as 'the point system,' meant that immigrants to Canada were increasingly from non-European societies"; this change was first completed in 1967.[27] Improving on this original change, a more multicultural concept of integration was adopted. The second change was formalized in 1971 and adopted by the federal government. It entailed accepting that many "immigrants will visibly and proudly express their identity, that imposes an obligation on the part of public institutions to accommodate these ethnic identities."[28] The original goals of the policy were to "assist all Canadian cultural groups that have demonstrated a desire and effort to continue to develop a capacity to grow and contribute to Canada"; to "assist members of all cultural groups to overcome cultural barriers to full participation in Canadian society"; to "promote creative encounters and interchange amongst all Canadian cultural groups"; and to "assist immigrants to acquire at least one of Canada's official languages in order to become full participants in Canadian society."[29] These four goals have remained, but there have been various changes over the years since 1971. In 1988, the policy was reaffirmed and given a statutory basis in the Canadian Multiculturalism Act of 1988.[30] It was also renewed in 1997, after twenty-five years of operation, following a "major policy review."[31] As a result of all this, the multiculturalism policy in Canada is ambiguous. As Banting and Kymlicka suggest, to refer to it can mean many things, such as "modest funding programmes administered by the multiculturalism directories," or the "federal commitment to promoting the goals of multiculturalism across all departments and agencies," all of which the policy encompasses.[32]

Benedict Anderson's notion of an "imagined community" provides a useful analytical framework to understand the role of print media in the search for Latin American nationalism in Canada. Importantly, a distinction must be made in that Anderson's argument does not mean that a nation does not exist or is unreal. Anderson is instead proposing that a nation is constructed. For example, Anderson argues it is imagined because the members of even the smallest nation will never know most of their fellow-members, meet them, or even hear of them, yet in the minds of each lives the image of their communion.[33]

Anderson's proposal redefines thinking about how institutions and nations are formed, as people "imagine" they are united and share a common set of beliefs and practices. Print-capitalism and newspapers, Anderson argues, can explain the simultaneous national experiences of people throughout history.[34] Significantly, each newspaper reader is well aware that the "ceremony" he performs by reading the newspaper is also replicated simultaneously by thousands (or millions) of others. The reader is confident in this concept, Anderson mentions, but he "has not the slightest notion" of the identity of his fellow readers.[35] By the same token, the newspaper reader is observing exact replicas of his own newspaper being consumed by "his subway, barbershop, or residential neighbours, [being] continually reassured that the imagined world is visibly rooted in everyday life."[36] In this respect, newspapers made it possible for people to think about themselves and relate to others in new ways. Occurrences were bonded together as national experiences, as people felt that everyone was reading the same thing. Anderson stated, the convergence of capitalism and print technology on the fatal diversity of human language created the possibility of a new form of imagined community, which in its basic morphology set the stage for the modern nation.[37]

Anderson attempts to disassemble pre-existing assumptions about nationality and how media communication, such as newspapers, can allow us to know our social group without ever meeting our "imagined communities." Nowadays, the idea of a "nation" is now "nestled firmly in virtually all print-languages; and nation-ness is virtually inseparable from political consciousness."[38] First presented by Anderson, this concept is best seen with *Correo Canadiense* and *Presencia Latina*. This chapter seeks to document and describe the making of two newspapers that have the diverse Latin American community that resides in Ontario in mind, and to explain what makes these newspapers *uniquely* Canadian.

The newspapers

The making of two newspapers that have the Latin American community in mind will begin with my interview with Freddy Velez of the *Correo Canadiense* newspaper. First and foremost, *Correo* is producing original journalism for the Hispanic community in the Greater Toronto Area, Hamilton, and Niagara.[39] In regard to *Correo*'s outreach, Velez believes that the GTA is more widespread in comparison to Montreal for Latin American people. This is important, because it shows the uniqueness of the "nation" of Latinos in the GTA, Hamilton, and Niagara, and how they are dispersed. Therefore, notions of an "imagined community" can arise because they [Latinos] are not physically visible to most. Velez made it clear however, that the location of Correo's office in Dufferin, an area of Toronto, is very Latino.[40] It is obvious that a Latin American newspaper for a diverse ethnic community would be located in an area of Toronto with a large Latino population. *Correo* is distributed four times a month, weekly, with a widespread area of distribution. Velez clarified that the paper's circulation reaches as far as St. Catharines - on occasion.[41] In total, *Correo* circulates 10,000 newspapers across Ontario.[42] Velez revealed that only about five to six people contribute, sending articles and pictures.[43] However, he did mention that an "army of volunteers" help him and that they "do their own work on the side as well."[44] Being a weekly paper that combines everything in the news in Canada and the Latino community, research is needed. This is best highlighted by the notion that, as a newspaper for Spanish people in Canada, "we try to also reach out to all Latinos [...] first generation, second generation, or those connected to Latinos [...] we go to Latin American cultural events in town."[45] This process Velez says can be difficult when you have no money for freelance work.[46] The editorial process *Correo* uses is best described by four qualifications: (1) there is something about sports every week; (2) photography is done by one person; (3) opinion columns are written by a lady who is a lawyer; and (4) an individual who has a PhD in theology is the person who writes about the Pope.[47] Velez adds, "[W]e covered the Pope when he was in Cuba [...] we have a connection there," in other words, *Correo's* coverage of the Pope in Cuba was a huge event in the Latino community.[48]

Velez was questioned if *Correo* participates in any other campaigns that help to further promote Latin culture. He mentions that *Correo* has contributed to social campaigns, for example, helping to raise $300,000 dollars once for a man who needed an arm.[49] In addition to this, he stated that they have started many campaigns, one of which included helping Latino immigrants gain status to get them into schools. At one point, Velez notes, the Latino community in the GTA sought to be part of the Catholic and Public School Boards.[50] Correo sought to establish policy that would prevent schools from asking parents for immigration papers. For this reason, many Latinos were not allowed in schools. Velez believes "they were scared to be reported" and "scared of going to schools without their papers."[51] Therefore, *Correo* decided to support this campaign until both school boards approved it. *Correo* has also helped support campaigns to raise the minimum wage.[52] Key to this interview, Velez mentioned that *Correo* does not want to make itself appear to be "leading."[53] What I mean by this is that its role is only to let people know of these campaigns in the community, not to lead them. In terms of advertisements, Velez said these were not from their own communities, but recognition was received from governments, school boards, as well as the City of Toronto.[54] Velez also said that *Correo* has advertised for the Nuit Blanche artistic event in Toronto and the Juno Awards, because many Latino artists participate in these events.[55] This demonstrates how *Correo* seeks to make itself visible to all Latinos, regardless of their social class and ethnicity.

The key to any successful enterprise is a curious matter to those on the outside. Velez believes that consistency is critical to their success and something that is needed when they are a weekly newspaper. Yet, *Correo* also faces many challenges. Velez mentions, "Print is difficult" because ad sponsors do not want to pay as much as in other media; breaking news is tough also because it could expire weekly, and digital campaigns are cheaper.[56] For example, Velez said once that *Correo* delayed their weekly printing because of soccer games. Velez and team sought to cover an Ecuador soccer game that was later in the day;[57] therefore, printing of that issue of *Correo* was delayed until the evening.[58] Usually, *Correo* editions would be done by midday; however, this edition was completed by 6:00 pm, with graphic design by 4:00 or 5:00 pm.[59] This instance illustrates the occasional struggle a weekly Latino newspaper would face. Velez says that although *Correo* focuses on original stories and journalism, the staff still have to put out news despite the lack of resources at times.[60] The driving motivation behind their newspaper is to connect all Hispanics in the GTA. Velez notes, however, "Always remember that some people don't have access to Internet [...] most still prefer the paper for news," a fact that will be attested to in the analysis later in this chapter, with support from scholarly sources.[61] Commenting on immigrants in general, Velez brought the concept of "living in a bubble" to light. This concept, he says, is related to the Hispanic community here in Canada, as he believes the "immigrant community still live in a 'bubble.' "[62] The immigrant people here, Velez proclaims, live in a sort of "limbo." This he explains as "body here, but souls in their countries."[63] It is technology and communication that makes them long to go back and cause them to wonder what is going on in their native country. Velez believes that when foreign-born individuals have migrated and created a new life in a "host society," they pay more attention to their native country than the actual people living there.[64] Therefore, newspapers such as *Correo* have the power to bring these feelings to those who are reading them and to act as a bridge between their native land and their new places of residence.

Correo Canadiense is a fairly recent newspaper dedicated to the Latino community in the Golden Horseshoe. The history of the newspaper dates back to 2001, when an Argentinian and a Chilean took their idea of opening a Spanish newspaper to the late Daniel Ianuzzi, the founder of Multimedia Nova Corporation.[65] Multimedia Nova is a Canada-based publisher of community newspapers and cultural publications, best known for the Italian Canadian newspaper *Corriere Canadese*. Velez mentions that Ianuzzi approved and thought it was a good idea. Velez was considerate of Ianuzzi's help in the project: "He [Ianuzzi] put a lot of money into this project [...]. He paid for ads in the *Globe and Mail* [...] people were excited by this."[66]

Correo Canadiense started not long after Ianuzzi's approval: their first edition was in June 2001. Velez says that they wish they had "real competition." Velez wishes he would be working harder with original journalism [...] he has no motives because there is no competition.[67] Although he noted that *Presencia Latina* was similar, he clarified that *Presencia* is monthly and smaller, and *Correo* is weekly. Further, he said Toronto has a larger Hispanic population that is spread out, allowing for more readership. Velez mentions that he came onboard in May 2001 and has been with them ever since.[68]

So, what is Velez's story? Well, he has been a journalist since 1981. He mentions that he was already contributing before then to a local newspaper in his home town in Colombia.[69] Velez believes that his talent can be connected "half to his university education and half to his experience."[70] He has been in Canada for fifteen years and started contributing to local diasporas with an internship for the *Hamilton Spectator*. During the internship, Velez comments that he started to find his own stories to write about. He started by writing an article about Israel Valderrama, a man who rode his bike from Medellín, Colombia, to Niagara-on-the-Lake for the World Boy Scouts Jamboree in 1955. Valderrama left Colombia in 1954 and biked to Toronto, arriving nine months after his journey began.[71] His bike is now located at the Niagara Historical Museum in Niagara-on-the-Lake. Importantly, many people enjoyed this story Velez wrote: it was a human story, something that, as Velez indicates, "kind of started my career." Thus commenced his quest to express the real stories of Latin Americans in Canada.[72]

Velez wrote several other articles during his time at the *Hamilton Spectator*. Another article that he wrote was about one gentleman who received a three-million-dollar grant to study an illness caused by mosquito feces.[73] This gentleman was from Hamilton, Ontario, and was supported by the World Health Organization. Additionally, he covered a Colombian man who brought Latin American markets to a steel company in Hamilton. Velez indicates that this man sold one million dollars in steel when this partnership was created.[74] Stories such as these are noted for helping Velez push his career forward and helping him increase his confidence. In regards to how Velez and McTavish knew one another and how they are connected in the Latino diaspora in Ontario, this is best explained by looking at Velez's internship at the *Hamilton Spectator*. Velez wrote a piece on McTavish because he believed him to be an interesting character. McTavish received a PhD in music, had his own Latin American radio show that played "Salsa Rhythms," and also had both English and Spanish programs.[75] This is noteworthy to Velez, who mentions that he thought this was unusual, given that McTavish was an Anglo Canadian. Nevertheless, Velez thought it was in his best interest to present McTavish's story to the readers of the *Hamilton Spectator*. At the end of his internship, Velez received an award for his fine efforts. Velez notes that the *Spectator* did not have the money to hire him at that time; thus, he went back to school to "prove that he could work in English."[76] Velez was still working for *Correo* from 2007 to 2008, when he went to Sheridan College for journalism. He believes that it was a time when journalism was becoming increasingly difficult. For instance, he comments that "there was a technology shift [...] less people were getting hired [...] it was competitive."[77]

From 2003 to 2010, Velez also worked as Toronto correspondent for the CBC/Radio Canada International's Latin American program. He told me that he talked about immigration and the belief of an "easy life" and the "(taking) advantage theory" often associated with immigrants.[78] Velez interviewed Latino immigrants to disprove notions that "immigrants don't pay taxes"; he did this for both *Correo* and the Radio-Canada program. The results he found were surprising. Velez comments: "their stories were sad [...] they were living in fear [...] people think they had an easy life"; he covered these stories to change popular thinking.[79] The most surprising results were that it was not only Canadians who believed the "advantage theory," but also Latino Canadians who believed in this "immigrant advantage theory."[80] In talking about his own career, Velez believes that there is something about Canadian culture that prevented him from being competitive in journalism. He believes that his name is judged, as happens to other ethnic minorities in Canada. Velez went so far as to say that he even considered changing his name.[81] Consequently today, Velez portrays himself as a Latin American specialist here in Canada. It is problematic trying to break into the mainstream Canadian media, as Velez states, because Canadian media prefers journalism from Latin America.[82] This conception proves that Canada is not doing enough to highlight its ethnic groups, especially Hispanics. Velez states that "Latin America is that big [...] there are many points of view, [Canadian media] don't know a thing about it."[83]

Interestingly enough, Velez also notes how Latinos in Latin America say that "Canada is not very unique [...] they see it as the United States [...] but not the United States"; they don't want to know much about Canada it seems.[84] This notion that many see Canada as the United States is fairly common, especially in regards to Latin Americans, and clarified best with Armony's studies. Latin America is made up of twenty-two countries, with many different people. Velez thinks that every community is a "micro community, inside another [...] it is difficult to say you know everything about them [...] it is hard to know all [Latinos] in the GTA."[85] Yet, these communities in the GTA have been connected through *Correo* through a process that is happening without the readers' awareness.

As the interview came to a close, I asked Velez if he thought *Correo* continues to fill an important gap, one left by mainstream media in Canada in respect to Latin Americans. He said, "Yes [...] Latin Americans want to have their own perspective."[86] Furthermore, I asked Velez what news is for him. He said that news can be understood best with the simple "belly button" analogy,[87] his belief is that everything in proximity to the belly button - (1) heart; (2) sex; and (3) money - is all news.[88] He did mention that nothing in *Correo* is about sex, however; sometimes they place photos of women in the newspaper to still have this "analogy" part of their newspaper.[89] These are three aspects that are part of the stories that *Correo* seeks to highlight. On Latinos in general, Velez stated that they are very opinionated and not as politically correct as Canadians. He clarified this by saying, "when doing journalism, you need to be opinionated [...] You have to adopt an opinion, whether positive or negative."[90] Opinions are important in presenting information to the Latino community. In addition, he proclaims that Latin Americans are more directed "by their heart than their brain [they struggle with] what it is, and what it should be [...] a balance of life [...]."[91] On the topic of Latino culture, Velez made a few points. He highlighted that companies in Canada have some outstanding Latin American professionals. According to him, Latinos have many skills: "they are trained; they are passionate; they are proud of what they achieve; they are resourceful; they have ideas and systems for how they could make these ideas work; they don't rely on much to make something happen; they take risks; and finally, they see more than the setting or the context in which they live."[92] All of these skills Velez thinks Latin Americans in Canada have and importantly, they should be recognized more, not just by employers but by other Latinos. In relation to many ethnic minorities, Velez thinks that Latin Americans have to create their own opportunities and have the power to do so.[93] The final thoughts during the interview focused on what Velez thinks about Canada and his own identity. He believes that he adopted "many things from this country, without even knowing it."[94] This is an interesting revelation, because other Latino communities in Canada can also similarly declare this, such as Quebec Latinos. Is this indicative of a uniquely Latino Canadian identity that is starting to emerge? The answer to that question is still far from reached. Velez thinks, "Canada is building its own identity," and with multiculturalism, Canada has the potential to create its own unique identity that is neither exclusively Canadian nor exclusively Latino, but a combination of both.[95] Despite so many years living in Canada, Velez has said that "he sees himself as more Latino than Canadian," something he clarifies as being "Latino Canadian."[96] What exactly does it mean to be "Latino Canadian"? And what does it mean to be "Latino Canadian" in the GTA, Hamilton, and Niagara? These are broad questions that still need answering. However, one thing is certain, as Velez mentions: "Latinos should stop believing they are here temporarily [...] be proud of their second home [...] and be the best they can be."[97] My interview with Freddy Velez closed with more inquiries than answers, but I was more inclined to view ethnic print media as an important factor in the process of creating a community of Latinos.

The *Presencia Latina* newspaper is a magazine-style newspaper that offers important news and information to the Hispanic community in and around the Greater Toronto Area, as well as in the Niagara region.[98] *Presencia* seeks to represent and showcase Latinos in Canada, Canadians, and Latino culture, and to promote a sense of community among all Hispanics.[99] *Presencia Latina* means "Latino Presence" in Spanish: the idea behind its name was to tell Canadians that there is, in fact, a Latino presence in Canada, according to McTavish.[100]

It is interesting to see the meanings behind the name given to the newspaper. Like many of the ethnic media outlets that focus on Latinos, there appears to be an interest from people not ethnically Latin American. For example, McTavish was first fascinated by Latino culture during his high school days, when he was left without other class options. He quickly came to realize that Spanish was much easier to learn than French and started to like it. He also started to enjoy the Latin culture, a mistake, he jokes, "that changed his life."[101] McTavish worked for *Presencia* for eight years, from its inception in 2005 until 2013. According to him, it was a very large part of what he was doing, and he devoted much time to it.[102] He also had experience with Latinos that allowed for such a wide-ranging and accurate newspaper. In the 1980s, McTavish helped with the settlement, translation, and other processes required for the scores of Central American immigrants who came to Canada.[103]

Following his time spent helping Latino immigrants, he decided to completely immerse himself in the culture by moving from Canada to Panama and lived there for 10 years. McTavish said that he had always had an interest in the media field in Panama.[104] When he came back to Canada, he began to teach Spanish at Niagara College and continued to promote Latino culture in the community and through *Presencia Latina*. McTavish also hosted a radio show in an effort to keep the media side going. It was a Spanish show that he ran for six years every Sunday on 101.5 FM from 12:00 to 2:00 p.m. out of the Mohawk College radio station.[105] The radio show, along with the newspaper, was another way in which McTavish brought Latino culture into view for both Canadians and Latinos in Canada. When asked if they have ever seen a Latino, the average Canadian thinks of a farm worker, especially in the Niagara Region.[106] Niagara has around 4,000 Mexican workers, and these are the most visible Latinos that Canadians in this area have seen. McTavish sought to change this notion by creating community events. *Presencia Latina* had the first Latin American Gala that gave the opportunity for Latinos to showcase their culture and feel good about themselves.

McTavish ran four galas in Hamilton while he was a part of the newspaper, in 2008, 2009, 2010, and 2011.[107] Each of the galas had four hundred in attendance, and usually about eighty of them were Canadians, the rest Latinos. According to McTavish, these galas allowed Canadians to see the large population of Latinos in the area, learn about their culture, and break down stereotypes.[108] *Presencia Latina* under McTavish also established the "Latino of the Year" award in which they polled the community on their website to nominate individuals who they thought were leaders in the Latino community.[109] McTavish compared the feeling of being at these gala award ceremonies to that of being at the Academy Awards.[110]

McTavish also stated his delight at knowing that the four people who won those years he was in charge of *Presencia* all went on to undertake significant projects to support the Latino community. Notable winners included a woman from Honduras who went on to start an organization called "Scholarship Fund" for Latino youth to help them study at college or university, and a man from Chile who started a new institute called the "Latin Fraternity Organization" that taught elder Latinos how to use computers and other skills necessary for success in Canada.[111] McTavish believes that the Latino of the Year Award inspired others to go and do good for their communities and also gave extra motivation to the winners. A more important result from the Latino Galas and "Latino of the Year" award was, in McTavish's view, the fact that Latino people were now more connected and were able to get to know each other better than before. It appears then that *Presencia Latina* was more than just news; as McTavish puts it, it was a "community growth process."[112]

The core demographic of readers for the *Presencia Latina* consists of adults between the ages of thirty-five and seventy-five who miss their language and culture living in Canada. McTavish pointed out that their readers were not kids or young adults, such as the twenty-year-olds, because many may not be bilingual.[113] Furthermore, I asked McTavish if *Presencia* talked about issues that were not discussed in common Canadian media. He replied by asserting that the whole idea of the newspaper was also to bring Latino news before the eyes of Latino Canadians. He said there was no use in reprinting news in Spanish that could already be seen in English.[114] Outstandingly, McTavish said that they did not write about what was happening in the news because everyone goes on their own favourite news website to see breaking news. They also were not printing what goes on in Latin America because many Latinos go on the Internet and read their own country's news, a trend that many Latino media outlets such as *La Jornada* and others in Canada concentrate on. *Presencia*, instead, sought to present news that was happening in the Latino community that the mainstream media was not talking about.[115] Specific attention was paid to people who were excellent in their field, such as sports, music, and professions. Further attention was paid to people who had done well for the community and were involved in many different projects. McTavish mentioned that *Presencia* was able to let people know certain positive aspects of the community that they never would have heard about in mainstream media.[116]

A particular strength of the *Presencia Latina* newspaper was the original journalism being accomplished by its team. As McTavish said, there are probably half a dozen Spanish newspapers in the Toronto area including *Correo Canadiense*, *La Jornada*, and magazines such as *Avenida*, but *Presencia* was the only Spanish medium in the areas of Halton, Hamilton, and Niagara, and the only newspaper - along with *Correo* - that did original journalism with a team of professionals.[117] In addition, he said that there is a tendency for most media in areas like Toronto, to be just a vehicle to sell advertising that has no real substance and to tell just a few stories that are mostly from the Internet. This was the main focus, i.e. giving exposure to people in the Latino community through this ethnic medium. McTavish believes that the ethnic niche market is one that will not disappear as quickly because "people are able to find stories they cannot get on regular print or digital."[118] In terms of circulation and distribution, he states that *Presencia* did it themselves, similar to *Correo*. *Presencia* would print 5,000 copies when McTavish was in charge, and they would not pick the papers up at the end of the month.[119] He mentions that they estimated some 20,000 people were reading their newspapers a month - that is, not including papers in communal spaces like doctors' offices.[120] I inquired about the process of creating a monthly *Presencia* issue. McTavish said that on any given issue, they would have one individual editing photos; another would be editing articles; McTavish would write one or two articles; four people would proofread; there would be one graphic designer; and there would be some people doing distribution.[121] In all, the core team comprised about six people doing hands-on work, plus others who would contribute articles monthly. McTavish notes, "It was not a money-making business," that is, most of the work was produced by passionate individuals in volunteer positions.[122] McTavish stated that oftentimes people on the street would come up and say that they would read the newspaper from cover to cover, complimenting him on its unique style and coverage.[123] The team tried to include every event pertaining to Latinos in the area - graduations, new business openings, etc. - and also interviewed newsmakers. They took all the photos for the newspaper themselves and made sure to build connections with the backbone of the Latino community.[124] *Presencia* truly had every avenue covered, with McTavish saying that they would even interview Canadian people as well so that they could talk about their own perspective and reach out to the Latino community. The importance of interviewing is seen with Presencia, expressed by McTavish: they were always conducted in person. He said that they wanted to build real connections with the community and that these connections would always help them when they needed something, such as sponsorship.[125]

It seems that the success of *Presencia* was also down to journalism and ample public relations work. McTavish highlighted that they did not do it for the money, but out of their passion for journalism, for writing, and for Latino culture.[126] *Presencia* under McTavish's leadership properly made people aware of Latinos and broke down certain stereotypes. The vast circulation of the newspaper, in various supermarkets and convenience stores, allowed for a large number of readers. According to McTavish, *Presencia* had a lot of Portuguese, Italian, and Canadian readers who expressed their pleasure in reading the paper.[127] The team behind *Presencia* always sought to present articles in a positive light, because of the negative portrayal and misinterpretation of Latin Americans in mainstream media. McTavish said that, in regard to the Latin American region, the mainstream media takes negative instances and perpetuates the idea that the whole area is unlivable.[128]

One major accomplishment of *Presencia Latina* was that it united all the Latinos. McTavish made this clear by explaining that Latin Americans have people all over the place - Central America, Caribbean, South America – and that there are 19 different countries in this one region in which they speak Spanish. For instance, the Italians have their group and the Germans have their group; when someone is talking about these European cultures, they are talking about one country. Conversely, Latin America is comprised of multiple countries, so naturally it is more challenging to understand what a Latino is. McTavish stated that each culture has its own celebrations and that people from different cultures did not know each other: Chileans and Mexicans did not know each other, for instance.[129] The whole idea of *Presencia Latina*, according to McTavish, was to have sort of an "umbrella presence," where all these different Latinos from all the diverse areas of the Latin American region could get to know each other and present themselves as one united Latino community.[130] *Presencia* had a leadership role in the Spanish-speaking community - it was a unifying project. The Latinos in Hamilton and Niagara had *Presencia* as a vehicle to unite them with strong bonds coming out of this, according to McTavish.[131] The common language shared by all Latino cultures allowed them to be brought together. Among many other successes, this feat is what McTavish felt most proud of, i.e. that *Presencia* was able to get all Latinos to connect and get to know each other.[132] He added that he was very happy to see the direction the newspaper was headed in and that although he has not been with the paper for a year and a half, it is continuing successfully on its path.

McTavish gave his advice on which three characteristics the media needs in order to be successful. The first was a good quality product, something he states that the team behind *Presencia Latina* could be proud of because of their quality of the Spanish language and their content.[133] The next was advertising and how many media outlets would be unsuccessful without it. According to McTavish, *Presencia Latina* was a hundred percent funded through the ads that it sold. *Presencia* represented Latinos attracting Latinos and also Canadians attracting Latinos, with ads from Scotia Bank and other businesses attempting to attract Latino clients. Finally, in order to be successful, any media needs to have a proper distribution system, McTavish said, and this is where many magazines and newspapers fail.[134] The difference between *Presencia* and other newspapers was that the team did the distribution themselves, similar to *Correo Canadiense*. The process was a lot of work and required driving to and from supermarkets, community centres, Latino businesses, and a mix of many places Latinos frequented. Nonetheless, McTavish remembered that this was a fun time of the month for the team at *Presencia* because they were reconnecting with the people. It was all about the physical connection, which is often missing with other forms of ethnic media. McTavish ended his talk about his three steps to finding success in media by saying that Latinos are very people-friendly and prefer face-to-face not email - human connection is important to them.[135] McTavish also described what *Presencia* is and what it is not. What I mean by this is that he gave some important characteristics about the newspaper; for example, he said that *Presencia* was not an advertisement newspaper and it was "high quality journalism."[136] Additionally, *Presencia* did not take political or religious sides: McTavish says, "No controversial subjects [...] no tabloid-style journalism [...] they did not want to slander anyone [...] always a positive spin on things [...] maintain friendship with all religions and businesses."[137]

Presencia newspapers were always produced with a positive relationship in mind. In the words of McTavish, *Presencia Latina* was a "labour of love," and he put much "heart and soul" into making it successful. McTavish also says the integration process was the success of the paper: it was the first generation who wanted to read in their own language.[138] He states that since Latinos are newer to Canada, they are still looking for something such as the *Presencia Latina* newspaper. McTavish believes that once Latinos are "integrated" they do not "need it anymore" and it might not be relevant.[139] The principle of less text and more photos was also behind *Presencia Latina*'s success, as the team would take hundreds of photos at Latino events and post them on their webpage. This is a strategy which, McTavish said, gave the webpage thousands of new visitors and traffic, as people could send the link back home to family.[140]

This phenomenon is also supported by scholarship with Mastro, McKinley, and Warber's "Social identity theory as a framework for understanding the effects of exposure to positive media images of self and other intergroup outcomes." In this study, these scholars examined how media images directly influence Latinos. The underrepresentation of Latinos in entertainment media for example, influenced their perceptions of self, social status, and relevance in American society.[141] They found that positive images of Latinos in music, performing arts, and media were motivational and inspired other Latinos to achieve similar success. It helped Latinos form a better self-concept than the misrepresentation- and stereotype-filled mainstream media.[142] *Presencia Latina*'s principle of "less text, more photos" had a great effect on the Latino readers. Seeing positivity in their community encouraged them to form a positive self-concept. The mainstream media had predominantly limited and stereo-typed, and portrayed Latinos in unfavorable ways in film, print, television, and advertising for many years; in fact, it is still happening today, according to Clara Rodriguez in *Latin Looks*.[143] Rodriguez states that, despite the positive progress over the years, mainstream media continues to portray Latinos in a negative light. There continues to be serious underrepresentation of Latinos and other minorities.[144] It is important that newspapers such as *Presencia Latina* exist and have been able to give proper representation and agency to Latino groups in Canada.

Analysis and Findings

The main questions that guided the analysis of *Correo Canadiense* and *Presencia Latina* were: What kind of ethnic community is this? What are these newspapers contributing to shaping? and What are the interests or concerns from the point of view of the editors or founders? One article stood out amongst many written about ethnic media in Canada: Tokunbo Ojo's article, "Ethnic print media in the multicultural nation of Canada." It focuses on ethnic print media in Canada, but through the lens of a black newspaper in Montreal. He examines how these ethnic media are "(re)constructing their own identities in contrast to their framed identities in the mainstream national print media such as the *Globe and Mail*, *National Post* and *Toronto Sun*."[145] Ojo notes that there are 250 ethnic newspapers in Canada and each of these can be used "as tools for cultural preservation and also at the same time, agents of assimilation of ethnic minority audiences to the dominant mainstream culture and values."[146] I would like to acknowledge Ojo's article because it represents a similar study to this one in that he chose to focus on an ethnic newspaper to challenge notions of identity construction. Several key findings from his study, such as the "assumption by managing editors at big media outlets in Canada that ethnic media is generally not considered to be "real" reporting and no real journalism," were instrumental in shaping the goals of this newspaper.[147] This notion is proven wrong in this study, as *Correo* and *Presencia* represent ethnic print media that are producing "real", that is, original journalism, similar to Ojo's case study. Moreover, Ojo's case study looks at how these ethnic print media outlets were established. He believes that they were created as a "response to the misrepresentation, under-representation and invisibility of visible minorities in the mainstream media."[148] Therefore, with ethnic media being an outlet for an alternative voice to the dominant discourse of mainstream media, it has the power to change. This power can "help mainstream audiences and journalists have a critical awareness of their positions in the construction and circulation of meaning through their works." They therefore have an important role to play in any ethnic community.[149]

The impression that immigrants rely on information media is not new. Luisa Veronis is one such scholar who has focused on this notion and presents her findings in a 2015 study of Ottawa. Essentially, Veronis states that immigrants rely on information media such as social networks, immigrant organizations, and various forms of media and communication technologies to access information, resources, and services they need to participate in economic, social, cultural and civic life of their new society.[150]

I find this particularly interesting because it confirms that Anderson's concept of "imagined communities" is still relevant today. Immigrants, such as Latin Americans to Canada, long to feel connected and can establish this connection to one another through ethnic information media. However, some studies have explained that mainstream media is becoming more important to immigrants and the ethnic-language newspapers are slowly deteriorating. Veronis mentions that the rate of ethnic-language newspaper usage is only twenty-one percent.[151] This could be indicating that second- to third-generation Latinos are not using ethnic media. For instance, Veronis' study of Ottawa did mention that "there is no community specific web-forum for Latin Americans [...] they commonly consulted the Facebook page of their local ethno-cultural community in Ottawa."[152] Therefore, can this explain the idea that second- to third-generation Latinos are not using print media as much as their parents?

Looking at some statistics, perhaps the answer can be found by using the United States as an example. A survey conducted in 2005 by Bendixen and Associates indicated that eighty-seven percent of Hispanic adults access Spanish newspapers on a regular basis.[153] Additionally, one-fifth of Hispanic adults reported at that time that they preferred Spanish-language newspapers to their English-language counterparts.[154] This study also confirmed Freddy Velez's notion that many Hispanics still cannot access the Internet: "Hispanics have very low access (24%) to the internet."[155] They have to rely on information from newspapers to stay updated on the Latino community and their native country. The study disclosed that adults from 40 to 60+ are the primary consumers of ethnic media, with 18- to 39-year-olds only using it at a rate of fifty-four percent.[156] Final findings were also that "Hispanics are the only group studied that prefer ethnic media to mainstream media for their information," and demographically, "53% who viewed ethnic media made under $30,000 a year."[157] These statistics in the United States can be used to assume the same to be true for Canada in regard to Latin Americans who use ethnic media. This helps add the appropriate data to the information presented by Velez and McTavish. The greatest problem today is the lack of sources and studies on Latin American ethnic media usage in Canada. Nevertheless, Latin Americans rely on ethnic print media because it helps immigrants adapt to a new culture and resolve some of the dilemmas of the immigrant experience.

Integration is an important area to address as a reason behind the success of Latino ethnic print newspapers. A concept that McTavish mentions is that new Latinos are increasingly turning to ethnic print media as a way to foster integration and keep connected. Likewise, "age" and "generation" play roles in the types of media used. In another study by Veronis with focus group participants, a key finding was presented: "there was more agreement that older generations are accustomed to using more traditional [print] media [...] as they did in their countries of origin, whereas younger generations are more familiar with new technologies."[158] Findings in her study of Ottawa's ethnic media reveal that many Latino immigrants thought their local ethnic media was not sufficient and that it should do more, such as "providing relevant information to assist settlement and integration process, instead of being only entertainment."[159] These findings expose a very different ethnic environment in Ottawa in comparison to the GTA, Hamilton, and Niagara. However, *Correo* and *Presencia* show that the information provided in their newspapers reflect real stories of Latinos in the area.

The notion of language as a barrier has also been tackled in scholarship. As a Latino, being an "English as a second language" individual in Canada is difficult. This is something that Velez mentions early with "wanting to change his name." In fact, language, in particular the accents of those who learned to speak the English language as adults, "is one of the most important markers of otherness and 'difference,' and of devaluation."[160] The importance of language and its effects on immigrants should not be overlooked. For Latinos, Spanish remains an important attribute of their identity: "Spanish-language products promote connection to Latino identity well beyond any English-language product [...] therefore, Latinos who desire to keep Spanish viable as a language in their personal life will derive more gratification from consuming Spanish-language news media."[161]

Spanish is equally important to Latinos in Canada in the process of integration. Scholars such as Ryan Salzman have proven that stronger language skills in both English and Spanish in immigrants and their children provide them with a better assimilation experience. In analyzing what McTavish says about the perception that Latin American acculturation is beginning, one finds that this process can also be related to language. Salzman makes this clear: "each new generation of Latinos living [...] should prefer English news more than the previous generation as their identities are more similar to the American public than any specific ethnic group."[162] Crucially, Salman's conclusions are that "a first-generation Latino is more closely tied to their Latin American culture and thus maintain a distinctly Latino identity, whereas a fourth-generation Latino is naturally more acculturated to American society."[163] Hence, McTavish was correct when he said *Presencia Latina* is mostly relevant to first-generation Latinos in Hamilton and Niagara.

Looking at the notions of identity construction first presented by Velez and McTavish, related scholarship can also support their beliefs. Velez and McTavish say that many Latinos in the GTA, Hamilton, and Niagara look back to their countries and stay updated on the news. To confirm this, Anna De Fina says, "This is the case with many diasporic communities, which maintain continuous economic, but also emotional and cultural ties, with their places of origin while living in a new host country."[164] De Fina also explains the role ethnic media plays in this concept: "[as] sources of information and orientation in the host country [...] for the communities that they address [...] play a central role in forging their [immigrants'] identities."[165] Just as Velez speaks about his identity being "Latino Canadian," many Hispanics prefer their family's country of origin to pan-ethnic terms. For example, a United States survey conducted from November to December 2011 by the Pew Hispanic Center demonstrates national findings. A survey of 1,220 Hispanic adults revealed that 51 percent say that most often they use their family's country of origin to describe their identity.[166] Moreover, when asked whether they prefer "Hispanic" or "Latino," most do not care; but among those who do, "Hispanic" is preferred.[167] It is interesting to compare this to the information given by Velez and McTavish regarding *Correo* and *Presencia*. This survey says that "most Hispanics do not see a shared common culture among US Hispanics."[168] Another result of the survey was that most Hispanics believe "in the efficacy of hard work [...] more so than the general public [...] 75% of Hispanics say most people can get ahead if they work hard."[169] Both Velez and McTavish made statements about the Latino people being known for their work ethic. Consequently, scholarship does exist that confirms the oral histories of Velez and McTavish.

It goes without saying that the scholarship for statistics used to analyze the interviews of Velez and McTavish is mostly from the United States; these are not statistics for Canada. However, there is a lack of visible sources and surveys on the Latin American population in Canada. This should not be the case in the next few years but for now, I have used American Latino statistics because they are the only ones that exist on a national level. Analysis of the interviews has shown unmistakably that building a common Latino identity is an issue for ethnic media in Canada. *Correo* and *Presencia* show that individuals such as Velez and McTavish have both made steps towards unifying all Latinos in an "imagined community" created by print media. But more work is still needed for this to happen on a physical level. According to De Fina,

> The great diversity in Latin Americans in terms of race, history, customs [...] is the source of historical divisions among the countries of the region, and as a result, nationally based identities can be a barrier and a source of conflict rather than unity among Latin Americans belonging to different countries.[170]

The main attempt that scholars, bureaucrats, and mainstream media made to counter this great diversity was the term "Latino."

A "Unifying" Term

While I have already shown that Latin America is many countries for many people, I have not explained the importance of the term "Latino." "Latino" is a unifying term, and it is turned into a unifying strategy by many in Canada and the United States. According to Veronis, "[i]n the eyes of the Canadian state, Latin Americans form a single, homogeneous community suggested by the categories 'Latin American' and 'Spanish-speaking' used in the Canadian Census."[171] Certainly, the question of whether we should even use the labels "Latino" or "Hispanic" in Canada, a question Victor Armony raised, should be researched fully. Are they too US-specific? This can be debated, as the United States has the most scholarship of any country on the Latin American diaspora. An analysis of the Latin American population in Canada must find its own footing and is also needed. Nevertheless, the goals of this unifying strategy are several and noteworthy.

The goals of putting all of these diversity terms under the umbrella of Latino can first be understood by the idea of collective organizing. Looking at another Veronis study, it is possible to see how Latino immigrants are actively participating in print media. She says researchers often use terms referring to "broad regional, national and cultural, linguistic, and/ or religious categories to describe immigrant groups."[172] The use of these terms suggests that these groups are consistent and homogeneous (omitting the internal complexity and diversity) as applied to Latin Americans in Canada. The issue in recent years has been the increasing diversity and emergence of new Latino immigrants in Canada, a change that makes it difficult to build a common voice and form a united community.[173] This is not to say that Latinos in certain areas have not united to form an "imagined community." Velez and McTavish's first-hand accounts of the history and making of *Correo* and *Presencia* provide a wealth of information proving the "imagined community" theory at work in the GTA, Hamilton, and Niagara. The unifying Latino strategy can also be seen with the Multiculturalism Act and it has its flaws. Many critics have pointed out that broad terms and categories "manage" diversity by "creating artificial and homogenized groups in addition to creating inequities between them."[174] Immigrant groups face dominant discourses and exclusion that is informed by multiculturalism - a notion presented by Veronis. I believe that Latin Americans form a community that is more "imagined" than real, and that the success of *Correo* and *Presencia* in their respective locations has a lot to do with Anderson's notions of how print media can inform national consciousness.

In a 2015 radio interview with the National Public Radio, American sociologist Christina Mora states, "Before ideas of us [Hispanics] coming together were even there, we were all our separate distinct nationalities."[175] For instance, in the 1960s, Mexicans had a different set of needs and wants in migration to the United States. Mora also attempts to answer the question of who was responsible for this notion. She believes that "the national consul was one of the first groups to lobby the census bureau to change the way to classify these [Hispanic] groups."[176] The reason behind this change has to do with the context at the time. Hispanics were labelled as whites in the 1960s and 1970s, and they were never able to have their own data to lobby the federal and provincial governments.[177] They had to create a category, "a broad Hispanic category," that would unite all those of Latin American origin.[178] Another factor in the idea of Hispanics under one umbrella was the media. Univision, for instance, created a Hispanic and Latino identity as well.[179] Mora argues, "They began to attach sounds, images and narratives to this idea of what a Hispanic really is."[180] Thus, marketing and advertising also had its role in the creation of the broad "Hispanic" category. The positives of having this notion of a pan-ethnic Latino community are worth noting. Mora thinks that when you have a sense of a powerful community, "you can create lots of things [...]. You can create organizations that help to reproduce the notion of a community."[181] Adding to this effect, Hispanics could use this Hispanic category for social justice and civil rights. Why is this all-important, you might ask? Well, it is clear the category of "Hispanics" or "Latinos" was man-made. Governments, organizations, and Hispanics themselves constructed it in an altered context for different purposes. Clearly, this notion of all Hispanic people living under one umbrella might be the case for the United States, but it is not and never has been for Canada.

Scholars have debated why this pan-ethnic strategy is still used in the present day. Victor Armony has asked the question of what purpose is served by speaking of Latin American migrants as a single group in a given host society. He attempts to solve this: "There is no question that Latin Americans express a strong sense of belonging to a larger community across nationalities."[182] Armony also argues, "They [Latinos] may question and give new meanings to that self-identification, but they nevertheless tend to show a persistent attachment to their cultural background."[183] There is no question that this strong sense of belonging has a role in how *Correo* and *Presencia* present themselves as ethnic print media. They have acted as a "third space" for Latin Americans to understand one another regardless of having a "physical" space in the GTA, Hamilton, and Niagara. Christina Mora also argues that "the Hispanic category became institutionalized as bureaucrats, activists, and media executives forged networks and worked together to build panethnic organizations that popularized the notion of a Hispanic identity."[184] She cautions, however, that the notion of Hispanics as a homogeneous community with little to no internal variation is dangerous. But Mora again argues more in favour of the Hispanic category: "We should not dismiss the social currents that are attempting to unify subgroups and the potential impact that Latino/Hispanic solidarity can have on American institutions."[185] Her findings reveal that, for future unity, the challenge of Hispanic/Latino organizations will be to honour their communities while emphasizing the community of focus' similarities with other organizations.[186] In this analysis I would argue that identity is a social construct. Ethnic print newspapers, such as *Correo* and *Presencia* can play a role in how the Latin American nationalities are presented to one another. Ethnic print newspapers have access to this power because of their unique niche with immigrants. This has brought to light the importance of ethnic print media. *Correo* and *Presencia* can, in fact, act as a "third space," as in Cassandra Eberhardt's thesis, according to which Latin American groups in the GTA, Hamilton, and Niagara have come together in an "imaginary" community.

The goal from the point of view of physical material (newspapers), I would argue, is to connect all Latinos in the GTA, Hamilton, and Niagara to one another. In doing so, they have, perhaps without realizing, acted as a "third space" in which Latinos can (re)construct their identity. The question of how to unite all of this Latino diversity has emerged in many scholarly studies. For example, David Spencer and Joseph Straubhaar state that "one of the issues facing Americas [...] is how to represent the diversity of cultures within and across nations in broadcasting and other media."[187] This has led to the theory of hybridity, which according to Spencer and Straubhaar is one of "the most influential theories to come out of Latin America" and "deals with this question of internal cultural diversity and its relation to outside cultures."[188] This theory suggests that dominant society has moved away from multiculturalism, in which the "other" is its own culture. Rather, it suggests that cultural practices are actually brought together in the host society. Hybrid spaces can also be formed in this host society. As noted earlier, Latinos in the GTA, Hamilton, and Niagara do not have a physical space in which their diverse cultures can mix and mingle. However, only this year Mexicans in Toronto finally opened their own "House of Cultures." An article from April 2015, in *La Portada* newspaper, highlights the opening of the "Casa Cultural Mexicana," Toronto's Mexican headquarters for its community.[189] It briefly states that the Cultural House, which is located on St. Clair Avenue in the Italian Quarter of Toronto, will be open to "all cultural expressions of Mexicans."[190] This highlights the fact that attempts are being made to unite the diversity of Hispanics in Toronto. Yet it reveals that, even after all these years, it has been difficult for Hispanics to find a "home" in the Greater Toronto Area. Hybrid spaces such as the "*Casa Cultural Mexicana*" do exist, and have become more prevalent recently. But physical hybrid spaces of Latinos do not exist yet in the GTA, Hamilton, and Niagara area. An "imaginary" space connects all Latino cultures through *Correo Canadiense* and *Presencia Latina*. The readers of these two newspapers, although they may not be aware of it, engage in simultaneously consuming *Correo* and *Presencia*, and both think of themselves, and relate to other Latinos, in new ways.

In comparison with other newspapers in the GTA, Hamilton, and Niagara region, community growth is a feature only some can officially announce. For example, the *La Jornada* Hispanic newspaper is strictly focused on news for the Latino Canadian audience.[191] This newspaper does not appear to participate in any Latino events or contribute to community growth. The *Avenida Latina*, on the other hand, contributes to the Toronto Latino youth community by participating and calling attention to events such as the *aluCine Latin Film and Arts Festival*, which presents unique works by Latino artists living in Canada and abroad.[192] Similarly, it calls attention to Latino youth who are making an effort to enhance the Latino culture or immigrant experience in Canada, as for instance, *Avenida's* event showcasing paintings by Alex Padulo, a young Argentinian whose abstract work has strong emotional content.[193] *La Portada Canadá* newspaper describes itself as being a "new Hispanic vision in Canada" and a means of "communication of greater Latin projection" in Canada, Toronto, and the world.[194] Striking, for me, is the fact that *La Portada Canadá* appears to take much of its news from other sources and photos from the Internet - the embodiment of what McTavish and Velez described as their competition. The half-dozen or so newspapers and magazines in the GTA, Hamilton, and Niagara area, in my view, cannot be placed in the same category as *Correo* and *Presencia*, newspapers that are producing original journalism. The only other comparable area in Canada with Latino print media is Quebec, specifically Montreal. As Victor Armony mentions, Latino-ness in different areas of Canada will probably take different shapes. Montreal and Ottawa also have several noteworthy Latino newspapers: *El Chasqui Latino* (Montreal) and *Eco Latino* (Ottawa) are both comparable to *Correo* and *Presencia*. *El Chasqui Latino* mentions that it is the largest circulated Latino weekly in Quebec province and also the most requested on the market.[195] The problem with accepting this as truth is that, taking a look through one edition of their newspaper, I noticed that most of their forty pages of content are simply advertisements.[196] It appears they are just selling advertisements of local Hispanic businesses as well as other Canadian businesses, basically a "tool to sell advertisements" for profit. This is a notion that McTavish and Velez have said places *Correo* and *Presencia* ahead on the spectrum.

The only other Latino newspaper that might be comparable with *Correo* and *Presencia* is *Eco Latino* in Ottawa. *Eco Latino* does not have a website, though Luisa Veronis mentions it. Veronis highlights the importance of *Eco Latino* in helping the immigrant experience in an interview with an adult Hispanic woman in Ottawa. She says,

[T]he language and the media play an important role in facilitating integration particularly for elderly people. The *Eco Latino* plays an important role, the radio plays an important role. The television with [...] the [program] "Spanish Roots," all of these [...] are helping them to facilitate integration [...] so if they don't have that access, depression and sadness for elderly people is possible.[197]

Eco Latino's role is very similar to that of *Correo* and *Presencia* in enabling Latino immigrants to feel connected and in integrating them into their new communities. I chose to focus on these two newspapers because I feel there is a lack of evidence that Latino newspapers in the GTA, Hamilton, and Niagara are also helping the Latino community feel a sense of belonging. In regard to *Presencia Latina*, McTavish says they changed considerably over their ten years of existence. For example, looking at a July 2006 issue, I became aware of a change in the content *Presencia* was offering. McTavish mentions that this was the first issue in which Canadians were presented to Latinos - an attempt to make them aware of each other.[198] For the year 2007, I noticed that the June issue included a page that had photos of Latinos on trips around the world[199] - perhaps a change that made other Latinos aware of the diversity in *Presencia* consumers, putting faces to the "imaginary" community. McTavish spoke of when they started on the Internet in 2008.[200] Their March 2008 issue appears to advertise their website, which would also include all of the photos of Latinos in the community.[201] A change, McTavish says, added 1000 new visitors a month, as Latinos would share the website link to their families in Latin America - connecting them beyond geography.[202] The July 2009 edition celebrates Canada Day and includes all the local politicians that support *Presencia*.[203] The September 2011 issue commemorates NDP leader Jack Layton after his death.[204] McTavish tells me that he took all of the photos from the article about Layton on various occasions[205] - a fact that did not surprise me, as it is evident the photos in *Presencia* are in-house photographs and not taken from the Internet. One of the final issues when McTavish was leading *Presencia* was the November 2012 issue. In this issue, they had stories about recent graduates from Niagara College who were Latino, and also a main article about the "Miss Universe Canada" contest in 2012 - in which a Latina won.[206] The breadth of the news and stories in *Presencia Latina* issues when McTavish was heading it is astounding.

Correo Canadiense also highlights the real stories in the Latino community in the GTA and around Canada. For instance, Velez mentions that in early November of 2015, he travelled to Ottawa for Prime Minister Justin Trudeau's induction ceremony.[207] On page four is seen a full-page article by Freddy Velez which has photos taken at the event, including photos of Mexican-Canadians and other Trudeau supporters.[208] Looking at a later November 2015 issue, there is an article on a Latino artist, Natalie Castro, who managed to gather $4000 for the Sick Kids Hospital in Toronto.[209] Many revealed that they are excited for next year's event as well.[210] These stories are from real life, emphasizing the efforts local Latinos are making in the GTA, Hamilton, and Niagara area that are not visible in the mainstream Canadian media. In fact, most individuals in Canada are completely unaware of the many positives Latinos bring to our country. I credit Velez and McTavish for their efforts in presenting content that is not visible anywhere else. The content in *Correo* and *Presencia* is giving a voice to Latinos in the GTA, Hamilton, and Niagara who are successful business people, winners of awards, and who are organizing events for the greater good of local communities. Looking to scholarly support, I began to look at what was coming out of these two newspapers and the kind of message that appeared.

These small numbers of Latinos in the GTA, Hamilton, and Niagara who are making a difference have encouraged others to take action. For instance, Hugh Hazelton touches upon this concept:

> [S]mall numbers of Latin Americans in Canada have encouraged people from different backgrounds to transcend national and cultural boundaries and define themselves linguistically [...] there is now a surprisingly high degree of integration and fertile cultural interchange between various Spanish-speaking nationalities.[211]

Hazelton looks at ten Latino writers in Canada who have sought to make it in the world of writing. His concept suggests that Latinos in Canada, whatever their occupation, have been able to encourage others directly through print media and/or various forms of communication and literature. This data also suggests that, although the broad concept of Latino is used as a unifying strategy, the group has engaged in print media and actively established an "imagined community" among the Latin American populations in the GTA, Hamilton, and Niagara. It serves Latin Americans' needs and represents their interests, an area that Luisa Veronis has explored in her 2010 study. In addition, other scholars have said that to recommend Latin/Hispanic as a unifying umbrella essentially implies "blurring and de-emphasizing distinctions between different nationalities and erasing traditional boundaries."[212] This strategy has resulted in the denationalization of Latin American immigrants in North America. *Correo* and *Presencia* have brought to light the differences in Latino populations in the GTA, Hamilton, and Niagara, but also sought to make them aware of each other and to find commonalities among them. They have not attempted to impose a pan-ethnic identity on all Latinos but rather to create understanding. In Canada, De Fina shows that the common media plays down the differences among Latin Americans and represents them as a community united "linguistically and culturally," a statement that *Correo* and *Presencia* have chosen to avoid.[213] Ethnic print media has the power to connect every Latin American culture in Canada by becoming a means for them to express their nationality or identity, based on their "print-language."

Latinos are connecting among their cultural silos but are not connecting greatly with Canadians. Could it be that reverse-acculturation is happening with Latinos in Niagara? I think that many are looking at their own culture and heritage and looking for a physical place or more recognition in Canadian society. Pamela Shoemaker, Stephen Reese, and Wayne Danielson look into this notion in their 1985 study of Spanish print media in the United States as an indicator of acculturation. They define acculturation as "an ethnic individual becoming acquainted with and adopting the norms and values of salient reference groups of the new society."[214] Interestingly, the results in their study show that the use of print media seems to be a better indicator of acculturation than that of any other form of media, such as broadcast media.[215] Although this is a dated article, it attempts to understand whether Hispanic Spanish-language print media use is actually an indicator of their level of acculturation into the United States culture. Shoemaker, Reese, and Danielson also make the case that "[i]f Hispanics are fully acculturated, then there is little reason for newspaper and magazine publishers to offer bilingual or Spanish monolingual editions."[216] Therefore, using this basis, *Correo* and *Presencia* are evidence that Latinos in the GTA, Hamilton, and Niagara are not fully acculturated. More of this study's findings point to age playing an important role: "young Hispanic adults may be more acculturated than their parents or grandparents," an idea I first saw in my interviews with Velez and McTavish.[217] Remarkably, this 1985 study proposed that the Hispanics surveyed showed that the Hispanic populations were in fact gradually becoming more acculturated and that the need for Spanish-language print media would "decrease over time."[218] It is not entirely true in present-day Latin American communities in the GTA, Hamilton, and Niagara - as *Correo* and *Presencia* show - that there is an increasing interest from Hispanics in their culture and language. Hispanic print media is still alive and well in the GTA, Hamilton, and Niagara. Shoemaker, Reese, and Danielson attempted to show that Hispanic acculturation in the United States as a linear process over a long period of time could have been a possibility in 1985. But by 2015, this was not the case: Hispanic acculturation is non-linear and difficult to predict. Latinos in Canada are a diverse group; some have experienced acculturation, but most are still searching for their own identities in Canada.

The fact that studies have not focused on Spanish-language media is perhaps another reason that this is relevant to Niagara. Meghan Storm points out that "these studies are limited and have largely addressed preference for media consumption, radio broadcasting, and small talk in Spanish-language news reporting in the U.S."[219] This hints that Latino print media in local areas has often been missed in studies. This chapter has hopefully contributed to correcting the lack of studies of local Latino newspapers by focusing on newspapers *Correo* and *Presencia*, which are distributed in the GTA, Hamilton, and Niagara. Similar to other scholars, Storm's findings express the fact that "newspaper consumption has decreased drastically in other markets since widespread access to internet ... [but] print media continue to be a viable source of news for the Latin community in the United States."[220] This same notion is true for Canada. This is important to the community of Niagara because we are seeing how Spanish-language print media is vital to how Latinos view themselves and others. What comes out of these newspapers in the Latino community in Canada is important. For instance, Storm has said there is an assumption that there is a "dialectal relationship between discourse and society."[221] Notions of social hierarchy are also an area that can emerge as Latino identities are constructed. In host societies, how these constructions can complicate traditional understanding should not be overlooked. Most importantly, because of the popularity of Latino print media in the GTA, Hamilton, and Niagara, Latino immigrants occupy a subordinate position in the social hierarchy. Storm thinks this is "produced by the past such as colonialism and imperialism," but comments, "Latinos have the greatest potential to dismantle this hierarchy by physically occupying the space of the dominant group."[222] This subordinate position follows as a consequence of the consumption of publications such as *Correo* and *Presencia* because Latinos are consuming a rather antiquated source "print-media" for their news, one that goes largely unobserved in mainstream media sources. Until Latinos are able to occupy a superior social position, they will continue to consume print media such as *Correo* and *Presencia*, thus occupying a subordinate role in the social hierarchy of their regions of residence in Canada. Then why is this relevant to the Niagara Region? These newspapers have the power to change society in Niagara. By reaching out and challenging subordinate positions of Latinos in Canada (in just the same way as *Correo* and *Presencia* have been doing), they can help Latinos gain recognition and unite the dispersed Latino cultural silos with Canadians. Latino print media can also have an impact on how these groups are perceived and how they are able to dismantle old hierarchies and present fresh new ideas to the old, imperial, Anglo Canadian societies.

The future of Latin Americans in Canada and Latino print media for Latinos in Canada is bright. For the most part, visible minorities such as Latinos in the Greater Toronto Area remain seriously underrepresented among leaders of the largest employment sectors according to some researchers. "Diversity and Leadership in Media," a 2010 study of the representation of ethnic minority groups in senior roles in the GTA and in the media content, revealed that only fourteen percent of GTA leaders were members of minorities, including Latinos.[223] Minority groups are also underrepresented among news and decision-makers, along with media leaders. Furthermore, minorities are underrepresented as experts, hosts, reporters, and stock images on newstime broadcasts and other media.[224] All of this was seen to have a negative effect on the groups who do not see themselves represented, and these included Latinos. According to Canadian census data, there are now over 700,000 Latin Americans residing in Canada, and some estimate that the number will soon be at one million.[225] According to a careful study presented by two scholars, Daniel Schugurensky and Jorge Ginieniewicz in their blog entry, Latinos are the third largest ethnic minority group in Canada and represent more than two percent of the population of Canada. Half of those Latinos are located in Montreal and the Greater Toronto Area,[226] and they represent a relatively new and rapidly-growing community. Compared to those of the United States, these numbers are not very substantial, but in Canada this is significant.

According to McTavish, while there are more Chinese, Indian and other Asian immigrants currently, their immigration rate has begun to drop. Latinos, however, have been the fastest-growing ethnic group in Ontario for the last few years, and many are coming to Canada from the United States as well.[227] McTavish reiterated that many Canadian companies want to do business in Latin America and that Spanish is the language of the business future.[228] Some challenges still need to be overcome, and these include both external and internal integration. Schugurensky and Ginieniewicz point out that the Latin American community in Canada is still experiencing difficulties in terms of socio-cultural, educational, economic, and political integration.[229] Furthermore, the problem of internal integration still persists and involves alienation, isolation, mistrust, and fragmentation. The diversity in Canada for Latinos has often left Latinos fragmented, as many activities develop inside each national or ethnic micro-community, with each of these separated into different sub-groups that rarely interact with each other.[230] However, as seen with *Correo Canadiense* and *Presencia Latina*, this is not always the case. Nonetheless, signs of hope have emerged. McTavish believes that the future of media is in the ethnic newspaper niche. This is because mainstream media is not read on paper anymore, but is read online for free.[231] Ultimately, ethnic newspapers have a future because the information they provide is not available elsewhere.

All of the evidence has shown an overabundance of information that has emphasized the uniqueness of Latino print media for Latinos in Canada. Certainly, a specific focus on Latino newspapers in the GTA, Hamilton, and Niagara has revealed that successful positive media outlets do exist that are changing the way Latinos see themselves and others. This study has shown that Latino print media, with a focus on *Correo Canadiense* and *Presencia Latina* newspapers, has acted as an umbrella under which Latin Americans in the GTA, Hamilton, and Niagara were unified in a larger, "imagined community" that might be invisible, but nonetheless is very real. They were able to construct a new, inclusive Latino identity that is uniquely Canadian and not fragmented.

This chapter has revealed a "gap in the understanding" of Latino media in which most scholars have overlooked the role ethnic print media can play in acculturation, identity creation, and community construction. The two newspapers of focus in this study show that they contribute to local, regional, and national issues within a broader perspective on Latin American Canadian and Latino American relations. The focus on *Correo Canadiense* and *Presencia Latina*, with the help of Velez and McTavish, exposes the fact that many studies are out of focus and that the success of Latino identity and community lie within plain sight in Canada. *Correo* and *Presencia*, under the leadership of John McTavish, who is Scottish Canadian and has a passion for Latino culture, and Freddy Velez, who is Colombian and a Latino specialist, show signs of hope for better integration of Latin Americans across Canada. In the Greater Toronto Area,

Hamilton, and Niagara, one thing is certain: Canadians now have a better understanding of Latino culture and Latinos have a greater appreciation, acceptance, and knowledge of one another. This newspaper represents only an area in Canada in which Latino media has allowed for a unified "imagined" cultural identity to be seen. There is no unified physical "Hispanic" community feeling in the GTA, Hamilton, and Niagara. Essential, however, is the fact that *Correo* and *Presencia* are involved in an attempt to do so. There is still a visible gap in scholarship on Latinos in Canada, and more research is still needed in order to differentiate Latino Canada and the United States. It is hoped that this study will allow for more interest, inquiry, and research into Latino media newspapers and vehicles for Latino expression across Canada.

Part 4
Hall of Mirrors

Chapter 12

El Sistema Up North: Re-Imagining Venezuela's Music-Education Program for Canada[1]

Victoria Wolff

I invite every music teacher in Canada... every member of the symphony orchestras in this country, to join this project, to give their support to the children
of Canada, so that every child in this country has free and full access to music and
so that we can turn our countries into a fraternal bond that will remain eternal.[2]
  José Antonio Abreu, Glenn Gould Prize Laureate, Toronto, Ontario, Canada

Introduction
The 2008 Glenn Gould Prize, through music, linked a cultural icon from
Canada to a cultural icon from Latin America. Glenn Gould, born in Toronto, Ontario, was an acclaimed concert pianist, recording artist, thinker,
and writer, with a professional interest in the intersections of mass media,
communication, technology, and music. The prize, established in Gould's
honour after his untimely death, is promoted in its literature as "the vital
connection between artistic excellence and the transformation of lives," and
"is awarded to an individual for a unique lifetime contribution that has enriched the human condition through the arts."[3] Chosen as the 2008 Laureate was Venezuelan politician, economist, and conductor, José Antonio
Abreu. Abreu was recognized by the Glenn Gould Foundation for establishing and developing *El Sistema*, a music-education program geared towards youth that strives, in the words of Abreu, to put "art at the service of
society."[4] This chapter contends that the Glenn Gould Prize was an important moment for the recognition and development of El Sistema in Canada.
I will describe the presence and development of Sistema-inspired programs
in Canada from Toronto 2008 to today, their cultural significance, and future implications for Canada in relation to *El Sistema* in Venezuela.

The sociology of music and performance studies
This discussion of "Latin America (re)made in Canada" through El
Sistema and Sistema-inspired programs will be examined through the the-
oretical perspectives of the sociology of music and performance studies.

One of the primary themes of the sociology of music is that there is an important relationship and correspondence between the structures of music and the structures of society. Ivo Supičić in *Music in Society: A Guide to the Sociology of Music* explains: "The fundamental goal of the sociology of music may be divided into two parts: first to examine the relationship of music to diverse global societies as well as to various social groups within those societies; second, to examine how music itself is a social phenomenon, or rather, to examine the social aspects within music."[5] In this chapter, we will see that El Sistema programs are arranged around the concept of the *núcleo*, or music-education centre, the orchestra ensemble, and, principally, classical or art music. El Sistema's central claim is that these musical structures directly mirror, reproduce, and feed back into social structures of community and family, and that music, therefore, has the potential to be an important tool for social transformation. These claims will be examined considering research compiled by Geoffrey Baker in *El Sistema: Orchestrating Venezuela's Youth*. Is classical music created in an orchestra setting an appropriate way to encourage social justice, inclusion, and community development in Canada?

A key figure in facilitating the interactions of music and society is the professional musician. One of the underlying assertions of *El Sistema* is that, in the twentieth and twenty-first centuries, the *maestro* now focuses less on musical genius and more on being a teacher, educator, innovator, community partner, and activist.[6] These claims will be examined through a comparison with the study entitled the "Social Obligations of the Emancipated Musician in the 19th Century," by Walter Salmen. Does the musician-figure conceptualized by El Sistema represent a fundamental shift in the social status of the professional musician? What is the role of the musician-figure in developing and directing Sistema-inspired programs in Canada? What is the relationship between the central, professional musician-figure and the young musicians that comprise the ensembles?

The sociology of music intersects with performance studies through the issue of the transmission of music. The transmission of music engages the continual tension of what scholar Diana Taylor calls "the archive" and "the repertoire." Taylor uses these concepts in *The Archive and the Repertoire: Performing Cultural Memory in the Americas* to discuss cultural practices of performance which may be either fixed in "supposedly enduring materials," such as written and printed texts, and/or ephemeral practices of embodied knowledge, such as dance and ritual, that persist and are transmitted through non-archival systems.[7]

One of the central features of classical or art music in the western tradition is its written form, which has allowed for its wide circulation and preservation, but also marginalizes the possibilities of improvisation and displaces other cultural forms. Performance is a central feature of El Sistema and Sistema-inspired programs. While the written form of music ensures its enduring legacy, it is the bringing of music into the repertoire through performance that purportedly makes it a transformative experience for both the participants in the program and the wider public.

New digital archival systems, specifically the Internet, have now become central to documenting and transmitting performance and information on El Sistema. By this means, José Antonio Abreu and his most famous protégé, Gustavo Dudamel, have become Hispanic global and cultural icons, and El Sistema has come into the mainstream as a captivating way to potentially address some of the complex relationships of music and society. However, Baker cautions that in Hispanic Baroque fashion, the spectacle of El Sistema has won over the hearts of global audiences, creating a sense of wonder while, at the same time, suppressing the mind.[8] What other connections to Hispanic culture are essential to our understanding of El Sistema? How will these cultural elements be received, adopted, or adapted in Canada?

The Foundational Fictions of José Antonio Abreu and El Sistema

This section discusses primary ideas and themes from Hispanic literature and culture that have influenced the perspectives of José Antonio Abreu and ultimately structured the philosophical framework upon which El Sistema was founded. These themes are based on spiritual, political, and artistic writing, thought, and action, and our understanding of them will be essential to our reflections on how El Sistema might be perceived and received in Canada.

In *Foundational Fictions: The National Romances of Latin America*, Doris Sommer shows the centrality of literature, specifically romantic novels, in the nineteenth-century nation-building projects of Latin America. Citing writer-statesmen such as Andrés Bello and José Martí, among others, Sommer argues that intellectuals of the time conceptualized nation alongside narration and felt strongly that "good novels could promote Latin American development."[9] I argue that artistic action or art in the service of nation-building continues to be an important trend in the twentieth and twenty-first centuries in Latin America (and beyond). However, the dominant narrative surrounding El Sistema promotes music, not literature, as the means by which development may occur. As literature was once a way to inspire reflection, so music, through El Sistema, has been constructed as a way to instill action. However, as we shall see, the narrative of El Sistema and its perception as an effective program through which to address issues of social justice, inclusion, and community development is still being constructed through the oral and written word.

The foundational narratives surrounding El Sistema have circulated in both traditional (print) and non-traditional (digital Internet) archival systems in both Latin America and North America. Key in constructing the El Sistema narrative has been Abreu's own speeches, which are widely available, viewed, transcribed, and translated on the Internet. In a speech labelled "The *El Sistema* Music Revolution" for the 2009 Ted Prize, Abreu documents the foundational fiction of El Sistema, which goes back to a Caracas garage in 1975:

> Since I was a boy, in my early childhood, I always wanted to be a musician, and, thank God, I made it. From my teachers, my family and my community, I had all the necessary support to become a musician. All my life I've dreamed that all Venezuelan children have the same opportunity that I had. For that desire and from my heart stemmed the idea to make music a deep and global reality for my country. From the very first rehearsal, I saw the bright future ahead, because the rehearsal meant a great challenge to me. I had received a donation of 50 music stands to be used by 100 children in that rehearsal. When I arrived at the rehearsal, only 11 kids had shown up, and I said to myself, "Do I close the program or multiply it by thousands?" I decided to face the challenge, and on that same night, I promised those 11 children that I would turn our orchestra into one of the leading orchestras in the world.[10]

Tunstall's chronicle has also been essential in crystallizing and transmitting the El Sistema foundational narrative, particularly for English-speaking audiences of North America. She writes,

> What he had, in fact, was an orchestra - a youth orchestra in a country where there had never been one before; an all-Venezuelan orchestra in a culture where orchestra players were, almost by definition, non-Venezuelan; a spontaneous, self-invented volunteer orchestra with no budget, no institutional affiliation, and no name. In an unaccountable collective act of faith, the young members of this orchestra continued to assemble and rehearse together day after day, for many hours a day, in an empty garage. How could such an orchestra possibly survive?[11]

In the speech by Abreu, we see that he attributes his musical success to a higher power - a Christian God - and describes, in an almost miraculous way how, true to his vision, he labours to develop a world-renowned music-education and performance program from nothing. This narrative is reproduced in Tunstall's published chronicle a few years later. In both texts, connections are apparent between the El Sistema foundational fiction and canonical biblical narratives of Jesus feeding the multitudes with a few loaves of bread and a few fishes. In the foundational fiction of El Sistema, Christian religious experience and spirituality are primary themes and must therefore be taken into consideration in relation to the development of El Sistema in Canada.

The spiritual foundations of a music-education program: The Jesuit heritage of the El Sistema "movement"

An examination of the biographical information of El Sistema founder José Antonio Abreu explains that he came to Caracas in 1957 to concurrently study music at the José Ángel Lamas Conservatory and economics at the Andrés Bello Catholic University. While the music conservatory has ties going back to the post-independence period of the first half of the nineteenth century, the Society of Jesus had only recently established the Andrés Bello Catholic University in 1953.[12] I argue that Abreu's Jesuit background, connecting back to sixteenth-century Spain, Ignatius Loyola, and the Society of Jesus' global campaign, provides the important spiritual foundations of what is frequently referred to as the "El Sistema movement."[13]

In Sistema-inspired music education, the spiritual exercises of meditation, prayer, and other forms of mental training are supplanted with the exercise, practice, and discipline of music. An example from his Ted Prize acceptance speech clearly demonstrates how Abreu links religious spirituality to art and education in the creation of what he perceives to be a more just society:

> A few years ago, historian Arnold Toynbee said that the world was suffering a huge spiritual crisis. Not an economic or social crisis, but a spiritual one. To confront such a crisis, it could be argued that only art and religion can give proper answers to humanity, to mankind's deepest aspirations, and to the historic demands of our times. Education - the synthesis of wisdom and knowledge - is the means to strive for a more perfect, more aware, more noble and more just society.[14]

It is no coincidence, then, that in both religious-academic and popular culture, discussions of Ignatius Loyola and the Jesuits, José Antonio Abreu, and El Sistema rely upon perceived connections of music and spirituality. In his discussion of "The Experience of Spiritual Exercises," Joseph Tetlow states, "Ignatius saw all grace coming from God into humankind through the church, broken and corrupted, as a whole symphony must come from an orchestra, however inattentive, unskilled, and ill-equipped."[15] In this quote, Tetlow describes the grace of God as (divine) music; the church is equated with the orchestra, while the orchestra musicians represent humankind. The musicians, no matter what level they are, strive to reproduce (musically) the grace of God and are brought together through the organizational structure of the orchestra. "Grace," therefore, embodies the twofold meaning of the word, both as a religious notion of God's favour or blessing and in the sense of elegance and refinement, which is the primary goal in learning, practicing, and performing music. In this view, an orchestra, such as El Sistema, is uniquely positioned as the mediator in the spiritual and social worlds of humankind.

If the orchestra is an important mediator for music and society, so too is the orchestra's leader. In a *New York Times* article, journalist Daniel Wakin calls Abreu the "Venerated High Priest and Humble Servant of Music Education."[16] Focusing on the parallels between Catholicism and Sistema-style music education, Wakin describes the orchestra as a way to gracefully elevate participants from sectors described as the most impoverished ones of Venezuelan society. He, too, highlights the foundational story and musical repertoire of El Sistema in religious terms and describes Abreu and his followers as "persistent evangelizers for El Sistema, proclaiming its advocacy of social justice with the zeal of missionaries."[17] Without a doubt, Abreu and his system of orchestras have a historical precedent in Ignatius Loyola, his Companions, and the vast network of Jesuit institutions around the world, and in fact makes continued references to them.

The key features of Ignatian spirituality present in El Sistema are 1) the perceived unification of ideals and action; 2) the importance of education and educational networks; and 3) the transatlantic nature of the movement. The diversity of contexts and multicultural dimensions within which Ignatian spirituality operated historically, and through which El Sistema functions currently, rely upon the notion of expansion. At a structural level, I see a direct connection between Abreu's *núcleos* and the historical Jesuit *reducciones* (settlements), since both are constructed as physical spaces and functional microcosms of what is perceived to be an ideal, utopian society.

On a spatial level, fundamental to *El Sistema*'s Jesuit-based belief system is the idea of expanding beyond national boundaries into new cultural and linguistic territories. In this regard, it is not surprising that Tunstall dedicates much of her book to El Sistema's expansion beyond Venezuela; and in his Glenn Gould Prize acceptance speech, Abreu calls upon Canadians to connect with Venezuela through *Sistema*-inspired music education.

On a cultural level, the interrelations of Jesuit heritage and music education through El Sistema may prove to be an important factor in the development of Sistema-inspired programs in the Canadian context. As in the Hispanic world, the Jesuits have had an enduring presence in what would later become the nation of Canada.[18] In effect, the history and development of the Society of Jesus is deeply interwoven into the foundational narratives of Canada, particularly in the provinces of Ontario and Quebec. I predict that this association, however, could prove to be problematic in an ethnically, culturally, and linguistically diverse Canada of the twenty-first century. Baker raises concerns that El Sistema's focus on the orchestra as a social organization and its use of the European canon reproduce hierarchical colonial dynamics and threaten local progressive and evidence-based cultural programs.[19] Baker explains: "Whatever benefits it may produce, a program that places European classical music on the highest pedestal and relegates the indigenous and African to distant margins has obvious colonial precedents - particularly when it promotes such music as cultural salvation for the Other."[20]

Without a doubt, the clear Jesuit heritage of El Sistema and the impetus to expand connects Latin America and Canada through a shared cultural legacy. However, this bond is weakened if what is touted as a progressive program is, in reality, what Baker calls "the past in disguise."[21] As Canada is still reconciling itself to its colonial past, particularly in relation to First Nations communities, cultural diversity in relation to music curriculum, pedagogy, and cultural and social development must be a central concern in considering this program of Latin American origin up North.

Political and historical foundations: Bolívar, the Bolivarian Revolution, and the El Sistema "struggle"

In addition to a (musical and spiritual) "movement," El Sistema has been constructed as both a "struggle" and a "revolution," also linking the program to Latin America's colonial and postcolonial history and political past.[22] The most obvious link comes from Spanish America's transition from colonial entity to network of independent but associated national bodies, primarily through the figure of Simón Bolívar. The original youth orchestra founded by Abreu in the 1970s was, in fact, christened the Simón Bolívar Youth Orchestra of Venezuela. As we shall see in this section, the connections between *fundador* (Abreu) and *libertador* (Bolívar) are also made evident in *El Sistema*'s foundational fiction. Furthermore, it is proposed that struggle and revolution may be reconciled through imagined pan-American communities.[23]

Through the connection of figures such as Bolívar and Abreu, nineteenth-century independence and twentieth and twenty-first century projects of nation-building and cultural construction are interwoven. In the history of musical nationalism in Spanish America, for example, the post-independence period inspired local artists to musically evoke the unique languages, sounds, stories, and landscapes of the Spanish-speaking Americas.[24] In the continued face of external political and cultural pressures from both Spain and North America, Spanish American musicians and composers sought to anchor their efforts in the shared history of the struggle for independence from Spain; from that point forward in their common history, they cultivated cultural connections and relationships in the development of uniquely Spanish American musical art forms. In other words, while the dream of Bolívar's pan-Americanism might have passed politically, the thought was that it could still be realized through the arts, particularly music.

As is evident in his Glenn Gould Prize speech, Abreu explicitly takes up the banner of pan-Americanism through music. However, instead of limiting his artistic vision to the Spanish-speaking countries of the Americas, Abreu makes direct appeals to other non-Spanish-speaking Latin American nations, the United States, and, ultimately, Canada:

> We started with our closer neighbors in Trinidad and Colombia, and through the years we have already developed a very wide network of orchestras through Latin America and the Caribbean, and we've managed in every country to have the state support them, not just financially, but recognizing and acknowledging them. When music is done as a collective practice, through choirs or orchestras, every choir and orchestra is a joyous community [...]. We have twenty buildings under construction for one million students and this is why we have come to Canada. This country has been a friend to Venezuela for many years.[25]

While on the one hand, Abreu promotes a pan-American-imagined community through music that transcends national and political boundaries, on the other, he also makes a clear association between the cultivation of *El Sistema* and Sistema-inspired music-education programs, and the state; in other words, the individual governments of the countries participating in the so-called El Sistema "revolution" continue to play a central role.

These foundational associations of politics and music have been extended in recent years to a new, potentially more problematic connection between El Sistema and the so-called "Bolivarian Revolution" of the late Venezuelan President Hugo Chávez. This has created what I would label as the first public, global debate on the program, played out in both news and social media.

Historically, and from its beginnings, Abreu has been the central figure of El Sistema in Venezuela. Both Tunstall and Baker note how Abreu's political and diplomatic machinations have allowed him to cultivate and maintain a series of governmental relationships in support of *El Sistema*, traversing the political spectrum of seven different Venezuelan presidents, including Hugo Chávez.[26] However, Baker outlines how the election of Chávez in 1998 coincides with a marked shift in El Sistema's rhetoric to music as social action. In Baker's estimation, "the linking of the arts and social inclusion - in Venezuela as elsewhere - might be understood primarily as an instrumental response to changing political priorities, economic circumstances, and cultural beliefs in the 1990s."[27]

The shift in discourse of El Sistema appealed to Chávez as a potential way to address poverty and other social problems in Venezuela. As a result, and in a move unprecedented in the history of the program, Chávez transferred the program to be under the control of the presidential office.[28] The explicit merging of cultural and political agendas - the spectacle of music (Abreu) and the spectacle of politics (Chávez) - was the beginning of the controversy surrounding the program both in Venezuela and abroad. Wakin in his *New York Times* article "Music Meets Chávez Politics, and Critics Frown" poses the following questions: "Should they [art and politics] remain separate? Should artists denounce politics they don't agree with? At what cost should culture be kept alive?"[29] Without a doubt, the controversy surrounding *El Sistema* in connection with the government and politics of the late president Hugo Chávez raises important issues of music, society, politics, and power.

The discussion of the primary narrative threads in the foundational fictions of José Antonio Abreu and El Sistema show that cultural beliefs and narratives, circulated in both print and non-print media, must be considered in relation to contemporary social and artistic projects and to their adoption and adaptation into other cultural contexts. How cultural systems developed in Latin America translate fully in the Canadian context is an important area of inquiry. In the section that follows, we shall look at the early phenomenon of El Sistema up North.

From South to North: The El Sistema effect in Canada

There are two essential points to keep in mind when discussing El Sistema in Canada: First, it is a recent phenomenon and second, it is in a perpetual state of flux.[30]

Petri's "A National Sistema Network in Canada: Feasibility Study and Strategic Plan" from 2013 states, "Taking their inspiration from the compelling Venezuelan experience, 22 Canadian centres are now operating with nearly half of them in their first year."[31] The report includes a graph, which shows that there were four "Sistema centres" founded in 2007, one in 2008, two in 2009, one in 2010, one in 2011, eight in 2012, and five in 2013.[32] In other words, after an initially strong establishment of four centres in 2007, there was modest but sustained growth in 2008, 2009, 2010, and 2011.

The year of greatest impact thus far has been 2012, with eight new centres. The report notes, "Centres are located in seven provinces and one territory, with the majority clustered in Ontario."[33] Looking at the report's findings, two related questions emerge: (1) Why did El Sistema develop in Canada at this particular moment in time? and (2) Why has most growth occurred in the province of Ontario? To answer these questions, I look again to the report's assertion that Canada's development of El Sistema was inspired by its "Venezuelan experience."

Five total centres were established in 2007 and 2008, and fifteen total centres in 2009, 2010, 2011, and 2012. In other words, if the 2008 Glenn Gould Prize awarded to Abreu by the jurors of the Glenn Gould Foundation in Toronto, Ontario, is used as a marker of "before" and "after," three times as many centres were founded after the Glenn Gould Prize as before. Canada's experience of Venezuela's El Sistema program is largely based on the events surrounding the 2008 Glenn Gould Prize. This award represented an important public recognition, an event, and a celebration of a program and its figurehead that in many ways contributed to what I would call the El Sistema effect.[34] This effect was most strongly felt in the province of Ontario, in which the celebration took place.

What is described in its own literature as "Canada's most exclusive arts award" was transformed into a much more inclusive series of community and cultural events.[35] Abreu brought the Simón Bolívar Youth Orchestra with him to Toronto for a week-long residency.[36] Not only did the Venezuelan musicians perform but they also served as ambassadors and representatives of the program to different community and arts groups, politicians, and youth in Canada. As is traditional, the Glenn Gould Foundation allowed the Laureate Abreu to name a protégé. The connections between El Sistema's past in Latin America and future in North America were solidified as Abreu selected the best-known musician developed under El Sistema in Venezuela, Gustavo Dudamel, who, at the time of the award, was about to become the Music and Artistic Director of the Los Angeles Philharmonic.

Lending intellectual weight to the celebrations was a series of keynote addresses, round-table discussions, and presentations by experts from a variety of disciplines, discussing the potential for music to positively affect early childhood development, prevent crime, assist in mental health strategies, stimulate the economy, promote citizenship, and foster the inclusion of minority communities. In the aftermath of the events surrounding the award, *Globe and Mail* reporter Robert Everett-Green writes,

> The Glenn Gould Foundation really hit the jackpot when it picked José Antonio Abreu as the latest winner of the $50,000 Glenn Gould Prize. None of the celebrated musicians who have claimed this honour in the past - including Oscar Peterson, Yehudi Menuhin and Pierre Boulez - created anything like the wave of public interest stirred by the Venezuelan music educator, who until recently was so little known that some of the Gould jurors, when they convened eight months ago, had to be told who he was. Since then, Abreu has ridden the fast escalator to world fame, thanks to the even quicker ascent of his star pupil, conductor Gustavo Dudamel, who made a glittering debut last month as the new director of the Los Angeles Philharmonic.[37]

As a result of the Glenn Gould Prize, the majority of the Canadian Sistema-inspired programs are located in Ontario. As of 2013, other centres can be found in the provinces of Alberta, British Columbia, Manitoba, New Brunswick, Quebec, and Saskatchewan, and in the territory of Nunavut.[38]

In the face of the growing presence of Sistema-inspired programs in Canada, the Canadian Music Educators' Association released an important statement of position in 2012. The association in principle supports the El Sistema movement in Canada since the core values and ideals of the program, as articulated in the post-1990s in Venezuela, resonate with the overall mandate and mission of the CMEA.[39] However, the report cautions that the establishment of what are largely grassroots, *Sistema-*

inspired programs in Canada should not lessen the responsibility of government at all levels to provide quality music education within school systems. In other words, El Sistema in Canada has been conceived as a community-based music-education program, but "does not, or should not, claim or position itself to be a replacement model for publicly funded school music education."[40]

Furthermore, the report cites that El Sistema's emphasis on social change is not currently part of any school music curriculum in Canada, nor does it meet any of the current curricular outcomes. According to the association, real deficits in Sistema-inspired programming include a lack of assessment of individual student learning, an absence of standardization of teacher qualifications, and no integration of technology into composition, practice, or performance.[41] Perhaps most importantly, "Most school systems have mandated objectives for inclusiveness and diversity that may not resonate with El Sistema objectives [...]. The strong emphasis by El Sistema on western European art music, as in the original Venezuelan model, does not reflect the broader reach of music education goals and specific curricula goals currently in practice in most school jurisdictions in Canada."[42]

Regarding the implementation of El Sistema in the Canadian context, the report recommends that El Sistema be included in the landscape of music education in Canada but not replace any current programming. Furthermore the report, recognizing the diverse communities within Canada, makes it clear that it is not sufficient to remake Latin America, or even Venezuela, in Canada: "El Sistema needs to be flexible and adaptive to the particular circumstances of a region taking into account local programming, local funding, local resources and specific needs of the identified community. A one-size-fits-all programming is not supported."[43] In the section that follows, we shall consider a Sistema-inspired program in relation to the specific needs and local circumstances of London, Ontario, Canada.

El Sistema Aeolian: Music education in a mid-size Ontario community

El Sistema Aeolian is housed at The Aeolian Music Hall at the intersection of Rectory and Dundas streets in London's Old East Neighborhood.[44] The building has a long and varied history beginning in 1882, and its transformations are interwoven with the development of the surrounding community. Once a town hall, fire station, court of law, public school, and library, among other things, the building first became a concert hall and was officially designated the "Aeolian" in 1947.[45]

In its most recent history, the Ontario-born concert pianist Clark Bryan purchased the building in 2004, expanding its mandate to include multi-genre music, art, and community events. In 2009, he changed its governance to a Registered Charity/Non-Profit Corporation called the Aeolian Musical Arts Association. By 2011, Bryan had transferred ownership of the building to the charity to ensure its future in the Public Trust.[46] That same year, Bryan also launched El Sistema Aeolian as a free music-education program (including musical instruments, instruction, and public performances) offered to children regardless of background or socio-economic limitations. In line with the shift in values of El Sistema in Venezuela during the 1990s, El Sistema Aeolian not only provides music education for youth but also emphasizes the development of social and life skills in the areas of communication, problem solving, and self-monitoring. It distinguishes itself as the only program in North America to offer complete, warm suppers for participants.

According to an early evaluation report of El Sistema Aeolian, the inaugural year was on a pilot basis. The music hall partnered with Lorne Avenue Public School, based primarily on proximity.[47] The school provided the student referrals and the music hall provided the space and administrative support.

The first cohort consisted of twenty grades five and six students, sixteen of whom finished the year as part of the program. Instruments and repertoire were solicited by the Aeolian from the community and were either donated or lent to the program. Local government (City of London) provided an initial grant of $10,000. A year later, a subsequent, provincial Trillium Foundation grant of $85,000 supported the program into the second and third years. For the first half of the initial year of the program, instruction was held after school, three days a week, from 3:30 to 6:00 p.m. Six total hours were dedicated to music instruction and the additional time was reserved for meals. In the second half of the program, a fourth day of class was added to the schedule for a total of 7.5 hours of music instruction per week. Participants had the option of signing up for an additional chamber ensemble on Fridays. After the academic year, optional two-week summer sessions were offered, one in July and the other in August. Twelve of the sixteen students participated in summer sessions.[48]

As in Venezuela, the orchestra and classical music are central to El Sistema Aeolian. However, the program has demonstrated some important re-considerations of popular culture, the orchestra ensemble, and cultural diversity in its practice and performance repertoire.

Of note is the fact that the program directors once asked for and were granted permission to use the popular Angry Birds video game theme song with the youth orchestra for practice and public performance.[49] Furthermore, the optional chamber ensemble offers an important alternative for collaborative playing through composition and improvisation that has the potential to go beyond simply playing together as an orchestra.[50] More significant to the daily running of the program is the fact that the Aeolian Music Hall houses and utilizes gamelan as a central feature of its music-education program.

Gamelan is the traditional ensemble music of Indonesia composed of percussive instruments, the most common being metallophones or tuned metal bars that are struck with mallets to produce sound. Other components include drums, xylophones, flutes, bowed instruments, and sometimes vocalists. Gamelan first came to influence Western music through its exhibition and performance during world's fairs, such as the Paris Exposition (1889) and the Columbian Exposition (1893) of Chicago.

Gamelan arrived in London, Ontario, through one of the El Sistema Aeolian program educators, Nur Intan Murtadza.[51] The use of gamelan is an important example of a way in which Sistema-inspired programs are adapting in order to diversify music education and experience in the Canadian context. Not only is gamelan effective in teaching music through distinctive instruments, and a different cultural conception of ensemble, but it also provides a unique opportunity for discussions of Javanese mythology, Indonesian history, dance, puppet performances, ritual, ceremony, and transatlantic cultural exchanges.

The connection between El Sistema in Latin America and El Sistema in London, Ontario, is through the Assistant Executive Director of the program, Minerva Figueroa. Originally from Mexico City, Figueroa is a classically-trained violinist who studied music at the National Conservatory. Figueroa first became involved in El Sistema as a teacher, conductor, and coordinator of a youth orchestra in Mexico City for four years. In 2008 Figueroa moved to London, Ontario. I sent Minerva Figueroa five key questions that touch upon central themes in this chapter. Her written responses are as follows.

Questions and answers with assistant executive director of El Sistema Aeolian, Minerva Figueroa[52]

Question 1: Based on your experience working in Mexico and Canada, compare and contrast Sistema-inspired music education programs in

Latin and North America. How are they similar? How do they differ? What are the unique features of El Sistema Aeolian?

Answer 1: The Sistema-inspired program I was involved with and the current programs in Mexico are similar to programs across North America in many regards. Programs have (1) always been free and addressed barriers to participation; (2) required a fair amount of commitment; (3) been organized around the orchestra and team experience; and (4) usually started with strings and developed to full orchestra. Relevant partnerships with other community players make the programs stronger.

The current version of the program is a collaborative project including a private foundation, the Education Ministry, Culture and Heritage bodies, and local governments. However, the Sistema-inspired programs in Mexico City have a different structure from many North American programs: It began as a nationwide program, run by a not-for-profit organization (with charitable status) named Orquestas y Coros Juveniles de México AC. Although it was a centralized program, it provided support to the setting up of programs when community members expressed interest in creating a local centre. Support consisted in providing musical instruments, repertoire materials, teacher training, and financial support for overall running of the program, teacher wages, and participation in regional and national conferences, workshops, and concerts. Usually local communities provided the spaces within community centres.

At the time I was involved with the program (1995-1999), it was not associated with the school system. Youth had the choice of joining only a choir or an orchestra. Snacks and meals were not included during regular sessions. Every year there were training opportunities for conductors and teachers during summer camps (two weeks long), with participants from all over the country. The camps included workshops, orchestra rehearsals, master classes, and concerts, as well as meals and accommodations for two weeks. Regional training sessions would take place over weekends in different cities. Every year there was at least one massive concert, bringing together participants from different regions and orchestras.

What I see as unique features of the El Sistema Aeolian program (ESA) is its association with Aeolian Hall. It offers the program participants and their families a very special experience, both as a privileged performance venue and as a space closely connected to the local community and issues. ESA participants have regular access to attending performances by renowned musicians, but they also have the opportunity to volunteer and learn about their community. Another unique feature of ESA is its association with the 88 Keys to Inspiration Program, which allows participant youth to receive, at no cost, a piano donated to the program by individuals in the larger community.

Question 2: How "connected" is El Sistema Aeolian with El Sistema Programs in Latin America? What about connections with other El Sistema and Sistema-inspired programs in Canada?

Answer 2: At the moment, the only connection between ESA and other Sistema programs in Latin America is my personal background, which, of course, colours the perspective I bring to El Sistema Aeolian. However, we are much more connected to other Canadian programs. There are amazing people running programs from Vancouver to New Brunswick, and there is so much to learn from each other. We are particularly connected to Sistema Toronto and Orkidstra Ottawa, with which ESA is in the process of spearheading a provincial association of Sistema-inspired programs.

Question 3: Some of the purported features of El Sistema and Sistema-inspired programs are flexibility and adaptability. How has *El Sistema* Aeolian adapted to the particular features of the Canadian context, the province of Ontario, and the community of London?

Answer 3: El Sistema Aeolian, as part of a global movement, shares philosophical principles with other Sistema-inspired programs. However, there are no two places that look exactly the same. Therefore, we all adapt philosophy and ideals in the practical aspects of implementing a program in our local reality. For instance, North America runs most of *Sistema*-inspired programs through partnerships with the school boards. Sistema New Brunswick runs programs in English and French. Serving a number of newcomer families, Sistema Toronto and El Sistema Aeolian open possibilities for parents to get involved and develop links to their new communities through their children, thus fostering the integration process.

El Sistema Aeolian had a wealth of expertise and a solid community network from its inception, since Aeolian Hall had already worked with the local community for years prior to launching ESA. However, every year we got through a flexibility exercise, redesigning the program after assessing it and then implementing the changes for another year before assessing it again, from the perspectives of the participant children, the volunteers, staff, etc., as well as current external circumstances.

Question 4: How has the role of the professional musician changed in light of El Sistema and Sistema-inspired programs? How do the professional musician-figures, performers, and educators facilitate connections between young musicians, the orchestra, and the community?

Answer 4: I see the role of the teachers involved in Sistema-inspired programs as community connectors who happen to be musicians and who facilitate music experiences for young learners.

Question 5: What do you see as the future of El Sistema and Sistema-inspired programs in Canada? What challenges have you faced and [do you] continue to face?

Answer 5: What I see as challenges shared by every Sistema-inspired program are recruitment of teachers that are highly flexible and that are able to balance the musical with the social goals of the program and development of funding strategies to ensure growth and sustainability in the long term. Regarding the future of Sistema-inspired programs, there are already a high number of incredibly committed people involved with Sistema programs across Canada. Their motivation stems from the genuine interest in providing a better future for children and youth. I can see Sistema-inspired programs becoming part of every community in Canada in the near future.[53]

Conclusion

In his study "Social Obligations of the Emancipated Musician in the 19th Century," Walter Salmen writes of the "place of honor" accorded to music in the nineteenth century, elevating it beyond all other arts forms.[54] The musician-figure also enjoyed a new status but now had to negotiate the tensions between the autonomous pursuit of his or her own art or music as the means for more humanitarian or utilitarian ends.[55] In the first instance, the musician-figure "take[s] the role of a prophesying priest, even a god-like one" and is aligned with the image propagated of and by José Antonio Abreu.[56] In the second case, we see the numerous musicians, educators, and program directors who appear to be genuinely interested in a socially determined art.

I conclude that El Sistema programs in Canada are inspired by the image of El Sistema in Venezuela and other Latin-American countries projected through internationally recognized cultural events and mass media but do not seek to reproduce the same model of music education. While El Sistema in Latin America is deeply invested in the structure of the classical music orchestra, Sistema-inspired programming in Canada is exploring other models of collaboration, practice, and performance, such as chamber ensembles, the use of popular music, and instruments from other cultures. Instead of musicians as teachers, as is the case of El Sistema in Latin America, Canadian programs envision their teachers as "community connectors" who use music as the way through which young individuals engage in a variety of experiences.

As more research and critical studies on El Sistema in Venezuela appear, "community connectors" in Canada will need to consider how closely associated they would like to be with the Latin American phenomenon. This study has shown some of the problematic connotations of El Sistema's cultural heritage in Canada. While association with El Sistema in Latin America might generate publicity about a similar endeavour in Canada, conversely any intense criticism or scandal related to the program in the media would be detrimental to any related project in Canada.

Central to *Sistema*-inspired programming is its flexibility and openness to change. Through the continual assessing, reassessing, and redesigning of the programs in Canada, the question remains, how far will they evolve from El Sistema in Latin America? Will the association with El Sistema in Venezuela even be necessary, or will Canada develop its own unique model and approach to music education and community?

In the instance of El Sistema Aeolian, Sistema-inspired programs are strongest in Ontario. With the impetus for a provincial association, this will continue to be the case. The 2008 Glenn Gould Prize laid the foundations for Sistema-inspired programming in Ontario and throughout Canada. Ontario will continue to be an important province in which to study the dynamics of El Sistema in Canada.

Chapter 13

Stammer and Rustle: Indisciplined Translations (Visual Essay)[1]

Dianne Pearce

Over the four years I studied in Mexico City and the ten years I subsequently taught art there, my artistic practice experienced a transformation that broke free of disciplines, crossing borders into new territories. Disciplinary institutions have organized careers as a process of subjectivation that re-affirms the existing order and distribution of power. But art by nature presupposes a close relationship with language, history, religion, philosophy, anthropology, sociology, and a myriad of other disciplines that include the visual within their own disciplinary parameters. To this end, the past thirty years or so have witnessed a trend of universities launching visual or cultural studies programs in which many disciplines are gathered under what is now known as *interdisciplinarity*, a kind of safe zone allowing unusual and un-locatable practices the opportunity of finding a respectable home. The downside is that these activities, which formerly challenged official culture, soon became comfortably accepted within the institution and forfeited their once transgressive qualities.

However, in an attempt to retain their transgressive nature, W.J.T. Mitchell mentions that, for him, it is not so much interdisciplinarity that interests him, but rather *indiscipline*, which he describes as the moment "of turbulence or incoherence at the inner and outer boundaries of disciplines. If a discipline is a way of insuring the continuity of a set of collective practices [...] 'indiscipline' is a moment of breakage or rupture, when the continuity is broken and the practice comes into question [...] that moment before the routine or ritual is reasserted, the moment of chaos or wonder when a discipline, a way of doing things, compulsively performs a revelation of its own inadequacy. [I] think of it as the 'anarchist' moment."[2]

Mitchell's "moment of chaos or wonder" compares to Henri Lefebvre's ideas of *la fête*, or *la fiesta* in Spanish. For him, a festival is much more than a party: "[I]t is the oppositional culture of the oppressed, a counter model of cultural production and desire. It offers a view of the official world as seen from below - not the mere disruption of etiquette but a symbolic, anticipatory overthrow of oppressive social structures."[3] These are moments of the everyday that allow for a critique of the everyday itself, and from within the everyday at that - and although fleeting, they offer the possibility of difference and change, interrupting the continuum of the present (Fig. 1). Thus, the festival presents a moment "Other" to the capitalist every day.

Julia Kristeva calls Mitchell's "moment of chaos and wonder" *jouissance*, which translates beautifully from French to joy, enjoyment, or pleasure. In her text on the abject (Other), she uses this term to discuss societal structures, and especially to comment on how they become skewed. The "Other" is thus the stray or vagabond who arrives only to catch the object (or individual) off guard and cast it into the "abominable real." It is important to emphasize that the real, horrific as it may be, remains inaccessible without the aid of such jouissance, "in which the subject is swallowed up but in which the Other, in return, keeps the subject from foundering by making it repugnant. One thus understands why so many victims of the abject are its fascinated victims - if not its submissive and willing ones."[4]

Expats living in foreign countries confront the Other, the "abominable real" that becomes accessible through *jouissance*: enjoyment that allows them to be swallowed up. But rather than sinking, the country keeps them afloat in its contrariness such that the expat becomes a willing participant. *Fiesta* and laughter are the vehicles: prominent in Mexican culture, they provided access to the abject Other that is, according to Kristeva, an in-between, ambiguous, and composite space. My artwork soon began to disrespect borders, subvert positions, and break rules as it, too, became in-between, ambiguous, and composite.

Kristeva's mentor, Mikhail Bakhtin, uses the word *carnival* to refer to similar notions of disruption, but his context is one of a generation earlier and of communist Russia. He posits "turning the world upside down" as the way to critical potential necessary for the dominated to respond to the dominating and says that *laughter* is the vehicle for this. Thus, for him, laughter has no place in the East; rather, it belongs to the West, for it is the language of subversion, satire, and parody, all of which are used by capitalist society to question, challenge, or undermine official discourse. Bakhtin describes carnival laughter as "first of all, a festive laughter [...] not an individual reaction to some [...] 'comic' event. [...] Second, it is universal in scope; it is directed at all and everyone [T]he entire world is seen in its droll aspect. [...] Third, this laughter is ambivalent; it is [...] triumphant, and at the same time mocking, deriding. It asserts and denies."[5]

Bakhtin's Russian heritage led me to the concept of *tusovka*, which refers to the artistic and intellectual community of the 1960s and 70s, forced underground to avoid persecution from the Communist Party. Although *tusovka* literally means "to shuffle," today it is used as slang for hanging out. The Café Saigon in Leningrad (1964 to December 1991) is one of the best-known tusovka cafés where intellectuals were able to create conceptual art and share Western writings that were not authorized by official culture and were, as such, illegal. They were places where otherwise-banned European books would be translated night after night: pages would be written by hand in Russian and passed among the *tusovchiks* (participants), or a reader would translate live. Elena Zdravomyslova calls this the "informal-public sphere"[6]: such cafés were symbolic locales for people (the urban intelligentsia) whose everyday practices were identified as representing an alternative to those accepted by officially-sanctioned public life (Fig. 2).

These were communicative meetings that included drinking sessions, informal and absurdist humour, and the arranging of events and performances - a meeting at the café was regarded as the starting point for a night of conviviality (more below regarding Ivan Illich's writings on conviviality). A humorous, light style typified communication and was a sign of alienation from the false seriousness of life regulated by the party-state. This absurdist humour was present in their storytelling as well as happenings, and the unpublished texts of the Leningrad absurdist literary school Obereu (1920-30s) were highly respected. Humour was therefore the essential practice that gave charm to the Café Saigon's discourse and was a means of escaping from wider society and one's personal life, rife with insufficiencies. By the late 1980s, many *tusovchiks* found their place in the emerging post-Soviet order of the non-subsidized market and democratic openings and soon entered the emerging public sphere. In late 1991, the Café Saigon had closed down and - ironically - been converted into a store selling toilets made in Italy, a symbol of the drastic social change taking place. As Zdravomyslova states, "[T]he Café Saigon tusovka has no possibility of existence in today's Russia [...] The marketisation and monetarisation of everyday life are not conducive to the Saigon lifestyle."[7]

My practice has long been installation-based, creating environments for people to do things like weaving shoelaces through enormous wooden puzzles, stamping rubber stamps, or walking through spirals. The *tusovkian* spaces created in my work are an extension of indiscipline and carnivalism in which my intention is precisely to inspire jouissance and laughter as a way of crossing boundaries and breaking the barriers of disciplines. Treating my practice as tusovkian meetings (Fig. 3) - gatherings that lack an apparently identifiable hierarchy for participants - means that whoever shows up at the exhibition, be they artist or not, is accepted as a tusovchik regardless of his or her background or artistic proposal. Likewise, my classes at post-secondary institutions such as the Escuela Nacional de Pintura, Escultura y Grabado "La Esmeralda" (ENPEG) and the Universidad Iberoamericana became transformed into *tusovkian* meetings that incorporated "indisciplined" exercises for artists and non-artists alike.

Cuban-born, Puerto Rican-raised, American-based artist Ernesto Pujol sheds a Hispanic light on these ideas with The Field School project. Although Pujol's artwork is performance-based and thus unrelated to my work *per se*, his teachings at various art institutes in the United States parallel my interests. He publicly fuses his site-specific performance practice with his studio instruction by way of intensive retreats akin to training workshops, mentoring environments, and, well, field schooling in ephemeral classroom settings. His sights are set on long-term pedagogical potential and social practice. Much like tusovka, he sees art in a socially critical role in the evolution of the democratic experiment, currently weakened worldwide: art schools must consider their institutional role in support of democracy. He follows Carol Becker's writings that we are witnessing a return of the artist to society, a return to the artist as citizen, and the return of art to society, and he believes the artist's creative critical thinking tools are pivotal to democracy. Art students need access to training in other disciplines, and this, he says, should be regarded as the beginning of a lifelong intellectual journey: "[T]his is about generating public intellectuals, visual scholars, and *artist citizens*: active cultural workers who participate in global society,"[8] and "art schools should be the conscience of the art world."[9] Pujol is no stranger to interdisciplinarity: he studied psychology and literature while doing undergrad work in the humanities and visual arts and went on to study Spanish art history and then philosophy at a seminary. He later pursued graduate work in education, art therapy, and communications and media theory, finishing with a master of fine art.

My interest in tusovka and The Field School were initiated by stories told to me of teenage life in the 1940s at rural boarding schools for peasants (*escuela normal rural*), especially the one in Tamazulapan, Oaxaca. Many students from that era then went on to attend government-funded Teacher's Colleges (*escuela normal para maestros*). The Federation of Socialist Peasant Students of Mexico (FECSM) is the oldest student organization in the country, the inheritor of Centralized Democracy, and the supporter of theories by Marx, Lenin, and Engels. The entity is currently fighting the closure of the seventeen remaining rural schools throughout the Mexican Republic.

But, for the students, it is not only a school: it is their "home, family, and educational opportunity; and more than that: an opportunity at life."[10] The schools have been swimming against the current since they were founded in 1922: governments have always eyed them with suspicion, often referring to them as "greenhouses for guerrilla activity," but FECSM (founded in 1934) maintains they teach critical, analytical, and reflexive thinking by revealing injustice and teaching peasants and workers about their rights. Peasants of the 1940s saw the boarding schools - complete with dining halls and full scholarships - as an opportunity for a better life (Fig. 4). They are essentially self-sufficient farms complete with poultry, swine, goats, and sheep; fields of corn, wheat, and sorghum, as well as orchards; carpentry and metal workshops; cultural clubs (*rondalla*, *trio*, tropical music groups, and dance); and sports activities (soccer, basketball, volleyball, track and field, and swimming). They seek to be sustainable, self-sufficient cooperatives, each having about sixty students who perform the work. Students study socialist economics, problems facing Mexican peasants, the critique of solutions from a socialist standpoint, socialist orientation, and worker-peasant legislation. However, when students leave as certified teachers, they do not merely teach villagers to read and write; rather, they also act as doctors, handypeople, farmers, carpenters, metalsmiths, and so on, depending on the need of the village.

The system rejects "assessors," so that older students mentor new ones in order to remain loyal to the structure and objectives; no one assesses them, neither teachers nor authorities. The prerequisite for admission is simple: you must be poor and come from a family that works in agriculture. Selection is carried out not only by provincial and federal educational authorities, but also by the students themselves, who ensure the newcomers fit the criteria; many of them are Indigenous or *mestizo*. Former students - now in their eighties and nineties - do not idealize their time there (they speak of long hours, hard work, and intermittent hunger), but many went on to teach at government elementary schools across the Republic. Many of the rural boarding schools were closed after the student uprisings in 1968 so, as of 2008, only seventeen have survived, with two of these currently being threatened.

The notions of Russian tusovka, Pujol's Field School and the rural peasant schools in Mexico, recall the brilliant yet polemical ideas of Ivan Illich: he advocated deinstitutionalization in favour of more *convivial forms* of education where celebration, open-endedness, and egalitarianism were paramount for lifelong learning. He vied for "engendering a lifestyle which will enable us to be spontaneous, independent, yet related to each other,"[11] and to this end, his life was dedicated to showing how institutionalized education has come to obscure and undermine the value of everyday or vernacular forms. He critiques the process of institutionalization, experts and expertise, commodification, and counter-productivity, in short, the messianic principle that schools and institutions can in fact educate.

Illich was no stranger to Mexico. He began as a priest in one of the poorest neighbourhoods of New York, home to many Puerto Ricans. He then worked in Puerto Rico before moving to Cuernavaca, Mexico, in 1961 to establish the *Centro Intercultural de Documentación* (Intercultural Documentation Centre), which was essentially part research centre offering language courses to missionaries and part free university for intellectual hippies from across the Americas. Although dispatched by the Vatican, Illich soon began teaching missionaries not to impose their cultural values but instead to identify themselves as guests in the host country. After ten years of critical analysis of the Church's actions, the Centre soon found itself in conflict with the Vatican and closed in 1976 in order to avoid the side effects of formal academia and institutionalization. By that time, Illich had left the priesthood but continued to be popular among leftist intellectuals.

The concepts fiesta (Bakhtin's carnival, Kristeva's jouissance), hanging out (tusovka), disciplines, boundaries, territories (Pujol's Field Schools, Mitchell's indiscipline), and conviviality (rural boarding schools, Illich's writings) all had a profound effect on both my artwork and teaching while in Mexico between 1991 and 1994, and then again between 1998 and 2007. Immersed in Spanish, I began working with language as a structure determining position and power, seeking to subvert its authority by creating installations that employed carnival, jouissance, and fiesta, in short, humour and unexpected plays on words. My installations have become gatherings that lack identifiable structures and hierarchies, and the work itself employs such popular supports as posters, flyers, and photocopies, laden with low-brow aesthetics. By creating convivial environments and applying the visual aesthetics of clip art and pop culture, I encourage a bit of "indiscipline" or, as Mitchell says, moments of "chaos and wonder." The environments I have created over the past ten years tend to look like parties or schoolrooms, and the pieces often invite the public to touch or interact with them (Fig. 5): weaving shoelaces through holes, eating apples provided free in bushels, stamping images with rubber stamps, or taking paper flyers home and then sending me an email. The public is *constructing* the piece with me. Indeed, as an art instructor, didactic-like materials with instructions riddle my work: my installations encourage a DIY philosophy akin to unschooling and autodidacticism.

Both Jean-François Lyotard and Suzi Gablik have written about heal-ing and *reconstruction*, respectively, in art, although Gablik has criticized Lyotard's fatalistic discourse on "hoping for nothing" (because the notion of hope is pointless, according to him). I nevertheless find some similarities between their ideas and feel that the *tusovkian* meeting, with its lack of hier-archical structure, allows for this positive response to the deconstruction so prevalent in the eighties and nineties. At one point, Lyotard says, "in these various invitations to suspend artistic experimentation, there is the same call to order, a desire for unity, identity, security, and popularity. [...] Artists and writers must be made to return to the fold of the community; or at least, if the community is deemed to be ailing, they must be given the responsibility of healing it."[12] Not only does this reinforce Pujol and Illich's ideas above, but it clearly ties in with Gablik's proposal for a reconstructive art that will reframe the world, one that will "make the transition from Eurocentric, patriarchal thinking [...] toward an aesthetics of interconnectedness, social responsibil-ity and ecological attunement."[13] She feels the new paradigm must be one of *participation* and of social relatedness (Fig. 6). Embracing this, my environ-ments were created to allow for harmonious interaction between disparate artistic proposals, one that remained open to all artistic investigations regard-less of theme, technique, or level of research.

Gilles Deleuze calls this being a *producer* rather than an author. He first catches our attention by quoting a Bob Dylan poem and commenting that, as a teacher, he would like to give a course in the same way Dylan organizes a song: as a producer rather than an author.[14] The latter, the author, is the model who regulates, recognizes, and judges - in short, an individual who ap-plies strategies to dominate outwardly from his site of power. Deleuze (and I) would rather be producers, those individuals who prepare at length but reject method, rules, and recipes in favour of finding, encountering, and stealing.

To support this, Deleuze ascertains that there are "no correct ideas, just ideas [...]. Just ideas: this is the encounter, the becoming, the theft and the nuptials [...]. You should not try to find whether an idea is just or correct. You should look for a completely different idea, elsewhere, in another area, so that something passes between the two, which is neither in one nor the other. Now, one does not generally find this idea alone; a chance is needed, or else someone gives you one. You don't have to be learned, to know or be familiar with a particular area, but to pick up this or that in areas which are very differ-ent."[15] Roland Barthes also does a pretty good job of de-throning the author, that great maestro whose genius is supposed to release a single theological meaning. He emphasizes that a "text consists of multiple writings, proceeding from several cultures and entering into *dialogue*, into parody, into contestation; but there is a site where this multiplicity is collected, and this site is not the author [...] but the reader [...] [T]he unity of a text is not in its origin but in its destination" [my emphasis].[16]

This becomes quite clear in the cultural environments where artists are "quoting" many sources, from art history to pop culture, from philosophy to flea markets. Nothing is new or original, everything is mixed and remastered, like the *post-production* ideas of Nicolas Bourriaud, like Bakhtin's writings on *dialogism*, like Kristeva's research on *intertextuality*. This last term is an activity that destabilizes narratives with its double-codedness, thereby blurring the line between what is true and what is not: fact can no longer be distinguished from fiction, nor constructed from the real. Thus, intertextuality implies *parody*, whose juxtaposition of styles and codes serves to question, disturb, and even subvert the dominance of established forms. What we see in the classroom is a play of styles and images that pervades the way students and artists speak and the art they produce, and indeed my own work emphasizes translations both literal and non-literal (Fig. 7).

In my work as a translator of Spanish to English between 1998 and 2006, finding the right words was key to creating a true yet non-literal translation. I tried to "rustle" rather than "stammer," concepts borrowed from Roland Barthes' *The Rustle of Language*: "the good functioning of the machine is displayed in a musical being: to rustle is to make audible the very evaporation of noise [...] rustle signifies that something, collectively, is working," whereas "stammering is a message spoiled twice over: it is the noise of language comparable to a motor that is not working properly."[17] Indeed, the entire paragraph of this quote became an interactive art piece, a spiral of porcelain letters that people could walk through and converse with (Fig. 8).

Bourriaud states that art today demands such a *conversation*. In fact, "the role of artworks is no longer to form imaginary and utopian realities, but to actually be ways of living and models of action within the existing real. [The artist] is a *tenant of culture*, to borrow Michel de Certeau's expression."[18] His writing on *relational aesthetics* is quite exciting as he proposes art as human interaction, a veritable de-throning of the work of art and subordination of the artist as genius. Bourriaud attributes this to the birth of a worldwide urban culture that has resulted in the urbanization of the artistic project in general. The gallery or museum space that was meant to be walked through has thus been transformed into a "period of time meant to be lived through,"[19] a place where being-together is a central concern for the devising of a collective meaning. Art, for Bourriaud, is a state of encounter. Isn't this

Russian *tusovka*, Pujol's Field School, Illich's conviviality at the Intercultural Documentation Centre, and even the Mexican rural peasant schools under ex-president Lázaro Cárdenas?

Steven H. Madoff defines artistic work in relation to social praxis and calls it *service aesthetics*. The practitioners of this art are not drawn to collective experience, but rather to the task of offering transactional sites that fill the landscape of the service economy: doctor's offices, clinics, hair salons, and shops. "The audience is not seen as an ad hoc participatory community [...] but each viewer is instead implicated as an individual participant [...] as a client to be served. [S]ervice aesthetics [...] attempts to rescue the service act from anonymity, standardization, and indifference through personal attention and [...] claims for the sovereignty of personal agency, individuality, and difference. [T]he establishment of an ethical transactional gesture remains at the core."[20] The priority for these artists is to render an actual service in order to counter the uniformity of experience by looking inside its bureaucracy, its commercially charged insincerity, and its indifference. Service aesthetics affirms a sense of self for the individual client and offers a restorative space opened up in the institutional recontextualization of the service enterprise, and it points to art's ability to transform the world by dissolving the distinction between the artist and any other worker.

Creators of the Mexico City art project *Pinto mi raya*, husband and wife team Víctor Lerma and Mónica Mayer had been doing service aesthetics long before the term was developed. They are predominantly performance artists trained in the seventies, Mónica having done a master's degree in sociology at Goddard College in the United States. In 1988, Víctor and Mónica formed *Pinto mi raya* - literally *I Draw My Line*, which refers to both drawing as an art medium while also referencing the sense of creating a limit. Finally, it is an idiomatic expression in both Spanish and English that means "I've had enough." A year later, Mónica began writing art reviews for *El Universal* newspaper, for which she still writes today, becoming a respected author in her own right and also publishing various books on art. As she began her career as an art critic, she wondered if anyone really read her columns; in fact, both she and Víctor noticed that a fair amount of art criticism was being written, but it was scattered throughout many newspapers. They decided to compile it all on a bi-weekly basis.

The largest achievement of this pair, among their many projects, is *Raya: Crítica y debate en las artes visuales* (Line: Critique and Debate in the Visual Arts). It is a bi-weekly publication that brings together between fifty and eighty critical texts on art published in twelve printed Mexican newspapers, as well as another eight online newspapers and blogs. In March of 1991, they produced the first two-week compilation of press clippings from all the newspapers, pasted on paper, photocopied, and bound into books. By May of that year - just three months later -, they had a system in place and were producing compilations every fortnight, then distributing them to libraries, museums, and art centres that had subscribed to their service. These included the Instituto de Investigaciones Estéticas de la UNAM, the Biblioteca de las Artes at the Centro Nacional de las Artes, Casa Lamm, Fundación Jumex, FEMSA, and the University of Monterrey. This shows the demand for art criticism (especially in Spanish) from cultural organizations and libraries, with their limited resources.

Over the years, they have come to know the writers, and their project remains strongly inclusive: they don't choose "good" or "bad" articles, but rather include everything related to visual arts so the reader can decide what is useful. With the change of millennium and a decade of newspaper clippings under their belts, in 2001 they decided to launch a research project called *Hurgando en el archivo* (Poking Through the Archive), in which they reviewed ten years of clippings to create compilations on different subjects: women artists, digital art, public art, photography, installation, art education, and performance, to name a few. This means that if someone is studying performance art, for example, that person will have information available, compiled by professionals, and won't have to sift through some 38,000 articles to compile it for him/herself. And they do indeed receive inquiries on a regular basis - in fact, many of their thematic compilations have resulted from such enquiries.

Why have they been doing this for twenty-three years? To "lubricate the art system"[21]: their archiving is intended to affect social intervention and boost education. *Raya: Crítica y debates en las artes visuales* functions thanks to the inefficiency of other institutions. In fact, they maintain that either the Biblioteca de las Artes at the Centro Nacional de las Artes or the Centro de Información y Documentación de Arte or the Instituto de Investigaciones Estéticas at the UNAM, all of which subscribe to their publication, should be allocating resources and finances to do this. Víctor does most of it virtually now, and on a part-time basis at that, so it is something these institutions could manage if they allocated resources to it.

Although they do not make money from the project, they do receive financial aid that ensures the majority of the population will have access to the archive: they apply for funding and have been supported by Bancomer and Canon to create specialized compilations. The former recently provided them with a large grant to digitize the compendiums, the objective being to donate them to twenty-five university art schools across the nation, they are pleased because it ensures the archive is dispersed throughout the country so people have access to it. Mónica states that *Pinto mi raya* is an act of resistance, a political act in response to the lack of information available in Mexico. It is an educational, non-profit project with a political message: it seeks to change the power relations within the guild and, in doing so, those in other guilds as well. It is a friendly questioning of power structures and a way of constructing a social fabric.

Mónica led performance workshops at the Escuela Nacional de Pintura, Escultura y Grabado "La Esmeralda" (ENPEG), located within the Centro Nacional de las Artes (CNA). She wrote reviews of my work and exhibitions, and therein began a relationship with *Pinto mi raya* and a great respect for the work they do. Their socialist interests in collective meaning-making and shared cultural experiences aligned with my art production and research into interdisciplinary activities, conviviality, tusovka, artist citizens, and carnivalism, all used to subvert official culture. Indeed, *Pinto mi raya* even harkened back to the rural peasant schools I learned about from fellow Mexicans.

In conclusion, Argentinian artists Roberto Jacoby's *Proyecto Venus* (*Venus Project*) sums up the concepts in this chapter. Born in 1944, he was one of the first in Latin America to form groups in which artists worked together. Between 2000 and 2006, Jacoby conceived of and developed a network of artists and non-artists brought together in the *Venus Project*. This was defined as a social experiment with a network of almost 500 people with diverse social backgrounds and education. Using a currency called the "venus," these people exchanged symbolic or material goods to undertake a variety of projects together.

The *Venus Project* drew its force from the conviction that collaboration between two or more people resulted in the formation of a post-individual identity, a collective intelligence that was richer in possibilities than the individual one. Toni Negri, upon learning of the project at a barbecue hosted by Jacoby in Buenos Aires in 2003, aptly called it a public lodge (a kind of tusovka): there are no prerequisites for taking part in the game; rather, the proposal is open to anyone willing to participate.

Much in the same way sociologist Roberto Jacoby's *Venus Project* encouraged the art of connecting people, my work interweaves artist and public, crossing symbolic borders and multiplying opportunities for fertile encounters. Jacoby called this a catalyst for global dialogue and coined it a "technology of friendship."

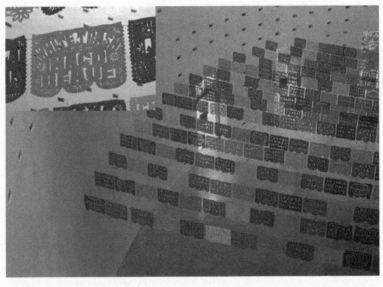

Figure 1. *Better Left Unsaid*, 2005, 15"x19", measurements variable. 48 distinct designs hand-cut from plastic banners, called punched plastic. Interactive element: banners are available for sale by the sheet for a nominal fee. Galería de la Universidad Iberoamericana, Mexico City, 2005. Photo by Andrés Olmos.

Papel picado is a traditional festive decoration in Mexico and, depending on the holiday, different images and/or words are cut out of the paper or plastic to create colourful banners. *Better Left Unsaid* looks festive, but upon reading the words on each banner, the viewer is bullied in Spanish, English, and French with double entendres. The desire is to celebrate those whose visions cross geographical, religious, gender, sexual, racial, and political borders - to transcend borders.

red skin piel roja peau rouge, indian red rojo indio, yellow chale jaune, half breed moreno café au lait, whitie cara blanca blanc bec, pinko socialo, black negrillo noire, red rojo rouge, brown noser sanguijuela lèche-cul, green verde vert, pigs judas flic, dog perra chienne, cow vaca grosse vache, coon pata rajada bur, frog franchute, bitch pute, chick chiquita souris, pussy gata chatte, chicken gallina poulemouillée, slut zorra pétasse, bunny conejo bimbo, dinks riquillo bourge, trailer-parker lumpen, blue-collar ganapan prolo, white trash naco beauf, chacha boniche, yuppie junior bobo, commie rojillo coco, yes-mn chupamedias lèche-bottes, tree hugger ecoloco ecolo, granola baba, right winger derechista facho, politico polaco, fairy puñal fifre, queen reina tante, queer mariposón folle, butch trailera camionneur, dyke tortillera lesbo, baby nen nana, little lady mujercita, gal tipa, witch bruja, doll muñeca poupée, dick verga bite, cunt concha garce, nosey metiche comère, asshole ojete trou du cul, cheapo codo radin.

Figure 2. *Polyphonic Novel (title after Bakhtin)*, 2006-07, variable dimensions. 516 rubber stamps produced with all images from Webster's Ninth New Collegiate Dictionary in English, stamp pads, paper, bulletin board, tacks. Interactive element: the public creates designs with the stamps, hangs some on the bulletin board, and takes others home. Ex-Teresa Arte Alternativo, Mexico City, 2007, second photo by Gerardo Toledo.

As a translator from Spanish to English, my favourite English dictionary is *Webster's Ninth New Collegiate Dictionary* because of its 516 drawings used to define lesser-known objects in a concise, didactic way. For *Polyphonic Novel*, a rubber stamp for each of the 516 drawings was produced. They were made available to the public to "construct" visual stories by stamping on coloured pieces of paper. This piece was shown on two occasions in Mexico, where Spanish-speaking audiences worked in English - an English lesson but with images. However, many of the images are also unknown to English speakers because they are images of objects that are difficult to define with just words.

Figure 3. *Tusovkian Meetings*, 2010, variable dimensions. Series of 10 colouring blocks containing 516 images from the Webster's Ninth New Collegiate Dictionary (multiple copies made so the public can take some away with them), wax crayons, tables and chairs, school-room environment. Interactive element: visitors sit at a table and colour the blocks, and then take one with them. Red Head Gallery, Toronto, 2010.

The effectiveness of the participant in tusovka meetings and projects is "achieved through individual flexibility and acceptance of the other."[22] In my installation *Tusovkian Meetings*, 516 images from the *Webster's Ninth New Collegiate Dictionary* were compiled in ten colouring books. Each of the 516 object words was translated into Spanish so that an anglophone audience - such as the one in Toronto where the piece was first exhibited - could learn another language while colouring. The dictionary's black and white line drawings lent themselves to a colouring book format, which alludes to leisure but also didactic workbooks for children. Visitors were encouraged to take a set of ten blocks with them so they would have the entire alphabet.

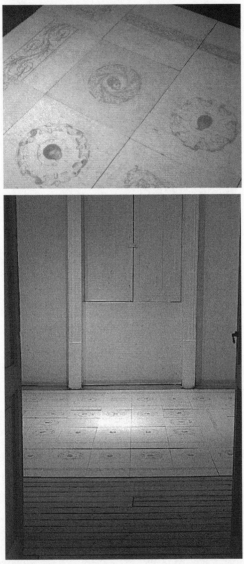

Figure 4. *Restricted to Those Pleasures and Desires Inscribed within the Encyclopaedia of Mandatory Good Taste (title after Oscar Wilde)*, 2002, 5'x9'. Floor covering made of 99 vinyl tiles mounted on wood, photographs from the 1950s and 60s (from the "Social" sections of Mexican newspaper archives, now sold to flea market vendors), photocopies, turpentine transfer. Interactive element: with proper fastening to the floor, people can remove their shoes and walk on this piece. MUCA-Roma, Mexico City, 2002.

On Sundays, the hundreds of vendors display wares in a Mexico City flea market called *La Lagunilla* (The Little Lagoon). In the antique section, there are defunct photographic archives from newspapers, especially photos from the "Social" sections. The photographs from the 50s and 60s showed beautiful women in bobs and beehives, black eyeliner, and taffeta. There were no names noted on the back. The photographs were displayed on fabric laid on the ground, which inspired me to work with vinyl tiles as a domestic floor surface. Using turpentine, their portraits were transferred to the tiles with Victorian decorative designs positioned around them so they became embellishments adorning a functional surface that people could walk on.

Figure 5. *Wallflowers*, 2003, variable dimensions. Handmade plaster filigree based on Colonial decoration in Mexican homes (silicon moulds made from wood filigree purchased at Home Mart, Mexico City). Interactive element: bins of plaster filigree are in the exhibition space so people can take pieces from them and add to the installation on the floor; people are also welcome to take a piece of filigree home with them. Ex-Teresa Arte Alternativo, Mexico City, 2007, Photo by Andrés Olmos.

Colonial houses in Mexico City have floral cornices running along the top of the walls. Today, many colonial buildings are in decay. American hardware chains have popped up all over Mexico City, and in the early twenty-first century, Mexicans began bypassing the *ferreterías* (family-owned, neighbourhood hardware shops) that once served people. At the larger chains, you can find wooden filigree that imitates the plaster floral cornices in Colonial homes - you simply glue it on and paint it white to look like plaster. Purchasing all the designs from Home Mart, I made silicon moulds and began a production line, essentially returning to the artisanal way of producing the decorations. *Wallflowers* covers walls and fills rooms with plaster flowers and leaves as if they were imposing their aristocratic status on old buildings. But upon closer inspection, the pieces are crumbling, alluding to past times and decaying infrastructures.

Figure 6. *Vast Regions of Domain (title after Michel de Certeau)*, 2011, each banner measures 48" x 36". Series of 20 digital drawings printed on vinyl scrim banners: surgical diagrams from the fifties and theoretical texts on language in three languages. Museo de Arte Moderno Chiloe, Castro, Chile, 2012. Interactive element: each of the 20 printed vinyl designs have also been printed on small sheets of papers as flyers; people can take a set of flyers home, read them, discover my email on them, and send me a note.

There is a rich printing tradition in Mexico (both offset and screen-printing), the Santo Domingo neighbourhood in the Colonia Centro being the hub for invitations and flyers. *Volantes*, or flyers, are handed out in the streets, placed on windshields, or put in mailboxes. They are typically used to advertise neighbourhood repair shops. At the same time, there is a strong tradition of painted signs and vinyl scrim banners. *Vast Regions of Domain* uses the flyer and banner to "advertise" the challenges of language and communication via these popular formats. On one side of the flyer are images of mouth, tongue, and neck surgeries taken from 1950s medical books found at used bookstores on Avenida Álvaro Obregón in the Colonia Roma. These surgical techniques allude to a preference for excision rather than curing: removal and elimination of contaminated matter rather than preventative approaches. The quotes on the back philosophize about language and meaning.

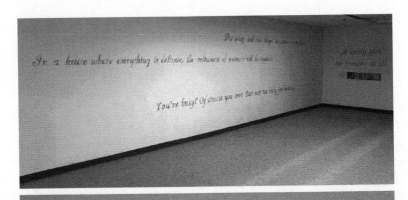

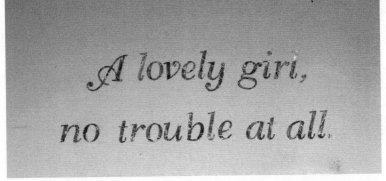

Figure 7. *Words of Wisdom and Verbal Abuse*, 2003-04, variable dimensions. Series of 4 wall texts from 4 books, letters cut from plastic Mexican tablecloths. DNA Art Space, London, Canada, 2013.

Texts read:

A lovely girl, no trouble at all. From Janet Frame. An Autobiography. New Zealand, 1955.

You're busy? Of course you are! But not too busy for beauty. From Kate Aitken. Lovely You. Toronto: Wm. Collins Sons & Co. Ltd., 1951.

But nobody could climb through that pattern - it strangles so. From Charlotte Perkins Gilman. "The Yellow Wallpaper" (1891). *Black Water 2*, Alberto Manguel, ed. Toronto: Lester & Orpen Dennys, 1990.

In a house where everything is delicate, the refinement of manners will be acquired. From Oscar Wilde. "Decoración doméstica" (1882). *Conferencia a los estudiantes de arte y otros ensayos. Mexico*: UNAM, 1986.

Floral oilcloths are used to cover tables in market food stalls, popular *cantinas, fondas* (small family luncheon places), and road-side food stalls. The tablecloths are sold by the metre in bright designs. The patterns reference the female domain and its connection to the home, and this in turn reveals social status, class, and good taste. The chosen texts are from writers Janet Frame and Charlotte Perkins Gilman - both encountering challenges in their time as women writers - as well as Oscar Wilde writing on good taste and Kate Aitken, on being a good housewife in the 50s. They are comments on the power of the word to create scripts for all to live by. The fonts of the four phrases were chosen for their curving, rounded lines, alluding to femininity and good penmanship. From afar, the scripts appear to be beautiful, scrolling decorations, but upon a closer look, we notice the phrases are cut from humble oilcloth, typical of the popular classes.

Figure 8. *Stammer and Rustle* (title after Roland Barthes), 2006-07, 20' diameter. Spiral on floor made of porcelain letters; the public can walk to the centre and make new words from the pile of letters. Interactive element: the public walks through the spiral and, upon arriving in the centre, can make words out of the pile of porcelain letters found there. Ex-Teresa Arte Alternativo, Mexico City, 2007, photos Gerardo Toledo and Andrés Olmos.

The spiral spells out a quote from Michel de Certeau's text on tactics versus strategies. The letters are made of natural white porcelain with a clear glaze, each letter measuring about eight inches high. The spiral is large enough to permit an adult to enter and walk to the centre of it. The spiral alludes to tornadoes and their all-consuming action, which I compare to the power of language. In contrast to the possible devastation of this natural phenomenon, the porcelain letters emphasize the fragility of the institution of language. The text spelt out is the following:

Speech is irreversible. What has been said cannot be unsaid, except by adding to it: to correct, here, is, oddly enough, to continue. In speaking, I can never erase, annul; all I can do is say "I am erasing, annulling, correcting," in short, speak some more. This annulation-by-addition I shall call 'stammering.' Stammering is a message spoiled twice over: it is the noise of language comparable to a motor that is not working properly. Similarly, the good functioning of the machine is displayed in a musical being: the rustle. The rustle is the noise of what is working well. The rustle denotes a limit-noise, an impossible noise, the noise of what has no noise; to rustle is to make audible the very evaporation of noise: the tenuous, the blurred. It trembles and rustles: in short, it works, and it works well and this rustle signifies that something, collectively, is working.[23]

Chapter 14

You Look at Me, I Look at You: Urban Space and Identity Reciprocity in the Work of Catherine Bodmer[1]

Nuria Carton de Grammont
Translated from the Spanish by Paula Secco Hoyos

Post-NAFTA imagined identities

Since the implementation of the North American Free Trade Agreement (NAFTA), not only have economic relations between Mexico and Canada been consolidated but cultural ties between the two nations have been strengthened as well. For twenty years, this partnership has promoted a cultural cooperation that encourages the mobility of artists from one country to the other and boosts attendance at festivals, book fairs, residencies, and other events. Such exchanges have set off a dialogue among institutions, artists, and audiences that brings face to face these countries' respective views of one another and contributes to the formation of a cultural identity that could be called "post-NAFTA," which has emerged in response to this new bloc of economic, political, and cultural power. In addition to the free movement of goods and capital, the agreement ushered in a new productive culture, while at the same time creating a flow of narratives driven by global dynamics that gave rise to a redefinition of identity in national projects.

According to Saskia Sassen, globalization brings not only the transmigration of capital, but at the same time it also opens a space for the transmigration of cultural forms and the reterritorialization of "local" subcultures.[2] A new debate arises in this context over whether the globalization and integration of North America would engender a loss of national identity via its creation of a homogenizing impulse, or just the opposite, i.e., strengthen local cultures. Since the signing of NAFTA, this question has been answered through numerous case studies; it is clear, however, that globalization has brought about a release from traditional identities, in turn generating new notions of belonging and community.[3] In this regard, Néstor García Canclini wondered what it might take to carry out the changes in identity and culture that our international integration will require at this stage of globalization.[4] To answer this, he examined the risks in moving beyond a tired museum culture, dusty from the changeless hush that comes with protecting the viewer from any sort of social confrontation: "There was a period when identity seemed to become trapped inside of the museums. Imitations of a complete and coherent presentation of each nation's culture were staged in them. The displays and galleries assigned an order to the scattered elements, erratic practices and dissident traditions, seemingly unifying them in a polite, amiable entity."[5] However, with the transnational circulation of culture and art, which are finding new exhibition spaces outside the traditional "white cube" museum gallery, the question initially raised by Canclini is revised through a post-NAFTA aesthetic that questions national imageries and sets out to redefine cultural identities.

In the post-NAFTA climate of cultural mobility, North America forms a bloc that strategically seeks to strengthen its cultural ties. Mexico has an intertwined historical relationship with the United States, to a large extent because of the shared border; but NAFTA created a relatively new relationship with Canada, involving new political challenges and economic responsibilities. On the one hand, Mexico stopped being part of the Latin American conglomerate in order to become an equal member, it was believed, of this powerful trio. On the other, for Canada this stage represented a departure from "occidentalism" in order to open doors to new regions, and particularly to the Southern Cone through Mexico, as suggested by Sarah Smith.[6] But beyond the use of art and culture from the perspective of diplomatic rapprochement, there emerged with mutual recognition a curiosity to know who these "other" neighbours were. In this context, the province of Quebec was chosen as a guest of honour at the 2003 Guadalajara International Book Fair (FIL). The honouring of the autonomy of this Canadian province and its francophone tradition helped to consolidate relations formed over several years of cultural rapprochement between the two nations, according to Culture Minister Diane Lemieux's declaration.[7] Not only was this a memorable occasion to present an overview of what the culture of the self-proclaimed "Latinos of the North" had to offer, but with it, too, as Lemieux added, "Mexico now occupies a prominent place in the imagination of Quebecers."[8]

Catherine Bodmer[9] was one of the artists to represent Quebec in the Vitae exhibition, held during the "Voilà Québec en México!" festival as part of the FIL's cultural activities. However, her installation sought to challenge the imaginary of the Canadian identity and what it represents overseas. To this versatile and multidisciplinary artist, the identity construction of the landscape would become a recurrent theme to be deconstructed and reconstructed through various media, particularly photography. Through the urban spaces of Mexico City, specifically the median strips that divide the wide avenues of the capital or the rooftops of buildings and houses, the artwork challenges the way we look at the Other from the viewpoint of globalization and makes us turn this gaze toward ourselves. Bodmer's work is this chapter's point of departure, a case study, reflecting on North-South cultural relations and the construction of national identities in the post-NAFTA era, that discusses the question of how "you view me and I view you" through this shared imagery.

Globalization and pine forests

In 2003, ten female artists from Quebec were invited to take part in a live exhibit in the rooms of the Hotel Isabel, a colonial-era building in the historic centre of Mexico City converted into an alternative exhibition space. For Janet Bellotto,[10] curator of the above-mentioned Vitae exhibition, the aim was to bring face to face the ideas of mobility and displacement in the experience of international artists whose production is continually carried out in a foreign context. How do you "make art" in a city you do not know? What resources are there? What can you say for a city that you are seeing for the very first time?

To answer these questions, Bodmer addresses cultural clichés that set nationalities into simplistic categories through her installation Desinfectado (2003) (Fig. 1). In international imagery, Canada embodies a vast, untamed nature, a virgin territory safeguarded by park rangers who look after the wild animals. Guided by this notion, she will transform her installation room into an artificial forest of aromatic pine trees using synthetic rear-view mirror air fresheners to mask the surrounding odours with their fragrance. Its scenery will be as artificial as the cultural stereotype it represents. Each pine tree will be carefully hung from the ceiling in a transparent plastic bag, into which Bodmer also inserts a pubic hair, noticeable at close range. The gesture undermines the politically correct mentality in Canadian imagery and strikes a blow at the conformist impulses of a context of aseptic modernity.

According to Catherine Bodmer, the excessive consumption of detergents, disinfectants, and air fresheners in Western culture reveals the fantasy of a fully controlled environment in which any risk of exposure to

Figure 1. Catherine Bodmer. *Desinfectado*. 2003. Photograph. Colour. Reproduced with permission of the artist.

foreign bodies is avoided, where cleanliness is mingled with moral and social values: "My attention is particularly directed toward daily rituals and obsessions concerned with cleaning and purifying as being significant for the construction of identity, not only on an individual level, but also as a culture or as a society."[11] Bodmer has scented galleries by vaporizing the room with the fresh clean smell of freshly-laundered clothes,[12] has transformed exhibition spaces into seas of soap powder,[13] and has even spread gold dust in abandoned hospitals, thus sanctifying their contaminated environment.[14] For art critic Jim Drobnick, the hygienic obsession questioned in Bodmer's work exposes our intolerance to bodily decomposition, to the Other who does not smell like me, toward the culturally unknown: "Conditions of purity - whether regarding laundry, gallery space, or a building's air conditioning apparatus - rely upon acts of exclusion, acts that easily drift towards intolerance if not also extermination, when physical or medical ideas of purification become the model for cleansing operations on moral or ethnic levels."[15]

Over the course of the exhibition's three weeks, the artists will sleep with their installations in their rooms at the Hotel Isabel. Nearly succumbing to intoxication from the scent of more than five hundred pine trees sponsored by the Car-Freshner Corporation - producer of the famous "Little Trees Air Freshener"[16] - Bodmer highlights with irony the political dimension of sanitizing identities, cleansed of all social and ethnographic conflict, which distort cultural subjectivity. The representation of these cultural stereotypes recreates the prefabricated imageries sold to foreign countries, while the pubic hair contaminates the space and apparent harmony of national identities. With her pine forest, Catherine Bodmer responds to the stereotyped contemplation of the Other upon its own self, upon its own culture, constructed out of the common space of global identities.

Interstitial spaces

Bodmer would return to Mexico seven years later: first, with a scholarship from the "Échanges d'artistes et d'ateliers-résidences Québec-Mexique" program, jointly overseen by the Conseil des arts et des lettres du Québec (CALQ, Quebec's arts council) and the Fondo Nacional para la Cultura y las Artes (FONCA, Mexico's National Fund for Culture and the Arts);[17] and second, with a four-month stay at the newly inaugurated arts and new media centre, Centro ADM, which is creating an international artist-in-residence program in Mexico City.[18] During these two residencies, Bodmer's objective was to produce a series of photographs that would capture the uniqueness of the urban landscape of this Mexican megalopolis.

La Casa del Escritor, where she stayed during her first residency, is located near the Casa Azul (Blue House), where Frida Kahlo was born and lived for several years with the muralist Diego Rivera, in the historic district of Coyoacán. More than anyone else, these two figures have embodied the representation of Mexico abroad with their avant-garde art, which teems with both folklore and suffering. Like the iconic Canadian forest and its roaming wild animals, Frida and Diego embody the picturesque Mexico of postcards with its colonial architecture; its craft markets and local food; and its squares and tree-lined cobblestone streets, with weeping willows and jacarandas. Bodmer slips away from this handy area of cultural heritage, instead focusing her residency on a variety of interstitial urban spaces supporting an uncertain but necessary use in everyday life in the city: the median strips, or camellones, which divide the expressways of Mexico City.[19] The typical Mexico fades away behind these seemingly anonymous and depersonalized public places, which might appear in any part of the world where urban modernization had been introduced via major road axes. The result of Bodmer's work will be published in her and Charron's book, *Catherine Bodmer: Mexico DF (détails)*.[20]

These stretches dividing the main roads of the capital represent small oases of trees and grasses amidst a desert of concrete, and their uses vary depending on the streets and neighbourhoods in which they are located. Some serve as walkways, while others are used as makeshift parks. Some of these spaces host transmission towers, while elsewhere access to them is prohibited for safety reasons due to traffic. Many are adorned with jacarandas, eucalyptus, coral trees, magueys, or other kinds of vegetation that can withstand the relentless hustle and bustle of cars passing at full speed on either side. Bodmer rescues these forsaken green interstices and examines these spaces as precarious habitats stranded between avenues.

Currently, these medians are intermediate spaces that elude the intransigent and accelerated rhythm of the city, the so-called "cult of speed," as Paul Virilio would say - parenthetical spaces in the empire of movement and capitalization of time that the motorist imposes.[21] They often represent a pause, a break, for the pedestrians crossing the streets, and are also places of congregation for informal business, of exchange between street vendors and motorists, of encounter and social tension. Neither transit route nor pedestrian walkway, they are places without a defined use, improvised instead in multiple ways, often at the margins of norms of urban regularization. For Bodmer, these urban interstices, deprived of any tourist significance or patrimonial heritage, would be the starting point to dust off the identities showcased in the context of post-NAFTA globalization, and to reflect upon the gaze of the One facing the Other.

The depopulated metropolis

In addition to her installations, Catherine Bodmer is recognized for her photography, which is characterized by elaborate, almost sculptural work in which she digitally alters the details of each composition in order to unfold a landscape distinct from the original.[22] In this manner, she has appropriated ordinary landscapes of every kind for use in constructing optical illusions that reflect impossible situations: fictional views of ice skaters, bicycles and water games,[23] depicted in infinite reproductions of Möbius strips.[24] Her compositions multiply like a kaleidoscope in diptychs, triptychs, and other kinds of mirror play wherein the landscape seems to be just what it is, while at the same time something else. Bodmer's photography represents a variable entity, a flexible, dynamic material that enables the creation of a new narrative about the places it represents. Through her postproduction process, she digitally denatures her photographs to give them a meaning that differs from the reality they represent.

In her *Río Churubusco (Circuito Interior)* (2010) series (Fig. 2),[25] Bodmer reclaims the median strip along *Avenida Churubusco*, also called the *Circuito Interior* (Inner Loop), which, in its forty-two-kilometre loop, is the only highway connecting neighbourhoods and districts in the central and southern sections of the Mexican capital. Initially, Bodmer captures three trees from different angles on the median dividing the avenue. Later, she manipulates the urban habitat, beginning with the trees' foliage, various advertisements, and the avenue itself, in order to transform the original nature of the space and create four versions of each tree. In this way, she achieves a syntax of twelve images, which bears a strange resemblance across the calculated medians to the well-balanced trees, the coordinated advertisements. With this effect, she recreates the landscape of Mexico City, and, like a city planner, designs her own master plan, erasing the contingencies, overseeing the details, and planning a new order. This strange, artificial harmony moves away from the documentary genre to create a fictitious landscape. The city is unrecognizable, now cleansed of the traffic, the noise, and the people who walk every day along this indispensable artery for metropolitan traffic and mobility. A paradox lies in the symmetrical relationship of an urbanism that, now freed from its regular agitation, seems as comfortable and effective as the imaginary of modernity that gave rise to it.

The Circuito Interior was built under Regent Ernesto P. Uruchurtu, who, during his administration (1952-66), sought to reform the city according to a modern urban plan. Modernity arrived in the country via what became known as the "Mexican miracle," with the aim of making the capital a model by which Mexico might project an image of economic and social stability abroad.[26] This modernization project promised to overcome urban anarchy through a choreography of avenues and main roads that would extend its tentacles throughout the city to ease transportation. To Rachel Kram Villarreal, Uruchurtu, also called the "Iron Regent,"[27] "sought to bring order to the chaos of the modern city

Figure 2. Catherine Bodmer. *Río Churubusco (Circuito Interior)*, detail. 2010. Series of photographs. Colour. Ink jet print. Reproduced with permission of the artist.

by imposing restrictions on building and through moralization and sanitation initiatives."[28] This sanitizing impulse embodied a national policy based on the quest for a modern identity using technology to bring about the domination of nature and remodelling of urban infrastructure. In Haussmannesque style, Uruchurtu's plan was unfaltering in applying an authoritarian urbanization, including the destruction of entire neighbourhoods, deforestation, and the disappearance of green areas, in order to build a system of wide avenues and main roads to lend the old Aztec capital an air of modernity. A spatial rearrangement was applied to modernize the city according to Louis Sullivan's famous slogan, "form follows function," envisioning a social order purged of chaos, folklore, poverty, and post-revolutionary idiosyncrasies.[29] The title of Bodmer's work, *Río Churubusco (Circuito Interior)* (2010), reminds us of the existence of a river that once passed by there, now "intubated" under the medians in the name of progress.[30]

Although at first sight Catherine Bodmer's landscapes seem consistent and effective, they contain inconsistencies that obfuscate the uses of the urbanism they represent. Marie-Ève Charron states, "While symmetrical effects seem to be part of urban planning, when introduced into the image, they create dysfunctional incongruities that deflect the intended usefulness of the facilities depicted."[31] Looking closely at the image, doubt inevitably sets in, bringing with it the question, is it possible for a city like this to exist? In an overpopulated city like Mexico, this deserted moonscape devoid of its daily life stands in contrast to the contemporary reality. In turn, Bodmer's images inject a synthetic and apparently functional urban plan, with her digitally in-balance trees or the artificial scent of her pine forest. Without the avenue's usual hubbub, the purified city appears cleansed of all social, ethnographic, and cultural conflict.

The landscape is constructed through an optical illusion that repeats itself and unfolds infinitely like a Möbius strip, bringing into focus a third setting that creates a crossroads between reality and fiction. As Rebecca E. Biron explains, "The scholar, traveller, or resident moves in a single moment and forms a single perspective into different levels and layers of the connections that destabilize the difference between the real city and the imagined city."[32] Under this particular epistemology, Bodmer transcends the original narratives of the urban space and of the photographic space in order to examine the perception of what one looks at and how one looks at it. The objective is to destabilize the preconceiving gaze of the viewer in order to challenge its place in the space of representation.

Uses and disuses

The median strips, which originally had a pragmatic function - to divide the large avenues, or to re-channel rivers - today possess a new urban identity, which marks the transition between the modern city as imagined by the Iron Regent, Ernesto Uruchurtu, and the explosion of the megalopolis in the context of the emergence of the "global city" as the terrain of a new economic order, according to Saskia Sassen.[33] Their repurposing is part of a neoliberal policy focused on the rehabilitation of abandoned spaces, industrial spaces, places inhabited by the poor, places of informal trade, and secluded areas sensitive to danger - a policy that has been imposed on various cities in the world.

In her series of *Camellones* (2010), Catherine Bodmer displays these passageways stranded between avenues - recreational parks with games, sport fields, walkways, and benches - to reveal their diverse social uses and the new dynamics of their reappropriation. In an era of urban overcrowding and lack of space, these interstices take on a new civic value and a potential for development to improve the living quality of large cities. So called "Pocket Parks," which maximize public, recreational, and green spaces in dense cities, have been converted into a successful export model.[34] Under

319

this model of urban recycling, the High Line park in Manhattan has reclaimed an old urban train line, in disuse since the 1980s, as the setting for an elevated park more than two kilometres long, allowing visitors to discover the city from its various historic sites, while boosting property development in the area.[35] This policy of gentrification of areas considered to be "deteriorating," which has also been applied to Mexico City, has transformed the capital's urban landscape in many ways.[36]

In Bodmer's images, however, such recycled spaces remain far from being tourist attractions, as they respond to the needs of self-urbanized, working-class neighbourhoods such as the Pedregal de Santo Domingo, where *Avenida Pedro H. Ureña (Eje 10 Sur)* (Fig. 3) is located,[37] where the median is set up as a walkway for the local community. This lower-class neighbourhood was built during what José Iñigo Aguilar Medina called "the largest invasion of urban land in Latin America,"[38] undertaken in the early 1970s by some one hundred families from the countryside who settled in Coyoacán, a volcanic area at the south end of Mexico City.[39] Relying on a social process of self-management and self-organization beyond the scope of state-planning policies, this mass of poor, homeless persons managed to urbanize this hostile, rugged territory, thought of as uninhabitable prior to their arrival. In his book *Autoconstrucción*, the artist Abraham Cruzvillegas, who settled in the area with his family as a child, claims that this "aesthetic of urgency" responds to a permanent improvisation inasmuch as it lacks any plans or models and aims at finding solutions to meet the demands of everyday life in situations of poverty.[40] The stretch of Avenida Pedro H. Ureña, together with its median arrived alongside social movements that fought for the political recognition of this informal urbanism and that managed to "legalize" these neighbourhoods and, thereby, the construction of their access road, the Eje 10 Sur.

Figure 3. Catherine Bodmer. *Avenida Pedro H. Ureña (Eje 10 Sur)*, detail. 2010. Series of photographs. Colour. Ink jet print. Reproduced with permission of the artist.

Catherine Bodmer frames this urgency in her work, this need of the inhabitants who gradually, by various strategies, took over these long passageways with their own modernizing ambitions. On *Avenida de las Torres (Eje 6 Sur)* (Fig. 4), which bisects Iztapalapa -one of the world's largest self-urbanized boroughs, with a population of two million-, an empty park constructed to fend off the deserted elements doubles as a makeshift clothesline and a space for erecting informal tents, suggesting uses other than merely recreational ones.

Figure 4. Catherine Bodmer. *Avenida de las Torres (Eje 6 Sur)*, detail. 2010. Series of photographs. Colour. Ink jet print. Reproduced with permission of the artist.

Further on, atop the median of that same avenue, is installed the so-called *Tianguis Luis Méndez (Eje 6 Sur)* (Fig. 5), also known as the "Tianguis de las Torres" - one of the Mexican megalopolis's largest *tianguis* (street markets) - and home to hundreds of vendors, thus representing an option for people with lower incomes who come to buy smuggled or pirated merchandise and all manner of objects recycled from the capital's landfills.

Figure 5. Catherine Bodmer. *Tianguis Luis Méndez (Eje 6 Sur)*, detail. 2010. Series of photographs. Colour. Ink jet print. Reproduced with permission of the artist.

In their exhibit, *Libre Comercio* (2011), the Montreal artistic duo Patrick Dionne and Miki Gingras compiled a photographic record of the street-vendor kiosks of this popular *tianguis*.⁴¹ But while their recording of the assembly and disassembly of the kiosks was prompted by the informal economy's architectural ingenuity, Bodmer shows the landscape during off-hours, with the clear stillness of the median after the overwhelming market dynamism subsides. What remains is the silence of the well-trodden gravel, people in the distance collecting the remnants of garbage, and a perspective dominated by monumental transmission towers with their hanging wires that supply power to the city. Just a few blocks away, she photographed the abstract geometry of the aisles and walkways of *Parque Deportivo Cuitláhuac (Eje 6 Sur)* (Fig 6), which for many years festered as an old garbage dump in the eastern part of the city, later converted to a recreational area for the community.⁴²

Figure 6. Catherine Bodmer. *Parque Deportivo Cuitláhuac (Eje 6 Sur)*, detail. 2010. Series of photographs. Colour. Ink jet print. Reproduced with permission of the artist.

With her minimalist, balanced landscapes, Catherine Bodmer calls on us to reflect upon the specificity of the urban space with its appropriations and cultural transformations. Her images reflect the vicissitudes of a neoliberal policy that reinvents the modern utopia with new urban rehabilitation programs that respond to the needs of underdevelopment but that also find ways of projecting a global identity onto the city as it seeks to insert itself into the exigencies of the contemporary world.

Bodmer's images also demonstrate how, under a totally informal system of organization, these spaces are taken over, via ingenuity and despite precarity, for conversion into various social, recreational, or commercial uses. The space rebels against institutional domestication, assumes multiple functions and is assigned new values according to what Emilio Duhau and Angela Giglia have termed "the rules of disorder," the informal appropriation of urban space based on everyday life.[43] Far from the supposed "chaos" or "ungovernability" of the city, they consider the existence of various social orders or practices that exist simultaneously: "To understand the (dis)order of the metropolis involves entering into the operating methods of these diverse orders."[44] In this regard, the digital reordering that Bodmer proposes reveals the close relationship maintained between the city and its users. What is left revealed is the part the citizen plays in producing the landscape and thus in asserting her/his power as a reactivating agent of the space.

Casas

In her latest series, *Casas* (2010), Catherine Bodmer shows how these changes, adaptations, and reconfigurations of the metropolis also take place in the home. During her stay in Mexico City, she collected images of the roofs of the houses of various people she met, titling each image with the name of the tenant who granted her access along with the number of floors of the building. In this megalopolis deprived of green spaces, the roof is often an improvised place of leisure and rest, as for example the third floor of Ramiro's house where chairs, tables, and beer bottles exist side by side with gas tanks and satellite dishes. In the case of Guillermo, it is an open space where one can contemplate a seventh-floor panoramic view of the city. Susana's, however, on the fifth floor, represents an extension of the home where daily chores are carried out, such as washing and hanging out clothes. Despite the absence of tenants, in this domestic space there are vestiges of the various social classes of the capital living side by side. These are domestic perspectives that show the economic paroxysms and social contrasts that exist alongside each other in the city every day. They also demonstrate a model of urban development characteristic of the globalization out of which it is born, as stated by Jordi Borja, a "perverse combination between globalized enclaves of excellence and urban fragments of low citizen profile."[45] Bodmer's *Casas* reflect the contrast between the creation of ultra-modern spaces and the marginal areas where a precarious urbanism prevails, thus revealing the "increasingly evident division between 'insiders and outsiders,' " "class struggle in the territory," and the "asymmetric conflict" generated in such metropolises.[46]

The visual artifice of roofs and medians exposes this social asymmetry, which sets the absence of users in contrast with the domestic and recreational needs of this underdeveloped urbanism. However, far from painting the megalopolis as an urban leviathan, Bodmer accesses the space through a poetic sensibility whereby urban silence possesses an internal dimension, a form of reflection where "the banal and the sublime coexist," as Pascale Beaudet suggests.[47] In these sometimes desolate scenes, she recalls everyday life through the presence of a stray soccer ball, plays with the zigzag of the pedestrian path, erases flowers from the trees, duplicates children's slides, and conveys a fascination with the monumentality of transmission towers. Yet, as Beaudet observes, "Catherine Bodmer applies herself to divesting the landscape of the romanticism which often pervades it. Instead of denying its presence, she removes it from its reality, a more judicious strategy."[48] This digital removal allows us to capture the footprint, the trace, and the material memory of humanity in the space, as a result of past and present actions. Each space has a story built and reinvented by society, as M. Christine Boyer states: "Not only does the city's structure shift with time, but its representational form changes as well. [...] [T]he city has been represented in different ways: that is, different structural logics, call them aesthetic conventions that have been imposed for various reasons and at separate times upon the city's imagined (imaged) form."[49] Each historic moment invents an urban narrative that expresses the city's temporal and spatial palimpsest. The reconfiguration of the landscape is an image under permanent construction. In this regard, rather than unpopulated medians or ceilings, Bodmer depicts venues for meetings and disagreements, spaces of social asymmetries, both common and individual, interstitial spaces where another process of city production takes place.

Conclusion

According to Roland Barthes, "photography is the advent of myself as another: a cunning dislocation of the awareness of identity."[50] That dislocation refers undoubtedly not only to the identity that forms in ourselves when looking at a picture, or even when producing one, but to how we look at the Other, how we capture through the lens an essence that supposedly characterizes it. In that sense, Catherine Bodmer's photographs question the viewers' preconceived ideas about what they are observing, restoring their ability to reflect on the meaning of their own perception and the places represented. She alters her photographs to question who looks at whom and to examine how this looking happens as part of an illusion that causes an encounter with the Other. This Made-in-Canada Mexico is presented as an optical illusion that repeats itself and unfolds infinitely like a Möbius strip. The virtual space of Bodmer's images creates a contrast between the real city and the imagined one, the global and the local city, prompting us to think of identity as a complex cultural process. The construction of an interwoven, post-NAFTA cultural identity has been achieved through the cultural relationship launched between Mexico and Canada. Doreen Massey raises the idea of "a global sense of place," inferring that the identity of any place is not rooted simply in itself but is built largely through interdependent relationships with other places.[51] The work of Catherine Bodmer is part of such a framework of flows, influences, exchanges, and post-NAFTA cultural imaginaries. Thus, she seeks to implement a critical, retrospective viewpoint in order to challenge national imaginaries and deconstruct the cultural stereotypes that regard one another from a single angle or frame through the museum's display case. She encourages the spectator to take a stand when facing reality and to question the manner in which it is observed, impelling us to participate in the cultural semantics that, according to Néstor Garcia Canclini, corresponds more to the idea of a "garage sale"[52] than to "museum appreciation" where one confronts the eclecticism of the objects in use and accepts that their diverse uses and correspondences form part of their value.

Notes

Introduction
Writing the Cultural History of Canadian-Latin American Relations Through a Cultural Production Lens

1 As a matter of convention, Latin America is made up of the sum total of the sovereign nation states that were born out of the Independence movements that spread like wildfire across North, Central and South America in the early 1800s. It includes Brazil and Spanish-speaking countries in the Caribbean that achieved independence following a different path throughout the 19th and early 20th century.

2 The repertoire of documented experiences that could have been included in this volume is sufficiently vast and heterogeneous as to merit a framing device premised on chronology such as the one proposed in this volume. We offer readers diversity instead of exhaustiveness.

3 One example of related research is Cassandra Eberhardt, "Hispanic (Hybridity) in Canada: The Making and Unmaking of a Diaspora" (Master's thesis, Queen's University, 2010).

4 Per Winfried Siemerling and Sarah Phillips Casteel, eds., *Canada and Its Americas: Transnational Navigations* (Montreal and Kingston: McGill-Queen's University Press, 2010), 4.

5 Our attempt at expanding Canadian history has been informed by Margaret Conrad et al., *Canadians and Their Pasts* (Toronto: University of Toronto Press, 2013); and Ruth W. Sandwell, ed., *To the Past: History Education, Public Memory, and Citizenship in Canada* (Toronto: University of Toronto Press, 2006).

6 Salimah Valiani, "The Articulation of an Independent Foreign Policy: Canada and Latin America in the Early Twentieth Century," *Latin American Perspectives* 39, no. 6 (November 2012): 165-80; Yasmine Shamsie and Ricardo Grispun, "Missed Opportunity: Canada's Reengagement With Latin America and the Caribbean," *Canadian Journal of Latin American and Caribbean Studies / Revue canadienne des études latino-américaines et caraïbes* 35, no. 69 (2010): 171-99.

7 For a study of Chileans' contribution to Canadian society and culture, see Francis Peddie, *Young, Well-Educated, and Adaptable: Chilean Exiles in Ontario and Québec, 1973-2010* (Winnipeg: University of Manitoba Press, 2014). As a point of comparison see Wisdom J. Tettey and Korbla P. Puplampu, eds., *The African Diaspora in Canada: Negotiating Identity and Belonging* (Calgary: University of Calgary Press, 2005); Kamala Elizabeth Nayer, *The Sikh Diaspora in Vancouver: Three Generations Amid Tradition, Modernity, and Multiculturalism* (Toronto: University of Toronto Press, 2004); Wing Chung Ng, *The Chinese in Vancouver: The Pursuit of Identity and Power* (Vancouver: University of British Columbia Press, 1999).

8 Maureen Moynagh, "Eyeing the North Star? Figuring Canada in Postslavery Fiction and Drama," in *Canada and Its Americas: Transnational Navigations*, eds. Winfried Siemerling and Sarah Philips Casteel (Montreal and Kingston: McGill-Queen's University Press, 2010), 12.

9 According to these authors, NAFTA in particular "triggered a process of discovery by Canadians of Mexico and Latin America unparalleled in post-1945 external relations" (Jean Daudelin and Edgar J. Dosman, eds., *Beyond Mexico: Changing Americas, Vol. 1* (Ottawa: Carleton University Press, 1995), 2).

10 By way of example, James Rochlin uses the term "discovery" in his "Introduction: Canada and the Americas: There's Still Much to Discover" (in *Canada Looks South: In Search of an Americas Policy*, ed. Peter McKenna (Toronto, Buffalo, London: University of Toronto Press, 2012), 3-26).

11 With respect to translation and interpretation in literature, see Norman Cheadle and Lucien Pelletier, eds., *Canadian Cultural Exchanges* (Waterloo: Wilfrid Laurier University, 2007).

12 José Antonio Giménez Micó, "Latin-Americanizing Canada," in *Canadian Cultural Exchanges*, eds. Norman Cheadle and Lucien Pelletier (Waterloo: Wilfrid Laurier University, 2007), 59-74.

13 J. C. M. Ogelsby, *Gringos from the Far North: Essays in the History of Canadian-Latin American Relations, 1866-1968* (Toronto: Macmillan of Canada, 1976), 7.

14 Ogelsby, *Gringos*, 294-95.

15 He explicitly referred to literature, poetry, art and music (Ogelsby, *Gringos*, 294-95).

16 Ogelsby, *Gringos*, 292.

17 Ogelsby, *Gringos*, 295.

18 Ogelsby, *Gringos*, 295.

19 Ogelsby, *Gringos*, 295.

20 Ogelsby, *Gringos*, 295-96.

21 This was, according to him, a pattern already in place at the time of the Canadian Confederation (Ogelsby, *Gringos*, 295).

22 Victor Armony, Martha Barriga, and Daniel Schugurensky, "Citizenship Learning and Political Participation: The Experience of Latin American Immigrants in Canada," *Canadian Journal of Latin American and Caribbean Studies* 29, no. 57-58 (2004): 17-38; Armony, "Introduction: Latin American Diasporas: Common Origins and Different Paths," *Canadian Ethnic Studies* 46, no. 3 (2014): 1-6; Armony, "Latin American Communities in Canada: Trends in Diversity and Integration," *Canadian Ethnic Studies* 46, no. 3 (2014): 7-34. For discussion of the Latin American diaspora in Toronto, see Luisa Veronis, "Strategic Spatial Essentialism: Latin Americans' Real and Imagined Geographies of Belonging in Toronto," *Social and Cultural Geography* 8, no. 3 (2007): 455-73; Veronis, "Immigrant Participation in the Transnational Era: Latin Americans' Experiences with Collective Organising in Toronto," *International Migration and Integration* 11, no. 2 (2010): 173-92; and Veronis, "The Canadian Hispanic Day Parade, or How Latin American Immigrants Practise (Sub)Urban Citizenship in Toronto," *Environment and Planning A: Economy and Space* 38, no. 9 (2006): 1653-71.

23 John C. Harles, "Immigrant Integration in Canada and the United States," *American Review of Canadian Studies*, 34, no. 2 (2004): 223-58; Patricia Landolt and Luin Goldring, "Immigrant Political Socialization as Bridging and Boundary Work: Mapping the Multi-Layered Incorporation of Latin American Immigrants in Toronto," *Ethnic and Racial Studies* 32, no. 7 (2009): 1226-47.

24 Kirsty Robertson et al., "'More a Diplomatic than an Esthetic Event': Canada, Brazil, and Cultural Brokering in the São Paulo Biennial and 'Isumavut,'" *Journal of Canadian Studies* 47, no. 2 (2013): 60-88. See also Edith-Anne Pageot, "Figure de l'indiscipline. Domingo Cisneros, un parcours artistique atypique," *RACAR* 42, no. 1 (2017): 5-21; and Mariza Rosales Argonza, *Vues transversales. Panorama de la scène artistique latino-québécoise* (Montreal: Éditions CIDIHCA/ LatinArte, 2018).

25 Hugh Hazelton, *Latinocanadá: A Critical Study of Ten Latin American Writers of Canada* (Montreal and Kingston: McGill-Queen's University Press, 2007); Natalie Alvarez, ed., *Latina/o Canadian Theatre and Performance* (Toronto: Playwrights Canada, 2013); Alvarez, ed., *Fronteras Vivientes: Eight Latina/o Canadian Plays* (Toronto: Playwrights Canada Press, 2013).

26 See Maurice Demers, *Connected Struggles: Catholics, Nationalists, and Transnational Relations between Mexico and Quebec, 1917-1945* (Montreal and Kingston: McGill-Queen's University Press, 2014); Fred Burrill and Catherine LeGrand, "Progressive Catholicism at Home and Abroad: The 'Double Solidarité' of Quebec Missionaries in Honduras, 1955-1975," in *With and Without the Nation: Canadian History as Transnational History*, eds. Karen Dubinsky, Adele Perry, and Henry Yu (Toronto: University of Toronto Press, 2015), 311-40.

27 This volume does not claim to cover the entire Canadian territory. Most of the examples presented are illustrative of experiences coming out of Ontario and Quebec, and have varying local, provincial, and national significance. Collectively, the chapters offer a balanced representation of heavily populated and agro-industrial urban centres.

28 The conceptualization of the outsider as an insider, and of the full realization of the outsider's potential at particular moments in the history of a nation's history is informed by Peter Gay's *Weimar Culture: The Outsider as Insider* (New York: Harper & Row, 1968).

29 Our approach to analyzing images and performances has been especially informed by the work of two authors: Peter Burke, *Eyewitnessing: The Uses of Images as Historical Evidence* (Ithaca: Cornell University Press, 2008); and Diana Taylor, *The Archive and the Repertoire: Performing Cultural Memory in the Americas* (Durham: Duke University Press, 2003).

Part I

Chapter 1
Representations of Brazil in Canadian Newspapers at the Turn of the Twentieth Century

1 *Brazil and Canada: Economic, Political, and Migratory Ties, 1820s to 1970s* (Lanham: Lexington, 2017), xiv-xv.

2 Marilyn Lake and Henry Reynolds, *Drawing the Global Colour Line: White Men's Countries and the International Challenge of Racial Equality* (Cambridge: Cambridge University Press, 2008), 7, 198.

3 *The Evening Star*, October 13, 1896.

4 See Cedric J. Robinson, *Black Marxism: The Making of the Black Radical Tradition* (Chapel Hill, N.C.: University of North Carolina Press, 2000); and Peter James Hudson, "Imperial Designs: The Royal Bank of Canada in the Caribbean," *Race and Class* 52, no. 1 (2010): 33-48.

5 See Barbosa, *Brazil and Canada*, 98-104, and John Zucchi, "Mad Flight? The Montreal Migration of 1896 to Brazil," *Journal of the Canadian Historical Association* 24, no. 2 (2013): 189-217.

6 Barbosa, *Brazil and Canada*, 98-99.

7 Barbosa, *Brazil and Canada*, 99.

8 See for instance: *Montreal Daily Herald*, September 14, 1896; *Le Monde*, September 14, 1896; *Montreal Daily Witness*, September 14, 1896, *La Presse*, September 14, 1896; nd *The Globe*, September 14, 1896.

9 Barbosa, *Brazil and Canada*, 105.

10 *La Presse*, September 14, 1896.

11 *The Evening Star*, September 15, 1896.

12 *The Evening Star*, October 13, 1896.

13 See for instance: Adonis Valder Fauth, *A Imigração suiço-valensana no Rio Grande do Sul* (Carlos Barbosa, RS: Associação Valensana do Brasil, 2000); Adriana Lopes, *De Cães a lobos-do-mar: súditos ingleses no Brasil* (São Paulo: Editora Senac, 2007); Marionilde Dias Brepohl de Magalhães, *Presença Alemã no Brasil* (Brasilia, DF: Editora UnB, 2004); and Gilson Justino da Rosa, *Imigrantes alemães, 1824-1853* (Porto Alegre: EST Edições, 2005).

14 Thomas H. Holloway, *Immigrants on the Land. Coffee and Society in São Paulo, 1886-1934* (Chapel Hill: University of North Carolina Press, 1980), 139.

15 See, for instance, Patrick Wilcken, *Empire Adrift. The Portuguese Court in Rio de Janeiro, 1808-1821* (London: Bloomsbury, 2004).

16 *The Evening Journal*, September 15, 1896.

17 *The Globe*, September 15, 1896.

18 *The Montreal Gazette*, September 17, 1896.

19 *The Globe*, September 26, 1896.

20 *The Evening Star*, October 13, 1896. See quote on page 2.

21 *The Globe*, December 14, 1896.

22 *The Globe*, December 14, 1896.

23 See, for example, Roderick J. Barman, *Citizen Emperor: Pedro II and the Making of Brazil, 1825-1891* (Stanford: Stanford University Press, 1999).

24 Lúcia Maria Bastos Pereira das Neves and Humberto Fernandes Machado, *O Império do Brasil* (Rio de Janeiro: Editora Nova Fronteira, 1999), 444-45.

25 Zucchi, "Mad Flight?" 192-93.

26 *The Montreal Daily Herald*, September 16, 1896. Cited in Barbosa, *Brazil and Canada*, 108.

27 Barbosa, *Brazil and Canada*, 108.

28 *The Montreal Gazette*, September 16, 1896. Cited by Barbosa, *Brazil and Canada*, 108.

29 Barbosa, *Brazil and Canada*, 88.

30 *The Evening Star*, November 15, 1896.

31 *The Globe*, February 9, 1901. Note that the newspaper refers to Pará as a city, but Pará is the state and the capital of it is Belém, also known as Belém do Pará.

32 *The Globe*, November 11, 1903.

33 *The Globe*, January 25, 1904.

34 Greg Grandin, *Fordlandia. The Rise and Fall of Henry Ford's Forgotten Jungle City* (New York: Picador, 2009), 32.

35 For more information, see Grandin, *Fordlandia*, and Elizabeth Esch, "Whitened and Enlightened. The Ford Motor Company and Racial Engineering in the Brazilian Amazon," in *Company Towns in the Americas: Landscape, Power, and Working-class Communities*, eds. Oliver J. Dinius and Angela Vergara (Athens: University of Georgia Press, 2011), 91-110.

36 See Barbosa, *Brazil and Canada*, 30-43, and Duncan McDowall, *The Light. Brazilian Traction, Light and Power Company Limited, 1899-1945* (Toronto: University of Toronto Press, 1988).

37 Cited in Barbosa, *Brazil and Canada*, 34.

38 *The Globe*, January 17, 1902.

39 *The Star*, January 18, 1902.

40 *The Globe*, March 1, 1902.

41 Cited in Barbosa, *Brazil and Canada*, 34.

42 *The Star*, April 30, 1902.

43 *The Globe*, May 1902.

44 *The Star*, October 10, 1903.

45 *The Star*, June 22, 1904.

46 *The Globe*, July 5,1902.

47 *The Globe*, November 10, 1902.

48 *The Globe*, November 17, 1902.

49 Antonio Bulhões, *Diário da Cidade Amada: Rio de Janeiro, 1922*, vol. 3 (Sextante-Artes: 2003), 16.

50 Barbosa, *Brazil and Canada*, 34-35, 41.

51 Hudson, "Imperial Designs," 38.

52 Robinson, *Black Marxism*, 2.

53 Lake and Reynolds, *Drawing*, 7.

Chapter 2
Depictions of Authenticity and Risk in Canadian Tourism Representations of Latin America

1 See William M. O'Barr, *Culture and the Ad: Exploring Otherness in the World of Advertising* (Boulder: Westview Press, 1994); and Nigel Morgan and Annette Pritchard, *Tourism Promotion and Power: Creating Images, Creating Identities* (Chichester: Wiley, 1998).

2 See Margaret Marshment, "Gender Takes a Holiday: Representation in Tourism Brochures," in *Gender, Work and Tourism*, ed. M. Thea Sinclair (London: Routledge, 1997), 15-32; and Graham Dann, "The People of Tourist Brochures," in *The Tourist Image: Myths and Myth Making in Tourism*, ed. Tom Selwyn (Chichester: John Wiley, 1996), 61-82.

3 In a 1996 study of British holiday brochures comprising 5172 brochure pictures, Graham Dann found that less than 10% of the images showed tourists mixing with members of the local population; the majority of images showed tourists on their own. Meanwhile, Morgan and Pritchard found that the prevalence of local people in tourism advertisements depends significantly on the region being marketed. They observe that the "exoticism and traditions of local peoples" play an integral role in promotional materials for South and Central America. The Caribbean, by contrast, is depicted as "an almost exclusively white, heterosexual playground" of beaches, swimming pools, and luxury hotels in which indigenous African Caribbeans hardly feature at all. See Morgan and Pritchard, *Tourism Promotion*, 220-22.

4 See Robert A. Britton, "The Image of the Third World in Tourism Marketing," *Annals of Tourism Research* 6, no. 3 (1979): 318-29; Ira Silver, "Marketing Authenticity in Third World Countries," *Annals of Tourism Research* 20, no. 2 (1993): 302-18; and Laurence Wai-Teng Leong, "Commodifying Ethnicity State and Ethnic Tourism in Singapore," in *Tourism, Ethnicity and the State in Asian and Pacific Societies*, eds. Michel Picard and Robert Everett Wood (Honolulu: University of Hawaii Press, 1997), 71-98.

5 The company changed its name from Gap Adventures to G Adventures in 2011 after losing a trademark infringement lawsuit with Gap Inc. clothing.

6 Interview by author with Rodrigo Esponda and Cesar Mendoza (Mexico Tourism Board), Vancouver, April 2014.

7 Interview by author with Mark Bernhardt (Sirens Communications), February-March 2014.

8 Email interview by author with A. Assoignon (G Adventures), February-March, 2014.

9 In 2010 G Adventures was segmenting its brochures by destination. In 2014, G Adventures was no longer segmenting its brochures by destination but by travel style.

10 Arthur Asa Berger, *Ads, Fads and Consumer Culture: Advertising's Impact on American Character and Society*. 4th ed. (Lanham: Rowan and Littlefield Publishers, 2011).

11 O'Barr, *Culture*, 8.

12 Statistics Canada, *Travel by Canadians to Foreign Countries, Top 15 Countries Visited*. 2000-2012 (Ottawa: Statistics Canada), http://www.statcan.gc.ca/tables-tableaux/sum-som/l01/cst01/arts37a-eng.htm.

13 Susan Crompton and Leslie Anne Keown, "Going on Vacation: Benefits Sought from Pleasure Travel," in *Canadian Social Trends* (2009): 42-51, https://www150.statcan.gc.ca/n1/pub/11-008-x/2009001/article/10850-eng.pdf.

14 "Three Travel Trends to Watch in 2014," Canadian Tourism Commission, accessed November 5, 2014, http://en-corporate.canada.travel/content/ctc_news/travel-trends-2014.

15 Gwen Dianne Reimer, "Packaging Dreams: Canadian Tour Operators at Work," *Annals of Tourism Research* 17 (1990): 501-12.

16 Interview by author with Rodrigo Esponda and Cesar Mendoza (Mexico Tourism Board), Vancouver, April 2014.

17 Annie Ruiz Andrews and Brad Miron, "Mexico and the Canadian Market: The Next 5 Years and Beyond," www.Itravel2000.com, 2007.

18 Interview by author with Rodrigo Esponda and Cesar Mendoza (Mexico Tourism Board), Vancouver, April 2014.

19 Interview by author with Mark Bernhardt (Sirens Communications), February-March 2014.

20 Silver, "Marketing Authenticity," 312.

21 Silver, "Marketing Authenticity," 312.

22 Adrian Swinscoe, "Do You Need to Change Your Organisational Structure to Improve Your Customer Experience?" *Forbes*, January 9, 2014, http://www.forbes.com/sites/adrianswinscoe /2014/01/09/do-you-need-to-change-your-organisational-structure-to-improve-your-customer-experience/.

23 *South and Central America* (Gap Adventures, 2010), 190.

24 Intrepid Travel, an Australian company which is G Adventures' biggest competitor, offers a similar travel philosophy to that of G Adventures, marketing sustainable travel for people "with a yearning to get off the beaten track." Its brochures are available at Travel Cuts. It offers 152 travel packages to Latin America, many of which include homestays in rural villages and farms, and claims to give its clients an opportunity to encounter "real people, real cultures and incredible real-life experiences."

25 "About Us," G Adventures, accessed 2010, 2014, https://www.gadventures.com/about-us/.

26 Delfín Pauchi was described as Gap's "poster boy" by a Gap Adventures employee in a presentation about the company I attended at a Travel Cuts fair at McGill University in November 2010.

27 *South and Central*, inside cover.

28 Bruce Poon Tip, *Looptail: How One Company Changed the World by Reinventing Business*. (Toronto: Collins, 2013).

29 http://www.travelandtransitions.com/interviews/preview_bruce_poon_tip.htm

30 Poon Tip, *Looptail*, 15.

31 Email interview by author with A. Assoignon (G Adventures), February-March, 2014.

32 Poon Tip, *Looptail*, 231.

33 Email interview by author with A. Assoignon (G Adventures), February-March, 2014.

34 Poon Tip, *Looptail*, 231.

35 *South and Central America* (Gap Adventures, 2010), 89.

36 Efforts to counter national stereotypes (i.e. explicitly addressing and rejecting a known national stereotype) are more frequent for European nations than they are for Latin American ones.

37 Peter Wade and Fredrick Pike's research focuses on the historical projection of sexually deviant natures onto Latin Americans in general, and blacks in particular (the image accompanying Brazil's description is of a black Capoeira dancer). See Frederik B. Pike, *The United States and Latin America: Myths and Stereotypes of Civilization and Nature* (Austin: University of Texas Press, 1992), 52; and Peter Wade, *Race and Ethnicity in Latin America* (Chicago: Pluto Press, 1997).

38 ap Adventures, accessed November 2010, https://www.gadventures.com.

39 Country profiles for Asia and Africa heavily feature local people as well; however, none of the Middle East country profiles do.

40 Gap Adventures, accessed November 2010, https://www.gadventures.com.

41 Wai-Teng Leong, "Commodifying Ethnicity," 72.

42 Wai-Teng Leong, "Commodifying Ethnicity," 71.

43 Silver, "Marketing Authenticity," 303.

44 "Travel Advisories," Government of Canada, accessed October 2014, http://travel.gc.ca /travelling/advisories.

45 Nigel Morgan, Annette Pritchard, and Roger Pride, *Destination Branding: Creating the Unique Destination Proposition* (Oxford: Elsevier Butterworth-Heinemann, 2004), 65.

46 Colombia Travel, accessed December 2010, http://www.colombia.travel/en.

47 Colombia Travel.

48 "Colombia," G Adventures, accessed November 2014, http://www.gadventures.com/ destinations/south-america/colombia/.

49 "Bolivia," G Adventures, accessed November 2014, http://www.gadventures.com/ destinations/south-america/bolivia/.

50 "Bolivia."

51 Reimer, "Packaging Dreams," 508.

52 Yvette Reisinger and Felix Mavondo, "Cultural Differences in Travel Risk Perception," *Journal of Travel and Tourism Marketing* 20, no. 1 (2006): 13-31.

53 The website for Nicaraguan Tourism Institute, http://www.visitanicaragua.com/ ingles/nicaragua.php, does not address recent histories of political turmoil.

54 World Tourism Organization and European Travel Commission. *Handbook on Tourism Destination Branding* (Madrid: World Tourism Organization, 2009).

55 "South America," Travel Cuts, accessed November 2014, http://www.travelcuts.com/destinations /south-america/.

56 *Latin America Travel* (Intrepid: 2014), 64.

57 Dean MacCannell, *The Tourist: A New Theory of the Leisure Class* (New York: Schocken Books, 1976), 14.

58 Heidi Dahles and Lou Keune, *Tourism Development and Local Participation in Latin America* (New York: Cognizant Communication Corporation, 2002), 147.

59 Charles Lindholm, *Culture and Authenticity* (Malden, MA: Blackwell Publishing, 2008), 5.

60 "Venezuela," G Adventures, accessed October 2010, http://www.gapadventures.com /destinations/south-america/venezuela/. (The description for Venezuela has changed since 2010, no longer referring to stone-age tribes).

61 *Latin America and Antarctica* (Intrepid: 2014), 69.

62 "Inland and Amazon," G Adventures, accessed November 2014. http://www.gadventures.com /trips/inland-and-amazon/EIA/2014/.

63 "South America," Travel Cuts, accessed November 2014. http://www.travelcuts.com /destinations/south-america/.

64 *South and Central*, 99.

65 "Guatemala," G Adventures, accessed November 2014. http://www.gadventures.com /destinations/central-america/guatemala/.

66 For more on this topic, see Martin Mowforth, Clive Charlton, and Ian Munt, *Tourism and Responsibility: Perspectives from Latin America and the Caribbean* (London: Routledge, 2008).

Chapter 3
Representations of the Latin American Diaspora in Quebec: Latino-Québécois Visions

1 Ramón de Elía, "La otra bahía de Hudson," *The Apostles Review* No. 7 (Winter 2011): 16-19. "Uno podría vivir tranquilamente poniéndose el disfraz de inmigrante cuando esto fuera necesario y sacándoselo cuando a uno le plazca, si no fuera porque para tener un diálogo productivo, inteligente y sincero con la sociedad que lo recibe se necesita conocerse mutuamente." All translations from texts originally in Spanish from here onwards are by Michael William Parker Stainback.

2 Zygmunt Bauman, *La cultura en el mundo de la modernidad líquida* (Mexico City: Fondo de Cultura Económica, 2011), 101.

3 An example of their work is the show entitled "Contextes fragmentés," presented from 31 March to 1 May 2011 at the Musée des maîtres et artisans du Québec in Montréal. In the show, artists explicitly evoked the immigration experience and experiences of cultural difference through a repertoire of figurative paintings linked to the muralism movement and the so-called Mexican school of painting.

4 See http://www.centreclark.com, http://www.atelier-circulaire.qc.ca/, http://www. mumtl.org/a-propos/vision/.

5 LatinArte is a cultural project begun in December 2009 with support from the Montreal Arts Council. See http://www.latinarte.ca.

6 See http://lacap.ca/home/.

7 The 1968 student movement was a social movement which, in addition to students from a number of universities, included participation on the part of professors, intellectuals, housewives, labourers and professionals in Mexico City. It was violently suppressed by the Mexican government on 2 October 1968 by means of a notorious massacre on the Plaza de las Tres Culturas in Tlatelolco. The killings occurred at the hands of a paramilitary group known as the Batallón Olimpia, Mexico's internal security agency (known as DFS in Spanish) and the Mexican Army, in opposition to protests organized by the Consejo Nacional de Huelga, the movement's oversight organization.

8 This college (1974-1976) was located in La Macaza and catered to Indigenous students.

9 In the 1970s, Domingo Cisneros directed the Arts and Communications Department at Manitou College, in the Laurentians, where he trained an entire generation of Québécois Indigenous artists.

10 Gerardo Mosquera, "El arte latinoamericano deja de serlo," *ARCO Latino* 1 (1996): 7-10.

11 Mosquera, "El arte latinoamericano."

12 UNESCO conventions for conserving intangible heritages recognize that communities, groups, and, in some cases, individuals play an important role in the production, conservation, maintenance, and re-creation of intangible heritages,

thus contributing to the enrichment of cultural diversity and human creativity (Paris, September 29-October 17, 2003), (http://www.unesco.org/culture/ich/index.php?lg= es&pg=00006, accessed March 12, 2014).

13 Hazelton, *Latinocanadá*, 3-9.

14 Colombia, Mexico, and Peru are among the 25 main countries of origin of all immigrants to the province of Quebec, according to statistics from the Ministry of Immigration and Cultural Communities that include immigrants from all admissions categories in the 2002-2011 period still present in 2013 (Table 5) (http://www.micc.gouv.qc.ca/publications/fr/recherches-statistiques/PUB_Presence2013_admisQc_02_11.pdf, accessed March 12, 2014).

15 Between 2008-2012, the Ministry of Immigration and Cultural Communities placed Colombia as the sixth nation of origin for immigrants categorized as "accepted qualified workers" in Quebec (Table "7 (suite)"). In the family reunification category, Mexico comes in at seventh place (Table "13 (suite)"). Colombia holds first place for the greatest number of refugees admitted between 2008 and 2012, followed by Mexico, which holds fourth place (Tableau "16 (suite)"). See Immigration et communautés culturelles Québec, *L'immigration permanente au Québec selon les catégories d'immigration et quelques composantes (2008-2012)* (Immigration et communautés culturelles Québec, July 2013), 32-33, 54-55, 64-65, http://www.micc.gouv.qc.ca/publications/fr/recherches-statistiques/Portraits_categories_2008_2012.pdf.

16 José Del Pozo, "L'immigration des latino-américains. Une histoire de réfugiés et d'immigrants," in *Histoires d'immigrations au Québec*, eds. Guy Berthiaume, Claude Corbo, and Sophie Montreuil (Montreal: Presses de l'Université du Québec, 2014), 173.

17 Del Pozo, "L'immigration," 172.

18 For example, the artist Domingo Cisneros, who lives in the Laurentians, or Giorgia Volpe, who lives outside Quebec City. Another example is the Université du Quebec à Chicoutimi (acronym in French: UQAC), where a number of artists of Latin American origin have been trained in part by the Colombia-born artist and professor, Constanza Camelo.

19 There is ample literature on Chicano studies. The following milestone works merit mention: Rodolfo Acuña, *Occupied America: A History of Chicanos* (New York: Harper and Row, 1972); Tomás Almaguer, "Race, Class and Chicano Oppression," in *Socialist Revolution* 25 (July-Sept. 1975): 71-99. From 1987 onwards: Almaguer, "Ideological Distortions in Recent Chicano Historiography: The Internal Model and Chicano Historical Interpretation," in *Aztlán* 18 (Spring 1987): 7-28; Gloria Anzaldúa, *Borderlands/La Frontera: The New Mestiza* (San Francisco: Ante Lute Press, 1987); Albert Camarillo, *Chicanos in a Changing Society* (Cambridge: Harvard University Press, 1979); Guillermo Flores, "Race, Culture in the Internal Colony: Keeping the Chicano in His Place," in *Structures of Dependency*, eds. Frank Bonilla and Robert Henriques Girling (Palo Alto: Stanford University Press, 1973), 189-95; Letticia Galindo and María Dolores Gonzales, eds., *Speaking Chicana: Voice, Power and Identity* (Tucson: University of Arizona Press, 1999); Juan Gómez Quiñones, *Chicano Politics, Reality and Promise, 1940-1990* (Albuquerque: University of New Mexico Press, 1990); Jorge A. Huerta, *Chicano Theater, Themes and Form* (Ypsilanti: Bilingual Press,

1982); David Maciel, ed., *La otra cara de México, el pueblo chicano* (Mexico City: Ediciones El Caballito, 1977); Carlos Muñoz, *Youth, Identity Power, the Chicano Movement* (London: Verso Press, 1989). Chicano Studies programs offered in the United States and Mexico, e.g., UC Davis, http://chi.ucdavis.edu/welcome-department-chicana-andchicano-studies?destination=node/1; an MA in Chicano Studies from the University of San Diego, as well as the Seminario Permanente de Estudios Chicanos y de Fronteras (SPEChF) del Área Sobre la Cuestión Nacional, Chicanos y Fronteras at Mexico's Instituto Nacional de Antropología e Historia's department of Ethnology and Social Anthropology, among others.

20 See http://www.diversiteartistique.org/en/, accessed December 6, 2016.

21 See http://m-a-i.qc.ca, accessed November 10, 2015.

22 Charles Taylor, "The Policy of Recognition," in *Multiculturalism: Examining the Politics of Recognition*, eds. Charles Taylor and Amy Gutman (Princeton: Princeton University Press, 1994), 88-89.

23 Néstor García Canclini, "Noticias recientes sobre la hibridación," *Trans - Revista Transcultural de Música* 7, no. 2 (2003), http://www.sibetrans.com/trans/articulo/209/noticias-recientes-sobre-la-hibridacion.

24 Néstor García Canclini, "De la diversidad a la interculturalidad," in *Conflictos interculturales*, eds. José Luis Brea and Néstor García Canclini (Mexico City: Gedisa, 2011), 110. "Es fácil declarar que todas las culturas, o modalidades culturales dentro de una nación, son legítimas; pero ¿vale lo mismo ser occidental que oriental, y dentro y fuera de Occidente, ser estadounidense, europeo o latinoamericano, y aun dentro de la variedad de culturas contenidas en cada una de estas regiones, pertenecer a una o a otra? Cuando preguntamos si valen lo mismo, necesitamos despojar la cuestión de cualquier esencialismo. No pienso en superioridades intrínsecas de una cultura o sociedad respecto a otras, sino de las condiciones que cada una otorga a sus miembros para desempeñarse en un mundo interconectado donde las comparaciones y confrontaciones de desarrollos socioculturales son constantes e inevitables."

25 Walter Mignolo, *Local Histories/Global Designs: Coloniality, Subaltern Knowledges and Border Thinking* (Princeton: Princeton University Press, 2000).

26 Homi Bhabha, *The Location of Culture* (London and New York: Routledge, 1994).

27 Walter Mignolo, *La idea de América Latina. La herida colonial y la opción decolonial* (Barcelona: Gedisa, 2007), 159.

28 John Ochoa, "El desafío de las fronteras," in *Bitácora de cruce*, ed. Guillermo Gómez Peña (Mexico City: Fondo de Cultura Económica, 2006), 22.

29 Pierre Ouellet, "Présentation," *Les écrits* 140 (2014): 8.

30 Fernando Ortiz, *Contrapunteo cubano del tabaco y el azúcar* (La Habana: Editorial Ciencias Sociales, 1991).

31 Néstor García Canclini, *Culturas híbridas* (Mexico City: Grijalbo, 1989).

32 Arjun Appadurai, *Modernity at Large: Cultural Dimensions of Globalization* (Minneapolis: University of Minnesota Press, 1996); Ulf Hannerz, "Borders," *International Social Science Journal* 49, no. 154 (1997): 537-548. https://doi.org/10.1111/j.1468-2451.1997.tb00043.x.

33 David Harvey, *The Condition of Postmodernity* (Oxford: Blackwell, 1989).

34 Michel Maffesoli, *La tajada del diablo. Compendio de subversión posmoderna* (Mexico City: Siglo XXI Editores, 2002).

35 Bhabha, *The Location.*

36 Gerardo Mosquera, coord. *Adiós identidad. Arte y cultura desde América Latina* (Madrid: Museo Extremeño e Iberoamericano de Arte Contemporáneo, 2001), 8.

37 Nelly Richard, "El régimen crítico-estético del arte en el contexto de la diversidad cultural y sus políticas de identidad," in *Real/virtual en la estética y la teoría de las artes*, ed. Simón Marchán, trans. Martha Pino Moreno (Buenos Aires: Paidós, 2006), 118-19.

38 José Jiménez, ed. *Una teoría del arte desde América Latina* (Madrid: Turner, 2011), 15.

39 See https://www.artsmontreal.org/en/search?search=diversité, accessed December 2017.

40 Taylor, "The Policy," 98.

41 Eduardo Galeano, *Memorias del fuego I. Los nacimientos* (Mexico City: Siglo Veintiuno Editores, 1991).

42 Major Meso-American cultures shared a use of clay urns to be placed within tombs.

43 George Yúdice, *El recurso de la cultura. Usos de la cultura en la era global* (Barcelona: Gedisa, 2002).

44 Ciudad Juárez, lying along the US-Mexico border, was characterized in 2009 as one of the most violent cities in the world for the second consecutive year, based on reports by the Centro Ciudadano para la Seguridad Pública, AC, ("Citizen Centre for Public Security;" acronym in Spanish: CCSP) in Mexico City as well as according to official data distributed in other countries. The recorded murder rate in Ciudad Juárez, Chihuahua, is 191 homicides per 100 thousand inhabitants, which comes in higher than the world's 49 most violent cities, ahead of such places as Kandahar, Afghanistan; San Pedro Sula, Honduras; and Baghdad. See http://seguridadjusticiaypaz.org.mx/sala-de-prensa/58-cd-juarez-por-segundo-ano-con-secutivo-la-ciudad-mas-violenta-del-mundo/, accessed March 12, 2014.

45 Ticio Escobar, "Acerca de la modernidad y del arte: un listado de cuestiones finiseculares," in *Adiós identidad, arte y cultura desde América Latina*, ed. Gerardo Mosquera (Badajoz: Museo Extremeño e Iberoamericano de Arte Contemporáneo, 2001), 38.

Part II

Chapter 4
Exhibiting Mexican Art in Canada: Histories of Cultural Exchange and Diplomacy in the Mid-Twentieth Century

1 "Places of Their Own" toured venues in Canada and the United States, including the McMichael Canadian Art Collection, the Santa Fe Museum of Fine Arts, the National Museum of Women in Art, and the Vancouver Art Gallery. "Baja to Vancouver" toured venues in Canada and the United States, including

the Seattle Art Museum, the Museum of Contemporary Art San Diego, the Vancouver Art Gallery, and the CCA Wattis Institute for Contemporary Arts.

2 "Panoramas" and "Perspectives" opened in 2001 and 2002 respectively. These online exhibitions were hosted by the Virtual Museum of Canada, administered by the Canadian Heritage Information Network, a special operating agency of the Department of Canadian Heritage. See Canadian Heritage Information Network, "What We Do."

3 I have explored these exhibitions and events in my larger research project. See Sarah E. K. Smith, *Art and the Invention of North America, 1985-2012.* (PhD diss., Queen's University, 2013).

4 US Department of State, "North American Partnership: Trilateral Ministerial Meeting Communiqué," online, accessed 10 June 2014, http://1997-2001.state.gov/www/regions/wha/uscanmex_trilat/000812_trilat_communique.html.

5 Such appearances by key state actors are more than perfunctory and contribute to the public representation of an event and its significance. National Gallery of Canada Archives (NGCA), National Gallery of Canada fonds, Exhibitions - Mexican Modern Art, 1998, "Communications, Special Events," vol. 8, Correspondence, Emily Tolot to Marie Claire Morin, February 15, 2000.

6 I argue that NAFTA led to a surge of cultural exchanges in North America, including exhibitions of Mexican art in Canada, as well as exhibitions articulating new narratives of North America. See Sarah E.K. Smith, "Visualizing the 'New' North American Landscape," in *Negotiations in a Vacant Lot: Studying the Visual in Canada*, eds. Lynda Jessup, Erin Morton, and Kirsty Robertson (McGill-Queen's University Press, 2014), 130-49; and Smith, "Cross-Border Identifications and Dislocations Visual Art and the Construction of Identity in North America." In *Parallel Encounters: Culture at the Canada-US Border*, eds. D.F. Stirrup and Gillian Roberts (Waterloo: Wilfrid Laurier University Press, 2013), 187-205.

7 Maria Teresa Gutiérrez Haces, "Canada-Mexico: The Neighbour's Neighbour," in *NAFTA in Transition*, eds. Stephen J. Randall and Herman W. Konrad (Calgary: University of Calgary Press, 1995), 57.

8 Joseph S. Nye Jr., *Soft Power: The Means to Success in World Politics* (New York: Public Affairs, 2004), xi, 6, 7, 31.

9 Judith Huggins Balfe, "Artworks as Symbols in International Politics," *International Journal of Politics, Culture, and Society* 1, no. 2 (Winter, 1987): 195, 210, 214-15.

10 I acknowledge the constructed nature of national identities, and in this chapter I examine representations of Canada and Mexico as specific constructions that different actors have a vested interest in contributing to. See Brian Wallis, "Selling Nations: International Exhibitions and Cultural Diplomacy," in *Museum Culture: Histories, Discourses, Spectacles*, eds. Daniel J. Sherman and Irit Rogoff (Minneapolis: University of Minnesota Press, 1994), 266.

11 José Springer, "Birds of a Feather: Canada, Mexico, NAFTA and Culture," *Fuse* 19, no. 3 (Spring 1996): 32.

12 In the United States, by contrast, audiences were introduced to Mexican art in the 1930s, though these exhibitions were no less politically motivated. A key show in this regard was Mexican Arts, a major survey of twelve hundred objects

curated by René d'Harnoncourt and circulated by the American Federation of the Arts between 1930 and 1932. For a detailed discussion of this exhibition, see Anna Indych, "Mexican Muralism without Walls: The Critical Reception of Portable Work by Rivera, Orozco and Siqueiros in the United States, 1927-1940" (PhD diss., New York University, 2003), and Anna Indych-López, *Muralism Without Walls: Rivera, Orozco and Siqueiros in the United States, 1927-1940* (Pittsburgh: University of Pittsburgh Press, 2009).

13 I did not consider exhibitions of Mexican art in Canada held in commercial galleries, regional museums, or artist-run centres.

14 "Insight into Mexican Life is Afforded by Art Exhibit," *Ottawa Journal*, July 17, 1943, Clippings, NGCA, Exhibitions - Mexican Art Today, 1943.

15 "About the Department," Foreign Affairs and International Trade Canada, 6 March 2013. Accessed 26 July 2013. http://www.international.gc.ca/about-a_propos/index.aspx?view=d.

16 Government of Canada, "Canada-Mexico Relations"; Gutiérrez Haces, "Canada-Mexico: The Neighbour's Neighbour," 60; Randall and Konrad, "Introduction."

17 "Mexican Art Today," File 2, NGCA, Exhibitions - Mexican Art Today, 1943.

18 The NGCA documentation does not speak about Amor's involvement; rather, it emphasizes the Mexican state's role, specifically that of the Dirección General de Educación Extraescolar y Estética in Mexico. For a discussion of Clifford and Amor's relationship and work on the first installation of this show in Philadelphia, see Rachel Kaplan, "*Mexican Art Today*: Inés Amor, Henry Clifford and the Shifting Practices of Exhibiting Modern Mexican Art," *Journal of Curatorial Studies* 3, no. 2-3 (2014): 264-88.

19 "Mexican Art Today Due Here Next Month," *Montreal Gazette*, August 21, 1943, Clippings, NGCA, Exhibitions - Mexican Art Today, 1943.

20 "Synopsis of Exhibition Mexican Art Today," April 29, 1943, Clippings, NGCA, Exhibitions - Mexican Art Today, 1943.

21 "To Open Exhibition Tonight of Mexican Art at Gallery," *Ottawa Citizen*, July 22, 1943, Clippings, NGCA, Exhibitions - Mexican Art Today, 1943.

22 "Mexican Paintings Arrive in Montreal," *Montreal Gazette*, August 28, 1943, Clippings, NGCA, Exhibitions - Mexican Art Today, 1943.

23 "Mexican Art Exhibition So Popular that Catalogue Shortage Exists," *Montreal Star*, September 20, 1943, Clippings, NGCA, Exhibitions - Mexican Art Today, 1943.

24 Luis Cardoza y Aragón, "Contemporary Mexican Painting," in *Mexican Art Today*, trans. Esther Rowland Clifford (Philadelphia: Philadelphia Museum of Art, 1943), 25.

25 Cardoza y Aragón, "Contemporary Mexican Painting," 26.

26 Cardoza y Aragón, "Contemporary Mexican Painting," 26.

27 Pearl McCarthy, "Latin Americans Give New Thrills," *Globe and Mail*, October 16, 1943, Clippings, NGCA, Exhibitions - Mexican Art Today, 1943.

28 Elizabeth Gairdner, "Modern Mexican Art Boldly Interprets Social Revolutions," *Standard*, September 18, 1943, Clippings, NGCA, Exhibitions - Mexican Art Today, 1943.

29 The WIB was established in August 1942, tasked, in part, with promoting Canada's image in the United States. The organization grew out of the Bureau of Public Information, a unit attached to the Prime Minister's Office that was created in 1939 by Mackenzie King. For more information on the historical development of the Wartime Information Board, see William R. Young, "Academics and Social Scientists versus the Press: The Policies of the bureau of Public Information and the Wartime Information Board, 1939 to 1945," *Historical Papers* 13, no. 1 (1978): 217-40; and Young, "Making the Truth Graphic: The Canadian Government's Home Front Information Structure and Programs During World War II" (PhD diss., University of British Columbia, 1978); "Many See Exhibit of Mexican Art," *Ottawa Journal*, July 23, 1943, Clippings, NGCA Exhibitions - Mexican Art Today, 1943.

30 "Mexican Art Exhibition Opens: Will Be on View Until Oct. 3," *Star*, September 10, 1943, Clippings, NGCA, Exhibitions - Mexican Art Today, 1943.

31 Correspondence, John Grierson to H.O. McCurry, May 20, 1943, File 1, NGCA, Exhibitions - Mexican Art Today, 1943.

32 "Correspondence from McCurry to A.S. Grigsby," September 10, 1943, File 2, NGCA, Exhibitions - Mexican Art Today, 1943.

33 "Art Exhibits Open at Gallery Today," *Globe and Mail*, October 15, 1943, Clippings, NGCA, Exhibitions - Mexican Art Today, 1943.

34 "Colour in Mexican Works is Magnificently Vital," *Toronto Telegram*, October 16, 1943, Clippings, NGCA, Exhibitions - Mexican Art Today, 1943.

35 "Mexican Art on exhibition at Gallery Starting July 22," *Ottawa Citizen*, July 17, 1943, Clippings, NGCA, Exhibitions - Mexican Art Today, 1943.

36 The same could be said of art exhibitions, with US interest in and knowledge of Mexican art firmly established with the 1940 blockbuster, "Twenty Centuries of Mexican Art," at the Museum of Modern Art.

37 "To Open Exhibition Tonight of Mexican Art at Gallery," *Ottawa Citizen*, July 22, 1943, Clippings, NGCA, Exhibitions - Mexican Art Today, 1943.

38 "Latin-American Exhibit Promises to be Popular," *Toronto Telegram*, October 2, 1943, Clippings, NGCA, Exhibitions - Mexican Art Today, 1943.

39 Valerie Conde, "Mexican Art Exhibit," *Daily Star*, September 4, 1943, Clippings, NGCA, Exhibitions - Mexican Art Today, 1943.

40 Dina Berger, "Goodwill Ambassadors on Holiday: Tourism, Diplomacy, and Mexico-U.S. Relations," in *Holiday in Mexico: Critical Reflections on Tourism and Tourist Encounters*, eds. Dina Berger and Andrew Grant Wood (Durham and London: Duke University Press, 2010), 107.

41 "Mexican Art on Exhibition at Gallery Starting July 22," *Ottawa Citizen*, July 17, 1943, Clippings, NGCA, Exhibitions - Mexican Art Today, 1943.

42 "Colour in Mexican."

43 "Mexico's Consul-General opens Fine Art Display," *Ottawa Citizen*, July 23, 1943, Clippings, NGCA, Exhibitions - Mexican Art Today, 1943; "To Open Exhibition Tonight of Mexican Art at Gallery," *Ottawa Citizen*, July 22, 1943, Clippings, NGCA, Exhibitions - Mexican Art Today, 1943.

44 "Many See Exhibit of Mexican Art," *Ottawa Journal*, July 23, 1943, Clippings, NGCA, Exhibitions - Mexican Art Today, 1943.

45 "Address given by Sr. C.A. Calderón, Consul-General of Mexico in Canada, upon the opening of the Exhibition of 'Mexican Art To-day' in the National Gallery of Canada," Ottawa, July 22, 1943, File 1, NGCA, Exhibitions - Mexican Art Today, 1943.

46 "Mexican Art."

47 "Mexican Art Exhibition."

48 "Sees Opening of Mexican Exhibit Educational for Both Countries," *Gazette*, September 10, 1943, Clippings, NGCA, Exhibitions - Mexican Art Today, 1943.

49 "Mexican Art Show at Gallery Friday," *Globe and Mail*, October 11, 1943, Clippings, NGCA, Exhibitions - Mexican Art Today, 1943.

50 Pearl McCarthy, "Mexican Painting Coming to City," *Globe and Mail*, October 2, 1943, Clippings, NGCA, Exhibitions - Mexican Art Today, 1943.

51 McCarthy, "Mexican Painting Coming."

52 Similar rhetoric around Mexican art occurred in the United States and other international locations in this period

53 Pearl McCarthy, "Latin Americans Give New Thrills," *Globe and Mail*, October 16, 1943, NGCA, Exhibitions - Mexican Art Today, 1943.

54 "Mexican Films to be Shown," *Star*, September 14, 1943, Clippings, NGCA, Exhibitions - Mexican Art Today, 1943.

55 "Mexican Art Will be Shown" *Star*, September 9, 1943, Clippings, NGCA, Exhibitions - Mexican Art Today, 1943.

56 "To Open Exhibition Tonight of Mexican Art at Gallery," *Ottawa Citizen*, July 22, 1943, Clippings, NGCA, Exhibitions - Mexican Art Today, 1943.

57 "To Open Exhibition."

58 "To Open Exhibition."

59 "Contemporary Mexican Painting," File 1, NGCA, Exhibitions - Mexican Painting (& Furniture), 1946.

60 "Mexican Exhibition," NGCA, Exhibitions - Mexican Painting (& Furniture), 1946.

61 "Mexican Exhibition."

62 Valerie Conde, "Mexican Art Exhibit," NGCA, Exhibitions - Mexican Painting (& Furniture), 1946.

63 Irene Baird, "Memorandum for the Ambassador on the Book Fair, Mexico City," June 12, 1945, Exhibitions - Mexican Book Fair Exhibition, NGCA, 1946, 3.

64 "Inter-Departmental Committee on Canadian Publicity in Latin America," NGCA, Exhibitions - Mexican Book Fair Exhibition, 1946.

65 Baird, "Memorandum," 1, 2.

66 "Memorandum for Mr. F.P. Cosgrove," March 19, 1946, NGCA, Exhibitions - Mexican Book Fair Exhibition, 1946.

67 Correspondence from H.O. McCurry to Arnold Tucker, February 28, 1946, NGCA, Exhibitions - Mexican Painting (& Furniture), 1946.

68 Correspondence from Arnold Tucker to H.O. McCurry, March 5, 1946, NGCA, Exhibitions - Mexican Painting (& Furniture), 1946; Correspondence from H.O. McCurry to S.D. Hemsley, April 29, 1946, NGCA, Exhibitions - Mexican Painting (& Furniture), 1946.

69 Correspondence to H.O. Tucker to Arnold McCurry, March 5, 1946.

70 Indych-López, *Muralism Without Walls*, 5; Salomon Grimberg, "Inés Amor and the Galería de Arte Mexicano," *Woman's Art Journal* 32, no. 2 (Fall/Winter 2011), 5.

71 I thank Adriana Ortega Orozco for bringing this to my attention. Kaplan also discusses Amor's U.S. connections, stating, "From its inception, the Galería de Arte Mexicano engaged foreign audiences by attracting art-minded tourists to Mexico and sending exhibitions to the United States" ("Mexican Art Today," 267). For more on Amor, see Jorge Alberto Manrique and Teresa del Conde, *Una mujer en el arte mexicano: memorias de Inés Amor*. 2nd ed. (Mexico City: Universidad Nacional Autónoma de México, Instituto de Investigaciones Estéticas, 2005).

72 Correspondence from H.O. Tucker to Arnold McCurry, March 16, 1946, NGCA, Exhibitions - Mexican Painting (& Furniture), 1946.

73 Likely Mexican Contemporary Paintings was a small show because it bypassed the Mexican state bureaucracy - a shortcut for the Canadian state, which would later have difficulties securing Mexican exhibitions through state channels.

74 Correspondence from Inés Amor to McCurry, June 17, 1946, NGCA, Exhibitions - Mexican Painting (& Furniture), 1946.

75 "Those Mexican Pictures," *Telegram*, October 26, 1947, NGCA, Exhibitions - Mexican Painting (& Furniture), 1946.

76 Correspondence from J.S. McLean to H.O. McCurry, October 23, 1946, NGCA, Exhibitions - Mexican Painting (& Furniture), 1946.

77 Correspondence from H.O. McCurry to J.S. McLean, October 24, 1946, NGCA, Exhibitions - Mexican Painting (& Furniture), 1946.

78 The NGC clippings file includes a note indicating that the original press clippings file was lost, which makes gauging the tone of the reception of the exhibition to the Canadian public difficult, as well as how much publicity it received.

79 Reciprocal exhibitions were not standard for Mexico at the time.

80 Correspondence from the Canadian Embassy in Mexico to H.O. McCurry, March 18, 1948, NGCA, Exhibitions - Mexican Art Ex. (Proposed), 1948-1954.

81 In the mid-twentieth century Mexico was focused on exhibiting its art in Paris, France. In 1952, the show Art mexicain du précolombien á nos jours was shown at the Musée national d'art moderne. The exhibition subsequently toured. Here, Mexico exerted artistic direction and curatorial control, demonstrating interest in creating a specific message for international audiences. For a discussion of the history of this exhibition and the promotion of Mexican art abroad, see Adriana Ortega Orozco, "México-Francia: una larga historia de exposiciones como herramientas diplomáticas," *IdeAs* 8 (Fall 2016/Winter 2017), accessed May 10, 2017, http://ideas.revues.org/1729.

82 My thanks to Debra Antoncic for bringing the 1951 Canada-First Trade Policy to my attention.

83 Correspondence from the Under-Secretary of State for External Affairs to the Canadian Embassy Mexico City, August 11, 1953, NGCA, Exhibitions - Mexican Art Ex. (Proposed), 1948-1954.

84 Correspondence from Charles S. Band to H.O. McCurry, December 6, 1949, NGCA, Exhibitions - Mexican Art Ex. (Proposed), 1948-1954.

85 Correspondence from H.O. McCurry to Martin Baldwin, August 19, 1952, NGCA, Exhibitions - Mexican Art Ex. (Proposed), 1948-1954; correspondence from Fernando Gamboa to Arthur Blanchette, September 28, 1951, NGCA, Exhibitions - Mexican Art Ex. (Proposed), 1948-1954.

86 Correspondence from H.O. McCurry to A.F. Key, August 13, 1951, NGCA, Exhibitions - Mexican Art Ex. (Proposed), 1948-1954.

87 Correspondence from H.O. McCurry to Paul Malone, February 2, 1954, NGCA, Exhibitions - Mexican Art Ex. (Proposed), 1948-1954.

88 Correspondence from C.P. Hébert to C.S. Band, July 22, 1950, NGCA, Exhibitions - Mexican Art Ex. (Proposed), 1948-1954.

89 Correspondence from Michael Forster to Kathleen, June 8, 1953, NGCA, Exhibitions - Mexican Art Ex. (Proposed), 1948-1954.

90 Correspondence from H.O. McCurry to Howard Gamble, January 8, 1954, NGCA, Exhibitions - Mexican Art Ex. (Proposed), 1948-1954.

91 Correspondence from H.O. McCurry to Howard Gamble, January 8, 1954.

92 Correspondence from Lupe Solórzano to the Canadian Ambassador to Mexico, April 7, 1956, NGCA, Exhibitions - Mexican Art Ex. (Proposed), 1956.

93 Correspondence from D.W. Buchanan to A.J. Andrew, June 7, 1956, NGCA, Exhibitions - Mexican Art Ex. (Proposed), 1956.

94 Correspondence from D.W. Buchanan to G.W.G. McConachie, June 8, 1956, NGCA, Exhibitions - Mexican Art Ex. (Proposed), 1956.

95 Correspondence from D.W. Buchanan to A.J. Andrew, June 7, 1956.

96 Correspondence from G.W.G. McConachie to D.W. Buchanan, June 13, 1956, NGCA, Exhibitions - Mexican Art Ex. (Proposed), 1956.

97 Correspondence from Jorge Rangel Guerra to D.W. Buchanan, June 18, 1956, NGCA, Exhibitions - Mexican Art Ex. (Proposed), 1956.

98 Correspondence from D.W. Buchanan to R.A. Keith, August 4, 1956, NGCA, Exhibitions - Mexican Art Ex. (Proposed), 1955.

99 Mexican President Adolfo López Mateos made an official visit in 1959 to Canada, where he met Canadian Prime Minister John Diefenbaker in Ottawa. As Jason Gregory Zorbas notes, it was his first state visit. "Diefenbaker, Latin America and the Caribbean: The Pursuit of Canadian Autonomy" (PhD diss., University of Saskatchewan, 2009), 98.

100 "Exhibition: Mexican Exchange Exhibition (Mexico to Canada)," vol. 4, NGCA, Exhibitions - Mexican Exchange Exhibition (Mexico to Canada), 1960.

101 Correspondence from Richard B. Simmins to William Dale, November 5, 1959, vol. 1, NGCA, Exhibitions - Mexican Exchange Exhibition (Mexico to Canada), 1960; "Mexican Art Exhibition," press release, p.1-3, January 2, 1961, vol. 3, NCGA, Exhibitions - Mexican Exchange Exhibition (Mexico to Canada), 1960.

102 "Preface," in *Mexican Art: From Pre-Columbian Times to the Present Day*, eds. Donald W. Buchanan and Jorge Olvera (Vancouver: The Keystone Press Limited, 1960), n.p.

103 Memorandum, D.W. Buchanan to Dr. Hubbard, June 1, 1960, vol. 3, NGCA, Exhibitions - Mexican Exchange Exhibition (Canada to Mexico), 1960.

104 While the exhibition was still in its nascent phase, both the Canadian ambassador to Mexico and the undersecretary of foreign affairs in Mexico decided that gov-

ernment officials and embassies should withdraw their involvement in the development of the exhibition. However, by 1960 the Canadian embassy was once again assisting with the show, advising the NGCA on their dealings with the INBA.

105 To contextualize, in the early 1950s Mexican art exhibitions toured Paris, Stockholm, and London. In 1959, another show, "Chefs d'oeuvre de l'art mexicain," travelled extensively, with displays in Zurich, Cologne, The Hague, West Berlin, Vienna, Moscow, Leningrad, Warsaw, Paris, Rome, and Los Angeles. I thank Adriana Ortega Orozco for bringing this touring exhibition to my attention. This context demonstrates the significant interest in Mexico and political will to circulate artwork abroad. As such, the Canadian exhibition should not be viewed in isolation but rather as a part of the larger Mexican state interest in cultural exchange.

106 D.W. Buchanan, "Memorandum to Mexican Exhibition File," June 17, 1957, vol. 1, NGCA, Exhibitions - Mexican Exchange Exhibition (Mexico to Canada), 1960.

107 Correspondence from Douglas S. Cole to D.W. Buchanan, July 25, 1957, vol. 1, NGCA, Exhibitions - Mexican Exchange Exhibition (Mexico to Canada), 1960; Richard B. Simmins, "Memorandum to the Director," July 22, 1960, vol. 2, NGCA, Exhibitions - Mexican Exchange Exhibition (Mexico to Canada), 1960.

108 Correspondence from Richard B. Simmins to Miguel Salas Anzures, October 14, 1960, vol. 3, NGCA, Exhibitions - Mexican Exchange Exhibition (Canada to Mexico), 1960.

109 Correspondence from Miguel Salas Anzures to D.W. Buchanan, February 15, 1960, vol. 1, NGCA, Exhibitions - Mexican Exchange Exhibition (Mexico to Canada), 1960; Correspondence from Jacques Asselin to Salas Anzures, January 7, 1960, vol. 1, NGCA, Exhibitions - Mexican Exchange Exhibition (Mexico to Canada), 1960.

110 "Remarks by the Minister, the Hon. Ellen Fairclough," January 6, 1961, vol. 3, NGCA, Exhibitions - Mexican Exchange Exhibition (Mexico to Canada), 1960; Correspondence from Charles F. Comfort to Hon. Ellen Fairclough, December 22, 1960, vol. 3, NGCA, Exhibitions - Mexican Exchange Exhibition (Mexico to Canada), 1960.

111 Buchanan and Olvera, "Preface," n.p.

112 In 1967, Canada used the anniversary of Confederation to position itself internationally, especially with Montreal's Expo 67. Notably, Fernando Gamboa, a key figure who organized numerous displays of Mexican culture abroad, including Mexico's pavilion in Venice in 1950, was also involved in coordinating Mexico's pavilion at Expo 67, which featured, amongst other elements, a mural by Rufino Tamayo.

113 Both Canada and Mexico incorporated indigenous cultural production into national narratives, something that did not happen as early or to the same extent in US exhibitions of Mexican art.

114 Translated correspondence from Miguel Álvarez Acosta to Douglas S. Cole, August 29, 1957, vol. 1, NGCA, Exhibitions - Mexican Exchange Exhibition (Mexico to Canada), 1960.

115 Translated correspondence from Miguel Álvarez Acosta to Douglas S. Cole, August 29, 1957.

116 Untitled document, October 1958, vol. 1, NGCA, Exhibitions - Mexican Exchange Exhibition (Mexico to Canada), 1960.

117 Richard B. Simmins, "Memorandum for D.W. Buchanan, Mexico-Canada Exchange Exhibitions," October 7, 1958, vol. 1, NGCA, Exhibitions - Mexican Exchange Exhibition (Mexico to Canada), 1960.

118 Correspondence from D.W. Buchanan to Martin Baldwin, October 18, 1957, vol. 1, NGCA, Exhibitions - Mexican Exchange Exhibition (Mexico to Canada), 1960.

119 Correspondence from D.W. Buchanan to Martin Baldwin, August 1, 1957, vol. 1, NGCA, Exhibitions - Mexican Exchange Exhibition (Mexico to Canada), 1960.

120 "Cartographies" was curated by Ivo Mesquita and organized by the Winnipeg Art Gallery (WAG). The WAG played a key role in introducing Latin American art to Canada in the late 1980s and early 1990s through the curator-in-residence program. Mesquita was the first to participate in this program, taking up residence at the institution in 1988. His work at the WAG resulted in "Cartographies," which toured five venues internationally between 1993 and 1995. Despite the success of these initiatives, the WAG's efforts to promote Latin American art were not sustained in the late 1990s.

Chapter 5
Economic Pilgrimage to Southern Ontario: Vincenzo Pietropaolo and the Photohistory of Mexican Farmhands, 1984-2006

1 Pietropaolo has published several photo essays on workers, immigrants, and the marginalized in Canada and Latin America. See Pietropaolo, *Celebration of Resistance: Ontario's Days of Action* (Toronto: Between the Lines, 1999); Pietropaolo, *Canadians at Work* (Toronto: CAW-Canada, 2000); Pietropaolo, *Not Paved with Gold: Italian-Canadian Immigrants in the 1970s* (Toronto: Between the Lines, 2006); *Harvest Pilgrims: Mexican and Caribbean Migrant Farm Workers in Canada* (Toronto: Between the Lines, 2009); *Invisible No More: A Photographic Chronicle of the Lives of People with Intellectual Disabilities.* (New Brunswick: Rutgers University Press, 2010); and Cecelia Lawless, *Making Home in Havana* (New Brunswick: Rutgers University Press, 2002). His work on the Italian community in Toronto and other buildings of the city have also been featured in Pietropaolo, *Ritual* (London: Black Dog Publishing, 2016); Satu Repo, *Marco and Michela*. 2nd ed. (Toronto: James Lorimer and Company, 1985); Penina Coopersmith, *Cabbagetown: The Story of a Victorian Neighbourhood* (Toronto: James Lorimer, 1998); Jean Cochrane, *Kensington* (Erin: Boston Mills Press, 2000); and Michiel Horn, *York University: The Way Must Be Tried* (Montreal and Kingston: McGill-Queen's University Press, 2009).

2 Pietropaolo, *Harvest Pilgrims*, 25.

3 There are seventy-nine photographs altogether in *Harvest Pilgrims*, thirteen of which were taken in Mexico. It is important to note that, while several of Pietropaolo's subjects were Caribbean workers, in this essay I only concentrate on his photographs of Mexican farmhands.

4 Taken from an interview in 2009 with Pietropaolo by the United Food and Commercial Workers Union Canada. See http://www.youtube.com/watch?v=1x-sW_iaJZs.

5 Since these photographs have not been assigned numbers in *Harvest Pilgrims*, to facilitate the reader I have referenced their page numbers in parentheses in the body of the essay.

6 Samuel Truett, "Introduction: Making Transnational History: Nations, Regions, and Borderlands," in *Continental Crossroads: Remapping U.S.-Mexico Borderlands History*, eds. Samuel Truett and Elliott Young (Durham: Duke University Press, 2004), 23.

7 The idea of "many Mexicos" was coined by Lesley Byrd Simpson in her book *Many Mexicos* (Berkeley: University of California Press, 1941). It is now more common, however, to recognize that the histories of Mexico and the United States - both the colonial and modern periods - need to be told together. See Colin M. MacLachlan and William H. Beezley, *El Gran Pueblo: A History of Greater Mexico*, 3rd ed. (Upper Saddle River: Prentice Hall, 2004); and Ida Altman, Sarah L. Cline, and Juan Javier Pescador, *The Early History of Greater Mexico* (Upper Saddle River: Prentice Hall, 2003).

8 Américo Paredes, *"With His Pistol in His Hand": A Border Ballad and Its Hero* (Austin: University of Texas Press, 1958), 129-30.

9 For comparisons between the Bracero Program and the CSAWP (also known as SAWP), see María Muñoz Neri, "The Mexican Temporary Agricultural Workers Program in Canada," *Revista Mexicana de Estudios Canadienses* 1, no. 1 (1999): 91-107; and Tanya Basok, "He Came, He Saw, He...Stayed: Guest Worker Programs and the Issue of Non-Return," *International Migration Review* 38, no. 2 (2000): 215-38.

10 For statistics on Mexican workers in the CSAWP, see Muñoz Neri, "The Mexican Temporary," 96; Leigh Binford et al., *Rumbo a Canadá. La migración canadiense de trabajadores agrícolas tlaxcaltecos* (Mexico City: Ediciones Taller Abierto, 2004), 50; and Maxwell Brem, "Migrant Workers in Canada: A Review of the Canadian Seasonal Agricultural Workers Program," Policy Brief (Ottawa: The North-South Institute, 2006), 2.

11 Ronald L. Mize and Alicia C.S. Swords, *Consuming Mexican Labor: From the Bracero Program to NAFTA* (Toronto: University of Toronto Press, 2011), xxxii.

12 Pietropaolo, *Harvest Pilgrims*, 6. Janet McLaughlin explores the "invisibility" of Mexican workers in the wineries of the Niagara Region in "The Hands behind the Harvest: Migrant Workers in Niagara's Wine Industry," in *The World of Niagara Wine*, eds. by Michael Ripmeester and Phillip Gordon Mackintosh (Waterloo: Wilfrid Laurier University Press, 2013), 109-22.

13 A review of the requirements of the program from the late 1990s and early 2000s can be found in Catherine Colby, "From Oaxaca to Ontario: Mexican Contract Labor in Canada and the Impact at Home," Report for the California Institute for Rural Studies (Davis: California Institute for Rural Studies, 1997); Tanya Basok, *Tortillas and Tomatoes: Transmigrant Mexican Harvesters in Canada* (Montreal and Kingston: McGill-Queen's University Press, 2002), 89-105; and Binford et al., *Rumbo a Canadá*, 48-55.

14 For the experiences of migrant Mexican women in the CSAWP, see Deborah Brandt, *Tangled Routes: Women, Work, and Globalization on the Tomato Trail.* 2nd ed. (Lanham: Rowman & Littlefield Publishers, 2008), 192-200; Kerry Preibisch, "Gender Transformative Odysseys: Tracing the Experiences of Transnational Migrant Women in Rural Canada," *Canadian Women Studies* 24, no. 4 (2005): 91-97; and Ofelia Becerril, "Gendered Politics of Labour: A Study of Male and Female Mexican Migrant Farm Workers in Canada," in *Organizing the Transnational: Labour, Politics, and Social Change,* eds. Luin Goldring and Sailaja Krishnamurti (Vancouver: University of British Columbia Press, 2007), 157-72.

15 Brem, "Migrant Workers," 2.

16 For Caribbean workers in Ontario, see R.G. Cecil and G.E. Ebanks, "The Human Condition of West Indian Migrant Farm Labour in Southwestern Ontario," *International Migration* 29, no. 3 (1991): 389-405; and Cecil and Ebanks, "The Caribbean Migrant Farm Worker Programme in Ontario: Seasonal Expansion of West Indian Economic Spaces," *International Migration* 30, no. 1 (1992): 19-37.

17 For health problems, see B. Singh Bolaria, "Farm Labour, Work Conditions, and Health Risks," in *Rural Sociology in Canada*, eds. David A. Hay and Gurcharn S. Basran (Oxford: Oxford University Press, 1992), 228-45; B. Singh Bolaria and Rosemary Bolaria, "Immigrant Status and Health Status: Women and Racial Minority Immigrant Workers," in *Racial Minorities, Medicine, and Health*, eds. B. Singh Bolaria and Rosemary Bolaria (Halifax: Fernwood Publishing, 1994), 149-68; Janet McLaughlin, "Migration and Health: Implications for Development: A Case Study of Mexican and Jamaican Migrants in Canada's Seasonal Agricultural Workers Program" (FOCAL, Policy Paper, October 2009), https://www.focal.ca/pdf/Migrant%20Health%20McLaughlin%202009.pdf; and McLaughlin, "Trouble in Our Fields: Health and Human Rights among Mexican and Caribbean Migrant Farm Workers in Canada" (PhD diss., University of Toronto, 2009). For working experiences, see Colby, "From Oaxaca"; Binford et al., *Rumbo a Canadá*, 145-81; and Leigh Binford, *Tomorrow We're All Going to the Harvest: Temporary Foreign Work Programs and Neoliberal Political Economy* (Austin: University of Texas Press, 2013), 65-92. For remittances, see Tanya Basok, "Obstacles to Productive Investment, Mexican Farm Workers in Canada," *International Migration Review* 34, no. 1 (2000), 79-97; Basok, "Mexican Seasonal Migration to Canada and Development: A Community-Based Comparison," *International Migration Review* 41, no. 2 (2003), 3-25; Gustavo Verduzco and María Isabel Lozano, "Mexican Farm Workers' Participation in Canada's Seasonal Agricultural Labour Market and Development Consequences in their Rural Home Communities" (Ottawa: The North-South Institute, 2003); and Leigh Binford, *Tomorrow We're All Going to the Harvest: Temporary Foreign Work Programs and Neoliberal Political Economy* (Austin: University of Texas Press, 2013), 116-45. For immigration policy, see Kerry Preibisch, "Local Produce, Foreign Labour: Labour Mobility Programs and Global Trade Competitiveness in Canada," *Rural Sociology* 72, no. 3 (2007): 418-49. For social exclusion, see Tanya Basok, "Post-National Citizenship, Social Exclusion and Migrants Rights: Mexican Seasonal Workers in Canada," *Citizenship Studies* 8, no. 1 (2004): 47-64; and Jenna L. Hennebry, *Permanently Temporary? Agricultural Mi-*

grant Workers and Their Integration in Canada (Montreal: Institute for Research on Public Policy, 2012); and for social inclusion, see Kerry Preibisch, "Migrant Agricultural Workers and Processes of Social Inclusion in Rural Canada: Encuentros and Desencuentros," *Canadian Journal of Latin American and Caribbean Studies* 29 (2004): 203-39; and Preibisch, "Globalizing Work, Globalizing Citizenship: Community-Migrant Worker Alliances in Southwestern Ontario," in *Organizing the Transnational: Labour, Politics, and Social Change*, eds. Luin Goldring and Sailaja Krishnamurti (Vancouver: University of British Columbia Press, 2007), 97-114.

18 See Ellen Wall, "Personal Labor Relations and Ethnicity in Ontario Agriculture," in *Deconstructing a Nation: Immigration, Multiculturalism and Racism in 90s Canada*, ed. Vic Satzewich (Halifax: Fernwood, 1992), 261-75; Tanya Basok, "Free to Be Unfree: Mexican Guest Workers in Canada," *Labour, Capital and Society* 32, no. 2 (1999): 192-221; Basok, *Tortillas and Tomatoes*, 3-16; Vic Satzewich, "The Economic Rights of Migrant and Immigrant Workers in Canada and the United States," in *Economic Rights in Canada and the United States*, eds. Rhoda E. Howard-Hessmann and Claude E. Welch Jr (Philadelphia: University of Pennsylvania Press, 2006), 169-85; Leigh Binford, "Campos agrícolas, campos de poder. El estado mexicano, los granjeros canadienses y los trabajadores temporales mexicanos," *Migraciones Internacionales* 3, no. 3 (2006): 54-80; Binford, "From Fields of Power to Fields of Sweat: The Dual Process of Constructing Temporary Migrant Labour in Mexico and Canada," *Third World Quarterly* 30, no. 3 (2009): 503-17; Binford, *Tomorrow*, 48-52; and Jenna L. Hennebry and Kerry Preibisch, "A Model for Managed Migration? Re-Examining Best Practices in Canada's Seasonal Agricultural Worker Program," *International Migration* 50, no. 1 (2010): 19-40.

19 For feudal serfs, see Harald Bauder, *Labor Movement: How Migration Regulates Labor Markets* (Oxford: Oxford University Press, 2006), 159. For subordination, see Janet McLaughlin, "Classifying the 'Ideal Migrant Worker': Mexican and Jamaican Transnational Farmworkers in Canada," *Focaal: Journal of Global and Historical Anthropology* 57 (2010): 79-94. For paternalism, see Basok, "Tortillas and Tomatoes," 124; Basok, "He Came," 229-30; and Wall, "Personal Labor Relations," 265. For racism, see Leigh Binford, "Social and Economic Contradictions of Rural Migrant Contract Labor between Tlaxcala, Mexico and Canada," *Culture and Agriculture* 24, no. 2 (2002): 1-19; and Binford, *Tomorrow*, 93-115. And for gender biases, see Becerril, "Gendered Politics," 157-72.

20 Nelson Ferguson, "Conversations with Eulogio: On Migration and the Building of a Life-Project in Motion," in *Human Nature as Capacity: Transcending Discourse and Classification*, ed. Nigel Rapport (New York: Berghahn Books, 2010), 31-53.

21 Pietropaolo, *Harvest Pilgrims*, 6.

22 For two studies on migrant workers in Ontario media, see Harald Bauder and Margot Corbin "Foreign Farm Workers in Ontario: Representations in the Newsprint Media" (Research Paper, University of Guelph, 2002); and Bauder, *Labor Movement*, 163-85.

23 Pietropaolo, *Harvest Pilgrims*, 21.

24 An interesting exception is the work of the Canadian artists Carol Condé and Karl Beveridge in their exhibition, Salt of the Earth (2008). See http://condebev-

eridge.ca/?projects=salt-earth-2008. In 2004, Katie Marie Hinnenkamp asked migrant workers in the Niagara Region to draw or choose other creative mediums to express their work experiences in Canada. For a sample of their work, see Hinnenkamp, "Bicycles Traveling in the Rain: A Participatory, Arts-Informed Account of Mexican Farmworkers in Canada" (Master's thesis, University of Toronto, 2007), 127-30.

25 No survey exists on the number of migrant workers with cameras, but researchers have noticed Mexicans using them to document their experiences in Canada. See Basok, "Tortillas and Tomatoes," 107; *El Contrato*, directed by Min Sook Lee (2003; Leamington: National Film Board of Canada), streaming media, 51:15, https://www.nfb.ca/film/el_contrato/; and Binford et al., *Rumbo a Canadá*, 151.

26 Since a large portion of studies on the CSAWP have appeared in academic journals, there are few accompanying photographs. For some notable exceptions, see María del Socorro Arana Hernández and José de Jesús Rogelio Rodríguez Maldonado, *Experiencias laborales de jornaleros tlaxcaltecas en Canadá* (Tlaxcala: Universidad Autónoma de Tlaxcala, 2006), 54-74; Benjamin López Xochihua and Silvia García Ramírez, "Programa de trabajadores agrícolas temporales México-Canadá (PTAT)" in *La migración de tlaxcaltecas en Estados Unidos y Canadá. Panorama actual y perspectivas*, eds. Raúl Jiménez Guillén and Adrián González Romo (San Pablo Apetatitlán: El Colegio de Tlaxcala; Tlaxcala: Universidad Autónoma de Tlaxcala; Tlaxcala: Sistema Estatal de Promoción del Empleo y Desarrollo Comunitario, 2008), 434-40; and Binford, *Tomorrow*, 55, 75, 137-38, 167, 173.

27 Pietropaolo, *Harvest Pilgrims*, 10.

28 Burke, *Eyewitnessing*, 14. Also useful for thinking about photographs as historical documents, specifically in the context of Latin America, is Robert M. Levine, *Images of History: Nineteenth and Early Twentieth Century Latin American Photographs as Documents* (Durham: Duke University Press, 1989).

29 Burke, *Eyewitnessing*, 21.

30 Pietropaolo, *Invisible No More*, 16; Pietropaolo, *Not Paved*, 4.

31 See John Mraz, "Más allá de la decoración. Hacía una historia gráfica de las mujeres en México," *Política y cultura* 1 (1992): 155-89; Mraz, "Photographing Mexico," *Mexican Studies/Estudios Mexicanos* 17, no. 1 (2001): 193-211; Mraz, "Mexican History: A Photo Essay," in *The Mexico Reader: History, Culture, Politics*, eds. Gilbert M. Joseph and Timothy J. Henderson (Durham: Duke University Press, 2002), 297-331; Mraz, "Picturing Mexico's Past: Photography and 'Historia Gráfica,'" *South Central Review* 21, no. 3 (2004): 24-45; Mraz, "Representing the Mexican Revolution: Bending Photographs to the Will of *Historia Gráfica*," in *Photography and Writing in Latin America: Double Exposures*, eds. Marcy E. Schwartz and Mary Beth Tierney-Tello (Albuquerque: University of New Mexico Press, 2006), 21-40; and Mraz, "¿Fotohistoria o historia gráfica? El pasado mexicano en fotografía," *Cuicuilco* 14, no. 41 (2007): 11-41.

32 Mraz, "Picturing Mexico's Past," 35.

33 John Mraz and Jaime Vélez Storey, *Uprooted: Braceros in the Hermanos Mayo Lens* (Houston: Arte Público Press, 1996), 4.

34 Pietropaolo, *Canadians at Work*, 10.

35 Pietropaolo, *Harvest Pilgrims*, 6; Pietropaolo, *Not Paved*, 1.

36 Pietropaolo, *Not Paved*, 4.

37 Pietropaolo, *Invisible No More*, 15.

38 Pietropaolo, *Not Paved*, 11. For an overview of the origins and development of documentary photography, see Beaumont Newhall, *The History of Photography from 1839 to the Present Day*, rev. ed. (New York: Museum of Modern Art, 1978), 135-50.

39 Pietropaolo, *Invisible No More*, 16. For a similar approach among migrant Mexican workers in California, see Rick Nahmias, *The Migrant Project: Contemporary California Farm Workers* (Albuquerque: University of New Mexico Press, 2008).

40 Pietropaolo, *Invisible No More*, 16. For a similar approach among migrant Mexican workers in California, see Nahmias, *The Migrant Project*.

41 In his use of the camera as a "research tool," Pietropaolo follows photographers from the 1930s who documented, in black and white, the living and working conditions of armhands in the wake of the Great Depression in the United States. See Erskine Caldwell and Margaret Bourke-White, *You Have Seen Their Faces* (New York: Modern Age Books, 1937); and Dorothea Lange and Paul Schuster Taylor, *An American Exodus: A Record of Human Erosion*, rev. ed. (New York: Arno Press, 1975).

42 Lewis W. Hine, *Men at Work: Photographic Studies of Modern Men and Machines*, rev. ed. (New York: Dover Publications, 1977), n.p.; Pietropaolo, *Harvest Pilgrims*, 26.

43 For a list of his solo or group exhibitions in both Canada and Mexico, see Pietropaolo, *Harvest Pilgrims*, 129.

44 Pietropaolo, *Harvest Pilgrims*, 6.

45 Naomi Rosenblum, *A World History of Photography* (New York: Abbeville Press, 1984), 508-12.

46 W. Eugene Smith and Aileen M. Smith, *Minamata* (New York: Holt, Rinehart and Winston, 1975), 138-39.

47 Pietropaolo, *Not Paved*, 79.

48 Elin Luque Agraz and Mary Michele Beltrán provide a nice overview of ex-votos in Mexico in "Imágenes poderosas. Exvotos mexicanos," in *Retablos y exvotos*, (Mexico City: Museo Franz Mayer, 2000), 32-53.

49 Some of the earliest ex-votos of the Virgin of Guadalupe can be viewed in Elin Luque Agraz and Mary Michele Beltrán, *El arte de dar gracias. Selección de exvotos pictóricos del Museo de la Basílica de Guadalupe* (Mexico City: Universidad Iberoamericana and Casa Lamm, 2003). Roberto Montenegro provides a sample of ex-votos from eighteenth-century New Spain in *Retablos de México/Mexican Votive Paintings*, trans. Irene Nicholson (Mexico City: Ediciones Mexicanas, 1950), 1-13. And Pilar Gonzalbo Aizpuru points out that "miraculous cures" were the most common themes of colonial ex-votos in "Lo prodigioso cotidiano en los exvotos novohispanos," in *Dones y promesas: 500 años de arte ofrenda (exvotos mexicanos)* (Mexico City: Fundación Cultural Televisa, 1996), 47-63.

50 For ex-votos in nineteenth-century Mexico, see Gloria Kay Giffords, *Mexican Folk Retablos: Masterpieces on Tin* (Tucson: University of Arizona Press, 1974); and Solange Alberro, "Retablos y religiosidad en el México del siglo XIX," in *Retablos y exvotos* (Mexico City: Museo Franz Mayer, 2000), 8-31.

51 For the work of a contemporary retablero, see Vilchis Roque, *Infinitas Gracias*. During a visit to Puebla in 2010, I encountered a retablero selling ex-voto paintings on the street together with other souvenirs. Retablos can also be found in La Ciudadela in Mexico City, a popular destination for artisanal crafts, and in the gift shops of museums like the Museo de Arte Popular, also located in the capital.

52 Jorge Durand and Douglas S. Massey, *Miracles on the Border: Retablos of Mexican Migrants to the United States* (Tucson: University of Arizona Press, 1995), 67. For other scholars who have taken similar approaches, see Mary Michele Beltrán and Elin Luque Agraz, "Where Past and Present Meet: The Ex-Votos of Mexican Immigrants," in *The Road to Aztlan: Art From a Mythical Homeland*, eds. Virginia M. Fields and Victor Zamudio-Taylor (Los Angeles: Los Angeles County Museum of Art, 2001), 318-31; Ana María Pineda, "Imágenes de Dios en el camino: Retablos, Ex-votos, Milagritos, and Murals," *Theological Studies* 65 (2004): 364-79; and Tijen Tunali, "Crossing the Border with Divine Assistance: Ex-voto Paintings of Mexican Immigrants to the United States" (Master's thesis, State University of New York at Buffalo, 2006).

53 Durand and Massey, *Miracles*, 120.

54 Pietropaolo, *Harvest Pilgrims*, 107.

55 McLaughlin records how one migrant worker, Pedro, performs an annual trip to the Basílica de Guadalupe in Mexico City both prior to departure and upon returning home from Canada, "Trouble in Our Fields," 168, 472.

56 Durand and Massey, *Miracles*, 134.

57 Muñoz Neri, "The Mexican Temporary," 100.

58 Brem, "Migrant Workers," 6.

59 Verduzco and Lozano, "Mexican Farm," 3.

60 Durand and Massey, *Miracles*, 142.

61 Pietropaolo, *Harvest Pilgrims*, 105.

62 For a visual tour of one house from the early 2000s in Leamington, see Lee, *El Contrato*. One can also view examples of other living conditions in the photographs of Arana Hernández and Rodríguez Maldonado, *Experiencias laborales*, 61-3, and McLaughlin, "Trouble," 338.

63 Basok, *Tortillas and Tomatoes*, 115. McLaughlin provides a detailed overview of living conditions in "Trouble," 327-39.

64 Preibisch, "Migrant Agricultural Workers," 203-39, and "Globalizing Work," 97-114. Josephine Smart found similar trends among migrant Mexican workers in Alberta in the 1990s, "Borrowed Men on Borrowed Time: Globalization, Labour Migration and Local Economies in Alberta," *Canadian Journal of Regional Science* 20, no. 12 (1997): 141-56.

65 Durand and Massey, *Miracles*, 146.

66 Pietropaolo, *Harvest Pilgrims*, 108.

67 Basok, "He Came," 215-38.

68 Durand and Massey, *Miracles*, 160.

69 Durand and Massey, *Miracles*, 179.

70 McLaughlin, "Trouble," 428-49.

71 Colby, "From Oaxaca," 15-16.

72 Kerry Preibisch and Stan Raper, "Forcing Governments to Govern in Defence of Noncitizen Workers: A Story about the Canadian Labour Movement's Alliance with Agricultural Migrants," in *Organizing the Transnational: Labour, Politics, and Social Change*, eds. Luin Goldring and Sailaja Krishnamurti (Vancouver: University of British Columbia Press, 2007), 119.

73 McLaughlin, "Trouble," 284-88.

74 McLaughlin, "Trouble," 347-52.

75 Durand and Massey, *Miracles*, 194.

76 McLaughlin, "Trouble," 480-84.

77 Hennebry, *Permanently Temporary?*, 3.

78 In a 2010 survey conducted by Hennebry and Preibisch, 60 percent of workers from Mexico and Jamaica expressed interest in permanent residency if given the opportunity. Hennebry, *Permanently Temporary?*, 13.

Chapter 6
Linguistic Landscape: Imagined Borders and Territories Made by/for Latin Americans in Canada

1 Robert Phillipson, *Linguistic Imperialism* (Oxford: Oxford University Press, 1992). Phillipson notes that in other contexts, LL is a marker of linguistic imperialism, showing the power of a foreign language over the local language (e.g. the use of English in the LLs of Mexico City). This power can be related to the economy, domination, global languages, and/or linguistic status.

2 Eliezer Ben-Rafael et al., "Linguistic Landscape as Symbolic Construction of the Public Space: The Case of Israel," *International Journal of Multilingualism* 3, no. 1 (2006): 7-30.; Durk Gorter, *Linguistic Landscape. A New Approach to Multilingualism* (Clevendon: Multilingual Matters, 2006); Huebner, "Bangkok's Linguistic Landscape 31-51; Rodrigue Landry and Richard Bourhis, "Linguistic Landscape and Ethnolinguistic Vitality: An Empirical Study," *Journal of Language and Social Psychology* 16, no. 23 (1997): 23-49; David Malinowski, "Authorship in the Linguistic Landscape: A Multilingual-Performative View," in *Linguistic Landscape: Expanding the Scenery*, ed. Elana Shohamy and Durk Gorter (New York: Routledge, 2009), 107-25.

3 Landry and Bourhis, "Linguistic Landscape," 23-49.

4 Statistics Canada, *The Latin American Community in Canada* (Ottawa: Statistics Canada, 2007), http://www.statcan.gc.ca/pub/89-621-x/89-621-x2007008-eng.htm.

5 Statistics Canada, *The Latin American*.

6 Statistics Canada, *The Latin American*.

7 Statistics Canada, *The Latin American*.

8 Statistics Canada. *The Latin American*.

9 Delphine Nakache and Paula J. Kinoshita, "The Canadian Temporary Foreign Worker Program: Do Short-Term Economic Needs Prevail Over Human Rights Concerns?" IRPP Study No. 5 (2010): 1-49.

10 Citizen and Immigration Canada, *Facts and Figures 2012 - Immigration Overview: Permanent and Temporary Residents*, http://www.cic.gc.ca/english/resources /statistics/facts2012/temporary/03.asp.

11 Citizen and Immigration Canada, *Annual Report to Parliament on Immigration*, 2009, http://www.cic.gc.ca/english/resources/publications/annualreport2009/index.asp.

12 Citizen and Immigration Canada, *Annual Report*.

13 Employment and Social Development Canada, *Temporary Foreign Worker Program Labour Market Opinion (LMO) Statistics Annual Statistics 2006-2009*, http://www.hrsdc.gc.ca/eng/workplaceskills/foreign_workers/stats/annual/table10a.shtml

14 Employment and Social Development Canada, *Seasonal Agricultural Worker Program*, http://www.esdc.gc.ca/eng/jobs/foreign_workers/agriculture/seasonal/.

15 Philip Martin, "Managing Labor Migration: Temporary Worker Programs for the 21st Century," *International Labour Organization (International Institute for Labour Studies)*, 2003, 1-33.

16 Manolo Abella, "Policies and Best Practices for Management of Temporary Migration," International Symposium on International Migration and Development, Population Division, Department of Economic and Social Affairs, United Nations Secretariat, Turin, Italy, June 28-30, 2006, https://www.un.org/en/development/desa/population/events/pdf/other/turin/P03_Abella.pdf and https://www.migrationpolicy.org/article/canadas-temporary-migration-program-model-despite-flaws.

17 Citizen and Immigration Canada, "Facts and Figures."

18 Secretaría de Trabajo y Previsión Social, "Programa de trabajadores agrícolas temporales México-Canadá."

19 Secretaría de Relaciones Exteriores, "Trabajadores Agrícolas Temporales (PTAT)," accessed March 14, 2014, http://www.sre.gob.mx/proteccionconsular/index.php/trabajadores-agricolas-en-canada.

20 Statistics Canada, *Focus on Geography Series, 2011 Census* (Ottawa: Statistics Canada), https://www12.statcan.gc.ca/census-recensement/2011/as-sa/fogs-spg/Facts-pr-eng.cfm?Lang=Eng&GC=47.

21 Municipality of Leamington, "About Leamington," https://www.leamington.ca/en/index.aspx

22 Statistics Canada, *Visual Census, 2006 Census* (Ottawa: Statistics Canada, 2006), http://www12.statcan.gc.ca/censusrecensement/2006/dppd/fsfi/index.cfm?Lang=ENG&TOPIC_ID=11&PRCODE=01.

23 Tanya Basok, Danièle Bélanger and Eloy Rivas, "Reproducing Deportability: Migrant Agricultural Workers in South-Western Ontario," *Journal of Ethnic and Migration Studies* 20, no. 9 (2014): 1-20.

24 Basok, Bélanger and Rivas, "Reproducing Deportability," 1-20.

25 María Eugenia De Luna, "Mexican Temporary Agricultural Workers in Canada: A Language and Migration Approach" (PhD diss., University of Western Ontario, 2011), http://ir.lib.uwo.ca/etd/257.

26 De Luna, "Mexican Temporary Agricultural."

27 Marie-Ève Hudon, *Official Languages in Canada: Federal Policy*, 2010, https://lop.parl.ca/sites/PublicWebsite/default/en_CA/ResearchPublications/201170E.

28 Hudon, *Official Languages*.

29 Minister of Justice, *Official Languages Act R.S.C., 1985, c. 31* (4th Supp.), 2014, accessed June 20, 2014, https://laws-lois.justice.gc.ca/eng/acts/O-3.01/.

30 Hudon, *Official Languages.*

31 Don J. DeVoretz, Holger Hinte, and Christiane Werner, "How Much Language Is Enough? Some Immigrant Language Lessons from Canada and Germany," IZA Discussion Papers Series no. 555, 2002, http://ftp.iza.org/dp555.pdf.

32 Thomas Ricento, "Models and Approaches in Language Policy and Planning," in *Language and Communication: Diversity and Change,* eds. Marlis Hellinger and Anne Pauwels (Berlin: Mouton de Gruyter, 2007), 177-207.

33 Services Ontario, *French Language Services Act,* 2013, accessed April 29, 2014, http://www.elaws.gov.on.ca/html/statutes/english/elaws_statutes_90f32_e.htm.

34 François Vaillancourt and Olivier Coche, *Official Language Policies at the Federal Level in Canada: Costs and Benefits in 2006* (Vanvouver: Fraser Institute, 2009).

35 Advertising Standards Canada, *The Canadian Code of Advertising Standards,* accessed May 19, 2014, http://www.adstandards.com/en/standards/canCodeOfAdStandards.aspx

36 Advertising Standards Canada, *The Canadian Code.*

37 Municipality of Leamington, "About Leamington."

38 Municipality of Leamington, "About Leamington."

39 Office québécois de la langue française, "Charter of the French Language," 2014, accessed October 25, 2014, http://www2.publicationsduquebec.gouv.qc.ca/dynamicSearch/telecharge.php ?type=2&file=/C_11/C11_A.html.

40 Office québécois de la langue française, "Charter."

41 Office québécois de la langue française, "Charter."

42 Landry and Bourhis, "Linguistic Landscape," 23-49.

43 Landry and Bourhis, "Linguistic Landscape," 4.

44 Thom Huebner, "Bangkok's Linguistic Landscape: Environmental Print, Codemixing and Language Change," in *Linguistic Landscape: A New Approach to Multilingualism,* ed. by Durk Gorter (Clevendon, England: Multilingual Matters Ltd., 2006), 31-51.

45 Huebner, "Bangkok's Linguistic Landscape," 5.

46 Durk Gorter, H.F. Marten and L. Van Mensel, *Minority Languages in the Linguistic Landscape* (Houndmills, Basingstoke, Hampshire: Palgrave Macmillan, 2012).

47 Florian Coulmas, *Sociolinguistics: The Study of Speakers' Choices* (New York: Cambridge University Press, 2005).

48 Landry and Bourhis, "Linguistic Landscape," 23-49.

49 Landry and Bourhis, "Linguistic Landscape," 6.

50 Landry and Bourhis, "Linguistic Landscape," 6.

51 Landry and Bourhis, "Linguistic Landscape," 7.

52 Jasone Cenoz and Duke Gorter, "El estudio del paisaje lingüístico," accessed October 2013, https://www.euskadi.eus/gobierno-vasco/contenidos/informacion/artik22_1_cenoz_08_03/es_cenoz/artik22_1_cenoz_08_03.html.

53 Cenoz and Gorter, "El estudio."

54 Cenoz and Gorter, "El estudio."

55 Diego Muñoz Carrobles, "Breve itinerario por el paisaje lingüístico de Madrid," Ángulo Recto. Revista de estudios sobre la ciudad como espacio plural 2, no. 2 (2010): 103-09.

56 Lola Pons-Rodríguez, "Hispanoamérica en el paisaje lingüístico de Sevilla," *Itinerarios* 13 (2011): 97-129.

57 Ron Scollon and Suzanne Scollon, *Discourses in Place: Language in the Material World* (London: Routledge, 2003).

58 Ben-Rafael et al., "Linguistic Landscape," 7-30.

59 Malinowski, "Authorship," 107-25.

60 De Luna, "Mexican Temporary Agricultural."

61 Landry and Bourhis, "Linguistic Landscape," 23-49; Huebner, "Bangkok's Linguistic Landscape," 31-51.

62 De Luna, "Mexican Temporary Agricultural." Saint-Rémi is located near Montreal; it is a small town, and it is mainly francophone. It has a small population, considered to be a visible minority; it has few ethnic enclaves, and therefore the LL is mainly in French, as De Luna explains.

63 Gorter and Van Mensel, *Minority Languages*, 1-15.

64 Muñoz Carrobles, "Breve itinerario," 103-09.

65 De Luna, "Mexican Temporary Agricultural."

66 Muñoz Carrobles, "Breve itinerario," 103-09.

67 Pons-Rodríguez, "Hispanoamérica," 97-129.

68 Ricento, "Models and Approaches," 177-207.

69 Municipality of Leamington, "About Leamington."

70 Landry and Bourhis, "Linguistic Landscape," 23-49.

71 John Bourhis and Mike Allen, "Meta Analysis of the Relationship between Communication Apprehension and Cognitive Performance." *Communication Education* 41, no. 1 (1992): 68-76.

72 Statistics Canada, Focus on Geography Series.

73 Pons-Rodríguez, "Hispanoamérica," 97-129.

74 Malinowski, "Authorship," 107-125.

75 Landry and Bourhis, "Linguistic Landscape," 23-49; Huebner, "Bangkok's Linguistic Landscape," 31-51; Gorter and Van Mensel, *Minority Languages*.

76 Huebner, "Bangkok's Linguistic Landscape," 31-51.

Chapter 7
Expatria: Natalia Lara Díaz-Berrio's Photographs on the Mexican Diaspora and the Domestic Space (Visual Essay)

1 The model for this essay was inspired by the visual essay by Maria del Carmen Suescun Pozas, "From Reading to Seeing. Doing and Undoing Imperialism in the Visual Arts," in *Close Encounters of Empire: Writing the Cultural History of U.S-Latin American Relations*, eds. Gilbert Joseph, Catherine LeGrand, and Ricardo Salvatore (Durham, NC: Duke University Press, 1998), 525-56.

2 Tzvetan Todorov, *La conquista de América: el problema del otro* (Mexico City: Siglo XXI Editores, 1999), 13. The quote given here was translated from the Spanish by Zuniga.

3 Jacques Rancière, *The Emancipated Spectator* (New York: Verso Books, 2014), 82.

4 Rancière, *The Emancipated Spectator*, 99.

5 This chapter was written in English, the interviews were conducted in Spanish, translated by the author, and revised by the translator Luz María Méndez. For this chapter, I chose five interviewees who, I found, were significant for their differences and who could reflect particular aspects of Mexican migration in Quebec. For one of the two chosen photographs, I asked the sitters to wear something that represented Mexico personally (or to choose a Mexican object if they didn't have any Mexican clothes). I was interested in the discrepancy that the diptychs revealed.

6 Robert Clarke, "Fe Fi Fo Fum...The Cultural Ambiguities of the Incomer," in *Art Education Discourses*, vol 1, *Root and Stem*, ed. Jacquie Swift (Birmingham: ARTicle Press, 1998), 37.

7 Susan Chevlowe, *The Jewish Identity Project, New American Photography* (New Haven: Yale University Press, 2005), 7.

8 Stuart Hall, *Modernity: An Introduction to Modern Societies* (Malden, MA: Blackwell Publishers, 1996), 614.

9 Raymond Williams, *Keywords: A Vocabulary of Culture and Society* (New York: Oxford University Press, 1983), 215.

10 Chevlowe, *The Jewish Identity*, 2.

11 Ashok Mathur, Jonathan Dewar, and Mike DeGagné, *Cultivating Canada: Reconciliation through the Lens of Cultural Diversity* (Ottawa: Aboriginal Healing Foundation, 2011), 127.

12 Mathur, Dewar, and DeGagné, *Cultivating Canada*, 128.

13 Peter Galassi, *Pleasures and Terrors of Domestic Comfort* (New York: Museum of Modern Art, 1991), 12.

14 Myria Georgiou, *Diaspora, Identity and the Media: Diasporic Transnationalism and Mediated Spatialities* (Cresskill, New Jersey: Hampton Press, 2006), 50.

15 Clarke, "Fe Fi Fo," 37.

16 Hall, *Modernity*, 617.

17 Maurice Berger, *Whiteness and Race in Contemporary Art* (Baltimore: University of Maryland Baltimore County, 2004), 45.

18 Berger, *Whiteness and Race*, 25.

19 Drucilla Cornell, *Moral Images of Freedom: A Future for Critical Theory* (Maryland: Rowman & Littlefield Publishers, 2008), 128.

20 Cornell, *Moral Images*, 128.

21 For the project *Expatria*, oral interviews were conducted in the domestic space. For this chapter, the conversation has been condensed. Questions were set up in a way that would allow the participant's responsiveness. They were open questions, promoting dialogue by expressing interest in Mexicans' perceptions and experiences. Some of the questions had to do with their expectations when they moved to Montreal and with their notion of contributing (or not) to the society where they live. Other questions had to do with their bond with Mexico and their perception of what defined them as Mexicans.

22 Cornell, *Moral Images*, 123.

23 Interviewees are presented by their first name only to respect their anonymity.

24 The support groups are: Todos a Québec (Everyone to Quebec) and *Aquí decidimos vivir* (This is where we decided to live). The group Aquí decidimos vivir has about 600 members and shares information with the permanent resident

Mexicans who have just arrived in Montreal (from basic needs to information on social insurance and health insurance).

25 He said he has a fondness for the country's history and the *charrería* (*charrería* is the national practice of riding and of the various forms of rodeo. It is also one of the most representative Mexican traditions; it shows the courage, bravery, and manhood of the charro (horseman), and the energy and image of the horse, with a celebration of music and colour). A clear reflection of this interest was his knowledge of these traditions and the Mexican clothes he brought to Canada (as shown in the second photograph).

26 The MUR group (Mexicans United for Legalization) was formed in 2011 from the need to support the large number of Mexicans who were being deported; it is a network of solidarity, self-management, and resistance. Its main conviction is that no one deserves more than others do. The group participated in the march to Ottawa on 2 November 2012 to demand the legalization of people without status and to express their disagreement over the free-trade agreements that do not allow the free movement of people. The agreement is effective as of 1 January 1994. The group organizes legal clinics to provide information to those who have applied for asylum or who have problems with their papers; they assist people who do not speak English or French when they go to their migration appointments, and support the families in different ways. MUR also publicizes individual cases of migrants in order to put pressure on the government. One of them was the case of the Reyes Méndez family (the father had been kidnapped three times and that is why they decided to leave the country). They tried to prevent the deportation of the family and obtained the support of Deputy Amir Khadir from the Solidaire party of Quebec, but they could not prevent the deportation.

Part III

Chapter 8
Culture for *la denuncia:* The Chilean Exile Community and the Political Goals of Cultural Expression, 1973-1980

1 Five of the twenty-one exiles I interviewed were brought to Canada on the state's initiative or sponsored by organizations working in solidarity with the persecuted in Chile. Carlos Torres, whose testimony appears in this essay, was sponsored by the government of Quebec as part of a programme for political prisoners.

2 Oñate and Wright have documented the presence of Chilean exiles in up to 140 countries. Rody Oñate and Thomas Wright, *La diáspora chilena a 30 años del golpe militar*, 2nd ed. (Mexico City: Urdimbre, 2002), 123.

3 One example of this is a hunger strike by Chilean exiles and sympathizers that took place in multiple countries in 1978. José Del Pozo, "Las organizaciones comunitarias de chilenos en la provincia de Québec, Canadá," in *Exiliados, emigrados y retornados: chilenos en América y Europa, 1973- 2004*, ed. José del Pozo (Santiago: RIL Editores, 2006), 134.

4 Gabrielle Etcheverry, "Ediciones Cordillera: A Study of Chilean Literary Production in Canada" (Master's diss., York University, 2005), 36.

5 Joan Simalchik, "The Material Culture of Chilean Exile: A Transnational Dialogue," *Refuge* 23, no. 2 (2006): 99, 104.

6 Fernando Allodi and Alejandro Rojas, "The Role of a Housing Coopera-tive Community in the Mental Health and Social Adaptation of Latin American Refugees in Toronto," *Migration World Magazine* 16, no. 3 (1988); Jorge Barudy, "A Programme of Mental Health for Political Refugees: Dealing with the Invis-ible Pain of Political Exile," *Social Science and Medicine* 28, no. 7 (1989); Liliana Muñoz, "Exile as bereavement: Socio-Psychological Manifestations of Chilean Exiles in Great Britain," *British Journal of Medical Psychology* 53 (1980): 227-232; Margarite M. Perez, "Exile: The Chilean Experience," *International Journal of Social Psychiatry* 30, no. 1-2 (Mar. 1, 1984): 157-161.

7 Only two of the people I interviewed arrived before the establishment of the Special Movement Chile in November 1973.

8 One such group was composed of Chilean students studying at the Univer-sity of Toronto, who were mentioned by several of the people I interviewed. They were part of a group that carried out a protest in Ottawa on 20 September 1973 to push for Canadian government action on the crisis in Chile. "Chilean students parade in Ottawa to protest junta," *Toronto Star*, September 21, 1973, A10.

9 For a detailed description and analysis of Canadian groups working in soli-darity with Chilean exiles, see Joan Simalchik, "Part of the Great Awakening: Canadian Churches and the Chilean Refugees, 1970-1979" (Master's thesis, University of Toronto, 1993).

10 Delegations representing a large number of organizations involved in the Chilean solidarity movement met with officials of the federal government on two occasions, in 1974 and in 1976. The written portion of their presentations can be found in the NACLA-ALA archive: "Canadian Policy Toward Chile. Brief to the Honourable Allan J. MacEachern, Secretary of State for External Affairs, and the Honourable Robert K. Andras, Minister of Manpower and Immigration," Octo-ber 9, 1974, Roll 14, File 67, Canada-Chile Relations: 1968-1974, NACLA-ALA, Chile; "Canada and the Rights of the Chilean People. A Brief Presented to the Can-adian Government by the Coalition on Canadian Policy Towards Chile," March 1976, Roll 14, File 67, Canada-Chile Relations: 1968-1974, NACLA-ALA, Chile.

11 The events leading up to the announcement of the SMC are described in George Hanff, Decision-Making Under Pressure: A Study of the Admittance of Chilean Refugees by Canada." *NS, North-South* 4, no. 8 (1979): 116-135.

12 Jaime Llambías-Wolff, *Notre exil pour parler: les Chiliens au Québec* (Mont-real: Fides, 1988), 121-22; Ana Vásquez and Ana María Araujo, *La maldición de Ulises: Repercusiones psicológicas del exilio* (Santiago: Sudamericana, 1990), 207.

13 Interview by author with Juan Núñez, Toronto, 21 November 2009. This quotation also appears as part of a longer quote in Francis Peddie, "Young, Well-Educated, and Adaptable People: Chilean Exiles, Identity and Daily Life in Can-ada, 1973 to the Present Day" (Ph.D. diss., York University, 2010), 19.

14 Interview by author with S.V.P., Toronto, 31 October 2008. She asked to be identified by her initials. This quotation also appears in Peddie, "Young, Well-Educated," 91.

15 Interview by author with Joan Simalchik, Toronto, 15 February 2010. This quo-tation also appears as part of a shorter quote in Peddie, "Young, Well-Educated," 87.

16 Del Pozo, "Las organizaciones comunitarias," 133-34. Del Pozo describes the objectives of both groups as denuncia and solidarity, and cites activities such

as protests, conferences, and fund-raising. La Asociación de chilenos de Montreal also took part in the 1978 global hunger strike in support of political prisoners and ran a Spanish-language special school to help ensure that children of exiles wouldn't lose their mother tongue.

17 A federal memorandum from 1974 discusses the policy of dispersing Chileans throughout the country for better access to jobs and resettlement assistance. A Manpower and Immigration official from the Prairies states that the "economic conditions, job vacancies and availability of language training along with the probable co-operation of the provinces were all positive factors" in the resettlement of Chileans in that region. "Notes - meeting held Dec. 27, 1974 in the Board Room of the ADM Immigration re: Special Program - Chile." RG 76, Vol. 986, File 5781-1, Refugees-Chilean Movement General, Library and Archives Canada.

18 Litzy Baeza Kallens, "Voces del exilio: testimonios orales del exilio chileno en Edmonton, Canadá" (Master's thesis, Universidad de Chile, 2004), 81.

19 Baeza Kallens, "Voces del exilio," 75.

20 Interview by author with Marlinda Freire, Toronto, 22 October 2008. Interview in Spanish.

21 Llambías-Wolff, *Notre exil*, 124.

22 Interview by author with Carlos Torres, Toronto, 21 October 2008. Interview in English.

23 Interview by author with S.V.P., Toronto, 31 October 2008. Interview in Spanish.

24 Interview by author with Nidia Rivera, Toronto, 9 November 2008. Interview in English. This quotation also appears in Peddie, "Young, Well-Educated," 95.

25 Interview by author with Willy Behrens, Ottawa, 17 February 2010. Interview in Spanish.

26 Interview by author with Jorge Etcheverry, Ottawa, 16 February 2010. Interview in Spanish. This quotation also appears in Peddie, "Young, Well-Educated," 95.

27 Etcheverry, "Ediciones Cordillera," 64-5.

28 Interview by author with Jeffry House, Toronto, February 11, 2010. Interview in English.

29 Baeza Kallens, "Voces del exilio," 66-70.

30 Perez, "Exile," 159.

31 Muñoz, "Exile as Bereavement," 231.

32 Oñate and Wright, *La diáspora chilena*, 61.

33 Barudy, "A Programme," 718, 725.

34 Allodi and Rojas, "The Role," 19.

35 Simalchik, "The Material Culture," 98-9.

36 Interview by author with Ana María Barrenechea, Toronto, 14 February 2010.

37 Interview by author with Marlinda Freire, Toronto, 22 October 2008. This quotation also appears as part of a longer quote in Peddie, "Young, Well-Educated," 112.

38 Interview by author with Juan Núñez, Toronto, 21 November 2009. Interview in Spanish.

39 Interview by author with Marlinda Freire, Toronto, 22 October 2008. This quotation also appears as part of a longer quote in Peddie, "Young, Well-Educated," 152.

40 Interview by author with Jorge Etcheverry, Ottawa, 16 February 2010. See also Etcheverry, "Ediciones Cordillera," 66.

41 Llambías-Wolff, *Notre exil*, 53.

42 Interview by author with Ana María Barrenechea, Toronto, 14 February 2010. Interview in Spanish and English.

43 Del Pozo, "Las organizaciones comunitarias," 135, 143.

44 Baeza Kallens, "Voces del exilio," 75.

45 Del Pozo, "Las organizaciones comunitarias," 139; Baeza Kallens, "Voces del exilio," 77.

46 Interview by author with Carlos Torres, Toronto, 21 October 2008.

47 Interview by author with Jorge Etcheverry, Ottawa, 16 February 2010; see also G. Etcheverry, "Ediciones Cordillera," 36-40, for the range of Ediciones Cordillera activities.

48 Interview by author with Patricia Godoy, Toronto, 31 October 2008. Interview in Spanish. This quotation also appears in Peddie, "Young, Well-Educated," 96.

Chapter 9
Theatre and the Building of a Latin American Identity in Canada

1 Vargas Llosa, *Letras Libres*. Unless otherwise indicated, all translations into English of Spanish texts are mine.

2 Fernando Ortiz Arellano, "Eduardo Galeano: América Latina cuenta con grandes reservas de dignidad," *Pueblos*, Dec. 1, 2005. http://www.revistapueblos.org/old/spip.php?article306.

3 Víctor Ramos, "La identidad latinoamericana: proceso contradictorio de su construcción-deconstrucción-reconfiguración dentro de contextos globales," *Universitas Humanística* 73 (2012): 15-58.

4 Ric Knowles and Ingrid Mündel, eds. "Ethnic," *Multicultural and Intercultural Theatre*, vol. 14 of *Critical Perspectives on Canadian Theatre in English* (Toronto: Playwrights Canada Press, 2009).

5 Knowles and Mündel, "Ethnic," 100

6 Douglas Kellner, "Brecht's Marxist Aesthetics," Illuminations: The Critical Theory Website (University of Texas at Arlington), accessed October 29, 2014, http://www.uta.edu/huma/illuminations/kell3.htm, first published in *Bertolt Brecht. Political Theory and Literary Practice*, ed. Betty Nance Weber and Hubert Heinen (Manchester: Manchester University Press, 1980), 29-42.

7 Manuel M. Martín Rodríguez, "El teatro chicano a través de los siglos: panorama crítico," *Revista Arrabal* (Universidad de Alicante) no. 7-8 (2010): 33. The original reads, "producto que es hoy en día bilingüe, multicultural, transnacional, fronterizo y, al mismo tiempo, decididamente original."

8 Rob Appleford, ed., *Aboriginal Drama and Theatre*. Vol. 1 of *Critical Perspectives on Canadian Theatre in English* (Toronto: Playwrights Canada Press, 2005).

9 Appleford, ed., *Aboriginal Drama*, iii.

10 Appleford, ed., *Aboriginal Drama*, x.

11 Appleford, ed., *Aboriginal Drama*.

12 Appleford, ed., *Aboriginal Drama*, 1.

13 Appleford, ed., *Aboriginal Drama*, 1.

14 Karen Shimakawa, "Enunciating Asian Canadian Drama," in *Asian Canadian Theatre*, eds. Nina Lee Aquino and Ric Knowles (Toronto: Playwrights Canada, 2011), 1-10.

15 Nina Lee Aquino and Ric Knowles, eds., *Asian Canadian Theatre*, 4. Vol. 1 of *New Essays on Canadian Theatre* (Toronto: Playwrights Canada Press, 2011).

16 Aquino and Knowles, eds., *Asian Canadian Theatre*, 4.

17 Aquino and Knowles, eds., *Asian Canadian Theatre*, 7.

18 This is a highly summarized overview of the history of Latin American immigration to Canada presented in order to provide context.

19 Cited in Pilar Riaño-Alcalá et al., *Forced Migration of Colombians. Colombia, Ecuador, Canada* (Vancouver: University of British Columbia, 2008).

20 Riaño-Alcalá et al., *Forced Migration*, 21.

21 Riaño-Alcalá et al., *Forced Migration*, 23.

22 For more recent data on immigration trends, on the Latin American community and comparisons with previous census, go to https://www120.statcan. gc.ca/stcsr/en/sr1/srs?fq=stclac:2&start=0&showSum=show2&q=populati on%20ethnic%20origin.

23 See https://www120.statcan.gc.ca/stcsr/en/sr1/srs?fq=stclac:2&start=0&s howSum=show2&q=population%20ethnic%20origin.

24 Hazelton, *Latinocanadá*, 30.

25 Hazelton, *Latinocanadá*, 30.

26 Eve Dumas, "Un vistazo al teatro latinoamericano en el Canadá," *Revista Conjunto* 125 (2002), 89-95. "Hoy, la presencia latinoamericana en el Canadá se debe en gran medida a los intercambios. De este modo, mexicanos, cubanos, chilenos, argentinos y otros, descubren las culturas canadiense y quebequense al mismo ritmo que canadienses y quebequenses disfrutan de la producción artística de la América Latina en todas sus sutilezas. Por demás una parte importante del teatro y de la realidad hispanoamericana nos llega a través del quehacer de chilenos, argentinos o salvadoreños exiliados en el Canadá desde hace muchos años," in the original.

27 See http://www.ontarioimmigration.ca/en/living/OI_HOW_LIVE_TO-RONTO.html

28 Aguirre was particularly shocked when Gass told her that there were no "superb" Latino actors in Canada. A summary of the controversy can be read in https://nowtoronto.com/news/dramatic-ending/.

29 By the time this essay was completed, Alameda Theatre has stopped their activities. Mariló Núñez worked as a General Manager for the Hamilton's Fringe Festival and currently is a freelance theatre artist and producer.

30 After closing the theatre company, Alameda Theatre, and the website, all the content and the work that was hosted there unfortunately disappeared. Mariló Núñez keeps part of the information in her own records.

31 To read more on the community aspect of theatre, go to Jorge Dubatti, *El convivio teatral: teoría y práctica del teatro contemporáneo* ["The convivial theatre: theory and practice of modern theatre," in a rough translation] (Buenos Aires: Atuel, 2003) (Spanish only).

32 Alvarez, *Latina/o Canadian Theatre*.

33 There are many stories about Joaquín Murieta that make him either a horse thief or a revolutionary. He has been called The Mexican Robin Hood or The Robin Hood of El Dorado and, thanks to a dime store novel written in the mid 1800s and translated into French, the story travelled to Europe. The facts about him are that there was a Mexican man named Joaquín Murrieta born in Hermosillo, Sonora, Mexico, in 1829, who married Rosita Feliz and travelled to California in 1849 to take part in the Gold Rush. He didn't succeed because of racism and the opposition of the miners that were already digging the site. Then he became a thief and raised a gang with family and friends that was considered among the most dangerous in the region. He was caught and beheaded in 1852 and his head was exhibited in travelling fairs until it was destroyed in the 1906 San Francisco earthquake. The myth of his early death (at 23), misfortune and the bad treatment he received from the Anglos made him a great character to use to oppose racism.

34 Lola Montez, whose real name was Eliza Rosana Gilbert, is another very well documented historical character. She was an Irish woman whose intense life took her from Ireland to England, India, France, the USA, Australia and back to the USA. She is an example of the Latin Lover cliché, because she chose her identity as Lola Montez the Spanish Dancer to build up a career on the stage. At some point she was better known for her beauty than for her dancing or acting and she lived as a courtesan. She ended up as an author of an *Autobiography* (edited by Charles Chauncey Burr including her lectures on "womanly" topics such as Heroines of History) and of a book called *The Arts of Beauty, Or, Secrets of a Lady's Toilet*. Chilean author Isabel Allende describes her in her novel *Hija de la fortuna* as the owner of "disturbing malignancy, [her] legendary beauty and [her] fiery temperament" (New York: HarperCollins, 1999), 189.

35 Mariló Núñez, *Three Fingered Jack and the Legend of Martín Murieta*, in *Fronteras Vivientes: Eight Latina/o Canadian Plays*, ed. Natalie Alvarez (Toronto: Playwrights Canada Press, 2013), 173-207.

36 Núñez, *Three Fingered Jack*, 195

37 Núñez, *Three Fingered Jack*, 204

38 Núñez, *Three Fingered Jack*, 205

39 This and the following quotations from Natalie Alvarez have been taken from my interview with Alvarez, Toronto, June 2014. The interview was conducted in Spanish, the translation is mine.

40 Interview with Alvarez.

41 This and the following quotations from Guillermo Verdecchia have been taken from my own Skype conversation with Verdecchia, June, 2014. The interview was conducted in Spanish, the translation is mine.

42 Alvarez, *Fronteras Vivientes*, 75-6

43 Alvarez, *Fronteras Vivientes*, 103

44 Alvarez, *Fronteras Vivientes*, 105

45 Alvarez, *Fronteras Vivientes*, 106

46 Alvarez, *Fronteras Vivientes*, 84

47 Interview with Verdecchia.

48 In Appleford, *Aboriginal Drama*, 108-09.

49 Interview with Verdecchia.

50 The following quotations come from my interview with Lorena Leija, Guelph (Ontario), July 2014. The interview was conducted in Spanish, the translation is mine.

51 Anne Nothof, "Soulpepper Theatre Company," *Canadian Theatre Encyclopedia*, last updated July 1, 2020, http://www.canadiantheatre.com/dict. pl?term=Soulpepper%20Theatre %.

Chapter 10
Perspectives of Exile in Twenty-First Century Hispano-Canadian Short Narrative

1 The excerpts from the short stories cited in this chapter were translated by Natalia Caldas from the Spanish.

2 Hugh Hazelton explains that political refugees made community centres in Toronto in which poems and stories that talked about the experience of war and exile were put on the walls. For further details consult Hazelton, *Latinocanadá*, 5.

3 According to Statistics Canada, Spanish occupies the third place within non-official languages that are most spoken in the country in the 2011 census. Likewise, it is among the languages used in the home that showed the largest growth from the last two censuses, reporting an increase of 32% between the 2006 and 2011 census. *Visual Census, 2011 Census* (Ottawa: Statistics Canada, 2012), http://www12.statcan.gc.ca/census-recensement/2011/dp-pd/vc-rv/index. cfm?Lang=ENG&TOPIC_ID=4&GEOCODE=01.

4 With the arrival of the Chilean immigration in the 1970s, the first Spanish-language publishing houses began to appear. Ediciones Cordillera (Ottawa), for example, founded in 1976 by the narrator Leandro Urbina and other Chilean authors, would publish the first anthology of Spanish-speaking authors in the country: *Literatura chilena en Canadá/Chilean Literature in Canada* (1982), edited by Naín Nómez. Also giving an account of the work by Chilean authors in favour of the production and dissemination of Hispano-Canadian literature in general are other publishing companies such as Split Quotation/La cita trunca (founded in 1996 by Jorge Etcheverry) and Verbum Veritas (opened by Luciano Díaz); El Dorado Cultural Workshop, where monthly works by Hispano-Canadian authors can be read; or the literary meetings known as Boreal. Among many others that still run or have closed their doors, there also exist small publishing presses established by authors of origins other than Chilean. White Dwarf Editions/Les Éditions de la Naine Blanche/Las Ediciones de la Enana Blanca, is a trilingual micro-publishing house founded in 1982 by Hugh Hazelton, a Montreal-based poet and translator. Amaranta Press began to publish in 2000 in Saskatoon and was founded by the Salvadorean Julio Torres-Recinos. It is important to note that small presses such as those mentioned, events, and reading workshops, in addition to print and online journals that promote works of Hispano-Canadian authors, have been created by members of the Hispanic community in Canada, many of whom have been connected to the universities of the country. Take for example the cases of Leandro Urbina, who obtained a master of literature degree from the University of Ottawa; Jorge Etcheverry, a Doctor of literature from the University of Montreal; Hugh Hazelton, professor emeritus of Spanish Translation and Latin American Civiliza-

tion at Concordia University in Montreal; and Julio Torres-Recinos, literature professor at the University of Saskatchewan.

5 Jorge Etcheverry attributes this subalternity to the production in English and French, to the necessity of guaranteeing the survival of culture and identity in Canada in the face of pressures from the diverse immigration that arrives in the country and the cultural pressures from the southern neighbour (US). Likewise, he points out that literature written in Spanish in Canada is more important if it is compared to other "transplanted literatures," i.e. written in other languages in the country. This takes into account both the quantity of its production and the quality. For more information on this topic, read Jorge Etcheverry's "Una literatura en castellano en un medio anglófono" at http://www.letras.mysite.com/je040405.htm.

6 Jorge Etcheverry, email to the author, December 15, 2013.

7 Both anthologies were dedicated in the new century in an exclusive manner to the short story, and it is for this reason that they have been the subjects of this study. *Las imposturas de Eros: cuentos de amor en la posmodernidad*, edited by Julio Torres-Recinos and Luis Molina-Lora and published by Lugar Común in 2009, is also composed only of short stories, but which are dedicated to the topic of love. Nevertheless, in *Imposturas* it is possible to find stories that depict the lives and experiences of the exile, for which reason its inclusion in a larger study is recommended. Likewise, numerous short stories with a migratory topic make up part of anthologies that present other genres too. It is recommended the reader consult *Otras Latitudes: Voces argentinas alrededor del Paralelo 49*, edited by Margarita Feliciano and published by Anthology of Contemporary Writers in 2013; *Borealis: Antología literaria de El Dorado* edited by Luciano Díaz and Jorge Etcheverry, and published by Verbum Veritas in 2011; and *Notas viajeras: Escritura de viajes y testimonio. Nuevos autores latino-canadienses*, edited by Andrés Arteaga and David Rozotto, and published by Broken Jaw Press in 2013. Finally, the in-depth study on exile in the Hispano-Canadian short story in the twenty-first century cannot leave out stories published online in literary journals such as *The Apostles Review* or *Qantati*.

8 Suffice it to mention canonical authors whose short stories form part of the universal literary heritage such as Jorge Luis Borges, Horacio Quiroga, Julio Cortázar, Juan Rulfo, or Augusto Monterroso, among many others.

9 Hugh Hazelton's book *Latinocanadá*. This book is the first in-depth approach to Hispano-Canadian literature produced in the country for more than four decades, and it is for this reason that it was chosen by Trish Van Bolderen as a milestone in her article "The Evolution of Hispanic-Canadian Literature: What's In (and Behind) the Anthologies?" *Interfaces Brasil/Canadá. Canoas*, 13, no. 2 (2013): 57-76, accessed December 14, 2013, http://www.revistas.unilasalle.edu.br/index.php/interfaces/article/view/1133/972.

10 Van Bolderen, "The Evolution."

11 Trish Van Bolderen organized a list that includes twenty-five Hispano-Canadian literary anthologies published between 1982 (the first of which is dedicated to Chilean literature in Canada) and 2013. Of the twenty-five published anthologies, four have been dedicated exclusively to the short story, twelve to poetry, while the other nine are a mix of distinct genres with the short story

included in seven of them. For more information, consult Van Bolderen, "The Evolution."

12 More precisely the word "transterrado" is a term coined by the Spanish philosopher José Gaos to discuss the transfer of the land of the country in which one was born to a new one: in other words, to extend to a new geographical territory, the customs, culture and language of the original society.

13 Etcheverry, "Ojeada preliminar sobre las revistas hispanocanadienses," *La cita trunca*, Sept. 30, 2012, http://etcheverry.info/hoja/catastro/notas/article_1662.shtml. "[L]a inmigración no debe verse como absolutamente separada del exilio, ya que la gente emigra por causas económicas, sociales y políticas bastante precisas, que en su forma extrema se concretizan en conflicto civil, dictadura o golpe de estado, provocan[do] el exilio."

14 Luis Torres, "Exile and Identity," in *Relocating Identities*, ed. Elizabeth Montes Garcés (Calgary: University of Calgary Press, 2007), 55-83.

15 Claude Duchet, "Para una socio-crítica o variaciones sobre un íncipit," in *Sociocríticas. Prácticas textuales/cultura de fronteras*, ed. M.-Pierrette Malcuzynski (Amsterdam: Editios Rodopi B.V., 1991), 31.

16 M.-Pierrette Malcuzynski, "A modo de introducción," in *Sociocríticas. Prácticas textuales/cultura de fronteras*, ed. M.-Pierrette Malcuzynski (Amsterdam: Editios Rodopi B.V., 1991), 22.

17 José Manuel Guzmán Díaz, "Panorama de las teorías sociológicas de la novela," *Cultura y representaciones sociales* 3, no. 5 (2008): 113.

18 Jorge Etcheverry and Hugh Hazelton have dedicated significant effort to the study of this literature. Hazelton's book, *Latinocanadá*, is now a classic in its approach to Spanish literary production in this country. Also, the topic has been an object of study for professors such as Norman Cheadle and Carol Stos of Laurentian University; Julio Torres-Recinos from the University of Saskatchewan; Luis Torres at the University of Calgary; Lady Rojas-Benavente and José Antonio Giménez Micó at Concordia University; and Elena Palmero González of Universidade Federal do Rio de Janeiro, among others.

19 The study of literature written in Spanish in Canada by authors with origins other than Hispanic-American or Spanish are of interest to the author of this text. Of particular interest is the production that touches on the topic of exile, even if the author cannot be classified as an immigrant in Canada; therefore, to place emphasis on "Hispano" makes sense. Additionally, the study of production by authors of Hispanic-American or Spanish origin in one of the two official languages is also of interest to the author. In this second case, the term "Hispano" incorporates the notion of ethnic origin, without the intention of homogenizing, but more with the intention of searching for a term that places more emphasis first on language, and then on the cultural complexity of those who are linked to the language by birth or language adoption.

20 For more information on the origins and uses of the terms "Hispanic" and "Latino"in the United States and Canada, consult the introduction of Natalie Alvarez's book *Fronteras vivientes*.

21 For more information on the subject, read Harles, "Immigrant Integration."

22 Andrew Machalski, *Hispanic Writers in Canada: A Preliminary Survey of the Activities of Spanish and Latin-American Writers in Canada* (Ottawa: Department of the Secretary of State of Canada, 1988), 3.

23 Etcheverry, "Poesía chilena en Canadá: historia e identidades," *Contexto: revista anual de estudios literarios*, no.17 (2011): 183.

24 Hugh Hazelton, "La soledad del exilio: marginalidad y aislamiento en la literatura latinocanadiense," *Poesias.cl*, accessed November 12, 2013, http://www.poesias.cl/latinocanadiense02.htm.

25 The reasons for the Spanish and Hispanic-American departures mention coincided with Canadian policies such as the refugee program (initiated in 1962), the system of points developed in 1967 to select skilled workers that contributed to the country's economy, or the immigration amnesty in 1973. For more detailed information of these different waves of migration and immigration policies in Canada from the time of its "discovery," consult Ninette Kelley and Michael Trebilcock, *The Making of the Mosaic. A History of Canadian Immigration Policy* (Toronto: University of Toronto Press Incorporated, 2010).

26 Hazelton, *Latinocanadá*, 6-7.

27 Hazelton, *Latinocanadá*, 6.

28 Hazelton, *Latinocanadá*, 20.

29 Hazelton, *Latinocanadá*.

30 Elena Palmero González, "Desplazamiento cultural y procesos literarios en las letras hispanoamericanas contemporáneas: la literatura hispano-canadiense," *Contexto: revista anual de estudios literarios* 17 (2011): 73.

31 Machalski, *Hispanic Writers*, 2.

32 Etcheverry, "Poesía chilena," 192. "[Q]ue experimenta un gran desarrollo y está presente en entornos con un cierto público en la comunidad hispanohablante, los estudios académicos hispánicos, el campo de la traducción literaria y la solidaridad internacional."

33 For more detail read the article by Monique Carcaud-Macaire, "Reflexiones Sociocríticas sobre la alteridad. El Otro modelo hegemónico y el tercer interpretante. Ejemplo de caso: entre imagen improbable y figura banalizada. El árabe en la cultura francesa," *Revista Káñina* 32, no. 1 (2008): 29-38.

34 Consult Edmond Cros, "De la independencia a los años 1960 en América Latina: los avatares de las conciencias de las identidades nacionales y culturales," last modified March 18, 2010, https://www.sociocritique.fr/?De-la-Independencia-a-los-anos-1960-en-America-Latina-los-avatares-de-las.

35 Cristina Elgue de Maritini, "La literatura como objeto social," *Invenio* 6, no. 11 (2003): 9-20.

36 Jorge Ramírez Caro, "Tres propuestas analíticas e interpretativas del texto literario: estructuralismo, semiótica y sociocrítica," *Revista Comunicación* 12, no. 2 (2002): n. p." "Dado que la práctica de la escritura es una práctica social, todo texto materializa las diversas voces y contradicciones sociohistóricas y socioculturales de las formaciones sociales e ideológicas que la originan."

37 Birgit Mertz-Baumgartner, "Imágenes del exilio y la migración en la literatura latinoamericana en Canadá," in *Migración y literatura en el mundo hispánico*,

ed. Irene Andrés-Suárez (Madrid: Editorial Verbum, 2004), 283. "[M]antienen un concepto de conflicto identitario dialéctico percibiendo y describiendo la experiencia migratoria como enfrentamiento de dos mundos culturales contrarios."

38 Torres, "Exile and Identity," 55.

39 Jorge Etcheverry, "El ojo escindido: autores latinos en Canadá," *Crítica.cl*, December 18, 2007, http://critica.cl/literatura/el-ojo-escindido-autores-latinos-en-canada.

40 Noé Jitrik, "La exclusión," in *Escrituras latinoamericanas en el siglo XXI*, ed. Noé Jitrik (Córdoba, Argentina: Alción Editora, 2006), 359.

41 Yoel Isaac Díaz León was born in Cuba in 1976 and emigrated to Canada in 2004, settling in Toronto. He writes narratives in general, but with an emphasis on short stories. "Miedo viejo" won the first prize of the contest Nuestra Palabra in 2005.

42 Isaac Yoel Díaz León, "Miedo viejo," in *Cuentos de nuestra palabra en Canadá*, eds. Guillermo Rose and Alex Zisman (Markham, Ontario: Editorial nuestra palabra, 2009), 46. "Nuestras conversaciones son las mismas de siempre: lo inaguantable de la situación y la conclusión inexorable de que hice bien en irme al menos yo; ellos para qué."

43 Díaz León, "Miedo viejo," 46. "[L]a tensión de la gente, sus groserías y violencias, el calor insoportable dentro de la guagua."

44 In addition to being a writer, Jorge Etcheverry (1945) studies and is a critic of Hispano-Canadian literature. He arrived in Canada in 1975 and obtained a doctorate in literature from the Université de Montréal. Author of novels, short stories, and, especially, poetry, he is also an artist. His works have been published in Chile and Canada, where he actively participates in Hispano-Canadian literature as a writer, editor, promoter, critic, and judge for competitions like Nuestra Palabra. His work has been largely anthologized in print and electronically. He resides in Ottawa. For more information on his literary works and criticism, visit http://etcheverry.info.

45 Etcheverry, "Metamorfosis II," 102. "[N]o parece producirse en nuestros países, no al menos en el mismo grado."

46 Etcheverry, "Metamorfosis II," 102. "[N]o es nunca el verdadero, rotundo poder, y lo mismo pasa con la cultura, un fruto ambiguo con raíces quién sabe dónde, pero cuyos injertos de elementos europeos resultan muchas veces grotescos para el hombre de mundo."

47 Rojas Primus (b. 1972) is a professor in the Department of Modern Languages and Linguistics at the Kwantlen Polytechnic University, Vancouver. She arrived in Canada from Chile in 1996 to study her Master's and, later, a doctorate at the University of Alberta. Her short story "La iniciación" obtained an honorary mention in the Nuestra Palabra contest in 2005.

48 Constanza Rojas Primus, "La iniciación," in *Cuentos de nuestra palabra en Canadá*, eds. Guillermo Rose and Alex Zisman (Markham, Ontario: Editorial nuestra palabra, 2009), 63. "Me imagino sus caras al saber que ya no soy la misma, ni tengo el mismo nombre, y que dicto los caminos de mi vida desde mis espíritus, mi muerto, mi ganga." Note that "ganga" denotes a box or cauldron that contains several small objects (including bones and sticks) where it is believed the spirit of the dead resides in. It is an important part of the Palo Monte religion.

49 Anita Junge-Hammersley (b. 1949) is a Chilean author who arrived in Canada in 1974 and resides in Ottawa. Her literary work is made up of narrative and poetry. In addition, she is an artist. The short story "Cerrado el círculo" (*Cuentos de nuestra palabra en Canadá*, eds. Guillermo Rose and Alex Zisman (Markham, Ontario: Editorial nuestra palabra, 2009), 104-08) won second place in the Nuestra Palabra contest in 2006. For more information her blog can be visited at http://anitajunge.blogspot.ca or her web page http://www.anitajungehammersley.com.

50 Carmen Rodríguez was born in Chile in 1948. She arrived in Canada in 1974 at the same time as other Chilean exiles due to the Pinochet regime. An author of short stories, novels, and poetry, she writes and publishes her works in English and Spanish. She taught Latin-American literature and translation at Simon Fraser University. Her work has been anthologized multiple times, especially in Canada, where she has contributed to various causes such as teaching reading and writing to adults. She resides in Vancouver. For more information her website can be visited at http://www.carmenrodriguez.ca.

51 Carmen Rodríguez, "Juegos y jugarretas," 231. "[E]stoy bajo otro cielo y otro sol, muy lejos del puerto [Valparaíso]. Mis padres, esperando al cartero en su casita de Quilpué y buscando a mi hermano, desaparecido desde el 11 de septiembre de 1973. Yo, aprendiendo a hablar de nuevo en el Canadá y tratando a toda costa de encontrarle algún sentido a la vida. Trabajo haciendo limpieza en un rascacielos del centro de Vancouver. Del piso 32 veo los barcos en la bahía, como los veíamos desde el cerro Bellavista, hace ya casi treinta años."

52 Díaz León, "Miedo viejo," 56.

53 Etcheverry, "Metamorfosis II," 100.

54 Casuso is a social communicator and was born in 1973 and works in e-business. Casuso writes short stories and novels, and his work has been recognized on various occasions in his native Peru. For "En la habitación," he obtained an honourable mention in the Nuestra Palabra contest in 2005.

55 Casuso, "En la habitación," in *Cuentos de nuestra palabra en Canadá*, eds. Guillermo Rose and Alex Zisman (Markham, Ontario: Editorial nuestra palabra, 2009), 70. "En Canadá los inmigrantes valen menos que los incendios."

56 Casuso, "En la habitación," 71. "[P]ara que pierdas tu visa, maldito inmigrante."

57 Of Nicaraguan origin, Pastor Valle-Garay (b. 1936) arrived in Canada in 1964 and settled in Toronto. Narrator and poet, he has also written articles for different medias in Canada and Cuba. He is a retired professor from the Department of Languages, Literatures, and Linguistics at York University. His short story "Mi arce en Arce" won an honourable mention in the Nuestra Palabra contest in 2005. In 1978, the volume *Doce poemas y una esperanza* was published in Toronto by the Nicaragua Human Rights Committee. He dedicates his time to photography, political analysis, and cultural consultancy.

58 Pastor Valle-Garay, "Mi arce en Arce (Maple, Ontario)," in *Cuentos de nuestra palabra en Canadá*, eds. Guillermo Rose and Alex Zisman (Markham, Ontario: Editorial nuestra palabra, 2009), 85. "[D]e casas en serie, arquitectura-a-la-carrera, monótonas residencias de indefinido diseño neocanadiense."

59 Valle-Garay, "Mi arce," 86.

60 Etcheverry, "Camas paralelas," 93. "[H]echos para gente alta, que sus manos no podían alcanzar."

61 Etcheverry, "Camas paralelas," 94. "[C] hiquillos rubios."

62 Etcheverry, "Camas paralelas," 94. "[L]as niñas gringas."

63 Saravia (b. 1962) is a journalist and writes prose and poetry. He arrived in Canada in 1986 and currently resides in Brossard, Québec. His work has been anthologized in various compilations, in particular his poetry and short stories. He is the author of two novels and six volumes of poetry. He writes in Spanish, English, and French. This Bolivian author is a journalist in Montreal and he studied literature at the Université de Montréal and the University of Ottawa.

64 Alejandro Saravia, "La orureña," in *Cuentos de nuestra palabra en Canadá*, eds. Guillermo Rose and Alex Zisman (Markham, Ontario: Editorial nuestra palabra, 2009), 111. "Urbe henchida, políglota. Por sus calles corrían los tranvías como musculosos caballos colorados. Ciudad de mil lenguas y cocinas. Olor de leones en el metro."

65 Saravia, "La orureña," 111. "[N]o se preocupe por el acento, nosotros no hablamos como españoles, ni los toronteños hablan como londinenses (...) Aquí todos tenemos acento, doña María."

66 Saravia, "La orureña," 113. "[L]os martes y los jueves por la mañana María Isabel continúa platicando con James, quien ineluctablemente va perdiendo la memoria. Ella le cuenta cómo era Oruro again and again. A veces le habla de la vasta ciudad de Toronto que ella va inventando en su nueva lengua. Y James va haciéndose orureño a fuerza de pasear por las mismas calles y acudir a las mismas fiestas."

67 Norman Cheadle, "El Canadá americano de Alejandro Saravia," *Contexto: revista anual de estudios literarios* 17 (2011), 106. "[C]on maestría."

68 Cheadle, "El Canadá americano," 106. "Tal dominio de las lenguas de uso canadiense va de la mano del empeño, también bastante único en su generación, con que Saravia se ha acercado a lo que es Canadá, adentrándose en su historia, sus literaturas y culturas."

69 Alejandro Saravia, "Los osos de Port Churchill," in *Cuentos de nuestra palabra en Canadá*, eds. Guillermo Rose and Alex Zisman (Markham, Ontario: Editorial nuestra palabra, 2009), 82. "[Q]ué tipo de animal era aquel que podía acomodar dos oseznos en los costados de la boca."

70 Saravia, "Los osos," 82. "[C]apaz de tragarse todas las posibilidades del lenguaje y devorar al mundo entero."

71 Anita Junge-Hammersley, "Carnaval cultural," 150. "[E]n Santiago, o en otro país latinoamericano."

72 Junge-Hammersley, "Carnaval cultural," 150. "[G]ente del mundo entero, rumiando chicles, escupiendo al suelo, mujeres con coches de guagua, todo en idiomas distintos y una variedad de vestimentas, el comportamiento cultural propio y los ademanes correspondientes."

73 Ramón de Elía was born in Argentina in 1964. Thirty years later he arrived in Canada to complete his doctorate at McGill University. Having settled in Montreal, this author writes short stories and poetry, and his work has been showcased in various printed and electronic anthologies. In 2004 he won the Nuestra Palabra contest with his short story "Estaciones," available in an English

translation by Cecilia Rose at http://dialogos. ca/2014/08/nuestra-palabra-2004-ramon-de-elia/.

74 Ramón De Elía, "Las doce noches," 80. "Levanté la vista y miré hacia el este: Pointe-aux-Trembles se encontraba en algún lado del horizonte, más allá de los humos de las refinerías, más allá de todo lo razonable, mucho más allá de lo que un inmigrante que dejó casi todo atrás esperaba encontrar en esta ciudad. Pensé en ella y en esa noche agónica que, como la descascarada pintura de un fresco renacentista, había sido restaurada a sus vivos y atroces colores originales. Pensé en esas doce noches que me habían sido devueltas sin haber siquiera ejercido mi derecho a elegir."

75 De Elía, "Las doce noches," 79. "[C]omo yo y como tantos otros -, o si renegarás, como algunos, de la posibilidad de saber cómo pasaron las cosas. Si esquivarás la responsabilidad que el futuro se parecerá irremediablemente (...) a ese pasado. Y que ese pasado sos vos."

76 Tarud was born in Chile in 1970, arriving in Canada in 2004 and working as a translator in Toronto. She writes short stories, poems, and plays. Her short story "La caja del falte" obtained an honourable mention in the Nuestra Palabra contest in 2008.

77 Denise Tarud, "La caja del falte," in *Cuentos de nuestra palabra en Canadá*, eds. Guillermo Rose and Alex Zisman (Markham, Ontario: Editorial nuestra palabra, 2009), 240. "Llegué a Toronto medio dormida, después de más de trece horas de vuelo. A pesar de haber tenido los tres asientos de la corrida del medio del avión para mí, poco había logrado dormir. Aquí estaba yo, otra emigrante en la familia. Venía en un cómodo avión, no en la tercera clase de un barco. Eran sólo trece horas, no meses, de viaje. En mi destino me esperaba un taxi, no una mula. Y no venía huyendo de guerra alguna."

Chapter 11
Ethnic Media in Canada: Latino Newspapers in the GTA, Hamilton, and Niagara, 2001-2015

1 A draft of this chapter was presented at the 2016 Canadian History of Education Association Conference, 30 October 2016 at Panel Session 32: "Thinking Niagara, Thinking Latin America: Expanding Canada's Cultural Heritage by Making History Together," Waterloo, Ontario, Canada. Armony, "Latin American Communities," 18.

2 Interview by Paloma Martínez with Maria del Carmen Suescun Pozas, *Radio Canada International*, 9 November 2015. http://www.rcinet.ca/es/2015/11/09/canada-y-america-latina-unidas-en-la-historia/.

3 Interview by Paloma Martínez with Suescun Pozas.

4 Benedict R. O'G. Anderson, *Imagined Communities: Reflections on the Origins and Spread of Nationalism* (London and New York: Verso, 1991), 6.

5 "Cultural Identity," Oxford Reference.

6 *Presencia Latina* 8, no. 2 (Nov. 1, 2012)

7 *Presencia Latina*

8 Consuelo Solar, "Media: Connecting Latinos," *Canadian Newcomer Magazine*, accessed December 10, 2015, http://www.cnmag.ca/issue-31/516-n09-media-connecting-latinos.

9 See Solar's description in "Media: Connecting Latinos."

10 Anna De Fina, "Top-Down and Bottom-Up Strategies of Identity Construction in Ethnic Media," *Applied Linguistics* 34, no. 5 (December 2013): 557.

11 Luisa Veronis and Rukhsana Ahmed, "The Role of Multicultural Media in Connecting Municipal Governments with Ethnocultural Communities: The case of Ottawa," *Global Media Journal - Canadian Edition* 8, no. 2 (2015): 75.

12 Veronis and Ahmed, "The Role," 75.

13 Veronis and Ahmed, "The Role," 75.

14 Veronis and Ahmed, "The Role," 76.

15 Eberhardt, "Hispanic (Hybridity)," 28.

16 Eberhardt, "Hispanic (Hybridity)," 28.

17 Armory, "Latin American Communities," 13.

18 Armory, "Latin American Communities," 8-9.

19 Armory, "Latin American Communities," 10.

20 Armory, "Latin American Communities," 11.

21 Victor Armory, "Settling North of the U.S. Border: Canada's Latinos and the Particular Case of Québec," *LASA Forum* XLVI, no. 4 (2015): 21.

22 Armory, "Settling North," 22.

23 Michael Dewing, "Canadian Multiculturalism" (Ottawa: Library of Parliament, 2009), 8, http://publications.gc.ca/collections/collection_2010/bdp-lop/prb/prb0920-eng.pdf.

24 Dewing, "Canadian Multiculturalism," 8.

25 Dewing, "Canadian Multiculturalism," 8.

26 Dewing, "Canadian Multiculturalism," 12.

27 Dewing, "Canadian Multiculturalism," 49.

28 Keith Banting and Will Kymlicka, "Canadian Multiculturalism: Global Anxieties and Local Debates." *British Journal of Canadian Studies* 23, no. 1 (2010): 49.

29 Banting and Kymlicka, "Canadian Multiculturalism," 50.

30 Banting and Kymlicka, "Canadian Multiculturalism," 50.

31 Banting and Kymlicka, "Canadian Multiculturalism," 50.

32 Banting and Kymlicka, "Canadian Multiculturalism," 51.

33 Anderson, *Imagined Communities*, 6.

34 Anderson, *Imagined Communities*, 35.

35 Anderson, *Imagined Communities*, 35.

36 Anderson, *Imagined Communities*, 35-36.

37 Anderson, *Imagined Communities*, 46.

38 Anderson, *Imagined Communities*, 135.

39 "Made in house, real journalism [...] cost us more than others because of this," said by Freddy Velez, in interview by Raimondo, 2015.

40 "Dufferin is very Latino," said by Velez, in interview by author.

41 "It is in St. Catharines sometimes," said by Velez, in interview by author.

42 Velez, interview by author.

43 "Only about five to six people contribute," said by Velez, in interview by author.

44 Velez, interview by author.

45 Velez, interview by author.
46 Velez, interview by author.
47 Velez, interview by author.
48 Velez, interview by author.
49 Velez, interview by author.
50 Velez, interview by author.
51 Velez, interview by author.
52 Velez, interview by author.
53 Velez, interview by author.
54 Velez, interview by author.
55 Velez, interview by author.
56 Velez, interview by author.
57 Velez, interview by author.
58 *Correo Canadiense*, 160 (October 16, 2015), accessed December 2015, https://www.correo.ca/.
59 Velez, interview by author.
60 Velez, interview by author.
61 Velez, interview by author.
62 Velez, interview by author.
63 Velez, interview by author.
64 Velez, interview by author.
65 Velez, interview by author.
66 Velez, interview by author.
67 Velez, interview by author.
68 Velez, interview by author.
69 Velez, interview by author.
70 Velez, interview by author.
71 "Life's a Ride for Israel Valderrama," *Hamilton Spectator*, October 26, 2007, Local sec., accessed December 21, 2015, http://www.thespec.com/newsstory/2089741-life-s-a-ride-for-israel-valderrama/.
72 Velez, interview by author.
73 Velez, interview by author.
74 Velez, interview by author.
75 Velez, interview by author.
76 Velez, interview by author.
77 Velez, interview by author.
78 Velez, interview by author.
79 Velez, interview by author.
80 Velez, interview by author.
81 Velez, interview by author.
82 Velez, interview by author.
83 Velez, interview by author.
84 Velez, interview by author.
85 Velez, interview by author.
86 Velez, interview by author.
87 Velez, interview by author.

88 Velez, interview by author.
89 Velez, interview by author.
90 Velez, interview by author.
91 Velez, interview by author.
92 Velez, interview by author.
93 Velez, interview by author.
94 Velez, interview by author.
95 Velez, interview by author.
96 Velez, interview by author.
97 Velez, interview by author.
98 *Presencia Latina.*
99 *Presencia Latina.*
100 John McTavish, interview by author, St. Catharines, ON, Winter 2015.
101 "Mistake that changed my life," McTavish, interview by author.
102 McTavish, interview by author.
103 "I had worked a lot with Latin immigrants in Canada back in the late 1980s, especially when many refugees came up from Salvador and Guatemala." McTavish, interview by author.
104 "I moved after and lived 10 years in Panama and was always interested in the media field there." McTavish, interview by author.
105 "I wanted to keep the media side going so we had the newspaper and a radio we ran for 6 years." McTavish, interview by author.
106 "Asking the average Canadian if they have ever seen a Latino, they might think of a farm worker that we have in the Niagara Region." McTavish, interview by author.
107 McTavish, interview by author.
108 "We also had the first Latin American Gala." McTavish, interview by author.
109 "We instituted Latino of the Year." McTavish, interview by author.
110 "Nobody knew who he or she were until the end when the trophy was handed out." McTavish, interview by author.
111 "The effort to recognize them as community leaders put an extra motivation on them that they really need to go out and do more things." McTavish, interview by author.
112 "*Presencia Latina* was more than just news, it was a community growth process." McTavish, interview by author.
113 McTavish, interview by author.
114 "Yes, that was the whole idea." McTavish, interview by author.
115 McTavish, interview by author.
116 McTavish, interview by author.
117 "We did real journalism too." McTavish, interview by author.
118 McTavish, interview by author.
119 McTavish, interview by author.
120 McTavish, interview by author.
121 McTavish, interview by author.
122 McTavish, interview by author.
123 McTavish, interview by author.

124 "We would interview Canadian people as well." McTavish, interview by author.
125 "Made real connections with the community." McTavish, interview by author.
126 "We didn't do it for the money, we did it for our passion for journalism and writing, and my passion for the Latin culture." McTavish, interview by author.
127 McTavish, interview by author.
128 "We always wanted to put things in a positive light." McTavish, interview by author.
129 "One thing the newspaper really did was unite the Latinos amongst each other." McTavish, interview by author.
130 "The whole idea of Presencia Latina was to have sort of an umbrella presence." McTavish, interview by author.
131 McTavish, interview by author.
132 "This was the big job that I felt proud of." McTavish, interview by author.
133 McTavish, interview by author.
134 McTavish, interview by author.
135 "It's all about people and connecting with people." McTavish, interview by author.
136 McTavish, interview by author.
137 McTavish, interview by author.
138 McTavish, interview by author.
139 McTavish, interview by author.
140 "Less text, more photos." McTavish, interview by author.
141 Dana Mastro, Christopher McKinley and Katie Warber, "Social Identity Theory as a Framework for Understanding the Effects of Exposure to Positive Media Images of Self and Other Intergroup Outcomes," *International Journal of Communication* 8 (2014), https://ijoc.org/index.php/ijoc/article/viewFile/2276/1116, 1015.
142 Mastro, McKinley and Warber, "Social Identity Theory," 1015.
143 Clara E. Rodriguez, *Latin Looks: Images of Latinas and Latinos in the U.S. Media* (Boulder: Westview Press, 1997), 235.
144 Rodriguez, *Latin Looks*, 235.
145 Tokunbo Ojo, "Ethnic Print Media in the Multicultural Nation of Canada," *Journalism* 7, no. 3 (August 2006): 344.
146 Ojo, "Ethnic Print Media," 353.
147 Ojo, "Ethnic Print Media," 350.
148 Ojo, "Ethnic Print Media," 350.
149 Ojo, "Ethnic Print Media," 350.
150 Veronis and Ahmed, "The Role," 75.
151 Veronis and Ahmed, "The Role," 82.
152 Veronis and Ahmed, "The Role," 82.
153 Bendixen and Associates, "The Ethnic Media," 15.
154 Bendixen and Associates, "The Ethnic Media," 15.
155 Bendixen and Associates, "The Ethnic Media," 15.
156 Bendixen and Associates, "The Ethnic Media," 15.
157 Bendixen and Associates, "The Ethnic Media," 5, 38.
158 Veronis and Ahmed, "The Role," 86.

159 Veronis and Ahmed, "The Role," 86.

160 Patricia Tomic, "The Colour of Language: Accent, Devaluation and Resistance in Latin American Immigrant Lives in Canada," *Canadian Ethnic Studies/ Études Ethniques au Canada* 45, no. 1-2 (2013): 11.

161 Salzman, "News or Noticias: A Social Identity Approach to Understanding Latinos' Preferred Language for News Consumption in the United States," *Mass Communication and Society* 17 (2014): 59.

162 Salzman, "News or Noticias," 60.

163 Salzman, "News or Noticias," 71.

164 De Fina, "Top-Down and Bottom-Up," 556.

165 De Fina, "Top-Down and Bottom-Up," 557.

166 Paul Taylor et al., "When Labels Don't Fit: Hispanics and Their Views of Identity," Pew Research Centers Hispanic Trends Project RSS, April 3, 2012, accessed December 10, 2015, http://www.pewhispanic.org/2012/04/04/when-labels-dont-fit-hispanics-and-their-views-of-identity/, 1.

167 Taylor et al., "When Labels Don't," 1.

168 Taylor et al., "When Labels Don't," 1.

169 Taylor et al., "When Labels Don't," 1.

170 De Fina, "Top-Down and Bottom-Up," 559.

171 Veronis, "Strategic Spatial Essentialism," 461.

172 Veronis, "Immigrant Participation," 176.

173 Veronis, "Immigrant Participation," 188.

174 Veronis, "Strategic Spatial Essentialism," 462.

175 G. Christina Mora, interview by National Public Radio.

176 Mora, interview by National Public Radio.

177 Mora, interview by National Public Radio.

178 Mora, interview by National Public Radio.

179 Mora, interview by National Public Radio.

180 Mora, interview by National Public Radio.

181 Mora, interview by National Public Radio.

182 Armony, "Introduction: Latin American," 3.

183 Armony, "Introduction: Latin American," 3.

184 G. Christina Mora, *Making Hispanics: How Activists, Bureaucrats and Media Constructed A New American* (Chicago: University of Chicago Press, 2014), xiii.

185 Mora, *Making Hispanics*, 169.

186 Mora, *Making Hispanics*, 169.

187 David R. Spencer and Joseph D. Straubhaar, "Broadcast research in the Americas: Revisiting the Past and Looking to the Future," *Journal of Broadcasting & Electronic Media* (2006): 376.

188 Spencer and Straubhaar, "Broadcast research," 376.

189 "Mexicanos en Toronto ya tienen su Casa de la cultura." *La Portada*, April 1, 2015. https://www.laportadacanada.com/noticia/mexicanos-en-toronto-ya-tiene-su-casa-de-la-cultura/2396

190 "Mexicanos en Toronto ya tienen su Casa de la cultura."

191 "About Us," *La Jornada*, https://news.lajornada.ca/quienes-somos/.

192 "Events," *Avenida Latina Magazine,* http://avenidamagazine.ca/en/events/.

193 "Events," *Avenida Latina Magazine.*

194 *La Portada Canadá,* accessed December 10, 2015, http://laportadacanada.com.

195 *El Chasqui Latino,* "Bienvenidos," https://elchasquilatino.com/.

196 *El Chasqui Latino,* November 19, 2015, no. 937.

197 Veronis and Ahmed, "The Role," 85.

198 *Presencia Latina* 1, no. 10 (July 2006).

199 *Presencia Latina* 2, no. 9 (June 2007).

200 McTavish, interview by author.

201 *Presencia Latina* 3, no. 6 (March 2008).

202 McTavish, interview by author.

203 *Presencia Latina* 4, no. 9 (July 2009).

204 *Presencia Latina* 6, no. 12 (September 2011).

205 McTavish, interview by author.

206 *Presencia Latina* 8, no. 2 (November 2012).

207 Velez, interview by author.

208 *Correo Canadiense* 163 (Nov. 6, 2015).

209 *Correo Canadiense* 165 (Nov. 20, 2015).

210 *Correo Canadiense* 165 (Nov. 20, 2015).

211 Hazelton, *Latinocanadá,* 4.

212 De Fina. "Top-Down and Bottom-Up," 559.

213 De Fina. "Top-Down and Bottom-Up," 570.

214 Pamela J. Shoemaker, Stephen D. Reese, and Wayne A. Danielson, "Spanish-Language Print Media Use as an Indicator of Acculturation," *Journalism Quarterly* 62, no. 4 (Winter 1985): 734.

215 Shoemaker, Reese, and Danielson, "Spanish-Language Print Media," 734.

216 Shoemaker, Reese, and Danielson, "Spanish-Language Print Media," 734.

217 Shoemaker, Reese, and Danielson, "Spanish-Language Print Media," 734.

218 Shoemaker, Reese, and Danielson, "Spanish-Language Print Media," 740.

219 Megan Strom, "Social Hierarchy in Local Spanish-Language Print Media: The Discursive Representation of Latino Social Actors in the United States," *Discourse & Society* no. 2 (2015): 233.

220 Strom, "Social Hierarchy," 235.

221 Strom, "Social Hierarchy," 236.

222 Strom, "Social Hierarchy," 247.

223 Wendy Cukier et al., "Diversity in Leadership and Media: A Multi-Perspective Analysis of the Greater Toronto Area, 2010," *DiverseCity Counts: A Snapshot of Diversity in the Greater Toronto Area* (2010): 11.

224 Cukier et al., "Diversity in Leadership," 11.

225 Daniel Schugurensky and Jorge Ginieniewicz, "The Latin American Community in Canada: Some Challenges Ahead," *Diálogos* (January 1, 2007), accessed December 2015, https://dialogos.ca/2007/07/the-latin-american-community-in-canada-some-challenges-ahead/.

226 Schugurensky and Ginieniewicz. "The Latin American."

227 McTavish, interview by author.

228 "Spanish is the language of the business future," McTavish, interview by author.

229 Schugurensky and Ginieniewicz, "The Latin American."

230 Schugurensky and Ginieniewicz, "The Latin American."

231 McTavish, interview by author.

Part IV

Chapter 12
El Sistema Up North: Re-Imagining Venezuela's Music-Education Program for Canada

1 This research was presented at the following venues: Colloquium Series, Department of Modern Languages and Literatures, The University of Western Ontario (2016); Latin America Made in Canada Virtual Workshop (2015); Conference of the American Association of Teachers of Spanish and Portuguese - Ontario Chapter, Wilfrid Laurier University (2015).

2 José Antonio Abreu quoted in Penny Johnson, "Promise of Music Symposium Wrap-Up," The Glenn Gould Foundation, Mar. 26, 2010, accessed on June 17, 2014, http://www.glenngould.ca/promise-of-music-symposium-wrap-up/. All translated quotes in this essay are from the original published source.

3 "The Glenn Gould Prize," The Glenn Gould Foundation, https://www.glenngould.ca/the-glenn-gould-prize/.

4 José Antonio Abreu, "The *El Sistema* Music Revolution," TED Prize speech, February 2009, https://www.ted.com/talks/jose_antonio_abreu_the_el_sistema_music_revolution.

5 Ivo Supičić, *Music in Society: A Guide to the Sociology of Music* (New York: Pendragon Press, 1988), 47-8.

6 Salmen, "Social Obligations of the Emancipated Musician in the 19th Century," in *The Social Status of the Professional Musician from the Middle Ages to the 19th Century*, ed. Walter Salmen, Herbert Kaufmann, and Barbara Reisner (Hillsdale, NY: Pendragon Press, 1983), 266.

7 Taylor, *The Archive*, 19-20.

8 Geoffrey Baker, *El Sistema: Orchestrating Venezuela's Youth* (Oxford and New York: Oxford University Press, 2014), 254.

9 Doris Sommer, *Foundational Fictions: The National Romances of Latin America* (Berkeley and Los Angeles: University of California Press, 1991), 9.

10 Abreu, "The El Sistema."

11 Tricia Tunstall, *Changing Lives: Gustavo Dudamel, El Sistema, and the Transformative Power of Music* (New York: W.W. Norton and Company, 2012), 59.

12 Tunstall, *Changing Lives*, 59. The 1950s and 1960s in Caracas, Venezuela, are described by Tunstall as a period of national consolidation through increased oil revenues; immigration from Germany, Italy, and Spain; tourism; and rapid modernization. All of these, together, greatly influenced the cultural scene.

13 Joseph Tetlow, *Introduction to Ignatius Loyola: Spiritual Exercises*, ed. Joseph Tetlow (New York: Crossroads Publishing Company, 1992), 18-30. Íñigo López

de Loyola, better known as Ignatius Loyola, was alive at the historical intersection of the end of the Reconquest and the beginnings of the Spanish colonization of the Americas. He lived in an age of religious fervour and reform as well as at a time that saw individuals of an endeavouring and pioneering spirit looking beyond the limits and constraints of the known world. The tensions of tradition and change in his time helped shape Loyola in such a way that he was able to overcome the limitations of his early life to provide service to the crown under various protectors at court. Frequently identified as a soldier, Loyola's transformative moment is said to have come when he was severely wounded in battle during the French incursion into Pamplona in 1521. Convalescing for a period of months, it was during this time that he began to read spiritual books and texts. Upon full recovery, his notion of heroic service shifted from crown to religion. He became a pilgrim, travelled widely, and eventually immersed himself n the study of theology. Education would become central to the reforming spirit of Ignatius Loyola and the Society of Jesus, which he would later found and lead. Loyola left an important textual legacy of his life and work, and his spirituality is detailed in numerous written documents, one of which is the well-known and widely used *Spiritual Exercises.*

14 Abreu, "The El Sistema."

15 Tetlow, *Introduction to Ignatius*, 35.

16 Daniel Wakin, "Venerated High Priest and Humble Servant of Music Education," *The New York Times*, March 1, 2012, http://www.nytimes.com/2012/03/04/arts/music/jose-antonio-abreu-leads-el-sistema-in-venezuela.html?pagewanted=all.

17 Wakin, "Venerated High Priest."

18 The Jesuits left an important textual legacy of their mission in documents such as *The Jesuit Relations* (Relations des Jésuites de la Nouvelle-France).

19 Baker, *El Sistema: Orchestrating*, 289-97.

20 Baker, *El Sistema: Orchestrating*, 291.

21 Baker, *El Sistema: Orchestrating*, 244.

22 Alberto Arvelo's documentary is entitled *Tocar y luchar* (2006). Tunstall calls one of her chapters "To Play and to Struggle: The Evolution of El Sistema," and the CBC links to a documentary on its website named "Sistema Revolution." As noted previously, Abreu's widely viewed TED Prize speech (2009) is labelled "The El Sistema Music Revolution."

23 Anderson, *Imagined Communities*, 44-6. My understanding of nationalism and how cultural products participate in the creation of national consciousness is informed by the work of Benedict Anderson. Anderson advances the idea that a nation "is an imagined political community" and suggests that nationalism, therefore, is not generated by the nation but rather invents the nation. Focusing on novels and newspapers, Anderson demonstrates the importance of the commercial development, reproduction, and dissemination of the printed word as a way to create national consciousness. Unique to the printed word is its permanence or "fixity," and the circulation of printed works functions to promote a unified form of communication and a cohesive outlook. In the case of El Sistema, we see that imagined communities go beyond the nation and are now conceived on a global scale.

24 Baker, *El Sistema: Orchestrating*, 36-7; and María Elena Kuss, "Nativistic Strains in Argentine Operas Premiered at the Teatro Colón (1908-1972)" (Ph.D diss., UCLA, 1976), 193-94.

25 Abreu quoted in Johnson, "Promise of Music."

26 Baker, *El Sistema: Orchestrating*, 35; and Tunstall, *Changing Lives*, 84.

27 Baker, *El Sistema: Orchestrating*, 167.

28 Tunstall, *Changing Lives*, 35.

29 Daniel Wakin, "Music Meets Chávez Politics, and Critics Frown," *The New York Times*, February 17, 2012, http://www.nytimes.com/2012/02/18/arts/music/venezuelans-criticize-hugo-chavezs-support-of-el-sistema.html?pagewanted=all&_r=0.

30 Programs in Canada may label themselves as either El Sistema or Sistema-inspired programs. Additionally, some long-standing music-education programs are transitioning into El Sistema or Sistema-inspired programs. Finally, some programs are adopting some, but not all, elements of El Sistema into their pedagogy.

31 Inga Petri, "A National Sistema Network in Canada: Feasibility Study and Strategic Plan," 7, accessed on February 9, 2015, pdf.s3.amazonaws.com/corporate/SistemaCanada_FeasibilityReport_en.pdf.

32 Petri, "A National Sistema."

33 Petri, "A National Sistema."

34 "Good Day, Columbus" in Michel-Rolph Trouillot, *Silencing the Past: Power and Production of History* (Boston: Beacon Press, 1995), 116, 113. As indicated by Trouillot, commemorations are single moments that attempt to create, define, and shape public meaning. The processual character of these events must also be taken into consideration as they are an important part of continuous mythmaking and the narrativization of history. The idea of an El Sistema effect recognizes the power, production, and performance of these singular events in relation to their ongoing aftermath.

35 "The Glenn Gould Prize," Glenn Gould Foundation.

36 "The Glenn Gould." Promoting the idea of an exchange, Abreu and El Sistema covered the orchestra's transportation costs to Canada and waived all the normal appearance fees, an estimated value of around $500,000. The Glenn Gould Prize is a $50,000 monetary award. Yamaha tripled the award for a value of $150,000. The money was used in Canada to purchase instruments, which returned to Venezuela with the orchestra.

37 Everett-Green, "Gustavo Dudamel," n. p.

38 Petri, "A National Sistema," 9.

39 CMEA ad hoc El Sistema committee, "El Sistema Position Paper," 1. Namely, music should be accessible and available to all, partnerships between music-education groups and community are essential, and music can be a way in which to engender positive social values on the levels of both the individual and the group.

40 CMEA ad hoc El Sistema committee, "El Sistema Position Paper," 2. http://cmea.ca/wp-content/uploads/2013/01/CMEA-El-Sistema-Position-Paper-Nov-2012-approved.pdf

41 CMEA ad hoc El Sistema committee, 2-3.

42 CMEA ad hoc El Sistema committee, 3.

43 CMEA ad hoc El Sistema committee, 3.

44 "Old East" is described as "an urban core area with lower-socio-economic demographic but a strong arts and culture community anchored by Aeolian Hall." Sattler, "El Sistema Aeolian Evaluation Report," 15.

45 "History of Aeolian Hall," The Aeolian Hall, https://aeolianhall.ca/.

46 "History of Aeolian."

47 Sattler, "El Sistema Aeolian Evaluation Report," 15. Lorne Avenue Public School has since been closed due to low enrollment.

48 Sattler, "El Sistema Aeolian," 8-9.

49 The composer is Helsinki-born video game musician and sound designer, Ari Pulkkinen.

50 Baker, *El Sistema: Orchestrating*, 218. Baker cautions that the orchestra ensemble has become more of a symbol of teamwork than a reality. Chamber music is one of a few alternatives he mentions that is more likely to foster the group over the individual and democracy over meritocracy.

51 "Nur Intan Murtadza: Gamelan," The Aeolian Hall. Intan Murtadza received her training from some of the great masters of gamelan in both Indonesia and the United States. She has an MA in Music Education from the University of Toronto. She is currently pursuing a doctorate specializing in Music Education. Her interests are teaching and learning as a social and cultural practice.

52 The question and answer interview was conducted in English.

53 Minerva Figueroa (Assistant Executive Director, El Sistema Aeolian, London, Ontario, Canada), in an interview in writing by the author, March 31, 2015. As of 2017, El Sistema Aeolian works with sixty young people, ranging in age from six to sixteen. While the program continues to be open to all, due to high demand there is now an application and wait list. Growth has necessitated a change in venue to the Bishop Cronyn Memorial Place, still in Old East and not far from the original Lorne Avenue Public School and Aeolian Music Hall locations. El Sistema Aeolian is led by an advisory committee, guided by a teaching team, and supported by a group of volunteers.

54 Salmen, "Social Obligations," 267.

55 Salmen, "Social Obligations," 281.

56 Salmen, "Social Obligations," 267.

Chapter 13
Stammer and Rustle: Indisciplined Translations (Visual Essay)

1 Title with a nod to Barthes' *The Rustle of Language*, 1986. Concepts in this manifesto were researched over a number of years, beginning in approximately 2005 and developing in conjunction with the art pieces presented here. Further artwork can be viewed at www.diannepearce.ca.

2 W.J.T. Mitchell, "Interdisciplinarity and Visual Culture," *Art Bulletin* 77, no. 4 (December 1995): 541.

3 Robert Stam cited in Ben Highmore, *Everyday Life and Cultural Theory* (London: Routledge, 2002), 123.

4 Julia Kristeva, *Powers of Horror: An Essay on Abjection*, trans. Leon S. Roudiez (New York: Columbia University Press, 1984), 6.

5 Mikhail Bakhtin, *The Dialogic Imagination*, trans. Caryl Emerson and Michael Holquist (Austin: University of Texas Press, 1981), 11-2.

6 Elena Zdravomyslova, "The Café Saigon *Tusovka*: One Segment of the Informal-Public Sphere of Late-Soviet Society," in *Biographical Research in Eastern Europe*, eds. Robin Humphrey, Robert Miller, and Elena Zdravomyslova (Hampshire: Aldershot, 2003), 143.

7 Zdravomyslova, "The Café Saigon," 174.

8 Ernesto Pujol, "On the Ground: Practical Observations for Regenerating Art Education," in *Art School: Propositions for the 21ª Century*, ed. Steven Henry Madoff (Cambridge: MIT Press, 2009), 6.

9 Pujol, "On the Ground," 9.

10 Zósimo Camacho and Julio César Hernández, "Resistencia de las Normales Rurales," *Revista Contralínea* 5: no. 99 (April 1, 2008), accessed January 25, 2014. http://www.contralinea.com.mx/archivo/2008/abril/htm/resistencia-normales-rurales.htm. My translation from the Spanish.

11 Ivan Illich, *Deschooling Society* (Harmondsworth: Penguin, 1973), 57.

12 Suzi Gablik, *The Re-Enchantment of Art* (New York: Thames and Hudson, 1991), 4.

13 Gablik, *The Re-Enchantment*, 22.

14 Gilles Deleuze and Claire Parnet, *Dialogues*, trans. Hugh Tomlinson and Barbara Habberjam (London: The Athlone Press, 1987), 8.

15 Deleuze, *Dialogues*, 9-10.

16 Barthes, *The Rustle*, 54.

17 Barthes, *The Rustle*, 76.

18 Bourriaud, *Relational Aesthetics*, 13-4.

19 Bourriaud, *Relational Aesthetics*, 15.

20 Madoff, "Service Aesthetics," 167.

21 Mayer, "Pinto mi raya."

22 Misiano, "An Analysis of 'Tusovka,'" 164.

23 Barthes, *The Rustle*, 76.

Chapter 14
You Look at Me, I Look at You: Urban Space and Identity Reciprocity in the Work of Catherine Bodmer

1 A condensed version of this chapter was published as "Catherine Bodmer: Espacio urbano e imaginarios identitarios post-TLCAN," *Oltreoceano. Rivista sulle migrazioni* 13 (2017), 51-64, http://riviste.forumeditrice.it/oltreoceano/article/view/807.

2 Saskia Sassen, *Globalization and Its Discontents* (New York: New Press, 1999), xxxiii.

3 Sassen, *Globalization*, xxxiii.

4 Néstor García Canclini, "Museos, aeropuertos y ventas de garage. La identidad ante el Tratado de Libre Comercio," in *Identidad: análisis y teoría, simbolismo, sociedades complejas, nacionalismo y etnicidad. III Coloquio Paul Kirchhoff*, eds. Leticia Irene Méndez y Mercado (Mexico City: UNAM, 1996), 91.

5 García Canclini, "Museos, aeropuertos," 94.

6 See chapter 4, in this volume.

7 Diane Lemieux, "À l'occasion de la conférence de presse."

8 Several public and private institutions have engaged in strengthening cultural ties through artistic work between Mexico and Quebec. Mexico's most important festivals have reserved a place of honour for the Canadian province in recent years: After "Voilà Québec en México!" in 2003, "Hola Québec!" was held to celebrate the 37th edition of the Festival Internacional Cervantino in 2009, and in 2012 Quebec was the guest of the Festival Cultural de Mayo, which takes place in various cities in the state of Jalisco, as well as of the Guadalajara International Film Festival in 2014. Meanwhile, to celebrate the bicentennial of its Independence, Mexico was the guest of honour at the Quebec International Book Fair in 2010 and the Montreal Poetry Festival in 2013.

9 Catherine Bodmer, of Swiss origin, has lived and worked in Montreal, Canada, since 1996. She studied at the Lucerne School of Art and Design in Switzerland and later obtained a master of fine arts (MFA) at the University of Quebec in Montreal (UQÀM) in 1999. Her artistic practice consists of installations, in-situ works, and photographs, which have been presented in Canada, as well as in Mexico City and Taiwan. She has also actively participated in several artist-run centres in Montreal, as the artistic coordinator at La Centrale Galerie Powerhouse (1999-2002), and at Articule (2004-09). Since 2013, she has been the coordinator of training and professional development at Le Regroupement des centres d'artistes autogérés du Québec (Quebec's association of artist-run centres, or RCAAQ). For more details on her career path, consult her website: http://www.catherinebodmer.com/.

10 Janet Bellotto is an artist and curator from Toronto who bases her practice and artistic reflections on engagements that are site-specific or take place in public space. For more details on her trajectory, consult her website, www.janetbellotto.com.

11 Catherine Bodmer, text of report: *Desinfectado*, 2003. Explanatory text about the work provided by the artist to the author, January 13, 2014.

12 Catherine Bodmer, *Bounce* (2002-03).

13 Catherine Bodmer, *Embruns* (1998).

14 Catherine Bodmer, *Or* (2001).

15 Drobnick, "*Airchitecture*," 153.

16 Interview by author with Catherine Bodmer, Montreal, November 29, 2013.

17 Launched in 1994 and running until 2014-15, the "Échanges d'artistes et d'ateliers-résidences Québec-Mexique" program had a binational institutional infrastructure that directly involved the Consulate General of Mexico in Montreal, the Government of Mexico, the Department for International Development and Intergovernmental Relations of the Ministry of Culture and Communications of Quebec, and the General Delegation of Quebec in Mexico. This institutional network was intended to receive, provide a framework for, and monitor the artists selected. This program was meant to establish permanent relations between cultural institutions in order to encourage artists in diverse media (visual arts, media arts, theatre, literature and music) to travel to Quebec and Mexico City reciprocally for artistic residencies of up to four months.

18 The history of post-NAFTA diplomacy would also see an unprecedented development of cultural events supported by private initiatives thanks to the de-

veloping market for Latin American art (broadly conceptualized). This cultural renaissance enabled many institutions to open their doors, including the Centro ADM, which aims to reflect on the world through contemporary art, photography, and digital media and communication.

19 According to the Royal Academy of the Spanish Language, the term *camellón* comes from *caballón* (ridge), "the lump between groove and furrow plowed land" in agriculture. See *Diccionario de la Lengua Española*, "caballón": Lomo de tierra, como el que queda entre surco y surco al arar un terreno o el que se levanta con la asada (http://dle.rae.es/?id=6OVKXe7).

20 Catherine Bodmer and Marie-Ève Charron, *Catherine Bodmer: Mexico DF (details)* (Alma: Sagamie Édition d'Art, 2012).

21 Paul Virilio, *Velocidad y Política* (Buenos Aires: La Marca, 2007).

22 Bodmer won the Duke and Duchess of York Prize in Photography from the Canada Council for the Arts in 2008.

23 *Lacs* (2005); *Narcisse* (2008); *Himmel und Hoelle (variation)* (2008); *Himmel und Hoelle (Marelle/Hopscotch)* (2005-08).

24 La bande de Moebius I, II et III (2008).

25 See the complete series here: http://www.catherinebodmer.com/projets_churubusco.html.

26 The "Mexican miracle" is the title given to the period of economic development which began in the 1940s and which was characterized by sustained growth achieved by restricting imports, thus enabling the country's industrialization and the development of an urban infrastructure.

27 The administrative office of regent existed between 1941 and 1993, when Mexico City held the status of a department of the Federal District and was, thus under the rule of the president of the republic, who appointed the regent to govern the capital on his behalf.

28 Rachel Kram Villarreal, "Gladiolas for the Children of Sanchez: Ernesto P. Uruchurtu's Mexico City, 1950-1968" (PhD diss., The University of Arizona, 2008), 51.

29 According to Enrique X. de Anda, what is referred to in Mexico as Functionalism and known in other countries as International Modernism begins making headway in the 1930s, not only in reconstructing a country faced with the destruction of much of its public infrastructure and weakened by the Mexican Revolution that shook the country in the early twentieth century, but also simply in meeting the needs of a growing country. De Anda, *Historia de la arquitectura mexicana* (Barcelona: Gustavo Gili, 2008), 182. Project of the Government of the City of Mexico, implemented by the head of government, Miguel Angel Mancera, in 2013.

30 The same occurred with several tributaries that now run through steel channels beneath the asphalt of the capital's highways, and whose existence today amounts to nothing more than the names of avenues: Río Churubusco, Río Mixcoac, Río Piedad, and Río San Joaquín.

31 Charron, "Urban Particles." In Bodmer and Charron, *Catherine Bodmer: Mexico D.F. (details)*, 73.

32 Rebecca E. Biron, *City/Art: Setting the Scene*, 23.

33 Saskia Sassen, "The Global City," p. 27.

34 Alison Blake, "Pocket Parks." Pocket Parks emerged in the 1960s in Philadelphia as a social movement that sought to provide the city with public spaces. Between 1961 and 1967, about sixty abandoned spaces, which up until then had been considered dangerous neighbourhood zones, were recovered to create small community parks as part of the Philadelphia Neighborhood Program. https://depts.washington.edu/open2100/Resources/2_OpenSpaceTypes/Open_Space_Types/pocket_parks.pdf

35 The High Line Park Project took shape under the administration of Mayor Michael Bloomberg, who in 2004 made the decision to finance the rehabilitation of an old railroad line built in the 1930s to connect the industrial districts on Manhattan's West Side. The project was developed in three stages: the first opened in 2009, the second in 2011, and the third in 2014. High Line also is an open-air museum that features several public art sculptures and is considered the world's longest green rooftop, as it allows the regeneration of nature in New York City. See http://www.thehighline.org/.

36 The Pocket Parks in Mexico City are part of the Public Spaces Recovery Project of the Government of the City of Mexico, implemented in 2013 by Miguel Angel Mancera, Head of Government of the Federal District (5 December 2012 - 29 March 2018).

37 According to Priscilla Connolly ("Evolución del problema habitacional en la Ciudad de México," in *La vivienda popular en la Ciudad de México. Características y políticas de solución a sus problemas. Conferencias y mesa redonda*, ed. Adrián Guillermo Aguilar (Mexico City: Instituto de Geografía-UNAM, 1985), 20), sixty percent of Mexico City is self-built, without any government help, in a disorderly, unregulated manner. This type of urban planning intensified in the 1940s due to the concentration of industrial resources in the capital, a population explosion, and migrations of Mexicans from rural to urban areas in search of better living conditions.

38 José Iñigo Aguilar Medina, *La ciudad que construyen los pobres* (Mexico City: Plaza y Valdés, 1996), 45.

39 Aguilar Medina, *La ciudad*, 45. On the night of September 1, 1971, and over a period of fifteen days, Santo Domingo was overtaken by hundreds of families arriving from the countryside in search of a place to settle in the city. The invasion was an important event that affected the entire area because it involved communal lands, so that it generated tensions between the invaders and the communal owners.

40 Abraham Cruzvillegas, *Autoconstrucción* (Glasgow: Centre for Contemporary Arts, 2008), 15.

41 The exhibit "Libre Comercio" is part of a larger project on the disparate architectures of street peddlers in Mexico City, carried out by the artistic duo during the summer of 2011 thanks to a Mexico-Quebec artistic residencies grant from the CALQ and FONCA. See http://patmiki.blogspot.mx/p/algorit.html.

42 In what was an area built out of "urgency," today there exists the Parque Ecológico Cuitláhuac, also known as the "people's park," which opened in 2012 and whose ninety-three acres make it one of the largest recreation areas in the eastern part of Mexico City.

43 Emilio Duhau and Angela Giglia, *Las reglas del desorden: habitar la metrópoli* (Mexico City: Siglo XXI Editores/Universidad Autónoma Metropolitana-Azcapotzalco, 2008).

44 Duhau and Giglia, *Las reglas*, 45.

45 Jordi Borja, "Revolución y contrarrevolución en la ciudad global: las expectativas frustradas por la globalización de nuestras ciudades," *Revista EURE* 33, no. 100 (2007): 42.

46 Borja, "Revolución y contrarrevolución," 46.

47 Pascale Beaudet, "Catherine Bodmer: Lacs," *Image and Imagination,* ed. Martha Langford (Montreal and Kingston: McGill-Queen's University, 2005), 6.

48 My translation from the original French. Beaudet, "Catherine Bodmer: Lacs," 6.

49 Christine M. Boyer, *The City of Collective Memory. Its Historical Imagery and Architectural Entertainments* (Cambridge: MIT Press, 1998), 32.

50 Roland Barthes, *La cámara lúcida. Nota sobre la fotografía* (Barcelona: Paidós Comunicación, 1989), 40.

51 Doreen Massey, "Lugar, identidad y geografías de la responsabilidad en un mundo en proceso de globalización," *Treballs de la Societat Catalana de Geografia,* 57 (2004), 77-84.

52 Massey, "Lugar, identidad," 14.

Bibliography

This bibliography is organized into two main parts: primary sources and secondary sources. The secondary sources, which are listed last, are organized alphabetically. They represent roughly three quarters of the bibliography, in terms of the number of pages they occupy. Since much of the material cited in this book nonetheless consists of primary sources, we have organized the bibliography to give prominence to the important role of these sources and to facilitate readers' access to such works. Primary sources are subdivided into 10 sections: archives, artwork, audiovisual, creative writing, online government sources, interviews, periodicals, travel brochures, websites, miscellaneous. Items listed under "Miscellaneous" include the likes of reports, press conference presentations, and advertising standards.

Primary sources

1. Archives
Centro de la Vicaría de la Solidaridad. "El derecho de vivir en su patria." *Foi et Développement*, 56, April 1978, p. 6 CDVS, Exilio, box 29.
The Library and Archives of the National Gallery of Canada, Ottawa.

2. Artwork
Bernal, Claudia. *Monumento a Ciudad Juárez, sólo aquellas que mueren de muerte violenta entrarán al paraíso.* 2002. Mixed media, installation.
Bodmer, Catherine. *Desinfectado.* 2003. Photograph, colour.
—. *Río Churubusco (Circuito Interior).* 2010. Series of photographs, colour, ink jet print.
—. *Avenida Pedro H. Ureña (Eje 10 Sur).* 2010. Series of photographs, colour, ink jet print.
—. *Avenida de las Torres (Eje 6 Sur).* 2010. Series of photographs, colour, ink jet print.
—. *Tianguis Luis Méndez (Eje 6 Sur).* 2010. Series of photographs, colour, ink jet print.
—. *Parque Deportivo Cuitláhuac (Eje 6 Sur).* 2010. Series of photographs, colour, ink jet print.
Cisneros, Domingo. *La Reconquista.* 2008. Mixed media, installation.
Lara Díaz-Berrio, Natalia. *Rafael in his living room wearing casual clothing.* 2010-2012. Digital photograph, colour.
—. *Rafael with the jersey of the Mexican national soccer team.* 2010-2012. Digital photograph, colour.
—. *Aida, husband, and son in their living room.* 2010-2012. Digital photograph, colour.
—. *Aida, husband, and son with a Mexican flag.* 2010-2012. Digital photograph, colour.

—. *Araceli wearing Mexican embroidered clothes.* 2010-2012. Digital photograph, colour.

—. *Araceli wearing Mexican embroidered clothes.* 2010-2012. Digital photograph, colour.

—. *Jorge enacting a mariachi, with his collection of Mexican hats.* 2010-2012. Digital photograph, colour.

—. *Jorge in his dining room, wearing casual clothing.* 2010-2012. Digital photograph, colour.

—. *Carmelo in his bedroom, wearing casual clothing.* 2010-2012. Digital photograph, colour.

—. *Carmelo swaddled in blanket with the Mexican flag.* 2010-2012. Digital photograph, colour.

Pearce, Dianne. *Better Left Unsaid,* 2005. Mixed media, Variable dimensions, installation. Galería de la Universidad Iberoamericana, Mexico City.

—. *Polyphonic Novel,* 2006-2007. Mixed media, variable dimensions. exTeresa Arte Alternativo, Mexico City.

—. *Tusovkian Meetings,* 2010. Mixed media, variable dimensions. Red Head Gallery, Toronto.

—. *Restricted to Those Pleasures and Desires Inscribed within the Encyclopaedia of Mandatory Good Taste* , 2002. Mixed media, variable dimensions. MUCA-Roma, Mexico City.

—. *Wallflowers,* 2003. Mixed media, variable dimensions. Ex-Teresa Arte Alternativo, Mexico City, 2007.

—. *Vast Regions of Domain.* 2011. Mixed media, variable dimensions. Museo de Arte Moderno Chiloe, Castro, Chile, 2012.

—. *Words of Wisdom and Verbal Abuse.* 2003-2004. Mixed media, variable dimensions. DNA Art Space, London, Canada, 2013.

—. *Stammer and Rustle.* 2006-2007. Mixed media, variable dimensions. Ex-Teresa Arte Alternativo, Mexico City, 2007.

Pietropaolo, Vincenzo. *Celebration of Resistance: Ontario's Days of Action.* Toronto: Between the Lines, 1999.

—. *Canadians at Work.* Toronto: CAW-Canada, 2000.

—. *Harvest Pilgrims: Mexican and Caribbean Migrant Farm Workers in Canada.* Toronto: Between the Lines, 2009.

—. *Invisible No More: A Photographic Chronicle of the Lives of People with Intellectual Disabilities.* New Brunswick: Rutgers University Press, 2010.

—. *Not Paved with Gold: Italian-Canadian Immigrants in the 1970s.* Toronto: Between the Lines, 2006.

—. *Ritual.* London: Black Dog Publishing, 2016.

—, and Cecelia Lawless. *Making Home in Havana.* New Brunswick: Rutgers University Press, 2002. Ramírez Castillo, Osvaldo. *Becerrillo.* 2008. Mixed media.

3. Audiovisual

Abreu, José Antonio. "The El Sistema Music Revolution." *TED.* Filmed February 2009. Video, 16.37. Accessed June 17, 2014. http://www.ted.com/talks/jose_abreu_on_kids_transformed_by_music ?language=en.

Arvelo, Alberto, dir. *Tocar y luchar*. Kingston, NY: Explorart Films, 2006. DVD.
Latour, Charles, dir. *Los mexicanos: The combat of Patricia Perez*. DVD. Montreal: Macumba, 2007.
Lee, Min-Sook, dir. *El Contrato*. National Film Board of Canada, 2003. Video, 51 min. https://www.nfb.ca/film/el_contrato/.
United Food and Commercial Workers Union Canada. "Vincenzo Pietropaolo: Witness to the Harvest Pilgrims." *YouTube*. Published October 21, 2009. Video, 10.14. http://www.youtube.com/watch?v=1x-sW_iaJZs.

4. Creative writing

Álvarez, Natalie, ed. *Fronteras Vivientes: Eight Latina/o Canadian Plays*. Toronto: Playwrights Canada Press, 2013.
—. *Latina/o Canadian Theatre and Performance*. Toronto: Playwrights Canada, 2013.
Casuso, Luis. "En la habitación." In *Cuentos de nuestra palabra. Primera hornada*, edited by Guillermo Rose and Alex Zisman, 69-73. Markham: Editorial Nuestra Palabra, 2009.
De Elía, Ramón. "La otra bahía de Hudson." *The Apostles Review* 7 (Hiver 2011): 16-19.
—. "Las doce noches." In *Retrato de una nube: primera antología del cuento hispano canadiense*, edited by Luis Molina Lora and Julio Torres-Recinos, 71-80. Ottawa: Editorial Lugar Común, 2008.
Díaz León, Yoel Isaac. "Miedo viejo." In *Cuentos de nuestra palabra. Primera hornada*, edited by Guillermo Rose and Alex Zisman, 45-47. Markham: Editorial Nuestra Palabra, 2009.
Etcheverry, Jorge. "Camas paralelas." In *Retrato de una nube: primera antología del cuento hispano canadiense*, edited by Luis Molina Lora and Julio Torres-Recinos, 93-96. Ottawa: Editorial Lugar Común, 2008.
—. "Metamorfosis II." In *Retrato de una nube: primera antología del cuento hispano canadiense*, edited by Luis Molina Lora and Julio Torres-Recinos, 100-103. Ottawa: Editorial Lugar Común, 2008.
Junge-Hammersley, Anita. "Cerrando el círculo." In *Cuentos de nuestra palabra. Primera hornada*, edited by Guillermo Rose and Alex Zisman, 103-107. Markham: Editorial Nuestra Palabra, 2009.
—. "Carnaval cultural." In *Retrato de una nube: primera antología del cuento hispano canadiense*, edited by Luis Molina Lora and Julio Torres-Recinos, 150-51. Ottawa: Editorial Lugar Común, 2008.
Molina Lora, Luis, and Julio Torres-Recinos, eds. *Retrato de una nube: primera antología del cuento hispano canadiense*. Ottawa: Editorial Lugar Común, 2008.
Rodríguez, Carmen. "Juegos y jugarretas." In *Retrato de una nube: primera antología del cuento hispano canadiense*, edited by Luis Molina Lora and Julio Torres-Recinos, 229-31. Ottawa: Editorial Lugar Común, 2008.
Rojas Primus, Constanza. "La iniciación." In *Cuentos de nuestra palabra. Primera hornada*, edited by Guillermo Rose and Alex Zisman, 59-63. Markham: Editorial Nuestra Palabra, 2009.

Rose, Guillermo, and Alex Zisman. *Cuentos de nuestra palabra. Primera hornada*. Markham: Editorial Nuestra Palabra, 2009.

Saravia, Alejandro. "Los osos de Port Churchill." In *Cuentos de nuestra palabra. Primera hornada*, edited by Guillermo Rose and Alex Zisman, 79-83. Markham: Editorial Nuestra Palabra, 2009.

——. "La orureña." In *Cuentos de nuestra palabra. Primera hornada*, edited by Guillermo Rose and Alex Zisman, 109-113. Markham: Editorial Nuestra Palabra, 2009.

Tarud, Denise. "La caja del falte." In *Cuentos de nuestra palabra. Primera hornada*, edited by Guillermo Rose and Alex Zisman, 237-241. Markham: Editorial Nuestra Palabra, 2009.

Valle-Garay, Pastor. "Mi arce en Arce (Maple, Ontario)." In *Cuentos de nuestra palabra. Primera hornada*, edited by Guillermo Rose and Alex Zisman, 85-89. Markham: Editorial Nuestra Palabra, 2009.

5. Online government sources

"What We Do." Canadian Heritage Information Network. Accessed June 15, 2014. http://www.rcip-chin.gc.ca/apropos-about/notre_mission-what_we_do-eng.jsp (site discontinued).

Citizenship and Immigration Canada. *Annual Report to Parliament on Immigration 2009*. Ottawa: Minister of Public Works and Government Services Canada, 2009. https://canucklaw.ca/wp-content/uploads/2020/02/2009.annual.immigration.report.to_.parliament.pdf.

——. *Canada Facts and Figures 2012. Immigration Overview: Permanent and Temporary Residents*. Ottawa: Minister of Public Works and Government Services Canada, 2012. https://qspace.library.queensu.ca/bitstream/handle/1974/8469/2012_CIC_Facts%20and%20Figures%20-%20Immigration%20Overview%20-%20Permanent%20and%20Temporary%20Residents.pdf?sequence=16&isAllowed=y.

——. *FW1 Foreign Worker Manual*. Accessed April 23, 2014. http://www.cic.gc.ca/english/resources/manuals/fw/fw01-eng.pdf (site discontinued).

Crompton, Susan, and Leslie-Anne Keown. "Going on Vacation: Benefits Sought from Pleasure Travel." Component of Statistics Canada Catalogue no. 11-008-X, *Canadian Social Trends*. Updated May 14, 2009. https://www150.statcan.gc.ca/n1/pub/11-008-x/2009001/article/10850-eng.htm.

Dewing, Michael. *Canadian Multiculturalism*. Ottawa: Library of Parliament, 2009. https://publications.gc.ca/collections/collection_2010/bdp-lop/prb/prb0920-eng.pdf.

Employment and Social Development Canada. *Seasonal Agricultural Worker Program*. Accessed April 23, 2014. http://www.esdc.gc.ca/eng/jobs/foreign_workers/agriculture/seasonal/ (site discontinued).

——. *Temporary Foreign Worker Program Labour Market Opinion (LMO) Statistics Annual Statistics 2006-2009*. Accessed April 23, 2014. http://www.hrsdc.gc.ca/eng/workplaceskills/foreign_workers/stats/annual/table10a.shtml (site discontinued).

Foreign Affairs and International Trade Canada. "About the Department," March 6, 2013. http://www.international.gc.ca/about-a_propos/index. aspx?view=d (site discontinued).

Government of Canada. *Canada-Mexico Relations.* Updated November 10, 2021. http://www.canadainternational.gc.ca/mexico-mexique/canmex. aspx?view=d.

—. "Travel Advisories," 2014. http://travel.gc.ca/travelling/advisories.

Hudon, Marie Eve. *Official Languages in Canada: Federal Policy.* Publication No. 08-44E, 2010. https://lop.parl.ca/sites/PublicWebsite/default/ en_CA/ResearchPublications/201170E.

Machalski, Andrew. *Hispanic Writers in Canada. A Preliminary Survey of the Activities of Spanish and Latin-American Writers in Canada.* Ottawa: Department of the Secretary of State of Canada, 1988.

Minister of Justice. *Official Languages Act R.S.C., 1985, c. 31* (4th Supp.). Accessed June 10, 2014. https://laws-lois.justice.gc.ca/eng/acts/O-3.01/.

Natural Resources Canada. *The Atlas of Canada-Toporama.* Accessed January 15, 2014. http://atlas.nrcan.gc.ca/site/english/toporama/index.html#.

Office Québécois de la Langue Française. *Charter of the French Language,* 2014. http://www2.publicationsduquebec.gouv.qc.ca/dynamicSearch/telecharge.php ?type=2&file=/C_11/C11_A.html (page no longer available).

Service Ontario. *French Language Services Act.* 2013. http://www.elaws.gov. on.ca/html/statutes/english/elaws_statutes_90f32_e.htm (site discontinued).

Secretaría de Relaciones Exteriores. *Trabajadores Agrícolas Temporales (PTAT).* Accessed March 14, 2014. http://www.sre.gob.mx/proteccionconsular/ index.php/trabajadores-agricolas-en-canada (page no longer available).

Statistics Canada. *Focus on Geography Series, 2011 Census.* Ottawa: Statistics Canada Catalogue no. 98-310-XWE2011004. Updated October 24, 2012. https://www12.statcan.gc.ca/census-recensement/2011/as-sa/fogs-spg/Facts-pr-eng.cfm?Lang=Eng&GC=47.

—. *Hispanic (Spanish Speaking) Population in Canada: A Special Report Prepared for the Canadian Hispanic Congress.* 2006. http://revistadebate.net/ global/attachments/article/2481/CENSUS%20REV%202006.pdf (page no longer available).

—. *Linguistic Characteristics of Canadians.* Accessed January 2013. http:// www12.statcan.gc.ca/census-recensement/2011/as-sa/98-314-x/98-314-x2011001-eng.cfm.

—. *The Latin American Community in Canada.* Ottawa: Statistics Canada, 2007. http://www.statcan.gc.ca/pub/89-621-x/89-621-x2007008-eng.htm.

—. *Travel by Canadians to Foreign Countries, Top 15 Countries Visite,* 2000-2012. http://www.statcan.gc.ca/tables-tableaux/sum-som/l01/cst01/ arts37a-eng.htm (site discontinued).

—. *Visual Census. 2006 Census.* Ottawa: Statistics Canada, December 7, 2010. Accessed September 2, 2014. http://www12.statcan.gc.ca/ censusrecensement/2006/dppd/fsfi/index.cfm?Lang=ENG&TOPIC_ ID=11&PRCODE=01 (site discontinued).

—. *Visual Census, 2011 Census*. Ottawa: Statistics Canada, October 2012. http://www12.statcan.gc.ca/census-recensement/2011/dp-pd/vc-rv/index.cfm?Lang=ENG&TOPIC_ID=4&GEOCODE=01.

Secretaría de Trabajo y Previsión Social. *Programa de trabajadores agrícolas temporales México-Canadá*. Mexico City: Secretaría del Trabajo y Previsión Social, 2013. Accessed February 14, 2014. http://www.stps.gob.mx/bp/secciones/conoce/areas_atencion/areas_atencion/servicio_empleo/trabajadores_agricolas.html (page no longer available).

United Nations High Commissioner for Refugees. *La situación de los refugiados en el mundo 2000*. Barcelona: Icaria Editorial, 2000.

U.S. Department of State. *North American Partnership: Trilateral Ministerial Meeting Communiqué*. Washington, DC: U.S. Department of State, August 12, 2000. https://1997-2001.state.gov/regions/wha/uscanmex_trilat/000812_trilat_communique.html.

World Tourism Organization and European Travel Commission. *Handbook on Tourism Destination Branding*. Madrid: World Toursim Organization, 2009.

6. Interviews

Álvarez, Natalie, interview by Andrea Ávila, Toronto, June 2014.

Assoignon, A. (G Adventures), interview by Madeleine de Trenqualye, February-March 2014.

Barrenechea, Ana María, interview by Francis Peddie, Toronto, February 14, 2010.

Behrens, Willy, interview by Francis Peddie, Ottawa, February 17, 2010.

Bernal, Claudia, interview by Mariza Rosales Argonza, 2012 and 2016.

Bernhardt, Mark (Sirens Communications), interview by Madeleine de Trenqualye, February-March 2014.

Bodmer, Catherine, interview by Nuria Carton de Grammont, November 29, 2013.

Cisneros, Domingo, interview by Mariza Rosales Argonza, 2011 and 2012.

Etcheverry, Jorge, interview by Francis Peddie, Ottawa, February 16, 2010.

—, interview by Andrea Ávila, December 15, 2013.

Esponda, Rodrigo (Mexico Tourism Board), interview by Madeleine de Trenqualye, Vancouver, April 2014.

Freire, Marlinda, interview by Francis Peddie, Toronto, October 22, 2008.

Godoy, Patricia, interview by Francis Peddie, Toronto, October 31, 2008.

House, Jeffry, interview by Francis Peddie, Toronto, February 11, 2010.

Leija, Lorena, interview by Andrea Ávila, Guelph, ON, July 2014.

McTavish, John (founder and former editor-in-chief of *Presencia Latina*), interview by John Raimondo, November 25, 2015.

Mendoza Cesar (Mexico Tourism Board), interview by Madeleine de Trenqualye, Vancouver, April 2014.

Mora, G. Christina, interview by National Public Radio, *National Public Radio*, May 22, 2015. http://www.npr.org/2015/05/22/408835942/making-hispanics.

Núñez, Juan, interview by Francis Peddie, Toronto, November 21, 2009.
Ramírez Castillo, Osvaldo, interview by Mariza Rosales Argonza, 2012 and 2014.
Rivera, Nidia, interview by Francis Peddie, Toronto, November 9, 2008.
Simalchik, Joan, interviewed by Francis Peddie, Toronto, February 15, 2010.
Suescun Pozas, Maria del Carmen, interview by Paloma Martinez, *Radio Canada International*, November 9, 2015. http://www.rcinet.ca/es/2015/11/09/canada-y-america-latina-unidas-en-la-historia/.
S.V.P., interview by Francis Peddie, Toronto, October 31, 2008.
Torres, Carlos, interview by Francis Peddie, Toronto, October 21, 2008.
Velez, Freddy (editor-in-chief of *Correo Canadiense*), interview by John Raimondo, November 24, 2015.
Verdecchia, Guillermo, interview by Andrea Ávila, June 2014.

7. Periodicals
Canadian Newcomer Magazine
Correo Canadiense
El Chasqui Latino
El Universal
Hamilton Spectator
La Jornada Hispanic Newspaper
La Portada Canada
La Presse
Le Monde
Maclean's Magazine
Ottawa Journal
Ottawa Citizen
Presencia Latina
Standard
The Evening Journal
The Evening Star
The Globe and Mail
The Montreal Daily Herald
The Montreal Daily Witness
The Montreal Gazette
The Montreal Star
The Star
Toronto Telegram
Toronto Star
Windsor Daily Star

8. Travel Brochures
Gap Adventures: The Adventure Travel Company. *South and Central America*, 2010.
Intrepid Travel. *Latin America*, 2010.

—. *Latin America and Antarctica*, 2014.
Travel Cuts. *Travel Cuts - Canada's Student Travel Experts*, 2010.

9. Websites
Aeolian. http://aeolianhall.ca.
Alameda Theatre Company. http://www.alamedatheatre.com/ (site discontinued).
Aluna Theatre. http://www.alunatheatre.ca/.
Catherine Bodmer. http://www.catherinebodmer.com/.
Canadian Hispanic Congress. https://canadianhispaniccongress.com/.
Canadian Theatre Encyclopedia. http://www.canadiantheatre.com/.
Casa Maíz. http://www.casamaiz.org/.
High Line Park Project. Accessed December 12, 2016. http://www.thehigh-line.org/.
Itravel2000. https://itravel2000.com/.
Municipality of Leamington. https://www.leamington.ca/en/index.aspx.
The Glenn Gould Foundation. https://www.glenngould.ca/.
Vividata. https://vividata.ca/.

10. Miscellaneous
Advertising Standards Canada. *The Canadian Code of Advertising Standards*. Accessed May 19, 2014. https://adstandards.ca/code/the-code-online/.
Canadian Music Educators' Association ad hoc El Sistema committee. "*El Sistema* Position Paper." Accessed February 9, 2015. http://cmea.ca/wp-content/uploads/2013/01/CMEA-El-Sistema-Position-Paper-Nov-2012-approved.pdf.
—. "El Sistema Position Paper." November 24, 2012. http://cmea.ca/wp-content/uploads/2013/01/CMEA-El-Sistema-Position-Paper-Nov-2012-approved.pdf.
Canadian Tourism Commission. *Three Travel Trends to Watch in 2014*. Accessed November 5, 2014. http://en-corporate.canada.travel/content/ctc_news/travel-trends-2014 (page no longer available).
Diversité Artistique de Montréal. *Guide des publics: Répertoire des ressources culturelles des communautés latino-américains hispanophones de Montréal*. Montreal: DAM, 2009.
Elementary Teachers' Federation of Ontario. "The Glenn Gould Prize Celebration of Music." http://www.etfo.ca/Pages/Home.aspx (page no longer available).
Lemieux, Diane. "À l'occasion de la conférence de presse annonçant la participation du Québec comme invité d'honneur à la Foire internationale du livre de Guadalajara." Address given at the press conference that announced Quebec's role as guest of honour at the 2003 Guadalajara International Book Fair, Guadalajara, December 8, 2002. http://www.mrif.gouv.qc.ca/document/SPDI/FondDoc/FDOC_alloc_1615_20021208_lemieux.htm.
Sattler, Peggy. "*El Sistema* Aeolian Evaluation Report." London, ON: Academica Group Inc., April 2013.

Secondary sources

Abella, Manolo. "Policies and Best Practices for Management of Temporary Migration." *International Symposium on International Migration and Development*, Population Division, Department of Economic and Social Affairs, United Nations Secretariat, Turin, Italy, June 28-30, 2006. https://www.un.org/en/development/desa/population/events/pdf/other/turin/P03_Abella.pdf.

Aguilar Medina, José Íñigo. *La ciudad que construyen los pobres*. Mexico City: Plaza y Valdés, 1996.

Alberro, Solange. "Retablos y religiosidad en el México del siglo XIX." In *Retablos y exvotos: colección uso y estilo*, 8-31. Mexico City: Museo Franz Mayer, 2000.

Alia, Valerie, and Simone Bull. *Media and Ethnic Minorities*. Edinburgh: Edinburgh University Press, 2005.

Allen, Graham. *Intertextuality*. London: Routledge, 2000.

Allende, Isabel. *Hija de la fortuna*. Barcelona: Plaza y Janes, 1999.

Allodi, Fernando, and Alejandro Rojas. "The Role of a Housing Cooperative Community in the Mental Health and Social Adaptation of Latin American Refugees in Toronto." *Migration World Magazine* 16, no. 3 (1988): 17-21.

Altman, Ida, Sarah L. Cline, and Juan Javier Pescador. *The Early History of Greater Mexico*. Upper Saddle River: Prentice Hall, 2003.

Anderson, Benedict R. O'G. *Imagined Communities: Reflections on the Origin and Spread of Nationalism*. London and New York: Verso, 1991.

—. *Imagined Communities: Reflections on the Origins and Spread of Nationalism*. Rev. ed. London and New York: Verso, 2006.

Anzaldúa, Gloria. *Borderlands/La frontera: The New Mestiza*. San Francisco: Aunt Lute Books, 1987.

Appadurai. Arjun. *Modernity At Large: Cultural Dimensions of Globalization*. Minneapolis: University of Minnesota Press, 1996.

Appleford, Rob, ed. *Aboriginal Drama and Theatre*. Toronto: Playwrights Canada Press, 2005.

Aquino, Nina Lee. *Love and Relasianships: A Collection of Contemporary Asian-Canadian Drama*, Vol. 2. Toronto: Playwrights Canada Press, 2009.

—, and Rick Knowles, eds. *Asian Canadian Theatre: New Essays on Canadian Theatre*, Vol. 1. Toronto: Playwrights Canada Press, 2011.

Arana Hernández, María del Socorro, and José de Jesús Rogelio Rodríguez Maldonado. *Experiencias laborales de jornaleros tlaxcaltecas en Canadá*. Tlaxcala: Universidad Autónoma de Tlaxcala, 2006.

Arellano Ortiz, Fernando. "Eduardo Galeano: América Latina cuenta con grandes reservas de dignidad." *Pueblos*, 1 December 2005. http://www.revistapueblos.org/old/spip.php?article306.

Armony, Victor. "Introduction: Latin American Diasporas: Common Origins and Different Paths." *Canadian Ethnic Studies Journal/Études Ethniques au Canada* 46, no. 3 (2014): 1-6.

—. "Latin American Communities in Canada: Trends in Diversity and Integration." *Canadian Ethnic Studies/Études Ethniques au Canada* 46, no. 3 (2014): 7-34.

—. "Settling North of the U.S. Border: Canada's Latinos and the Particular Case of Québec." *LASA Forum* XLVI, no. 4 (2015): 20-22.

—, Martha Barriga, and Daniel Schugurensky. "Citizenship Learning and Political Participation: The Experience of Latin American Immigrants in Canada." *Canadian Journal of Latin American and Caribbean Studies* 29 (2004): 17-38.

Backhaus, P. *Linguistic Landscapes: A Comparative Study of Urban Multilingualism in Tokyo*. Clevendon: Multilingual Matters, 2007.

Baeza Kallens, Litzy. "Voces del exilio: testimonios orales del exilio chileno en Edmonton, Canadá." Master's thesis, Universidad de Chile, 2004.

Baker, Geoffrey. *El Sistema: Orchestrating Venezuela's Youth*. Oxford and New York: Oxford University Press, 2014.

Bakhtin, Mikhail. *The Dialogic Imagination*. Translated by Caryl Emerson and Michael Holquist. Austin: University of Texas Press, 1981.

Balfe, Judith Huggins. "Artworks as Symbols in International Politics." *International Journal of Politics, Culture, and Society* 1, no. 2 (Winter 1987): 195-217.

Banting, Keith, and Will Kymlicka. "Canadian Multiculturalism: Global Anxieties and Local Debates." *British Journal of Canadian Studies* 23, no. 1 (2010): 43-72.

Barbosa, Rosana. *Brazil and Canada: Economic, Political and Migratory Ties, 1820s to 1970s*. Lanham: Lexington Books, 2017.

Barman, Roderick. *Citizen Emperor. Pedro II and the Making of Brazil, 1825-1891*. Stanford: Stanford University Press, 1999.

Barthes, Roland. *The Rustle of Language*. Translated by Richard Howard. New York: Hill and Wang, 1986.

—. *La cámara lúcida. Nota sobre la fotografía*. Barcelona: Paidós Comunicación, 1989.

Barudy, Jorge. "A Programme of Mental Health for Political Refugees: Dealing with the Invisible Pain of Political Exile." *Social Science and Medicine* 28, no.7 (1989).

Basok, Tanya. "Free to Be Unfree: Mexican Guest Workers in Canada." *Labour, Capital and Society* 32, no. 2 (1999): 192-221.

—. "Obstacles to Productive Investment: Mexican Farm Workers in Canada." *International Migration Review* 34, no. 1 (2000): 79-97.

—. "He Came, He Saw, He…Stayed: Guest Worker Programs and the Issue of Non-Return." *International Migration Review* 38, no. 2 (2000): 215-38.

—. *Tortillas and Tomatoes: Transmigrant Mexican Harvesters in Canada*. Montreal: McGill-Queen's University Press, 2002.

—. "Mexican Seasonal Migration to Canada and Development: A Community-Based Comparison." *International Migration Review* 41, no. 2 (2003): 3-25.

—. "Post-national Citizenship, Social Exclusion and Migrants Rights: Mexican Seasonal Workers in Canada." *Citizenship Studies* 8, no. 1 (2004): 47-64.

Basok, Tanya, Danièle Bélanger, and Eloy Rivas. "Reproducing Deportability: Migrant Agricultural Workers in South-Western Ontario." *Journal of Ethnic and Migration Studies* 20, no. 9 (2014): 1-20.

Baud, Michel, and Johanna Louisa Ypeij, eds. *Cultural Tourism in Latin America: The Politics of Space and Imagery*. Leiden; Boston: Brill, 2009.

Bauder, Harald. *Labor Movement: How Migration Regulates Labor Markets*. Oxford: Oxford University Press, 2006.

—, and Margot Corbin. "Foreign Farm Workers in Ontario: Representations in the Newsprint Media." University of Guelph, 2002. http://www.geography.ryerson.ca/hbauder/Immigrant%20Labour/foreign-farm-workers.pdf.

Bauman, Zygmunt. *La cultura en el mundo de la modernidad líquida*. Mexico City: Fondo de Cultura Económica, 2011.

Beaudet, Pascale, "Catherine Bodmer: Lacs." *Image and Imagination*, Le Mois de la Photo à Montréal 2005, edited by Martha Langford, 244-48. Montreal and Kingston: McGill-Queen's University, 2005.

Becerril, Ofelia. "Gendered Politics of Labour: A Study of Male and Female Mexican Migrant Farm Workers in Canada." In *Organizing the Transnational: Labour, Politics, and Social Change*, edited by Luin Goldring and Sailaja Krishnamurti, 157-72. Vancouver: University of British Columbia Press, 2007.

Beltrán, Michele M., and Elin Luque Agraz. "Where Past and Present Meet: The Ex-Votos of Mexican Immigrants." In *The Road to Aztlan: Art From a Mythical Homeland*, edited by Virginia M. Fields and Victor Zamudio-Taylor, 318-31. Los Angeles: Los Angeles County Museum of Art, 2001.

Ben-Rafael, Eliezer, Muhammad Hasan Amara, Nira Trumper-Hecht, and Elana Shohamy. "Linguistic Landscape as Symbolic Construction of the Public Space: The Case of Israel." *International Journal of Multilingualism* 3, no. 1 (2006): 7-30.

Bendixen and Associates, "The Ethnic Media in America: The Giant Hidden in Plain Sight. Final Report." 2005. Accessed December 23, 2015. https://legacy.npr.org/documents/2005/jul/ncmfreport.pdf.

Berger, Arthur Asa. *Ads, Fads and Consumer Culture: Advertising's Impact on American Character and Society*. 4th ed. Lanham: Rowman and Littlefield Publishers, 2011.

—. *Deconstructing Travel: Cultural Perspectives on Tourism*. Walnut Creek, CA: Altamira Press, 2004

Berger, Dina. "Goodwill Ambassadors on Holiday: Tourism, Diplomacy, and Mexico-U.S. Relations." In *Holiday in Mexico: Critical Reflections on Tourism and Tourist Encounters*, edited by Dina Berger and Andrew Grant Wood, 107-29. Durham and London: Duke University Press, 2010.

Berger, Maurice. *Whiteness and Race in Contemporary Art*. Baltimore: University of Maryland Baltimore County, 2004.

Bhabha, Homi. "El compromiso con la teoría." Translated by Ana Romero. Accessed March 7, 2014. https://red.pucp.edu.pe/wp-content/uploads/biblioteca/4.pdf. Originally published as "The Commitment to Theory" (in *The Location of Culture*, London: Routledge, 1994).

——. *The Location of Culture*. London and New York: Routledge, 1994.

Binford, Leigh. "Social and Economic Contradictions of Rural Migrant Contract Labor between Tlaxcala, Mexico and Canada." *Culture and Agriculture* 24, no. 2 (2002): 1-19.

——. "Campos agrícolas, campos de poder. El estado mexicano, los granjeros canadienses y los trabajadores temporales mexicanos." *Migraciones Internacionales* 3, no. 3 (2006): 54-80.

——. "From Fields of Power to Fields of Sweat: The Dual Process of Constructing Temporary Migrant Labour in Mexico and Canada." *Third World Quarterly* 30, no. 3 (2009): 503-17.

——. *Tomorrow We're All Going to the Harvest: Temporary Foreign Work Programs and Neoliberal Political Economy*. Austin: University of Texas Press, 2013.

——, Guillermo Carrasco Rivas, and Socorro Arana Hernández. *Rumbo a Canadá. La migración canadiense de trabajadores agrícolas tlaxcaltecos.* Mexico City: Ediciones Taller Abierto, 2004.

Biron, Rebecca E. "City/Art: Setting the Scene." Introduction to *City/Art: The Urban Scene in Latin America*, 1-34. Durham and London: Duke University Press, 2009.

Black, Jerome H., and Christian Leithner. "Immigrants and Political Involvement in Canada: The Role of The Ethnic Media." *Canadian Ethnic Studies* 20, no. 1 (January 1988): 1-20.

Blake, Alison. "Pocket Parks." University of Washington. https://depts.washington.edu/open2100/pdf/2_OpenSpaceTypes/Open_Space_Types/pocket_parks.pdf.

Bodmer, Catherine, and Marie-Ève Charron. *Catherine Bodmer: Mexico DF (détails)*. Alma: Sagamie Édition d'Art, 2012.

Bolaria, B. Singh. "Farm Labour, Work Conditions, and Health Risks." In *Rural Sociology in Canada*, edited by David A. Hay and Gurcharn S. Basran, 228-45. Oxford: Oxford University Press, 1992.

——, and Rosemary Bolaria. "Immigrant Status and Health Status: Women and Racial Minority Immigrant Workers." In *Racial Minorities, Medicine, and Health*, edited by B. Singh Bolaria and Rosemary Bolaria, 149-168. Halifax: Fernwood Publishing, 1994.

Borges, Jorge Luis. *Selected Poems*. Edited by Alexander Coleman. London: Penguin Books, 2000.

Borja, Jordi. "Revolución y contrarrevolución en la ciudad global: las expectativas frustradas por la globalización de nuestras ciudades." *Revista EURE* 33, no. 100 (2007): 35-50.

Bourhis, John, and Mike Allen. "Meta Analysis of the Relationship between Communication Apprehension and Cognitive Performance." *Communication Education* 41, no. 1 (1992): 68-76.

Bourriaud, Nicolas. *Postproduction. Culture as Screenplay: How Art Reprograms the World*. New York: Lucas and Sternberg, 2002.

——. *Relational Aesthetics*. Dijon: Les presses du réel, 2001.

Boyer, M. Christine. *The City of Collective Memory. Its Historical Imagery and Architectural Entertainments*. Cambridge, MA: MIT Press, 1998.

Braidotti, Rosi. *Transpositions: On Nomadic Ethic*. Cambridge: Polity Press, 2006.

Branco, Catullo. *Energia Elétrica e Capital Estrangeiro no Brasil*. São Paulo: Editora Alfa Omega, 1975.

Brandt, Deborah. *Tangled Routes: Women, Work, and Globalization on the Tomato Trail*. 2nd ed. Lanham: Rowman and Littlefield Publishers, 2008.

Brem, Maxwell. "Migrant Workers in Canada: A Review of the Canadian Seasonal Agricultural Workers Program." Ottawa: The North-South Institute, 2006. http://www.nsi-ins.ca/wp-content/uploads/2012/10/2006-Migrant-Workers-in-Canada-A-review-of-the-Canadian-Seasonal-Agricultural-Workers-Program.pdf.

Britton, Robert A. "The Image of the Third World in Tourism Marketing." *Annals of Tourism Research* 6, no. 3 (1979): 318-29.

Buchanan, Donald W., and Jorge Olvera. "Preface." In *Mexican Art: From Pre-Columbian Times to the Present Day*. n.p. Vancouver: The Keystone Press Limited, 1960.

Bulhões, Antônio. *Diário da Cidade Amada do Rio de Janeiro, 1922*, Vol. 3. Rio de Janeiro: Sextante-Artes, 2003.

Burke, Peter. *Eyewitnessing: The Uses of Images as Historical Evidence*. Ithaca: Cornell University Press, 2008. First published 2001 by Cornell University Press (Ithaca, NY).

Burr, C. Chauncey. *Autobiography and Lectures of Lola Montez*. Charleston: Nabu Press, 2011.

Burrill, Fred and Catherine Legrand. "Progressive Catholicism at Home and Abroad: The 'Double Solidarité' of Quebec Missionaries in Honduras, 1955-1975." In *With and Without the Nation: Canadian History as Transnational History*, edited by Karen Dubinsky, Adele Perry, and Henry Yu, 311-340. Toronto: University of Toronto Press, 2015.

Caldwell, Erskine, and Margaret Bourke-White. *You Have Seen Their Faces*. New York: Modern Age Books, 1937.

Camacho, Zósimo, and Julio César Hernández. "Resistencia de las Normales Rurales." *Revista Contralínea* 5, no. 99 (April 1, 2008). Accessed January 25, 2014. http://www.contralinea.com.mx/archivo/2008/abril/htm/resistencia-normales-rurales.htm (page no longer available).

Carcaud-Macaire, Monique. "Reflexiones Sociocríticas sobre la AlIteridad. El Otro Modelo Hegemónico y el Tercer nterpretante. Ejemplo de Caso: Entre Imagen Improbable y Figura Banalizada. El Árabe en la Cultura Francesa," *Revista Káñina*, 32, no. 1 (2008): 29-38.

Cardoza y Aragón, Luis. "Contemporary Mexican Painting." Translated by Esther Rowland Clifford. In *Mexican Art Today*, Philadelphia: Philadelphia Museum of Art, 1943.

Cecil, R.G., and G.E. Ebanks. "The Human Condition of West Indian Migrant Farm Labour in Southwestern Ontario." *International Migration* 29, no. 3 (1991): 389-405.

—. "The Caribbean Migrant Farm Worker Programme in Ontario: Seasonal Expansion of West Indian Economic Spaces." *International Migration* 30, no. 1 (1992): 19-37.

Cenoz, Jasone, and Duke Gorter. "El estudio del paisaje lingüístico." Accessed October 2013. https://www.euskadi.eus/gobierno-vasco/contenidos/informacion/artik22_1_cenoz_08_03/es_cenoz/artik22_1_cenoz_08_03.html.

Certeau, Michel de. "De las prácticas cotidianas de oposición." In *Modos de hacer*, edited by Paloma Blanco, Jesús Carrillo, Jordi Claramonte, and Marcelo Expósito, 391-425. Salamanca: Ediciones Universidad de Salamanca, 2001.

—, ed. *The Practice of Everyday Life. Volume 2: Living and Cooking*. Minneapolis: University of Minnesota Press, 1998.

Chabaud Magnus, Jaime. "Teatro e identidad nacional (1790-1840)." *Revista Casa del Tiempo* 25 (November 2009): 113-116. Accessed September 6, 2014. http://www.uam.mx/difusion/casadeltiempo/25_iv_nov_2009/casa_del_tiempo_eIV_num25_113_116.pdf.

Charron, Marie-Ève. "Urban Particles." In *Catherine Bodmer, Mexico DF (détails)*, by Catherine Bodmer and Marie-Ève Charron, 72-75. Alma: Sagamie Édition d'Art, 2012.

Cheadle, Norman. "El Canadá Americano de Alejandro Saravia." *Contexto: revista anual de estudios literarios* 17 (2011): 105-29.

—. "Emerging from a Cloud: The Inter-American Discursive Position of Hispano-Canadian Literature." *Interfaces Brasil/Canadá. Canoas* 13, no. 2 (2013): 17-55.

—, and Lucien Pelletier, eds. *Canadian Cultural Exchanges*. Waterloo, ON: Wilfrid Laurier University. 2007.

Chevlowe, Susan. *The Jewish Identity Project, New American Photography*. New Haven, CT: Yale University Press, 2005.

Chorba, Carrie C. *Mexico, from Mestizo to Multicultural: National Identity and Recent Representations of the Conquest*. Nashville: Vanderbilt University Press, 2007.

Clarke, Robert. "Fe Fi Fo Fum…The Cultural Ambiguities of the Incomer." In *Root and Stem* (Vol. 1 of *Art Education Discourses*), edited by Jacquie Swift, 15-43. Birmingham: ARTicle Press, 1998.

Clifford, James. *The Predicament of Culture: Twentieth-Century Ethnography, Literature, and Art*. Cambridge, MA: Harvard University Press, 1988.

Cochrane, Jean. *Kensington*. Erin, ON: Boston Mills Press, 2000.

Coffee, Mary K. *How a Revolutionary Art Became Official Culture: Murals, Museums and the Mexican State*. Durham: Duke University Press, 2012.

Cohen, Robin, ed. *The Cambridge Survey of World Migration*. Cambridge: Cambridge University Press, 1995.

Colby, Catherine. "From Oaxaca to Ontario: Mexican Contract Labor in Canada and the Impact at Home." Davis: California Institute for Rural Studies, 1997.

Condé, Carol, and Karl Beveridge. *Salt of the Earth*, 2008. https://condebeveridge.ca/project/salt-of-the-earth-2008/.

Connolly, Priscilla. "Evolución del problema habitacional en la Ciudad de México." In *La vivienda popular en la Ciudad de México. Características y políticas de solución a sus problemas. Conferencias y mesa redonda*, edited by Adrián Guillermo Aguilar, 13-27. Mexico City: Instituto de Geografía-UNAM, 1985.

Conrad, Margaret, Kadriye Ercikan, Gerald Friesen, Jocelyn Létourneau, Delphin Muise, David Northrup, and Peter Seixas. *Canadians and Their Pasts*. Toronto: University of Toronto Press, 2013.

Coopersmith, Penina. *Cabbagetown: The Story of a Victorian Neighbourhood*. Toronto: James Lorimer, 1998.

Cornell, Drucilla. *Moral Images of Freedom: A Future for Critical Theory*. Maryland: Rowman and Littlefield Publishers, 2008.

Coulmas, Florian. *Sociolinguistics: The Study of Speakers' Choices*. New York: Cambridge University Press, 2005.

Cros, Edmond. "De la independencia a los años 1960 en América Latina: los avatares de las conciencias de las identidades nacionales y culturales." Posted December 21, 2009. https://www.sociocritique.fr/?De-la-Independencia-a-los-anos-1960-en-America-Latina-los-avatares-de-las.

Cruzvillegas, Abraham. *Autoconstrucción*. Glasgow: Centre for Contemporary Arts, 2008.

Cukier, Wendy, John Miller, Kristen Aspevig, and Dale Carl. "Diversity in Leadership and Media: A Multi-Perspective Analysis of the Greater Toronto Area, 2010." *Proceedings for the 11th International Conference on Diversity in Organisations, Communities and Nations, South Africa, June 20-22, 2011*. https://www.ryerson.ca/content/dam/diversity/academic/Diversity%20in%20Leadership%20and%20Media_2011.pdf.

Dahles, Heidi, and Lou Keune. *Tourism Development and Local Participation in Latin America*. New York: Cognizant Communication Corporation, 2002.

Dann, Graham. "The People of Tourist Brochures." In *The Tourist Image: Myths and Myth Making in Tourism*, edited by Tom Selwyn, 61-82. Chichester: John Wiley.

Daudelin, Jean and Edgar J. Dosman, eds. *Beyond Mexico*. Vol. 1 of *Changing Americas*. Ottawa: Carleton University Press, 1995.

De Anda, Enrique X. *Historia de la arquitectura mexicana*. Barcelona: Gustavo Gili, 2008.

De Fina, Anna. "Top-Down and Bottom-Up Strategies of Identity Construction in Ethnic Media." *Applied Linguistics* 34, no. 5 (December 2013): 554-73.

De Luna, María Eugenia. "Mexican Temporary Agricultural Workers in Canada: A Language and Migration Approach." PhD diss., University of Western Ontario, 2011. http://ir.lib.uwo.ca/etd/257.

Del Pozo, José. "Las organizaciones comunitarias de chilenos en la provincia de Québec, Canadá." In *Exiliados, emigrados y retornados: chilenos en América y Europa, 1973- 2004*, edited by José del Pozo, 127-47. Santiago: RIL Editores, 2006.

—. *Les Chiliens au Québec. Immigrants et réfugiés, de 1955 à nos jours*. Montreal: Boréal, 2009.

—. "L'immigration des latino-américains. Une histoire de réfugiés et d'immigrants." In *Histoires d'Immigrations au Québec*, edited by Guy Berthiaume, Claude Corbo, and Sophie Montreuil, 162-179. Montreal: Presses de l'Université du Québec, 2014.

—, ed. *Exiliados, emigrados y retornados: chilenos en América y Europa, 1973-2004*. Santiago: RIL Editores, 2006.

Deleuze, Gilles and Claire Parnet. *Dialogues*. Translated by Hugh Tomlinson and Barbara Habberjam. London: The Athlone Press, 1987.

Demers, Maurice. *Connected Struggles: Catholics, Nationalists, and Transnational Relations between Mexico and Quebec, 1917-1945*. Montreal and Kingston: McGill-Queen's University Press, 2014.

DeVoretz, Don J., Holger Hinte, and Christiane Werner. "How Much Language is Enough? Some Immigrant Language Lessons from Canada and Germany." IZA Discussion Papers Series no. 555, August 2002. http://ftp.iza.org/dp555.pdf.

Doña-Reveco, Cristián, and Amanda Levinson. "Chile: A Growing Destination Country in Search of a Coherent Approach to Migration." *Migration Policy Institute Country Profile*, June 6, 2012. https://www.migrationpolicy.org/article/chile-growing-destination-country-search-coherent-approach-migration.

Drobnick, Jim, "Airchitecture: Guarded Breaths and the [Cough] Art of Ventilation." In *Art, History and the Senses*, edited by Patrizia di Bello and Gabriel Koureas, 147-66. London: Ashgate, 2010.

Dubatti, Jorge. *El convivio teatral*. Buenos Aires: Atuel, 2003.

Duchet, Claude. "Para una socio-crítica o variaciones sobre un íncipit." In *Sociocríticas. Prácticas textuales/cultura de fronteras*, edited by M.-Pierrette Malcuzynski, 29-41. Amsterdam: Editios Rodopi B.V., 1991.

Duhau, Emilio, and Angela Giglia. *Las reglas del desorden: habitar la metrópoli*. Mexico City: Siglo XXI Editores/Universidad Autónoma Metropolitana-Azcapotzalco, 2008.

Dumas, Eve. "Un vistazo al teatro latinoamericano en el Canadá." *Revista Conjunto* 125 (2002): 89-95.

Durand, Jorge, and Douglas S. Massey. *Miracles on the Border: Retablos of Mexican Migrants to the United States*. Tucson: University of Arizona Press, 1995.

Durand, Régis. *La Part de l'ombre. Essais sur l'expérience photographique*. Paris: La Différence, 1990.

Eberhardt, Cassandra "Hispanic (Hybridity) in Canada: The Making and Unmaking of a Diaspora." Master's thesis, Queen's University, 2010.

Edwards, Elizabeth. "Beyond the Boundary: A Consideration of the Expressive in Photography and Anthropology." In *Rethinking Visual Anthropology*, edited by Marcus Banks and Howard Morphy, 53-80. London: Yale University Press, 1997.

Elgue de Maritini, Cristina. "La literatura como objeto social." *Invenio* 6, no. 11 (2003): 9-20.

Ember, Melvin, Carol R. Ember, and Ian Skoggard, eds. *Encyclopedia of Diasporas: Immigrant and Refugee Cultures Around the World*. Vol. 2 of *Diaspora Communities*. New York: Kluwer Academic/Plenum Publishers, 2004.

Esch, Elizabeth. "Whitened and Enlightened. The Ford Motor Company and Racial Engineering in the Brazilian Amazon." In *Company Towns in the Americas Landscape, Power, and Working-class Communities*, edited by Oliver J Dinius and Angela Vergara, 91-110. Athens: University of Georgia Press, 2011.

Escobar, Ticio. "Acerca de la modernidad y del arte: un listado de cuestiones finiseculares." In *Adiós identidad, arte y cultura desde América Latina*, edited by Gerardo Mosquera, 23-41. Badajoz: Museo Extremeño e Iberoamericano de Arte Contemporáneo, 2001.

Etcheverry, Gabrielle. "Ediciones Cordillera: A Study of Chilean Literary Production in Canada." Master's thesis, York University, 2005.

Etcheverry, Jorge. "El ojo escindido: autores latinos en Canadá." *Crítica.cl*, published December 18, 2007, http://critica.cl/literatura/el-ojo-escindi-do-autores-latinos-en-canada.

—. "Identidad, globalidad y escritores aleatorios." *La cita trunca*, published January 16, 2013, http://etcheverry.info/hoja/catastro/notas/article_1682.shtml (site discontinued).

—. "Ojeada preliminar sobre las revistas hispanocanadienses." *La cita trunca*, published September 30, 2012. http://etcheverry.info/hoja/catastro/no-tas/article_1662.shtml (site discontinued).

—. "Poesía chilena en Canadá: historia e identidades." *Contexto: revista anual de estudios literarios* 17 (2011): 183-199.

Fauth, Adonis Valder. *A Imigração suiço-valensana no Rio Grande do Sul*. Carlos Barbosa, RS: Associação Valensana do Brasil, 2000.

Ferguson, Nelson. "Conversations with Eulogio: On Migration and the Building of a Life-Project in Motion." In *Human Nature as Capacity: Transcending Discourse and Classification*, edited by Nigel Rapport, 31-53. New York: Berghahn Books, 2010.

Fletcher, Harrell. *Thek's Teaching Notes*. Portland: Publication Studio, 2010.

Fréchette, Carol. *Les Quatre Morts de Marie*. Montreal: Les Herbes Rouges, 1995.

Freidus, Marc. *Typologies, Nine Contemporary Photographers*. Newport Beach and New York: Newport Harbor Art Museum/Rizzoli, 1991.

Frohlick, Susan. *Sexuality, Women, and Tourism: Cross-Border Desires through Contemporary Travel*. New York: Routledge, 2013.

Gablik, Suzi. *The Re-Enchantment of Art*. New York: Thames and Hudson, 1991.

Galassi, Peter. *Pleasures and Terrors of Domestic Comfort*. New York: Museum of Modern Art, 1991.

Galeano, Eduardo. *Memoria del fuego I. Los nacimientos*. Mexico City: Siglo Veintiuno Editores, 1991.

Galerie Push. *Osvaldo Ramírez Castillo*. Montreal: Push, 2009.

Gallo, Rubén. *New Tendencies in Mexican Art*. New York: Palgrave Macmillan, 1994.

García Canclini, Néstor. *Culturas híbridas*. Mexico City: Grijalbo, 1989.

——. "Museos, aeropuertos y ventas de garage. La identidad ante el Tratado de Libre Comercio." In *Identidad: análisis y teoría, simbolismo, sociedades complejas, nacionalismo y etnicidad*, edited by Leticia Irene Méndez y Mercado, 89-97. Mexico City: UNAM, 1996.

——. *Latinoamérica buscando lugar en este siglo*. Buenos Aires: Paidós, 2002.

——. "De la diversidad a la interculturalidad." In *Conflictos interculturales*, edited by José Luis Brea and Néstor García Canclini, 103-12. Mexico City: Gedisa, 2011.

——. "Noticias recientes sobre la hibridación." *Trans: Revista Transcultural de Música* 7, no. 2 (2003). Accessed February 14, 2014. http://www.sibetrans.com/trans/articulo/209/noticias-recientes-sobre-la-hibridacion.

Gay, Paul, and Hall, Stuart, eds. *Questions of Cultural Identity*. London: Sage Publications, 1996.

Gay, Peter. *Weimar Culture: The Outsider as Insider*. New York: Harper & Row, 1968.

Georgiou, Myria. *Diaspora, Identity and the Media: Diasporic Transnationalism and Mediated Spatialities*. Cresskill, New Jersey: Hampton Press, 2006.

Giffords, Gloria Kay. *Mexican Folk Retablos: Masterpieces on Tin*. Tucson: University of Arizona Press, 1974.

Giménez Micó, José Antonio. "Estudios hispánicos canadienses: estableciendo vínculos intramuros y extramuros." *Hispanic Issues Online* 2 (Fall 2007): 89-94. https://conservancy.umn.edu/handle/11299/182542.

——. "Latin-Americanizing Canada." In *Canadian Cultural Exchanges*, edited by Norman Cheadle and Lucien Pelletier, 59-74. Waterloo, ON: Wilfrid Laurier University Press, 2007.

Giménez Romero, Carlos. "Pluralismo, multiculturalismo e interculturalidad. Propuesta de clarificación y apuntes educativos." *Educación y Futuro* 8 (2003): 9-26.

Giménez, Gilberto. "Relación simbiótica entre cultura e identidad." Mexico City: Consejo Nacional para la Cultura y las Artes, 2005.

Gómez-Peña, Guillermo. *Bitácora de cruce*. Mexico City: Fondo de Cultura Económica, 2006.

Gonzalbo Aizpuru, Pilar. "Lo prodigioso cotidiano en los exvotos novohispanos." In *Dones y promesas: 500 años de arte ofrenda (exvotos mexicanos)*, 47-63. Mexico City: Fundación Cultural Televisa, 1996.

Gorter, Durk, H.F. Marten, and L. Van Mensel. *Minority Languages in the Linguistic Landscape*. Houndmills, Basingstoke, Hampshire: Palgrave Macmillan, 2012.

——. *Linguistic Landscape. A New Approach to Multilingualism*. Clevendon: Multilingual Matters, 2006.

Grande Rosado, María de los Ángeles. "Hacia un teatro global. Cultura e identidad en el teatro contemporáneo." *Teatro: revista de estudios teatrales*, 13/14 (1998-2001): 185-97.

Grandin, Greg. *Fordlandia. The Rise and Fall of Henry Ford's Forgotten Jungle City*. New York: Picador, 2009.

Grimberg, Salomon. "Inés Amor and the Galería de Arte Mexicano." *Woman's Art Journal* 32, no.2 (Fall/Winter 2011): 3-13.

Gutiérrez Háces, Maria Teresa. "Canada-Mexico: The Neighbour's Neighbour." In *NAFTA in Transition*, edited by Stephen J. Randall and Herman W. Konrad, 57-76. Calgary: University of Calgary Press, 1995.

Guzmán Díaz, José Manuel. "Panorama de las teorías sociológicas de la novela." *Cultura y representaciones sociales* 3, no. 5 (2008): 88-124.

Habermas, Jürgen. *The Structural Transformation of the Public Sphere: An Inquiry into a Category of Bourgeois Society*. Cambridge, MA: MIT Press, 1989.

Hall, Stuart. *Modernity: An Introduction to Modern Societies*. Malden, MA: Blackwell Publishers, 1996.

—. *The Fateful Triangle: Race, Ethnicity, Nation*. Cambridge, MA: Harvard University Press, 2017.

Hanff, George. "Decision-Making Under Pressure: A Study of the Admittance of Chilean Refugees by Canada." *NS: North-South* 4, no. 8 (1979): 116-35.

Hannerz, Ulf. "Borders." *International Social Science Journal* 49, no. 154 (1997): 537-48. https://doi.org/10.1111/j.1468-2451.1997.tb00043.x

Harbron, John D. "Canada Draws Closer to Latin America: A Cautious Involvement." In *Latin America's New Internationalism: The End of Hemispheric Isolation*, edited by Roger W. Fontaine and James D. Theberge, 109-142. New York: Praeger, 1976.

Harles, John C. "Immigrant Integration in Canada and the United States." *American Review of Canadian Studies* 34, no. 2 (2004): 223-58.

Harvey. David. *The Condition of Postmodernity*. Oxford: Blackwell, 1989.

—. *Justice, Nature, and the Geography of Difference*, Oxford: Blackwell, 1996.

Hazelton, Hugh. *Latinocanadá. A Critical Study of Ten Latin American Writers of Canada*. Montreal and Kingston: McGill-Queen's University Press, 2007.

—. "La soledad del exilio: marginalidad y aislamiento en la literatura latinocanadiense." *Poesias.cl*. Accessed November 12, 2013. http://www.poesias.cl/latinocanadiense02.htm (site discontinued).

Hennebry, Jenna L. *Permanently Temporary? Agricultural Migrant Workers and Their Integration in Canada*. Montreal: Institute for Research on Public Policy, 2012.

—. and Kerry Preibisch. "A Model for Managed Migration? Re-Examining Best Practices in Canada's Seasonal Agricultural Worker Program." *International Migration* 50, no. 1 (2010): 19-40.

Hernández, Ellie. "Re-Thinking Margins and Borders: An Interview with Gloria Anzaldúa." *Discourse: Journal for Theoretical Studies in Media and Culture* 18, no. 1-2 (Fall and Winter 1995-96): 7-15.

Heulwen Jenkins, Olivia. "Tourist Destination Images and Stereotypes: A study of Backpacker Images of Australia." PhD diss., University of Queensland, 2000.

Highmore, Ben. *Everyday Life and Cultural Theory*. London: Routledge, 2002.

Hine, Lewis W. *Men at Work: Photographic Studies of Modern Men and Machines*. New York: Dover Publications, 1977. First published 1932 by The Macmillan Company (New York).

Hinnenkamp, Katie Marie. "Bicycles Traveling in the Rain: A Participatory, Arts-Informed Account of Mexican Farmworkers in Canada." Master's thesis, University of Toronto, 2007.

Holloway, Thomas. *Immigrants on the Land. Coffee and Society in São Paulo, 1886-1934*. Chapel Hill: University of North Carolina Press, 1980.

Horn, Michiel. *York University: The Way Must Be Tried*. Montreal and Kingston: McGill-Queen's University Press, 2009.

Hudson, Peter James. "Imperial Designs: The Royal Bank of Canada in the Caribbean." *Race and Class* 52, no. 1 (2010): 33-48.

Huebner, Thom. "Bangkok's Linguistic Landscape: Environmental Print, Codemixing and Language Change." In *Linguistic Landscape: A New Approach to Multilingualism*, edited by Durk Gorter, 31-51. Clevendon, England: Multilingual Matters, 2006.

Husband, Charles. "Diasporic Identities and Diasporic Economies: The Case of Minority Ethnic Media." In *Diversity in the City*, edited by Marco Martiniello and Brigitte Piquard. Bilbao: Deusto, 2002.

Illich, Ivan. *Deschooling Society*. Harmondsworth: Penguin, 1973.

Indych, Anna. "Mexican Muralism without Walls: The Critical Reception of Portable Work by Rivera, Orozco and Siqueiros in the United States, 1927-1940." PhD diss., New York University, 2003.

Indych-López, Anna. *Muralism Without Walls: Rivera, Orozco and Siqueiros in the United States, 1927-1940*. Pittsburgh: University of Pittsburgh Press, 2009.

Institut de recherche et d'informations socio-économiques. "L'intégration des immigrants et immigrantes au Québec," November 27, 2012. https://cdn.iris-recherche.qc.ca/uploads/publication/file/Note-immigration-web.pdf.

International Organization for Migration, Chile. *Las migraciones internacionales: análisis y perspectivas para una política migratoria*. Santiago, Chile, 2003.

Jiménez, José, ed. *Una teoría del arte desde América Latina*. Madrid: Turner, 2011.

Jitrik, Noé. "La exclusión." In *Escrituras latinoamericanas en el siglo XXI*, edited by Noé Jitrik, 357-73. Córdoba, Argentina: Alción Editora, 2006.

Johnson, Melissa A. "Constructing a New Model of Ethnic Media: Image-Saturated Latina Magazines as Touchstones." In *A Companion to Media Studies*, 272-92. Oxford: Wiley-Blackwell, 2007.

Johnson, Penny. "Promise of Music Symposium Wrap-Up." *The Glenn Gould Foundation*. March 26, 2010. http://www.glenngould.ca/promise-of-music-symposium-wrap-up/.

Kaplan, Rachel. "Mexican Art Today: Inés Amor, Henry Clifford and the Shifting Practices of Exhibiting Modern Mexican Art." *Journal of Curatorial Studies* 3, no. 2-3 (2014): 264-88.

Karim, Karim H. *The Media of Diaspora*. London: Routledge, 2003.

Kelley, Ninette, and Michael Trebilcock. *The Making of the Mosaic. A History of Canadian Immigration Policy*. Toronto: University of Toronto Press, 2010.

Kellner, Douglas. "Brecht's Marxist Aesthetics." *Illuminations: The Critical Theory Website*. Arlington: University of Texas at Arlington. Accessed October 29, 2014. http://www.uta.edu/huma/illuminations/kell3.htm (page no longer available). Now available at https://www.cddc.vt.edu/illuminations/ kell3.htm. First published as "Brecht's Marxist Aesthetics: The Korsch Connection." In *Bertolt Brecht. Political Theory and Literary Practice*, edited by Betty Nance Weber and Hubert Heinen, 29-42. Manchester: Manchester University Press, 1980.

Knowles, Ric, and Ingrid Mündel, eds. "Ethnic," *Multicultural and Intercultural Theatre*. Vol. 14 of *Critical Perspectives on Canadian Theatre in English*. Toronto: Playwrights Canada Press, 2009.

Kram Villarreal, Rachel. "Gladiolas for the Children of Sanchez: Ernesto P. Uruchurtu's Mexico City, 1950-1968." PhD diss., The University of Arizona, 2008.

Kristeva, Julia. *Powers of Horror: An Essay on Abjection*. Translated by Leon S. Roudiez. New York: Columbia University Press, 1984.

Kujundzic, Dragan. "Laughter as Otherness in Bakhtin and Derrida." In "Bakhtin and Otherness," edited by Robert S. Barsky and Michael Holquist. Special issue, *Discours Social Discourse* 3, no. 1-2 (Spring-Summer 1990): 271-93.

Kuss, María Elena. *Nativistic Strains in Argentine Operas Premiered at the Teatro Colón (1908-1972)*. PhD diss., UCLA, 1976.

Lake, Marilyn, and Henry Reynolds. *Drawing the Global Colour Line: White Men's Countries and the International Challenge of Racial Equality*. Critical Perspectives on Empire. Cambridge: Cambridge University Press, 2008.

Landolt, Patricia, and Luin Goldring. "Immigrant Political Socialization as Bridging and Boundary Work: Mapping the Multi-Layered Incorporation of Latin American Immigrants in Toronto." *Ethnic and Racial Studies* 32, no. 7 (2009): 1226-47.

Landry, Rodrigue, and Richard Bourhis. "Linguistic Landscape and Ethnolinguistic Vitality: An Empirical Study." *Journal of Language and Social Psychology* 16, no. 23 (1997): 23-49.

Lange, Dorothea, and Paul Schuster Taylor. *An American Exodus: A Record of Human Erosion*. New York: Arno Press, 1975. First published 1939 by Reynal and Hitchcock (New York).

Lawless, Cecelia Elizabeth Burke. *Making Home in Havana*. New Brunswick: Rutgers University Press, 2002.

Leal, Cirilo. "Teatro e Identidad." *Cuadernos del Ateneo de la Laguna* (La Laguna, Tenerife) 1 (1996): 103-106.

Lee, Anthony W. *Painting on the Left: Diego Rivera, Radical Politics and San Francisco's Public Murals*. Berkeley: University of California Press, 1999.

Levine, Robert M. *Images of History: Nineteenth and Early Twentieth Century Latin American Photographs as Documents*. Durham: Duke University Press, 1989.

411

Lindholm, Charles. *Culture and Authenticity*. Malden, MA: Blackwell Publishing, 2008.

Llambías-Wolff, Jaime. *Notre Exil pour Parler: Les Chiliens au Québec*. Montreal: Fides, 1988.

Lopes, Adriana. *De Cães a lobos-do-mar: súditos ingleses no Brasil*. São Paulo: Editora Senac, 2007.

López Xochihua, Benjamín, and Silvia García Ramírez. "Programa de trabajadores agrícolas temporales México-Canadá (PTAT)." In *La migración de tlaxcaltecas en Estados Unidos y Canadá. Panorama actual y perspectivas*, edited by Raúl Jiménez Guillén and Adrián González Romo, 431-440. San Pablo Apetatitlán: El Colegio de Tlaxcala; Tlaxcala: Universidad Autónoma de Tlaxcala; Tlaxcala: Sistema Estatal de Promoción del Empleo y Desarrollo Comunitario, 2008.

Lugones, María. "Playfulness, 'World'-Travelling, and Loving Perception," *Hypatia* 2, no. 2 (Summer, 1987): 3-19.

Lumsdon, Les, and Jonathan Swift. *Tourism in Latin America*. London: Continuum, 2001.

Lundstrom, Jan-Erik, and Uta Grosenick. *Photo Art: The New World of Photography*. London: Thames & Hudson, 2008.

Luque Agraz, Elin, and Mary Michele Beltrán. "Imágenes poderosas. Exvotos mexicanos." In *Retablos y exvotos*, 32-53. Mexico City: Museo Franz Mayer, 2000.

—. *El arte de dar gracias. Selección de exvotos pictóricos del Museo de la Basílica de Guadalupe*. Mexico City: Universidad Iberoamericana and Casa Lamm, 2003.

Lyotard, Jean-François. *The Postmodern Explained. Correspondence 1982-1985*. Translated by Julian Pefanis and Morgan Thomas. Minneapolis: University of Minnesota Press, 1993.

MacCannell, Dean. "Staged Authenticity: Arrangements of Social Space in Tourist Settings." *The American Journal of Sociology* 79, no. 3 (1973): 589-603.

—. *The Tourist: A New Theory of the Leisure Class*. New York: Schocken Books, 1976.

MacLachlan, Colin M., and William H. Beezley. *El Gran Pueblo: A History of Greater Mexico*. 3rd ed. Upper Saddle River: Prentice Hall, 2004.

Madoff, Steven Henry. "Service Aesthetics: Steven Henry Madoff on Personal Transactions in Art." *Artforum International* 47, no. 1 (2008): 165ff. Accessed January 31, 2014. http://www.mutualart.com/OpenArticle/Service-Aesthetics /78DAFE2E6583FA94.

—. ed. *Art School: Propositions for the 21st Century*. Cambridge, MA: MIT Press, 2009.

Maffesoli, Michel. *La tajada del diablo. Compendio de subversión posmoderna*. Mexico City: Siglo XXI Editores, 2002.

Magalhães, Marionilde Dias Brepohl de. *Presença Alemã no Brasil*. Brasilia, DF: Editora UnB, 2004.

Malcuzynski, M.-Pierrette. "A modo de introducción." In *Sociocríticas. Prácticas textuales/cultura de fronteras*, edited by M.-Pierrette Malcuzynski, 11-27. Amsterdam: Editios Rodopi B.V., 1991.

Malinowski, David. "Authorship in the Linguistic Landscape: A Multilingual-Performative View." In *Linguistic Landscape: Expanding the Scenery*, edited by Elana Shohamy and Durk Gorter, 107-25. New York: Routledge, 2009.

Manrique, Jorge Alberto and Teresa del Conde. *Una mujer en el arte mexicano: memorias de Inés Amor.* 2nd ed. Mexico City: Universidad Nacional Autónoma de México, Instituto de Investigaciones Estéticas, 2005.

Marchan, Simón, ed. *Real/virtual en la estética y la teoría de las artes.* Buenos Aires: Paidós Estéticas, 2006.

Marshment, Margaret. "Gender Takes a Holiday: Representation in Holiday Brochures." In *Gender, Work and Tourism*, edited by M. Thea Sinclair. 15-32. London: Routledge, 1997.

Martín Barbero, Jesús. "From Latin America: Diversity, Globalization and Convergence." *Westminster Papers In Communication & Culture* 8, no. 1 (March 2011): 39-64.

Martín Rodríguez, Manuel M. "El teatro chicano a través de los siglos: panorama crítico." *Revista Arrabal* 7-8 (2010): 27-33.

Martin, Philip. *Managing Labor Migration: Temporary Worker Programs for the 21st Century.* Geneva: International Labour Organization (International Institute for Labour Studies), 2003.

Massey, Doreen. "Lugar, identidad y geografías de la responsabilidad en un mundo en proceso de globalización." *Treballs de la Societat Catalana de Geografia*, 57 (2004): 77-84.

Mastro, Dana, Christopher McKinley, and Katie Warber. "Social Identity Theory as a Framework for Understanding the Effects of Exposure to Positive Media Images of Self and Other Intergroup Outcomes." *International Journal of Communication* 8 (2014): 1049-68. https://ijoc.org/index.php/ijoc/article/viewFile/2276/1116.

Mata, Fernando. "Latin American Immigration to Canada: Some Reflections on the Immigration Statistics." *Canadian Journal of Latin American and Caribbean Studies* 10, no. 20 (1985): 27-42.

Mathur, Ashok, Jonathan Dewar, and Mike DeGagné. *Cultivating Canada: Reconciliation through the Lens of Cultural Diversity.* Ottawa: Aboriginal Healing Foundation, 2011.

Mayer, Mónica. "Raya: Crítica y debate en las artes visuales." *Pala: Revista virtual de arte contemporáneo*, February 7, 2006. Accessed February 2, 2014. http://la-pala.com/articulos/item/132-raya-cr%C3%83%C2%ADtica-y-debate-en-las-artes-visuales.html.

—. "Pinto mi raya: un espacio donde los artes visuales suenan." *De archives y redes: un proyecto artístico sobre la integración y reactivación de archivos*, May 5, 2014. Accessed February 2, 2014. https://www.pintomiraya.com/pmr/8-textos-pmr/performance-proyectos/46-suenan.

McDowall, Duncan. *The Light. Brazilian Traction, Light and Power Company Limited, 1899-1945.* Toronto: University of Toronto Press, 1988.

413

McLaughlin, Janet. "Migration and Health: Implications for Development. A Case Study of Mexican and Jamaican Migrants in Canada's Seasonal Agricultural Workers Program." Ottawa: FOCAL, October 2009. https://www.focal.ca/pdf/Migrant%20Health%20McLaughlin%202009.pdf.

——. "Classifying the 'Ideal Migrant Worker': Mexican and Jamaican Transnational Farmworkers in Canada." *Focaal: Journal of Global and Historical Anthropology* 57 (2010): 79-94.

——. "The Hands behind the Harvest: Migrant Workers in Niagara's Wine Industry." In *The World of Niagara Wine*, edited by Michael Ripmeester and Phillip Gordon Mackintosh, 109-122. Waterloo, ON: Wilfrid Laurier University Press, 2013.

——. "Trouble in Our Fields: Health and Human Rights among Mexican and Caribbean Migrant Farm Workers in Canada." PhD diss., University of Toronto, 2009.

Mertz-Baumgartner, Birgit. "Imágenes del exilio y la migración en la literatura latinoamericana en Canadá." In *Migración y literatura en el mundo hispánico*, edited by Irene Andrés-Suárez, 280-94. Madrid: Editorial Verbum, 2004.

Mignolo, Walter. *Local Histories/Global Designs: Coloniality, Subaltern Knowledges and Border Thinking*. Princeton: Princeton University Press, 2000.

——. *La idea de América Latina. La herida colonial y la opción decolonial.* Barcelona: Gedisa, 2007.

Minh-ha, Trinh T. *Elsewhere, Within Here: Immigration, Refugeeism and the Boundary Event*. New York: Routledge, 2011.

Misiano, Viktor. "An Analysis of '*Tusovka*': Post-Soviet Art of the 1990s." In *Art in Europe 1990-2000*, edited by Gianfranco Maraniello, 161-77. Milan: Skira, 2002.

Mitchell, W. J. T. "Interdisciplinarity and Visual Culture." *Art Bulletin* 77, no. 4 (December 1995): 540-44.

Mize, Ronald L., and Alicia C.S. Swords. *Consuming Mexican Labor: From the Bracero Program to NAFTA*. Toronto: University of Toronto Press, 2011.

Montenegro, Roberto. *Retablos de México/Mexican Votive Paintings*. Translated by Irene Nicholson. Mexico City: Ediciones Mexicanas, 1950.

Montez, Lola. *The Arts of Beauty, Or, Secrets of a Lady's Toilet*. New York: Dick & Fitzgerald, 1858. Available at https://archive.org/details/artsbeautyorsec00montgoog.

Mora, G. Christina. *Making Hispanics: How Activists, Bureaucrats and Media Constructed A New American*. Chicago: University of Chicago Press, 2014.

Morgan, Nigel, Annette Pritchard, and Roger Pride. *Destination Branding: Creating the Unique Destination Proposition*. Oxford: Elsevier Butterworth-Heinemann, 2004.

Morgan, Nigel, and Annette Pritchard. *Tourism Promotion and Power: Creating Images, Creating Identities*. Chichester: Wiley, 1998.

Mosquera, Gerardo. "El arte latinoamericano deja de serlo." Madrid: ARCO Latino, 1996.

——, ed. *Adiós identidad. Arte y cultura desde América Latina*. Madrid: Museo Extremeño e Iberoamericano de Arte Contemporáneo, 2001.

Mowforth, Martin, Clive Charlton, and Ian Munt. *Tourism and Responsibility: Perspectives from Latin America and the Caribbean.* London: Routledge, 2008.

Moynagh, Maureen. "Eyeing the North Star? Figuring Canada in Postslavery Fiction and Drama." In *Canada and Its Americas: Transnational Navigations,* edited by Winfried Siemerling and Sarah Phillips Casteel, 135-47. Montreal and Kingston: McGill-Queen's University Press; 2010.

Mraz, John. "Más allá de la decoración. Hacía una historia gráfica de las mujeres en México." *Política y cultura* 1 (1992): 155-89.

——. "Photographing Mexico." *Mexican Studies/Estudios Mexicanos* 17, no. 1 (2001): 193-211.

——. "Mexican History: A Photo Essay." In *The Mexico Reader: History, Culture, Politics,* edited by Gilbert M. Joseph and Timothy J. Henderson, 297-331. Durham: Duke University Press, 2002.

——. "Picturing Mexico's Past: Photography and 'Historia Gráfica.'" *South Central Review* 21, no. 3 (2004): 24-45.

——. "Representing the Mexican Revolution: Bending Photographs to the Will of Historia Gráfica." In *Photography and Writing in Latin America: Double Exposures,* edited by Marcy E. Schwartz and Mary Beth Tierney-Tello, 21-40. Albuquerque: University of New Mexico Press, 2006.

——. "¿Fotohistoria o historia gráfica? El pasado mexicano en fotografía." *Cuicuilco* 14, no. 41 (2007): 11-41.

——. *Looking for Mexico: Modern Visual Culture and National Identity.* Durham: Duke University Press, 2009.

Mraz, John, and Jaime Vélez Storey. *Uprooted: Braceros in the Hermanos Mayo Lens.* Houston: Arte Público Press, 1996.

Muñoz Carrobles, Diego. "Breve itinerario por el paisaje lingüístico de Madrid," *Ángulo Recto. Revista de estudios sobre la ciudad como espacio plural* 2, no. 2 (2010): 103-9.

Muñoz Neri, María. "The Mexican Temporary Agricultural Workers Program in Canada." *Revista Mexicana de Estudios Canadienses* 1, no. 1 (1999): 91-107.

Muñoz, Liliana. "Exile as Bereavement: Socio-Psychological Manifestations of Chilean Exiles in Great Britain." *British Journal of Medical Psychology* 53 (1980): 227-32.

Nahmias, Rick. *The Migrant Project: Contemporary California Farm Workers.* Albuquerque: University of New Mexico Press, 2008.

Nakache, Delphine, and Paula J. Kinoshita. "The Canadian Temporary Foreign Worker Program: Do Short-Term Economic Needs Prevail Over Human Rights Concerns?" *IRPP Study No. 5* (2010): 1-49.

Nayer, Kamala Elizabeth. *The Sikh Diaspora in Vancouver: Three Generations Amid Tradition, Modernity, and Multiculturalism.* Toronto: University of Toronto Press, 2004.

Neves, Lúcia Maria Bastos Pereira das, and Humberto Fernandes Machado. *O Império do Brasil.* Rio de Janeiro: Editora Nova Fronteira, 1999.

Newhall, Beaumont. *The History of Photography from 1839 to the Present Day*. Rev. ed. New York: Museum of Modern Art, 1978.

Ng, Wing Chung. *The Chinese in Vancouver: The Pursuit of Identity and Power*. Vancouver: University of British Columbia Press, 1999.

Núñez, Mariló. "Three-Fingered Jack and the Legend of Joaquín Murieta." In *Fronteras Vivientes: Eight Latina/o Canadian Plays*, edited by Natalie Alvarez, 173-207. Toronto: Playwrights Canada Press, 2013.

Nye, Joseph S., Jr. *Soft Power: The Means to Success in World Politics*. New York: Public Affairs, 2004.

O'Barr, William M. *Culture and the Ad: Exploring Otherness in the World of Advertising*. Boulder: Westview Press, 1994.

Ochoa, John. "El desafío de las fronteras." Prologue to *Bitácora de cruce* by Guillermo Gómez-Peña. Mexico City: Fondo de Cultura Económica, 2006.

Ogelsby, J. C. M. *Gringos from the Far North: Essays in the History of Canadian-Latin American Relations, 1866-1968*. Toronto: Macmillan of Canada, 1976.

Ojo, Tokunbo. "Ethnic Print Media in the Multicultural Nation of Canada." *Journalism* 7, no. 3 (August 2006): 343-61.

Oñate, Rody, and Thomas Wright. *La diáspora chilena a 30 años del golpe militar*. 2nd ed. Mexico City: Urdimbre, 2002.

Ortega Orozco, Adriana. "México-Francia: una larga historia de exposiciones como herramientas diplomáticas." *IdeAs* 8 (Fall 2016/Winter 2017). https://doi.org/10.4000/ideas.1729.

Ortiz, Fernando. *Contrapunteo cubano del tabaco y el azúcar*. La Habana: Editorial Ciencias Sociales, 1991. First published 1940 by Jesús Montero (Havana).

Ouellet, Pierre. "Présentation." *Les écrits* 140 (2014).

Pageot, Edith-Anne. "Figure de l'indiscipline. Domingo Cisneros, un parcours artistique atypique." *RACAR* 42, no. 1 (2017): 5-21.

Palmero González, Elena. "Desplazamiento cultural y procesos literarios en las letras hispanoamericanas contemporáneas: la literatura hispano-canadiense." *Contexto: revista anual de estudios literarios* 17 (2011): 57-81.

Paredes, Américo. *"With His Pistol in His Hand": A Border Ballad and Its Hero*. Austin: University of Texas Press, 1958.

Paz, Octavio. *The Labyrinth of Solitude and Other Writings*. New York: Grove Press Inc, 1985.

Peddie, Francis. "Young, Well-Educated and Adaptable People: Chilean Exiles, Identity and Daily Life in Canada, 1973 to the Present Day." PhD diss., York University, 2010.

—. *Young, Well-Educated, and Adaptable: Chilean Exiles in Ontario and Quebec, 1973-2010*. Winnipeg: University of Manitoba Press, 2014.

Pérez Firmat, Gustavo. *Literature and Liminality: Festive Readings in the Hispanic Tradition*. Durham: Duke University Press, 1985.

Perez, Margarite M. "Exile: The Chilean Experience." *International Journal of Social Psychiatry* 30, no. 1-2 (March 1, 1984): 157-61.

Petri, Inga. *A National Sistema Network in Canada: Feasibility Study and Strategic Plan*. August 9, 2013. Accessed on February 9, 2015. https://

naccna-pdf.s3.amazonaws.com/corporate/SistemaCanada_FeasibilityReport_en.pdf.

Phillipson, Robert. *Linguistic Imperialism.* Oxford: Oxford University Press, 1992.

Pike, Fredrik B. *The United States and Latin America: Myths and Stereotypes of Civilization and Nature.* Austin: University of Texas Press, 1992.

Pineda, Ana María. "Imágenes de Dios en el camino: Retablos, Ex-votos, Milagritos, and Murals." *Theological Studies* 65 (2004): 364-79.

Pons-Rodríguez, Lola. "Hispanoamérica en el paisaje lingüístico de Sevilla." *Intinerarios* 13 (2011): 97-129.

Poon Tip, Bruce. *Looptail: How One Company Changed the World by Reinventing Business.* Toronto: Collins, 2013.

Preibisch, Kerry. "Migrant Agricultural Workers and Processes of Social Inclusion in Rural Canada: Encuentros and Desencuentros." *Canadian Journal of Latin American and Caribbean Studies* 29 (2004): 203-39.

—. "Gender Transformative Odysseys: Tracing the Experiences of Transnational Migrant Women in Rural Canada." *Canadian Women Studies* 24, no. 4 (2005): 91-97.

—. "Globalizing Work, Globalizing Citizenship: Community-Migrant Worker Alliances in Southwestern Ontario." In *Organizing the Transnational: Labour, Politics, and Social Change,* edited by Luin Goldring and Sailaja Krishnamurti, 97-114. Vancouver: University of British Columbia Press, 2007.

—. "Local Produce, Foreign Labour: Labour Mobility Programs and Global Trade Competitiveness in Canada." *Rural Sociology* 72, no. 3 (2007): 418-49.

—. "Interrogating Managed Migration's Model: A Counternarrative of Canada's Seasonal Agricultural Workers Program." In *Migrants and Migration in Modern North America: Cross-Border Lives, Labor Markets, and Politics,* edited by Dirk Hoerder and Nora Faires. Durham: Duke University Press, 2011.

—, and Stan Raper. "Forcing Governments to Govern in Defence of Noncitizen Workers: A Story about the Canadian Labour Movement's Alliance with Agricultural Migrants: Interview with Stan Raper by Kerry Preibisch." In *Organizing the Transnational: Labour, Politics, and Social Change,* edited by Luin Goldring and Sailaja Krishnamurti, 115-28. Vancouver: University of British Columbia Press, 2007.

Pujol, Ernesto. "On the Ground: Practical Observations for Regenerating Art Education." In *Art School: Propositions for the 21st Century,* edited by Steven Henry Madoff, 1-14. Cambridge, MA: MIT Press, 2009.

Ramírez Caro, Jorge. "Tres propuestas analíticas e interpretativas del texto literario: estructuralismo, semiótica y sociocrítica." In *Revista Comunicación* 12, no. 2 (2002): n.p.

Ramos, Víctor. "La identidad latinoamericana: proceso contradictorio de su construcción-deconstrucción-reconfiguración dentro de contextos globales." *Universitas Humanística* 73 (2012): 15-58.

Rampley, Matthew. "La cultura visual en la era poscolonial: El desafío de la Antropología," *Revista Estudios Visuales. Ensayo, teoría y crítica de la cultura visual y el arte contemporáneo* 3 (2006): 186-211.

Rancière, Jacques. *The Emancipated Spectator*. New York: Verso Books, 2014.

Randall, Stephen J., and Herman W. Konrad, eds. "Introduction." In *NAF-TA in Transition*, edited by Stephen J. Randall and Herman W. Konrad, 1-11. Calgary: University of Calgary Press, 1995.

Reimer, Gwen Dianne. "Packaging Dreams: Canadian Tour Operators at Work." *Annals of Tourism Research* 17 (1990): 501-12.

Reisinger, Yvette, and Felix Mavondo. "Cultural Differences in Travel Risk Perception." *Journal of Travel and Tourism Marketing* 20, no. 1 (2006): 13-31.

Repo, Satu. *Marco and Michela*. 2nd ed. Toronto: James Lorimer and Company, 1985.

Retta, Edward, and Cynthia Brink. "Latino or Hispanic Panic: What Term Should We Use?" Preprint, submitted 2007. https://web.archive.org/web/20120807224426/http://www.crossculturecommunications.com/latino-hispanic.pdf.

Riaño-Alcalá, Pilar, Martha Colorado, Patricia Díaz, and Amantina Osorio. *Forced Migration of Colombians. Colombia, Ecuador, Canada*. Vancouver: University of British Columbia, 2008.

Ricento, Thomas. "Models and Approaches in Language Policy and Planning." In *Language and Communication: Diversity and Change*, edited by Marlis Hellinger and Anne Pauwels. 177-207. Berlin: Mouton de Gruyter, 2007.

Richard, Nelly. "El régimen crítico-estético del arte en el contexto de la diversidad cultural y sus políticas de identidad." Translated by Martha Pino Moreno. In *Real/virtual en la estética y la teoría de las artes*, edited by Simón Marchán Fiz, 115-26. Buenos Aires: Paidós, 2006.

Riding, Alan. *Distant Neighbors: A Portrait of the Mexicans*. Toronto: Random House of Canada, 1984.

Robertson, Kirsty, Stephanie G. Anderson, Elizabeth Diggon, Ahlia Moussa, and Sarah E. K. Smith. "'More a Diplomatic than an Esthetic Event': Canada, Brazil, and Cultural Brokering in the São Paulo Biennial and 'Isumavut.'" *Journal of Canadian Studies* 47, no. 2 (2013): 60-88.

Robinson, Cedric J. *Black Marxism: The Making of the Black Radical Tradition*. Chapel Hill: University of North Carolina Press, 2000. https://libcom.org/files/Black%20Marxism-Cedric%20J.%20Robinson.pdf.

Rochlin, James A. *Discovering the Americas: Evolution of Canadian Foreign Policy towards Latin America*. Vancouver: University of British Columbia Press, 1993.

Rochlin, James. "Introduction: Canada and the Americas: There's Still Much to Discover." In *Canada Looks South: In Search of an Americas Policy*, edited by Peter McKenna, 3-26. Toronto: University of Toronto Press, 2012.

Rodriguez, Clara E. *Latin Looks: Images of Latinas and Latinos in the U.S. Media*. Boulder: Westview Press, 1997.

Rodríguez, Orlando. "El teatro latinoamericano en el exilio." *Nueva Sociedad* (Fundación Friedrich Ebert Stiftung) 58 (January/February 1982): 55-66.

Rosa, Gilson Justino da. *Imigrantes alemães, 1824-1853*. Porto Alegre: EST Edições, 2005.

Rosales Argonza, Mariza, ed. *Vues transversales. Panorama de la scène artistique latino-québécoise.* Montreal: Éditions CIDIHCA/LatinArte, 2018.

Rosenblum, Naomi. *A World History of Photography.* New York: Abbeville Press, 1984.

Rugoff, Ralph, ed. *Baja to Vancouver: The West Coast and Contemporary Art.* San Francisco: CCA Wattis Institute for Contemporary Arts, 2003.

Said, Edward. *Orientalism.* New York: Pantheon Books, 1978.

Salmen, Walter. "Social Obligations of the Emancipated Musician in the 19th Century." In *The Social Status of the Professional Musician from the Middle Ages to the 19th Century,* edited by Walter Salmen, Herbert Kaufmann, and Barbara Reisner, 266-81. Hillsdale, NY: Pendragon Press, 1983.

Salzman, Ryan. "News or Noticias: A Social Identity Approach to Understanding Latinos' Preferred Language for News Consumption in the United States." *Mass Communication and Society* 17 (2014): 54-73.

Sandwell, Ruth W., ed. *To the Past: History Education, Public Memory, and Citizenship in Canada.* Toronto: University of Toronto Press, 2006.

Sartre, Jean-Paul. *Being and Nothingness.* New York: Pocket Books, 1992.

Sassen, Saskia. *Globalization and its Discontents.* New York: New Press, 1999.

—. "The Global City: Introducing a Concept." *Brown Journal of World Affairs* 11, no. 2 (Winter/Spring 2005): 27-43.

Satzewich, Vic. "The Economic Rights of Migrant and Immigrant Workers in Canada and the United States." In *Economic Rights in Canada and the United States,* edited by Rhoda E. Howard-Hessmann and Claude E. Welch Jr, 169-85. Philadelphia: University of Pennsylvania Press, 2006.

Schugurensky, Daniel, and Jorge Ginieniewicz. "The Latin American Community in Canada: Some Challenges Ahead." *Diálogos,* July 15, 2007. Accessed December 2015. https://dialogos.ca/2007/07/the-latin-american-community-in-canada-some-challenges-ahead/.

Scollon, Ron, and Suzanne Scollon. *Discourses in Place: Language in the Material World.* London: Routledge, 2003.

Serrano Deza, Ricardo. "El hispanismo canadiense: descripción, dinámica, bibliometría." *Arbor* 576 (1993): 69-102.

Shamsie, Yasmine, and Ricardo Grispun. "Missed Opportunity: Canada's Reengagement with Latin America and the Caribbean." *Canadian Journal of Latin American and Caribbean Studies / Revue canadienne des études latino-américaines et caraïbes* 35, no. 69 (2010): 171-99.

Shayne, Julie D. *They Used to Call Us Witches: Chilean Exiles, Culture, and Feminism.* Lanham, MD: Rowman and Littlefield Publishers, 2009.

Shimakawa, Karen. "Enunciating Asian Canadian Drama." In *Asian Canadian Theatre,* edited by Nina Lee Aquino and Ric Knowles, 1-10. Toronto: Playwrights Canada, 2011.

Shoemaker, Pamela J., Stephen D. Reese, and Wayne A. Danielson. "Spanish-Language Print Media Use as an Indicator of Acculturation." *Journalism Quarterly* 62, no. 4 (Winter 1985): 734-40, 762.

Siemerling, Winfried, and Sarah Phillips Casteel, eds. *Canada and Its Americas: Transnational Navigations.* Montreal and Kingston: McGill-Queen's University Press, 2010.

Silver, Ira. "Marketing Authenticity in Third World Countries." *Annals of Tourism Research* 20, no. 2 (1993): 302-18.

Simalchik, Joan. "Part of the Great Awakening: Canadian Churches and the Chilean Refugees, 1970-1979." Master's thesis, University of Toronto, 1993.

—. "The Material Culture of Chilean Exile: A Transnational Dialogue." *Refuge* 23, no. 2 (2006): 95-105.

Simpson, Lesley Byrd. *Many Mexicos*. Berkeley: University of California Press, 1941.

Smart, Josephine. "Borrowed Men on Borrowed Time: Globalization, Labour Migration and Local Economies in Alberta." *Canadian Journal of Regional Science* 20, no. 12 (1997): 141-56.

Smith, Sarah E.K. "Art and the Invention of North America, 1985-2012." PhD diss., Queen's University, 2013.

—. "Cross-Border Identifications and Dislocations: Visual Art and the Construction of Identity in North America." In *Parallel Encounters: Culture at the Canada-US Border*, edited by D.F. Stirrup and Gillian Roberts, 187-205. Waterloo, ON: Wilfrid Laurier University Press, 2013.

—. "Visualizing the 'New' North American Landscape." In *Negotiations in a Vacant Lot: Studying the Visual in Canada*, edited by Lynda Jessup, Erin Morton, and Kirsty Robertson, 130-49. Montreal and Kingston: McGill-Queen's University Press, 2014.

Smith, W. Eugene, and Aileen M. Smith. *Minamata*. New York: Holt, Rinehart and Winston, 1975.

Solar, Consuelo. "Media: Connecting Latinos." *Canadian Newcomer Magazine*. Accessed December 10, 2015. http://www.cnmag.ca/issue-31/516-n09-media-connecting-latinos (page no longer available).

Sommer, Doris. *Foundational Fictions: The National Romances of Latin America*. Berkeley and Los Angeles: University of California Press, 1991.

Spencer, David R., and Joseph D. Straubhaar. "Broadcast Research in the Americas: Revisiting the Past and Looking to the Future." *Journal of Broadcasting & Electronic Media* 50 , no. 3 (2006): 368-82.

Spivak, Gayatri. *The Post-Colonial Critic: Interviews, Strategies, Dialogues*. London: Routledge, 1990.

Springer, José. "Birds of a Feather: Canada, Mexico, NAFTA and Culture." *Fuse* 19, no. 3 (Spring 1996): 31-38.

Strom, Megan. "Social Hierarchy in Local Spanish-Language Print Media: The Discursive Representation of Latino Social Actors in the United States." *Discourse & Society* 2 (2015): 230-52.

Suescun Pozas, Maria del Carmen. "From Reading to Seeing: Doing and Undoing Imperialism in the Visual Arts." In *Close Encounters of Empire: Writing the Cultural History of U.S-Latin American Relations*, edited by Gilbert Joseph, Catherine LeGrand, and Ricardo Salvatore, 525-56. Durham: Duke University Press, 1998.

Supičić, Ivo. *Music in Society: A Guide to the Sociology of Music*. New York: Pendragon Press, 1988.

Swinscoe, Adrian. "Do You Need to Change Your Organisational Structure to Improve Your Customer Experience?" *Forbes*. January 9, 2014. http://www.forbes.com/sites/adrianswinscoe/2014/01/09/do-you-need-to-change-your-organisational-structure-to-improve-your-customer-experience/.

Sznajder, Mario, and Luis Roniger. "Exile Communities and their Differential Institutional Dynamics: A Comparative Analysis of the Chilean and Uruguayan Political Diasporas." *Revista de Ciencia Política* 27, no. 1 (2007): 43-66. http://dx.doi.org/10.4067/S0718-090X2007000200003.

Taylor, Charles. "The Politics of Recognition." In *Multiculturalism: Examining the Politics of Recognition*, edited by Charles Taylor and Amy Gutman, 25-74. Princeton: Princeton University Press, 1994.

—. *Imaginarios sociales modernos*. Translated by Ramon Vilà Vernis. Barcelona: Ediciones Paidós Ibérica, 2006.

—. "La política del reconocimiento." In *El multiculturalismo y "la política del reconocimiento,"* written by Charles Taylor, translated by Mónica Utrilla de Neira, Liliana Andrade Llanas and Gerard Vilar Roca, 43-107. Mexico City: Fondo de Cultura Económica, 2009.

Taylor, Diana. *The Archive and the Repertoire: Performing Cultural Memory in the Americas*. Durham: Duke University Press, 2003.

Taylor, Paul, Mark Hugo Lopez, Jessica Martinez, and Gabriel Velasco. "When Labels Don't Fit: Hispanics and Their Views of Identity." Pew Research Centers Hispanic Trends Project RSS. April 4, 2012. Accessed December 10, 2015. http://www.pewhispanic.org/2012/04/04/when-labels-dont-fit-hispanics-and-their-views-of-identity/.

Tetlow, Joseph. "Introduction." In *Ignatius Loyola: Spiritual Exercises*, edited by Joseph Tetlow, 18-30. New York: Crossroads Publishing Company, 1992.

Tettey, Wisdom J., and Korbla P. Puplampu, eds. *The African Diaspora in Canada: Negotiating Identity and Belonging*. Calgary: University of Calgary Press, 2005.

Todorov, Tzvetan. *La conquista de América: el problema del otro*. Mexico City: Siglo XXI Editores, 1999.

Tomic, Patricia. "The Colour of Language: Accent, Devaluation and Resistance in Latin American Immigrant Lives in Canada." *Canadian Ethnic Studies/Études Ethniques au Canada* 45, no. 1-2 (2013): 1-21.

Torres, Luis. "Exile and Identity." In *Relocating Identities*, edited by Elizabeth Montes Garcés, 55-83. Calgary: University of Calgary Press, 2007.

Trouillot, Michel-Rolph. *Silencing the Past: Power and Production of History*. Boston: Beacon Press, 1995.

Truett, Samuel. "Introduction: Making Transnational History: Nations, Regions, and Borderlands." In *Continental Crossroads: Remapping U.S.-Mexico Borderlands History*, edited by Samuel Truett and Elliott Young, 1-32. Durham: Duke University Press, 2004.

Tunali, Tijen. "Crossing the Border with Divine Assistance: Ex-voto Paintings of Mexican Immigrants to the United States." Master's thesis, State University of New York at Buffalo, 2006.

Tunstall, Tricia. *Changing Lives: Gustavo Dudamel, El Sistema, and the Transformative Power of Music*. New York: W.W. Norton and Company, 2012.

Vaillancourt, François, and Olivier Coche. *Official Language Policies at the Federal Level in Canada: Costs and Benefits in 2006*. Vancouver: Fraser Institute, 2009.

Valiani, Salimah. "The Articulation of an Independent Foreign Policy: Canada and Latin America in the Early Twentieth Century." *Latin American Perspectives* 39, no. 6 (November 2012): 165-80.

Van Bolderen, Trish. "The Evolution of Hispanic-Canadian Literature: What's In (and Behind) the Anthologies?" *Interfaces Brasil/Canadá. Canoas* 13, no. 2 (2013): 57-76.

Vargas Llosa, Mario. "Dentro y Fuera de América Latina." *Letras Libres* (Mexico City) 84 (December 2005): 62-66.

Vásquez, Ana, and Ana María Araujo. *La maldición de Ulises: Repercusiones psicológicas del exilio*. Santiago: Sudamericana, 1990.

Vatz-Laaroussi, Michèle. *Mobilités, réseaux et résilience: le cas des familles immigrantes et réfugiées au Québec*. Quebec City: Presses de l'Université du Québec, 2009.

Verdecchia, Guillermo. "Fronteras Americanas/American Borders." In *Fronteras Vivientes: Eight Latina/o Canadian Plays*, edited by Natalie Alvarez, 55-107. Toronto: Playwrights Canada Press, 2013.

Verduzco, Gustavo, and María Isabel Lozano. "Mexican Farm Workers' Participation in Canada's Seasonal Agricultural Labour Market and Development Consequences in their Rural Home Communities." Ottawa: The North-South Institute, 2003.

Veronis, Luisa. "The Canadian Hispanic Day Parade, or How Latin American Immigrants Practise (Sub)Urban Citizenship in Toronto." *Environment and Planning A: Economy and Space* 38, no. 9 (2006): 1653-71.

—. "Strategic Spatial Essentialism: Latin Americans' Real and Imagined Geographies of Belonging in Toronto." *Social & Cultural Geography* 8, no. 3 (2007): 455-73.

—. "Immigrant Participation in the Transnational Era: Latin Americans' Experiences with Collective Organising in Toronto." *International Migration and Integration* 11, no. 2 (2010): 173-92.

Veronis, Luisa, and Rukhsana Ahmed. "The Role of Multicultural Media in Connecting Municipal Governments with Ethnocultural Communities: The Case of Ottawa." *Global Media Journal: Canadian Edition* 8, no. 2 (2015): 73-95.

Vilchis Roque, Alfredo. *Infinitas Gracias: Contemporary Mexican Votive Paintings*. Translated by Elizabeth Bell. Foreword by Victoire and Hervé Di Rosa. San Francisco: Chronicle Books, 2004.

Villenas, Sofia. "The Colonizer/Colonized Chicana Ethnographer: Identity, Marginalization, and Co-optation in the Field." *Harvard Educational Review* 66, no. 4 (December 1996): 711-32.

Virilio, Paul. *Velocidad y política*. Buenos Aires: La Marca, 2007.

Wade, Peter. *Race and Ethnicity in Latin America*. Chicago: Pluto Press, 1997.

Wai-Teng Leong, Laurence. "Commodifying Ethnicity: State and Ethnic Tourism in Singapore." In *Tourism, Ethnicity and the State in Asian and Pacific Societies*, edited by Michel Picard and Robert Everett Wood, 71-98. Honolulu: University of Hawai'i Press, 1997.

Wakin, Daniel. "Music Meets Chávez Politics, and Critics Frown." *The New York Times*, February 17, 2012. http://www.nytimes.com/2012/02/18/arts/music/venezuelans-criticize-hugo-chavezs-support-of-el-sistema.html?pagewanted=all&_r=0.

—. "Venerated High Priest and Humble Servant of Music Education." *The New York Times*, March 1, 2012. http://www.nytimes.com/2012/03/04/arts/music/jose-antonio-abreu-leads-el-sistema-in-venezuela.html?pagewanted=all.

Wall, Ellen. "Personal Labor Relations and Ethnicity in Ontario Agriculture." In *Deconstructing a Nation: Immigration, Multiculturalism and Racism in 90s Canada*, edited by Vic Satzewich, 261-75. Halifax: Fernwood, 1992.

Wallis, Brian. "Selling Nations: International Exhibitions and Cultural Diplomacy." In *Museum Culture: Histories, Discourses, Spectacles*, edited by Daniel J. Sherman and Irit Rogoff, 265-81. Minneapolis: University of Minnesota Press, 1994.

Weisbrot, Mark. "Irregularities Reveal Mexico's Election Far from Fair." *The Guardian*, July 9, 2012.

Wilcken, Patrick. *Empire Adrift. The Portuguese Court in Rio de Janeiro, 1808-1821*. London: Bloomsbury, 2004.

Williams, Raymond. *Keywords: A Vocabulary of Culture and Society*. New York: Oxford University Press, 1983.

Yilorm Barrientos, Yasla. "El exilio y el quiebre de la identidad nacional en El jardín de al lado, de José Donoso." *Documentos Lingüísticos y Literarios UACh* 26/27 (2003-2004). Accessed October 27, 2014. http://revistadll.cl/index.php/revistadll/article/view/279/409.

Young, William R. "Making the Truth Graphic: The Canadian Government's Home Front Information Structure and Programs During World War II." PhD diss., University of British Columbia, 1978.

—. "Academics and Social Scientists versus the Press: The Policies of the Bureau of Public Information and the Wartime Information Board, 1939 to 1945." *Historical Papers* 13, no. 1 (1978): 217-40.

Yúdice, George. *El recurso de la cultura. Usos de la cultura en la era global*. Barcelona: Gedisa, 2002.

Zdravomyslova, Elena. "The Café Saigon Tusovka: One Segment of the Informal-Public Sphere of Late-Soviet Society." In *Biographical Research in Eastern Europe*, edited by Robin Humphrey, Robert Miller and Elena Zdravomyslova, 141-77. Hampshire: Aldershot, 2003.

Zorbas, Jason Gregory. "Diefenbaker, Latin America and the Caribbean: The Pursuit of Canadian Autonomy." PhD diss., University of Saskatchewan, 2009.

Zucchi, John. "Mad Flight? The Montréal Migration of 1896 to Brazil." *Journal of the Canadian Historical Association* 24, no. 2 (2013): 189-217.

Contributors

A journalist and actress, **Andrea Ávila** has a bachelor's degree from UNAM FES Acatlán (1995), a master's in Humanities from the Universidad Anahuac (2003), a master's in Modern Literature (specialization in Drama) from the Universidad Iberoamericana (2008), and a PhD in Hispanic Studies from Western University in London, Ontario (2012). Her research focuses on the influence and transformative power of technology on the performing arts. Her doctoral dissertation, "Teatralidad, globalidad y tecnología en el siglo XXI" [Theatricality, totality and technology in the 21st century] (2012), examines Cirque du Soleil, Robert Lepage, and La Fura dels Baus as examples of how computers, lighting and virtual reality are used in contemporary theatre. Dr. Ávila has worked for such national print news media in Mexico as *El Universal* and *Contenido*, and has recently published a book of creative non-fiction, *Con dolor en el termostato* (Lugar Común Editorial, 2017). Her short story, "Primer día de clases," appeared in two 2019 anthologies: *México en Canadá* and *Relatos entrecruzados* (both published by Editorial Mapalé). Since obtaining her PhD, she has worked as a personal support worker, as an interpreter for Spanish-speaking newcomers to Canada, as a simulated patient and standardized patient for students at Fanshawe College and Western University, and as a cultural connector for the City of London (Canada). Her primary pursuit, however, is acting in London, Ontario theatre productions. Through these varied activities, Dr. Ávila has gained important knowledge about Canadian society and the positive role played by immigrants. She is keen to continue engaging with the community, helping other Hispanic-Canadians find their own ways of belonging within a diverse and ever-changing society.

Rosana Barbosa is Associate Professor in the Department of History at Saint Mary's University, in Halifax, Nova Scotia. Since her appointment in 2004, she has taught a variety of courses, including: Forced and Free Migration in Latin America; Race and Racism in Brazil; Latin American Revolutions; Pop Culture in Latin America; and Soccer: A History of Brazil, which was listed by the *Huffington Post* in 2014 as one of the "coolest classes" offered at a post-secondary institution in Canada. Dr. Barbosa completed her Bachelor of Arts at the Universidade Santa Úrsula in her hometown of Rio de Janeiro, and her master's and PhD at the University of Toronto. She is the author of a number of publications, including two books: *Brazil and Canada: Economic, Political, and Migratory Ties, 1820s to 1970s* (Lexington Books, 2017), and *Immigration and Xenophobia: Portuguese Immigrants in Early Nineteenth-Century Rio de Janeiro* (University Press of America, 2009). She has presented lectures and papers not only across Canada but also in the United States, France, Chile, Costa Rica, Belgium, Japan and Portugal, and at a number of Brazilian universities. She is now working on a manuscript about the early social history of soccer in Brazil. Since her arrival in Canada, she has been deeply involved in the

Brazilian community. From 1986 to 1995, she was a member, a board member, and ultimately the coordinator of the Grupo Brazil of Ontario, the oldest Brazilian community group in Canada. From 2000 to 2002, she was a founding member of the Grupo Comunitário de Informação Brasil/Angola, and she is currently a supporter of the newly created Casa Brazil Club Association of Nova Scotia.

Nuria Carton de Grammont is an art historian, curator and adjunct professor at Concordia University, specializing in contemporary Latin American and Latino-Canadian art. She received her PhD in Art History from Concordia in 2012. She did two postdoctoral fellowships at the Université de Montréal, the first at the Montreal Centre for International Studies (CÉRIUM), and the second in the Department of Geography. Dr. Carton de Grammont arrived in Quebec in 2004 to complete a master's at the Université du Québec à Montréal (UQAM). She completed an undergraduate degree in History at the Universidad Nacional Autónoma de México (UNAM). Her undergraduate thesis was awarded the Marcos y Celia Maus prize (2004-2005) by the Faculty of Philosophy and Literatures/UNAM. From 2013 to 2016, she coordinated CÉRIUM's Research Network on Latin America (RÉAL). As a curator, Dr. Carton de Grammont has organized different contemporary art exhibits in Mexico and Canada, such as "Milpa, ritual imprescindible" at the botanical garden of the UNAM (2016); Gilberto Esparza's "Plantas autofotosintéticas" at the Galerie de l'UQAM (2017); and "Un, dos, tres por mí y mis compañeras" at OPTICA, centre d'art contemporain (2020). She also co-curated the artistic installation "Objets personnels/Personal belongings/Objetos personales" for the permanent collection of the Americas at the Montreal Museum of Fine Arts, where she was a specialized consultant for the Arts of One World collection. She has served as a jury member for OPTICA; the Centre des arts actuels Skol; the Fonderie Darling; Montréal, arts interculturels; and La Centrale Powerhouse. She also serves on the executive committee of the Galerie de l'UQAM (2019-2021) and the board of directors for OPTICA (since 2018). She is the artistic director of artist Stanley Février's MAC-Invisible project, and of Skol. Dr. Carton de Grammont has been invited to participate in various national and international conferences and has published specialized articles in a number of scholarly venues, such as *Fractal, Esse arts + opinions, Inter: Art Actuel, Les Cahiers ALHIM, Artediseño, Oltreoceano*, and *Archée*. She also co-edited the book *Politics, Culture and Economy in Popular Practices in the Americas* (Peter Lang, 2016).

Ana Chiarelli works as an International Learning Coordinator at Western University (London, Ontario), where she is in charge of exchanges, and of research and study abroad opportunities in Europe. She is very interested in academic mobility and participated in the international exchange program for employees at Western. Ana completed bachelor's and postgraduate degrees in Caracas, in her home country of Venezuela: the first was in Journalism at the Andrés Bello Catholic University (1998), the second was in Business Management at the Simón Bolívar University (2004). She holds a PhD in Hispanic Studies and Migration and Ethnic Relations from Western (2015), receiving an Ontario

Graduate Scholarship in 2013 to support her PhD research and writing. Her research focuses on Hispanic-American migrant literature of the 21st century and, especially, on Spanish-language works written in Canada. Her publications in these areas include "Echoes of the Venezuelan Diaspora. One Novel, Two Realities" (*Changes, Conflicts and Ideologies in Contemporary Hispanic Culture*, Cambridge Scholars Publishing, 2014) and "Crónicas de un nómada: El humor como estrategia del recuerdo" (2013), published in Scholarship@Western, an online academic repository supported by the Western University library system. While in Venezuela, she had the opportunity to work as a journalist for the national daily newspaper, *El Nacional*, as well as in higher education. More recently, she has found great fulfillment in teaching Spanish as a lecturer at Western. In addition to pursuing academic work, Ana is committed to animal welfare, contributing as much as possible to this cause worldwide, including devoting significant personal time to the rescue and rehabilitation of dogs when she lived in Venezuela.

Jason Dyck is a historian of colonial religion, missionary work, and the craft of sacred history in the early modern Spanish world. He obtained a Bachelor of Arts degree in History and Philosophy from Brock University (2002), a master's in History from Queen's University (2003), and a PhD in History from the University of Toronto (2012). His publications focus on baroque religious practices and scholarship in New Spain, and have appeared in the *Colonial Latin American Review*, the *Florida Historical Quarterly*, and *Estudios de Historia Novohispana*. He also focuses on the transcription of colonial manuscript histories, specifically the writings of the Jesuits Francisco de Florencia (1620-1695) and Juan de Albizuri (1601-1651). Jason has lectured on the history of Latin America and of medieval and early modern Europe at various universities in southern Ontario. He has also been a research fellow in several rare book libraries in the United States, such as the John Carter Brown, Huntington, Newberry, and Beinecke Libraries. He has volunteered as an archives assistant at the St. Catharines Museum and initially developed his interest in colonial history while working with migrant Mexican farmhands over the course of thirteen seasons at a local nursery in the Niagara Region. Jason is currently a Lecturer in History at Western and Carleton Universities.

Natalia Lara Diaz-Berrio is a visual artist, photographer and teacher. She currently lives in Valencia (Spain), where she works as a one-on-one photography teacher, a writer, and a photographer for the arts magazine *Art-facto*. She is also presently engaged in a personal project about flamenco. From 2008 to 2010, Natalia studied Studio Arts at the Universidad Nacional Autónoma de México (UNAM) and simultaneously pursued an undergraduate education in Teaching French as a Second Language at the Universidad Pedagógica Nacional (Mexico City) and the Université de Bourgogne (France), obtaining her degree in 2012. In 2010, she moved to Montreal, where she furthered her Studio Arts studies at Concordia University, completing this undergraduate degree in 2014, with distinction. In 2013 and 2014, respectively, she took complementary photography courses at the Université du Québec à Montréal (analog photography) and the Université de Montréal (photojournalism). Natalia has taught photography at the Concordia Students Union (2011-2013), has written for newspapers such as *The Link*, *The Concordian* and *Le Délit* (2011-2014), and has done video and photography work for the Art Matters and Montreal Fringe festivals (2013-2014). As an artist, she has participated in exhibitions such as *Who is Looking at Who?* at Gallery X in Montreal (2011), *Emerg-Art* at Montreal's Gallery 514 (2011), *Reanimando lo obsoleto* at the Romerías de Mayo festival in Havana, Cuba (2011), and *Reconstrucción del* álbum *familiar* in the Arte Las Condes cultural centre in Santiago, Chili (2015). In 2012, she held two artist residencies: one at OZU residential culture and arts centre in Italy, the other with Halka Sanat Projesi (the Halka art project) in Turkey. Her photography project "Expatria" was presented in eight countries between 2012 and 2014, including in exhibitions at La ruche d'art (Montreal, 2013) and the Espacio México at the Mexican Consulate in Montreal (March & April 2014). She has also worked on two exhibitions as a curator: *Time to Act/Temps d'Agir?* at the Eastern Bloc gallery in Montreal (2016), and *Sin puntos cardinales: Time to Think*, at the Espacio Fidencia cultural centre in Mexico City (2017). From 2016 to 2019, Natalia lived between Chile and Mexico City, photographing and writing for several magazines, such as *Arte al límite*, *Artishock*, *Revolver* and *Città*. Over the years, she has collaborated with a range of other photographers, including Zony Maya, Gonzalo Donoso, Sebastián Utreras and Álvaro de la Fuente, and has been awarded scholarships from the Université de Montréal, Concordia University, UNAM, and the Gouvernement du Québec.

María Eugenia de Luna Villalón has been Assistant Lecturer of Spanish in the School of Modern Languages and Cultures at the University of Hong Kong (HKU) since 2017. Prior to that, she worked at the University of Waterloo, at Wilfrid Laurier University (both in Canada), and at Alvernia University in the United States. She holds a PhD in Hispanic Studies from Western University (2011), a master's in Applied Linguistics from the Universidad de las Américas Puebla (UDLAP) in Mexico (2007), a diploma in Business Administration from the Instituto Tecnológico de Monterrey-ITESM (Mexico, 2001), and a bachelor's degree in Communication Sciences from UDLAP (1990). Dr. de Luna Villalón's research focuses on sociolinguistics and, specifically, on themes related to language and migration. For her master's thesis, she worked with Mexican immigrants in Winnipeg (Manitoba), studying home-literacy practices to understand language use, maintenance and/or change in the case of different family members. Her PhD thesis, "Mexican Temporary Migrants in Canada: A Language and Migration Approach," involved compiling and analyzing sociolinguistic facts related to the situation of temporary agricultural migrants from Mexico who came to Canada through the Seasonal Agricultural Workers Program. She has since researched linguistic landscapes, with a view to understanding the use of Spanish in context in Canada, and is currently exploring linguistic ideologies in the teaching and learning of Spanish as a Foreign Language in higher education in Hong Kong. In addition to publishing in and acting as a reviewer for various scholarly and specialized journals, Dr. de Luna Villalón was involved with Western University's *Entrehojas: Revista de Estudios Hispánicos*, serving on the design team and as Editor-in-Chief from 2010 to 2011. She was also the content designer of the Spanish vocabulary app, *Spanish VocApp*, and co-wrote, co-directed and co-produced *San Pablito Cuna del Amatl*, an ethnographic documentary that was part of "Muestra Retrospectiva de México" (Espacio Audiovisual CONACYT) and was selected to participate in the 1988 Festival international du film scientifique in Palaiseau, France. She has experience in community service learning and community outreach, and was the coordinator of an access-to-university program for non-traditional learners, jointly run by Wilfrid Laurier University and the not-for-profit organization, The Working Centre (TWC). She has also been a volunteer with not-for-profit organizations in Canada that work with refugees, such as Reception House, the Mennonite Coalition for Refugee Support, and Speak English Café at TWC. In Hong Kong, she has volunteered with the Guestroom at ImpactHK, an NGO that provides support to homeless people. In 2006, Dr. de Luna Villalón was awarded the North American Mobility grant between UDLAP and the University of Manitoba. That same year, she was a Graduate Fellow/ Visiting Scholar for the Transnational Literacy Researchers Work Group in the Center for the Americas at Vanderbilt University. She has experience teaching Spanish language courses at all levels, including Spanish for Professionals, and content courses in linguistics, literature and culture.

Francis Peddie is Associate Professor at the Graduate School of International Development (GSID), Nagoya University, Japan. In 1994, he completed two bachelor's degrees from York University in Toronto: a Bachelor of Arts with Honours in History from Glendon College, and a Bachelor of Education. He earned a maestría en Historia (de México) from the Facultad de Filosofía y Letras of the Universidad Nacional Autónoma de México in 2005, and in 2012, completed his PhD in York University's Department of History, specializing in Latin American History and Canadian Social History. His publications on the Chilean community in Canada are *Young, Well-Educated and Adaptable: Chilean Exiles in Ontario and Quebec, 1973-2010* (University of Manitoba Press, 2014); "La política migratoria de Canadá: los refugiados del bloque comunista y la dictadura chilena, 1945-1976" (*La Guerra Fría y las Américas*, Universidad de Colima and Universidad Michoacana de San Nicolás de Hidalgo, 2014); and "Shaming an Unwilling Host: The Chilean solidarity movement, Fall 1973" (*Left History*, 17:2, 2014). At GSID, Dr. Peddie teaches in the Peace and Governance program, offering courses entitled International Politics and Global Governance, and conducting two specialist seminars: Migration and Truth, and Reconciliation Commissions. His current research includes investigations into motivations and destinations for labour migration from the rural town of Rizal, Laguna Province, the Philippines; changes to Japanese immigration policy and its Technical Intern Trainee Program; and the involvement of civil society organizations in reconciliation measures in post-conflict societies. He is a member of the Japanese Association for Latin American Studies, the Japanese Society for International Development, and the Japanese Association for Migration Studies, where he also serves on the editorial board.

Dianne Pearce is Cultural Coordinator for the Town of Oakville. She holds a Bachelor of Fine Arts from the Nova Scotia College of Art and Design, and a Master of Fine Arts from the Universidad Nacional Autónoma de México. Over the years, she has received grants from the Secretaría de Relaciones Exteriores de México, the Fondo Nacional para la Cultura y las Artes (Mexico), Foreign Affairs Canada (now Global Affairs Canada (GAC)), the Canada Council for the Arts, the Ontario Arts Council, the Conseil des arts et des lettres du Québec, and the Bank of Missions (International Academic Relations Program, Department of Foreign Affairs and International Trade (now GAC)). Dianne has participated in two artist residencies at the Banff Centre for the Arts, and has exhibited extensively in artist-run centres in her native Canada, as well as in museums in both Canada and Mexico. Internationally, she has shown her work in Paris, Madrid, Marbella, Milan, Miami, Chile and Argentina. She curated *Anatomical Permutations: Ten Canadian Artists* for the 1998 Festival Internacional Cervantino (Guanajuato) and *Sticks and Stones* (2005) for the Universidad Iberoamericana in Mexico City. She also co-curated *Trans-AMERICAS: A sign, a symbol, a situation* (2016) for Museum London. This last exhibition showed the work of fourteen Latin American artists now living and working in Canada and the United States. Dianne has presented papers at various conferences organized by the Universities Art Association of Canada, with many talks focusing on Latin American art, and others focused on alternative learning and teaching systems. She taught post-secondary art for ten years at the Escuela Nacional de Pintura, Escultura y Grabado "La Esmeralda" (Mexico City), and subsequently spent eight years as Curator of Public Programs at Museum London (Ontario, Canada).

John-Alexander Raimondo is an architecture student in the Toronto studio of the Royal Architectural Institute of Canada (RAIC) Syllabus program. He is also working for Raimondo + Associates Architects in Niagara Falls as part of the process of obtaining his architect licensure. He was born and raised in the Niagara Region and currently lives in St. Catharines. He holds both bachelor's and master's degrees in History from Brock University, where he focused his major research project on digital history and the potential for a virtual deep-map narrative to serve as an innovative genre for expressing history. He created a virtual deep map of the National Historic Willowbank Estate in Queenston, Ontario, Canada. His research interests include digital history, architecture, deep maps, spatial narratives, memory, and space and place studies. He was influential in re-launching the Brock University Historical Society in 2016. That same year, he spearheaded the first-ever Brock undergraduate history journal, *The General*. John volunteers with the Niagara Society of Architects and his publications include "Niagara Falls Rises: Entertainment Architecture in a Tourist Mecca" (*OAA Perspectives: The Journal of the Ontario Association of Architects*, 24: 3, Fall 2016, issue entitled "The Architecture of Entertainment") and "How the Niagara Region used Fellowship to raise the profile of architects" (RAIC Bulletin, September 2019), in collaboration with Ian Ellingham.

Alena Robin is Associate Professor in the Department of Visual Arts at Western University. She completed her Bachelor of Arts in Humanistic Studies at McGill University (1997), continuing on with a master's (2002) and PhD (2007) in Art History at the Universidad Nacional Autónoma de México (UNAM), where she specialized in religious art from New Spain (Colonial Mexico). She did a postdoctoral fellowship at the Université de Montréal, receiving funding from the Fonds québécois de la recherche sur la société et la culture (now Fonds de recherche du Québec — Société et Culture). Her research focuses on the presence of Latin American art in Canada and on the representation of the Passion of Christ in New Spain, in different artistic expressions, mostly during the 17th and 18th centuries. Other fields of interest and specialization are theories of art and artistic literature in Spain and Latin America, the historiography of painting in New Spain, and issues surrounding the conservation and restoration of cultural heritage. Her book, *Las capillas del Vía Crucis de la ciudad de México. Arte, patrocinio y sacralización del espacio* (2014), was published by the Instituto de Investigaciones Estéticas/UNAM. In 2013, she co-edited with Luis de Moura Sobral a special issue on Latin American Art for *RACAR: revue d'art canadienne/ Canadian Art Review*. Dr. Robin has also published in scholarly journals such as *Latin American and Latinx Visual Culture*, *Philostrato: Revista de Historia y Arte*, *RACAR*, *Goya*, *Anales del Instituto de Investigaciones Estéticas*, *Atrio: Revista de historia del arte*, and *Vía Spiritus: Revista de História da Espiritualidade e do Sentimento Religioso*. A collaborator with the Museo Regional de Guadalajara on the catalogue of their collection of Early Modern paintings, Dr. Robin is presently revisiting 18th-century paintings in New Spain, for which she has previously received Social Sciences and Humanities Research Council (SSHRC) Insight Development Grant (IDG) funding. She currently holds a SSHRC IDG to study art from Latin America in Canadian collections.

Mariza Rosales Argonza is a visual artist, independent researcher and cultural mediator. She received her Bachelor of Arts from the Universidad Nacional Autónoma de México in 1997 and went on to complete a master's in Art History and a PhD in Modern and Contemporary Art at the Centro de Cultura Casa Lamm in Mexico City. Her research is primarily oriented toward Chicano and Latino-Québécois art from a decolonial perspective, and she has a deep interest in the relationship between art and society, particularly in intercultural contexts. She received a postdoctoral fellowship at UQAM, was coordinator of what is now known as the Centre de recherche Cultures-Arts-Sociétés (CÉLAT) at UQAM from 2012 to 2015, and has published essays on art and cultural diversity in numerous journals. In 2018, she edited *Vues transversales: Panorama de la scène artistique latino-québécoise*, a collection of essays including diverse forms of visual and literary art, published in Montreal by CIDIHCA-LatinArte. Her own multidisciplinary artistic work includes photography, drawings, paintings, installations and performances, and has been exhibited in Europe and the Americas. At present, she is in charge of cultural mediation and co-creation projects in visual and media arts in the Accès culturel network, sponsored by the city of Montreal and various community organizations. She recently coordinated IN-

TER@MÉRIQUES, a program accompanying digital arts projects by artists of the Americas, which was funded by the Canada Council for the Arts. Since 2015, she has also been the artistic director and curator of exhibitions by Latino-Québécois artists in the annual LatinArte Festival in Montreal.

Sarah E. K. Smith is a scholar and curator based in Ottawa. Her research addresses modern and contemporary art in Canada, Mexico and the United States, as well as the topics of exhibitions, museums, and cultural policies. She works as Assistant Professor in Communication and Media Studies at Carleton University. She is also Affiliated Faculty in the Bachelor of Global and International Studies program, where she contributes to the Specialization in Global Media and Communication. Additionally, she is a fellow of the Canadian Global Affairs Institute. In 2017, Sarah co-founded the North American Cultural Diplomacy Initiative—a transdisciplinary research network addressing cultural diplomacy that includes academics, policymakers and practitioners from North America and beyond. Prior to joining the faculty at Carleton, Sarah held the 2015 Fulbright Visiting Research Chair in Public Diplomacy at the University of Southern California. She also held a postdoctoral fellowship with the Transnational Studies Initiative at Harvard University's Weatherhead Center for International Affairs, and a Banting Postdoctoral Fellowship in the Department of English and Film Studies at the University of Alberta. Sarah has experience in the museum sector and was Curator of Contemporary Art at the Agnes Etherington Art Centre in Kingston, Ontario. In 2016, her monograph *General Idea: Life & Work* was published by the Art Canada Institute. Sarah's curatorial projects include: *Sorting Daemons: Art, Surveillance Regimes and Social Control* (2010-11), co-curated with Jan Allen; *I'm Not Myself At All: Deirdre Logue and Allyson Mitchell* (2015); and *From Remote Stars: Buckminster Fuller, London, and Speculative Futures* (2020), co-curated with Kirsty Robertson.

Maria del Carmen Suescun Pozas is Associate Professor in the Department of History at Brock University and founding editor of the Huitzil Series with Lugar Común Editorial. She completed her Bachelor of Fine Arts at Concordia University in 1994, continuing on with a master's in Art History (1996), and a Joint PhD in History and Art History at McGill University (2005), and a postdoctoral research position in History at the Université de Montréal (2007). She is former president of the Canadian Association for Latin American and Caribbean Studies (CALACS), and founder of the Seedling for Change in History teaching and research collective, Seedling for Change in Society and Environment, The History Lab, and The Changhthang High Altitude Nomadic Research Institute. In terms of scholarly print projects, her previous collaborations include the publication of Michael Small's *El A.B.C. de una paz olvidada: Tiempo de medicación en Canadá, 1914* (Lugar Común Editorial, 2019; translated by Christel Kopp), originally published in English; *The Art of Solidarity: Visual and Performative Politics in Cold War Latin America* (University of Texas Press, 2018); a special issue of *Revista de Estudios Sociales y Culturales* (Universidad de los Andes, 2010), which was devoted to the cultural history of Colombia in the 1930s and 1940s; and the journal article "Corporate Social Responsibility and Extractive Industries in Latin America and the Caribbean: Perspectives from the Ground" (*The Extractive Industries and Society*, 2015). She also co-organized CALACS's first virtual forum— "Corporate Social Responsibility and Extractive Industries in Latin America and the Caribbean: A Multi-Stakeholder View from the LAC Region"—as part of the Association's 41st Congress, and she has collaborated extensively with artists on publication, exhibition, and multicultural projects. Dr. Suescun Pozas is a member of the Réseau d'études latino-americaines de Montréal, Le Laboratoire interdisciplinaire des études latino-américaines (at the Université du Québec à Montréal), and the Centre for Oral History and Digital Storytelling (Concordia University). Over the years, she has received the following funding: a Max Stern Museum Fellowship; a postdoctoral fellowship from the Fonds québecois de recherche sur la société et la culture (now Fonds de recherche du Québec — Société et Culture); a Social Sciences and Humanities Research Council Insight Development Grant; an International Visiting Scholar grant from the Programa de Pós-Graduação em Estudos de Fronteira, at the Universidade Federal do Amapá (UNIFAP) in Macapá, Brazil; a TELUS Scholarship for the Non-for-Profit Governance Essentials Program, awarded by the Institute of Corporate Directos; as well as grants from the Niagara Falls Cultural Development Fund, and the Government of Ontario's Multicultural Community Capacity Program. In 2012, Dr. Suescun Pozas was nominated for the "10 Most Influential Hispanic Canadians" annual national awards, and in 2018 she was a finalist in the Community Spirit category of the Greater Niagara Chamber of Commerce's Women in Business Awards.

Madeleine de Trenqualye is the Editorial Communications Manager for the Faculty of Arts at the University of British Columbia (UBC), where she writes news stories about research in the humanities, social sciences, and creative arts. She also works as a historical researcher, currently freelancing with Parks Canada, writing reports for them about places that have been nominated for heritage status; and previously providing support to the Vancouver Heritage Foundation, the Museum of Vancouver, and the Saturna Island Heritage Centre. Her research work also includes writing, digital storytelling, and community consultation. She is Vice-President of the Vancouver Historical Society and a member of the City of Vancouver's Civic Asset Naming Committee. Born in Santiago, Chile, she grew up in the United Kingdom and Canada. She studied Canadian History at UBC (Bachelor of Arts, 2007) and McGill University (Master of Arts, 2010) and lives in Vancouver.

Victoria F. Wolff is Associate Professor of Hispanic Studies at Western University in London, Ontario. She received her PhD in Hispanic Studies from McGill University (2008), her master's in Latin American Studies from the University of New Mexico (2002), and her bachelor's degree in Romance Languages (Spanish) from the University of North Carolina at Chapel Hill (1999). She specializes in interdisciplinary and transatlantic studies, focusing on the intersections between music and literature in the Hispanic world (both

Spain and Spanish America). The main body of her research centres on literary works that have been rewritten and adapted as libretti for musico-dramatic performance by writers, librettists and composers. She has also written on the use of music in the writing of Peruvian author José María Arguedas, and she studied the El Sistema music education program. Her scholarly articles have been published in such outlets as *Decimonónica: Journal of Nineteenth Century Hispanic Cultural Production*, *Ars Lyrica: Journal of the Lyrica Society for Word-Music Relations*, and *Hispanic Journal*. Dr. Wolff has taught a wide variety of graduate and undergraduate courses in both Peninsular and Latin American literature and culture. She is Affiliated Faculty in the Migration and Ethnic Relations specialization at Western and has twice received the Community Service-Learning Award. Prior to entering academia, she was a licensed secondary school teacher of Spanish and English as a Foreign Language in New Mexico. In addition to being an academic, Dr. Wolff is also a proud mother.

Index

A

Aboriginality, Aboriginal people, 184-185, 189, 199-200, 203-204. *See also* Indigeneity

Aboriginal-Canadian theatre, 184-185, 189, 199, 200, 203

Aboriginal Drama and Theatre (Appleford), 184, 189

Abreu, José Antonio, 9, 265, 267-275, 281, 381n22, 382n36

Acculturation, 181, 231, 250, 258-259, 261

Activism, activist: 85, 88, 156, 163, 166, 171, 176-177, 253, 266; feminist activism, 165; human rights activist, 165; political activism, 167, 169, 171; social activist, 49, 88, 101

Adaptation, 15, 116, 123, 126, 137, 143, 154, 180, 185, 192, 201, 204-205, 211, 223, 226-227, 249, 267, 273, 278, 280, 323. *See also* Integration

Adoption: 215, 233, 273, 368n19; adopted society, 213, 219; adoptive society, 206, 233. *See also* Host

Advertising Standards Canada, 118

Aeolian Musical Arts Association. *See* Association

Aesthetic of urgency, 320

Agency, 136, 247, 291

Aguilar, Jorge Iñigo, 47, 320

Aguirre, Carmen, 190-191

Air Canada, 30,

Airport, 97-99, 106, 217, 227

Alfaro Siqueiros, David, 71, 76

Alameda Theatre, 191, 199-200

Alemán, Miguel, 79

Aluna Theatre, 191, 195-196, 199-200

Alberta, 113-114, 169, 172, 174, 176, 275, 354n64, 370n47

Allende, Salvador, 161, 169, 174, 186, 211, 217. *See also* Salvador Allende School

Almario, Paolo, 47

Alterity, 212

aluCine Latin Film and Arts Festival, 255

Alvarado, David, 47

Álvarez Acosta, Miguel, 83

Alvarez, Natalie, 189-190, 192, 194-196, 199

Amazon, The, 17-18, 20-21, 30, 32, 42

Amazon River, The, 18, 20

América *invertida*, 1-2, 11

AMIGAS Latin American Women's Society, 176

Amnesty International, 131
Amor, Inés, 71, 77-78, 342n18, 345n71
Andean Wave, 186
Anderson, Benedict, 230-231, 234-235, 248, 252, 381n23
Andrés Bello Catholic University, 269
Angelo Fiorita & Co., 16
Anglo-Mexican Institute for Cultural Relations, 80
Anti-racism. *See* Race
Anxiety, 98-99, 162
Appropriation, 45, 55, 181, 183, 194, 316, 319, 323
Aquino, Juan, 47
Arabic, 115, 126-128
Archives, 7, 9, 70, 110, 164, 229, 266-268, 292-293, 300-301, 361n10
Argentina, Argentinians, 18, 19, 20, 32, 37, 41, 50, 74, 114, 177, 186-188,
    192, 196, 200, 208, 211, 225, 237, 255, 293, 373n73
Armony, Victor, 232, 233, 239, 251, 253, 255
Art, artist: 1-3, 6-10, 27, 36-37, 45-64, 65-84, 86, 89, 93, 95, 97, 103, 107,
    109, 133-138, 140, 142-145, 147, 162, 164, 166, 171, 181-185, 187-
    195, 198-206, 208, 214, 218, 236, 246, 255, 265-267, 269, 272-277,
    281, 283-286, 288-293, 296, 302-304, 306, 308, 311-315, 318, 320-
    323, 330n15, 337n3, 337n5, 337n9, 338n18, 340n1, 341n6, 341n12,
    342n13, 343n36, 345n71, 345n81, 348n120, 352n24, 364n29,
    365n34, 370n44, 371n49, 383n44, 383n1, 385n9, 385n10, 385n17,
    386n18, 386n22, 387n35, 387n41; Indigenous art, artist, 49, 337n9;
    international artist, 313, 315; Latino, Latin American art, artist, 45-46,
    48-51, 53-57, 63-64, 190-192, 195-196, 198-199, 202, 204, 236, 255,
    257, 337n5, 338n18, 384n120, 386n18; Mexican art, artist, 8, 67-84,
    341n6, 341n12, 342n13, 342n18, 343n36, 344n52, 345n81, 347n105,
    347n113, 385n17, 387n41; performance art, artist, 183, 189, 199, 291
Art Association of Montreal. *See* Association
Art Gallery of Toronto (AGT), 70, 76, 78-79
Art of Latin America, 73-74
Arte Canadiense, 82
Artistic residency, 10, 275, 311, 315-316, 348n120, 385-386n17, 387-
    388n41
Asian Canadian theatre, 185, 189, 204
Asian Canadian Theatre (Aquino and Knowles), 189
Asociación de chilenos del Quebec. See Association
Asociación de chilenos de Montreal. See Association
Assimilation, 57, 112, 142, 210, 231-232, 247, 250
Association: 164, 166, 168-172, 175-176, 275, 280, 282; Aeolian Musical
    Arts Association, 277; *Asociación de chilenos del Quebec*, 176; *Asociación
    de chilenos de Montreal*, 169, 176, 362n16; Art Association of Montreal,
    70, 76; Canadian Inter-American Association (CIAA), 72; Canadian
    Music Educators' Association (CMEA), 275; exile association, 166, 171;
    Ottawa Chilean Association, 171

borderland, 62-63, 87, 110; border studies, 54; Canada-US border, 87, 98; cross-border art, artist, 48, 55, 64; cross-border perspective, vision, 53, 55; cross-border strategy, 45, 48; (cross-)border thinking, 53-54, 63; cultural border, boundary, 8, 46, 59-60, 63, 68, 257; de-bordering, 55; geographical border, boundary, 133, 135, 230; ideological border, 55; imagined, imaginary border, boundary, 4, 111-130; international border, 206; linguistic border, 112, 116, 130; Mexico-US border, 62, 87, 98, 110, 340n44; national border, boundary, 5, 11, 54, 166, 271-272; physical border, 50, 63, 118, 130, 223; political boundary, 133, 272, 295. *See also Fronteras Americanas/American Borders*; *Miracles on the Border*
Bourgeoisie, 182
Bracero Program, 87, 88, 349n9
Brascan, 21
Brazil, Brazilians, 8, 15-24, 35, 37, 74, 113, 114, 179, 186, 329n1, 335n37
Brazilian Traction, Light and Power Company, 15, 21, 23
Brecht, Bertolt, 182
Bridge, 53, 56, 146, 194, 207, 213, 218, 221, 223, 237
Britain. *See* Great Britain
British: 16, 17, 18, 19, 80, 132, 334n3; British Commonwealth, 6; British Council, 72, 80; British Empire, 15, 24, 79. *See also* Great Britain
British Caribbean, 24
British Columbia (BC), 27, 113-114, 202, 275
Brookfield Asset Management, 21
"Brown group," 200
Buenos Aires, 18, 196, 293

C
Cahoots Theatre, 202
Calderón, Carlos A., 74
Calgary, 30, 113, 187
California, 98, 184, 193, 202, 353n39, 353n40, 365n33
Calle, Marcela, 47
Camelo, Constanza, 47, 338n18
Canadian Broadcasting Corporation (CBC), 76, 239. *See also Société Radio-Canada*
Canadian Business, 80
Canadian Census. *See* Census
Canadian Confederation, 83, 330n21, 347n112
Canadian Information Service, 76
Canadian Inter-American Association (CIAA). *See* Association
Canadian Mosaic. *See* Mosaic
Canadian Music Educators' Association (CMEA). *See* Association
Canadian Order of United Workmen, 19
Canadian Pacific Air Lines, 81
Canadian Seasonal Agricultural Workers Program. *See* Seasonal agricultural worker

Canadian Theatre Encyclopedia, 189-190, 199
Canadian Tourism Commission, 28
Caracas, 268-269, 381n12
Carbajal, Federico, 48
Cardoza y Aragón, Luis, 71
Caribbean, 2, 85, 87-88, 110, 177, 216, 245, 272, 329n1, 334n3, 348n3, 350n16
Carr, Emily, 67, 77
Cartographies: 14 Artists from Latin America, 84, 348n120
Casuso, Luis, 208, 219, 371n54
CCA Wattis Institute for Contemporary Arts, 340-341n1
Central America, Central Americans, 27, 29, 36, 50, 87, 186, 232, 241, 245, 334n3
Central American Wave, 186
Census: in Canada, 112-113, 115, 128, 186, 229, 251, 260, 364n22, 366n3; in the United States, 252
Charter of Rights and Freedoms. *See* Rights
Charter of the French Language. *See* Bill 101
Cheadle, Norman, 221
Chávez, Hugo, 273
Chicanos, 51, 54, 134, 183-184, 202-203, 338n19
Chicano theatre, 183-184, 202
Chicoutimi, 51, 338n18
Child, childhood, 32, 41, 52, 57, 93, 102, 106-107, 116, 146, 169, 171, 174, 178, 197, 200, 219, 220, 250, 265, 268, 275, 277, 280-281, 299, 324, 362n16
Chile, Chileans, 9, 19, 36, 37, 41, 50, 74, 112, 114, 161-178, 180, 186, 187, 188, 190, 192, 193, 194, 208, 210, 216, 217, 218, 222, 223, 225, 237, 242, 245, 304, 329n7, 360n1, 360n2, 360n3, 361n7-11, 362n16, 362n17, 365n34, 366n4, 368n11, 370n44, 370n47, 371n49, 371n50, 373n76
Chilean-Canadian Community of Edmonton. *See Comunidad chileno-canadiense de Edmonton*
Chile Democrático, 169
Chilenidad, Chilean-ness: 162-165, 167, 170-175, 177; performance of *chilenidad*, 163, 167
Church, 85, 93, 95-96, 101, 169, 178, 270, 288, 361n9
Cirque du Soleil, 182
Cisneros, Domingo, 46-49, 59-61, 337n9, 338n18
Ciudad Juárez, 49, 61-63, 340n44
Clark Centre for Contemporary Artists, 48
Class struggle, 54, 324
Classical music, 266, 271, 277, 281
Clemente Orozco, José, 71, 80
Cole, Douglas S., 83,

Coyoacán, 315, 320
Crisis, 131, 137, 141, 168, 186, 269, 361n8
Cros, Edmond, 212, 369n34
Cuba, Cubans, 26, 28, 32, 37, 74, 113, 188, 208, 215, 218, 236, 286, 370n41, 371n57
Cueca, 162, 169-173
Cuentos de nuestra palabra (Rose and Zisman), 206, 209, 219, 371n49
Cult of speed, 316
Culture: 1-4, 6, 8, 10, 25-29, 32-33, 37, 39, 41-57, 59-61, 63-64, 67-84, 87, 91, 101, 114, 117, 124, 126, 130, 132-133, 135-136, 138-140, 142-144, 146, 152, 161-178, 179, 181, 184, 188-191, 195-196, 198, 200-203, 205, 207, 210, 212-214, 216, 219, 221-222, 224, 226-227, 230-233, 236-237, 241-243, 245, 247-250, 252-254, 258, 260-261, 265-268, 271-273, 278-279, 282-283, 285-288, 290-293, 311-315, 319, 323, 325; Canadian culture, 6, 28, 47, 78, 83, 188, 200-201, 204-205, 211, 227, 233, 239, 329n7, 335n24, 337n3, 337n5, 338n14, 368n12, 367n5, 368n12, 368n19, 371n57, 381n12, 383n44, 385n8, 385-386n17, 386n18; Chilean culture, 9, 163, 172, 174-175, 177; cultural activity, event, 48, 161, 165, 167, 170, 235, 274, 281, 312, 386n18; cultural heritage, 4, 30, 47, 50, 227, 282, 316; cultural policy, 47, 51, 64, 232; cultural practice, 5, 50-51, 125, 181, 201, 254, 266, 383n51; cultural preservation, 31-32, 44, 169; cultural product, production, 1-5, 8-11, 46, 52, 54, 71, 75, 83, 201, 283, 381n23; cultural studies, 3, 46, 62, 283; culture of exile, exile culture, 172, 174-177; dominant culture, 46, 52, 184-185; global culture, 50; Indigenous culture, 36, 39, 42, 59, 61, 347n113; Latino/Latin American culture(s), 26, 32, 35, 44, 50, 141, 179, 200, 231, 235, 240-242, 244-245, 250, 254-255, 258, 261-262, 377n126; local culture, 26-27, 32-33, 49, 51, 311; material culture, 91, 143, 164; Mexican culture, 74-75, 79-80, 136, 146, 150, 284, 347n112; Québécois culture, 49, 51-52, 55, 64, 183, 188, 233; visual culture, 7, 10, 70. *See also* Acculturation; Border; Diversity; Expression; History; Identity; Multiculturalism; Performance; Popular culture; Stereotype; Transculturation
Cuzco, 32

D
Daily Star (Windsor), 73
Dance, 107, 161-162, 169, 171, 175, 177, 182-183, 197, 266, 278, 287, 335n37, 365n34. *See also* Cueca
Darlington, William, 19
De Colores Festival of New Works, 191
Deconstruction, 10, 48, 54, 61, 289, 313, 325
Deforestation, 318
Democracy: 44, 52, 55, 57, 73, 162, 164, 285, 286, 383n50; democratization, 55

E

Eco Latino, 255-256

Ecuador, Ecuadorians, 30, 32, 37, 41-42, 113-114, 186, 188, 236

Ediciones Cordillera, 171, 174, 176, 366n4

Edmonton, 81, 164, 169, 176, 187

Education, educator, 9, 23, 27-28, 35, 50-52, 88, 114, 116, 118, 143, 154, 163, 180, 182, 196, 208, 210, 238, 261, 265-282, 286-288, 292-293, 373n1, 381n13, 382n30, 382n39, 383n51. *See also* Teacher

El Barrio, 191

El Chasqui Latino, 255

Elía, Ramón de, 45, 64, 208, 222-223, 337n1, 373n73, 373n74, 373n75

El Salvador, Salvadoreans, 35, 37-38, 48, 50, 57, 112, 114, 127, 176-177, 187-188, 203, 211, 364n26, 366n4, 376n103

El Sistema Aeolian. *See* El Sistema

El Sistema: 265-282, 381n22, 381-382n23, 382n30, 382n34, 382n36, 382n39, 383n53; OrKidstra Ottawa, 280; El Sistema Aeolian, 276-280, 282, 383n53; El Sistema effect, 274, 382n34; "El Sistema Music Revolution," 268; Sistema Toronto, 288; and foundational fiction, 267-269, 272-273; and foundational narrative, foundational story, 268, 270-271; and spiritual foundation, 269; and Venezuela, 265-266, 268, 270-277, 281-282

Emigration, emigrants, 6, 16-20, 23, 50, 207, 214-215, 223, 370n41. *See also* Immigration; Migration; Transmigration

Empanada, 162, 169-170, 172-173

England, 135, 195, 365n34

English: English language, 3, 16, 18, 28, 48, 98, 111-112, 115, 117-122, 124-128, 148, 154, 156, 164, 179, 182-183, 185, 187, 191, 199, 201-202, 208, 220-221, 229, 233, 238, 243, 248-250, 168, 280, 290-291, 295-297, 355n1, 359n5, 360n26, 367n5, 371n50, 372n63, 373n73, 383n52; English Canada, 51-52, 163, 183, 195, 198, 201-202, 233; English culture, 117, 201-202; English (of/from England), 16-17, 22, 201-202

Escuela Salvador Allende. *See* Salvador Allende School

Essex County, 88

Etcheverry, Jorge, 171, 174, 176, 207-208, 214-216, 218, 220, 366-367n4, 367n5, 367n7, 368n18, 370n44

Ethnic media. *See* Media

Ethnicity, 50, 59, 68, 111-112, 115-116, 118-121, 123, 126, 128-129, 131, 135, 140, 161, 170-172, 177, 184, 189, 200-202, 211, 213, 229-233, 235-236, 239-241, 243, 246-251, 253-254, 258, 260-261, 271, 315, 358n62, 368n19

Ethnography, 124, 133, 136-137, 216, 222, 226, 315, 319

Europe, Europeans, 6, 8-9, 15-17, 19-20, 22, 24, 28, 30, 33, 35-37, 41-42, 50, 53, 59, 71, 79, 83-84, 92, 101, 110, 112, 139, 186, 216, 232-233, 245, 271, 276, 285, 335n36, 365n33

FONCA (Fondo Nacional para la Cultura y las Artes), 315, 387-388n41
Ford, Henry, 21
Foundational fictions. *See* El Sistema
Foundational narrative, foundational story. *See* El Sistema
France, 28, 33, 80, 135, 211, 345n81, 365n34
Francophone, 51-52, 55, 111, 118-119, 221, 312, 358n62
Freedom, 88, 145, 175, 197, 283, 317. *See also* Charter of Rights and Freedoms
Free trade agreements. *See* North American Free Trade Agreement
Freire, Marlinda, 170, 174
French: French language, 3, 16, 28, 48-49, 52, 98, 111, 115, 117-119, 121, 127-128, 148, 152, 154, 156, 179-180, 182-183, 187, 201-202, 208-209, 212, 221, 233, 241, 280, 284, 295, 358n62, 360n26, 365n33, 367n5, 372n63; French Canada, French Canadian(s), 18, 51, 82, 152, 182, 201-202; French culture, 117, 152-201, 202, 212; French (of or from France), 132, 152, 180, 201-202, 212, 381n13
French Language Services Act (FLSA), 118
French West Indies, 113
Friends, friendship: 73, 83, 102, 146, 162, 166, 173, 177, 180, 197, 215, 217, 219, 222-223, 246, 272, 293, 365n31; friendliness, 35, 38, 70, 72, 152, 246, 293
Fringe Festival (Hamilton), 364n29
Fronteras Americanas/American Borders, 192, 196-197
Fundraising, 161-162, 164, 166-168, 171, 177

G
G Adventures, 25-27, 29-36, 38-39, 42-43, 334n5, 334n9, 335n24
Gablik, Suzi, 289
Gadsden Purchase, 87
García Canclini, Néstor, 46, 52-55, 200, 311-312, 325
Galeano, Eduardo, 59, 179, 189
Galería de Arte Mexicano, 77, 345n71
Gallegos, Elsa, 47
Gamelan, 278, 383n51
Gang, 37-38, 193, 197, 219, 224, 365n33
Gaos, José, 368n12
Gap Adventures. *See* G Adventures
Gatineau, 51
Gender, 27, 62-63, 88-89, 91, 133, 176, 185, 193, 199, 295
Generation, 47, 51-52, 63, 106, 118, 167, 174, 180, 185, 192, 194, 199, 201, 208, 210, 221, 224, 235, 246, 248-250, 284, 337n9
Germans, Germany, 17, 28, 33, 73, 115, 121, 126-128, 135, 245, 381n12
Gilbert, Eliza Rosana. *See* Montez, Lola
Giménez, Gilberto, 189
Giménez Micó, José Antonio, 5, 368n18
Gingras, Miki, 322

449

Global, The: 24, 32, 45, 52, 56, 59, 268, 311; global campaign, 269; global capitalism, 92; global city, 319, 325; global debate, 273; global economy, 27; global icon, 267; global movement, 280; global payment service company, 116, 123; global sense of place, 325; global society, 131, 266, 286; global south, 11, 29. *See also* Audience; Culture; Dialogue; Identity

Global Affairs Canada. *See* Department of External Affairs

Globalization, 26, 40-41, 43, 50, 55, 120, 122, 125, 180, 311-313, 316, 324

Globe, The, 17-18, 20, 22-23

Globe and Mail, The, 74, 237, 247, 275

God, 22, 96, 268-270, 281

Godoy, Patricia, 177

Gorostiza, Celestino, 82

Gould, Glenn: 265; Glenn Gould Prize, 265, 271-272, 274-275, 282, 382n36; Glenn Gould Foundation, 274-275

Governance: 19, 277; self-governance, 79; ungovernability, 323

Government, 3, 15, 16, 18-19, 23, 31, 37, 49-50, 67-68, 70, 72-74, 76, 78-79, 81-82, 88, 99, 100, 103, 108, 116-120, 123, 129, 141, 154, 161, 164, 168-169, 172, 175-176, 182, 186, 200-201, 210, 220, 232-233, 236, 252-253, 273, 276-277, 279, 286-287, 337n7, 346-347n104, 360n26, 360n1, 361n8, 361n10, 385-386n17, 386n29, 387n36, 387n37. *See also* Non-governmental organization

Granby Rubbers, 21

Great Britain, 11, 22, 72, 133, 173

Greater Mexico, 8, 86-87, 90, 94, 96, 98, 108, 110

Greater Toronto Area (GTA), 9, 229-262

Grierson, John, 73

Grigsby, A.S., 72

Gringo, 168, 202

Groundswell Festival, 194

Guadalajara, 82, 212

Guadalajara International Book Fair, FIL, 312

Guadalajara International Film Festival, 385n8

Guanajuato, 99, 102, 107

Guatemala, 31, 37, 43, 50, 113-114, 127, 211

Guyana, 114, 179

H

Haeghe, Vander, 16

Haiti, Haitians, 113, 179

Halifax, 16

Hamilton, 9, 229-232, 235, 238, 241-243, 245, 249-250, 252-262

Hamilton Fringe Festival, 364n29

Hamilton Spectator, The, 238

Harry Love, 193

Harvest pilgrims, *Harvest Pilgrims*, 85-98, 100-101, 104, 108, 110, 348n3, 349n5

I

Ibero-Americanism: 179; Universidad Iberoamericana, 286, 294

Identity: 45, 51-52, 54-56, 59, 84, 91, 111, 129, 131-132, 134-140, 142-145, 162, 167, 169, 172-176, 179-204, 212-213, 215, 218, 231, 233-234, 240, 246, 249-250, 253, 258-259, 289, 311-312, 315-316, 318, 325, 365n34, 367n5; Chicano identity, 184; Chilean identity, 172, 174-175; class identity, 182; collective identity, 122, 129-130, 175, 216, 218-219, 225, 229; conceptual identity, 215; cultural identity, 43, 122, 129, 136, 195, 230, 262, 311-312, 325; ethnic identity, 111, 120-121, 233, 258; French Canadian identity, 182; global identity, 315, 323; gregarious identity, 215; group identity, 165, 173; Hispanic identity, 253; identity (re)building, construction, creation, 45, 60, 180, 182, 240, 247, 250-251, 261, 313; identity crisis, 137; identity marker, 181-183, 194, 198; identity politics, 135, 195; identity reciprocity, 311-325; inherited identity, 179; Latino, Latin American identity, 9, 46, 176, 179-204, 230, 240, 249-252, 259, 261; linguistic identity, 51; living identity, 179; Mexican identity, 9, 143; national identity, 9, 139-140, 142, 162, 167, 173-175, 180, 183, 212, 311, 313, 315, 341n10; personal, individual identity, 163, 180, 293; urban identity, 319

Illegal: armed group, 37; drug trafficking, 37; (im)migrants, 87, 101, 103, 107, 183-184, 203; writing, 285

Illich, Ivan, 285, 287, 288, 289, 291

Illustration, 164

Imagery, 86, 93, 313

Imaginary: 53, 54, 313, 317; geography, 3; letter, 85; map, 56; space, 254; reality, 290; community, 230, 254, 256; artistic imaginary, 59; cultural and linguistic imaginary, 8, 141; national imaginary, 10, 325; Québécois imaginary, 55; social imaginary, 52. See also Border

Imagined community, 139, 230-231, 234-235, 248, 251, 252, 257, 261, 272, 381-382n23

Immigration, immigrants: 5, 7, 9, 15-20, 23-24, 45-48, 50-52, 54, 83, 88, 91-92, 101-102, 111-115, 117-118, 122, 125, 130-140, 142-143, 146-147, 150, 156, 163, 165, 168, 175, 183-184, 186-187, 189, 198, 200-208, 210-211, 213-216, 218-227, 229, 231-233, 236-237, 239, 241, 248-250, 252, 254-255, 259-260; Latino, Latin American immigration, immigrants, 50, 186-187, 190, 200, 203-204, 236, 239, 241, 249, 252, 255-257, 259. See also Emigration; Migration; Transmigration

Inca Trail, 31-32

Inclusion, 5, 47, 53, 64, 84, 88, 101, 108, 122, 208, 217, 230, 266, 268, 273, 275, 367n7

Independence: 181, 272, 329n1; Mexican independence, 83, 96, 385n8; post-independence, 212, 269, 272

Indigeneity: 16, 30, 36, 41-43, 45, 48-49, 54, 59-61, 181, 231, 271, 287, 334n3, 337n8; Indigenous culture, 36, 41-42, 59, 61, 83, 347n113; Indigenous art, artist, craft, 36, 49, 60, 81-82, 337n9. See also Aboriginality; First Nations; Inuit; Métis; Native

Indiscipline, 283, 285-286, 288
Inequity, 162
Injustice. *See* Justice
Innovation, innovator, 16, 32, 57, 191, 266
Insider, 8, 65, 136, 141-142, 199, 324, 331n28. *See also* Outsider
Installation, 49, 60-63, 134, 285, 288, 292, 299, 302, 312-313, 315-316, 342n18, 385n9
Instituto Nacional de Bellas Artes (INBA), 68, 81-82,
Institution, (de)institutionalization, 3, 64, 67, 70-72, 77-80, 82, 117-118, 120-121, 124, 126, 129, 141, 187-188, 233-234, 253, 268, 270, 283, 286-288, 291-292, 309, 311, 323, 348n120, 385n8, 385-386n17, 386n18
Inter-American Development Bank, 31
Interculturalism, 37, 51-53, 64, 143, 189, 221, 227, 232-233, 288, 291
Inter-Departmental Committee on Canadian Publicity in Latin America, 76
Interdiscursivity, 207, 212, 224
Interdisciplinarity, interdisciplinary, 206, 283, 286, 293. *See also* Indiscipline
Integration, 42, 46, 50-53, 55, 57, 61, 64, 68, 76, 101, 118, 127, 142, 146, 148, 150, 170, 176, 182, 185, 202-203, 208, 210, 212, 224-225, 227, 229, 231-233, 246, 249-250, 256-257, 261, 276, 280, 311-312. *See also* Adaptation
International solidarity network, 211
International Book Fair in Mexico City, 76, 80
Internet, 237, 243, 248, 255-256, 259, 267-268
Interview, 17, 27, 45-46, 89, 92, 99, 123-124, 126, 135-138, 143-144, 146, 163-164, 168-170, 177, 188, 190, 229-231, 235-236, 239-241, 244, 251-252, 255, 258, 359n5, 359n21, 359n23
Inti-Illimani, 166
Intrepid Travel, 26-27, 29-30, 32-33, 40, 42, 335n24
Inuit, 60, 82
Ireland, Irish, 365n34
Italy, Italians, 16, 28, 73, 85, 91-93, 115, 121, 126-127, 177, 237, 244-245, 254, 348n1, 381n12

J
Jackson, A.Y., 77
Jamaica, Jamaicans, 88, 112, 355n78
Japan, Japanese, 84, 93, 115, 135, 185
Jesuits, Society of Jesus, 42, 181, 269-271, 381n13
Jornada, La, 243, 255
Journalism, journalist, 16, 85, 163, 208, 230, 235, 237-240, 243-244, 246-248, 255, 270, 372n63, 374n39, 376n117
Junge-Hammersley, Anita, 208, 217-218, 222, 227, 371n49
Junta, 164, 361n9
Justice: 18, 174-175, 182; injustice, 30, 176, 182, 287; social justice, 92, 133, 177, 253, 266, 268, 270

K

Kahlo, Frida, 71, 315
Keenleyside, H.K., 74

L

Labour, labourer, 16-17, 51, 86-87, 89, 92, 99, 102, 108, 110, 113-114,
    142, 148, 186, 210, 232, 246, 269, 337n7
Land, 261-264, 270, 272
Landscape: 1, 33, 36, 37, 38, 44, 67, 75, 80, 86, 132, 142, 189, 221, 229,
    272, 276, 291, 313, 316-320, 322-324; urban landscape, 315, 320. *See
    also* Linguistic landscape
Language: 3, 5-6, 9-10, 27, 46, 55, 64, 68, 85, 92, 99, 101, 104, 111-113,
    115-130, 143, 162, 164-166, 169, 171, 174, 176, 178-185, 187, 201-
    202, 210, 213, 220-222, 224, 226-227, 233-235, 243, 245-246, 248-
    250, 256, 258-260, 272, 283-284, 288, 290, 299, 304-305, 309, 355n1,
    362n16, 362n17, 366n3, 366n4, 367n5, 368n12, 368n19, 370n47,
    371n57, 383n1, 386n19; language policy, 117-119, 123; minority lan-
    guage, 111, 115-117, 121, 126-127; (non-)official language, 98, 111,
    115, 117, 121, 123-124, 126-129, 205, 225, 233, 366n3, 368n19
Latina/o Canadian Theatre and Performance, 189, 194
Latin America, Latin Americans, 2-11, 24-29, 31-32, 35-37, 39-41, 43-51,
    53-57, 59, 61, 69-70, 73-74, 76, 84, 110-115, 123-130, 140-141, 152,
    162-167, 170-171, 176, 179-181, 183-192, 194-195, 197-200, 202-
    204, 209, 212, 222, 227, 229-235, 238-245, 248-254, 256-258, 260-
    261, 265, 267-268, 271-272, 274-276, 278, 280-282, 293, 312, 320,
    329n1, 330n9, 330n22, 335n24, 335n36, 335n37, 338n18, 348n120,
    348n1, 352n28, 364n18, 364n22, 366n4, 371n50, 376n108, 380n1,
    364n18, 386n18. *See also* Art, Diaspora; Literature; Newspaper; Plays;
    Theatre.
LatinArte, LatinArte festival, 48, 337n5
Latinas, Latinos, Latinx: 7, 51, 193-194, 196, 198-200, 203, 229-232, 235-
    236, 239-262, 376n106, 377n129; Latino Galas, 242
Latinidad, Latino-ness, 9, 180, 193, 198, 204, 255
Latino (terminology), 209-210, 230, 250-251, 253, 257, 369n20
Latinocanadá (Hazelton), 187, 189, 367n9, 368n18
Latino Canada, Latino-Canadians, 192, 194, 199, 229, 239-241, 243, 250,
    262
Latino, Latin American community, 50-51, 129, 167, 190, 195, 230-232,
    235-237, 240, 242-245, 248, 253, 256, 259, 261
"Latino of the Year," 242, 376n109
Latino-Hispanic studies, 7
Latino population, 188, 196, 235, 242, 258
"Latinos of the North," 312
Latino Youth Initiative, 191
Lau, Manuel, 47
Lead Wave, 186

454

Leamington, 101, 112, 114-118, 123-128, 130, 354n62
Legalization, 320
Leija, Ana Lorena, 190, 199-200, 366n50
Lepage, Robert, 183
Lerma, Víctor, 291
Linguistic landscape (LL), 9, 111-130, 355n1
Literature: 3, 5-7, 27, 51, 86, 88-89, 123, 152, 162, 166, 171, 174, 176, 181,
    185, 189, 192, 205-214, 218, 221, 224, 227, 231, 257, 265, 267-268,
    274, 285-286, 330n11, 330n15, 338n19, 366-367n4, 367n5, 367n9,
    368n11, 368n18, 368n19, 370n44, 371n57, 372n63, 380n1, 386n17;
    exile literature, 213; Hispano-Canadian literature, 205-227, 366-367n4,
    367n7, 367n9, 368n11, 370n44; Latino, Latin American literature, 176,
    189, 209, 212; 371n50
Local city, 325
Loi 101. *See* Bill 101
London (England), 347n105
London (Ontario), Londoners, 81, 102, 221, 276, 277, 278, 280, 306
Loyola, Ignatius, 269-270, 381n13
Lyotard, Jean-François, 289

M
Macias, Pilar, 47
Mackenzie, Alexander, 21
MacKinnon, J.A., 74
Maclean, Allan, 18-19
Madoff, Steven H., 291
Mainstream, 191-192, 202, 204, 267. *See also* Media
Malleability, 139, 184
Manitoba (MB), 114, 275
March. *See* Demonstration
Marginalization, 54, 161, 168, 196, 203, 267, 324, 348n1
Martin Franco, Helena, 48
Mata, Fernando, 186
Maya, 42
Maya Anda, Alejandro, 47
Mayer, Mónica, 291
McLean, J.S., 77-78
McConachie, G.W.G., 81
McCurry, H.O., 72, 74, 77-80
McTavish, John, 230, 238, 241-246, 249-252, 255-258, 260-261, 376n101,
    376n103, 376n104, 376n105, 376n106, 376n108, 376n109, 376n110,
    376n111, 376n112, 376n114, 376n117, 376n124, 377n125, 377n126,
    377n128, 377n129, 377n130, 377n132, 377n135, 377n140, 380n228
Media: 1, 4, 7, 16, 17, 21, 27, 38, 58, 62, 76, 89, 139, 163, 169, 170, 183,
    229-262, 282, 286, 313, 315, 351n22, 371n57, 376n104, 376n105,

385-386n17, 386n18; Canadian media, 37-38, 239, 243, 257; ethnic media, 229-262; Latino media, 229-230, 243, 259, 260-262; mainstream media, 147, 240, 243-244, 246-249, 251, 259, 261; mass media, 45, 265, 281; social media, 31, 273. *See also* Print media

Median, median strip, 313, 316-322, 324

Mediator, 132, 214, 270

Megalopolis, 315, 319, 321, 323, 324

Melbourne, 30

Memorias del fuego (Galeano), 59

Memory, 46, 49, 55-56, 59-62, 64, 139, 192, 215, 217-218, 221-222, 225-227, 266, 324. *See also* Commemoration

Métis, 60, 199

Metropolis, 220, 316, 323-324,

Mexican-American War, 87

Mexican art. *See* Art

Mexican Arts, 341-342n12

Mexican Art Today, 70, 72-78, 80

Mexico, Mexicans, 8-10, 26, 28-29, 36, 38, 41-42, 47-48, 50-51, 56, 62, 67-94, 96-110, 112-116, 124, 127, 129, 131, 134-141, 143-157, 170, 180, 183-184, 186, 188, 190, 193-194, 199-200, 202-203, 212, 220, 245, 252, 254, 257, 278-279, 284, 286-288, 291, 293, 295, 297, 300, 302-303, 305-306, 311-312, 315-317, 319, 321, 325, 330n9, 337n3, 337n7, 338n14, 338n15, 338-339n19, 340n44, 341n5, 341n6, 341n10, 341n12, 342n13, 342n18, 343n36, 344n52, 345n71, 345n73, 345n78, 345n81, 346n99, 346n104, 347n105, 347n112, 347n113, 348n3, 349n7, 349n9, 349n10, 349n12, 350n14, 352n25, 353n39, 353n40, 353n43, 353n48, 354n50, 354n51, 354n64, 355n78, 359n5, 359n21, 360n24, 360n25, 360n26, 365n33, 385n8, 385n17, 386n26, 386n27, 386n29, 387n36, 387n37, 387-388n41. *See also* Greater Mexico; Mexico City; Mexican Temporary Agricultural Workers

Mexican Contemporary Paintings. See Painting

Mexican Revolution, 71-72, 386n29

Mexican Temporary Agricultural Workers (MTAW), 115-116, 124-126, 128-130

Mexico City, 10, 49, 63, 71, 76-77, 81-82, 85, 88-99, 101-102, 141, 148, 150, 154, 188, 278-279, 283, 291, 294, 296, 300-303, 308, 313, 315-317, 320, 323, 337n7, 340n44, 354n51, 354n55, 355n1, 385n9, 386n17, 386n27, 387n36, 387n37, 387n41, 388n42

Mexico Tourism Board, 27, 29, 38

Migration, migrants, 7-8, 20, 50, 85-86, 88-89, 91, 94, 96, 101, 104, 106, 110-111, 113, 122, 124-126, 130, 132, 137-138, 142-144, 146-148, 150, 152, 154, 156, 167, 175, 205, 206-209, 211-214, 223-224, 227, 237, 252. *See also* Emigration; Immigration; Transmigration

Military: alliance, 80; dictatorship, 161, 168, 175; leader, 162; regime, 162, 164, 166-167, 171-172, 174-177; repression, 169; rule, 161; takeover, 168. *See also* Paramilitary

197, 205, 219-220, 238, 243, 246, 265-282, 287, 290, 309, 330n15, 360n25, 381n22, 382n30, 382n39, 383n49, 383n50, 383n51, 383n53, 385-386n17; music education, 9, 265-282, 382n30, 382n39, 383n51

Mussolini, 73

N

NAFTA. *See* North American Free Trade Agreement

Narrative: 3, 5, 8, 62, 75, 92, 99, 133, 136, 185, 187, 252, 267, 268-269, 273, 290, 311, 317, 319, 324; colonial narrative, 83; immigrant narrative, 132; national narrative, 84, 139, 347n113; personal narrative, 137; short narrative, 99, 205-227. *See also* Short story

Nation, nationalism, nationality: 3-4, 6-7, 33, 38, 40, 46, 50, 53, 55, 69-70, 72-75, 83, 132-133, 139-140, 144, 163, 165, 179, 184, 188, 199, 207-208, 214-216, 229, 234-235, 247, 252-254, 257-258, 267, 271-272, 279, 293, 311-313, 381-382n23, 331n28, 335n36, 338n15; Latin American nation, nationalism, nationality, 40, 48, 73, 163, 176, 234, 253; Metis Nations, 199; musical nationalism, 272; nation-building, 267, 272; *nationem*, 139; nationhood, nation-ness, 5, 235; nation state, 87, 110, 232, 329n1; pan-nationalism, 165; Spanish-speaking nationality, 257; third nation, 54. *See also* Border; Denationalization; First Nations; Identity; Imaginary; Internationalism; Narrative; Patriotism; Tourism; Tradition; Transnationalism

National anthem, 96, 173

National Day (Chile), 174, 176

National Film Board of Canada (NFB), 76

National Fund for Culture and the Arts. *See* FONCA

National Gallery of Canada (NGC), 67, 68, 70-72, 74, 76-84

National Gallery of Canada Archives (NGCA), 70, 342n18, 346-347n104

National Museum of Canada, 82

National Museum of Women in Art, 340n1

National Post, The, 247

Native, 8, 32, 139-140, 181, 184, 201, 203, 221-222. *See also* Indigeneity

Native country, native land, 187, 207, 218, 237, 248. *See also* Birth country; Homeland; Motherland; Origin.

Negotiation, 4, 33, 52, 54-55, 64, 68, 79-80, 132, 134-136, 181, 281

Neocolonialism, 8, 13, 43, 54. *See also* Colonialism; Postcolonialism; Recolonization

Neo-expressionism, 59

Neoliberalism, 87, 108, 110, 175, 319, 323

Neruda, Pablo: 173, 193; Centro Pablo Neruda, 169

Network, 30, 101-102, 165-166, 169, 196, 230, 253, 270-272, 274, 280, 293, 341n2, 360n26, 385-386n17. *See also* Social network

New Brunswick, 114, 275, 280

Newcomer, new arrival, 131-132, 162-165, 168, 172, 175-176, 180, 199, 201, 204, 214, 280, 287

New Mexico, 67, 98
New Spain, 87, 181, 353n49
Newspaper: 8-9, 15-25, 89, 93, 229-262, 291-292, 300-301, 333n31,
376n105, 377n129, 381-382n23; Latino newspaper, 229-262. *See also*
Correo Canadiense; *Presencia Latina*
New York, 17, 22, 30, 73, 92, 164, 288, 387n35
New York Times, 270, 273
Niagara, Niagara Region, 9, 88, 229-262, 349n12, 352n24, 376n106
Niagara College, 231, 241, 256
Niagara Historical Museum, 238
Niagara-on-the-Lake, 231, 238
Nicaragua, Nicaraguans, 31, 37-39, 50, 113-114, 176, 186, 208, 219,
371n57
"Noble Savage" myth, 42
Non-governmental organization (NGO): 31, 72, 124, 126, 178; interna-
tional NGO, 131
North America, North Americans, 8, 23, 30-31, 48, 51, 67-69, 73-74, 76,
86, 88, 116, 152, 188, 193-194, 197, 216, 218, 232, 257, 268, 272, 275,
277, 279-280, 311-312
North American Congress on Latin America-Archive of Latin Americana
(NACLA-ALA), 164, 361n10
North American Free Trade Agreement (NAFTA), 68, 87, 311, 329n9, n6,
341n18
Norton Gunsaulus, Edwin, 22
Nostalgia, 33, 54, 138, 180, 187, 197, 204, 213
Not-for-profit, 191, 279
Núcleo (El Sistema music-education centre), 266, 270
Nuestra Palabra (contest), 209, 220, 370n41, 370n44, 370n47. *See also*
Cuentos de nuestra palabra
Nueva Voz, 191
Nunavut, 275
Núñez, Mariló, 191-194, 201, 364n29, 364n30

O
Official language, 98, 111, 115, 124, 127, 129, 130, 205, 225, 233, 366n3,
368n19
Official Languages Act (OLA), 117
Ogilvie, Will A., 77
Ontario, 16, 21-22, 76, 80-81, 85-90, 92-93, 95-97, 100, 103-110, 112-
115, 117-118, 125, 127-128, 142, 163-164, 169, 181, 187, 191, 199-
200, 202, 219, 232-233, 235, 238, 260, 265, 271, 274-278, 280, 282,
331n27, 350n16, 351n22, 380n1
Ontario Health Insurance Plan (OHIP), 103-104
Optical illusion, 316, 319, 325
Orchestra, 265-266, 268, 270-272, 274-275, 277-279, 281, 382n36,
383n50

Order of United Workmen. *See* Canadian Order of United Workmen
Orientation, disorientation, reorientation, 1, 47, 116, 123, 133, 138, 164, 168-169, 172, 207, 250, 287. *See also Miss Orient(ed)*
Origin: country of origin, 113, 135, 162, 167, 173, 180, 207, 211, 213, 215, 222-223, 250; place of origin, 129, 156, 213; society of origin, 206. *See also* Birth country; Homeland; Motherland; Native country
OrKidstra Ottawa. *See El Sistema*
Orquestas y Coros Juveniles de México AC, 279
Ortiz-Apuy, Juan, 48
Ottawa, 16, 70-72, 74, 80, 82-83, 118, 163, 171, 176, 187, 208, 216, 222, 248-249, 255-256
Ottawa Chilean Association. *See* Association
Ottawa Citizen, 73, 75
Ottawa Journal, 17, 70
Outdoor Life Network, 30
Outsider, 8, 42, 65, 126, 136, 142, 324, 331n28. *See also* Insider

P
Painting, painter: 47-48, 67, 71, 76, 80-83, 93-94, 105, 162, 197, 223, 255, 303, 305, 324, 337n3; Canadian painting, 77; *ex-voto* painting, 86, 93-94, 102, 105, 108, 354n51; *Mexican Contemporary Paintings*, 77, 345n73; Mexican painting, 71, 76-78, 80-81, 345n73
Palma, Julian, 47
Panama, 42, 113-114, 241, 376n104
Pan-Americanism, 272. *See also Festival Rutas Panamericanas/Panamerican Routes*
Pará, 20-21, 333n31
Paraguay, 37, 42, 113-114
Paramilitary, 337n7. *See also* Military
Paris, 79, 278, 345n81, 347n105
Park, 42, 120, 313, 316, 319-320
Partnership, 30-31, 70, 238, 279-280, 311, 382n39
Party (social): 35, 148, 162, 171, 221, 283, 288; political party, 141, 166, 168, 171, 173, 177, 285, 360n26
Patriotism, 96, 106, 144, 162, 214
Pauchi, Delfín, 30, 32, 335n26
Peasant, 42, 99, 184, 286-287, 291, 293. *See also* Federation of Socialist Peasant Students of Mexico (FECSM)
Peña, 162, 164, 169-171, 173, 177
Peru, Peruvians, 30-32, 37, 50, 74, 112-114, 208-209, 211, 219, 338n14, 371n54
Performance, performer, 7, 9, 11, 49, 61, 63, 163-164, 166, 171-172, 182-184, 191-192, 194, 200, 202-203, 266-267, 269, 276-279, 281, 285-286, 292-293, 331n29, 382n34; cultural performance, 161-162; performance of subordination, 89; performance studies, 265-266; puppet

performance, 278; public performance, 163, 277-278; performative, 10, 139. *See also* Art; Drama; *Chilenidad*; *Latina/o Canadian Theatre and Performance*; Race; Rehearsal; Theatre

Pernambuco, 22

Philadelphia Museum of Art, 71

Photography, photographer, 8-9, 28, 36, 40, 67, 70-71, 81, 85-110, 124, 131-157, 162, 235, 256, 292, 300-301, 313-322, 325, 348n3, 345n5, 352n26, 352n28, 353n38, 353n41, 354n62, 359n5, 360n25, 371n57, 385n9, 386n18, 386n22

Pietropaolo, Vincenzo, 85-110, 348n1, 348n3, 349n4, 353n41

Pimpilala, 30

Pinochet, Augusto, 173, 371n50

Pinto mi raya, 291, 293

Plays, playwright: 182-184, 187-194, 196-198, 200-202, 204, 373n76; Aboriginal playwright, 184; Chilean playwright, 192; Korean playwright, 185; Latino/a, Latin American plays, playwright, 188, 190-192, 194. *See also* Drama; Theatre

Poem, poetics, poetry, poet, 4, 10, 62, 162, 170-172, 176, 187, 206-208, 210, 220, 324, 350n15, 366n4, 368n11, 370n44, 371n49, 371n50, 371n57, 372n63, 373n73, 385n8

Political correctness, 37, 240, 313

Politics: 7, 56, 71-72, 134-135, 138, 171, 195, 210, 273; political goals, 69, 161-178; political message, 163-164, 166, 172, 293; political prisoner, 161-162, 166, 170, 177, 360n1, 362n16. *See also* Activism; Exchange; Exile; Refugee; Violence

Popular culture, 91, 139, 141, 170, 270, 277, 288, 290

Portugal, Portuguese, 17, 24, 115, 126-127, 169, 179-180, 209, 244

Postcolonialism, 8, 46, 53-55, 62, 271. *See also* Colonialism; Neocolonialism; Re-colonization

Poster, 30, 119, 164, 170, 288

Postmodernism, 63

Pozo, José del, 164-165, 169-170, 174, 176-177, 362n16

Pre-text, 207

Presencia Latina, 230-231, 235, 237, 241-243, 245-247, 250, 254, 256, 261, 376n112, 377n130

Presse, La, 16

Print media: 231, 234, 247-249, 251-252, 257-259; ethnic print media, 231, 241, 247, 249, 253-254, 258, 261; Latino print media, 229-230, 255, 259-261; non-print media, 273; Spanish-language print media, 258-259

Protest. *See* Demonstration

Psychiatry, psychiatrist, 167, 172-174

Public Library and Art Museum (London, Ontario), 81

Puerto Rico, Puerto Ricans, 13, 286, 288

Pujol, Ernesto, 286-289, 291

Q
Quebec (province), *Québécois*, Quebecers/Quebeckers, 16, 45-57, 63-64, 76, 113-114, 118-120, 123, 125, 127, 132, 134, 143, 146, 152, 163-165, 169-170, 174, 176, 183, 188, 198, 202, 232-233, 240, 271, 255, 275, 312-313, 315, 331n27, 337n3, 337n9, 338n14, 338n15, 338n18, 359n5, 360n24, 360n26, 360n1, 372n63, 385n8, 385n9, 385-386n17, 387-388n41
Quebec City, 51, 169, 176, 190, 232, 338n18
Quebec International Book Fair (*Salon international du livre de Québec*), 385n8
Quilapayún, 166

R
Race: 15, 24, 27, 91, 118, 133, 135-136, 139, 143-144, 215, 233, 251; anti-racism, 117; performance of race, 136; racism, 8, 75, 89, 143-145, 193-194, 351n19, 365n33
Radio, 156, 229, 238, 241-242, 252, 256, 259, 376n105. *See also Société Radio-Canada*
Ramírez Castillo, Osvaldo, 46-49, 57-59
Ramos, Víctor, 180
Reappropriation. *See* Appropriation
Reciprocity, 69, 78-79, 82-84, 311-325, 345n79, 385-386n17
Recognition, 9, 43, 52-57, 59-60, 80, 87, 92, 106, 110, 133, 144-146, 181, 189, 194-195, 197, 199, 205-206, 209, 231, 236, 240, 258, 260, 265, 272, 274, 276, 281, 289, 312, 316, 320, 337-338n12, 349n7, 371n54, 376n111, 382n34
Re-colonization, 194. *See also* Colonialism; Neocolonialism; Postcolonialism
Reconquista, La (Cisneros), 49, 59-61
Reconstruction, 48, 57, 63, 91, 169, 173, 289, 313, 386n29
Recycling, 156, 320-321
Refugee: 50, 131, 154, 168, 176, 180, 186, 190, 205, 211, 231, 338n15, 369n25, 376n103; political refugee, 186, 208, 225, 366n2
Refugee Hotel, The, 190-191
Regime, 50, 134, 138, 161-162, 164, 166-168, 171-177, 186, 371n50
Rehearsal, 192, 200, 268, 279. *See also* Performance
Rejection, 4, 30, 33, 139, 172, 203, 223, 287, 289, 335n36
Relation, relationship: 1-3, 5-7, 15, 26-28, 41, 43, 46-47, 51-53, 55, 57, 60, 64, 68-69, 70, 72-73, 75, 77, 79-81, 84, 89, 134, 136, 142-144, 148, 154, 163, 166, 188, 197-198, 212, 220-221, 224, 226, 246, 254, 259, 261, 266-267, 271, 273, 276, 283, 290, 293, 312, 317, 323, 325, 330n9, 342n18, 385-386n17; bilateral, 68, 79, 81-82; Canada-Mexico, 10, 69-70; Canadian-Latin American, 1-11; cultural, 50-51, 69, 80, 82, 227, 272, 313, 325; diplomatic, 73; economic, 69, 95, 218, 311; family, 187; international, 6-7; political, 210, 218; power, 25, 293; public, 38, 244; social, 85, 91, 110, 134, 214; state, 68, 77-78; trade, 7, 70; transnational, 224, 226

Religion, 3, 6, 61, 68, 71, 86, 93, 96, 116, 120, 123, 126, 131, 140, 143, 150, 168, 179, 181, 216, 246, 252, 269-270, 283, 295, 370-371n48, 381n13
Relocation, 48, 167, 171
Representation: 2, 15-24, 25-44, 45-64, 70, 75-77, 84, 91, 111-112, 129, 208, 212, 214-216, 218-219, 221, 224-226, 230, 260, 315, 319, 324; misrepresentation, 230, 246, 247; underrepresentation, 230, 246, 247, 260
Repression, 49, 145, 161-162, 169, 174, 176-177, 211
Residency, 15, 47, 100, 150, 154, 164, 237, 260, 355n78. *See also* Artistic residency
Resistance, 59, 71, 133, 135, 144, 233, 293, 360n26
Retablo, retablero, 86, 93-94, 96, 98-99, 101, 103-105, 107, 353n49, 354n51
Reterritorialization, 311
Retrato de una nube, 206, 209
Revolution, 19, 39-40, 44, 71-72, 94, 141, 168-169, 268, 271-273, 318, 365n33, 386n29
Rights: 22, 108, 117, 126, 156, 164, 194, 210, 233, 287; Charter of Rights and Freedoms, 117; civil rights, 253; human rights, 37, 53, 131, 162, 164-165, 371n57; Latino rights, 194
Río Churubusco (Bodmer), 317-318, 386-387n30
Rio de Janeiro, 16-17, 21-23, 368n18
Rivera, Diego, 71, 76, 80, 315
Rivera, Isidro Rosas, 99
Rivera, Nidia, 170
Roberts, Goodridge, 77
Rodrigues Alves, Francisco de Paula, 23
Rodríguez, Carmen, 208, 217-218, 371n50
Rojas-Benavente, Lady, 368n18
Rojas, Carlos, 47
Rojas-Primus, Constanza, 208, 216
Roof, rooftop, 40, 105, 313, 323-324
Rules of disorder, 323

S
Saint-Rémi, 125-126, 358n62
Salas, Andrés, 47
Santa Fe Museum of Fine Arts, 340n1
Santiago de Chile, 163, 171, 217, 222
São Paulo, 8, 15-18, 21-23
Salmen, Walter, 266, 281
Salon international du livre de Québec. See Quebec International Book Fair
Salvador Allende School, 169, 174
Salvadoreans. *See* El Salvador
Saravia, Alejandro, 208, 213, 220-224, 226-227, 372n63, 372n64
Saskatchewan, 114, 275, 366n4, 368n18

Saskatoon, 366n4
Schmidt, Francisco, 17
Seasonal agricultural worker: 8; Canadian Seasonal Agricultural Workers
    Program (CSAWP, SAWP), 9, 86-91, 98-100, 102, 104, 106, 108, 110,
    112, 114, 349n9, 349n10, 350n14, 352n26
Seattle Art Museum, 340-341n1
Self-governance. *See* Governance
Self-identification, self-naming, 2, 136, 161, 163, 195-196, 203, 208, 215,
    226, 253
Separation, separateness, 4, 7-9, 51, 57, 75, 105-106, 134, 137, 162, 166-
    167, 207, 220, 252, 261, 273, 324
Service aesthetics, 291
Shaw Festival, 196, 202
Short story, 9, 205-209, 213-216, 218-225, 227, 367n7, 367n8, 368n11,
    370n41, 370n44, 370n47, 371n49, 371n50, 371n54, 371n57, 372n63,
    373n73, 373n76. *See also* Narrative
Simalchik, Joan, 164-165, 167, 169-170, 173-174
Simcoe County, 88
Simón Bolívar Youth Orchestra, 272, 274
Simon Fraser University, 371n50
Skilled labour, labourer, worker. *See* Labour
Soccer, 149-150, 170, 175, 236, 287, 324
Social discourse. *See* Discourse
Social justice. *See* Justice
Social intervention, 292
Social network, 218, 248
Société Radio-Canada (SRC), 239
Society: 27, 33, 44-45, 47, 50-53, 59, 63, 71, 88, 93, 122, 130-131, 136,
    139-141, 145, 148, 156, 163, 165, 167, 170, 173-174, 180, 202-203,
    205-208, 212-216, 218-221, 224-227, 231-233, 237, 246, 248, 250,
    253-254, 258-260, 265-267, 269-270, 273, 284-286, 314, 324, 359n21,
    368n12; Canadian society, 9-10, 85, 88, 91, 93, 100-101, 117, 144, 150,
    165, 205, 208, 210, 218, 220-221, 223-224, 226, 229, 231, 233, 258,
    260, 329n7; Chilean society, 172, 174; Toronto Chilean Society, 168-
    171
Society of Jesus. *See* Jesuits
Sociocriticism, 207-208, 211-212, 214, 219, 224
Sociology of music, 265-266
Socio-text, 208
Solidarity: 5, 92, 161-162, 164, 166-173, 175-177, 211, 253, 360n26,
    360n1, 361n9, 361n10, 362n16; International Solidarity Movement,
    166; solidarity campaign, 162, 164, 171, 176
Sommer, Doris, 267
Song, singing, 96, 171, 173, 182, 219, 278, 289
Sonora, 48, 365n33
Sottolichio, Rafael, 47

Three Fingered Jack and the Legend of Joaquin Murieta (Nuñez), 192-195

Tianguis, 321-322

Tonnancour, Jacques de, 77

Toronto, Torontonian, 9, 16, 18, 21-22, 30, 41, 48, 50, 70, 73-74, 77-78, 80-81, 91-93, 97-98, 108, 111, 113, 125, 163, 168-171, 173-174, 177, 181, 187, 190-191, 195, 198-200, 202, 208, 219-221, 223, 230-232, 235-239, 241, 243, 247, 254-255, 257, 260-261, 265, 274-275, 280, 298-299, 306

Toronto Star, The, 18

Toronto Sun, The, 247

Torres, Carlos, 170, 176, 360n1, 366-367n4

Torres-García, Joaquín, 1-3, 11

Torres, José Luis, 47, 214, 368n18

Torres-Recinos, Julio, 206, 209, 367n7, 368n18

Tourism, tourists: 8, 25-44, 113, 121-122, 125, 334n3, 381n12; community tourism, 26, 31; cultural, 26, 41; national, 36-39, 44; international, 29, 38. *See also* Travel

Tradition: 32, 41, 44, 55-56, 63, 87, 139, 143, 146, 150, 176, 180, 182, 185, 191-192, 196, 198, 201, 203, 267, 305, 312, 334n3, 360n25, 381n13; cultural tradition, 42, 198; Latin-American tradition, 4, 10, 55; national tradition, 100, 162, 172; religious tradition, 61, 93; theatre, theatrical tradition, 183, 194-196, 202-203

Transculturation, 5, 56

Translation, translator, 46, 119, 137, 164, 169, 178, 181, 183, 188, 199, 208, 211, 241, 268, 274, 283-285, 290, 297, 299, 330n11, 365n33, 366-367n4, 371n50, 373n73, 373n76

Translocality, 208, 212, 218

Transmigration, transmigrants, 311. *See also* Emigration; Immigration; Migration

Transmission tower, 316, 322, 324

Transnationalism, 1, 4-5, 7, 45-46, 50, 53, 57, 63-64, 67, 85-87, 89, 91, 96, 106, 108, 110, 164-166, 184, 195, 208, 212, 218, 224, 226, 312

Transterramiento, 207, 368n12

Trauma, 162, 172-173

Travel, traveller, 8-9, 25, 27-33, 37-44, 49, 70, 80-82, 84, 92, 98-99, 101, 103, 135-137, 183, 186, 188, 192, 200, 256, 319, 334n9, 335n24, 347n105, 365n33, 381n13, 385-386n17. *See also* Tourism

Travel Cuts, 25, 27, 29, 40, 42, 335n24, 335n26

Tree, 17, 61, 87, 104, 219-220, 222, 227, 295, 313, 315-317, 319, 324

Trois-Rivières, 51

Tucker, Arnold, 77

Tunstall, Tricia, 268-269, 271, 273, 381n12, 381n22

Tusovka, tusovchik, tusovkian, 284-289, 291, 293, 298-299

U

Ungovernability. *See* Governance

Unidad Popular (UP), 161, 164, 166, 168-169, 171, 174

United Nations (UN), 356n16

United States (U.S.), 6, 8, 20, 29, 50-51, 53, 67-73, 86-88, 92, 94, 98-103, 105-108, 183, 193-194, 203, 210, 229-230, 232, 239, 248-253, 258-260, 262, 272, 286, 291, 312, 338-339n19, 340n1, 341-342n12, 343n29, 344n52, 345n71, 349n7, 353n41, 369n20, 383n51

Universidad Iberoamericana. *See* Ibero-Americanism

Université du Québec à Montréal, University of Quebec at Montreal (UQÀM), 49, 385n9,

Université de Montréal, 370n44, 372n63

University of Quebec in Montreal (UQÀM), 385n9

University of Toronto, 190, 361n8, 383n51

Unskilled labourer. *See* Labour

Urbanism, urbanization: 92, 290, 317-318, 320, 324; self-urbanization, 320-321; urban centre, 70, 280, 331n27; urban space, 311, 313, 316, 319, 323. *See also* Landscape

Uruchurtu, Ernesto P., 317-318

Uruguay, Uruguayans, 1, 36-37, 50, 113-114, 177, 186-187, 211

V

Valle-Garay, Pastor, 208, 219-220, 371n57

Van Bolderen, Trish, 206, 367n9, 368n11

Vancouver, 27, 30, 48, 50, 67, 72, 81, 83, 111, 113, 125, 165, 187, 208, 217, 280, 340-341n1, 370n47, 371n51

Vancouver Art Gallery, 72, 81, 340-341n1

Van der Wens, C.H., 23

Velez, Freddy, 230-231, 235-241, 248-252, 255-258, 261, 374n39, 375n40, 375n41, 375n43

Vélez Storey, Jaime, 91

Venezuela, Venezuelans, 35, 42, 113-114, 186, 188, 265-266, 268, 270-277, 281-282, 336n60, 381n12, 382n36. *See also* Caracas; El Sistema

Venice Biennale, 80

Verdecchia, Guillermo, 181, 190, 192, 196-199, 201-202, 365n41

Veronis, Luisa, 231, 248-249, 251-252, 255, 257

Villasin, Nadine, 185

Violence: 37-39, 44, 49, 54, 59, 62-63, 132, 152, 154, 173, 175, 177, 211, 215, 217-219, 224-225, 337n7, 340n44; political violence, 19, 26, 40

Virgin of Guadalupe, 96, 184, 353n49

Virtual Museum of Canada, 341n2

Visa, 98, 101, 148, 186, 219

Vitae exhibition, 312-313

"Voilà Québec en México!" festival, 312, 385n8

Volpe, Giorgia, 47, 338n18

W
Wagstaff, George, 16
Walkway, 316, 319-320, 322
War of Canudos, 19
Wartime Information Board, 72, 343n29
Weather, 187, 203
Wheatley, 87
Wideload, 197-198
Willistead Art Gallery, 76
Windsor, 73, 76, 80
Winnipeg, 81, 187, 348n120
Women, 11, 32, 62-63, 67, 88, 90, 94, 124, 136, 140, 165, 169, 176-177, 185, 191, 193, 199, 208, 220, 222, 240, 292, 301, 307, 340-341n1, 350n14
Writer, 1, 9, 20, 54, 123, 162, 171, 184, 187, 190-192, 198, 204, 209, 211, 214, 265, 267, 289, 292, 307, 367n7, 370n44; Latino-Québécois writer, 64, 198, 257. *See also* Author; Plays; Poet
Writing, 205, 285-286, 288-290
Writing retreat, 188

Y
Yes Yoko Solo (Yoon), 185
Yoon, Jean, 185
Youth orchestra, 268, 272, 274-275, 278. *See also* Simón Bolívar Youth Orchestra

Z
Zócalo, 63